NUMBER TWO HUNDRED AND FOUR

The Old Farmer's Almanac

Calculated on a new and improved plan for the year of our Lord

1996

Being LEAP YEAR and (until July 4)
220th year of American Independence

FITTED FOR BOSTON AND THE NEW ENGLAND STATES, WITH SPECIAL
CORRECTIONS AND CALCULATIONS TO ANSWER FOR ALL THE UNITED STATES.

Containing, besides the large number of Astronomical Calculations
and the Farmer's Calendar for every month in the year, a variety of
NEW, USEFUL, AND ENTERTAINING MATTER.

ESTABLISHED IN 1792
by Robert B. Thomas

*There is so much good in the worst of us,
And so much bad in the best of us,
That it hardly becomes any of us
To talk about the rest of us.*
– EDWARD WALLIS HOCH

COPYRIGHT 1995 BY YANKEE PUBLISHING INCORPORATED

COVER T.M. REGISTERED
IN U.S. PATENT OFFICE

ISSN 0078-4516

LIBRARY OF CONGRESS
CARD NO. 56-29681

Address all editorial correspondence to
THE OLD FARMER'S ALMANAC, DUBLIN, NH 03444

Contents
The Old Farmer's Almanac • 1996

Features

18 Consumer Tastes & Trends for 1996

46 Ready or Not, Here Comes the Millennium

80 "Never Take No Cutoffs"

90 Yes, Virginia, There IS an Aphrodisiac That Really Works

98 Getting Rid of Paper Clutter

page 80

104 The Father of All Traffic Laws

110 Who's Smarter: Cats, Dogs, or Human Beings?

page 110

116 The Heat Wave That Melted Dentures

148 The Beauty of Boxwood

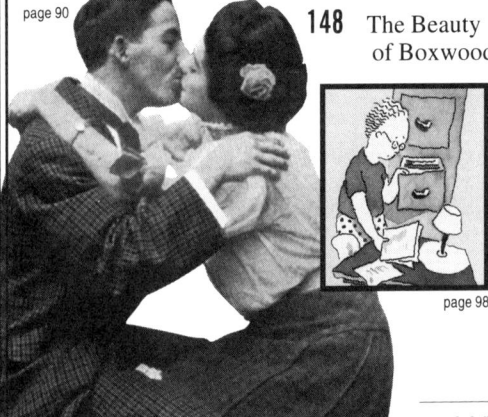
page 90

page 98

Weather

36
Forecast Methods

118
General U.S. Forecast

119
Map of U.S. Regions
Summer Olympics Forecast

120-147
Regional Forecasts

1. New England 120
2. Greater New York–New Jersey 122
3. Middle Atlantic Coast 124
4. Piedmont & Southeast Coast 126
5. Florida 128
6. Upstate New York . . . 130
7. Greater Ohio Valley 132
8. Deep South 134
9. Chicago & Southern Great Lakes 136
10. Northern Great Plains–Great Lakes 138
11. Central Great Plains 140
12. Texas–Oklahoma 142
13. Rocky Mountains . . . 144
14. Southwest Desert 145
15. Pacific Northwest 146
16. California 147

continued on page 4

1 **Northern Exposure.** Perfect for cool, short-season areas.

2 **Big Girl® Hybrid VF.** Perfect for slicing or wedges.

3 **Supersteak Hybrid VFN.** Extra-meaty 1-2 lb. fruits.

4 **Super Sweet 100 Hybrid.** Long season, extra sweet.

5 **Burpee's Early Pick.** Bears early, sets bumper crops all summer!

6 **Delicious.** Its seed grew the world's largest tomato!

7 **Winter Red Hybrid.** Keeps up to three months!

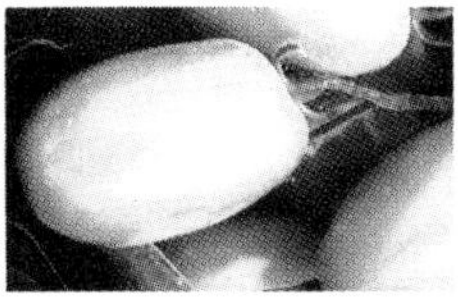

8 **Viva Italia Hybrid.** Tastes great fresh and in sauces.

9 **Gardener's Delight.** An old time favorite cherry.

10 **Tumbler Hybrid.** Very early, great for containers!

11 **Yellow Pear.** Mild and pleasing, great for salads.

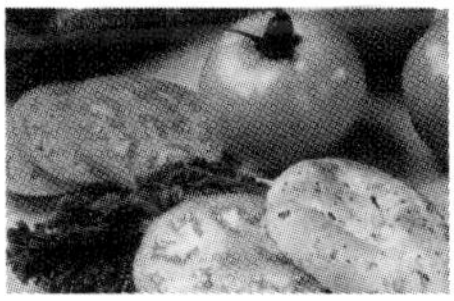

12 **Super Tasty™ Hybrid.** The best in our company's history.

12 Juicy Reasons to Send for a FREE 1996 Burpee Gardens Catalogue!

Tomatoes! Burpee's 1996 Garden Catalogue features 31 different tomato varieties! Early ones, late ones, big beauties and bite-sized gems. All packed full of garden-fresh flavor and *guaranteed* to satisfy. You will be able to choose from over 300 varieties of vegetables and over 400 varieties of flowers. Plus fruit trees, bulbs, shrubs, garden supplies. Your new catalogue will arrive in early January.

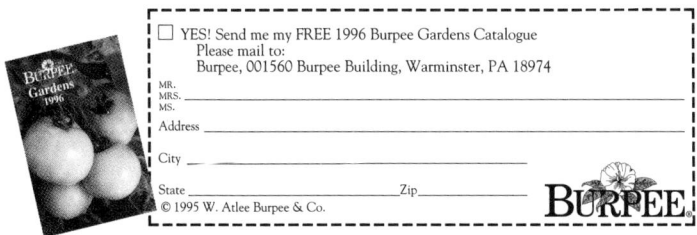

☐ YES! Send me my FREE 1996 Burpee Gardens Catalogue
  Please mail to:
  Burpee, 001560 Burpee Building, Warminster, PA 18974

MR.
MRS. _____
MS.
Address _____

City _____

State _____ Zip _____

© 1995 W. Atlee Burpee & Co.

BURPEE®

CONTENTS

continued from page 2

Features

- **156** Is It a Fruit? Or Is It a Vegetable?
- **164** The Pure Pleasures of Country Cooking
- **168** What You Can Eat to Achieve True Peace of Mind
- **188** The True Story of a Hero
- **194** Ready, Set, Go!
- **220** The Grandfather Paradox: Is Travel to the Past Possible?

page 188

225

Special Bookstore Supplement:
In Praise of Local Heroes, 1996, **PLUS** A Compendium of Useful and Unusual Reference Matter

Charts, Tables, and Departments

30
☞ How to Use This Almanac

Anecdotes and
   Pleasantries **212**
Aphelion, Earth at **34**
Astrological Timetable **186**
Calendar Pages **52-79**
Calendars, 1995-1997.. **224**
Chronological Cycles .. **33**
Church Holy
   Days **33, 36, 53-79**
Classified Advertising **205**
Conjunctions, Astronomical
   .... **34, 40, 53-79**
Dawn and Dark...... **201**
Day, Length of .. **30, 52-78**
Daylight Saving
   Time **30, 62, 74**
Earthquakes......... **33**
Eclipses............ **42**
Eras **33**
Essay Contest....... **176**
Fishing, Best Days for **204**
Foreword, To Patrons ... **6**
Frosts and Growing
   Seasons **160**
Glossary **38**
Holidays and
   Observances....... **36**
Key Letters **30, 196**
Meteor Showers **42**

Moon:
   Astrological Place .. **187**
   Astronomical
     Place **30, 52-78**
   Full, 1996-2000 .... **42**
   Gardening by.. **162, 187**
   Phases of....... **52-78**
   Rise and Set .. **30, 52-78**
Perihelion, Earth at **34**
Planets: Rise and Set ... **40**
   Symbols for **34**
Planting Tables .. **162, 187**
Recipe Contest **174**
Seasons **33**
Stars, Bright **44**
Sun: Declination ... **52-78**
   Rise and Set .. **30, 52-78**
Sun Fast **30, 52-78**
Sundials **30**
Tidal Glossary **201**
Tides, Boston ... **30, 52-79**
Tides, Correction
   Tables **202**
Time Correction
   Tables **196**
Twilight, Length of ... **201**
Weights and Measures **14**
Windchill Table **88**
Zodiac............ **184**

12 Great Reasons to Own a Mantis Tiller

1. Weighs just 20 pounds. Mantis is a joy to use. It starts easily, turns on a dime, lifts nimbly over plants and fences.

2. Tills like nothing else. Mantis bites down a full 10" deep, churns tough soil into crumbly loam, prepares seedbeds in no time.

3. Has patented "serpentine" tines. Our patented tine teeth spin at up to 240 RPM— twice as fast as others. Cuts through tough soil and vegetation like a chain saw through wood!

4. Weeds faster than hand tools. Reverse its tines and Mantis is a precision power weeder. Weeds an average garden in 20 minutes.

5. Digs planting furrows. With the Planter/Furrower, Mantis digs deep or shallow furrows for planting. Builds raised beds, too!

6. Cuts neat borders. Use the Border Edger to cut crisp edges for flower beds, walkways, around shrubs and trees.

7. Dethatches your lawn. Thatch on you lawn prevents water and nutrients from reaching the roots. The Dethatcher quickly removes thatch.

8. Aerates your lawn, too. For a lush, health carpet, the Aerator slices thousands of tine slits in you lawn's surface.

9. Trims bushes and hedges! Only Mantis has a optional 24" or 30" trimmer bar to prune and trim your shrubbery and small trees.

10. The Mantis Promise Try any product that you buy directly from Mantis with **NO RISK!** If you're not completely satisfied, send it back to us within one year for a complete, no hassle refund.

11. Warranties. The entire tiller is warranted for two full years. The tines are quaranteed forever against breakage.

12. Fun to use. The Mantis Tiller/Cultivator is so much fun to use gardeners everywhere love their Mantis tillers.

**Learn more about Mantis today!
For free details, call
TOLL FREE 1-800-366-6268.**

FREE BORDER EDGER WITH EARLY ORDERS

Mantis® 1028 Street Road Dept. 9268
Southampton, Pa 18966

☑ **YES!** Please send FREE information about the Mantis Tiller/Cultivator.

Name _____
Address _____
City _____ State _____ Zip _____

©1995 Mantis

P To ATRONS

What, exactly, is an "almanac," anyway?

Not many people today are certain just what constitutes an "almanac." This is because the word is so often misused in today's catalogs, book titles, and such to imply simply an assortment of information. But a look at all the possible origins of the word indicate that a true almanac has to be more than that. George P. Putnam of Massachusetts, a contributor to this Almanac during the middle years of the last century, maintained it is a Saxon or Old English word. He pointed out that the first almanacs were kept on carved sticks, which were called *al-moon-heed,* meaning the observation of all moon phases.

Other scholars go back further, saying that "Al" is from the Arabic article meaning *the,* and "manac" from the Greek word *mēnæus,* meaning a lunar cycle or the course of months. Among the hundreds of letters we received from readers last year was one from L. R. D. of Pittsburgh, who says he learned that "almanac" is derived from the Hebrew word, *Manach,* to count — or *mana,* a reckoning. He went on to say that a rough translation of "almanac" in the ancient Arabic language is "a calendar of the heavens."

So it's obvious that this publication cannot accurately be described as merely an assortment of varied information (the vast amount of exactly that on the following pages notwithstanding). It must also present the structure of the forthcoming days, weeks, months, and year — astronomically speaking (versus *astrologically* speaking, which is another matter). That is, if it is to call itself an "almanac."

That astronomical structure of the forthcoming year is always contained on the 28 pages known as the "Calendar Pages," two pages for each month plus four extra for November and December of the year preceding, included so readers don't have to refer back to last year's edition for those months. It is these 28 pages that have changed the least since we first appeared on the American scene in the fall of 1792, when George Washington was in his second term. Same look. Same astronomical symbols. Same sort of information — and more of it per square inch than you'll find anywhere. All of it 100 percent accurate, too, even though most are truly "predictions" of how the Earth, Sun, Moon, planets, and certain stars will be on each of the next 365 days. (We can all thank our consultant, Dr. George Greenstein, for that consistent 100 percent accuracy rate.)

To be sure, maybe half of our mail has to do with an entirely different section that, while important and part of our 204-year-old tradition, is not the core or, if you will, the *soul* of the Almanac as are the Calendar Pages. This other popular section comprises the 18 pages (15 in the Canadian edition) that present our long-range weather forecasts. Letters about them, we find, come in two varieties: from people who think our forecasts are uncannily accurate (many of these came from California and the West last year), and from those who think our forecasts are (to paraphrase them politely) no better than "guessing" (last year those voices came from the Northeast!). Maybe the truth is somewhere in between — like in the Midwest! In other words, our forecasts are not uncannily accurate (although we're working on significant improvements), but they are, year in and year out, definitely far better than guessing.

When we receive letters about the Calendar Pages, they are usually from longtime Almanac readers, who, it would appear, peruse those pages carefully. In fact, far *more* carefully, it would seem, than people who read the weather-prediction pages.

(continued on page 9)

ATTENTION PEOPLE WHO HAVE HIGH BLOOD PRESSURE OR ANGINA

Cardizem CD and *CardiSense*® May Help You Live Well

Cardizem CD plus *CardiSense* may give you an opportunity to lead a healthier life.

Cardizem CD gives:

- Effective control of high blood pressure or angina for many people
- Once-daily dosing
- A free quarterly newsletter, *CardiSense*, with timely information on nutrition, exercise, and maintaining a healthy lifestyle.

In clinical studies with Cardizem CD, the most common side effects, seen in less than 5.5% of patients, have been headache, dizziness, slow heart rate, heartbeat irregularities, and swelling of the ankles. Cardizem CD is not appropriate for all people, especially those with certain serious heart rhythm conditions. Make sure your health care professional knows about your medical history, including heart, liver, and kidney problems. Tell your health care professional about other medications you are taking because of possible drug interactions which could result in other potentially serious side effects.

95383401

Talk to your doctor or health care professional about Cardizem CD. Only a health care professional authorized to prescribe Cardizem CD can evaluate the potential risks and benefits of Cardizem CD for you.

Call for a free brochure on high blood pressure or angina, plus one free copy of *CardiSense*.

1-800-537-4994

ONCE-A-DAY
CARDIZEM® CD
(diltiazem HCl) 120-, 180-, 240-, 300-mg Capsules

See important additional information on adjacent page.

0832E5

Brief Summary of
Prescribing Information as of April 1993
CARDIZEM® CD
(diltiazem HCl)
Capsules

CONTRAINDICATIONS
CARDIZEM is contraindicated in (1) patients with sick sinus syndrome except in the presence of a functioning ventricular pacemaker, (2) patients with second- or third-degree AV block except in the presence of a functioning ventricular pacemaker, (3) patients with hypotension (less than 90 mm Hg systolic), (4) patients who have demonstrated hypersensitivity to the drug, and (5) patients with acute myocardial infarction and pulmonary congestion documented by x-ray on admission.

WARNINGS
1. **Cardiac Conduction.** CARDIZEM prolongs AV node refractory periods without significantly prolonging sinus node recovery time, except in patients with sick sinus syndrome. This effect may rarely result in abnormally slow heart rates (particularly in patients with sick sinus syndrome) or second- or third-degree AV block (13 of 3290 patients or 0.40%). Concomitant use of diltiazem with beta-blockers or digitalis may result in additive effects on cardiac conduction. A patient with Prinzmetal's angina developed periods of asystole (2 to 5 seconds) after a single dose of 60 mg of diltiazem.
2. **Congestive Heart Failure.** Although diltiazem has a negative inotropic effect in isolated animal tissue preparations, hemodynamic studies in humans with normal ventricular function have not shown a reduction in cardiac index nor consistent negative effects on contractility (dp/dt). An acute study of oral diltiazem in patients with impaired ventricular function (ejection fraction 24% ± 6%) showed improvement in indices of ventricular function without significant decrease in contractile function (dp/dt). Worsening of congestive heart failure has been reported in patients with preexisting impairment of ventricular function. Experience with the use of CARDIZEM (diltiazem hydrochloride) in combination with beta-blockers in patients with impaired ventricular function is limited. Caution should be exercised when using this combination.
3. **Hypotension.** Decreases in blood pressure associated with CARDIZEM therapy may occasionally result in symptomatic hypotension.
4. **Acute Hepatic Injury.** Mild elevations of transaminases with and without concomitant elevation in alkaline phosphatase and bilirubin have been observed in clinical studies. Such elevations were usually transient and frequently resolved even with continued diltiazem treatment. In rare instances, significant elevations in enzymes such as alkaline phosphatase, LDH, SGOT, SGPT, and other phenomena consistent with acute hepatic injury have been noted. These reactions tended to occur early after therapy initiation (1 to 8 weeks) and have been reversible upon discontinuation of drug therapy. The relationship to CARDIZEM is uncertain in some cases, but probable in some. (See PRECAUTIONS.)

PRECAUTIONS
General
CARDIZEM (diltiazem hydrochloride) is extensively metabolized by the liver and excreted by the kidneys and in bile. As with any drug given over prolonged periods, laboratory parameters of renal and hepatic function should be monitored at regular intervals. The drug should be used with caution in patients with impaired renal or hepatic function. In subacute and chronic dog and rat studies designed to produce toxicity, high doses of diltiazem were associated with hepatic damage. In special subacute hepatic studies, oral doses of 125 mg/kg and higher in rats were associated with histological changes in the liver which were reversible when the drug was discontinued. In dogs, doses of 20 mg/kg were also associated with hepatic changes; however, these changes were reversible with continued dosing. Dermatological events (see ADVERSE REACTIONS section) may be transient and may disappear despite continued use of CARDIZEM. However, skin eruptions progressing to erythema multiforme and/or exfoliative dermatitis have also been infrequently reported. Should a dermatologic reaction persist, the drug should be discontinued.

Drug Interactions
Due to the potential for additive effects, caution and careful titration are warranted in patients receiving CARDIZEM concomitantly with other agents known to affect cardiac contractility and/or conduction. (See WARNINGS.) Pharmacologic studies indicate that there may be additive effects in prolonging AV conduction when using beta-blockers or digitalis concomitantly with CARDIZEM. (See WARNINGS.)
As with all drugs, care should be exercised when treating patients with multiple medications. CARDIZEM undergoes biotransformation by cytochrome P-450 mixed function oxidase. Coadministration of CARDIZEM with other agents which follow the same route of biotransformation may result in the competitive inhibition of metabolism. Especially in patients with renal and/or hepatic impairment, dosages of similarly metabolized drugs, particularly those of low therapeutic ratio, may require adjustment when starting or stopping concomitantly administered diltiazem to maintain optimum therapeutic blood levels.

Beta-blockers. Controlled and uncontrolled domestic studies suggest that concomitant use of CARDIZEM and beta-blockers is usually well tolerated, but available data are not sufficient to predict the effects of concomitant treatment in patients with left ventricular dysfunction or cardiac conduction abnormalities.
Administration of CARDIZEM (diltiazem hydrochloride) concomitantly with propranolol in five normal volunteers resulted in increased propranolol levels in all subjects and bioavailability of propranolol was increased approximately 50%. In vitro, propranolol appears to be displaced from its binding sites by diltiazem. If combination therapy is initiated or withdrawn in conjunction with propranolol, an adjustment in the propranolol dose may be warranted. (See WARNINGS.)

Cimetidine. A study in six healthy volunteers has shown a significant increase in peak diltiazem plasma levels (58%) and area-under-the-curve (53%) after a 1-week course of cimetidine at 1200 mg per day and a single dose of diltiazem 60 mg. Ranitidine produced smaller, nonsignificant increases. The effect may be mediated by cimetidine's known inhibition of hepatic cytochrome P-450, the enzyme system responsible for the first-pass metabolism of diltiazem. Patients currently receiving diltiazem therapy should be carefully monitored for a change in pharmacological effect when initiating and discontinuing therapy with cimetidine. An adjustment in the diltiazem dose may be warranted.

Digitalis. Administration of CARDIZEM with digoxin in 24 healthy male subjects increased plasma digoxin concentrations approximately 20%. Another investigator found no increase in digoxin levels in 12 patients with coronary artery disease. Since there have been conflicting results regarding the effect of digoxin levels, it is recommended that digoxin levels be monitored when initiating, adjusting, and discontinuing CARDIZEM therapy to avoid possible over- or under-digitalization. (See WARNINGS.)

Anesthetics. The depression of cardiac contractility, conductivity, and automaticity as well as the vascular dilation associated with anesthetics may be potentiated by calcium channel blockers. When used concomitantly, anesthetics and calcium blockers should be titrated carefully.

Cyclosporine. A pharmacokinetic interaction between diltiazem and cyclosporine has been observed during studies involving renal and cardiac transplant patients. In renal and cardiac transplant recipients, a reduction of cyclosporine dose ranging from 15% to 48% was necessary to maintain cyclosporine trough concentrations similar to those seen prior to the addition of diltiazem. If these agents are to be administered concurrently, cyclosporine concentrations should be monitored, especially when diltiazem therapy is initiated, adjusted, or discontinued.
The effect of cyclosporine on diltiazem plasma concentrations has not been evaluated.

Carbamazepine. Concomitant administration of diltiazem with carbamazepine has been reported to result in elevated serum levels of carbamazepine (40% to 72% increase), resulting in toxicity in some cases. Patients receiving these drugs concurrently should be monitored for a potential drug interaction.

Carcinogenesis, Mutagenesis, Impairment of Fertility
A 24-month study in rats at oral dosage levels of up to 100 mg/kg/day and a 21-month study in mice at oral dosage levels of up to 30 mg/kg/day showed no evidence of carcinogenicity. There was also no mutagenic response in vitro or in vivo in mammalian cell assays or in vitro in bacteria. No evidence of impaired fertility was observed in a study performed in male and female rats at oral dosages of up to 100 mg/kg/day.

Pregnancy
Category C. Reproduction studies have been conducted in mice, rats, and rabbits. Administration of doses ranging from five to ten times greater (on a mg/kg basis) than the daily recommended therapeutic dose has resulted in embryo and fetal lethality. These doses, in some studies, have been reported to cause skeletal abnormalities. In the perinatal/postnatal studies, there was an increased incidence of stillbirths at doses of 20 times the human dose or greater.
There are no well-controlled studies in pregnant women; therefore, use CARDIZEM in pregnant women only if the potential benefit justifies the potential risk to the fetus.

Nursing Mothers
Diltiazem is excreted in human milk. One report suggests that concentrations in breast milk may approximate serum levels. If use of CARDIZEM is deemed essential, an alternative method of infant feeding should be instituted.

Pediatric Use
Safety and effectiveness in children have not been established.

ADVERSE REACTIONS
Serious adverse reactions have been rare in studies carried out to date, but it should be recognized that patients with impaired ventricular

CARDIZEM® CD
(diltiazem HCl)

function and cardiac conduction abnormalities have usually been excluded from these studies.

The following table presents the most common adverse reactions reported in placebo-controlled angina and hypertension trials in patients receiving CARDIZEM CD up to 360 mg with rates in placebo patients shown for comparison.

CARDIZEM CD Capsule Placebo-Controlled Angina and Hypertension Trials Combined

Adverse Reactions	Cardizem CD (n=607)	Placebo (n=301)
Headache	5.4%	5.0%
Dizziness	3.0%	3.0%
Bradycardia	3.3%	1.3%
AV Block First Degree	3.3%	0.0%
Edema	2.6%	1.3%
ECG Abnormality	1.6%	2.3%
Asthenia	1.8%	1.7%

In clinical trials of CARDIZEM CD capsules, CARDIZEM tablets, and CARDIZEM SR capsules involving over 3200 patients, the most common events (ie, greater than 1%) were edema (4.6%), headache (4.6%), dizziness (3.5%), asthenia (2.6%), first-degree AV block (2.4%), bradycardia (1.7%), flushing (1.4%), nausea (1.4%), and rash (1.2%).

In addition, the following events were reported infrequently (less than 1%) in angina or hypertension trials:

Cardiovascular: Angina, arrhythmia, AV block (second- or third-degree), bundle branch block, congestive heart failure, ECG abnormalities, hypotension, palpitations, syncope, tachycardia, ventricular extrasystoles
Nervous System: Abnormal dreams, amnesia, depression, gait abnormality, hallucinations, insomnia, nervousness, paresthesia, personality change, somnolence, tinnitus, tremor
Gastrointestinal: Anorexia, constipation, diarrhea, dry mouth, dysgeusia, dyspepsia, mild elevations of SGOT, SGPT, LDH, and alkaline phosphatase (see hepatic warnings), thirst, vomiting, weight increase
Dermatological: Petechiae, photosensitivity, pruritus, urticaria
Other: Amblyopia, CPK increase, dyspnea, epistaxis, eye irritation, hyperglycemia, hyperuricemia, impotence, muscle cramps, nasal congestion, nocturia, osteoarticular pain, polyuria, sexual difficulties

The following postmarketing events have been reported infrequently in patients receiving CARDIZEM: alopecia, erythema multiforme, exfoliative dermatitis, extrapyramidal symptoms, gingival hyperplasia, hemolytic anemia, increased bleeding time, leukopenia, purpura, retinopathy, and thrombocytopenia. In addition, events such as myocardial infarction have been observed which are not readily distinguishable from the natural history of the disease in these patients. A number of well-documented cases of generalized rash, characterized as leukocytoclastic vasculitis, have been reported. However, a definitive cause and effect relationship between these events and CARDIZEM therapy is yet to be established.

Prescribing Information as of April 1993

Marion Merrell Dow Inc.
Kansas City, MO 64114

ccdb0493r

(Did all of you in the Northeast, for instance, notice that our prediction for last winter was for "above-normal" temperatures? Just as actually happened?)

There have been those who've suggested that the information contained in the Calendar Pages is irrelevant today. "Your stories, recipes, gardening advice — even your weather forecasts — are useful and fun to read," wrote B. F. R., a new reader from Baltimore, "but why do you include 28 pages of little numbers, symbols, and odd religious days? I can't make head nor tail of that stuff. Why?" Well, B. F. R., not only because we're the oldest, continuously published periodical in North America and, as such, feel an obligation to maintain some sort of continuity with our past, but also because we're an "almanac." That's why.

So, please, B. F. R., do us a favor. Take a few minutes tomorrow, in the early morning before everyone else in the house is up, to peruse once again the Calendar Pages to see what the day will be like in our universe. Where is the Moon in its cycle? When will the Sun set? What are those two bright stars near the horizon? Is one of them a planet? How many hours and minutes of daylight will there be? Notice how orderly and precise all the heavenly bodies, including our own, are in relation to each other. Know that we could accurately predict those relationships on a day ten or 20 years from now. To within seconds.

Now try to think of yourself as an integral part of that amazing order, as most certainly you are. Perhaps then the problems of your day will not be quite as confusing as your past day-to-day experiences might indicate they'd be. Just perhaps then you'll find this information useful and relevant. Write us again and let us know. *J. D. H.* (June 1995)

However, it is by our works and not our words that we would be judged. These, we hope, will sustain us in the humble though proud station we have so long held in the name of,

Your obedient servant,

The Old Farmer's Almanac Joins the Internet

Yes, folks, you can find *The Old Farmer's Almanac* (or at least pieces of it) on the Internet. As of last spring, we are officially wired to the Internet's World Wide Web. The web site (**"http://www.nj.com/weather"**) is the initial offering of New Jersey On-Line, a local Internet service being developed by Newhouse Newspapers New Media. The site features famous bits of Almanac wit and wisdom, current weather conditions, and at-a-glance short-term weather forecasts.

Although the general content of the meteorological section focuses on the New Jersey and Philadelphia areas, short-term **weather forecasts** for 25 other cities across the United States are also included. This information is updated hourly, 24 hours a day.

Readers who enjoy the bits of historical information on our Right-Hand Calendar pages, a feature of the Almanac for all of its 204 years of publication, can get their daily dose of trivia electronically, if they prefer. For example, there's a **daily word of advice** ("Experience is what you get when you expected something else"), a **famous event** (Ben Franklin invented bifocals, May 23, 1785), and a **peek at meteorological history** (27" snow, N.J., March 12, 1888).

Readers can click to other pages for the Almanac's famous **weather predictions** and **astronomical information**, including a day-by-day look at the Moon's phase. Readers may also use the site to **send a letter or a question** to the Almanac's editors. Or you can send us a message directly to **OFA1792@aol.com**. Go ahead, get online — we'd love to hear from you.

Web site: http://www.nj.com/weather
Internet address: OFA1792@aol.com

THE 1996 EDITION OF
THE OLD FARMER'S ALMANAC
Established in 1792 and published every year thereafter
ROBERT B. THOMAS (1766-1846)
FOUNDER

EDITOR *(12th since 1792)*: JUDSON D. HALE SR.
MANAGING EDITOR: SUSAN PEERY
EXECUTIVE EDITOR: TIM CLARK
ART DIRECTOR: MARGO LETOURNEAU
WEATHER PROGNOSTICATOR: DR. RICHARD HEAD
WEATHER GRAPHICS: ©ACCU-WEATHER, INC., 1995
ASTRONOMER: DR. GEORGE GREENSTEIN
COPY EDITOR: LIDA STINCHFIELD
ASSOCIATE EDITORS: MARE-ANNE JARVELA,
DEBRA SANDERSON
ASSISTANT EDITORS: ANNA LARSON, MAUDE SALINGER,
JODY SAVILLE, MARY SHELDON
ARCHIVIST: LORNA TROWBRIDGE
CONTRIBUTING EDITORS: JAMIE KAGELEIRY,
CASTLE FREEMAN JR., *Farmer's Calendar;*
FRED SCHAAF, *Astronomy*
PRODUCTION DIRECTOR: SUSAN GROSS
PAGE PRODUCTION MANAGER: DAVID ZIARNOWSKI
PRODUCTION ASSISTANT: CLARE INNES
SENIOR PRODUCTION ARTIST: LUCILLE RINES
PRODUCTION ARTISTS: CHRIS SIMARD, JILL SHAFFER
PRODUCTION SYSTEMS COORDINATOR: STEVE MUSKIE

GROUP PUBLISHER: JOHN PIERCE
PUBLISHER *(23rd since 1792)*: SHERIN WIGHT
ADMINISTRATIVE ASSISTANT: SARAH DANFORTH
MAIL ORDER MARKETING MANAGER: DEB WALSH
DIRECT SALES MANAGER: CINDY SCHLOSSER
DIRECTOR OF NEW MEDIA: JAMIE TROWBRIDGE
SPECIAL MARKETS DIRECTOR: RONDA KNOWLTON
MARKETING RESEARCH MANAGER: MARTHA BENINTENDE
ADVERTISING PRODUCTION: RITA KLAPES, *Manager;* VALERIE BURGOS, MARY ANN FARREN
NEWSSTAND CIRCULATION:
PUBLISHER'S SINGLE COPY SALES SERVICE

EDITORIAL, ADVERTISING, AND PUBLISHING OFFICES:
P.O. BOX 520, DUBLIN, NH 03444
PHONE: 603-563-8111 • FAX: 603-563-8252

YANKEE PUBLISHING INC., MAIN ST., DUBLIN, NH 03444

JOSEPH B. MEAGHER, *President;* JUDSON D. HALE SR., *Senior Vice President;* BRIAN PIANI, *Vice President* and *Chief Financial Officer;* JODY BUGBEE, BROOKS FISHER, JAMES H. FISHMAN, JOHN PIERCE, and JOE TIMKO, *Vice Presidents.*

The Old Farmer's Almanac cannot accept responsibility for unsolicited manuscripts and will not return any manuscripts that do not include a stamped and addressed return envelope.

The newsprint in this edition of *The Old Farmer's Almanac* consists of 23 percent recycled content. All printing inks used are soy-based. This product is recyclable. Consult your local recycling regulations for the right way to do it. **PRINTED IN U.S.A.**

Collectible tractors from *The Old Farmer's Almanac* Limited-edition replicas... heritage quality by **ERTL**

Special Offer

SAVE EVEN MORE. BUY BOTH FOR ONLY $74.95.

Massey-Harris Twin Power Challenger, die-cast metal in 1/16th-scale.   #OF92TRB
Was $49.95, **now only $44.95**

Cockshutt 770 with original details and moving parts, die-cast metal in 1/10th-scale.   #OF94TRC
Was $49.95, **now only $44.95**

ORDER NOW WHILE SUPPLIES LAST. CALL (800) 223-3166 S950TRX

A Cheerful Fire & A Warm Home...

There is almost nothing as delightful as a crackling fire, or as comfortable as the soothing warmth of soapstone. Soapstone is nature's most beautiful, durable, and efficient stove material. It absorbs twice as much heat as metal, and radiates steady warmth, even after the fire has died.

Woodstock Soapstone Stoves offer both traditional and contemporary styling, and the latest in clean-burning technology. An internal catalytic combustor boosts heat output and virtually eliminates pollution.

Our financing plan makes it easy to own a Woodstock Soapstone Stove at low monthly terms. Send for free catalog, or call 800-866-4344 for free catloag *and* video.

As low as $52.50 per mo.

FREE COLOR CATALOG
Name_____
Address_____
City/State/Zip_____
Phone (daytime) (___)_____
Phone (evening) (___)_____

Woodstock Soapstone Co., Inc.
66 Airpark Rd., Dept. 398, W. Lebanon, NH 03784

Order free video by phone only.

FREE CATALOG & VIDEO   1-800-866-4344   FASTEST SERVICE!

☞ Catalog Emporium

FREE 1995 SEED CATALOG

STOKES SEEDS
1036 Stokes Building
Box 548, Buffalo NY 14240-0548

Name _____

Address _____

_____ Zip _____

Make your house a home with affordable gifts and home accessories from Terry's Village. Charming dolls, colorful windsocks, decorative birdfeeders and terra cotta pots and planters... a world of treasure awaits you.
Call 1-800-200-4400
and ask for Dept. 456.

Send us 25¢ and you'll get a packet of Walla Walla Onion Seeds plus a FREE 88-page color catalog, featuring:

- Vegetables • Fruits • Flowers
- Shade Trees • Garden Helpers

All with a One-Year Guarantee!

☐ Rush me my catalog and here's 25¢ for my Walla Walla Onion seeds.

Name _____
Street _____
City _____
State _____ Zip _____

U.S. residents, but please, no Hawaii or Alaska requests

HenryField's
SEED & NURSERY CO.
Dept. 71-2133, 415 N.Burnett St.
Shenandoah, IA 51602

Send for your FREE catalog and 25¢ pkt. of seeds— our famous

Stakeless TOMATO

Just one of our top-quality varieties! Try Gurney's for

- *flowers & vegetables*
- *fruit & shade trees*
- *cold-hardy shrubs*
- *garden supplies*

Over 2,000 items to choose — all priced right and backed by a full-year guarantee.

just **25¢** per pkt.

Name _____
Address _____
City _____
State _____ Zip _____

GURNEY'S
SEED & NURSERY CO.
110 Capital ▪ Dept. 85-3846 ▪ Yankton, SD 57079
Residents of the 48 Contiguous States Only, Please

☞ Catalog Emporium

NEW OFFER!

Miller's Spring '96 catalogs offer more planting information, more varieties to choose from than ever before. Page after page is chock-full of fruits, nuts, ornamentals, David Austin and Meidiland roses — and more. Miller's Canandaigua Quality (CQ), sets the standard for hardiness where plant hardiness counts. Comes the fall, you automatically get our Fall '96 edition with special planting offers too good to miss.
Don't miss our new Fraser Fir wreaths!

miller NURSERIES
J.E. Miller, Dept. 100
5060 West Lake Road
Canandaigua, NY 14424

Take Advantage of a Great View!

A Deltec circular home is an excellent way to bring nature inside the home, a way to take full advantage of your view and to make more efficient use of the sun with this passive solar design. Prebuilt packages provide a unique building system of floors, walls, decks, windows, doors, and exterior trim. Assemble it yourself or an authorized builder can do it for you. A planbook and video showcase exhibit how satisfying a Deltec Home can be.

Planbook: **$10.00**/Video Showcase: **$14.95**
(both only **$19.95**) • Visa/MC accepted
**Call or write us today at:
800-642-2508 or 704-253-0483
Deltec, 604 College St.,
Asheville, NC 28801**

MUSSER TREE CATALOG

Largest selection available of Evergreen and Hardwood Tree Seedlings, Native Plants, Landscape Shrubs, Ground Covers. Free color catalog with cultural descriptions for each variety. We ship throughout U.S. and Canada.

PLEASE PRINT
NAME _____
ADDRESS _____
CITY, STATE, ZIP _____

MUSSER FORESTS, INC. DEPT. 9-95
PO BOX 340 • INDIANA, PA 15701-0340
(412) 465-5685 • FAX (412) 465-9893

Northern
Where the Pros and Handymen Shop

FREE CATALOG!

Send today for your Catalog and save on...
• Air, Hand and Power Tools
• Pumps and Pressure Washers
• Lawn and Garden Accessories
• Generators and Engines
• Trailer Parts and Much MORE!

Call Toll Free! 1-800-533-5545
Name: _____
Address: _____
City: _____ State: ___ Zip: ___
Key Code **87790**

Table of Measures

Apothecaries'
1 scruple = 20 grains
1 dram = 3 scruples
1 ounce = 8 drams
1 pound = 12 ounces

Avoirdupois
1 ounce = 16 drams
1 pound = 16 ounces
1 hundredweight = 100 pounds
1 ton = 2,000 pounds
1 long ton = 2,240 pounds

Cubic Measure
1 cubic foot = 1,728 cubic inches
1 cubic yard = 27 cubic feet
1 cord = 128 cubic feet
1 U.S. liquid gallon = 4 quarts = 231 cubic inches
1 Imperial gallon = 1.20 U.S. gallons = 277.420 cubic inches
1 board foot = 144 cubic inches

Dry Measure
2 pints = 1 quart
4 quarts = 1 gallon
2 gallons = 1 peck
4 pecks = 1 bushel

Liquid Measure
4 gills = 1 pint
2 pints = 1 quart
4 quarts = 1 gallon
63 gallons = 1 hogshead
2 hogsheads = 1 pipe or butt
2 pipes = 1 tun

Linear Measure
1 foot = 12 inches
1 yard = 3 feet
1 rod = 5½ yards
1 mile = 320 rods = 1,760 yards = 5,280 feet
1 nautical mile = 6,076.1155 feet
1 knot = 1 nautical mile per hour
1 furlong = ⅛ mile = 660 feet = 220 yards
1 league = 3 miles = 24 furlongs

1 fathom = 2 yards = 6 feet
1 chain = 100 links = 22 yards
1 link = 7.92 inches
1 hand = 4 inches
1 span = 9 inches

Square Measure
1 square foot = 144 square inches
1 square yard = 9 square feet
1 square rod = 30¼ square yards = 272¼ square feet
1 acre = 160 square rods = 43,560 square feet
1 square mile = 640 acres = 102,400 square rods
1 square rod = 625 square links
1 square chain = 16 square rods
1 acre = 10 square chains

Household Measures
120 drops of water = 1 teaspoon
60 drops thick fluid = 1 teaspoon
2 teaspoons = 1 dessertspoon
3 teaspoons = 1 tablespoon
16 tablespoons = 1 cup
2 cups = 1 pint
2 pints = 1 quart
4 quarts = 1 gallon
3 tablespoons flour = 1 ounce
2 tablespoons butter = 1 ounce
2 cups granulated sugar = 1 pound
3¾ cups confectioners' sugar = 1 pound
2¾ cups brown sugar = 1 pound
3½ cups wheat flour = 1 pound
5⅓ cups dry coffee = 1 pound
4 cups cocoa = 1 pound
6½ cups dry tea = 1 pound
2 cups shortening = 1 pound
1 stick butter = ½ cup
3 cups cornmeal = 1 pound
2 tablespoons sugar = 1 ounce
2⅜ cups raisins = 1 pound
3½ cups walnuts (chopped) = 1 pound
9 eggs = 1 pound
8 egg whites = 1 cup

16 egg yolks = 1 cup
1 ounce yeast = 1 scant tablespoon
3 cups fresh, sliced peaches = 1 pound
60 pounds potatoes = 1 bushel
52 pounds onions = 1 bushel
24 pounds string beans = 1 bushel
56 pounds tomatoes = 1 bushel
55 pounds turnips = 1 bushel
54 pounds sweet potatoes = 1 bushel
45 pounds parsnips = 1 bushel
50 pounds carrots = 1 bushel
60 pounds beets = 1 bushel
60 pounds beans = 1 bushel
48 pounds apples = 1 bushel
196 pounds flour = 1 barrel

Metric
1 inch = 2.54 centimeters
1 centimeter = 0.39 inch
1 meter = 39.37 inches
1 yard = 0.914 meters
1 mile = 1,609.344 meters = 1.61 kilometers
1 kilometer = .62 mile
1 square inch = 6.45 square centimeters
1 square yard = 0.84 square meter
1 square mile = 2.59 square kilometers
1 square kilometer = 0.386 square mile
1 acre = 0.40 hectare
1 hectare = 2.47 acres
1 cubic yard = 0.76 cubic meter
1 cubic meter = 1.31 cubic yards
1 liter = 1.057 U.S. liquid quarts
1 U.S. liquid quart = 0.946 liter
1 U.S. liquid gallon = 3.78 liters
1 gram = 0.035 ounce
1 ounce = 28.349 grams
1 kilogram = 2.2 pounds
1 pound avoirdupois = 0.45 kilogram

Sand, cat-hairs, dust and dust-mites...
Nothing gets by the 8-lb. ORECK XL!

The favorite vacuum of over 50,000 hotels and more than 1 million professional and private users. Now you can use this powerful vacuum to clean your home better than ever before.

Exclusive Filter System assures hypo-allergenic cleaning with Germastat. Ideal for those who suffer from dust-related or allergic discomforts. There's virtually no after dust. Its unique top-fill action carries the litter up through the handle and deposits it on the inside top of the bag. Yesterday's dirt can't seep out. And the metal-tube top-fill performance works without hoses to crack, leak or break... ever.

The lightest full-size vacuum available. It weighs just 8 pounds. So stairs are a snap. It's super-powerful, with amazing cleaning power: the fast, double helical brushes revolve at an incredible 6,500 times a minute.

ORECK's Helping Hand® handle designed on the principles of ergonomics is available. No need to squeeze your hand or bend your wrist. A godsend for people with hand or wrist problems.

Exclusive New Microsweep® gets bare floors super clean, without any hoses, attachments or adjustments.

A full 10-year Guarantee against breakage or burnout of the housing PLUS a full 3-year Warranty on the extended life motor. We'll let you try the ORECK XL in your home for 15 days. If you don't love it, you don't keep it.

Made in the USA

For a free brochure call toll-free
1-800-989-4200 Ext. 80236
Or mail coupon today. No salesperson will visit.

FREE with purchase

Super Compact Canister
The 4-lb. dynamo you've seen on TV. The motor's so powerful it lifts a 16-lb. bowling ball! Hand-holdable and comfortable. Cleans under refrigerators... car seats... books... ceilings... even typewriter, computer and piano keys. With 8 accessories. Yours FREE when you purchase an ORECK XL upright. Offer limited, so act now.

ORECK CORPORATION   80236
100 Plantation Road, New Orleans, LA 70123

☐ **Yes!** I want to learn how the ORECK XL Hotel Vacuum can help me clean my home faster, easier and more effectively. Please send me your FREE information kit, without cost or obligation.
I understand I will receive absolutely FREE a Super Compact Canister, with the purchase of the ORECK XL Hotel Vacuum.

☐ Also include details of ORECK's Extended Payment Plan with No Interest or Finance Charge.

Name _____
(please print)
Address _____
City _____ State ____ Zip _____
Telephone(_____) _____
area code   (optional)

A-1

Hello, my name is Tom Lee, President of Bierhaus International, Inc.

If you're tired of paying $12-$18 a case for beer, I don't blame you.

That's why I'd like to show you an amazing *new* way to brew your own superb lager for as little as $6.00 per case. You actually SAVE up to $10 on EACH CASE OF BEER. And wait until you taste the beer. Compare it to the finest premium beers. Referring to this method of making beer, the *New York Times* stated, "...the quality of the beer may surprise many people. Wait two to four weeks and friends may be placing orders."

The secret is in an anaerobic mini-brewery that lets YOU make up to 6 gallons of ALL NATURAL BEER, using only the finest barley malt and hops. No chemicals. No preservatives. You can brew several cases of beer in about 25-30 minutes. And everything you'll need (except the bottles and a little household sugar) comes with your mini-brewery.

IS IT EASY TO MAKE?

Using the Bierhaus Mini-Brewery, you can brew beer in just 27 minutes on your kitchen stove. Let it ferment for seven days, bottle it, and you're done. Aging takes 3-5 weeks.

- No more late night trips to the carryout
- No more lugging empty beer cases
- No more chemistry set taste.
- No more standing in line to pay $12-$18 per case of beer.

Just brew what you need when you need it... for as little as 19 cents a bottle.

WHAT ABOUT ALCOHOLIC CONTENT?

You can make a super light beer (1.8%-2% alcohol), regular strength (4.5%-5%), or a European-style lager, ranging as high as 7.5% alcohol.

CAN I MAKE DIFFERENT KINDS OF BEER?

Certainly. Just vary the ingredients and recipes according to the instructions supplied with each kit. You can make...
- **LIGHT LAGER.** Comparable to most Canadian premium beers and some light European lagers.

I'll send you $5.00 FREE if you don't agree my ALL NATURAL beer is better than any commercial beer you've ever tasted.

- **BAVARIAN DARK LAGER.** Full bodied, yet not bitter. The head is incomparable—rich and creamy.
- **STOUT.** Rich in body with a hearty, robust flavor. In the finest tradition of grand Irish Stouts.
- **ALE.** Popular with American home brewers. From England's favorite hoppy, dry "bitter" ales, to the sweeter brown ales enjoyed in fine European pubs.

IS IT LEGAL?

You can make up to 200 gallons of beer per year — tax free — and you don't need a federal license of any kind.

I realize you may still be skeptical, and I don't blame you — that's why we're offering our unheard-of **$5.00 FREE GUARANTEE.**

> Try your mini-brewery. Keep it for up to 6 months. Make the beer at your leisure. If you don't agree that this is the best beer you've ever tasted in your life, we'll buy the kit back.
> What's more, we'll pay the return postage (by regular UPS or Parcel Post rates) and send you an extra $5.00 for your time and trouble. No conditions. No excuses.

CUSTOMER COMMENTS

"My friends and I had tours of duty in Europe and were looking for that "old country" flavor and body. Your Bavarian Dark has it all."
—Lt. Fred Frances, Texas

"Your Continental Amber is as close to a perfect beer as I have ever consumed."
—Dwayne Staner, Iowa

"I no longer wonder whether I prefer the best commercial beer or your beer which I made. NO QUESTION, YOURS IS THE BEST."
—Ed Pearson, New York

WHERE DO I GET SUPPLIES ONCE I GET THE KIT?

Just call us to reorder ingredients. Bierhaus is among the largest mail order suppliers of equipment and ingredients in the U.S.A. You can choose from over 50 different malts from countries all over the world. We also carry a wide range of brewing supplies and accessories... everything you need to brew the best beer you ever tasted.

We have sold more than 95,000 beer kits since 1978 and some of our first customers are still brewing with their original equipment. Remember, your equipment is guaranteed unconditionally for one full year from date of purchase.

Your new Bierhaus Mini-Brewery contains an FDA foodgrade 7½ gallon fermentation tank with lid and airlock, a 7½ gallon priming vessel complete with siphon unit, bottle capper and caps, hydrometer, bottle brush, brewing guide, and ingredients to make 5 gallons (2+ cases) of American style premium lager.

$5.00 FREE

Serve the beer to your family and friends. If everyone doesn't agree it's far better than commercial beer, simply return the kit. I'll pay the return postage and send you a check for your full purchase price. Plus I'll send you an EXTRA $5.00 for your time and trouble.

©1995 Bierhaus International, Inc.

Bierhaus International, Inc.
3723 West 12th Street, Dept. FA-3
Erie, Pennsylvania 16505

Please send me the following mini-brewery:

☐ **Exp. Basic Kit** (as described above)
$49.95 plus $7.50 S&H (UPS) continental USA only

☐ **Super Kit** (includes Basic Kit, brewing spoon, thermometer, additional lid with airlock, plus double ingredients for 10 gallons of beer.
$69.95 plus $9.90 S&H (UPS) continental USA only

NAME _____
ADDRESS _____
CITY _____ STATE ___ ZIP ___
PHONE _____
☐ Check enclosed
☐ Charge to: ☐ MasterCard ☐ VISA ☐ Discover
Acct. # _____
Expires _____ (PA residents add 6% sales tax)

FOR EXTRA FAST SERVICE Call us at **814-833-7747** from 8:30 a.m.-5:00 p.m. EST weekdays and charge to MasterCard, VISA or Discover.

TESTED! PROVEN! IT WORKS!

Miracle hormone makes plants ZOOOM!

INDOOR & OUTDOOR PLANTS GO WILD YEAR ROUND!

100% EFFECTIVE

A LEADING NATIONAL MAGAZINE reports the magic hormone contained in DYNOGEN is causing a plant revolution. This miracle hormone acts to promote the healthy growth, development and reproduction processes of plants, including:

- *Plants grow into giants even under the worst light and moisture conditions*
- *Plants that bloom rarely, now flower constantly!*
- *Rose bushes climb 3 times normal height!*
- *Young trees double or triple in size in 3 weeks!*

LEADING RESEARCH ACADEMIES have all acclaimed this hormone as being the most important development in horticulture.

DYNOGEN is more than just a plant food.

DYNOGEN is a plant hormone which contains the basic building blocks of life itself.

DYNOGEN GIVES PLANTS NEW VIGOR AND RESISTANCE TO DISEASE AND PESTS.

House Plants Go Wild For Dynogen!

You simply won't recognize your houseplants. Independent Laboratory Test reports you can can actually see an improvement within hours. African Violets, Geraniums, Orchids bloom magnificently! You get longer, earlier blooms, with bigger flowers, and more luxuriant foliage. Sick plants come alive. Propagating becomes a breeze.

HUNDREDS OF SATISFIED DYNOGEN USERS WRITE TO US REGULARLY:

"It's terrific"— Mrs. A.R., Plantation, Fla. "Faster bud setting, more vivid flowers... more vigorous growth... bigger leaf size... no more problems with pests." — Mrs. T.S. Ricacho, N.M. "Roses, trees, shrubs, and houseplants showed many new leaves and increased growth in 3 days." E.M., Lexington, Ohio "From practically dead to vibrantly alive." — W.Y., Entoka, Ga.

From Practically Dead...

Before *To Vibrantly Alive!!!* **After**

Outdoor Gardens Love It Too!
See Geraniums and Hydrangeas grow into giants...Roses turn into prize winners...huge Chrysanthemums bloom far ahead of time...bushes and shade trees zoom dramatically...Fuschias, Dahlias, Asters explode with vibrant color, and much, much more.

DYNOGEN PROMOTES YEAR-ROUND GROWTH EVEN UNDER POOR LIGHT AND MOISTURE CONDITIONS

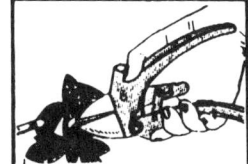

FREE With the purchase of 3 or more cans

Ratchet-Action shears with Teflon-coated cutting blade. **($12.95 value)** Cuts branches, twigs, etc., "like paper" Include 95¢ S&H.

UNCONDITIONAL MONEY-BACK GUARANTEE

Send To: Rush Industries, Dept. DS223SA
75 Albertson Avenue, Albertson, NY 11507

Special! ☐ New Double Size Dynogen Concentrate Can Only $8.95 plus $2.95 shipping & handling.
☐ 2 Double Size Cans Only $15.95 + $3.95 S&H.
Extra Bonus! ☐ 3 Double Size Cans Only $21.95 + $4.95 S&H.
Super Saver! ☐ Treat Your Entire Garden!
5 Double Size Cans Only $29.95 + $4.95 S&H.

Enclosed is $ _____ Sorry, no COD's. Or:
Charge It! ☐ Visa ☐ Master Exp. Date _____
Acct. No. _____
Name _____
Address _____
City _____
State _____ Zip _____

CONSUMER Tastes & Trends
FOR · 1996

GOOD NEWS

Cabbage Heads, Rejoice!
If you are very large headed, take heart: A new study shows that you are less likely to have **"impaired thinking ability"** later in life than those with very small heads.

Happiness Has a Long Shelf Life
Trying to recapture youth because you think it will make you happier? Don't bother. It's a myth that older people are more depressed than younger people. A recent study of 10,000 people found the **elders were just as happy as youth,** but for different reasons. As a matter of fact, when researchers looked at the total U.S. population, the "best" year was 50.

Dropouts Drop Off
According to the Census Bureau, the **high-school dropout rate** went from 21.9 percent in 1980 to 10.5 percent in 1993.

BAD NEWS

The "Bah, Humbug" Index
Joel Waldfogel, a professor of economics at Yale, got two cribbage boards for Christmas one year. "Since I don't play cribbage," he told *The American Economic Review*, "the first one I received was of little value to me, and the second one of no value at all." Being an economist (and a bit of a Scrooge?), Waldfogel decided to tally up the "deadweight loss" to the economy of unwanted Christmas gifts. Waldfogel, who sees the $20 cost of the cribbage board as **money that has been obliterated by the gift-giving transaction,** was able to calculate the Christmas loss at between four and 13 billion dollars.

The Pinocchio Factor
As you age, your ears will stretch and your nose will grow, not from lying, but from **subjecting your face to gravity** year after year, according to the Johns Hopkins School of Medicine.

THE MOOD

It's a busy world — even cat ownership is up because cats are such low-maintenance pets. Anything that makes life a little easier is welcome. Watch for such conveniences as phone-in postage (one method: postage may be faxed to you in bar-code form).

Flea markets are booming. Said one flea-market shopper, "This gives you a chance to reclaim some of the things you had years ago and that you knew worked."

Two-four-six-eight, what do we appreciate? Cheerleading! It's hotter than ever.

There's a definite backlash against Political Correctness, and even cigar-smoking is enjoying a little boom.

BEST New Way to Save Money, 1996

■ A typical low-fat diet (30 percent or less of total calories coming from fat) costs 75¢ less per person per day than a higher-fat diet, potentially saving a family of four $1,100 a year.

WORST New Way to Save Money, 1996

■ At the Annual Mosquito Cook-Off in Walcott, Arkansas, cooks whip up crushed mosquito cookies (the bugs are boiled first to get rid of diseases), mosquito meat pie, and chili con 'skeeter.

PET NEWS

Findings from a recent survey by the American Animal Hospital Association:

☞ Sixty-nine percent of **dog owners** give their pets as much attention as they give their children.

☞ Fifty-seven percent of **cat owners** sleep with their pets (though only 32 percent of dog owners do).

☞ Pets are more likely to **have human names** ("Robert") than pet names ("Puffy").

☞ Fifty-seven percent of dog owners spend more than an hour a day **playing with their pets** (most cat owners said that after several minutes of play, cats became bored and stalked away).

Food TRENDS

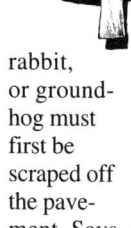

Coffee Backlash will take two forms: **ONE**, it's getting harder to find "just a regular cup of joe" amid all the *lattes*, espressos, and cappucinos. Look for an increased interest in **diner-type coffee**. In fact, we predict that it will soon be more fashionable to drink the plain stuff than the fancy beverages.

TWO, some people are forsaking the bean altogether, opting for tea or no stimulant at all. There's even a **"Caffeine Anonymous"** 12-step program in Portland, Oregon.

Beef consumption is at a five-year high (5.2 billion hamburgers were ordered in U.S. restaurants last year) and will go even higher in 1996. On the other hand, "SnackWell's," a line of reduced-fat cookies and crackers, now outsell America's favorite cookie, the Oreo.

Roadkill cuisine: Let's call it a mini-trend. You can **stew it, grill it, bake, or sauté it,** but to be true roadkill, the possum, squirrel, rabbit, or groundhog must first be scraped off the pavement. Says roadkill "Galloping Gourmet" Jeff Eberbaugh, who speaks in rhymed couplets, "The reason hillbillies are so strong and stout is they know what roadkill nutrition's about." (We'll stick to burgers and Oreos, thanks.)

Pink foods, such as pink grapefruit, pink juice, and pink guava puree (mixed into yogurt, pastry filling, and baby food) will take up more space on grocery shelves. **Blue foods** (such as gelatin and blue tortilla chips) are fading fast.

X-Tenda Fork, a new telescoping fork that **reaches up to two feet,** just made dessert-sharing easier. It's only $10 (about the cost of three desserts in a decent restaurant) in kitchen stores.

Consumer Tastes & Trends for 1996

Sure Shopping

The HOT COLLECTIBLES in 1996

Barbie: Old Barbie or GI Joe dolls in good shape can be **worth up to $400** apiece. Actually, anything that reminds consumers of their youth, such as Lone Ranger or Star Trek memorabilia, is collectible.

Gardening Equipment: Painted watering cans fetch up to $75; **iron gnome lawn ornaments** from 1900 get $500; and 19th-century lawnmowers sell for thousands.

Fishing Tackle: Hand-tied flies are now coveted.

Cans of Tennis Balls: The old "key-wind" cans that once contained white tennis balls **sell for up to $300** (with or without the balls inside).

Credit Cards: If you're thinking of just cutting them all up and throwing them out the window, think twice! An original **1958 American Express card** (made of cardboard) is worth about $500. That would pay some bills! Old plastic ones are also valuable.

Vintage Kitchenware: Early 19th-century apple parers are worth up to $200; **old cherry pitters** can bring $100. Other valuables: turn-of-the-century muffin pans, cast-iron hollowware (especially those that say **"Erie"** or **"Griswold"**), and mixing bowls and rolling pins decorated with advertising slogans.

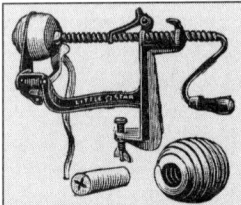

"I Wish I Hadn't Thrown That Away" Department: Transistor radios are the latest in the field of **electronic and industrial collectibles.** (Last year it was old computers.) The small radio from the 1950s and 1960s is seen as "one of the first distinctive emblems of the emerging postwar youth culture, integral as it was to the issues of defiance, sex, freedom, music, and mobility," according to Roger Handy, the author of a collectibles book.

Plus, **they're fun to look at,** especially novelty radios in the forms of flying saucers, beetles, or grasshoppers, or the "Charlie Tuna" or Dick Tracy transistors. Are eight-tracks next?

Another Myth Bites the Dust

"Birth order is radically oversold to parents as a way to explain behavior and personality," says Joseph Lee Rogers, a psychology professor at the University of Oklahoma, who has been studying birth order for years.

Home, Sweet Home, 1996

☞ Items, colors, and styles you may see more of in the next year:

Comfy: Sales of luxury beddings have jumped way up, as people indulge themselves and feather their nests.

Green is still the decorating color of choice, but all-white kitchens will be popular. Look for South Seas touches in furniture: rattan chairs, tropical plant prints on slipcovers, and relaxed lines. Fabrics on classic sofas and chairs will include plaids, ginghams, even denim. Also popular will be renditions of classic designs, such as Empire tables, in more casual materials, such as pine.

Three-Car Garages are growing in number.

(continued)

WE GUARANTEE TO END YOUR FOOT PAIN

...and We'll Prove it to You ...RISK-FREE!

The coupon below will bring you a Free Fact Kit about an amazing foot support, that for 40 years has brought blessed relief to more than 3,000,000 foot pain sufferers worldwide. No other foot support has ever given such long – lasting relief to so many people.

Did you know that most foot problems are caused by a misalignment of the bones in your feet? Such a misalignment can occur for many reasons... advancing age, improper shoes, lack of exercise or long hours on your feet.

Foot pain begins when the foot's balance and natural support is gone. Corns, calluses, bunions, even hammertoes can develop. Toe cramps, fallen arches, burning skin, tender blisters, flaking and chafing result. Ankle, leg, knee, hip – even lower back pain, can result from improper foot alignment. When your feet hurt you hurt all over.

Now! End foot pain instantly with the remarkable European discovery... *Flexible Featherspring*® Foot Supports. They help restore the natural support and balance of your feet... Something that pills, powders, salts, lotions or soaking can never do!

It doesn't matter how old you are or how long you've had foot pain, because Featherspring Foot Supports are custom-formed for your feet – and for your feet only!

Custom-formed Flexible Feathersprings help restore and maintain the elastic support you had when you were younger. And that's the key to Feathersprings.

Furthermore, you can stand all day, walk, dance, jog or even run in total comfort. Your feet, ankles, legs, knees, hips – even your back – can find relief. You see, Feathersprings actually support your feet. And they do so while absorbing shock and relieving pain.

The claims we make about Flexible Featherspring Foot Supports are not exaggerated! 3,000,000 satisfied customers are proof positive. If you are bothered by aches and pains of the feet, legs or lower back, we state firmly that Feathersprings will bring you relief instantly **or you risk nothing.**

Mail Today. Free Fact Kit.

Please, do not turn the page with the idea that you will come back to it later. Cut out the coupon now and mail it today. Make us prove our statements. You have nothing to lose but your foot pain.

© FEATHERSPRING, 712 No. 34th St., Seattle, WA 98103-8881

One pair of Feathersprings is all you'll ever need. And you can wear them anywhere, anytime – even with sandals and high heels. When worn they are virtually invisible under your feet!

Send today for your FREE Fact Kit which explains everything about proven Featherspring Foot Supports. Then, if you decide to try a pair, we will give you a full 60 days to test them with our full money-back guarantee!

FREE! SEND NO MONEY

FEATHERSPRING INTERNATIONAL, INC.
712 No. 34th St., Dept. OF-096
Seattle, WA 98103-8881

❏ **Yes!** I'm interested in ending my foot pain. Please rush, at no risk, the **FREE FACT KIT** that tells me all about Flexible Featherspring Foot Supports. I understand there is no obligation and no salesman will call. I will look for a **LARGE PINK ENVELOPE** containing all the details.

Print Name _____

Address _____

City _____ State _____ Zip _____

Fashion TRENDS

Men's suits this fall and winter will feature jackets with peaked lapels and a bit more padding in the shoulders; pants will be narrower in the leg, without pleats. More styles will use corduroy and velvet.

Watch for women's styles to look more "feminine" this year. Good-bye combat boots, hello spike heels, "wonderbras," and clingy dresses. Not everyone will be wearing the five-inch red patent-leather spikes featured in a recent *Vogue* spread (price: $455), but if you do opt for the spikes, Dr. Scholl's has come out with a "Toe Squish Preventer," a cushion to insert in the toe of the shoe.

Look for classic sweater sets, even for dressy events. Dresses are fitted in the bodice with a flared skirt (ending at the knee) and a slender belt cinching the waist (very fifties). Suit jackets will have a tight-waisted 1940s look.

Black is still the best bet, but some designers are showing wild colors such as cerise, mango, berry, and purple.

For casual wear, both men and women will be wearing **fewer western styles** (cowboy-boot sales have dropped 15 percent) and more woodsy "Oregon Logger" type gear. Those big clunky work boots and plaid shirts will be around for a while.

Dress-down backlash: Those casual Fridays have become so widespread that some employees, not wanting to conform, are wearing suits on those days, according to *The Wall Street Journal*.

A new fiber called Tencel, made from wood pulp, may eventually replace rayon. It looks and feels like silk, has the absorbency of cotton and the strength of polyester, and it's washable. Top designers such as **Armani** and **Versace** have already started using it.

THE DIFFERENCES Between Men and Women *in* 1996

WOMEN used to complain that their husbands just weren't listening to them. Now it appears that men just aren't *hearing*. The National Institute on Aging says that men experience "age-related hearing loss" earlier in life and at twice the rate that women do. Men start to lose hearing in their twenties; women in their thirties.

MEN are more apt to drive "well over" the speed limit than women. Ironically, men believe they are better drivers: Fifty percent of men surveyed said their own driving ability was "excellent," and 80 percent thought they drove "better than most" other drivers on the road. Only 34 percent of women thought they were excellent drivers, and 61 percent thought they drove better than others.

RESEARCHERS at the University of Illinois studied the daily emotional status of 110 husbands and wives, all employed and all with children. They found that the men were happier when they could stay at home with the kids, and the women were happier out on the job. Because men felt obliged to "bring home the bacon," they were happier when they could choose not to, just as women felt a freedom in the workplace.

(continued)

ADVERTISEMENT

Atlanta Housewife Investigated And Almost Arrested For Losing 73 Pounds

By Kathleen Ann Maldoney

Did you ever notice that when you're fat, people actually stare at you while you eat. It's as if they want to tap you on the shoulder and say, "If you wouldn't eat that stuff, you wouldn't be so fat!"

Hello. My name is Kate Maldoney. You don't know me from Adam. But I'm a real person. I live near Sandy Springs, Georgia. And, up until two years ago, I was the fat lady that everyone was staring at.

I was too tired to go out with my friends at night. I was even embarrassed to go out on weekends by myself. I waddled when I walked. I sweat when I ate. I wore anything loose that would hang straight down and wouldn't cling. I couldn't even cross my legs. I wasn't just "overweight." I was fat. I was 5'4" and weighed 202 pounds.

I went to my doctor for help. But I wasn't optimistic. During the past seven years I had tried 16 *different* diets. One by one. And I failed at all of them.

My doctor listened to me very carefully and then recommended an entirely different program. This wasn't a "diet." It was a unique new weight-loss program researched by a team of bariatric physicians — specialists who treat the severely obese. The program itself was developed by Dr. James Cooper of Atlanta, Georgia.

I started the program on May 17th. Within the first four days, I only lost three pounds. So I was disappointed. But during the three weeks that followed, my weight began to drop. Rapidly. Within the next 196 days, I went from 202 pounds to 129 pounds.

The reason the program worked was simple: I was *always* eating.

I could eat *six times every day*. So I never felt deprived. Never hungry. I could snack in the afternoon. Snack before dinner. I could even snack at night while I was watching TV.

How can you eat so much and still lose weight?

The secret is not in the amount of food you eat. It's in the *prescribed combination* of foods you eat in each 24-hour period. Nutritionally dense portions of special fiber, unrefined carbohydrates, and certain proteins that generate a calorie-burning process that continues all day long ... a complete 24-hour fat-reduction cycle.

Metabolism is evened out, so fat is burned away around the clock. Not just in unhealthy spurts while many diets. That's why it lets you shed pounds so easily. Without hunger. Without nervousness.

And it's all good wholesome food. No weird stuff. You'll enjoy a variety of meats, chicken, fish, vegetables, potatoes, pasta, sauces — plus your favorite snacks. Lots of snacks.

This new program must be the best kept secret in America. Because, up until now, it's *only been available to doctors*. No one else. In fact, the Clinic-30 Program has been used by 142 doctors in the U.S. and Canada to treat more than 9,820 patients. So it's doctor-tested. And proven. This is the first time it's been available to the public.

There are other benefits too ...

• There are no amphetamines. No drugs of any kind.

• No pills. No powders. No chalky-tasting drinks to mix. Everything's at your local supermarket. No special foods to buy.

• There's no strenuous exercise program.

• You don't count calories. Just follow the program. It's easy.

• It's low in sodium, so you don't hold water.

• You eat the foods you really enjoy. Great variety. Great taste.

• You can dine out.

• There's no ketosis. No bad breath odor.

But *here's* the best part ...

Once you lose the weight, you can keep it off. Permanently! Because you're not hungry all the time.

Let's face it. We all have "eating lifestyles." Our eating habits usually include three meals a day. Plus two or three snacks. We all love snacks. Especially at night.

But most diets force us to change all that.

And that's why they fail!

The Clinic-30 Program lets you *continue your normal eating lifestyle*. You can eat six times a day. You can snack when you wish. So, when you lose the weight, you can keep it off. For good. Because no one's forcing you to change.

Here are some other patients from Georgia who entered Dr. Cooper's Clinic-30 Program with me ...

• Reverend Donald F. is a 42-year-old minister who went from 227 to 179 in just four months.

"In spite of church suppers, I've lost almost 50 pounds in four months and I'm not having a rebound gain."

• Renate M. was a G.I. bride from Germany who went from 212 to 140.2 in 8½ months.

"I believe I was a participant in every weight-reducing plan there ever was. Then, about two years ago, I started the Clinic-30 Program. And I haven't regained a pound."

And then there's me. About 4 months ago I was stopped by a policeman for not using my turning signal. When he looked at my driver's license he claimed it wasn't mine. He said it had someone else's picture on it.

After he called for a computer check, he came back to the car smiling. "You must have lost a lot of weight. This picture doesn't even look like you." I agreed. In a way, it was one of the nicest "warnings" I'd ever received.

Obviously, I'm excited about the program. This is the first time it's been available outside of a clinical setting. Dr. Cooper has asked Green Tree Press, Inc. to distribute it.

We'll be happy to send you the program to examine for 31 days. Show it to your doctor. Try it. There's *no obligation*. In fact, your check won't be cashed for 31 days. You may even postdate it 31 days in advance if you wish.

Choose a day and start the program. If you don't begin losing weight within five days — and continue losing weight — we'll promptly return your *original uncashed check*. No delays. No excuses.

Or keep it longer. Try it for six months. Even then, if you're not continuing to lose weight on a regular basis, you'll receive a full refund. Promptly. And without question. This is the fairest way we know to prove to you how well this new program works.

To order, just send your name, address and postdated check for $12.95 (plus $3.00 shipping/handling) to The Clinic-30 Program, c/o Green Tree Press, Inc., Dept. 845, 3603 West 12th Street, Erie, PA 16505.

AN IMPORTANT REMINDER
As *your weight begins to drop, do not allow yourself to become too thin.*
It's also very important to consult your physician before commencing any weight-loss program. Show him this program. And be sure to see him periodically if you intend to take off large amounts of weight.

Green Tree Press is a member of the Erie, Pennsylvania Chamber of Commerce. Bank and business references are available upon request.

© 1995 Green Tree Press, Inc.

What's GOOD for You in 1996

Writing: When people who have undergone stressful events **write about the experience,** their immune cells increase, researchers tell us.

Music: Last year we wrote that listening to Mozart makes college students smarter. **Here's more good news:** Three-year-olds who were given weekly keyboard and daily singing lessons scored 47 percent better on "spatial" IQ tests than before their lessons.

Workers in stressful environments who listen to music improve their performance. A study done on 50 doctors showed that not only were they faster and more accurate at a set of math problems when music was playing, but they also performed even better when they selected the music themselves.

Hope: Middle-aged men who are hopeful about their futures and about achieving their goals are **far less likely to die** early than are equally healthy but less hopeful men. The men who are least hopeful, according to a study by the Human Population Laboratory in Berkeley, California, were almost twice as likely to die of heart attacks and also had a higher rate of accidental death.

Annual Olive Oil Award: It seems some new benefit of olive oil is discovered every year. Harvard University and University of Athens researchers have found that women who **consume olive oil** at more than one meal a day (such as the 2,400 Greek women studied) have 25 percent less chance of getting breast cancer. High consumption of vegetables and fruits also significantly lowers risk.

What's BAD for You

Tight Pants: A Stamford, Connecticut, physician has discovered what he's calling **"Tight Pants Syndrome"** in a patient (who shall be nameless) who insisted on wearing trousers three inches too small in the waist. Symptoms of TPS, in addition to derogatory remarks from a spouse and popping buttons, include bloating and chest pains.

Cultural BAROMETERS
⋅≼| 1996 |≽⋅

The Weirdness Index
■ The British *Fortean Times* (which specializes in chronicling strange events such as frog showers, spontaneous human combustions, and flying goats) reports that world weirdness was down two percent last year. (The previous year had seen a jump of 3.5 percent in overall strangeness.) Crop circles, water monsters, and both genius and stupidity were down. Reports of big cat sightings, new animal species, and cults were up; miracles, poltergeists, and prophecies were also on the rise. Hoaxes, panics, close encounters, and alien abductions held steady.

The Donkey Index
■ This informal gauge of holiday retail sales was up last year. By mid-December, glitzy retailer Neiman Marcus had sold six live donkeys (at $1,300 to $9,000 apiece) from its upscale Christmas catalog. They had also sold three $14,000 humidors (fancy cigar boxes) and three electric gondolas.

The False Teeth and Eyeballs Index
■ Hotel guests are showing an "alarming increase in forgetfulness," according to hoteliers. Not only are guests forgetting false teeth (the most commonly left-behind item in Hyatt Hotels worldwide), but they're also leaving shoes, rabbits in shoeboxes, contact lenses, and at the Hyatt Regency in Birmingham, England, a bag of glass eyeballs.

(continued)

DISCOVER AMERICA'S #1 "OFF-LAWN" MOWER!

Send for your FREE CATALOG on the amazing TROY-BILT® Sickle Bar Mower!

If you own an acre or more of property, the TROY-BILT® Sickle Bar Mower is the perfect "OFF-LAWN" Mower for cutting tall grass and weeds of any height — practically anywhere you can walk!

Now with power steering for greater maneuverability!

Comfortable, vibration-absorbing handlebars!

Powered wheels just roll over rugged terrain!

3 Models up to 5HP, 42" cut!

Mow Anything...Anywhere!
- **Clear overgrown areas** with far less effort.
- **Amazingly fast...** clears an acre in just 1 hour!
- **Cut your tallest weeds** — thorny brambles, sumac, goldenrod — even brush and saplings up to 1" thick.
- **Blaze trails** for walking, riding, skiing or snowmobiling!
- **Enjoy your property more** by making it useful & attractive!

BEFORE

Easily mow 2,800 square feet of tall weeds in less than 5 minutes with this amazing "Off-Lawn" Mower!

AFTER

For a FREE CATALOG, Call
1-800-221-2200 Dept. 4850
or send coupon today!

America's Backyard Legend

NEW!

Troy-Bilt Mfg. Dept. A4850   3 17
102nd St. & 9th Ave.
Troy, NY 12180
❏ **YES!** Please send me your FREE Catalog on how the TROY-BILT® Sickle Bar Mower can increase the beauty and value of my property. (For a free copy of the 7-Year Warranty, write to the address above.)

Name _____
Address _____
City _____
State _____ Zip _____

Product available in Canada!   ©1996 Garden Way Inc.

Why Didn't We Think of That BEFORE?

Fake Poop

How do diaper manufacturers test their products? They use such **stand-ins for the real thing** as mashed potatoes or canned pumpkin pie filling (the real thing being "objectionable" to researchers, biologically hazardous, and difficult to obtain). But the substitutes had problems, too. Eureka! Patent #5,356,626, granted to Kimberly-Clark, has solved the problem. The synthetic product is as close to the real thing as possible and smells like . . . nothing!

Antisnoring Device

Snorers' tongues flap back into their mouths, narrowing the breathing passageway and making that sound. A new pacifier-like object uses suction to **hold the tongue** in the front of mouth, keeping the snorer sleeping silently.

Breakfast Express

If you have not yet purchased an antisnoring device for your noisy spouse, you may feel awfully groggy when you wake up. Breakfast Express might help. **Set the timer** on this single appliance and it will brew coffee, make toast, and cook you two eggs, sunny-side up. Too bad it can't iron your trousers for you!

Trouser-Ironing Device

Take one pair of wet cotton trousers; hang them from a hanger. Put a plastic disk in the waist of the pants, close off the legs with clamps, and place a hair dryer in a hole in the disk. *Voilà!* Twenty minutes later: dried, **wrinkle-free pants**, courtesy of inventor John Dahman.

Talking Car Alarm

If you're walking through a parking lot, try not to violate "the personal space" of a car equipped with a new talking car alarm. Instead of those monotonous wails that everyone now ignores, these devices shout, **"YOU ARE TOO CLOSE TO THE VEHICLE; PLEASE MOVE AWAY!"** at 127 decibels (a typical jet plane at takeoff is 100 decibels). This *should* scare off car thieves or vandals. If it *doesn't* (and New York City police say hardened New Yorkers will just ignore it), then you can rely on the **"Smoke Defense Machine,"** which fills a car with smoke if it is broken into, rendering it impossible to drive.

Texas Two-Step Alarm

You've been trying to perfect your country-dancing form, but something just isn't clicking. **You need Les Burns's invention.** "It tells you whether your spins and pivots are vertical or whether you done blew it (at which point it will beep at you) and you're leaning hopelessly to one side or another," said Mr. Burns, who in addition to being in the country-dancing-alarm business is a private investigator.

Why Is Weather So Weird?

"The world is simply more erratic," says Elwynn Taylor, climatologist at Iowa State University, who has concluded that the variability of the world's weather from season to season is much greater now than 30 or 40 years ago.

(continued)

Poetry Contest
$24,000 in Prizes

The National Library of Poetry to award 250 total prizes in coming months

---

Owings Mills, Maryland – The National Library of Poetry has just announced that $24,000 in prizes will be awarded over the next 12 months in the North American Open Amateur Poetry Contest. The contest is open to everyone and entry is free.

"We're especially looking for poems from new or unpublished poets," indicated Howard Ely, spokesperson for The National Library of Poetry, "we have a ten year history of awarding large prizes to talented poets who have never before won any type of writing competition."

How To Enter
Anyone may enter the competition simply by sending in one original poem, any subject, any style to:

The National Library of Poetry
11419 Cronridge Drive
PO Box 704-6481
Owings Mills, MD 21117

The Coming of Dawn, featured above, is one of the National Library of Poetry's recent deluxe hardbound anthologies.

The poem should be no more than 20 lines, and the poet's name and address must appear on the top of the page. "Each poem received will be acknowledged, usually within seven weeks," indicated Mr. Ely.

Possible Publication
Many submitted poems will also be considered for inclusion in one of The National Library of Poetry's forthcoming hardbound anthologies. Anthologies published by the organization have included, *On the Threshold of a Dream*, *Days of Future's Past*, *Of Diamonds and Rust*, and *Moments More to Go*, among others.

Consumer Tastes & Trends for 1996

SOME MANNERS FOR 1996

INVITATIONS: It's OK to fax an invitation to a friend, if you've tried unsuccessfully to contact her by phone first, according to *The Amy Vanderbilt Complete Book of Etiquette* (rewritten for the nineties).

CELLULAR PHONES: It's still not OK to use a cell phone in a movie theater, at a table in a restaurant, or in a pew at church.

THE INTERNET has such a developed etiquette, it even has its own name — 'Netiquette. On-line manners seem to divide along gender lines. For instance, women will seldom "flame" (issue a statement designed to provoke or insult). But most 'Netiquette watchers agree that it is acceptable for all "Mouse Potatoes" (those, mostly men, who spend a lot of time on-line) to do so.

Agricultural News

Cotton on the New York Commodities Exchange reached $1.15 a pound recently, the highest price since the Civil War (when it hit $1.90). This will mean **high prices** on cotton clothing, probably by spring or summer of 1996. Fruit of the Loom (which produces 1.2 billion undergarments a year) says this means about a 25¢ increase on a $3 package of men's briefs.

Canadian geneticists have produced coho salmon that reach their normal adult weight of ten pounds in two years (it takes four years in the wild). **Fast-growing fish** will be a boon to aquaculturists. Taste tests are a couple of years away.

They don't look like cows, and they don't sound like cows or even walk like cows. But the American Ostrich Association says red meat from ostriches sure tastes like beef, and to top it off, it has **40 percent less fat.** There are already 3,500 ostrich ranchers in the U.S. Watch for feather boas to make a comeback.

The family farm: In the decade from 1992 to 2002, 500,000 older American farmers will leave the farm sector, to be replaced by only 250,000 new young farmers. In an effort to **keep the family farm alive,** many states have founded programs to match up retiring farmers with younger people wanting to get into farming but lacking the financial resources. In Iowa the program is called "Farm-On"; in Nebraska it's "Land-Link." The older farmer teaches the younger and may share in the profits.

DEMOGRAPHICA

Not Quite Over the Hill

■ These days, more people (16.7 million between 1994 and 1997) are **turning 40** than ever before, and middle age is becoming downright fashionable. Even teenagers now define "old" as being 50 for a man, 45 for a female (it used to be closer to 40 and 35).

Really Old

■ According to census figures, 37,300 Americans today are **over 100 years old,** and by the year 2040, there will be over one million centenarians. Look for a boom in retirement communities.

Not Just South of the Border

■ Though Florida still draws more retirees than any other state, **more folks are looking at college towns** like Oberlin, Ohio; Ithaca, New York; and Bloomington, Indiana. These communities offer cultural events, good health care, low crime, and an appealing mix of age groups. Today's senior citizens are also drawn to communities where outdoor activities are stressed, such as Guntersville, Alabama, and Catawba Island, Ohio. Another popular destination is Las Vegas, Nevada.

Consumer Tastes & Trends for 1996

HERE'S TO YOUR HEALTH 1996

Cast Off: A new "bone paste" called **Norian SRS** can be injected directly into broken bones. It hardens in ten minutes and becomes as strong as a real bone in 12 hours, so there's no need for a cast.

Gene guns are the newest weapon in the fight against cancer. The gun **inserts pure DNA** directly into cells in seconds. The DNA prods the cells to create a substance that provokes the body's immune system to attack the tumor.

A new study has suggested that high cholesterol doesn't pose an important risk for the healthy elderly. Dr. Harlan Krumholz of Yale School of Medicine thinks that people with relatively **high cholesterol** who survive into their late seventies without symptoms of heart disease may be resistant to cholesterol's effects.

Cow tongues contain a natural antibiotic (called peptides) that can **kill bacteria and viruses**. Researchers are hoping to find a way to use peptides to defeat viruses (such as herpes and HIV) that attack mucous membrane tissue.

The Planetree Movement, based on principles of compassion and family support, may be the biggest breakthrough in hospital care in ten years. In the two dozen or so Planetree centers in hospitals around the country, patients can **walk through atriums** and listen to live musical performances. Just as important, too, is the **open communication** between patients and caregivers. Results? Patients are happier (which usually means healthier) with their stays in these alternative units.

So Long, Farewell, Adios

PENNIES: Tim Jones, a "Garbologist" at the University of Arizona, thinks that about seven million pennies a day get thrown away, and most of the rest of the three billion dollars' worth of the cents in circulation are "in curation" (meaning they're being stored in jars). It won't be long, say the folks at the Coin Coalition in Washington, until pennies are a thing of the past.

THE LOCH NESS MONSTER: In 1934, Robert Wilson took the famous photograph of the long-necked serpent, while his mate shouted, "My God, it's the monster!" Well, the last of the group of hoaxers told the truth on his deathbed: He built a foot-high model, put it on a toy submarine, and took it to Scotland to be photographed. Alas.

GARBAGE: With all the composting and recycling, some people are producing no garbage at all.

COMING HOME TO A COLD, DARK HOUSE: Now you can call your house on the way home and, via phone, turn up the heat, turn on the lights, maybe tune in a little soft music. Pick up a pizza on the way, and you can settle right in. Now that's the kind of high tech we like.

How to Use This Almanac
Anywhere in the U.S.A.

Annually, for the interest and pleasure of our readers, *The Old Farmer's Almanac* provides a variety of astronomical data calculated for the upcoming year. The data cover a wide range of phenomena — the rising and setting times of the Sun and Moon; the declination of the Sun; the astronomical age and placement of the Moon and its monthly phases; the rising and setting times of the visible planets; solar and lunar eclipses; dates and times of meteor showers; rising and setting times of the bright stars; and a monthly summary of astronomical highlights.

The Left-Hand Calendar Pages
(Pages 52-78)

Much of the data is contained in the Left-Hand Calendar Pages (pages 52-78). For the enlightenment of our readers, part of a sample page is reproduced below, with an explanatory text summarizing the individual entries.

☞ **Please note** that all the times given in this edition of the Almanac are calculated for **Boston, Massachusetts.** However, Key Letters accompany much of the data. They are provided so that readers may correct the Boston times to those of their own localities. Several examples are given below to clarify this procedure. (**Eastern Standard Time is used throughout the Almanac.** One hour should be added for Daylight Saving Time between April 7 and October 27.)

Sample Left-Hand Calendar Page
(from November 1995 — page 52)

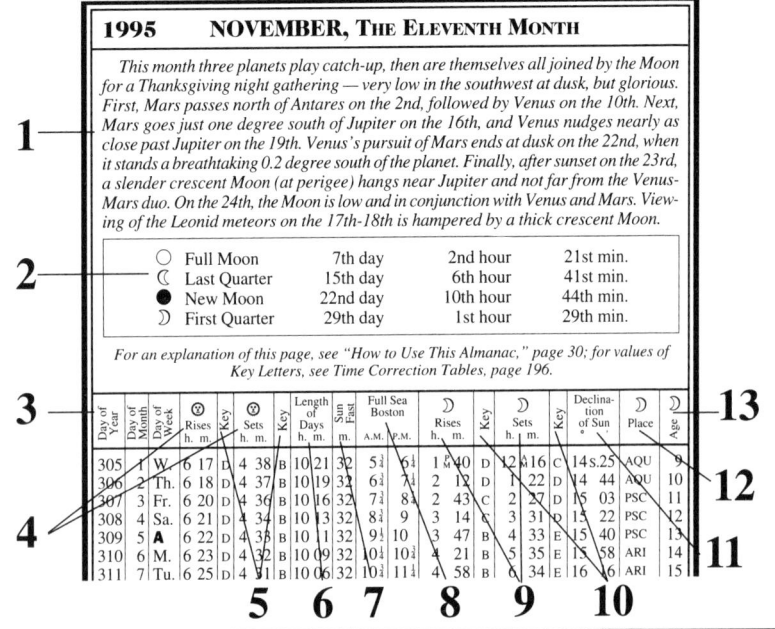

1. The text heading the calendar page is a summary of the sky sightings for the month. These astronomical highlights appear on each month's calendar page.

2. The dates and times of the Moon's phases for the month. (For more details, see Glossary, page 38.)

3. The days of the year, month, and week are listed on each calendar page. The traditional ecclesiastical calendar designation for Sunday — the Dominical Letter — A for 1995, G/F for 1996 — is used by the Almanac. (For further explanation, see Glossary, page 38.)

4. Sunrise and sunset times (EST) for Boston for each day of the month.

5. Key Letter columns. The letters in the two columns marked "Key" are designed to correct the sunrise/sunset times given for Boston to other localities. Note that each sunrise/sunset time has its Key Letter. The values (that is, the number of minutes) of these Key Letters are given in the **Time Correction Tables**, page 196. Simply find your city, or the city nearest you, in the tables, and locate the figure in the appropriate Key Letter column. Add, or subtract, those minutes to the sunrise or sunset time given for Boston. (Because of the complexities of calculation for different locations, times may not be precise to the minute.)

Example:

To find the time of sunrise in Cincinnati, Ohio, on November 1, 1995:

Sunrise, Boston, with Key Letter D (p. 30)	6:17 A.M., EST
Value of Key Letter D for Cincinnati (p. 197)	+ 48 minutes
Sunrise, Cincinnati	7:05 A.M., EST

Use the same process for sunset. (Add one hour for Daylight Saving Time between April 7 and October 27.)

6. Length of Days. This column denotes how long the Sun will be above the horizon in Boston for each day of the month. To determine the length of any given day in your locality, follow the procedure outlined in #5 above to determine the sunrise and sunset times for your city. Then, add 12 hours to the time of sunset, subtract the time of sunrise, and you will have the length of day.

Example:

Sunset, Peoria, Illinois, Nov. 1	4:54
Add 12 hours	+ 12:00
	16:54
Subtract sunrise, Peoria, Nov. 1	− 6:28
Length of day, Peoria, Nov. 1 (10 hrs., 26 min.)	10:26

– Beth Krommes

7. The Sun Fast column is designed to change sundial time into clock time in Boston. A sundial reads natural, or Sun, time, which is neither Standard nor Daylight time except by coincidence. Simply *subtract* the minutes given in the Sun Fast column to get Boston clock time, and use Key Letter C in the Time Correction Tables (page 196) to correct the time for your city. (Add one hour for Daylight Saving Time between April 7 and October 27.)

Example:

To change sundial time into clock time in Atlanta, Georgia, on November 1, 1995:

Sundial reading, Nov. 1	12:00
Subtract Sun Fast (p. 30)	− 32 minutes
Clock time, Boston	11:28 A.M., EST
Use Key C for Atlanta (page 196)	+ 53 minutes
Clock time, Atlanta	12:21 P.M., EST

8. The times of daily high tides in Boston, for morning and evening, are recorded in this column. ("5¾" under "Full Sea Boston, A.M." on November 1 means that the high tide that morning will be at 5:45 — with the number of feet of high tide shown for some of the dates on the Right-Hand Calendar Pages. Where a dash is shown under Full Sea, it indicates that time of high water has occurred on or after midnight, and so is recorded on the next date.) Tide corrections for some localities can be found in the **Tide Correction Tables** on page 202.

9. Moonrise and moonset times (EST) for Boston for each day of the month. (Dashes indicate that moonrise or moonset has occurred on or after midnight and so is recorded on the next date.)

10. Key Letter columns. These columns designate the letters to be used to correct the moonrise/moonset times for Boston to other localities. As explained in #5, the same procedure for calculating "Sunrise/sunset" is used *except* that an additional correction factor based on longitude (see table below) should be used. For the longitude of your city, consult the Time Correction Tables, page 196.

Longitude of city	Correction minutes
58°- 76°	0
77°- 89°	+1
90°-102°	+2
103°-115°	+3
116°-127°	+4
128°-141°	+5
142°-155°	+6

Example:

To determine the time of moonrise in Little Rock, Arkansas, on November 7, 1995:

Moonrise, Boston, with Key Letter B (page 30)	4:58 P.M., EST
Value of Key Letter B for Little Rock (page 198)	+ 35 minutes
Correction for Little Rock longitude 92° 17'	+ 2 minutes
Moonrise, Little Rock	5:35 P.M., CST

Use the same procedure for moonset. (Add one hour for Daylight Saving Time between April 7 and October 27.)

11. This column denotes the declination of the Sun (angular distance from the celestial equator) in degrees and minutes, at *noon,* EST.

12. The Moon's Place denoted in this column is its *astronomical* place, i.e., its *actual* placement, in the heavens. (This should not be confused with the Moon's *astrological* place in the zodiac, as explained on page 184.) *All* **calculations in this Almanac, except for the astrological information on pages 184-187, are based on astronomy, not astrology.**

In addition to the 12 constellations of the astronomical zodiac, five other abbreviations appear in this column: Auriga (AUR), a northern constellation between Perseus and Gemini; Cetus (CET), which lies south of the zodiac, just south of Pisces and Aries; Ophiuchus (OPH), a constellation primarily north of the zodiac, but with a small corner between Scorpius and Sagittarius; Orion (ORI), a constellation whose northern limit first reaches the zodiac between Taurus and Gemini; Sextans (SEX), which lies south of the zodiac except for a corner that just touches it near Leo.

13. The last column lists the Moon's age, i.e., the number of days since the previous new Moon. (The lunar month is 29.53 days.)

Further astronomical data may be found on page 42, which lists the eclipses for the upcoming year, the principal meteor showers, and dates of the full Moon over a five-year period.

The Visible Planets (page 40) lists the rising and setting times for Venus, Mars, Jupiter, and Saturn for 1996; page 44 carries the rising and setting and transit times of the Bright Stars for 1996. Both feature Key Letters, designed to convert the Boston times given to those of other localities (see #5 and #10 above).

Also, on page 201, can be found "The Twilight Zone," a chart that enables you to calculate the length of time of dawn and dark in your area.

THE RIGHT-HAND CALENDAR PAGES
(Pages 53-79)

These pages are a combination of astronomical data; specific dates in mainly the Anglican church calendar, inclusion of which has always been traditional in American and English almanacs (though we also include some other religious dates); tide heights at Boston (the Left-Hand Calendar Pages include the daily times of high tides; the corrections for your locality are on page 202); quotations; anniversary dates; appropriate seasonal activities; and a rhyming version of the weather forecasts for New England. (Detailed forecasts for the entire country are presented on pages 118-147.)

The following details some of the entries from the Right-Hand Calendar Pages, together with a sample (the first part of November 1995) of a calendar page explained. Also, following the Almanac's tradition, the Chronological Cycles and Eras for 1996 are listed.

MOVABLE FEASTS AND FASTS FOR 1996
Septuagesima Sunday .... Feb. 4
Shrove Tuesday .... Feb. 20
Ash Wednesday .... Feb. 21
Palm Sunday .... Mar. 31
Good Friday .... Apr. 5
Easter Day .... Apr. 7
Rogation Sunday .... May 12
Ascension Day .... May 16
Whit Sunday-Pentecost .... May 26
Trinity Sunday .... June 2
Corpus Christi .... June 6
1st Sunday in Advent .... Dec. 1

THE SEASONS OF 1995-1996
Fall 1995 .... Sept. 23, 7:13 A.M., EST
Winter 1995 ..... Dec. 22, 3:17 A.M., EST
Spring 1996 ..... Mar. 20, 3:03 A.M., EST
Summer 1996 ... June 20, 9:24 P.M., EST
Fall 1996 .... Sept. 22, 1:00 P.M., EST
Winter 1996 ..... Dec. 21, 9:06 A.M., EST

CHRONOLOGICAL CYCLES FOR 1996
Golden Number (Lunar Cycle) 2
Epact 10
Solar Cycle.. 17
Dominical Letter .... G/F
Roman Indiction 4
Year of Julian Period 6709

Era	Year	Begins
Byzantine	7505	Sept. 14
Jewish (A.M.)*	5757	Sept. 13
Roman (A.U.C.)	2749	Jan. 14
Nabonassar	2745	Apr. 24
Japanese	2656	Jan. 1
Grecian (Seleucidae)	2308	Sept. 14 (or Oct. 14)
Indian (Saka)	1918	Mar. 21
Diocletian	1713	Sept. 11
Islamic (Hegira)*	1417	May 18
Chinese (Lunar) (Rat)	4694	Feb. 19

*Year begins at sunset

DETERMINATION OF EARTHQUAKES
☞ Note, on right-hand pages 53-79, the dates when the Moon (☾) "rides high" or "runs low." The date of the high begins the most likely five-day period of earthquakes in the Northern Hemisphere; the date of the low indicates a similar five-day period in the Southern Hemisphere. You will also find on these pages a notation for Moon on the Equator (☾ on Eq.) twice each month. At this time, in both hemispheres, is a two-day earthquake period.

NAMES AND CHARACTERS OF THE PRINCIPAL PLANETS AND ASPECTS

☞ Every now and again on these Right-Hand Calendar Pages, you will see symbols conjoined in groups to tell you what is happening in the heavens. For example, ♂♄☽ opposite November 2, 1995, (see below) means that Saturn ♄ and the Moon ☽ are on that date in conjunction ♂ or apparently near each other.

— Beth Krommes

Here are the symbols used ...

☉	Sun	♂	Mars
○●☽	Moon	♇	Pluto
☿	Mercury	♃	Jupiter
♄	Saturn	♂	Conjunction, or in the same degree
♀	Venus		
⛢	Uranus	☊	Ascending Node
⊕	Earth	☋	Descending Node
♆	Neptune	☍	Opposition, or 180 degrees

EARTH AT APHELION AND PERIHELION 1996

☞ The Earth will be at Perihelion on January 4, 1996, when it will be 91,400,005 miles from the Sun. The Earth will be at Aphelion on July 5, 1996, when it will be 94,512,258 miles from the Sun.

SAMPLE RIGHT-HAND CALENDAR PAGE
(from November 1995 — page 53)

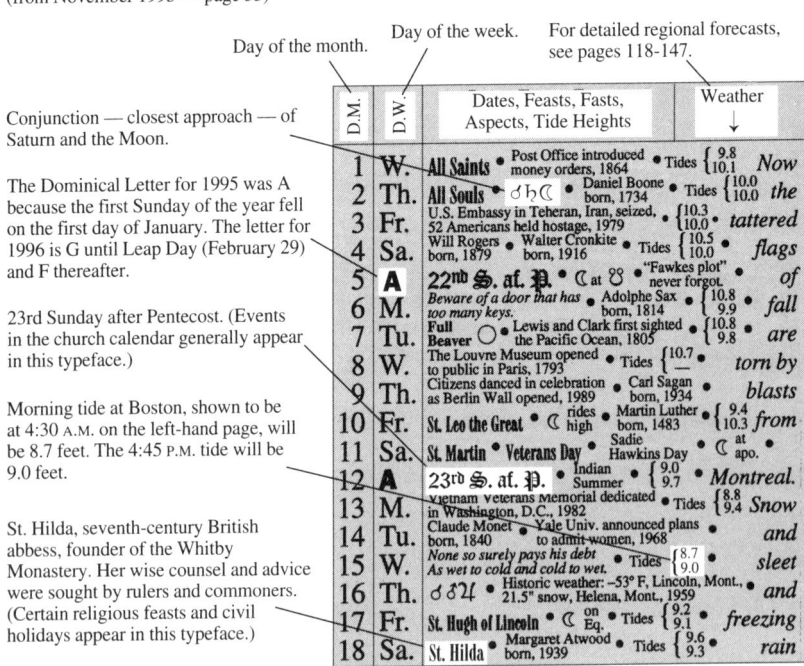

Day of the month. Day of the week. For detailed regional forecasts, see pages 118-147.

Conjunction — closest approach — of Saturn and the Moon.

The Dominical Letter for 1995 was A because the first Sunday of the year fell on the first day of January. The letter for 1996 is G until Leap Day (February 29) and F thereafter.

23rd Sunday after Pentecost. (Events in the church calendar generally appear in this typeface.)

Morning tide at Boston, shown to be at 4:30 A.M. on the left-hand page, will be 8.7 feet. The 4:45 P.M. tide will be 9.0 feet.

St. Hilda, seventh-century British abbess, founder of the Whitby Monastery. Her wise counsel and advice were sought by rulers and commoners. (Certain religious feasts and civil holidays appear in this typeface.)

For a more complete explanation of terms used throughout the Almanac, see Glossary, page 38.

ESSIAC®

The Resperin Corporation

The Original Rene Caisse

Health Enhancing Herbal Remedy

Acclaimed Since 1922

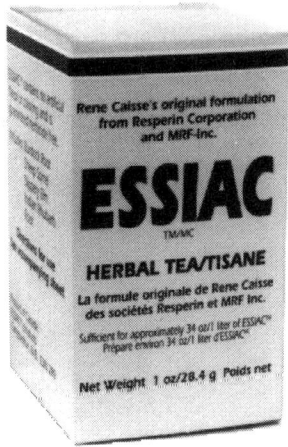

BEWARE OF COUNTERFEITS

- Non-Toxic
- Drug Free
- Detoxifies Body
- Cleanses Blood
- Effective Immune System Modulator

for Information:
Tel: 613-820-9311
Fax: 613-820-8455

Authorized by

Rene M. Caisse
1888–1978

ESSIAC® International
OTTAWA, ONT, CANADA

SUFFERING FROM
COLD SORES?
HAY FEVER?
SINUSITIS?
SKIN IRRITATION?

RELIEF CAN BE YOURS WITH

SINCE 1906

BOROLEUM®

IT WORKS and it's mild!

SINCLAIR PHARMACAL CO., INC.
Fishers Island, N.Y. 06390

If not available at your Pharmacy, call us directly, or send for:
2 Tubes - $8.00; 6 Tubes - $22.00
Send $1.00 for Postage & Handling.   Tel. 1-516-788-7210

THE CARROUSEL

What a delight to our senses.... and we've captured it's special sound on this beautiful "Collection Of Old-Time Favorite Songs", (marches, waltzes etc.) - Authentic Wurlitzer Merry-Go-Round Organ. 1 hour CD $14.95, or cassette $9.95.; add $1 shipping to **CARROUSEL MUSIC, BOX 231, DEPT F, CHAMBERSBURG, PA 17201**
(717) 264-5800   Mastercard or VISA

HEARING AIDS
UP TO 60% SAVINGS

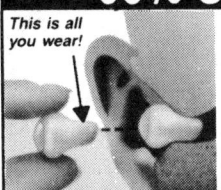

This is all you wear!

30-DAY TRIAL

TRY BEFORE YOU BUY

GUARANTEED LOWEST PRICES!
- ALL MAKES & MODELS   • TERMS ARRANGED
- 30 YRS. EXPERIENCE   • ALL MAKE REPAIRS
- CUSTOM INSTRUMENT SPECIALISTS •

FOR FREE INFORMATION CALL:

1-800-323-1212

We're the oldest, biggest and best

LLOYDS, DEPT. OF, BOX 1645, ROCKFORD, IL 61110

HOLIDAYS AND OBSERVANCES, 1996

(*) Recommended as holidays with pay for all employees
(**) State observances only

Jan. 1 (*) New Year's Day
Jan. 15 (*) Martin Luther King Jr.'s Birthday *(observed)*
Jan. 19 (**) Robert E. Lee's Birthday *(Ark., Fla., Ga., La., S.C., Tenn., Tex.)*
Feb. 2 Groundhog Day
Feb. 12 (**) Abraham Lincoln's Birthday
Feb. 14 Valentine's Day
Feb. 19 (*) Presidents Day
Feb. 20 (**) Mardi Gras *(Ala., La.)*
Feb. 22 George Washington's Birthday
Mar. 2 (**) Texas Independence Day
Mar. 15 (**) Andrew Jackson Day *(Tenn.)*
Mar. 17 (**) St. Patrick's Day; Evacuation Day *(Boston and Suffolk Co., Mass.)*
Apr. 2 (**) Pascua Florida Day
Apr. 13 (**) Thomas Jefferson's Birthday *(Ala., Okla.)*
Apr. 15 (**) Patriots Day *(Me., Mass.)*
Apr. 26 Arbor Day *(except Alaska, Ga., Kans., Va., Wyo.)*
May 1 May Day
May 8 (**) Truman Day *(Mo.)*
May 12 Mother's Day
May 18 Armed Forces Day
May 20 Victoria Day *(Canada)*
May 27 (*) Memorial Day *(observed)*
June 5 World Environment Day
June 11 (**) King Kamehameha I Day *(Hawaii)*
June 14 Flag Day
June 16 Father's Day
June 17 (**) Bunker Hill Day *(Boston and Suffolk Co., Mass.)*
June 20 (**) West Virginia Day
July 1 Canada Day
July 4 (*) Independence Day
July 24 (**) Pioneer Day *(Utah)*
Aug. 12 (**) Victory Day *(R.I.)*
Aug. 16 (**) Bennington Battle Day *(Vt.)*
Aug. 26 Women's Equality Day
Sept. 2 (*) Labor Day
Sept. 9 (**) Admission Day *(Calif.)*
Sept. 12 (**) Defenders Day *(Md.)*
Oct. 9 Leif Eriksson Day
Oct. 14 (*) Columbus Day *(observed)*; Thanksgiving *(Canada)*; (**) Native Americans Day *(S. Dak.)*
Oct. 18 (**) Alaska Day
Oct. 31 Halloween; (**) Nevada Day
Nov. 4 (**) Will Rogers Day *(Okla.)*
Nov. 5 Election Day
Nov. 11 (*) Veterans Day
Nov. 19 (**) Discovery Day *(Puerto Rico)*
Nov. 24 (**) John F. Kennedy Day *(Mass.)*
Nov. 28 (*) Thanksgiving Day
Dec. 10 (**) Wyoming Day
Dec. 25 (*) Christmas Day
Dec. 26 Boxing Day *(Canada)*

RELIGIOUS OBSERVANCES

Epiphany .... Jan. 6
First Day of Ramadan .... Jan. 22
Ash Wednesday .... Feb. 21
Palm Sunday .... Mar. 31
First Day of Passover .... Apr. 4
Good Friday .... Apr. 5
Easter Day .... Apr. 7
Orthodox Easter .... Apr. 14
Islamic New Year .... May 19
Whit Sunday-Pentecost .... May 26
Rosh Hashanah .... Sept. 14
Yom Kippur .... Sept. 23
First Day of Chanukah .... Dec. 6
Christmas Day .... Dec. 25

HOW THE ALMANAC WEATHER FORECASTS ARE MADE

Our weather forecasts are determined by the use of a secret formula devised by the founder of this Almanac in 1792, enhanced by the most modern scientific calculations based on solar activity. We believe nothing in the universe occurs haphazardly; there is a cause-and-effect pattern to all phenomena, including weather. It follows, therefore, that we believe the weather is predictable. It is obvious, however, that neither we nor anyone else has as yet gained sufficient insight into the mysteries of the universe to predict weather with anything resembling total accuracy.

The Cook's Garden

Seeds & Supplies for the New American Kitchen Garden

The ultimate resource for kitchen gardeners, our expanded 112 page catalog features heirloom and speciality vegetables, salad greens, sunflowers, edible and fragrant flowers as well as climbers and everlastings. You can depend on our seeds to perform. We also carry a broad line of books, equipment and supplies for the kitchen gardener, including hard-to-find items for environment conscious organic gardeners. Send for your FREE Spring 1996 catalog today!

The Cook's Garden

Post Office Box 535   Londonderry, Vermont 05148

☑ A FREE Catalog is in the mail to:

Please Print: HZ160

Name _____

Address _____ Apmt. _____

City _____

State _____ Zip _____

GLOSSARY

Aph. – Aphelion: Planet reaches point in its orbit farthest from the Sun.
Apo. – Apogee: Moon reaches point in its orbit farthest from the Earth.
Celestial Equator: The plane of the Earth's equator projected out into space.
Conj. – Conjunction: Time of apparent closest approach to each other of any two heavenly bodies. **Inf. – Inferior:** Conjunction in which the planet is between the Sun and the Earth. **Sup. – Superior:** Indicates that the Sun is between the planet and the Earth.
Declination: Measurement of angular distance of celestial object perpendicularly north or south of celestial equator. The Almanac gives the Sun's declination at noon EST.
Dominical Letter: Used for the ecclesiastical calendar and determined by the date on which the first Sunday of the year falls. If Jan. 1 is a Sunday, the Letter is A; if Jan. 2 is a Sunday, the Letter is B; and so on to G. In leap year the Letter applies through February and then takes the Letter before.
Eclipse, Lunar: Occurs when the Moon, at full phase, enters the shadow of the Earth. There are three kinds: **Total:** The Moon passes completely into the umbra (central dark part) of the Earth's shadow. **Partial:** Only part of the Moon passes through the umbra. **Penumbral:** The moon passes through only the penumbra (an area of partial darkness which surrounds the umbra).
Eclipse, Solar: Occurs when the Moon passes between the Earth and the Sun, and all three bodies are aligned in the same plane. **Annular:** The Moon appears silhouetted against the Sun, with a ring of sunlight showing around it.
Epact: A number from 1 to 30 to harmonize the lunar year with the solar year; used for the ecclesiastical calendar.
Eq. – Equator: A great circle of the Earth equidistant from the two poles.
Equinox, Autumnal: Sun passes from Northern to Southern Hemisphere. **Vernal:** Sun passes from Southern to Northern Hemisphere.
Evening Star: A planet that is above the horizon at sunset and less than 180 degrees east of the Sun.
Golden Number: The year in the 19-year cycle of the Moon. The Moon phases occur on the same dates every 19 years.

Greatest Elongation (Gr. El.): Greatest apparent angular distance of a planet from the Sun as seen from the Earth.
Moon Rides High or Runs Low: Day of month Moon is highest or lowest above the south point of the observer's horizon.
Moon's Age: The number of days since the previous new Moon.
Moon's Phases: First Quarter: Right half of Moon illuminated. **Full Moon:** Moon reaches opposition. **Last Quarter:** Left half of Moon illuminated. **New Moon:** Sun and Moon in conjunction.
Morning Star: A planet that is above the horizon at sunrise and less than 180 degrees west of the Sun in right ascension.
Node: Either of the two points where the Moon's orbit intersects the ecliptic.
Occn. – Occultation: Eclipse of a star or planet by the Moon or another planet.
Opposition: Time when the Sun and Moon or planet appear on opposite sides of the sky (el. 180 degrees).
Perig. – Perigee: Moon reaches point in its orbit closest to the Earth.
Perih. – Perihelion: Planet reaches point in its orbit closest to the Sun.
Roman Indiction: A cycle of 15 years established Jan. 1, A.D. 313, as a fiscal term. Add 3 to the number of years in the Christian era and divide by 15. The remainder is Roman Indiction – no remainder is 15.
Solar Cycle: A period of 28 years, at the end of which the days of the month return to the same days of the week.
Solstice, Summer: Point at which the Sun is farthest north of the celestial equator. **Winter:** Point at which the Sun is farthest south of the celestial equator.
Stat. – Stationary: Halt in the apparent movement of a planet against the background of the stars just before the planet comes to opposition.
Sun Fast: The column in the Left-Hand Calendar Pages designed to change sundial time into clock time.
Sunrise & Sunset: Visible rising and setting of the Sun's upper limb across the unobstructed horizon of an observer whose eyes are 15 feet above ground level.
Twilight: Begins or ends when stars of the sixth magnitude appear or disappear at the zenith; or when the Sun is about 18 degrees below the horizon.

CAN'T SLEEP?
TRY
DORMIN
THE NIGHTTIME SLEEP-AID

FAST
SAFE
EFFECTIVE
MONEY BACK
GUARANTEE

The original non-prescription sleep-aid. Quality and value since 1952.

IF NOT AVAILABLE AT YOUR PHARMACY
SEND $5.00 for 32 SIZE (+50¢ Postage, Handling)
TO: RANDOB LABS
P.O. Box 440
Cornwall, NY 12518

TAKE DORMIN and SLEEP TONIGHT...

KEEP THE BUGS AWAY!
with the GENUINE Bug Baffler®

GET COMPLETE UPPER BODY / HEAD PROTECTION

- durable 100% nylon screening - Olive Green
- generously sized, lightweight, chemical-free

SHIRT with attached Headnet
Sizes: S/M, L/XL $34.50
XXL + (235 lb. + up) $39.50

Money-Back Guarantee!

To get yours FASTER use MC or VISA
Call 1-800-662-8411
OR Send check or money order to: **Bug Baffler**
P.O. Box 444, Goffstown, NH 03045

Add $4.50 S/H per order
Order Code: FA

CHOIR ROBES
EXPERT TAILORING $26⁹⁵ UP

Finest Fabrics including Permanent Press and Wash & Wear. Superior Quality. Free Color Catalog and Fabric Swatches on Request. *Guaranteed Satisfaction.*

Toll Free 1-800-826-8612

REGENCY
CAP & GOWN CO
P.O. Box 8988-FM
Jacksonville, Florida 32211

Own A Wood-Mizer® PORTABLE SAWMILL

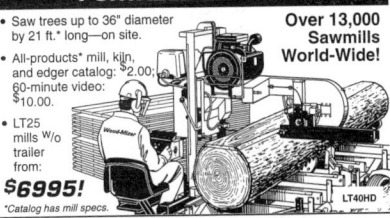

- Saw trees up to 36" diameter by 21 ft.* long—on site.
- All-products* mill, kiln, and edger catalog: $2.00; 60-minute video: $10.00.
- LT25 mills w/o trailer from: **$6995!**

*Catalog has mill specs.

Over 13,000 Sawmills World-Wide!

LT40HD

1-800-553-0219
Wood-Mizer Products, Inc.
8180 West 10th Street Dept. BH9
Indianapolis, IN 46214-2400

Do You Need Pea and Bean Shelling Equipment?

Whether you're a small gardener or a professional grower, the famous "Little Sheller" or one of our commercial hullers will take the work out of your pea and bean shelling. These machines are efficient, smooth running, and easy to operate.

FOR FREE BROCHURE WRITE:

TAYLOR MANUFACTURING CO., INC. OFA 96
P.O. BOX 625-MOULTRIE, GEORGIA 31776-0625 (912) 985-5445

Home of the "Little Sheller" for over 34 years

THE VISIBLE PLANETS, 1996

The times of rising or setting of the planets Venus, Mars, Jupiter, and Saturn on the 1st, 11th, and 21st of each month are given below. The approximate time of rising or setting of these planets on other days may be found with sufficient accuracy by interpolation. For an explanation of Key Letters (used in adjusting the times given here for Boston to the time in your town), see page 30 and pages 196-200. Key Letters appear as capital letters beside the time of rising or setting. (For definitions of morning and evening stars, see page 38.)

VENUS is a brilliant object in the evening sky from the beginning of the year until midway through the first week of June, when it becomes too close to the Sun for observation. During the middle of June it reappears in the morning sky, where it stays until the end of the year. Venus is in conjunction with Saturn on February 2, with Mercury on June 23, and with Mars on June 29 and September 4.

MARS is too close to the Sun for observation until mid-May, when it appears in the morning sky. Its westward elongation gradually increases, moving from Aries into Taurus in early June and into Gemini in late July. It then continues through Cancer, Leo, and into Virgo, where, after mid-December, it can be seen for more than half the night. Mars is in conjunction with Mercury on May 31 and June 14 and with Venus on June 29 and September 4.

Boldface — P.M.   Lightface — A.M.

Jan. 1 ...... set **7:00** A	July 1 ...... rise 2:36 A	Jan. 1 ...... set **5:25** A	July 1 ...... rise 2:20 A
Jan. 11 .... " **7:26** B	July 11 .... " 2:05 A	Jan. 11 .... " **5:25** A	July 11 .... " 2:07 A
Jan. 21 .... " **7:50** B	July 21 .... " 1:43 A	Jan. 21 .... " **5:27** A	July 21 .... " 1:55 A
Feb. 1...... " **8:16** B	Aug. 1...... " 1:27 A	Feb. 1...... " **5:29** B	Aug. 1...... " 1:44 A
Feb. 11.... " **8:39** C	Aug. 11... " 1:19 A	Feb. 11.... " **5:31** B	Aug. 11... " 1:35 A
Feb. 21.... " **9:00** D	Aug. 21... " 1:19 A	Feb. 21.... " **5:32** B	Aug. 21... " 1:26 A
Mar. 1...... " **9:20** D	Sept. 1...... " 1:25 A	Mar. 1...... " **5:34** B	Sept. 1...... " 1:18 A
Mar. 11.... " **9:40** D	Sept. 11... " 1:36 A	Mar. 11 ... rise 6:05 C	Sept. 11... " 1:10 A
Mar. 21.... " **9:59** E	Sept. 21... " 1:50 B	Mar. 21.... " 5:43 C	Sept. 21... " 1:02 A
Apr. 1...... " **10:18** E	Oct. 1 ...... " 2:08 B	Apr. 1...... " 5:18 C	Oct. 1 ...... " 12:54 A
Apr. 11.... " **10:30** E	Oct. 11 .... " 2:28 B	Apr. 11.... " 4:56 B	Oct. 11 .... " 12:46 A
Apr. 21.... " **10:34** E	Oct. 21 .... " 2:48 B	Apr. 21.... " 4:33 B	Oct. 21 .... " 12:37 B
May 1 ...... " **10:28** E	Nov. 1 ...... " 3:12 C	May 1 ...... " 4:12 B	Nov. 1 ...... " 12:25 B
May 11 .... " **10:08** E	Nov. 11... " 3:35 C	May 11 .... " 3:51 B	Nov. 11 .... " 12:14 B
May 21 .... " **9:29** E	Nov. 21... " 3:58 D	May 21 .... " 3:30 B	Nov. 21 .... " 12:01 B
June 1 ...... " **8:22** E	Dec. 1 ...... " 4:22 D	June 1 ...... " 3:09 A	Dec. 1 .... rise **11:45** A
June 11 ... rise 4:07 A	Dec. 11 ... " 4:47 D	June 11 ... " 2:51 A	Dec. 11 .... " **11:29** A
June 21 ... rise 3:18 A	Dec. 21 ... " 5:11 E	June 21 ... rise 2:35 A	Dec. 21 .... " **11:10** A
	Dec. 31 ... rise 5:34 E		Dec. 31 .. rise **10:49** B

JUPITER rises just before sunrise in Sagittarius, in which constellation it remains throughout the year. Its westward elongation gradually increases, and from the second week of April it can be seen for more than half the night. It is at opposition on July 4, when it is visible throughout the night. Its eastward elongation then decreases, and from the beginning of October until the end of the year, it can be seen only in the evening sky.

SATURN can be seen in the evening sky in Aquarius until late February, when it becomes too close to the Sun for observation. In early April it reappears in the morning sky in Pisces. It passes into Cetus in early June and again into Pisces in early September, where it remains for the rest of the year. On September 26 it is at opposition and visible throughout the night. Its eastward elongation then decreases until, in the second half of December, it can be seen only in the evening sky. Saturn is in conjunction with Venus on February 2.

Boldface — P.M.	Lightface — A.M.		Boldface — P.M.	Lightface — A.M.
Jan. 1 ...... rise 6:29 E	July 1 ...... rise 7:26 E	Jan. 1 ...... set 10:05 B	July 1 ...... rise 11:31 C
Jan. 11 ... " 5:59 E	July 11 ... set 3:50 A	Jan. 11 ... " 9:30 B	July 11 ... " 10:53 C
Jan. 21 ... " 5:29 E	July 21 ... " 3:05 A	Jan. 21 ... " 8:55 B	July 21 ... " 10:14 C
Feb. 1...... " 4:56 E	Aug. 1..... " 2:16 A	Feb. 1...... " 8:17 B	Aug. 1..... " 9:30 C
Feb. 11 .... " 4:25 E	Aug. 11 ... " 1:33 A	Feb. 11.... " 7:44 B	Aug. 11... " 8:50 C
Feb. 21.... " 3:53 E	Aug. 21... " 12:51 A	Feb. 21.... " 7:10 B	Aug. 21... " 8:10 C
Mar. 1..... " 3:24 E	Sept. 1..... " 12:06 A	Mar. 1..... " 6:40 B	Sept. 1..... " 7:26 C
Mar. 11 ... " 2:51 E	Sept. 11... set 11:23 A	Mar. 11 ... " 6:07 C	Sept. 11... " 6:45 C
Mar. 21... " 2:16 E	Sept. 21... " 10:46 A	Mar. 21 ... rise 5:49 C	Sept. 21... " 5:59 C
Apr. 1...... " 1:38 E	Oct. 1 ..... " 10:10 A	Apr. 1...... " 5:09 C	Oct. 1 ...... set 5:19 C
Apr. 11..... " 1:02 E	Oct. 11..... " 9:35 A	Apr. 11..... " 4:33 C	Oct. 11 ..... " 4:36 C
Apr. 21 ... " 12:25 E	Oct. 21.... " 9:02 A	Apr. 21... " 3:56 C	Oct. 21.... " 3:53 C
May 1..... rise 11:43 E	Nov. 1..... " 8:26 A	May 1 ..... " 3:19 C	Nov. 1..... " 3:07 C
May 11 ... " 11:03 E	Nov. 11... " 7:55 A	May 11 ... " 2:42 C	Nov. 11... " 2:25 C
May 21 ... " 10:22 E	Nov. 21... " 7:25 A	May 21 ... " 2:05 C	Nov. 21... " 1:44 C
June 1 ..... " 9:37 E	Dec. 1 ..... " 6:55 A	June 1 ..... " 1:24 C	Dec. 1 ..... " 1:04 C
June 11 ... " 8:54 E	Dec. 11 ... " 6:26 A	June 11 ... " 12:46 C	Dec. 11 ... " 12:25 C
June 21... rise 8:10 E	Dec. 21.... " 5:58 A	June 21 ... rise 12:08 C	Dec. 21 ... set 11:43 C
	Dec. 31 ... set 5:30 A		Dec. 31 ... set 11:06 C

MERCURY can be seen only low in the east before sunrise or low in the west after sunset. It is visible mornings between these approximate dates: January 25-March 19, May 24-July 4, and September 25-October 20. The planet is brighter at the end of each period (best viewing conditions in northern latitudes occur from early to mid-October). It is visible evenings between these approximate dates: January 1-13, April 6-May 5, July 19-September 11, and November 19-December 27. The planet is brighter at the beginning of each period (best viewing conditions in northern latitudes occur from mid-April to a few days before the end of that month).

DO NOT CONFUSE 1) Venus with Saturn from late January to early February, with Mars from late June to early July and late August to mid-September, and with Mercury the fourth week of June; Venus is always the brighter object. 2) Mercury with Mars in the last week of May to the end of the third week of June; Mercury is the brighter object except for the last week of May. 3) Jupiter with Mercury around mid-December when Jupiter is the brighter object.

ECLIPSES FOR 1996

There will be four eclipses in 1996, two of the Sun and two of the Moon. One of the solar eclipses will not be visible from the United States or Canada. The others will be seen in certain locations, as specified below. Lunar eclipses technically are visible from the entire night side of the Earth; solar eclipses are visible only in certain areas.

1. Total eclipse of the Moon, April 3. The beginning of the umbral phase will be visible in extreme eastern North America. The end will be visible in eastern and central regions of the United States and Canada. The Moon enters penumbra at 4:16 P.M., EST; totality begins and ends respectively at 6:27 P.M. and 7:53 P.M., EST; the Moon leaves penumbra at 10:04 P.M., EST.

2. Partial eclipse of the Sun, April 17. This eclipse will not be visible from the United States or Canada.

3. Total eclipse of the Moon, September 26-27. The beginning of the umbral phase will be visible in eastern and central regions of the United States and Canada. The end will be visible in North America (except for extreme western Alaska) and Hawaii. The Moon enters penumbra at 7:12 P.M., EST (4:12 P.M., PST), on the 26th; totality begins and ends respectively at 9:19 P.M. and 10:29 P.M., EST (6:19 P.M. and 7:29 P.M., PST); the Moon leaves penumbra at 12:36 A.M., EST, on the 27th (9:36 P.M., PST, on the 26th).

4. Partial eclipse of the Sun, October 12. This eclipse will be visible only in northeastern Canada. The eclipse begins and ends at 7:00 A.M., EST, and 11:05 A.M., EST, respectively.

FULL MOON DAYS

	1996	1997	1998	1999	2000
Jan.	5	23	12	1/31	20
Feb.	4	22	11	—	19
Mar.	5	23	12	2/31	19
Apr.	3	22	11	30	18
May	3	22	11	30	18
June	1/30	20	9	28	16
July	30	19	9	28	16
Aug.	28	18	7	26	15
Sept.	26	16	6	25	13
Oct.	26	15	5	24	13
Nov.	24	14	4	23	11
Dec.	24	13	3	22	11

PRINCIPAL METEOR SHOWERS

Shower	Best Hour (EST)	Radiant Direction*	Date of Maximum**	Approx. Peak Rate (/hr.)	Associated Comet
Quadrantid	5 A.M.	N.	Jan. 4	40-150	—
Lyrid	4 A.M.	S.	Apr. 21	10-15	1861 I
Eta Aquarid	4 A.M.	S.E.	May 4	10-40	Halley
Delta Aquarid	2 A.M.	S.	July 30	10-35	—
Perseid	4 A.M.	N.	Aug. 11-13	50-100	1862 III
Draconid	9 P.M.	N.W.	Oct. 9	10	Giacobini-Zinner
Orionid	4 A.M.	S.	Oct. 20	10-70	Halley
Taurid	midnight	S.	Nov. 9	5-15	Encke
Leonid	5 A.M.	S.	Nov. 16	5-20	1866 I
Andromedid	10 P.M.	S.	Nov. 25-27	10	Biela
Geminid	2 A.M.	S.	Dec. 13	50-80	—
Ursid	5 A.M.	N.	Dec. 22	10-15	—

* Direction from which the meteors appear to come.
** Date of actual maximum occurrence may vary by one or two days in either direction.

For a Healthy Digestive System
VITAMOL™ Tablets

Q WHAT DOES IT DO?
- A Helps prevent constipation.
- A Keeps your intestines healthy.
- A Promotes proper digestion.

Q WHY SHOULD I TAKE IT?
- A You should know that the secret to good health is proper elimination. Vitamol Tablets help prevent congestion and crowding of the vital organs caused by a distended stomach and bowels filled with gas and fecal matter that should be discharged daily.

Q WHAT IS IN IT?
- A Vitamol Tablets are composed of roots, moss, seaweed and certain parts of milk, grain and yeast. All of which are nutritionally beneficial for a healthy digestive system.

100% Money Back Guarantee! Try Vitamol tablets for just 30 days. If you don't feel Vitamol has made you feel better... just return the unused portion for a complete refund. No questions asked!

Before
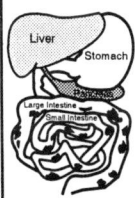

The dark spots in the illustration show decayed refuse lying in pockets in the folds of the intestines. Often these pockets become enlarged and the refuse matter is held there for weeks - polluting the system and congesting and irritating the surrounding organs - causing adhesions and all sorts of ailments. Note also how refuse matter passes through intestines in small, concentrated lumps.

After
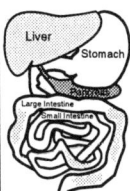

The shaded portions in the illustration show how Vitamol Tablets add bulk to the refuse in the intestines, filling the folds and pockets evenly, thus preventing their distortion and enlargement and producing full and complete evacuations.

☐ **YES!** I want to try Vitamol Tablets for 30 days. Please send me: VTI

Tablets	Cost	Shipping	Total
100	$9.95	$2.00	
200	$18.50	$3.00	
400	$32.50	$4.00	

Payment Method: (Check One)
☐ Check ☐ Money Order ☐ Visa
☐ Mastercard ☐ Discover

Expiration date: ____/____/____
Card # _____

Send to: Indiana Botanic Gardens, Inc. P.O. Box 5 Dept. OFMO, Hammond, IN 46325

Name_____
Address_____
City_____
State_____ Zip_____

"Keeping America Healthy Since 1910"

Bright Stars, 1996

The upper table shows the Eastern Standard Time when each star transits the meridian of Boston (i.e., lies directly above the horizon's south point there) and its altitude above that point at transit on the dates shown. The time of transit on any other date differs from that on the nearest date listed by approximately four minutes of time for each day. For a place outside Boston the local time of the star's transit is found by correcting the time at Boston by the value of Key Letter "C" for the place. (See footnote.)

Star	Constellation	Magnitude	Jan. 1	Mar. 1	May 1	July 1	Sept. 1	Nov. 1	Alt.
					Time of Transit (EST) Boldface — P.M. Lightface — A.M.				
Altair	Aquila	0.8	12:52	8:56	4:56	12:56	**8:48**	**4:48**	56.3
Deneb	Cygnus	1.3	**1:42**	9:47	5:47	1:47	**9:39**	**5:39**	92.8
Fomalhaut	Psc. Austr.	1.2	**3:57**	**12:01**	8:01	4:01	**11:54**	**7:54**	17.8
Algol	Perseus	2.2	**8:08**	**4:12**	**12:12**	8:12	4:08	12:09	88.5
Aldebaran	Taurus	0.9	**9:35**	**5:39**	**1:39**	9:39	5:36	1:36	64.1
Rigel	Orion	0.1	**10:13**	**6:17**	**2:18**	10:18	6:14	2:14	39.4
Capella	Auriga	0.1	**10:15**	**6:19**	**2:19**	10:20	6:16	2:16	93.6
Bellatrix	Orion	1.6	**10:24**	**6:28**	**2:28**	10:29	6:25	2:25	54.0
Betelgeuse	Orion	var. 0.4	**10:54**	**6:58**	**2:58**	10:58	6:55	2:55	55.0
Sirius	Can. Maj.	–1.4	**11:44**	**7:48**	**3:48**	11:48	7:44	3:45	31.0
Procyon	Can. Min.	0.4	12:42	**8:42**	**4:42**	**12:42**	8:38	4:38	52.9
Pollux	Gemini	1.2	12:48	**8:48**	**4:48**	**12:48**	8:44	4:44	75.7
Regulus	Leo	1.4	3:11	**11:11**	**7:11**	**3:11**	11:07	7:07	59.7
Spica	Virgo	var. 1.0	6:27	2:31	**10:27**	**6:27**	**2:23**	10:24	36.6
Arcturus	Bootes	–0.1	7:18	3:22	**11:18**	**7:18**	**3:14**	11:15	66.9
Antares	Scorpius	var. 0.9	9:31	5:35	1:35	**9:31**	**5:27**	**1:27**	21.3
Vega	Lyra	0.0	11:38	7:42	3:42	**11:38**	**7:35**	**3:35**	86.4

– Beth Krommes

Risings and Settings

The times of the star's rising and setting at Boston on any date are found by applying the interval shown to the time of the star's transit on that date. Subtract the interval for the star's rising; add it for its setting. The times for a place outside Boston are found by correcting the times found for Boston by the values of the Key Letters shown. (See footnote.) The directions in which the star rises and sets shown for Boston are generally useful throughout the United States. Deneb, Algol, Capella, and Vega are circumpolar stars — this means that they do not appear to rise or set, but are above the horizon.

Star	Interval hr. m.	Rising Key	Rising Dir.	Setting Key	Setting Dir.
Altair	6:36	B	EbN	E	WbN
Fomalhaut	3:59	E	SE	D	SW
Aldebaran	7:06	B	ENE	D	WNW
Rigel	5:33	D	EbS	B	WbS
Bellatrix	6:27	B	EbN	D	WbN
Betelgeuse	6:31	B	EbN	D	WbN
Sirius	5:00	D	ESE	B	WSW
Procyon	6:23	B	EbN	D	WbN
Pollux	8:01	A	NE	E	NW
Regulus	6:49	B	EbN	D	WbN
Spica	5:23	D	EbS	B	WbS
Arcturus	7:19	A	ENE	E	WNW
Antares	4:17	E	SEbE	A	SWbW

NOTE: The values of Key Letters are given in the Time Correction Tables (pages 196-200).

T☆WINKLE, T☆WINKLE L☆ITTLE...?

Why is the North Star also known as "Polaris"? Who decided to call the star at the tail of the swan "Deneb"? Where did "Betelgeuse" get its name? The origins of star names are often as complex as they are ancient. There are about 100 well known stars named by ancient Arabic, Chinese, Euphrates, Greek or Roman astronomers. Through the centuries, there have been more than 20 different listings of the stars created by astronomers all over the world. Most of these listings do not include specific star names, but list the stars numerically by size and location. In 1979 the International Star Registry was founded and began its first compilation of star names. The central world office is in Ingleside, Illinois with branch offices in London, Paris, Hamburg, Milano, Toronto and Tokyo. For a $45 fee, the International Star Registry will assign and register a person's name to one of the million unnamed stars in the sky. Although this is not the type of listing used by astronomers, naming a star in the sky is a special way to symbolize our own desire for immortality. In addition to being romantic and unique, star naming is also a novel way to introduce children to the miracle of astronomy. The person you choose to honor will receive a beautiful 12" x 16" parchment certificate with their name and the telescopic coordinates of the star, plus two sky charts and a booklet about astronomy. The star names are then copyrighted with their telescopic coordinates in a book for future generations to refer to and enjoy. To date, more than 500,000 individuals have had stars named for them. The cost of naming a star is $45 plus shipping and handling. Framing of the certificate is an additional fee. If you would like to name a star for someone special, call **800-282-3333** or write for a free brochure.

International Star Registry • 34523 Wilson Road • Ingleside, IL 60041

Bargain Books

Save up to 80% on publishers' overstocks, remainders. Thousands of books, from yesterday's best sellers to rarely seen titles. Gardening, Nature, History, Biography, Arts & Crafts, Fiction, Politics—over 40 subjects. Write for **FREE CATALOG.**
HAMILTON Box 15-147, Falls Village CT 06031

A catalog printed for the Amish

But they won't mind if we send you just one copy! Our old-timey hardware store is in the heart of the world's largest Amish settlement. Our 1000 item catalog is sent to Amish families in other areas. Filled with things you thought they'd quit making. **LEHMAN'S**

Rush me your country catalog. I am enclosing $2.00.
Mail to Lehman's, Box 41, Dept. 1-ZFG, Kidron, OH 44636

Name _____
Address _____
Zip _____

Of Ships & Sea

Cape Cod Weather Glass

Predict the weather-changes hours in advance with this Cape Cod Weather Glass. A hand-blown reproduction of weather-glasses used on many an old Clipper Ship.
Comes complete with black wrought-iron bracket and teak mounting-board. Detailed instructions. 11-1/4" x 3-1/2" x 3-1/2" Price: $29.95 ppd.

Fully illustrated 112-page catalog shows hundreds of decorative, nautical ideas for the home.

Also shown are ship models and kits, striking ship's clock, figureheads, ship's wheels, nautical lamps, and scores of famous marine paintings.

Send for free catalog to: **PRESTON'S**
21-E Main St. Wharf, Greenport, NY 11944
NYS residents please add Sales Tax

MILLENNIUM COUNTDOWN For 1996

READY OR NOT, HERE COMES THE MILLENNIUM

It's true. The year 2000 is now only four years away. While it may be a disappointment in some respects — let's face it, underwater cities, flying cars, and pills that make you smart are not going to arrive for a while yet — any event that happens only once in a thousand years is worth some thought. But what (and when) is the millennium, anyway? The answers may surprise you.

Enjoy yourself, it's later than you think,
Enjoy yourself, while you're still in the pink.
The years go by as quickly as a wink.
So enjoy yourself, enjoy yourself, it's later than you think.

Most people, if they thought about it for a moment, would probably say that the arrival of the year 2000 will mark the arrival of the 21st century, and the 2,000th anniversary of Christ's birth. Almost, but not quite. According to the accepted Christian chronology, Christ was born late in the year 1 B.C., with the following year — the first full calendar year following His birth — being designated A.D. 1. (A.D., incidentally, stands for anno Domini, or year of our Lord.) And the 2,000th anniversary of the year 1 is not the year 2000, of course, but 2001. Celebrants who usher in the new millennium on New Year's Eve of 1999 will actually be a full year early. Or will they

BY JON VARA

Revolutionary "2-in-1" TRIMMER/MOWER!

Takes the place of both your hand-held trimmer and steel-bladed rotary mower!

• The **DR® TRIMMER/MOWER** rolls "light as a feather" on two BIG WHEELS!

• **TRIMS** far easier, better, more precisely than hand-held trimmers. Plus, **MOWS** everything from whole lawns (even wet!) to tough, waist-high growth with ease!

• Rocks, roots, stumps, etc., do it no harm because the "DR®" has no steel blade to bend or dull.

• Perfect for *ALL* mowing and trimming around smaller properties, vacation homes, etc., or for finish-up mowing and trimming after riding mowers on larger parcels. A delight for *anyone* to use!

"Your machine is all you say it is. 75% quicker than a hand-held trimmer because of the extra power and heavier cord that enables me to wade right thru heavy grass and weeds. There is NO heavy load to swing back and forth tiring your arms and shoulders. It makes weed wacking 'duck soup'!"
-- Tom Lawrence, Somerville, NJ

CALL TOLL FREE
1(800) 215-1600

Please mail coupon today for FREE DETAILS about the Revolutionary DR® TRIMMER/MOWER!

YES! Please rush complete **FREE DETAILS** of the Revolutionary **DR® TRIMMER/MOWER** including prices and specifications of Manual, Electric-Starting and Professional Models, with "Off-Season" Savings now in effect. There is no obligation.

Name_____ ALM

Address_____

City_____ State_____ ZIP_____

To: **COUNTRY HOME PRODUCTS®**, Dept. 577, Ferry Road, Box 89, Charlotte, VT 05445

© 1995 CHP, Inc.

be late? The plain truth is that although we don't know precisely when Christ was born, we can be fairly certain that the traditional year of His birth — and the dating system based upon it — is seriously at odds with historical fact. Modern historians believe that Christ's birth actually occurred in what we now mistakenly call 6 B.C. In a strict, literal sense, this is not 1996 at all, but 2001 or so. Have you ever looked forward to the odometer in your car rolling over at 100,000 miles, then been distracted and missed it? It just happened again.

And although it *is* later than you think, the dating system itself is more recent than you might guess. It was devised in the sixth century A.D. by a Scythian monk named Dionysius Exiguus, whose real objective was to work out a system for determining the date of Easter. He did so, but rather than date it from the era of the fiercely anti-Christian Emperor Diocletian, as was then customary, he renumbered the years from what he believed to be the

ACCURATE PREDICTION

☞ **East German statesman Walter Ulbricht once delivered a ringing speech on the future of his nation in which he declared that "the millennium is on the horizon." When an aide later complimented him on the speech and asked if the millennium were truly on the horizon, Ulbricht confidently asserted that it was: "Don't you know the dictionary defines 'horizon' as an imaginary line that recedes as you approach it?"**

HOW LONG IS A THOUSAND YEARS?

A millennium may seem like a long time, but it takes surprisingly few human lifetimes to fill one. A baker's dozen lifetimes carry us from the year 1000 to the first decade of the 20th century — well into the lifetimes of several million octogenarian-plus Americans who will be here to celebrate in the year 2000.

1 Berenger of Tours, Christian scholar, 1000-1089
2 Suger, Abbot of Saint-Denis, leading French churchman, ca. 1081-1151
3 Maimonides, Jewish philosopher and theologian, 1135-1204
4 Simon de Montfort, English baronial leader, ca. 1208-1265
5 Dante Alighieri, Italian poet, 1265-1321
6 Sir John Hawkwood, English mercenary, 1320-1394
7 Donatello, Italian sculptor, 1386-1466
8 Leonardo da Vinci, Italian artist and inventor, 1452-1519

Leonardo da Vinci — Culver Pictures

9 Gerardus Mercator, Flemish cartographer, 1512-1594
10 Thomas Hobbes, English philosopher, 1588-1679
11 Jonathan Swift, English satirist, 1679-1754
12 Daniel Boone, American pioneer, 1734-1820
13 Florence Nightingale, English hospital administrator, 1820-1910

Florence Nightingale — Culver Pictures

From Forest to Jungle in Ten Centuries "A thousand years ago, Constantinople was considered the crossroads

birth of Christ. Considering the fact that he was dating an event that had taken place better than five centuries earlier, he didn't miss by much.

Interestingly enough, Dionysius himself did not use the new chronology in dating his own letters. Gradually, however, it caught on. England took up the new system late in the seventh century, with Spain and Gaul following suit shortly thereafter. The Church itself adopted the new chronology some three centuries later. By the 11th century it was in use throughout most of Europe, although it did not catch on in Greece until the 15th century. The arrival of the second millennium, in the year 1000, seems to have passed largely unnoticed — not surprising in an age when very few people could read, write, or count, let alone care about a newfangled method of numbering the years.

In short, the widespread awareness of the dawning of the third millennium — whenever it is — has no historical precedent. We're free to make of it what we will — and by all early indications, there won't be any shortage of ideas.

THE MORE THINGS CHANGE

A lot has changed in the past thousand years, but humankind's attitude toward taxation does not seem to be one of them. In 1086 — two decades after masterminding a cross-channel invasion and installing himself as King of England — William the Conqueror ordered a census of all land, livestock, population, and other resources of the realm, the better to assess taxes. The resulting tax roll came to be known as the *Doomsday Book,* and it is still a valuable source of information about everyday life in the 11th century. Scholars claim that the word *doomsday* simply reflected the idea of an economic "day of judgment," but they may be missing the point. Can it be coincidence that William the Conqueror was also known as William the Bastard?

THE Millentrepreneurial SPIRIT

Technically, at least, the millennium can be considered a religious celebration, which is probably why retailers are approaching it with the sort of thoughtful reverence ordinarily associated with Christmas. If you're the practical sort who likes to get your holiday shopping done early, you will want to consider:

☞ **Millennium tires from the Yokohama Tire Corp.**

☞ **Millennium wall coverings from Morton Jonap Co., Inc.**

☞ **Millennium wheelchairs from Everest & Jennings Inc.**

☞ **Millennium wood flooring from Manington Wood Floors Co.**

☞ **Millennium fabrics from Milliken & Co.**

☞ **Millennium computers and electronics equipment from Mega Drive Systems Inc.**

☞ **Millenia (sic) car from Mazda**

Too practical and impersonal? Not to worry. As the millennium draws

---

of the world. Today it's Times Square. A thousand years ago, Times Square was nothing but a forest."
– Gretchen Dykstra, president of the Times Square Business Improvement District

nearer, we will be able to choose from an ever-growing selection of gift items — items that anyone would be proud to give or receive at least once every thousand years, including:

A bottle of Millennium wine from Washington's Columbia Winery. According to vintner David Lake, this 1979 Cabernet — a big, intense wine — should be fully mature by the year 2000, which is more than can be said for a lot of 21-year-olds. There are only a few dozen cases left, and they won't last long at $75 a bottle.

The Millennium Planner, billed by Viking Studio Books as "your personal guide to the year 2000." It includes an illustrated book of stunning predictions, a handsome wall calendar, a "personal time capsule," and a contest form that makes entrants eligible to win vacations sponsored by Thomas Cook Travel. The cost is $24.95.

Or do you find that the very idea of millennium shopping irritates you? If so, you may want to try some Millennium 2000 Topical Ointment from Millennium 2000 in Whittier, California.

HEY, WE ALL MAKE MISTAKES

On New Year's Day of 1900, banner headlines in many American newspapers mistakenly hailed the arrival of the 20th century a full year too soon. Among those that did *not* was the mighty *New York Times*, which maintained a lofty silence on the subject. (Its first mention of the new

— courtesy Marie-Anne Jarvela

year was buried on page 2, in a careful allusion to holiday celebrations that ". . . ushered in the new year which ends the 20th century.")

The newspaper itself will no doubt get the millennium right as well, but the organizers of the upcoming turn-of-the-millennium celebration in Times Square have already dropped the ball. The festivities are scheduled for New Year's Eve of 1999, although the exact nature of the celebration has not yet been determined. The Times Square Business Improvement District held a contest in 1995 to design the perfect millennium celebration. (The deadline, alas, was September 1, 1995.) No word on the winner yet — if you're planning to spend the night of December 31, 1999, in Times Square, check next year's *Old Farmer's Almanac* for more information.

Contest organizers did report that a fourth of the mail they received took them to task for their blunder in choosing the date. So much for a new era of peace and understanding.

CAN'T YOU Just Push "Reset"?

Computer technicians have only a few years to eradicate a computer bug lurking in

---

The Advice of the Century "We had too many ideologies in the 20th century. The 21st should be governed by common sense."
– Lev Z. Kopelev, former Soviet dissident and publisher of the monthly journal *Forum XXI*

many of the world's 45,000 corporate mainframe computers. Most computer programs written during the 1960s — when most large corporations changed over to computerized record keeping — identified the year only by its last two digits. To the computer, "00" means "1900." And since many computers continue to use often-updated "legacy software," that limitation is now so deeply embedded that an industry-wide fix may cost as much as $75 billion.

But experts warn that the cost of not addressing the problem could go much higher. When confronted with "00" in the date line four years from now, computers using uncorrected software may freeze in their tracks like a deer caught in headlights or begin spewing gibberish. One software developer calculates that a $15 credit-card charge made on December 15, 1999, could lead to a bill, early in January, for 99 years of 21% compound interest — something over $1 billion.

IMMORTALITY
FOR SALE

☞ For a mere $35, Third Millennium Research in Seattle will bottle a small sample of your DNA for the edification of posterity. Dr. James Bicknell of Third Millennium says, "I'm not promising resurrection. It's a good memento, if nothing else." Address: Third Millennium Research, 5739 33rd Ave. N.E., Seattle, WA 98105.

SIGNS OF THE TIMES

Not everyone expects the millennium to usher in a time of peace and happiness. Gloomier predictions abound, including that of a Michigan group, which maintains that the United States is soon to be overwhelmed by forces under the control of the Royal Institute for International Affairs. (The day-to-day business of running the new government will fall to the Federal Emergency Management Agency.) Those who resist will be tossed into massive prison camps located on highways delineated by cryptic markings on the backs of road signs.

According to folklorist Ted Daniels, editor of the *Millennial Prophecy Report,* which tracks the activities of many such groups, the sign markings are real, although their purpose is not particularly sinister: They are instructions to highway line-painting crews. ☐☐

WANTED:
READERS' PLANS AND PREDICTIONS

☞ Please write to *The Old Farmer's Almanac* with your ideas about the Millennium: What are your personal plans for celebrating, and what activities are being planned in your town or region? What are your predictions for the new Millennium? We'll continue the Millennium Countdown, including information from readers, in the 1997 edition of the Almanac. Send information to "Millennium Countdown," *The Old Farmer's Almanac,* P.O. Box 520, Dublin, NH 03444. Internet address:

OFA1792@aol.com

Ain't it funny, how time slips away?

1995 NOVEMBER, THE ELEVENTH MONTH

This month three planets play catch-up, then are themselves all joined by the Moon for a Thanksgiving night gathering — very low in the southwest at dusk, but glorious. First, Mars passes north of Antares on the 2nd, followed by Venus on the 10th. Next, Mars goes just one degree south of Jupiter on the 16th, and Venus nudges nearly as close past Jupiter on the 19th. Venus's pursuit of Mars ends at dusk on the 22nd, when it stands a breathtaking 0.2 degree south of the planet. Finally, after sunset on the 23rd, a slender crescent Moon (at perigee) hangs near Jupiter and not far from the Venus-Mars duo. On the 24th, the Moon is low and in conjunction with Venus and Mars. Viewing of the Leonid meteors on the 17th-18th is hampered by a thick crescent Moon.

○	Full Moon	7th day	2nd hour	21st min.
☾	Last Quarter	15th day	6th hour	41st min.
●	New Moon	22nd day	10th hour	44th min.
☽	First Quarter	29th day	1st hour	29th min.

For an explanation of this page, see "How to Use This Almanac," page 30; for values of Key Letters, see Time Correction Tables, page 196.

Day of Year	Day of Month	Day of Week	☉ Rises h. m.	Key	☉ Sets h. m.	Key	Length of Days h. m.	Sun Fast m.	Full Sea Boston A.M.	Full Sea Boston P.M.	☽ Rises h. m.	Key	☽ Sets h. m.	Key	Declination of Sun ° '	☽ Place	☽ Age
305	1	W.	6 17	D	4 38	B	10 21	32	5¾	6¼	1 P.M. 40	D	12 A.M. 16	C	14s.25	AQU	9
306	2	Th.	6 18	D	4 37	B	10 19	32	6¾	7¼	2 12	D	1 22	D	14 44	AQU	10
307	3	Fr.	6 20	D	4 36	B	10 16	32	7¾	8¼	2 43	C	2 27	D	15 03	PSC	11
308	4	Sa.	6 21	D	4 34	B	10 13	32	8¾	9	3 14	C	3 31	D	15 22	PSC	12
309	5	**A**	6 22	D	4 33	B	10 11	32	9½	10	3 47	B	4 33	E	15 40	PSC	13
310	6	M.	6 23	D	4 32	B	10 09	32	10¼	10¾	4 21	B	5 35	E	15 58	ARI	14
311	7	Tu.	6 25	D	4 31	B	10 06	32	10¾	11¼	4 58	B	6 34	E	16 16	ARI	15
312	8	W.	6 26	D	4 30	A	10 04	32	11½	—	5 38	B	7 31	E	16 34	TAU	16
313	9	Th.	6 27	D	4 29	A	10 02	32	12	12¼	6 22	B	8 25	E	16 51	TAU	17
314	10	Fr.	6 28	D	4 27	A	9 59	32	12¾	12¾	7 10	B	9 15	E	17 08	TAU	18
315	11	Sa.	6 30	D	4 26	A	9 56	32	1½	1½	8 01	B	10 00	E	17 25	ORI	19
316	12	**A**	6 31	D	4 25	A	9 54	32	2¼	2¼	8 55	B	10 41	E	17 41	GEM	20
317	13	M.	6 32	D	4 24	A	9 52	31	3	3	9 51	B	11 18	E	17 57	GEM	21
318	14	Tu.	6 33	D	4 23	A	9 50	31	3¾	4	10 48	C	11 A.M. 52	D	18 13	CAN	22
319	15	W.	6 35	D	4 23	A	9 48	31	4½	4¾	11 P.M. 48	C	12 P.M. 23	D	18 28	LEO	23
320	16	Th.	6 36	D	4 22	A	9 46	31	5½	5¾	— —	–	12 54	D	18 44	SEX	24
321	17	Fr.	6 37	D	4 21	A	9 44	31	6¼	6½	12 A.M. 49	D	1 24	D	18 58	LEO	25
322	18	Sa.	6 38	D	4 20	A	9 42	31	7	7½	1 52	D	1 55	C	19 13	VIR	26
323	19	**A**	6 39	D	4 19	A	9 40	30	7¾	8¼	2 58	E	2 29	C	19 27	VIR	27
324	20	M.	6 41	D	4 19	A	9 38	30	8¾	9¼	4 07	E	3 06	B	19 41	VIR	28
325	21	Tu.	6 42	D	4 18	A	9 36	30	9½	10	5 17	E	3 49	B	19 54	LIB	29
326	22	W.	6 43	D	4 17	A	9 34	30	10¼	10¾	6 28	E	4 38	B	20 08	LIB	0
327	23	Th.	6 44	D	4 16	A	9 32	29	11	11¾	7 37	E	5 35	B	20 20	OPH	1
328	24	Fr.	6 45	D	4 16	A	9 31	29	—	12	8 40	E	6 39	B	20 32	SAG	2
329	25	Sa.	6 47	D	4 15	A	9 28	29	12½	12¾	9 36	E	7 47	B	20 44	SAG	3
330	26	**A**	6 48	D	4 15	A	9 27	29	1½	1¾	10 24	E	8 57	C	20 56	SAG	4
331	27	M.	6 49	E	4 14	A	9 25	28	2½	2¾	11 06	D	10 06	C	21 07	CAP	5
332	28	Tu.	6 50	E	4 14	A	9 24	28	3¼	3¾	11 A.M. 43	D	11 P.M. 14	C	21 18	CAP	6
333	29	W.	6 51	E	4 13	A	9 22	28	4½	4¾	12 P.M. 16	D	— —	–	21 28	AQU	7
334	30	Th.	6 52	E	4 13	A	9 21	27	5½	5¾	12 P.M. 47	C	12 A.M. 20	D	21s.38	PSC	8

NOVEMBER hath 30 days. 1995

The geese honked overhead
I ran to catch the skein
To watch them as they fled
In a long wavering line.
– May Sarton

D. M.	D. W.	Dates, Feasts, Fasts, Aspects, Tide Heights	*Weather* ↓
1	W.	All Saints • Post Office introduced money orders, 1864 • Tides {9.8 / 10.1	*Now*
2	Th.	All Souls • ☌♄☾ • Daniel Boone born, 1734 • Tides {10.0 / 10.0	*the*
3	Fr.	U.S. Embassy in Teheran, Iran, seized, 52 Americans held hostage, 1979 • {10.3 / 10.0 •	*tattered*
4	Sa.	Will Rogers born, 1879 • Walter Cronkite born, 1916 • Tides {10.5 / 10.0 •	*flags*
5	**A**	**22nd S. af. P.** • ☾ at ☋ • "Fawkes plot" never forgot. •	*of*
6	M.	*Beware of a door that has too many keys.* • Adolphe Sax born, 1814 • {10.8 / 9.9 •	*fall*
7	Tu.	**Full Beaver** ○ • Lewis and Clark first sighted the Pacific Ocean, 1805 • {10.8 / 9.8 •	*are*
8	W.	The Louvre Museum opened to public in Paris, 1793 • Tides {10.7 / — •	*torn by*
9	Th.	Citizens danced in celebration as Berlin Wall opened, 1989 • Carl Sagan born, 1934 •	*blasts*
10	Fr.	St. Leo the Great • ☾ rides high • Martin Luther born, 1483 • {9.4 / 10.3	*from*
11	Sa.	St. Martin • Veterans Day • Sadie Hawkins Day • ☾ at apo. •	
12	**A**	**23rd S. af. P.** • Indian Summer • {9.0 / 9.7 •	*Montreal.*
13	M.	Vietnam Veterans Memorial dedicated in Washington, D.C., 1982 • Tides {8.8 / 9.4	*Snow*
14	Tu.	Claude Monet born, 1840 • Yale Univ. announced plans to admit women, 1968 •	*and*
15	W.	*None so surely pays his debt As wet to cold and cold to wet.* • Tides {8.7 / 9.0 •	*sleet*
16	Th.	☌♂♃ • Historic weather: –53° F, Lincoln, Mont., 21.5" snow, Helena, Mont., 1959 •	*and*
17	Fr.	St. Hugh of Lincoln • ☾ on Eq. • Tides {9.2 / 9.1 •	*freezing*
18	Sa.	St. Hilda • Margaret Atwood born, 1939 • Tides {9.6 / 9.3 •	*rain*
19	**A**	**24th S. af. P.** • ☌♀♃ • Tides {10.2 / 9.7 •	*glaze*
20	M.	☾ at ☊ • President Lincoln delivered Gettysburg Address, 1863 • {10.8 / 10.1 •	*the*
21	Tu.	*Only the mediocre are always at their best.* • Tides {11.4 / 10.4 •	*glowing*
22	W.	♄ stat. • **New** ● • ☌♀♂ • {11.9 / 10.6	*windowpane.*
23	Th.	Thanksgiving Day • ☿ in sup. ☌ • ☾ at perig. • ☌♃☾ •	
24	Fr.	☾ runs low • ☌♂☾ • ☌♀☾ • Tides {— / 12.3 •	*Let's*
25	Sa.	Dinner for two at Delmonico's, New York, cost 25¢, 1834 • Tides {10.7 / 12.1 •	*say*
26	**A**	**25th S. af P.** • ☌♆☾ • ☌♅☾ • {10.6 / 11.7 •	*a*
27	M.	Curtis P. Brady received first permit to drive a car through Central Park, N.Y., 1889 •	*blessing,*
28	Tu.	Friedrich Engels born, 1820 • Coffee rationing began, 1942 • {10.2 / 10.7 •	*and*
29	W.	Lord Carnarvon and Howard Carter discovered tomb of King Tutankhamen, 1922 •	*pass the*
30	Th.	St. Andrew • ☾ on Eq. • ☌♄☾ • {10.0 / 9.7 •	*dressing!*

And now you're married, you must be good
And keep your wife in kindling wood. – Hearth and Home, 1875

Farmer's Calendar

The job of setting things about the place to rights for winter holds a telescope up to the spring and summer just past, a telescope that you look through at the wrong end. Events, individuals, mishaps, ideas, plans of May through September appear as if at a great distance through the lens of late-autumn chores. It's an effect that stands the Theory of Relativity on its head: Time speeds up, rushes more quickly into the past for the observer who is busy around his home in the fall.

The windowpane that I dislodged in swatting a fly in June, as I fix it in place now, seems to have been knocked loose years ago. When I tear out the frost-killed marigolds, a dank, tough tangle the height of my knee, I remember in spring planting their seeds like tiny porcupine quills; it feels as though that happened in another life. I promised I'd mend that fence. Today the project is as remote as the quest for the Northwest Passage. The lawn chairs must be lugged down to the cellar. The company who sat on them in the August heat have returned to distant cities. Now the air feels not far off snow. That visit might have happened to somebody else, in a former age.

Why should this be? In the spring when you're planting, setting out, opening up, you don't see a sharp image of the winter before receding into the past. You're looking forward then, I guess, letting your life expand. In the fall, however, you're moving inward, seeking warmth and light rather than joy. There's a certain pleasure in doing so, a certain security — but there's also a certain regret. Hence, perhaps, the feeling of remoteness of the life just past that comes in preparing your place for winter.

1995 DECEMBER, THE TWELFTH MONTH

Jupiter and Mars get lost in the Sun's glare, but Venus appears higher in the southwest. By midevening, the Northern Cross pattern of Cygnus the Swan is standing upright on the northwest horizon. Overhead is the constellation Perseus and the Pleiades cluster. High in the southeast, the arrowhead of the Hyades star cluster and orange Aldebaran outline Taurus the Bull's face, while following Orion the Hunter up the southeast sky are Procyon and the brightest star of all: Sirius. High in the east, yellow Capella flickers in Auriga; Gemini (the Twins) is low in the east. Look for Geminid meteors after midnight on the 12th and 13th, despite the glare from a gibbous Moon.

○	Full Moon	6th day	20th hour	28th min.
☾	Last Quarter	15th day	0 hour	33rd min.
●	New Moon	21st day	21st hour	24th min.
☽	First Quarter	28th day	14th hour	7th min.

For an explanation of this page, see "How to Use This Almanac," page 30; for values of Key Letters, see Time Correction Tables, page 196.

Day of Year	Day of Month	Day of Week	☉ Rises h. m.	Key	☉ Sets h. m.	Key	Length of Days h. m.	Sun Fast m.	Full Sea Boston A.M.	Full Sea Boston P.M.	☽ Rises h. m.	Key	☽ Sets h. m.	Key	Declination of Sun ° '	☽ Place	☽ Age
335	1	Fr.	6 53	E	4 13	A	9 20	27	6½	7	1 P.M. 18	C	1 A.M. 24	D	21 s.48	PSC	9
336	2	Sa.	6 54	E	4 12	A	9 18	27	7½	8	1 49	C	2 26	E	21 57	PSC	10
337	3	**A**	6 55	E	4 12	A	9 17	26	8¼	8¾	2 22	B	3 27	E	22 05	PSC	11
338	4	M.	6 56	E	4 12	A	9 16	26	9	9½	2 57	B	4 27	E	22 13	ARI	12
339	5	Tu.	6 57	E	4 12	A	9 15	25	9¾	10¼	3 36	B	5 24	E	22 21	TAU	13
340	6	W.	6 58	E	4 12	A	9 14	25	10½	11	4 18	B	6 19	E	22 28	TAU	14
341	7	Th.	6 59	E	4 12	A	9 13	25	11	11¾	5 05	B	7 10	E	22 35	TAU	15
342	8	Fr.	7 00	E	4 11	A	9 11	24	11¾	—	5 55	B	7 57	E	22 42	ORI	16
343	9	Sa.	7 01	E	4 11	A	9 10	24	12¼	12½	6 47	B	8 40	E	22 49	GEM	17
344	10	**A**	7 02	E	4 12	A	9 10	23	1	1	7 43	B	9 18	E	22 54	GEM	18
345	11	M.	7 03	E	4 12	A	9 09	23	1¾	1¾	8 39	C	9 53	E	22 59	CAN	19
346	12	Tu.	7 04	E	4 12	A	9 08	22	2½	2½	9 37	C	10 25	D	23 04	CAN	20
347	13	W.	7 05	E	4 12	A	9 07	22	3	3¼	10 36	D	10 55	D	23 08	LEO	21
348	14	Th.	7 05	E	4 12	A	9 07	21	4	4	11 P.M. 37	D	11 25	D	23 12	SEX	22
349	15	Fr.	7 06	E	4 12	A	9 06	21	4¾	5	— —	–	11 A.M. 54	D	23 16	LEO	23
350	16	Sa.	7 07	E	4 13	A	9 06	20	5½	6	12 A.M. 39	D	12 P.M. 26	C	23 19	VIR	24
351	17	**A**	7 08	E	4 13	A	9 05	20	6¼	6¾	1 44	E	12 59	C	23 21	VIR	25
352	18	M.	7 08	E	4 13	A	9 05	19	7¼	7¾	2 52	E	1 38	B	23 23	VIR	26
353	19	Tu.	7 09	E	4 14	A	9 05	19	8	8¼	4 01	E	2 23	B	23 24	LIB	27
354	20	W.	7 09	E	4 14	A	9 05	18	9	9½	5 11	E	3 15	B	23 25	LIB	28
355	21	Th.	7 10	E	4 14	A	9 04	18	9¾	10½	6 18	E	4 16	B	23 25	OPH	0
356	22	Fr.	7 11	E	4 15	A	9 04	17	10¾	11½	7 20	E	5 23	B	23 25	SAG	1
357	23	Sa.	7 11	E	4 15	A	9 04	17	11½	—	8 14	E	6 35	B	23 25	SAG	2
358	24	**A**	7 11	E	4 16	A	9 05	16	12¼	12½	9 01	E	7 48	C	23 25	CAP	3
359	25	M.	7 12	E	4 17	A	9 05	16	1¼	1½	9 41	D	8 59	D	23 23	AQU	4
360	26	Tu.	7 12	E	4 17	A	9 05	15	2	2¼	10 17	D	10 08	D	23 21	AQU	5
361	27	W.	7 12	E	4 18	A	9 06	15	3	3¼	10 50	D	11 P.M. 14	D	23 19	PSC	6
362	28	Th.	7 13	E	4 19	A	9 06	14	4	4¼	11 22	C	— —	–	23 16	PSC	7
363	29	Fr.	7 13	E	4 19	A	9 06	14	5	5½	11 A.M. 53	C	12 A.M. 18	E	23 13	PSC	8
364	30	Sa.	7 13	E	4 20	A	9 07	13	6	6½	12 P.M. 25	B	1 20	E	23 09	PSC	9
365	31	**A**	7 13	E	4 21	A	9 08	13	7	7½	12 P.M. 59	B	2 A.M. 20	E	23 s.05	ARI	10

DECEMBER hath 31 days. 1995

Christmas is coming, the geese are getting fat,
Please to put a penny in the old man's hat;
If you haven't got a penny, a ha'penny will do,
If you haven't got a ha'penny, God bless you!
– Beggar's Rhyme

D. M.	D. W.	Dates, Feasts, Fasts, Aspects, Tide Heights	Weather ↓
1	Fr.	Rosa Parks arrested for refusing to give up her bus seat to a white man, 1955 • {10.1 / 9.5 •	*Shop*
2	Sa.	☾ at ☋ • Barney Clark received first artificial heart, 1982 • {10.2 / 9.4 •	*early,*
3	**A**	**1st S. in Advent** • Tides {10.3 / 9.3 •	*dearie —*
4	M.	*The pure and simple truth is rarely pure and never simple.* • Tides {10.4 / 9.3 •	*soon*
5	Tu.	Prohibition repealed, 1933 • Walt Disney born, 1901 •	*you will*
6	W.	**St. Nicholas** • Full Cold ○ • Ira Gershwin born, 1896 • Tides {10.5 / 9.3 •	*be*
7	Th.	**St. Ambrose** • Japanese attacked and devastated Pearl Harbor, Hawaii, 1941 •	*winter-*
8	Fr.	☾ rides high • U.S. and Britain declared war on Japan, 1941 • {10.4 / — •	*weary.*
9	Sa.	☾ at apo. • Clarence Birdseye born, 1886 • Tides {9.2 / 10.2 •	*For*
10	**A**	**2nd S. in Advent** • "The Gift of the Magi" published, 1905	*though*
11	M.	Fiorello La Guardia born, 1882 • Joe DiMaggio retired, 1951 • Tides {9.0 / 9.8 •	*the*
12	Tu.	Beethoven paid 19¢ for his first music lesson from Haydn, 1792 •	*temperature's*
13	W.	**St. Lucy** • *An American in Paris* opened in New York, 1928 • {8.9 / 9.3 •	*above*
14	Th.	*Better a dry morsel and quietness therewith, than a house full of feasting, with strife.* •	*average,*
15	Fr.	☾ on Eq. • Bill of Rights ratified, 1791 • Canadian flag adopted, 1964 •	*so's the*
16	Sa.	☌♀♆ • Earthquake, New Madrid, Mo., changed course of Mississippi River, 1811	*snow,*
17	**A**	**3rd S. in Advent** • ☾ at ☊ • Tides {9.9 / 9.1 •	*and*
18	M.	☌♃☉ • Ty Cobb born, 1886 • Betty Grable born, 1916 • {10.4 / 9.4 •	*winds*
19	Tu.	Women awarded Rhodes Scholarships for the first time, 1976 • Tides {10.9 / 9.8 •	*are*
20	W.	☌♀♅ • Ember Day • Branch Rickey born, 1881 • Tides {11.5 / 10.1	*savage.*
21	Th.	**St. Thomas** • New ● • Joseph Stalin born, 1879 • {12.0 / 10.5 •	*Pray*
22	Fr.	☾ runs low • ☾ at perig. • Winter Solstice • Ember Day • {12.3 / 10.7 •	*we*
23	Sa.	☌☿☾ • ☌♂☾ • ☌♆☾ • ☌♅☾ • ☌☿♂	Ember Day
24	**A**	**4th S. in Advent** • ☌♀☾ • Halcyon Days {10.9 / 12.2	*now,*
25	M.	**Christmas Day** • *A green Christmas, a white Easter.* •	*both*
26	Tu.	**St. Stephen** • James H. Nason patented coffee percolator, 1865 • {10.7 / 11.2 •	*dudes*
27	W.	**St. John** • ☾ on Eq. • ☌♄☾ • ☌☿♆ • {10.5 / 10.6 •	*and*
28	Th.	**Holy Innocents** • Comet Kohoutek made closest approach to Sun, 1973 •	*hicks,*
29	Fr.	*The future is made of the same stuff as the present.* • Tides {10.1 / 9.3 •	*for a*
30	Sa.	–50° F, Bloomfield, Vermont, 1933 • Bo Diddley born, 1928 • {9.9 / 8.9 •	*peaceful*
31	**A**	*Begin the new year square with every man.* (Robert B. Thomas) • Tides {9.9 / 8.7 •	*'96.*

Farmer's Calendar

From a safe distance, anything that's possible looks easy. It's the theoretical point of view: If you *can* do a thing, you will. Then experience intervenes, and you learn that the street of reality has high curbs.

Nowhere is the gap between the possible and the practical wider than in the beliefs of those who move to the country from places having more complete amenities. Your house is without a modern stove? No problem: There's a wood-burning range with an oven. We'll cook the turkey in that. How hard can it be? Need six cords of wood to heat the house in the winter? No problem: We'll cut it on the weekend; after all, there are trees all around. It'll be fun.

You learn fast. I remember the first time a winter storm knocked out our electricity and left us without running water. I took it well at first because there were a couple of feet of fresh snow on the ground. What is snow, I reflected, but water? We don't really need running water; we'll just melt snow. I wasn't wrong, of course, but reality is in the ratios, and the water-to-snow ratio is not favorable to the comfort I felt in the fact that snow is nothing but water. I found that the five-gallon pot, our largest, which we use for lobsters, yielded about a quart of water when filled with snow and heated. That's good news if all you need is a cup of tea, but it's not much help if you want to bathe, do a wash, clean up the dirty dishes. Yes, you *could* melt, say, 1,000 gallons of snow, but you won't. You'll do what I did: Wait disconsolately for the power to come back on and reflect on the difference between the way you know things to be and the way they are.

1996 JANUARY, THE FIRST MONTH

Venus shines brightly in the southwest at nightfall. The less bright planet to its upper left, to which it draws closer all month, is Saturn (a telescope shows Saturn's rings as only a thin dark line now). For the first week, Mercury can be glimpsed far to the lower right of Venus after sundown. After midnight on the 23rd, the Moon is near Venus and near Saturn the same evening. At midevening, when all these planets have set, the south sky is dominated by the bright constellations Taurus, Auriga, Gemini, Canis Minor, Canis Major, and Orion the Hunter. The Great Square of Pegasus sets in the west. Jupiter begins to emerge from morning twilight, posing by a thin crescent Moon low in the southeast on the 18th. Earth is at perihelion on the 4th.

○ Full Moon	5th day	15th hour	52nd min.
☾ Last Quarter	13th day	15th hour	47th min.
● New Moon	20th day	7th hour	51st min.
☽ First Quarter	27th day	6th hour	15th min.

For an explanation of this page, see "How to Use This Almanac," page 30; for values of Key Letters, see Time Correction Tables, page 196.

Day of Year	Day of Month	Day of Week	☉ Rises h. m.	Key	☉ Sets h. m.	Key	Length of Days h. m.	Sun Fast m.	Full Sea Boston A.M.	Full Sea Boston P.M.	☽ Rises h. m.	Key	☽ Sets h. m.	Key	Declination of Sun ° '	☽ Place	☽ Age
1	1	M.	7 13	E	4 22	A	9 09	13	7¾	8½	1 P.M. 36	B	3 A.M. 18	E	23s.01	ARI	11
2	2	Tu.	7 14	E	4 23	A	9 09	12	8¾	9¼	2 17	B	4 14	E	22 55	TAU	12
3	3	W.	7 14	E	4 24	A	9 10	12	9½	10	3 02	B	5 06	E	22 50	TAU	13
4	4	Th.	7 14	E	4 25	A	9 11	11	10	10¾	3 50	B	5 55	E	22 44	AUR	14
5	5	Fr.	7 14	E	4 25	A	9 11	11	10¾	11¼	4 42	B	6 39	E	22 38	GEM	15
6	6	Sa.	7 14	E	4 26	A	9 12	10	11½	—	5 36	B	7 19	E	22 31	GEM	16
7	7	**G**	7 13	E	4 27	A	9 14	10	12	12	6 33	C	7 55	E	22 24	CAN	17
8	8	M.	7 13	E	4 28	A	9 15	9	12½	12¾	7 30	C	8 29	D	22 16	CAN	18
9	9	Tu.	7 13	E	4 30	A	9 17	9	1¼	1¼	8 29	C	8 59	D	22 07	LEO	19
10	10	W.	7 13	E	4 31	A	9 18	9	1¾	2	9 28	D	9 29	D	21 59	SEX	20
11	11	Th.	7 13	E	4 32	A	9 19	8	2½	2¾	10 28	D	9 58	D	21 49	LEO	21
12	12	Fr.	7 12	E	4 33	A	9 21	8	3¼	3½	11 P.M. 31	D	10 28	C	21 40	VIR	22
13	13	Sa.	7 12	E	4 34	A	9 22	7	4	4½	— —	–	10 59	C	21 30	VIR	23
14	14	**G**	7 12	E	4 35	A	9 23	7	4¾	5¼	12 A.M. 35	E	11 A.M. 34	B	21 20	VIR	24
15	15	M.	7 11	E	4 36	A	9 25	7	5¾	6¼	1 41	E	12 P.M. 14	B	21 09	LIB	25
16	16	Tu.	7 11	E	4 37	A	9 26	6	6¾	7¼	2 48	E	1 00	B	20 58	LIB	26
17	17	W.	7 10	E	4 39	A	9 29	6	7¾	8¼	3 55	E	1 55	B	20 46	OPH	27
18	18	Th.	7 10	E	4 40	A	9 30	6	8¾	9¼	4 58	E	2 57	B	20 34	SAG	28
19	19	Fr.	7 09	E	4 41	A	9 32	5	9½	10¼	5 56	E	4 06	B	20 22	SAG	29
20	20	Sa.	7 08	E	4 42	A	9 34	5	10½	11¼	6 48	E	5 19	C	20 09	SAG	0
21	21	**G**	7 08	E	4 43	A	9 35	5	11½	—	7 33	D	6 34	C	19 56	AQU	1
22	22	M.	7 07	E	4 45	A	9 38	4	12	12¼	8 12	D	7 46	D	19 43	AQU	2
23	23	Tu.	7 06	D	4 46	A	9 40	4	12¾	1¼	8 48	D	8 56	D	19 29	AQU	3
24	24	W.	7 06	D	4 47	A	9 41	4	1¾	2	9 22	C	10 04	D	19 15	PSC	4
25	25	Th.	7 05	D	4 48	A	9 43	4	2½	3	9 54	C	11 P.M. 09	D	19 00	PSC	5
26	26	Fr.	7 04	D	4 50	A	9 46	3	3½	4	10 27	C	— —	–	18 45	PSC	6
27	27	Sa.	7 03	D	4 51	A	9 48	3	4½	4¾	11 01	B	12 A.M. 11	E	18 30	ARI	7
28	28	**G**	7 02	D	4 52	A	9 50	3	5¼	6	11 A.M. 37	B	1 11	E	18 14	ARI	8
29	29	M.	7 01	D	4 54	A	9 53	3	6¼	7	12 P.M. 17	B	2 07	E	17 58	TAU	9
30	30	Tu.	7 00	D	4 55	A	9 55	2	7¼	8	1 00	B	3 01	E	17 42	TAU	10
31	31	W.	7 00	D	4 56	A	9 56	2	8¼	8¾	1 P.M. 47	B	3 A.M. 51	E	17s.26	TAU	11

JANUARY hath 31 days. 1996

Late lies the wintry sun a-bed,
A frosty, fiery sleepy-head;
Blinks but an hour or two; and then,
A blood-red orange, sets again.
– Robert Louis Stevenson

D. M.	D. W.	Dates, Feasts, Fasts, Aspects, Tide Heights	Weather ↓
1	M.	**New Year's Day** • **Circumcision** • ☌♂♆ •	
2	Tu.	☿ Gr. Elong. (19° E.) • Isaac Asimov born, 1920 • {10.0 8.8}	*Glacial —*
3	W.	Yerba Buena, pop. 200, renamed San Francisco, 1847 • {10.1 8.9}	*if yer toes*
4	Th.	⊕ at perihelion • ☾ rides high • Utah became 45th state, 1896 •	*don't*
5	Fr.	☾ at apo. • **Full Wolf** ○ • Twelfth Night • Tides {10.2 9.1} •	*freeze*
6	Sa.	**Epiphany** • New Mexico became 47th state, 1912 •	*yer facial.*
7	**G**	**1st S. af. Ep.** • ☌♂♅ • {9.2 10.2} •	*Muddy*
8	M.	Plough Monday • *Talk is cheap because supply exceeds demand.* • Tides {9.2 10.1} •	*and*
9	Tu.	☿ stat. • First women's golf tournament organized in Scotland, 1811 •	*floody,*
10	W.	Blizzard, Fargo, N.D.; wind chill of -98° F, 1982 • Tides {9.3 9.7} •	*stay in*
11	Th.	☾ on Eq. • Canada's first prime minister, John A. Macdonald, born, 1815 •	*your*
12	Fr.	☌☿♂ • John Singer Sargent born, 1856 • Tides {9.4 9.2} •	*study.*
13	Sa.	**St. Hilary** • ☾ at ☊ • *Bad luck is fertile.* • {9.5 9.0} •	*Flakes*
14	**G**	**2nd S. af. Ep.** • Propitious day for birth of women. • {9.7 8.9} •	*get*
15	M.	**Martin Luther King Jr.'s Birthday** • ☌♆☉ •	*caked*
16	Tu.	U.S. issued ban on travel to Cuba, 1961 • Dizzy Dean born, 1911 • {10.4 9.2} •	*with*
17	W.	Benjamin Franklin born, 1706 • *Necessity never made a good bargain.* •	*crust,*
18	Th.	☾ runs low • ☌♃☾ • ☿ in inf. ☌ •	*we trust.*
19	Fr.	☾ at perig. • Robert E. Lee born, 1807 • Tides {11.8 10.4} •	*Melt-*
20	Sa.	**St. Fabian** • New ● • Favorable day for birth of men. •	*down;*
21	**G**	**3rd S. af. Ep.** • **St. Agnes** • ☌♅☉ •	*watch*
22	M.	**St. Vincent** • *The Crucible* premiered on Broadway, 1953 • Tides {11.1 12.1} •	*it*
23	Tu.	☌♀☾ • ☌♄☾ • First episode "Roots" aired, 1977 •	*pelt*
24	W.	☾ on Eq. • Sir Winston Churchill died, 1965 • Tides {11.0 11.2} •	*down!*
25	Th.	**Conversion of Paul** • ☾ at ☋ • {10.8 10.5} •	*Above*
26	Fr.	**Sts. Timothy & Titus** • Michigan became 26th state, 1837 •	*freezin'*
27	Sa.	*Visits always give pleasure; if not the arriving, so the departing.* • {10.0 9.1} •	*hardly*
28	**G**	**4th S. af. Ep.** • **St. Thomas Aquinas** •	*season-*
29	M.	UCLA won 88th consecutive basketball game, 1974 • W.C. Fields born, 1880 •	*able.*
30	Tu.	☿ stat. • "The Lone Ranger" made radio debut, 1933 • {9.4 8.3} •	*Un-*
31	W.	☾ rides high • Jackie Robinson born, 1919 •	*reasonable!*

Farmer's Calendar

What do we want from the weather? Maybe not quite what we think. In my bailiwick at this time last year, winter was called off for a week in the warmest, longest January thaw anybody could remember. Afternoon temperatures went to 60° F or better day after day, it seemed. Kids turned up on bikes. People moved outdoors, put off their coats, let their stoves and furnaces go out. Most of the snow went away, then all of it. As though it had slipped a cog, the year jumped in a week from New Year's to May Day.

Winter repealed! Were we glad? For half the year we complain about the winter and for the other half we dread it. Now it had ended before it had begun. Did we like that? For my part, I think I liked it for about two days. Then I became uneasy. I wanted not more snow and cold, exactly, but not this fake May, either. Others I know felt the same way. For none of us was fooled. People aren't stupid. We knew it was no real May we were in. The air, though warm, was hard. The ground was frozen solid, and the exposed grass, though green, didn't grow. Above all, the days were dark and short. For all its softness, the season's nights came down like an ax at half past three: January's nights, never May's. Spring without light is no spring at all.

When around Groundhog Day it snowed a foot and the temperature dove for the negative integers, we were more than halfway pleased. We thought what we wanted from the weather was relief, mercy; whereas what we really wanted was almost the opposite: discipline, rigor, logic. We want the weather to do the right thing, and we know what that is.

1996 FEBRUARY, THE SECOND MONTH

Venus tremendously outshines Saturn, but the two make a spectacular pair early in the month, especially when closest to each other on Groundhog Day; they can be seen in the southwest after sunset. A telescope will show Saturn seemingly ringless until the 11th when the rings are edgewise. In the nights that follow, they appear as a razor-thin bright line (the last time until 2009). The Moon is near Jupiter in the southeast before dawn on the 15th and might be glimpsed as a marvelously thin crescent low in the west after sunset on the 19th. At dusk on the 20th the Moon shines near Saturn and near Venus on the 21st. Sirius, brightest of all stars, can be seen in the south at midevening, to the lower left of Orion.

○ Full Moon	4th day	10th hour	59th min.
☾ Last Quarter	12th day	3rd hour	38th min.
● New Moon	18th day	18th hour	31st min.
☽ First Quarter	26th day	0 hour	53rd min.

For an explanation of this page, see "How to Use This Almanac," page 30; for values of Key Letters, see Time Correction Tables, page 196.

Day of Year	Day of Month	Day of Week	☉ Rises h. m.	Key	☉ Sets h. m.	Key	Length of Days h. m.	Sun Fast m.	Full Sea Boston A.M.	Full Sea Boston P.M.	☽ Rises h. m.	Key	☽ Sets h. m.	Key	Declination of Sun ° '	☽ Place	☽ Age
32	1	Th.	6 59	D	4 58	A	9 59	2	9	9½	2 P.M. 37	B	4 A.M. 37	E	17s.09	GEM	12
33	2	Fr.	6 57	D	4 59	A	10 02	2	9¾	10¼	3 30	B	5 18	E	16 52	GEM	13
34	3	Sa.	6 56	D	5 00	A	10 04	2	10½	11	4 26	C	5 56	E	16 34	CAN	14
35	4	**G**	6 55	D	5 01	A	10 06	2	11	11½	5 24	C	6 31	D	16 17	CAN	15
36	5	M.	6 54	D	5 03	A	10 09	2	11¾	—	6 22	C	7 03	D	15 59	LEO	16
37	6	Tu.	6 53	D	5 04	A	10 11	2	12¼	12¼	7 22	D	7 33	D	15 41	SEX	17
38	7	W.	6 52	D	5 05	A	10 13	2	12¾	1	8 22	D	8 02	D	15 22	LEO	18
39	8	Th.	6 51	D	5 07	B	10 16	1	1¼	1½	9 23	D	8 32	C	15 03	VIR	19
40	9	Fr.	6 49	D	5 08	B	10 19	1	2	2¼	10 26	E	9 03	C	14 44	VIR	20
41	10	Sa.	6 48	D	5 09	B	10 21	1	2¾	3	11 P.M. 30	E	9 36	B	14 24	VIR	21
42	11	**G**	6 47	D	5 11	B	10 24	1	3½	4	— —	–	10 13	B	14 05	LIB	22
43	12	M.	6 46	D	5 12	B	10 26	1	4¼	5	12 A.M. 35	E	10 55	B	13 45	LIB	23
44	13	Tu.	6 44	D	5 13	B	10 29	1	5¼	6	1 39	E	11 A.M. 44	B	13 25	SCO	24
45	14	W.	6 43	D	5 14	B	10 31	1	6¼	7	2 42	E	12 P.M. 40	B	13 05	OPH	25
46	15	Th.	6 42	D	5 16	B	10 34	1	7¼	8	3 41	E	1 44	B	12 45	SAG	26
47	16	Fr.	6 40	D	5 17	B	10 37	1	8¼	9	4 34	E	2 53	C	12 24	SAG	27
48	17	Sa.	6 39	D	5 18	B	10 39	1	9¼	10	5 21	E	4 06	C	12 03	CAP	28
49	18	**G**	6 37	D	5 20	B	10 43	2	10¼	10¾	6 03	E	5 19	C	11 42	AQU	0
50	19	M.	6 36	D	5 21	B	10 45	2	11¼	11¾	6 42	D	6 31	D	11 21	AQU	1
51	20	Tu.	6 35	D	5 22	B	10 47	2	—	12	7 17	D	7 42	D	10 59	PSC	2
52	21	W.	6 33	D	5 23	B	10 50	2	12½	12¾	7 51	C	8 49	D	10 38	PSC	3
53	22	Th.	6 32	D	5 25	B	10 53	2	1¼	1¾	8 25	C	9 55	E	10 16	PSC	4
54	23	Fr.	6 30	D	5 26	B	10 56	2	2	2½	8 59	B	10 57	E	9 54	PSC	5
55	24	Sa.	6 29	D	5 27	B	10 58	2	3	3¼	9 36	B	11 P.M. 57	E	9 32	ARI	6
56	25	**G**	6 27	D	5 28	B	11 01	2	3¾	4¼	10 14	B	— —	–	9 10	TAU	7
57	26	M.	6 25	D	5 30	B	11 05	2	4¾	5¼	10 57	B	12 A.M. 53	E	8 47	TAU	8
58	27	Tu.	6 24	D	5 31	B	11 07	3	5½	6¼	11 A.M. 42	B	1 44	E	8 25	TAU	9
59	28	W.	6 22	D	5 32	B	11 10	3	6½	7¼	12 P.M. 31	B	2 32	E	8 02	ORI	10
60	29	Th.	6 21	D	5 33	B	11 12	3	7½	8¼	1 P.M. 23	B	3 A.M. 15	E	7s.39	GEM	11

FEBRUARY hath 29 days. 1996

A sparrow enters the tree
Whereon immediately
A snow-lump thrice his own slight size
Descends on him and showers his head and eyes.
– *Thomas Hardy*

D. M.	D. W.	Dates, Feasts, Fasts, Aspects, Tide Heights	*Weather* ↓
1	Th.	St. Brigid • ☾ at apo. • Tides {9.6 / 8.6 •	*Groundhog*
2	Fr.	Candlemas • **Purif. of Mary** • Groundhog Day • ☌♀♄ •	
3	Sa.	Buddy Holly, the Big Bopper, and Ritchie Valens killed in plane crash, 1959 •	*scurries,*
4	**G**	**Septuagesima** • **Full Snow** ○ • {10.1 / 9.3	*chased by*
5	M.	St. Agatha • Hank Aaron born, 1934 • Roger Staubach born, 1942	*flurries.*
6	Tu.	*If February give much snow, A fine summer it doth foreshow.* • Tides {9.5 / 10.2 •	*Rising*
7	W.	☾ on Eq. • Laura Ingalls Wilder born, 1867 • Tides {9.6 / 10.1 •	*drifts*
8	Th.	*The Saturday Evening Post* published last issue, 1969 • Jules Verne born, 1828 •	*crowd*
9	Fr.	☾ at ☊ • The Beatles appeared on "The Ed Sullivan Show," 1964 • {9.8 / 9.7 •	*the*
10	Sa.	First fire extinguisher patented, 1863 • Mark Spitz born, 1950 • {9.9 / 9.5 •	*lifts.*
11	**G**	**Sexagesima** • ☿ Gr. Elong. (26° W.) • ☌☿♆ •	*While*
12	M.	Abraham Lincoln born, 1809 • Charles Darwin born, 1809 •	*skiddering*
13	Tu.	Snowflakes recorded farthest south, Ft. Myers, Fla., 1899 • Tides {10.1 / 8.9 •	*in*
14	W.	St. Valentine • **Sts. Cyril & Methodius** • ☾ runs low •	*freezing*
15	Th.	☌♃☾ • *If you wish to live and thrive, let a spider run alive.* • {10.7 / 9.5	*rain,*
16	Fr.	☌♆☾ • ☌☿♅ • ☌♅☾ • Tides {11.1 / 10.1 •	*we're*
17	Sa.	☌☿☾ • ☾ at perig. • Winter's back breaks. •	*considering*
18	**G**	**Quinquagesima** • **New** ● • {11.8 / 10.9 •	*a move*
19	M.	Kansas adopted statewide prohibition, 1881 • Tides {11.9 / 11.2 •	*to Spain.*
20	Tu.	Shrove Tuesday • ☾ on Eq. • ☌♄☾ •	*Northeast*
21	W.	Ash Wednesday • Occn. ♀☾ • Malcolm X assassinated, 1965	*blast*
22	Th.	☾ at ☋ • George Washington born, 1732 • Tides {11.2 / 10.9 •	*that*
23	Fr.	*The best honey isn't got by squeezing.* • Rotary Club International founded, 1905	*doesn't*
24	Sa.	St. Matthias • -18° F Valley Head, Alabama, 1905 • {10.4 / 9.5 •	*last —*
25	**G**	**1st S. in Lent** • 91.6° F Los Angeles, California, 1921 •	*where*
26	M.	**Pure Monday** • Grand Canyon National Park in Arizona established, 1919 •	*are the*
27	Tu.	Oscar Hammerstein patented cigar-rolling machine, 1883 • Tides {9.2 / 8.2 •	*winters*
28	W.	☾ rides high • Ember Day • Mario Andretti born, 1940 • {9.1 / 8.1 •	*of our*
29	Th.	☾ at apo. • Hattie McDaniel became first black actress to win an Oscar, 1940 •	*past?*

Part of the secret of success in life is to eat what you like and let the food fight it out inside.
– Mark Twain

Farmer's Calendar

As the midwinter sun surmounts its daily arc, the leak above my kitchen windows comes to life with the chipper regularity of the flute line in a Bach concerto. *Blip, blip, blip-lip, blip-lip.* Some years ago we had skylights let into the pitch of the roof to admit light to what was a gloomy kitchen. They worked even better than we had hoped, admitting not only plenty of light but also a fair amount of water. Not rainwater. The roof doesn't leak in the rain. Leaking around here is a winter sport. Ice builds up above the skylights, and when it melts, the roof leaks.

Or it doesn't. Winter roof leaks, as far as I can tell, are like certain wildlife — deer, say, or upland gamebirds: Their behavior exhibits general patterns that are well known and clearly accounted for; nevertheless, exactly what they do, how, and when is unpredictable and sometimes quite mysterious. At a particular time of day, deer move to water; at another time they bed. But that doesn't mean you'll find them at the brook if you go there, and it doesn't mean they won't turn up in your backyard eating your roses. Similarly, whole winters have passed with ice on our roof and never a *blip,* and I have known a leak to turn up in the middle of a subzero night when the roof ought to have been frozen dry.

Nobody wants a leaky roof, of course, but if you have one anyway, there are innocent pleasures to be had from it. We have outwitted our leaks with pots and pans and, once, with a preposterous jury-rigged aqueduct of tin cans, wire, a soap-bubble blower, duct tape, and plastic tubing. It took most of an afternoon to get it hung just right. Then the next morning the leak sprang someplace else.

1996 MARCH, The Third Month

At month's end Venus sits near the pinnacle of this, the highest-reaching evening display in its eight-year cycle of appearances. The majestic planet sets several hours after the Sun. Jupiter is well up in the east by morning twilight; before dawn on the 6th, telescopes will show it approaching a star a little brighter than its moons and—while still dark on the West Coast—passing in front of the star (a very rare event). After dusk, the Big Dipper is ascending in the northeast, Orion descending in the southwest. Venus is at greatest elongation east (46 degrees) on the 31st; look for it in the west in the evenings. Vernal equinox is at 3:03 A.M., EST, on the 20th.

○ Full Moon	5th day	4th hour	24th min.
☾ Last Quarter	12th day	12th hour	16th min.
● New Moon	19th day	5th hour	46th min.
☽ First Quarter	26th day	20th hour	32nd min.

For an explanation of this page, see "How to Use This Almanac," page 30; for values of Key Letters, see Time Correction Tables, page 196.

Day of Year	Day of Month	Day of Week	☉ Rises h. m.	Key	☉ Sets h. m.	Key	Length of Days h. m.	Sun Fast m.	Full Sea Boston A.M.	Full Sea Boston P.M.	☽ Rises h. m.	Key	☽ Sets h. m.	Key	Declination of Sun ° '	Place	☽ Age
61	1	Fr.	6 19	D	5 35	B	11 16	3	8½	9	2 P_M18	B	3 A_M55	E	7s.17	GEM	12
62	2	Sa.	6 17	D	5 36	B	11 19	3	9¼	9¾	3 15	C	4 30	E	6 54	CAN	13
63	3	F	6 16	D	5 37	B	11 21	4	10	10½	4 13	C	5 04	D	6 31	CAN	14
64	4	M.	6 14	D	5 38	B	11 24	4	10½	11	5 13	D	5 35	D	6 08	LEO	15
65	5	Tu.	6 13	D	5 39	B	11 26	4	11¼	11½	6 14	D	6 05	D	5 44	LEO	16
66	6	W.	6 11	D	5 41	B	11 30	4	11¾	—	7 16	D	6 35	C	5 21	VIR	17
67	7	Th.	6 09	D	5 42	B	11 33	5	12¼	12½	8 19	D	7 06	C	4 58	VIR	18
68	8	Fr.	6 08	D	5 43	B	11 35	5	12¾	1¼	9 23	E	7 39	B	4 35	VIR	19
69	9	Sa.	6 06	D	5 44	B	11 38	5	1½	2	10 28	E	8 15	B	4 11	VIR	20
70	10	F	6 04	D	5 45	B	11 41	5	2¼	2¾	11 P_M32	E	8 55	B	3 48	LIB	21
71	11	M.	6 02	C	5 46	B	11 44	6	3	3½	—	—	9 42	B	3 24	SCO	22
72	12	Tu.	6 01	C	5 48	B	11 47	6	4	4½	12 A_M34	E	10 34	B	3 00	OPH	23
73	13	W.	5 59	C	5 49	B	11 50	6	5	5½	1 32	E	11 A_M33	B	2 37	SAG	24
74	14	Th.	5 57	C	5 50	B	11 53	6	6	6¾	2 26	E	12 P_M38	B	2 13	SAG	25
75	15	Fr.	5 56	C	5 51	B	11 55	7	7	7¾	3 14	E	1 47	B	1 50	SAG	26
76	16	Sa.	5 54	C	5 52	B	11 58	7	8	8¾	3 57	D	2 57	C	1 26	AQU	27
77	17	F	5 52	C	5 53	B	12 01	7	9	9¾	4 36	D	4 08	D	1 02	AQU	28
78	18	M.	5 50	C	5 55	B	12 05	7	10	10½	5 12	D	5 18	D	0 38	AQU	29
79	19	Tu.	5 49	C	5 56	C	12 07	8	11	11¼	5 46	D	6 27	D	0s.15	PSC	0
80	20	W.	5 47	C	5 57	C	12 10	8	11¾	—	6 20	D	7 35	D	0N.09	PSC	1
81	21	Th.	5 45	C	5 58	C	12 13	8	12	12½	6 55	D	8 39	E	0 32	PSC	2
82	22	Fr.	5 43	C	5 59	C	12 16	9	12¾	1¼	7 31	B	9 42	E	0 56	ARI	3
83	23	Sa.	5 42	C	6 00	C	12 18	9	1½	2	8 09	B	10 40	E	1 20	ARI	4
84	24	F	5 40	C	6 01	C	12 21	9	2¼	2¾	8 51	B	11 P_M35	E	1 43	TAU	5
85	25	M.	5 38	C	6 03	C	12 25	10	3	3¾	9 36	B	—	—	2 07	TAU	6
86	26	Tu.	5 37	C	6 04	C	12 27	10	4	4½	10 24	B	12 A_M25	E	2 30	ORI	7
87	27	W.	5 35	C	6 05	C	12 30	10	5	5½	11 A_M15	B	1 10	E	2 54	GEM	8
88	28	Th.	5 33	C	6 06	C	12 33	10	5¾	6½	12 P_M09	B	1 51	E	3 17	GEM	9
89	29	Fr.	5 31	C	6 07	C	12 36	11	6¾	7½	1 04	B	2 28	E	3 41	CAN	10
90	30	Sa.	5 30	C	6 08	C	12 38	11	7¾	8¼	2 02	B	3 02	D	4 04	CAN	11
91	31	F	5 28	B	6 09	C	12 41	11	8½	9	3 P_M01	B	3 A_M34	D	4N.27	LEO	12

MARCH hath 31 days. 1996

Over the land freckled with snow half-thawed
The speculating rooks at their nests cawed,
And saw from elm-tops, delicate as flowers of grass,
What we below could not see, Winter pass.
– Edward Thomas

D. M.	D. W.	Dates, Feasts, Fasts, Aspects, Tide Heights	*Weather* ↓
1	Fr.	St. David • Ember Day • Ohio became 17th state, 1803 • {9.3 8.6 •	*A*
2	Sa.	Ember Day • Puerto Rico became U.S. territory, 1917 • Tides {9.6 8.9 •	*teaser,*
3	**F**	**2nd S. in Lent** • **Sunday of Orthodoxy** •	*then*
4	M.	☌ ♂ ☉ • Old Inauguration Day • Vermont became 14th state, 1791 •	*back*
5	Tu.	**Full Sap** ○ • Town Meeting Day, Vermont • Josef Stalin died, 1953 • {10.2 9.9 •	*in*
6	W.	☾ on Eq. • The Alamo fell, 1836 • Toronto, Canada, incorporated, 1834 •	*the*
7	Th.	St. Perpetua • ☾ at ☊ • ♇ stat. •	*freezer.*
8	Fr.	*Time is nature's way of keeping everything from happening at once.* • Tides {10.3 10.1 •	*It's*
9	Sa.	Charles Graham of New York City patented artificial teeth, 1822 •	*dreary 'n'*
10	**F**	**3rd S. in Lent** • U.S. issued first paper money, 1862 •	*Siberian.*
11	M.	Johnny Appleseed died, 1847 • Bank of Canada opened, 1935 • {10.4 9.4 •	*A*
12	Tu.	St. Gregory • FDR delivered first fireside chat,1933 •	*Shakespearean*
13	W.	☾ runs low • Discovery of Pluto announced, 1930 • Tides {10.2 9.1 •	*might*
14	Th.	☌ ♃ ☾ • U.S. authorized first issue of war bonds, 1812 •	*remark:*
15	Fr.	☌ ♆ ☾ • ☌ ♅ ☾ • Tides {10.4 9.6 •	*"Beware*
16	Sa.	☾ at perig. • *If you are standing upright, do not fear a crooked shadow.* • {10.7 10.1	*the*
17	**F**	**4th S. in Lent** • St. Patrick • ☌ ♄ ☉ •	*tides*
18	M.	☾ on Eq. • Schick, Inc., marketed first electric razor, 1931 • Tides {11.3 11.1 •	*of*
19	Tu.	St. Joseph • **New** ● • Clear today betides a fertile year. •	*March."*
20	W.	☾ at ☋ • **Vernal Equinox** • Mister Rogers born, 1928 •	*Dance*
21	Th.	Persia renamed Iran, 1935 • Pocahontas died, 1617 • Tides {11.3 10.9 •	*a fling,*
22	Fr.	☌ ♂ ♄ • ☌ ♀ ☾ • YMHA founded New York City, 1874 •	*ye*
23	Sa.	☌ ☿ ♄ • ☌ ☿ ♂ • Fannie Farmer born, 1857 • {10.8 10.0 •	*lads*
24	**F**	**5th S. in Lent** • Passion • Tides {10.4 9.4 •	*and*
25	M.	Annunciation • Washington planted pecan trees at Mount Vernon, 1775 •	*lasses —*
26	Tu.	☾ rides high • Sandra Day O'Connor born, 1930 • Robert Frost born, 1874 •	*is*
27	W.	☾ at apo. • 91 mph winds, New York City, 1913 • Tides {9.1 8.2 •	*this*
28	Th.	☿ in sup. ☌ • Series of accidents began at Three Mile Island, 1979 •	*spring?*
29	Fr.	*Friendship is a plant we must often water.* • Cy Young born, 1867 • Tides {8.9 8.4 •	*Or*
30	Sa.	John Hinckley Jr. wounded President Ronald Reagan, 1981 •	*greenhouse*
31	**F**	**Palm Sunday** • ♀ Gr. Elong. (46° E.) • {9.3 9.2 •	*gases?*

Farmer's Calendar

In the tropics there are no evenings. The Sun goes down in a hurry and night arrives abruptly, with little or none of the long, thoughtful fading of the light that people in other latitudes rely on. The difference has to do with the apparent path of the Sun relative to the horizon at different points on Earth. Evening occurs because the light of the Sun remains visible above the horizon after the Sun has passed below it, until the Sun has gone a certain distance below the horizon. Near the equator, the Sun appears to set on a track perpendicular to the horizon, a track that takes it by the shortest course through the zone in which its light still reaches the horizon. The Sun sinks out of sight like a stone dropped into a pool. In the north, the Sun's apparent path is at an angle to the horizon. The Sun slips below the horizon obliquely, on a track that keeps it in the lighted zone for a longer time. Hence the prolonged twilight of the higher latitudes.

In those same latitudes, however, the Sun at any angle is scarce for half the year. Here in the North in winter, when it seems to rise and set furtively down in the southern corner of the sky, evening, though present in astronomical terms, doesn't count for much. That's part of the charm of the weeks around the Vernal Equinox. Especially after a stretch of bad weather, a clear day will suddenly be seen to have a fifth act, an envoi, a caboose, so to speak. By the second week of March, where I live, six in the afternoon — which only lately was as dark as midnight — is a daylight hour again, almost. The day resumes its fullness. We have the evening back for another year.

APRIL, THE FOURTH MONTH

A total lunar eclipse occurs on the 3rd, but is seen in its entirety only in extreme eastern North America. The partial solar eclipse on the 17th will not be seen in the United States. Early in the month peerlessly bright Venus is brushing past the very edge of the lovely Pleiades star cluster. Mercury gives its best evening showing of the year, appearing well to the lower right of Venus around the 23rd, its day of greatest elongation east (20 degrees). The Moon is near Venus early on the 21st and sets by late evening to allow viewing of the Lyrid meteors from high in the east. Daylight Saving Time begins at 2:00 A.M. on the 7th, Easter Sunday.

○	Full Moon	3rd day	19th hour	8th min.
☾	Last Quarter	10th day	18th hour	37th min.
●	New Moon	17th day	17th hour	50th min.
☽	First Quarter	25th day	15th hour	42nd min.

ADD 1 hour for Daylight Saving Time after 2 A.M., April 7th.

For an explanation of this page, see "How to Use This Almanac," page 30; for values of Key Letters, see Time Correction Tables, page 196.

Day of Year	Day of Month	Day of Week	☉ Rises h. m.	Key	☉ Sets h. m.	Key	Length of Days h. m.	Sun Fast m.	Full Sea Boston A.M.	Full Sea Boston P.M.	☽ Rises h. m.	Key	☽ Sets h. m.	Key	Declination of Sun ° '	☽ Place	☽ Age
92	1	M.	5 26	B	6 10	C	12 44	12	9¼	9¾	4 P.M. 01	D	4 A.M. 05	D	4N.50	SEX	13
93	2	Tu.	5 24	B	6 12	C	12 48	12	10	10½	5 03	D	4 35	C	5 13	LEO	14
94	3	W.	5 23	B	6 13	C	12 50	12	10¾	11	6 07	D	5 06	C	5 36	VIR	15
95	4	Th.	5 21	B	6 14	D	12 53	13	11½	11¾	7 12	E	5 39	C	5 59	VIR	16
96	5	Fr.	5 19	B	6 15	D	12 56	13	—	12	8 18	E	6 14	C	6 22	VIR	17
97	6	Sa.	5 18	B	6 16	D	12 58	13	12¼	12¾	9 24	E	6 54	B	6 44	LIB	18
98	7	**F**	5 16	B	6 17	D	13 01	13	1	1½	10 28	E	7 39	B	7 07	LIB	19
99	8	M.	5 14	B	6 18	D	13 04	14	1¾	2½	11 P.M. 28	E	8 30	B	7 29	OPH	20
100	9	Tu.	5 13	B	6 19	D	13 06	14	2¾	3¼	— —	–	9 28	B	7 51	SAG	21
101	10	W.	5 11	B	6 21	D	13 10	14	3½	4¼	12 A.M. 23	E	10 30	B	8 13	SAG	22
102	11	Th.	5 09	B	6 22	D	13 13	14	4¾	5½	1 11	E	11 A.M. 37	C	8 35	SAG	23
103	12	Fr.	5 08	B	6 23	D	13 15	15	5¾	6½	1 55	E	12 P.M. 45	C	8 57	AQU	24
104	13	Sa.	5 06	B	6 24	D	13 18	15	6¾	7½	2 34	D	1 54	D	9 19	CAP	25
105	14	**F**	5 04	B	6 25	D	13 21	15	8	8½	3 10	D	3 03	D	9 40	AQU	26
106	15	M.	5 03	B	6 26	D	13 23	16	9	9¼	3 44	C	4 10	D	10 02	PSC	27
107	16	Tu.	5 01	B	6 27	D	13 26	16	9¾	10¼	4 17	C	5 17	E	10 23	PSC	28
108	17	W.	5 00	B	6 28	D	13 28	16	10¾	11	4 51	C	6 22	E	10 44	PSC	0
109	18	Th.	4 58	B	6 30	D	13 32	16	11½	11¾	5 26	B	7 26	E	11 05	ARI	1
110	19	Fr.	4 56	B	6 31	D	13 35	16	—	12¼	6 04	B	8 26	E	11 26	ARI	2
111	20	Sa.	4 55	B	6 32	D	13 37	17	12¼	1	6 44	B	9 23	E	11 46	TAU	3
112	21	**F**	4 53	B	6 33	D	13 40	17	1	1½	7 28	B	10 16	E	12 07	TAU	4
113	22	M.	4 52	B	6 34	D	13 42	17	1¾	2½	8 15	B	11 04	E	12 27	TAU	5
114	23	Tu.	4 50	B	6 35	D	13 45	17	2½	3¼	9 05	B	11 P.M. 47	E	12 47	GEM	6
115	24	W.	4 49	B	6 36	D	13 47	17	3¼	4	9 58	B	— —	–	13 07	GEM	7
116	25	Th.	4 47	B	6 38	D	13 51	18	4¼	5	10 53	C	12 A.M. 26	E	13 26	CAN	8
117	26	Fr.	4 46	B	6 39	D	13 53	18	5¼	5¾	11 A.M. 49	C	1 01	E	13 45	CAN	9
118	27	Sa.	4 45	B	6 40	D	13 55	18	6	6¾	12 P.M. 47	C	1 33	D	14 04	LEO	10
119	28	**F**	4 43	B	6 41	D	13 58	18	7	7½	1 46	D	2 04	D	14 23	SEX	11
120	29	M.	4 42	B	6 42	D	14 00	18	7¾	8¼	2 47	D	2 34	D	14 42	LEO	12
121	30	Tu.	4 40	B	6 43	D	14 03	18	8¾	9	3 P.M. 50	D	3 A.M. 04	C	15N.00	VIR	13

APRIL hath 30 days. 1996

And all the woods are alive with the murmur and sound of Spring,
And the rose-bud breaks into pink on the climbing briar,
And the crocus-bed is a quivering moon of fire
Girdled round with the belt of an amethyst ring.

– Oscar Wilde

D. M.	D. W.	Dates, Feasts, Fasts, Aspects, Tide Heights	Weather ↓
1	M.	**All Fools** • U.S. began wartime rationing of meats, cooking oils, cheese, 1943 • {9.6 / 9.6} •	*It's*
2	Tu.	☾ on Eq. • First White House Easter egg roll, 1877 • Tides {9.9 / 10.0}	*raining*
3	W.	☾ at ☊ • **Full Sprouting Grass** ○ • Eclipse ☾ •	
4	Th.	**First day of Passover** • Linus Yale born, 1821 • {10.3 / 10.7} •	*buckets*
5	Fr.	**Good Friday** • Booker T. Washington born, 1856 •	*from*
6	Sa.	*Buy what you don't need and you'll sell what you can't spare.* • {11.0 / 10.3} •	*Maine to*
7	**F**	**Easter** • Daylight Saving Time begins, 2 A.M. • {11.1 / 10.2}	*Nantucket.*
8	M.	O. Raymond Knight, "Father of Canadian Rodeo," born 1872 • Pablo Picasso died, 1973 •	*In*
9	Tu.	☾ runs low • Astrodome opened in Houston, Texas, 1965 •	*Greenwich*
10	W.	☌ ♃ ☾ • ☾ at perig. • ASPCA founded 1866 •	*they're*
11	Th.	☌ ♆ ☾ • ☌ ♅ ☾ • Tides {10.4 / 9.5} •	*dreenwiched,*
12	Fr.	Yuri Gagarin became first man in space, 1961 • Space shuttle *Columbia* made first flight, 1981 •	*and*
13	Sa.	*While we consider when to begin, it becomes too late.* • Tides {10.2 / 9.9} •	*it's*
14	**F**	**1st S. af. Easter** • **Orthodox Easter** •	*coming*
15	M.	☾ on Eq. • ☌ ♄ ☾ • *The wages of sin are unreported.* •	*down*
16	Tu.	☾ at ☋ • Charlie Chaplin born, 1889 • {10.7 / 11.1} •	*torrents*
17	W.	New ● • Eclipse ☉ • First issue of *Stars and Stripes* published, 1942 •	*in*
18	Th.	First "washateria" opened, Fort Worth, Texas, 1934 • {10.6 / 11.2} •	*Lawrence.*
19	Fr.	☌ ☿ ☾ • Grace Kelly married Prince Rainier of Monaco, 1956 •	*At*
20	Sa.	*A vacant mind is open to all suggestions, as a hollow building echoes all sounds.* • {11.0 / 10.1} •	*last*
21	**F**	**2nd S. af. Easter** • **St. Anselm** • ☌ ♀ ☾ •	*it's*
22	M.	☾ rides high • First Oklahoma land rush began, 1889 • {10.4 / 9.3} •	*dry out*
23	Tu.	☿ Gr. Elong. (20° E.) • William Shakespeare born, 1564; died, 1616 • {10.0 / 8.9} •	*for*
24	W.	☾ at apo. • Library of Congress established, 1800 • Robert B. Thomas born, 1766	*Little*
25	Th.	**St. Mark** • Ella Fitzgerald born, 1918 • Tides {9.2 / 8.5} •	*League*
26	Fr.	John Wilkes Booth killed, 1865 • John James Audubon born, 1785 •	*tryouts.*
27	Sa.	*The devil can cite Scripture for his purpose.* • Tides {8.9 / 8.7} •	*Spoke*
28	**F**	**3rd S. af. Easter** • Lionel Barrymore born, 1878 •	*too*
29	M.	**St. Catherine** • ☾ on Eq. • ♆ stat. • {9.1 / 9.5} •	*soon —*
30	Tu.	Engineer Casey Jones died in train wreck, 1900 • Willie Nelson born, 1933	*monsoon!*

It is easier to fight for one's principles than to live up to them.

Farmer's Calendar

"Mud Time," we say, a simple, single idea, and so in our careless way we dismiss a substance that is fundamentally intellectual, even spiritual. Mud is not merely inconvenient stuff that happens to turn up each year around this time. On the contrary, mud is a complex, changing medium full of suggestion.

Consider how the mud of a single spring day transforms itself. In the morning, when you start off to work, the muddy road you drive will have frozen in the night. It will be bumpy but hard, offering no real obstacle to progress. "Piece of cake," you will say. If your sortie comes a couple of hours later, however, taking you to the store or the post office, the top inch or so of mud will have thawed out and turned to grease. You'll find yourself slipping along like a lump of bacon fat on a hot griddle, but the road will still be hard, the track fast.

At the end of the day, when you make your homeward trip, you will meet the mud at its best, its worst. The bottom will have fallen out of the road. All day the mud has been growing softer, deeper, and now it's prime. You find your way home has turned into a landscape in a dream, one of those long, weary, futile dreams just this side of nightmare in which you run or stumble along, evidently in pursuit of something ahead but never gaining on it, never making headway at all, really, for somehow the faster you run, the slower you go. It occurs to you that your life has gone profoundly but obscurely wrong and that your present ordeal is in some vague way an atonement — but for what? Were you a trifle overconfident this morning when you went down this same road? *Piece of cake,* indeed!

1996 MAY, THE FIFTH MONTH

Venus blazes to greatest brilliancy on the 4th, but also begins to set dramatically sooner after the Sun. By late in the month, as seen by telescope, it has become a remarkably thin and long crescent. On the evening of the 7th, the Moon is near Jupiter in the southwest; at dawn on the 13th it is near Saturn in the southeast. As dusk fades, the Big Dipper is pouring its imaginary contents onto the North Star and Little Dipper; extending the arc of its handle outward leads to the brilliant orange star Arcturus and onward to Virgo's brightest star, Spica. Compact Corvus the Crow flies not far to the lower right of Spica. Very dim Pluto appears at its best on the 22nd.

○	Full Moon	3rd day	6th hour	49th min.
☾	Last Quarter	10th day	0 hour	5th min.
●	New Moon	17th day	6th hour	47th min.
☽	First Quarter	25th day	9th hour	15th min.

ADD 1 hour for Daylight Saving Time.

For an explanation of this page, see "How to Use This Almanac," page 30; for values of Key Letters, see Time Correction Tables, page 196.

Day of Year	Day of Month	Day of Week	☼ Rises h. m.	Key	☼ Sets h. m.	Key	Length of Days h. m.	Sun Fast m.	Full Sea Boston A.M.	Full Sea Boston P.M.	☽ Rises h. m.	Key	☽ Sets h. m.	Key	Declination of Sun ° '	☽ Place	☽ Age
122	1	W.	4 39	B	6 44	D	14 05	18	9½	9¾	4 P.M. 55	E	3 A.M. 36	C	15N.18	VIR	14
123	2	Th.	4 38	B	6 45	D	14 07	19	10¼	10½	6 01	E	4 10	C	15 36	VIR	15
124	3	Fr.	4 36	A	6 46	D	14 10	19	11	11¼	7 09	E	4 49	B	15 54	LIB	16
125	4	Sa.	4 35	A	6 48	D	14 13	19	11¾	—	8 16	E	5 32	B	16 11	LIB	17
126	5	**F**	4 34	A	6 49	D	14 15	19	12	12½	9 19	E	6 23	B	16 28	OPH	18
127	6	M.	4 33	A	6 50	D	14 17	19	12¾	1¼	10 18	E	7 19	B	16 45	OPH	19
128	7	Tu.	4 31	A	6 51	D	14 20	19	1½	2¼	11 10	E	8 22	B	17 01	SAG	20
129	8	W.	4 30	A	6 52	D	14 22	19	2½	3¼	11 P.M. 56	D	9 29	B	17 17	SAG	21
130	9	Th.	4 29	A	6 53	D	14 24	19	3½	4	— —	–	10 37	C	17 33	CAP	22
131	10	Fr.	4 28	A	6 54	D	14 26	19	4½	5¼	12 A.M. 36	D	11 A.M. 46	C	17 49	CAP	23
132	11	Sa.	4 27	A	6 55	D	14 28	19	5½	6¼	1 12	D	12 P.M. 54	D	18 04	AQU	24
133	12	**F**	4 26	A	6 56	D	14 30	19	6½	7¼	1 46	D	2 00	D	18 19	PSC	25
134	13	M.	4 24	A	6 57	D	14 33	19	7¾	8¼	2 19	C	3 06	D	18 33	PSC	26
135	14	Tu.	4 23	A	6 58	E	14 35	19	8¾	9	2 51	C	4 11	E	18 48	PSC	27
136	15	W.	4 22	A	6 59	E	14 37	19	9½	9¾	3 25	B	5 14	E	19 02	PSC	28
137	16	Th.	4 21	A	7 00	E	14 39	19	10¼	10½	4 01	B	6 15	E	19 16	ARI	29
138	17	Fr.	4 20	A	7 01	E	14 41	19	11	11¼	4 39	B	7 13	E	19 29	TAU	0
139	18	Sa.	4 20	A	7 02	E	14 42	19	11¾	—	5 22	B	8 08	E	19 43	TAU	1
140	19	**F**	4 19	A	7 03	E	14 44	19	12	12½	6 08	B	8 58	E	19 55	TAU	2
141	20	M.	4 18	A	7 04	E	14 46	19	12½	1¼	6 57	B	9 43	E	20 08	ORI	3
142	21	Tu.	4 17	A	7 05	E	14 48	19	1¼	2	7 49	B	10 24	E	20 20	GEM	4
143	22	W.	4 16	A	7 06	E	14 50	19	2	2¾	8 43	B	11 00	E	20 31	GEM	5
144	23	Th.	4 15	A	7 07	E	14 52	19	2¾	3½	9 39	C	11 P.M. 33	E	20 43	CAN	6
145	24	Fr.	4 15	A	7 08	E	14 53	19	3½	4¼	10 35	C	— —	–	20 54	CAN	7
146	25	Sa.	4 14	A	7 09	E	14 55	19	4½	5	11 A.M. 33	D	12 A.M. 04	D	21 05	LEO	8
147	26	**F**	4 13	A	7 10	E	14 57	19	5¼	6	12 P.M. 32	D	12 34	D	21 15	LEO	9
148	27	M.	4 13	A	7 11	E	14 58	18	6¼	6¾	1 33	D	1 03	D	21 25	VIR	10
149	28	Tu.	4 12	A	7 12	E	15 00	18	7¼	7½	2 36	D	1 33	C	21 35	VIR	11
150	29	W.	4 11	A	7 12	E	15 01	18	8	8¼	3 41	E	2 06	C	21 44	VIR	12
151	30	Th.	4 11	A	7 13	E	15 02	18	8¾	9¼	4 48	E	2 42	B	21 52	VIR	13
152	31	Fr.	4 10	A	7 14	E	15 04	18	9¾	10	5 P.M. 56	E	3 A.M. 23	B	22N.01	LIB	14

MAY hath 31 days. 1996

In the great gardens, after bright spring rain,
We find sweet innocence come once again,
White periwinkles, little pensionnaires
With muslin gowns and shy and candid airs.
– Edith Sitwell

D. M.	D. W.	Dates, Feasts, Fasts, Aspects, Tide Heights	Weather ↓
1	W.	**Sts. Philip & James** • ☾ at ☊ • Tides {9.7 / 10.5 •	*This*
2	Th.	**St. Athanasius** • Dr. Benjamin Spock born, 1903 •	*month's*
3	Fr.	**Full Flower** ○ • Invention of the Cross • Pete Seeger born, 1919 •	*name*
4	Sa.	☿ stat. • ♀ Greatest Brilliancy • ♃ stat. • Tides {10.4 / — •	*is*
5	**F**	**4th S. af. Easter** • Spencer Tracy born, 1900 • {11.6 / 10.5	*truly*
6	M.	☾ runs low • ☾ at perig. • Willie Mays born, 1931 •	*fitting —*
7	Tu.	☌♃☾ • *The same fire purifies gold and consumes straw.* • {11.5 / 10.3 •	*may*
8	W.	☌♆☾ • ⛢ stat. • Over 6" snow, Indiana to New England, 1803 •	*be*
9	Th.	**St. Gregory of Nazianzus** • ☌⛢☾ • Tides {10.9 / 10.0	*sunny,*
10	Fr.	Nelson Mandela sworn in as first black president of South Africa, 1994 • {10.5 / 10.0 •	*may*
11	Sa.	Salvador Dali born, 1904 • **Three** • Bob Marley died, 1981 • {10.2 / 10.1 •	*be*
12	**F**	**Rogation S.** • ☾ on Eq. • **Chilly** •	*spitting.*
13	M.	☌♄☾ • First U.S. airmail stamps, 1918 • **Saints** •	*May*
14	Tu.	☾ at ☋ • ☿ in inf. ☌ • Gabriel Fahrenheit born, 1686 • {10.0 / 10.8	*be*
15	W.	☌♂☾ • First nylon stockings sold, 1940 • Tides {10.0 / 10.9	*hot,*
16	Th.	**Ascension** • First "Oscars" awarded, 1929 • Henry Fonda born, 1905 •	*may*
17	Fr.	**New** ● • Aristides won first Kentucky Derby, 1875 • Tides {9.9 / 10.9 •	*be*
18	Sa.	*"If" and "when" were planted, and "nothing" grew.* • Tides {9.8 / — •	*not.*
19	**F**	**1st S. af. Asc.** • **St. Dunstan** • ☌♀☾ •	*May*
20	M.	☾ rides high • ♀ stat. • Victoria Day (Canada) • {10.6 / 9.4	*changes*
21	Tu.	President Grant's daughter, Nellie, married at the White House, 1874 • {10.3 / 9.2	*moods*
22	W.	♇ at ☍ • ☾ at apo. • Tides {10.0 / 9.1 •	*just*
23	Th.	**Orthodox Ascension** • South Carolina became 8th state, 1788 •	*like*
24	Fr.	**Shavuot** • Bob Dylan born, 1941 • Tides {9.4 / 8.8 •	*a baby:*
25	Sa.	**St. Bede** • *No country or age has a monopoly on human folly.* •	*Someone*
26	**F**	**Whit S.** • **Pentecost** • **St. Augustine of Canterbury**	
27	M.	**Memorial Day** • ☾ on Eq. • ☿ stat. • Tides {8.9 / 9.4	*should*
28	Tu.	☾ at ☊ • 97° F at San Francisco, 1887 • Tides {9.0 / 9.8	*have*
29	W.	Ember Day • Bob Hope born, 1903 • John F. Kennedy born, 1917 •	*named*
30	Th.	*Good words without good deeds are rushes and reeds.* • Tides {9.5 / 10.8 •	*it*
31	Fr.	**Visit. of Mary** • ☌☿♂ • Ember Day •	*"maybe."*

Farmer's Calendar

In May 1791 Thomas Jefferson, U.S. Secretary of State, made a journey to New York, the upper Hudson River, and Lake Champlain. It was Jefferson's only trip to the interior of the North, and he eagerly observed the region's plants and animals and compared them with those of his home in Virginia. Writing from Bennington, Vermont, he noted the abundant pines, firs, and sugar maples, all rarities in the South. Jefferson also described as new to him a "small red squirrel of the color of our fox-squirrel, with a black stripe on each side, weighing about 6 oz. generally. . . ."

Jefferson's novel squirrel sounds like the common red squirrel of the northern woods, which is the size he suggests and which in summer shows black on its sides. Jefferson ought to have known this squirrel, which is also found in the mountains of Virginia, but he didn't recognize it. Why not?

We can only guess, but history tells us that squirrels weren't the only new things found on that northern tour. Although Jefferson blandly referred to the trip as a "botanizing excursion," it turned out that a certain amount of highly effective politicking got done that spring. For according to American political legend, the Virginian's visit to the North was intended to make an alliance between the planters of the South and the growing industrial populations of New York, an alliance that would oppose what Jefferson saw as the dangerous machinations of Alexander Hamilton and the old Federalists. The result was the party that, as the Democrats, dominated American politics for 100 years. If Jefferson failed to know that squirrel, it may have been because he had other things on his mind.

1996 — JUNE, THE SIXTH MONTH

As June's long evening twilights fade, Leo is approaching the west horizon, and the Summer Triangle of Vega, Deneb, and Altair is coming up in the east. High in the south shines bright Arcturus and its kite-shaped constellation, Bootes. Climbing the southeast sky is Scorpius, whose heart-star is the ruddy and bright Antares. Jupiter rises big and brilliant at evening's end; on the night of the 30th-July 1st, the month's second full Moon is near Jupiter. Venus is at inferior conjunction on the 10th; late in the month, the planet springs up just before dawn, passing near fainter Mercury on the 23rd. Summer solstice arrives at 9:24 P.M., EST, on the 20th.

○	Full Moon	1st day	15th hour	48th min.
☾	Last Quarter	8th day	6th hour	6th min.
●	New Moon	15th day	20th hour	37th min.
☽	First Quarter	24th day	0 hour	25th min.
○	Full Moon	30th day	22nd hour	59th min.

ADD 1 hour for Daylight Saving Time.

For an explanation of this page, see "How to Use This Almanac," page 30; for values of Key Letters, see Time Correction Tables, page 196.

Day of Year	Day of Month	Day of Week	☉ Rises h. m.	Key	☉ Sets h. m.	Key	Length of Days h. m.	Sun Fast m.	Full Sea Boston A.M.	Full Sea Boston P.M.	☽ Rises h. m.	Key	☽ Sets h. m.	Key	Declination of Sun ° '	☽ Place	☽ Age
153	1	Sa.	4 10	A	7 15	E	15 05	18	10½	10¾	7 P.M. 03	E	4 A.M. 10	B	22N.09	SCO	15
154	2	**F**	4 09	A	7 16	E	15 07	18	11¼	11½	8 06	E	5 05	B	22 16	OPH	16
155	3	M.	4 09	A	7 16	E	15 07	18	—	12¼	9 03	E	6 07	B	22 23	SAG	17
156	4	Tu.	4 09	A	7 17	E	15 08	17	12½	1	9 53	E	7 14	B	22 30	SAG	18
157	5	W.	4 08	A	7 17	E	15 09	17	1¼	2	10 36	E	8 24	C	22 37	CAP	19
158	6	Th.	4 08	A	7 18	E	15 10	17	2¼	3	11 15	E	9 35	C	22 43	AQU	20
159	7	Fr.	4 08	A	7 19	E	15 11	17	3¼	3¾	11 P.M. 50	D	10 45	D	22 49	AQU	21
160	8	Sa.	4 07	A	7 19	E	15 12	17	4¼	4¾	— —	–	11 A.M. 53	D	22 54	PSC	22
161	9	**F**	4 07	A	7 20	E	15 13	16	5¼	5¾	12 A.M. 22	D	12 P.M. 59	D	22 59	PSC	23
162	10	M.	4 07	A	7 21	E	15 14	16	6¼	6¾	12 55	C	2 03	D	23 03	PSC	24
163	11	Tu.	4 07	A	7 21	E	15 14	16	7¼	7¾	1 27	C	3 06	E	23 07	PSC	25
164	12	W.	4 07	A	7 22	E	15 15	16	8¼	8¾	2 02	B	4 07	E	23 11	ARI	26
165	13	Th.	4 07	A	7 22	E	15 15	16	9¼	9½	2 39	B	5 06	E	23 15	ARI	27
166	14	Fr.	4 07	A	7 23	E	15 16	15	10	10¼	3 19	B	6 02	E	23 18	TAU	28
167	15	Sa.	4 07	A	7 23	E	15 16	15	10¾	11	4 03	B	6 53	E	23 20	TAU	0
168	16	**F**	4 07	A	7 23	E	15 16	15	11½	11½	4 51	B	7 40	E	23 22	ORI	1
169	17	M.	4 07	A	7 24	E	15 17	15	—	12¼	5 42	B	8 23	E	23 23	GEM	2
170	18	Tu.	4 07	A	7 24	E	15 17	15	12¼	12¾	6 35	B	9 01	E	23 24	GEM	3
171	19	W.	4 07	A	7 24	E	15 17	14	1	1½	7 30	C	9 35	D	23 25	CAN	4
172	20	Th.	4 07	A	7 24	E	15 17	14	1½	2¼	8 26	C	10 06	D	23 25	CAN	5
173	21	Fr.	4 07	A	7 24	E	15 17	14	2¼	3	9 23	C	10 36	D	23 25	LEO	6
174	22	Sa.	4 08	A	7 25	E	15 17	14	3	3½	10 21	C	11 05	D	23 25	SEX	7
175	23	**F**	4 08	A	7 25	E	15 17	13	3¾	4½	11 A.M. 20	D	11 P.M. 34	D	23 24	LEO	8
176	24	M.	4 08	A	7 25	E	15 17	13	4¾	5¼	12 P.M. 20	D	— —	–	23 23	VIR	9
177	25	Tu.	4 09	A	7 25	E	15 16	13	5½	6	1 23	E	12 A.M. 05	C	23 21	VIR	10
178	26	W.	4 09	A	7 25	E	15 16	13	6½	6¾	2 27	E	12 38	C	23 19	VIR	11
179	27	Th.	4 09	A	7 25	E	15 16	13	7¼	7¾	3 34	E	1 15	B	23 16	LIB	12
180	28	Fr.	4 10	A	7 25	E	15 15	12	8¼	8½	4 41	E	1 58	B	23 13	LIB	13
181	29	Sa.	4 10	A	7 25	E	15 15	12	9¼	9½	5 46	E	2 48	B	23 10	OPH	14
182	30	**F**	4 11	A	7 25	E	15 14	12	10	10¼	6 P.M. 47	E	3 A.M. 46	B	23N.07	SAG	15

JUNE hath 30 days. 1996

Rainbows; and the blue bitter smoke of wood;
And radiant raindrops couching in cool flowers;
And flowers themselves, that sway through sunny hours;
Dreaming of moths that drink them under the moon.
– Rupert Brooke

D. M.	D. W.	Dates, Feasts, Fasts, Aspects, Tide Heights	Weather ↓
1	Sa.	Full Rose ○ • Kentucky became 15th state, 1792 • Ember Day •	*Showers*
2	F	**Trinity** • **Orthodox Pentecost** • Tides {10.4 / 12.0}	*ending,*
3	M.	☾ runs low • ☾ at perig. • Silver eliminated from U.S. dimes and quarters, 1965 •	*chill*
4	Tu.	☌♃☾ • ☌♆☾ • Tides {12.1 / 10.7} •	*descending.*
5	W.	**St. Boniface** • ☌♅☾ • Robert F. Kennedy assassinated, 1968 •	*Ditch*
6	Th.	**Corpus Christi** • American Lung Assoc. held first meeting, 1904 • {11.6 / 10.6} •	*the*
7	Fr.	*The harder you fall, the higher you bounce.* • Tides {11.1 / 10.5} •	*sweater;*
8	Sa.	☾ on Eq. • Ives W. McGaffey of Chicago patented vacuum cleaner, 1869 • {10.6 / 10.4} •	*it's*
9	F	**2nd S. af. P.** • **Orthodox All Saints** • ☌♄☾ •	
10	M.	☾ at ☋ • ☿ Gr. Elong. (24° W.) • ♀ in inf. ☌ •	*warmer*
11	Tu.	**St. Barnabas** • Mount Pinatubo erupted, 1991 •	*(and wetter).*
12	W.	Baseball Hall of Fame dedicated, 1939 • Tides {9.4 / 10.5} •	*Caps and*
13	Th.	☌☿☾ • ☌♂☾ • Tides {9.4 / 10.6} •	*gowns and*
14	Fr.	**St. Basil** • ☌☿♂ • Flag Day • {9.4 / 10.6} •	*farewell*
15	Sa.	New ● • Arkansas became 25th state, 1836 • {9.4 / 10.6} •	*kisses —*
16	F	**3rd S. af. P.** • ☾ rides high • Tides {9.3 / 10.6} •	*what a*
17	M.	Battle of Bunker Hill, 1775 • Igor Stravinsky born, 1882 •	*shining*
18	Tu.	*Laziness travels so slowly that poverty soon overtakes him.* • Tides {10.4 / 9.3}	*moment*
19	W.	☾ at apo. • Guy Lombardo born, 1902 • Tides {10.3 / 9.3} •	*this is!*
20	Th.	Summer Solstice • West Virginia became 35th state, 1863 • {10.1 / 9.2} •	*Gardens*
21	Fr.	90° F Nantucket, Mass., 1923 • Jean Paul Sartre born, 1905 •	*bake in*
22	Sa.	**St. Alban** • Anne Morrow Lindbergh born, 1906 • {9.5 / 9.2} •	*vernal*
23	F	**4th S. af. P.** • ☾ on Eq. • ☌☿♀ • {9.3 / 9.3} •	*heat,*
24	M.	**Nativ. John the Baptist** • ☾ at ☊ • Midsummer Day •	
25	Tu.	Rose O'Neill, creator of Kewpie doll, born, 1874 • Tides {9.0 / 9.7} •	*bringing*
26	W.	Pearl S. Buck born, 1892 • *A closed mouth catches no flies.* • Tides {9.0 / 10.1} •	*forth*
27	Th.	"Captain Kangaroo" (Bob Keeshan) born, 1927 • Helen Keller born, 1880 • {9.1 / 10.5}	*good*
28	Fr.	Battle of Monmouth fought "in sweltering heat — 96° F in the shade," 1778 •	*things*
29	Sa.	**Sts. Peter & Paul** • ☌♀♂ • Tides {9.8 / 11.5} •	*to*
30	F	**5th S. af. P.** • ☾ runs low • Full Strawberry ○ •	*eat.*

We don't know what we want, but we are ready to bite somebody to get it. – Will Rogers

Farmer's Calendar

Having made the necessary measurements and finished a series of computations, I have discovered that by summer's end, I will have walked, in the course of cutting the grass in my backyard, a distance of a little over seven miles. I worked that out by mapping the yard, finding its area, measuring the swath cut by my mower, figuring out how many passes the mower took to cut the whole area of the yard, dividing, multiplying. The result, 7.3 miles, seemed insufficiently remarkable, however, so I extrapolated it over a lifetime of mowing and arrived at a prospective total of miles walked by me in pushing a lawn mower around my yard: 292, or the distance from this house to Havre de Grace, Maryland. *That's more like it*, I thought.

I decided to go through the process just recounted for the sake of applying to my own humble life the kind of grandiose statistical translation so common in journalism, in which, for example, we learn that the current National Debt of the United States, taken in one-dollar bills laid end-to-end, would reach from Washington, D.C., to Jupiter. The best thing about these elaborate comparisons is how easy they are to execute; buy a dime-store calculator and the universe is yours. I have discovered that in driving my kids to the bus through their careers in school, we traveled the distance from home to Tokyo. Not bad.

In the end, though, I found, arrived a certain ennui. Havre de Grace is a long way to push a mower, Jupiter longer still. These majestic comparisons are offered by clever writers who wish to make abstract mathematical facts accessible to peasants, but in the end they don't tell us anything that helps. They only make us tired.

1996 JULY, THE SEVENTH MONTH

Jupiter reaches opposition on the 4th and is visible all night long at its brightest and (in telescopes) biggest. It rises in the southeast at sunset and burns in Sagittarius at the south end of the summer Milky Way. Venus climbs higher in the east before sunrise each day, reaching its greatest brilliancy on the 17th. Saturn's rings are their most tilted for the year, but the planet is not high until near dawn, when it is the brightest point of light in the south. The Moon is near Venus on the 12th and near Jupiter on the 28th. Vega is high in the east and Arcturus high in the west these evenings. Earth is at aphelion on the 5th.

☾	Last Quarter	7th day	13th hour	56th min.
●	New Moon	15th day	11th hour	16th min.
☽	First Quarter	23rd day	12th hour	50th min.
○	Full Moon	30th day	5th hour	37th min.

ADD 1 hour for Daylight Saving Time.

For an explanation of this page, see "How to Use This Almanac," page 30; for values of Key Letters, see Time Correction Tables, page 196.

Day of Year	Day of Month	Day of Week	☉ Rises h. m.	Key	☉ Sets h. m.	Key	Length of Days h. m.	Sun Fast m.	Full Sea Boston A.M.	Full Sea Boston P.M.	☽ Rises h. m.	Key	☽ Sets h. m.	Key	Declination of Sun ° '	☽ Place	☽ Age
183	1	M.	4 11	A	7 25	E	15 14	12	11	11¼	7 P.M. 42	E	4 A.M. 52	B	23N.03	SAG	16
184	2	Tu.	4 12	A	7 25	E	15 13	12	11¾	—	8 30	E	6 03	B	22 58	SAG	17
185	3	W.	4 12	A	7 24	E	15 12	11	12	12¾	9 12	D	7 16	C	22 53	AQU	18
186	4	Th.	4 13	A	7 24	E	15 11	11	1	1¾	9 50	D	8 29	D	22 48	CAP	19
187	5	Fr.	4 14	A	7 24	E	15 10	11	2	2½	10 25	D	9 40	D	22 42	AQU	20
188	6	Sa.	4 14	A	7 23	E	15 09	11	2¾	3½	10 58	C	10 49	D	22 36	PSC	21
189	7	**F**	4 15	A	7 23	E	15 08	11	3¾	4½	11 P.M. 31	C	11 A.M. 55	D	22 30	PSC	22
190	8	M.	4 16	A	7 23	E	15 07	11	4¾	5½	— —	–	12 P.M. 59	E	22 23	PSC	23
191	9	Tu.	4 16	A	7 22	E	15 06	10	6	6½	12 A.M. 05	B	2 01	E	22 15	ARI	24
192	10	W.	4 17	A	7 22	E	15 05	10	7	7¼	12 41	B	3 01	E	22 08	ARI	25
193	11	Th.	4 18	A	7 21	E	15 03	10	8	8¼	1 20	B	3 57	E	21 59	TAU	26
194	12	Fr.	4 19	A	7 21	E	15 02	10	8¾	9	2 02	B	4 49	E	21 51	TAU	27
195	13	Sa.	4 19	A	7 20	E	15 01	10	9¾	9¾	2 48	B	5 38	E	21 42	AUR	28
196	14	**F**	4 20	A	7 20	E	15 00	10	10½	10½	3 37	B	6 22	E	21 33	GEM	29
197	15	M.	4 21	A	7 19	E	14 58	10	11	11¼	4 30	B	7 01	E	21 23	GEM	0
198	16	Tu.	4 22	A	7 18	E	14 56	10	11¾	11¾	5 24	B	7 37	E	21 13	CAN	1
199	17	W.	4 23	A	7 18	E	14 55	9	—	12½	6 20	B	8 10	D	21 03	CAN	2
200	18	Th.	4 24	A	7 17	E	14 53	9	12½	1	7 16	C	8 40	D	20 53	LEO	3
201	19	Fr.	4 24	A	7 16	E	14 52	9	1¼	1¾	8 14	C	9 09	D	20 42	SEX	4
202	20	Sa.	4 25	A	7 15	E	14 50	9	1¾	2½	9 12	D	9 38	C	20 30	LEO	5
203	21	**F**	4 26	A	7 14	E	14 48	9	2½	3	10 10	D	10 07	C	20 19	VIR	6
204	22	M.	4 27	A	7 14	E	14 47	9	3¼	3¾	11 A.M. 11	D	10 38	C	20 06	VIR	7
205	23	Tu.	4 28	A	7 13	E	14 45	9	4	4½	12 P.M. 13	E	11 12	B	19 54	VIR	8
206	24	W.	4 29	A	7 12	E	14 43	9	5	5¼	1 16	E	11 P.M. 51	B	19 41	LIB	9
207	25	Th.	4 30	A	7 11	D	14 41	9	5¾	6¼	2 21	E	— —	–	19 28	LIB	10
208	26	Fr.	4 31	A	7 10	D	14 39	9	6¾	7¼	3 26	E	12 A.M. 36	B	19 15	SCO	11
209	27	Sa.	4 32	A	7 09	D	14 37	9	7¾	8¼	4 28	E	1 29	B	19 02	OPH	12
210	28	**F**	4 33	A	7 08	D	14 35	9	8¾	9	5 26	E	2 29	B	18 48	SAG	13
211	29	M.	4 34	A	7 07	D	14 33	9	9¾	10	6 18	E	3 37	B	18 34	SAG	14
212	30	Tu.	4 35	A	7 06	D	14 31	9	10¾	11	7 04	D	4 50	C	18 19	CAP	15
213	31	W.	4 36	A	7 04	D	14 28	9	11½	11¾	7 P.M. 45	D	6 A.M. 04	C	18N.04	CAP	16

JULY hath 31 days. 1996

In the dewy fields the cattle lie
Chewing the cud 'neath a fading sky.
Dobbin at manger pulls his hay:
Gone is another summer's day.
– Walter de la Mare

D. M.	D. W.	Dates, Feasts, Fasts, Aspects, Tide Heights	*Weather* ↓
1	M.	Canada Day • ☌♃☾ • ☾ at perig. • ♀ stat. •	*Linger*
2	Tu.	☌♆☾ • ☌♅☾ • Amelia Earhart disappeared, 1937 •	*late*
3	W.	Dog Days begin. • *Dog Days bright and clear, indicate a happy year.* • {12.3 / 11.0 •	*on*
4	Th.	Independence Day • ♃ at ☍ • Tides {12.1 / 11.1	*summer*
5	Fr.	⊕ at aphelion • Hail storm killed 16 horses, Rapid City, S.D., 1891 •	*porches,*
6	Sa.	☾ on Eq. • 121° F Steele, N.D., 1936 • Tides {11.2 / 10.8	*contemplate*
7	F	6th S. af. P. • ☾ at ☋ • ☌♄☾ •	*those*
8	M.	First public reading of the Declaration of Independence, Philadelphia, Pa., 1776 • {9.9 / 10.4	*fiery*
9	Tu.	Elias Howe, inventor of sewing machine, born, 1819 • Tides {9.4 / 10.3 •	*torches,*
10	W.	Arthur Ashe born, 1943 • Wyoming became 44th state, 1890 • {9.1 / 10.2 •	*crystal*
11	Th.	☿ in sup. ☌ • E. B. White born, 1899 • Tides {9.0 / 10.2 •	*patterns*
12	Fr.	☌♀☾ • ☌♂☾ • U.S. minimum wage 40 cents per hour, 1933 •	*in*
13	Sa.	☾ rides high • Electrical blackout, New York City, 1977 • Tides {9.0 / 10.2 •	*the*
14	F	7th S. af. P. • Bastille Day • Woody Guthrie born, 1912 •	*sky.*
15	M.	St. Swithin • New ● • Rain today means 40 more days of rain. •	*When*
16	Tu.	☾ at apo. • Comet Shoemaker-Levy crashed into Jupiter, 1994 • Tides {9.1 / 10.3 •	*the*
17	W.	♀ Greatest Brilliancy • Disneyland opened, Anaheim, Calif., 1955 • {— / 9.3 •	*rain*
18	Th.	♆ at ☍ • John Glenn born, 1921 • Nelson Mandela born, 1918 •	*comes,*
19	Fr.	♄ stat. • *Be slow to make a promise but swift to keep it.* • {10.1 / 9.4 •	*feel a*
20	Sa.	☾ on Eq. • Supreme Court Justice William Brennan resigned, 1990 •	*frisson;*
21	F	8th S. af. P. • ☾ at ☊ • 10° F, Painter, Wyoming, 1911 •	*go*
22	M.	St. Mary Magdalene • Rose Kennedy born, 1890 • {9.4 / 9.6 •	*inside*
23	Tu.	First U.S. swimming school opened, Boston, Mass., 1827 • Don Drysdale born, 1936 •	*to*
24	W.	*When all else is lost, the future still remains.* • Bella Abzug born, 1920 • {9.0 / 9.9 •	*bed*
25	Th.	St. James • ♅ at ☍ • Cornscateous air is everywhere. •	*and*
26	Fr.	St. Ann • New York became 11th state, 1788 • Tides {9.1 / 10.6 •	*listen*
27	Sa.	Leo Durocher born, 1906 • H.J. Heinz Co. incorporated, 1900 • Tides {9.4 / 11.1 •	*to*
28	F	9th S. af. P. • ☾ runs low • ☌♃☾ • {9.8 / 11.6	*the*
29	M.	Sts. Mary & Martha • ☌♆☾ • ☌♅☾ •	*drum-*
30	Tu.	☾ at perig. • Full Thunder ○ • Tides {10.7 / 12.2 •	*beat*
31	W.	*Education is a better safeguard of liberty than a standing army.* • {11.1 / — •	*of July.*

Farmer's Calendar

Long past midnight, from the hill to the south, now nearby, now far off, comes the demented tumult of the barred owl, invisible wind section of the woods: trumpet, oboe, tuba, sax, and kazoo in one package. There are two of them calling most nights, I think, but it's hard to tell. Sometimes it sounds as though a whole family of owls has moved in next door, a boisterous family given to loud argument and probably to drink.

The call of this owl that you mostly hear is the well-known eight-note phrase that sounds like *Who cooks for you? Who cooks for you-all?* The owl may give this call as a low guttural mutter, or it may belt it out as a cry that echoes over the woods and fields. Even in its conventional utterances, then, it insists on variety. But it also has a repertoire of other noises, all thoroughly weird — a bedlam of groans, shrieks, cackles, and yowls so various that you hardly credit they all come from the same bird. It's a precocious and quite insane mimic. Barking dogs, sick cats, sheep, hens, even a third-rate opera diva with a bad cold may visit the owner of woods where the barred owl holds forth.

In 20 years' attendance at the nocturnal performances of this owl, I have seen the star only once, at evening, perched on a limb over a little-used road in the woods. He looked at me. I looked at him. Then he opened his wings and drifted off into the trees, leaving me with the impression of a big bird, more brown than gray, with an enormous round head and broad wings. He made no sound; no hoot, no barnyard squawk, no madhouse caterwaul. Like so many other antic performers, I guess, the owl is a shy thing when he's not working.

1996 AUGUST, The Eighth Month

After midnight on the 11th and 12th, the Perseid meteors are at their peak, streaking out of the north with no significant interference from moonlight. On the 19th, Venus reaches its greatest elongation west (46 degrees), a magnificent sight in the east before dawn. Jupiter dominates the evening sky from its position in the southeast near the Teapot figure of Sagittarius. Brilliant Scorpius crawls into the southwest while high in the north, dimmer Draco the Dragon extends his compact head toward the zenith. The Moon is near Saturn before dawn on the 3rd, close to Venus at dawn on the 10th (with Mars nearby), and near Jupiter the evening of the 24th.

☾ Last Quarter	6th day	0 hour	26th min.
● New Moon	14th day	2nd hour	35th min.
☽ First Quarter	21st day	22nd hour	38th min.
○ Full Moon	28th day	12th hour	53rd min.

ADD 1 hour for Daylight Saving Time.

For an explanation of this page, see "How to Use This Almanac," page 30; for values of Key Letters, see Time Correction Tables, page 196.

Day of Year	Day of Month	Day of Week	☉ Rises h. m.	Key	☉ Sets h. m.	Key	Length of Days h. m.	Sun Fast m.	Full Sea Boston A.M.	Full Sea Boston P.M.	☽ Rises h. m.	Key	☽ Sets h. m.	Key	Declination of Sun ° '	Place	☽ Age
214	1	Th.	4 37	A	7 03	D	14 26	9	—	12½	8 P M 22	D	7 A M 19	D	17 N. 49	AQU	17
215	2	Fr.	4 38	A	7 02	D	14 24	9	12¾	1¼	8 58	C	8 31	D	17 33	PSC	18
216	3	Sa.	4 39	A	7 01	D	14 22	9	1½	2¼	9 32	C	9 41	D	17 17	PSC	19
217	4	**F**	4 40	A	7 00	D	14 20	10	2½	3	10 06	B	10 48	D	17 01	PSC	20
218	5	M.	4 41	A	6 58	D	14 17	10	3½	4	10 42	B	11 A M 52	E	16 45	PSC	21
219	6	Tu.	4 42	A	6 57	D	14 15	10	4½	5	11 P M 20	B	12 M 53	E	16 28	ARI	22
220	7	W.	4 43	A	6 56	D	14 13	10	5½	5¾	—		1 51	E	16 11	TAU	23
221	8	Th.	4 44	A	6 55	D	14 11	10	6½	6¾	12 A M 02	B	2 45	E	15 54	TAU	24
222	9	Fr.	4 45	A	6 53	D	14 08	10	7½	7¾	12 46	B	3 35	E	15 37	TAU	25
223	10	Sa.	4 46	A	6 52	D	14 06	10	8½	8¾	1 34	B	4 20	E	15 20	GEM	26
224	11	**F**	4 47	A	6 50	D	14 03	10	9¼	9½	2 25	B	5 01	E	15 02	GEM	27
225	12	M.	4 48	A	6 49	D	14 01	11	10	10¼	3 19	B	5 38	E	14 44	CAN	28
226	13	Tu.	4 50	A	6 48	D	13 58	11	10¾	10¾	4 14	C	6 12	D	14 25	CAN	29
227	14	W.	4 51	B	6 46	D	13 55	11	11¼	11½	5 11	C	6 43	D	14 07	LEO	0
228	15	Th.	4 52	B	6 45	D	13 53	11	—	12	6 08	C	7 13	D	13 48	LEO	1
229	16	Fr.	4 53	B	6 43	D	13 50	11	12	12½	7 06	D	7 42	D	13 29	LEO	2
230	17	Sa.	4 54	B	6 42	D	13 48	12	12¾	1	8 04	D	8 11	C	13 10	VIR	3
231	18	**F**	4 55	B	6 40	D	13 45	12	1¼	1¾	9 04	D	8 41	C	12 50	VIR	4
232	19	M.	4 56	B	6 39	D	13 43	12	2	2½	10 04	E	9 14	B	12 30	VIR	5
233	20	Tu.	4 57	B	6 37	D	13 40	12	2¾	3	11 A M 06	E	9 50	B	12 11	VIR	6
234	21	W.	4 58	B	6 36	D	13 38	12	3½	4	12 P M 09	E	10 31	B	11 51	LIB	7
235	22	Th.	4 59	B	6 34	D	13 35	13	4½	4¾	1 12	E	11 A M 19	B	11 30	LIB	8
236	23	Fr.	5 00	B	6 32	D	13 32	13	5½	5¾	2 13	E	—	—	11 10	OPH	9
237	24	Sa.	5 01	B	6 31	D	13 30	13	6½	6¾	3 11	E	12 A M 14	B	10 50	SAG	10
238	25	**F**	5 02	B	6 29	D	13 27	13	7½	7¾	4 04	E	1 16	B	10 29	SAG	11
239	26	M.	5 03	B	6 28	D	13 25	14	8½	8¾	4 52	E	2 25	B	10 08	SAG	12
240	27	Tu.	5 04	B	6 26	D	13 22	14	9½	9¾	5 36	D	3 37	C	9 47	AQU	13
241	28	W.	5 05	B	6 24	D	13 19	14	10¼	10¾	6 15	D	4 52	C	9 26	PSC	14
242	29	Th.	5 07	B	6 23	D	13 16	15	11¼	11½	6 52	D	6 05	D	9 05	AQU	15
243	30	Fr.	5 08	B	6 21	D	13 13	15	—	12	7 28	C	7 18	D	8 43	PSC	16
244	31	Sa.	5 09	B	6 19	D	13 10	15	12½	12¾	8 P M 03	C	8 A M 28	E	8 N. 21	PSC	17

AUGUST hath 31 days. **1996**

Many swarms of wild bees descended on our fields:
Stately stood the wheatstalk with head bent high:
Big of heart we laboured at storing mighty yields,
Wool and corn, and clusters to make men cry!
– George Meredith

D. M.	D. W.	Dates, Feasts, Fasts, Aspects, Tide Heights	Weather ↓
1	Th.	**Lammas Day** • Colorado became 38th state, 1876 • Tides {12.3 / 11.3 •	*Build*
2	Fr.	☾ on Eq. • President Warren G. Harding died, 1923 • {12.0 / 11.4 •	*a*
3	Sa.	☾ at ☋ • ☌ ♄ ☾ • American Canoe Assoc. founded, 1880 •	*castle,*
4	**F**	**10th S. af. P.** • U.S. Dept. of Energy created, 1977 • {11.0 / 11.0	*comb*
5	M.	*One man with courage makes a majority.* • Neil Armstrong born, 1930 • {10.3 / 10.6 •	*a*
6	Tu.	**Transfiguration** • Lucille Ball born, 1911 • Tides {9.7 / 10.3 •	*beach;*
7	W.	**Name of Jesus** • Snowfall, Haverill and Amesbury, Mass., 1893 •	*summer's*
8	Th.	**St. Dominic** • President Nixon announced his resignation, 1974 • {8.8 / 9.8	*ripe*
9	Fr.	☌ ♀ ☾ • Nagasaki bombed, 1945 • Jean Piaget born, 1896 •	*as*
10	Sa.	**St. Laurence** • ☾ rides high • ☌ ♂ ☾ • Tides {8.7 / 9.8 •	*any*
11	**F**	**11th S. af. P.** • **St. Clare** • Dog Days end. •	*peach.*
12	M.	☾ at apo. • First issue *Sports Illustrated,* 1954 • Tides {9.0 / 10.1 •	*Lightning*
13	Tu.	♇ stat. • Annie Oakley born, 1860 • Alfred Hitchcock born, 1899 •	*crack*
14	W.	**New ●** • *If you do not hear Reason, She will rap your knuckles.* • {9.4 / 10.2 •	*and*
15	Th.	**Assumption** • India gained independence, 1947 • {10.2 / 9.6 •	*thunder*
16	Fr.	☌ ☿ ☾ • Rain delayed the start of Battle of Bennington, 1777 •	*rumble —*
17	Sa.	☾ on Eq. • ☾ at ☊ • Cat Nights begin. • Tides {10.1 / 9.8	*rainy*
18	**F**	**12th S. af. P.** • Nineteenth Amendment ratified, 1920 •	*days*
19	M.	♀ Gr. Elong. (46° W.) • Gene Roddenberry born, 1921 • Tides {9.7 / 9.9	*make*
20	Tu.	*Most people would succeed in small things if they were not troubled by great ambitions.* •	*renters*
21	W.	☿ Gr. Elong. (27° E.) • American Bar Assoc. founded, 1878 •	*grumble.*
22	Th.	Teddy Roosevelt became first president to ride in an automobile, 1902 • {9.1 / 10.1 •	*Moms*
23	Fr.	Gene Kelly born, 1912 • Contruction workers paid 2 shillings a day, Mass., 1630 •	*lead*
24	Sa.	**St. Bartholomew** • ☾ runs low • ☌ ♃ ☾ • {9.2 / 10.6	*lives*
25	**F**	**13th S. af. P.** • ☌ ♆ ☾ • Tides {9.5 / 11.0 •	*of*
26	M.	☌ ♅ ☾ • First televised baseball games, WXBS-TV, New York City, 1939 •	*quiet*
27	Tu.	☾ at perig. • Hurricane Cleo battered south Florida, 1964 •	*desperation*
28	W.	**St. Augustine of Hippo** • **Full Sturgeon** ○ • {11.1 / 12.0	*in the*
29	Th.	Billy "Pop" Schriver caught ball dropped from Washington Monument, 1894 •	*last days*
30	Fr.	☾ on Eq. • ☾ at ☋ • ☌ ♄ ☾ • Tides {12.0 / 11.6 •	*of*
31	Sa.	*No one needs a vacation so much as the person who has just had one.* • {11.7 / 11.6	*vacation.*

Farmer's Calendar

With every step you take through the dry, late-summer meadows, grasshoppers spring out of your way. You can hear the little snap they make as they leap from the hard grass stalks; you might be walking through a field of tiny mousetraps. These are the common brown and green grasshoppers with short antennae, cousins of the katydids. They have been around all summer, but until now they were growing and they lay low. Now they're adult. A big one might be two inches long. And they're on the march.

Suddenly grasshoppers seem to be everywhere, popping out of the flowers, out of the gardens, out of the lawn, into your lap, and away, in a mild reprise of the hordes of locusts that the Lord sent to help Pharaoh make up his mind at last to let the Children of Israel depart out of Egypt. Those Egyptian grasshoppers, the Book says, were blown by "a mighty strong west wind" clear into the Red Sea. But you needn't wait for divine intervention to rid you of August's influx. After the first couple of hard frosts, you won't find a solitary grasshopper.

The best thing about grasshoppers, though, is seen not by marveling at their numbers but by catching one and examining it closely. Look at its profile, the most human in the insect world. All insects have eyes and most have a mouth, but the grasshopper has a face. It's a long, rather horselike face with large, candid eyes beneath a noble brow — a refined face but not an aristocratic one. Rather, it's the face of a sober Puritan divine. I have always thought grasshoppers looked like the poet Milton, author of *Paradise Lost,* though no doubt it would be more historical, if less flattering, to say Milton looked like a grasshopper.

1996 SEPTEMBER, THE NINTH MONTH

The full Moon (Harvest Moon) of the 26th is totally eclipsed that evening. The beginning will be visible in eastern and central regions of the U.S. and Canada; the end will be visible in North America (except for extreme western Alaska) and Hawaii. As the Moon darkens, Saturn brightens dramatically nearby. (Saturn reaches opposition that day and is brightest for 1996.) Jupiter is brilliant in the south at nightfall. At dawn on the 4th, Venus and Mars have a close conjunction. The crescent Moon joins them four days later, and late in the month Mercury comes into view, well to the lower left of Venus. The autumnal equinox occurs at 1:00 P.M., EST, on the 22nd.

☾	Last Quarter	4th day	14th hour	7th min.
●	New Moon	12th day	18th hour	9th min.
☽	First Quarter	20th day	6th hour	24th min.
○	Full Moon	26th day	21st hour	52nd min.

ADD 1 hour for Daylight Saving Time.

For an explanation of this page, see "How to Use This Almanac," page 30; for values of Key Letters, see Time Correction Tables, page 196.

Day of Year	Day of Month	Day of Week	☉ Rises h. m.	Key	☉ Sets h. m.	Key	Length of Days h. m.	Sun Fast m.	Full Sea Boston A.M.	Full Sea Boston P.M.	☽ Rises h. m.	Key	☽ Sets h. m.	Key	Declination of Sun ° '	☽ Place	☽ Age
245	1	**F**	5 10	B	6 18	D	13 08	16	1¼	1¾	8 P.M. 40	B	9 A.M. 36	E	8N.00	PSC	18
246	2	M.	5 11	B	6 16	D	13 05	16	2¼	2½	9 18	B	10 40	E	7 38	ARI	19
247	3	Tu.	5 12	B	6 14	D	13 02	16	3	3½	9 59	B	11 A.M. 41	E	7 16	TAU	20
248	4	W.	5 13	B	6 12	D	12 59	17	4	4¼	10 43	B	12 P.M. 38	E	6 53	TAU	21
249	5	Th.	5 14	B	6 11	D	12 57	17	5	5¼	11 P.M. 30	B	1 30	E	6 31	TAU	22
250	6	Fr.	5 15	B	6 09	D	12 54	17	6	6¼	— —	–	2 17	E	6 09	ORI	23
251	7	Sa.	5 16	B	6 07	D	12 51	18	7	7¼	12 A.M. 21	B	3 00	E	5 46	GEM	24
252	8	**F**	5 17	B	6 06	C	12 49	18	8	8¼	1 13	B	3 38	E	5 24	GEM	25
253	9	M.	5 18	B	6 04	C	12 46	18	8¾	9	2 08	B	4 13	D	5 01	CAN	26
254	10	Tu.	5 19	B	6 02	C	12 43	19	9½	9¾	3 04	C	4 45	D	4 38	CAN	27
255	11	W.	5 20	B	6 00	C	12 40	19	10	10¼	4 01	C	5 16	D	4 15	LEO	28
256	12	Th.	5 21	B	5 59	C	12 38	19	10¾	11	4 59	C	5 45	D	3 52	LEO	0
257	13	Fr.	5 22	B	5 57	C	12 35	20	11¼	11½	5 58	D	6 15	C	3 29	VIR	1
258	14	Sa.	5 23	B	5 55	C	12 32	20	—	12	6 57	D	6 45	C	3 06	VIR	2
259	15	**F**	5 24	B	5 53	C	12 29	20	12¼	12½	7 58	E	7 17	C	2 43	VIR	3
260	16	M.	5 26	B	5 51	C	12 25	21	1	1¼	9 00	E	7 52	B	2 20	VIR	4
261	17	Tu.	5 27	B	5 50	C	12 23	21	1½	1¾	10 02	E	8 31	B	1 57	LIB	5
262	18	W.	5 28	B	5 48	C	12 20	21	2¼	2½	11 A.M. 04	E	9 16	B	1 34	LIB	6
263	19	Th.	5 29	C	5 46	C	12 17	22	3¼	3½	12 P.M. 05	E	10 07	B	1 10	OPH	7
264	20	Fr.	5 30	C	5 44	C	12 14	22	4	4½	1 02	E	11 P.M. 05	B	0 47	SAG	8
265	21	Sa.	5 31	C	5 43	C	12 12	22	5	5½	1 55	E	— —	–	0 24	SAG	9
266	22	**F**	5 32	C	5 41	C	12 09	23	6¼	6½	2 44	E	12 A.M. 09	B	0N.01	SAG	10
267	23	M.	5 33	C	5 39	C	12 06	23	7¼	7½	3 28	D	1 17	C	0S.22	CAP	11
268	24	Tu.	5 34	C	5 37	C	12 03	24	8¼	8½	4 08	D	2 28	C	0 46	CAP	12
269	25	W.	5 35	C	5 36	C	12 01	24	9	9½	4 46	D	3 41	D	1 09	AQU	13
270	26	Th.	5 36	C	5 34	C	11 58	24	10	10½	5 22	C	4 53	D	1 32	PSC	14
271	27	Fr.	5 37	C	5 32	B	11 55	25	10¾	11¼	5 57	C	6 04	D	1 55	PSC	15
272	28	Sa.	5 38	C	5 30	B	11 52	25	11½	—	6 34	B	7 14	E	2 19	PSC	16
273	29	**F**	5 39	C	5 29	B	11 50	25	12	12½	7 12	B	8 21	E	2 42	ARI	17
274	30	M.	5 41	C	5 27	B	11 46	26	1	1¼	7 P.M. 53	B	9 A.M. 25	E	3S.05	ARI	18

SEPTEMBER hath 30 days. 1996

Give me the splendid silent sun with all his beams full-dazzling,
Give me juicy autumnal fruit ripe and red from the orchard,
Give me a field where the unmowed grass grows,
Give me an arbor, give me the trellised grape.
– Walt Whitman

D. M.	D. W.	Dates, Feasts, Fasts, Aspects, Tide Heights	Weather ↓
1	**F**	**14th S. af. P.** • First woman telephone operator, Boston, Mass., 1878 •	*Too*
2	M.	**Labor Day** • 400 killed in Labor Day hurricane, Florida Keys, 1935 • {10.7 11.0	*darn*
3	Tu.	♃ stat. • ☿ stat. • Ferdinand Porsche, inventor of the Volkswagen, born, 1875 •	*hot —*
4	W.	☌ ♀ ♂ • Barney Flaherty became first newspaper boy, 1833 • {9.4 10.0 •	*a*
5	Th.	Eleven members of Israel's Olympic team killed at Munich, 1972 • {8.9 9.6 •	*spot*
6	Fr.	☾ rides high • After 67 years as Leningrad, U.S.S.R., historic name of St. Petersburg restored, 1991	*of*
7	Sa.	*Good words cost nothing, but are worth much.* • Tides {8.5 9.4 •	*rain*
8	**F**	**15th S. af. P.** • ☌ ♀ ☾ • ☾ at apo. • ☌ ♂ ☾ •	
9	M.	Abraham Lincoln received license to practice law, 1836 • Tides {8.9 9.7 •	*wouldn't*
10	Tu.	Arnold Palmer born, 1929 • Roger Maris born, 1934 • Tides {9.2 9.9 •	*come*
11	W.	*Politeness is one half good nature and the other half good lying.* • Tides {9.5 10.0	*amiss.*
12	Th.	**New** ● • Four-time Olympic gold medalist (1936) Jesse Owens born, 1913 •	*Bliss!*
13	Fr.	☾ on Eq. • Army physician Walter Reed born, 1851 • {10.0 —	*Topping*
14	Sa.	**Holy Cross** • **Rosh Hashanah** • ☾ at ☊ • {10.2 10.1	*then*
15	**F**	**16th S. af. P.** • Agatha Christie born, 1890 •	*sopping,*
16	M.	6" snow, Stuart, Iowa, 1881 • Selective Service (the draft) started, 1940 •	*mostly*
17	Tu.	☿ in inf. ☌ • Hank Williams born, 1923 • Tides {9.8 10.3	*coastly.*
18	W.	Ember Day • *The school of life is a compulsory education that no one escapes.* •	*A pox*
19	Th.	A quiet week before the autumnal equinox and after, the temperature will continue higher into winter. •	*on*
20	Fr.	☾ runs low • Ember Day • Guy Lafleur born, 1951 • Tides {9.2 10.3 •	*the*
21	Sa.	**St. Matthew** • ☌ ♃ ☾ • Ember Day • {9.2 10.3	*equinox!*
22	**F**	**17th S. af. P.** • **Autumnal Equinox** • ☌ ♆ ☾ • ☌ ♅ ☾ •	
23	M.	**Yom Kippur** • Planet Neptune discovered, 1846 • {9.8 10.8 •	*No foolin',*
24	Tu.	☾ at perig. • Discovery of tetracycline reported, 1953 •	*it's coolin'.*
25	W.	☿ stat. • Barbara Walters born, 1931 • Tides {10.9 11.4 •	*Apples*
26	Th.	☾ on Eq. • ♄ at ☍ • **Full Harvest** ○ • Eclipse ☾ • ☌ ♄ ☾ •	
27	Fr.	**St. Vincent de Paul** • ☾ at ☋ • Tides {11.6 11.5 •	*are*
28	Sa.	**Succoth** • Ed Sullivan born, 1902 • Louis Pasteur died, 1895 • {11.7 —	*ripe,*
29	**F**	**18th S. af. P.** • **St. Michael** • {11.2 11.6 •	*children*
30	M.	**St. Jerome** • Babe Ruth hit 60th home run of season, 1927 •	*gripe.*

There is no pleasure in having nothing to do; the fun is in having lots to do and not doing it.

Farmer's Calendar

The hop hornbeam *(Ostrya virginiana)* is a small or middling tree related to the birches, a "serviceable and self-effacing" species, as D. C. Peattie writes in his rich and well-loved book on the American trees. It's fairly common in the foothills where I live; indeed there is quite a little grove of hornbeams on a wooded knoll a quarter mile from my house. None of the trees up there is more than 35 to 40 feet tall, few or none is a foot thick. Their bark is brown and scaly, their leaves oval, toothed, birchlike.

The wood of the hop hornbeam, I read, is nearly the hardest in the northern forest, hence the tree's other common name, ironwood. As you'd expect of a hard, heavy wood, it makes good fuel, although I have always found it hard to split because the grain seems often to twist. Maybe that's why the wood is so tough.

The fruit of this species is curious. I have one before me. It's a hanging cluster, two inches long, of 20 seeds arranged like overlapping scales. Each scale is a flimsy sac within which the seed itself is about the size and shape of a small apple seed. The fruit as a whole looks like the flower of the hop, that ancient vine whose greasy, bitter blossoms yield an oil used in brewing. This resemblance, which is striking, has always seemed to me odd. What does it do? We expect resemblance in nature to be based on advantage, as in the famous pair of like butterflies, the one poisonous, the other harmless but protected from predators who mistake it for its bitter twin. Where's the advantage to the hornbeam in having its fruit resemble the hop? No place, perhaps. Are we too serious in our science? In our explanation of nature do we forget to admit caprice?

1996 OCTOBER, The Tenth Month

Mercury gives its best dawn showing of the year for a number of mornings before and after its greatest elongation west from the Sun (18 degrees) on the 3rd; look for it before sunrise well to the left of more brilliant Venus. The Moon is near Venus on the evening of the 8th, near Jupiter in the southwest after dusk on the 18th. At midevening, Saturn shines in the southeast between the low star Fomalhaut and the higher-up Great Square of Pegasus. The Orionid meteors fly from the south before morning on the 21st and 22nd. The partial solar eclipse on the 12th will be visible only in northeastern Canada. Daylight Saving Time ends at 2:00 A.M. on the 27th.

☾	Last Quarter	4th day	7th hour	6th min.
●	New Moon	12th day	9th hour	16th min.
☽	First Quarter	19th day	13th hour	10th min.
○	Full Moon	26th day	9th hour	12th min.

ADD 1 hour for Daylight Saving Time until 2 A.M., October 27th.

For an explanation of this page, see "How to Use This Almanac," page 30; for values of Key Letters, see Time Correction Tables, page 196.

Day of Year	Day of Month	Day of Week	☉ Rises h. m.	Key	☉ Sets h. m.	Key	Length of Days h. m.	Sun Fast m.	Full Sea Boston A.M.	Full Sea Boston P.M.	☽ Rises h. m.	Key	☽ Sets h. m.	Key	Declination of Sun ° '	Place	☽ Age
275	1	Tu.	5 42	C	5 25	B	11 43	26	1¾	2	8ᴍ37	B	10ᴀ26	E	3s.29	TAU	19
276	2	W.	5 43	C	5 23	B	11 40	26	2½	2¾	9 23	B	11ᴀ21	E	3 52	TAU	20
277	3	Th.	5 44	C	5 22	B	11 38	27	3½	3¾	10 13	B	12ᴍ11	E	4 15	ORI	21
278	4	Fr.	5 45	C	5 20	B	11 35	27	4½	4¾	11ᴍ05	B	12 56	E	4 38	GEM	22
279	5	Sa.	5 46	C	5 18	B	11 32	27	5¼	5½	—	—	1 36	E	5 01	GEM	23
280	6	F	5 47	C	5 16	B	11 29	27	6¼	6½	12ᴀ00	B	2 12	E	5 24	CAN	24
281	7	M.	5 48	C	5 15	B	11 27	28	7¼	7½	12 55	C	2 46	D	5 47	CAN	25
282	8	Tu.	5 49	C	5 13	B	11 24	28	8	8¼	1 52	C	3 17	D	6 10	LEO	26
283	9	W.	5 51	C	5 11	B	11 20	28	8¾	9	2 49	D	3 46	D	6 33	SEX	27
284	10	Th.	5 52	C	5 10	B	11 18	29	9½	9¾	3 48	D	4 16	D	6 56	LEO	28
285	11	Fr.	5 53	C	5 08	B	11 15	29	10	10½	4 48	D	4 46	C	7 18	VIR	29
286	12	Sa.	5 54	C	5 07	B	11 13	29	10¾	11¼	5 49	D	5 18	C	7 41	VIR	0
287	13	F	5 55	D	5 05	B	11 10	29	11¼	11¾	6 51	E	5 52	B	8 03	VIR	1
288	14	M.	5 56	D	5 03	B	11 07	30	—	12	7 54	E	6 31	B	8 25	LIB	2
289	15	Tu.	5 57	D	5 02	B	11 05	30	12½	12¾	8 58	E	7 14	B	8 47	LIB	3
290	16	W.	5 59	D	5 00	B	11 01	30	1¼	1½	9 59	E	8 04	B	9 09	OPH	4
291	17	Th.	6 00	D	4 59	B	10 59	30	2	2¼	10 58	E	8 59	B	9 31	OPH	5
292	18	Fr.	6 01	D	4 57	B	10 56	30	3	3	11ᴀ52	E	10 01	B	9 53	SAG	6
293	19	Sa.	6 02	D	4 55	B	10 53	31	3¾	4	12ᴍ41	E	11ᴍ06	B	10 15	SAG	7
294	20	F	6 03	D	4 54	B	10 51	31	4¾	5¼	1 26	D	—	—	10 36	CAP	8
295	21	M.	6 05	D	4 52	B	10 47	31	6	6¼	2 06	D	12ᴍ14	C	10 57	AQU	9
296	22	Tu.	6 06	D	4 51	B	10 45	31	7	7¼	2 43	D	1 24	D	11 18	AQU	10
297	23	W.	6 07	D	4 49	B	10 42	31	8	8¼	3 18	D	2 34	D	11 39	PSC	11
298	24	Th.	6 08	D	4 48	B	10 40	31	8¾	9¼	3 53	C	3 44	D	12 00	PSC	12
299	25	Fr.	6 09	D	4 47	B	10 38	31	9¾	10¼	4 28	C	4 53	E	12 21	PSC	13
300	26	Sa.	6 11	D	4 45	B	10 34	32	10½	11	5 05	B	6 01	E	12 42	PSC	14
301	27	F	6 12	D	4 44	B	10 32	32	11¼	11¾	5 45	B	7 07	E	13 02	ARI	15
302	28	M.	6 13	D	4 42	B	10 29	32	—	12	6 28	B	8 10	E	13 22	TAU	16
303	29	Tu.	6 14	D	4 41	B	10 27	32	12½	12¾	7 14	B	9 08	E	13 42	TAU	17
304	30	W.	6 15	D	4 40	B	10 25	32	1¼	1½	8 03	B	10 02	E	14 01	TAU	18
305	31	Th.	6 17	D	4 38	B	10 21	32	2	2¼	8ᴍ55	B	10ᴀ50	E	14s.21	GEM	19

OCTOBER hath 31 days. 1996

On random wires the rows of summer swallows
Wait for their liftoff. They will soon be gone
Before All Saints and before All Hallows
The changing time when we are most alone.
– May Sarton

D. M.	D. W.	Dates, Feasts, Fasts, Aspects, Tide Heights	*Weather* ↓
1	Tu.	**St. Remigius** • First rural free delivery of mail, 1896 •	*Autumn*
2	W.	*Much rain in October, much wind in December.* • Groucho Marx born, 1890 • {9.7 / 10.3	*seizes*
3	Th.	☾ rides high • ☿ Gr. Elong. (18° W.) • Johns Hopkins Univ. opened, 1876 •	*the*
4	Fr.	**St. Francis of Assisi** • 82° F Seattle, Wash., 1932 • Tides {8.8 / 9.4	*terrain*
5	Sa.	First radio broadcast of World Series game, 1921 • Tides {8.6 / 9.2 •	*with*
6	**F**	**19th S. af. P.** • ♆ stat. • ☾ at apo. • {8.6 / 9.1 •	*its*
7	M.	☌ ♂ ☾ • Cape Cod Canal in Massachusetts opened, 1915 •	*regiments*
8	Tu.	☌ ♀ ☾ • Great fire of Chicago began, 1871 • Tides {9.0 / 9.4 •	*of*
9	W.	♅ stat. • Jacques Tati, famous French film director, born, 1908 •	*rain.*
10	Th.	☾ on Eq. • Helen Hayes born, 1900 • *Words are good but hens lay eggs.* •	*But*
11	Fr.	☾ at ☊ • First accurate adding machine patented, 1887 • Tides {10.1 / 10.0	*when*
12	Sa.	**New** ● • Eclipse ☉ • Robert E. Lee died, 1870 • {10.4 / 10.1	*the*
13	**F**	**20th S. af. P.** • First issue *(Old) Farmer's Almanac* on sale, 1792 •	*Sun*
14	M.	**Columbus Day** • Thanksgiving Day (Canada) • Tides {10.1 / 10.8 •	*bursts*
15	Tu.	John Kenneth Galbraith born, 1908 • Lee Iacocca born, 1924 • {10.1 / 10.9 •	*out*
16	W.	*Nothing so needs reforming as other people's habits.* • Noah Webster born, 1758 •	*of*
17	Th.	**St. Ignatius of Antioch** • ☾ runs low • Tides {9.8 / 10.7	*cloud,*
18	Fr.	**St. Luke** • ☌ ♃ ☾ • St. Luke's little summer. • {9.6 / 10.6 •	*the*
19	Sa.	☌ ♆ ☾ • ☌ ♅ ☾ • Dow Jones average fell 508 points, 1987 •	*quilted*
20	**F**	**21st S. af. P.** • Mickey Mantle born, 1931 • {9.5 / 10.3 •	*hills*
21	M.	Guggenheim Museum of Art, New York City, opened, 1959 • Dizzy Gillespie born, 1917 •	*all*
22	Tu.	☾ at perig. • Metropolitan Opera House opened, 1883 • {10.1 / 10.5	*shout*
23	W.	☾ on Eq. • Swallows leave San Juan Capistrano • Tides {10.6 / 10.7 •	*aloud.*
24	Th.	☾ at ☋ • ☌ ♄ ☾ • United Nations founded, 1945 • {11.0 / 10.8	*Trick*
25	Fr.	**St. Crispin** • -10° F, Bismarck, N.D., 1919 • Pablo Picasso born, 1881 •	*and*
26	Sa.	**Full Hunter's** ○ • *It's twice as hard to crush a half truth as a whole lie.* •	*treat —*
27	**F**	**22nd S. af. P.** • Daylight Saving Time ends, 2 A.M. • {11.6 / 10.6 •	*a*
28	M.	**Sts. Simon & Jude** • Statue of Liberty dedicated, 1886 •	*howling*
29	Tu.	Forest fire at Concord, N.H., drenched by man-made rain, 1947 • Tides {10.3 / 11.1 •	*gale,*
30	W.	Orson Welles broadcast "War of the Worlds," 1938 • Charles Atlas born, 1893 • {9.9 / 10.6	*then*
31	Th.	**All Hallows Eve** • ☾ rides high • Tides {9.5 / 10.2 •	*sweet.*

Farmer's Calendar

Columbus Day. Warm, air steeped in dust and amber sunlight like tea. In the afternoon I walked through the woods to the southern side of the hill where the land is steep and broken and nobody much goes. Along the ridge up there you are in an open woods with a few big old oaks growing right on bare ledge, it seems, and there are mossy places good for sitting. In front of you the hill falls off sharply, and down the pitch is a tree in which somebody has rigged a little platform for deer hunting, a tree stand. The platform is fixed 20 feet up on the trunk and there are no branches below it. He must climb to it using those boot spikes the linemen use on their poles. The deer, when they come, don't look up. They never know he's there. Long work, though, sitting in a tree waiting for the deer.

The leaves were down. They lay everywhere ankle deep, brown and brittle and dry as bone, no rain having fallen for a week. You couldn't take a step without making a great crash and rattle in the leaves. I finally stopped and sat because I was sick of the noise I made walking. Presently a terrific racket broke out among the leaves on my right. Something was coming through the woods, evidently something big from the commotion it made in the leaves. I thought the deer hunter must be coming to inspect his tree stand. What would I say to him? The rustling came closer. Then the piled leaves burst apart and a chipmunk rushed by. Only a chipmunk that could sit in your hand. Thrashing in the dry October leaves, it sounded like a giant. The fallen leaves magnified it. They acted as an alarm. You couldn't move quietly in those woods even if you were a harmless rodent. A good day, therefore, to hunt by being still.

1996 NOVEMBER, The Eleventh Month

The Great Square of Pegasus is high in the southwest at midevening, trailing from its upper left corner the lines of stars that form Andromeda. Orion the Hunter is rising due east. Higher and visible earlier in the evening is Taurus the Bull with the big V-shaped Hyades cluster and orange Aldebaran, and the beautiful dipper-shaped Pleiades cluster. To the upper left of the Pleiades are the bright star Capella and bright constellation Perseus. High above the North Star, the compact zigzag of stars that is Cassiopeia shines bright. Jupiter sets soon after dusk; Venus rises soon before dawn. Saturn shines in the south all evening. Watch for possibly more Leonid meteors than usual from the south before morning twilight on the 17th.

☾ Last Quarter	3rd day	2nd hour	52nd min.
● New Moon	10th day	23rd hour	17th min.
☽ First Quarter	17th day	20th hour	10th min.
○ Full Moon	24th day	23rd hour	11th min.

For an explanation of this page, see "How to Use This Almanac," page 30; for values of Key Letters, see Time Correction Tables, page 196.

Day of Year	Day of Month	Day of Week	☼ Rises h. m.	Key	☼ Sets h. m.	Key	Length of Days h. m.	Sun Fast m.	Full Sea Boston A.M.	Full Sea Boston P.M.	☽ Rises h. m.	Key	☽ Sets h. m.	Key	Declination of Sun ° '	☽ Place	☽ Age
306	1	Fr.	6 18	D	4 37	B	10 19	32	3	3	9 49 ᴾ ᴹ	B	11 33 ᴬ ᴹ	E	14s.40	GEM	20
307	2	Sa.	6 19	D	4 36	B	10 17	32	3¾	4	10 44	B	12 11 ᴾ ᴹ	E	14 59	CAN	21
308	3	F	6 20	D	4 35	B	10 15	32	4¾	5	11 40 ᴾ ᴹ	B	12 45	D	15 17	CAN	22
309	4	M.	6 22	D	4 33	B	10 11	32	5½	5¾	—	—	1 17	D	15 36	LEO	23
310	5	Tu.	6 23	D	4 32	B	10 09	32	6½	6¾	12 37 ᴬ ᴹ	C	1 47	D	15 54	LEO	24
311	6	W.	6 24	D	4 31	B	10 07	32	7¼	7¾	1 35	D	2 16	D	16 12	LEO	25
312	7	Th.	6 25	D	4 30	A	10 05	32	8	8½	2 34	D	2 45	C	16 30	VIR	26
313	8	Fr.	6 27	D	4 29	A	10 02	32	8¾	9¼	3 35	D	3 16	C	16 47	VIR	27
314	9	Sa.	6 28	D	4 28	A	10 00	32	9½	10	4 37	E	3 50	C	17 04	VIR	28
315	10	F	6 29	D	4 27	A	9 58	32	10¼	10¾	5 41	E	4 27	B	17 21	VIR	0
316	11	M.	6 30	D	4 26	A	9 56	32	10¾	11¼	6 46	E	5 09	B	17 37	LIB	1
317	12	Tu.	6 32	D	4 25	A	9 53	31	11½	—	7 50	E	5 58	B	17 54	SCO	2
318	13	W.	6 33	D	4 24	A	9 51	31	12	12¼	8 51	E	6 52	B	18 09	OPH	3
319	14	Th.	6 34	D	4 23	A	9 49	31	1	1	9 49	E	7 53	B	18 25	SAG	4
320	15	Fr.	6 35	D	4 22	A	9 47	31	1¾	2	10 40	E	8 58	B	18 40	SAG	5
321	16	Sa.	6 37	D	4 21	A	9 44	31	2½	2¾	11 26 ᴬ ᴹ	E	10 06	C	18 55	CAP	6
322	17	F	6 38	D	4 20	A	9 42	31	3½	3¾	12 07 ᴾ ᴹ	D	11 15 ᴬ ᴹ	C	19 09	AQU	7
323	18	M.	6 39	D	4 19	A	9 40	30	4½	5	12 44	D	—	—	19 23	PSC	8
324	19	Tu.	6 40	D	4 19	A	9 39	30	5½	6	1 19	D	12 24 ᴬ ᴹ	D	19 37	AQU	9
325	20	W.	6 42	D	4 18	A	9 36	30	6¾	7	1 53	C	1 32	D	19 51	PSC	10
326	21	Th.	6 43	D	4 17	A	9 34	30	7½	8	2 27	C	2 39	D	20 04	PSC	11
327	22	Fr.	6 44	D	4 17	A	9 33	30	8½	9	3 02	B	3 46	E	20 17	PSC	12
328	23	Sa.	6 45	D	4 16	A	9 31	29	9¼	10	3 39	B	4 52	E	20 29	ARI	13
329	24	F	6 46	D	4 15	A	9 29	29	10¼	10¾	4 20	B	5 55	E	20 41	ARI	14
330	25	M.	6 47	D	4 15	A	9 28	29	10¾	11½	5 05	B	6 55	E	20 53	TAU	15
331	26	Tu.	6 49	E	4 14	A	9 25	28	11½	—	5 53	B	7 51	E	21 04	TAU	16
332	27	W.	6 50	E	4 14	A	9 24	28	12¼	12¼	6 44	B	8 42	E	21 15	ORI	17
333	28	Th.	6 51	E	4 14	A	9 23	28	1	1	7 38	B	9 28	E	21 26	GEM	18
334	29	Fr.	6 52	E	4 13	A	9 21	27	1¾	1¾	8 33	B	10 08	E	21 36	GEM	19
335	30	Sa.	6 53	E	4 13	A	9 20	27	2½	2½	9 29 ᴾ ᴹ	B	10 44 ᴬ ᴹ	E	21s.46	CAN	20

NOVEMBER hath 30 days. 1996

"What do you hunt, Orion,
This starry night?"
"The Ram, the Bull and the Lion,
And the Great Bear," says Orion.
– Robert Graves

Farmer's Calendar

On front porches, doorsteps, and frost-bitten lawns, Halloween jack-o'-lanterns, undiscarded, contemplate with degrees of chagrin their fate: They're stuck in the wrong festival, they have outlived their time and now show faces full of regret to a world for which they are unprepared. The icon of All Hallows' Eve, a feast of misrule derived no doubt from pagan hell-raising far older than Christianity, ought not to endure to Thanksgiving, that mild and pious exercise in Puritan merrymaking — but it does.

My jack-o'-lantern is never thrown out. I haven't the heart. I simply leave it where it is, on the step. I then watch over the succeeding weeks as it softens and transforms. The manic grin I carved on October 31 sags and settles. It decays into a mask of pain and finally, by the end of November, becomes a hollow rictus of despair. In the features of the pumpkin, spread over a month or more, are all the changes that pass in a few seconds over the face of the man who walks into the wrong bar and finds, where he expected the chamber of commerce dinner, the outlaw Angels in full leather, chains, and hair.

Sad mortality. The eyes drop, the mouth falls at the corners, the skin draws in, the whole pumpkin seems to spread at the equator, flattening, corrupting into a slack and pathetic wreckage — the vegetable equivalent of an idle marchioness come to the end of a long life of self-indulgence.

It's not a pretty sight. Each year as the season turns past Thanksgiving and into the winter storms, I'm relieved to find my poor old friend's decline covered at last with a decent blanket of snow.

1996 DECEMBER, The Twelfth Month

After nightfall, Orion and Gemini tilt up in the east, the former offering the bright stars Rigel and Betelgeuse, the latter containing also bright Pollux and Castor. Above Gemini, Auriga the Charioteer is crowned with radiant Capella, and above Orion is Taurus, with its bright Bull's Eye star, Aldebaran. Procyon rises below Gemini and peerless Sirius below Orion around midevening. On the evenings of the 12th and 13th, Geminid meteors stream out, at peak as plentiful as a meteor a minute. Jupiter is becoming lost in evening twilight, Venus in morning twilight. The Moon is full on Christmas Eve to guide Santa's way. Winter begins on the 21st at 9:06 A.M., EST.

☾	Last Quarter	3rd day	0 hour	7th min.
●	New Moon	10th day	11th hour	58th min.
☽	First Quarter	17th day	4th hour	31st min.
○	Full Moon	24th day	15th hour	41st min.

For an explanation of this page, see "How to Use This Almanac," page 30; for values of Key Letters, see Time Correction Tables, page 196.

Day of Year	Day of Month	Day of Week	☉ Rises h. m.	Key	☉ Sets h. m.	Key	Length of Days h. m.	Sun Fast m.	Full Sea Boston A.M.	Full Sea Boston P.M.	☽ Rises h. m.	Key	☽ Sets h. m.	Key	Declination of Sun ° '	☽ Place	☽ Age
336	1	F	6 54	E	4 12	A	9 18	27	3¼	3¼	10 25 P	C	11 17 A M	D	21s.55	CAN	21
337	2	M.	6 55	E	4 12	A	9 17	26	4	4¼	11 22 P M	B	11 47 A M	D	22 03	LEO	22
338	3	Tu.	6 56	E	4 12	A	9 16	26	4¾	5	—	—	12 16 P M	D	22 12	LEO	23
339	4	W.	6 57	E	4 12	A	9 15	25	5¾	6	12 20 A M	D	12 45	D	22 19	VIR	24
340	5	Th.	6 58	E	4 12	A	9 14	25	6½	7	1 19	D	1 15	C	22 27	VIR	25
341	6	Fr.	6 59	E	4 12	A	9 13	25	7¼	7¾	2 19	E	1 46	C	22 34	VIR	26
342	7	Sa.	7 00	E	4 12	A	9 12	24	8	8½	3 22	E	2 21	B	22 41	VIR	27
343	8	F	7 01	E	4 12	A	9 11	24	8¾	9½	4 26	E	3 00	B	22 47	LIB	28
344	9	M.	7 02	E	4 12	A	9 10	23	9½	10¼	5 32	E	3 46	B	22 53	LIB	29
345	10	Tu.	7 03	E	4 12	A	9 09	23	10¼	11	6 36	E	4 39	B	22 58	OPH	0
346	11	W.	7 04	E	4 12	A	9 08	22	11¼	11¾	7 37	E	5 39	B	23 03	SAG	1
347	12	Th.	7 04	E	4 12	A	9 08	22	—	12	8 34	E	6 45	B	23 07	SAG	2
348	13	Fr.	7 05	E	4 12	A	9 07	21	12½	12¾	9 24	E	7 54	C	23 11	SAG	3
349	14	Sa.	7 06	E	4 12	A	9 06	21	1½	1¾	10 08	E	9 05	C	23 15	AQU	4
350	15	F	7 07	E	4 12	A	9 05	21	2¼	2½	10 47	D	10 15	D	23 18	CAP	5
351	16	M.	7 07	E	4 12	A	9 05	20	3¼	3½	11 23	D	11 24 P M	D	23 20	AQU	6
352	17	Tu.	7 08	E	4 13	A	9 05	20	4¼	4¾	11 57 A M	D	—	—	23 22	PSC	7
353	18	W.	7 09	E	4 14	A	9 05	19	5¼	5¾	12 30 P M	C	12 31 A M	D	23 24	PSC	8
354	19	Th.	7 09	E	4 14	A	9 05	19	6¼	6¾	1 04	C	1 38	E	23 25	PSC	9
355	20	Fr.	7 10	E	4 14	A	9 04	18	7¼	7¾	1 40	B	2 42	E	23 25	CET	10
356	21	Sa.	7 10	E	4 14	A	9 04	18	8¼	8¾	2 18	B	3 45	E	23 25	ARI	11
357	22	F	7 11	E	4 15	A	9 04	17	9	9¾	3 00	B	4 46	E	23 25	TAU	12
358	23	M.	7 11	E	4 16	A	9 05	17	9¾	10½	3 46	B	5 43	E	23 25	TAU	13
359	24	Tu.	7 12	E	4 17	A	9 05	16	10½	11¼	4 35	C	6 36	E	23 23	AUR	14
360	25	W.	7 12	E	4 17	A	9 05	16	11¼	11¾	5 28	C	7 23	E	23 22	GEM	15
361	26	Th.	7 12	E	4 18	A	9 06	15	—	12	6 23	B	8 06	E	23 19	GEM	16
362	27	Fr.	7 13	E	4 19	A	9 06	15	12½	12½	7 18	C	8 44	E	23 17	CAN	17
363	28	Sa.	7 13	E	4 19	A	9 06	14	1¼	1¼	8 15	C	9 18	D	23 14	CAN	18
364	29	F	7 13	E	4 20	A	9 07	14	2	2	9 11	C	9 49	D	23 10	LEO	19
365	30	M.	7 13	E	4 21	A	9 08	13	2½	2¾	10 08	D	10 19	D	23 06	SEX	20
366	31	Tu.	7 13	E	4 22	A	9 09	13	3¼	3½	11 06 A M	D	10 47 A M	C	23s.02	LEO	21

DECEMBER hath 31 days. 1996

Hark, how all the welkin rings,
'Glory to the King of kings';
Peace on earth, and mercy mild,
God and sinners reconciled.
– *Charles Wesley*

D. M.	D. W.	Dates, Feasts, Fasts, Aspects, Tide Heights	Weather ↓
1	**F**	**1st S. in Advent** • ☾ at apo. • Tides {8.9 9.3 •	*Rain*
2	M.	Bill Valverde caught a 279-pound alligator gar in Texas, 1951 • {8.8 9.0 •	*changing*
3	Tu.	☌ ♂ ☾ • Illinois became 21st state, 1818 • Tides {8.8 8.8 •	*to*
4	W.	☾ on Eq. • ♄ stat. • *Diligence is the mother of good luck.* •	*snow,*
5	Th.	☾ at ☊ • Phi Beta Kappa, first U.S. scholastic fraternity, organized, 1776 •	*then*
6	Fr.	**St. Nicholas** • **First day of Chanukah** • {9.6 8.9 •	*melting*
7	Sa.	**St. Ambrose** • Pearl Harbor attacked, 1941 • Microwave oven patented, 1945 •	*in*
8	**F**	**2nd S. in Advent** • ☌ ♀ ☾ •	*sunglow.*
9	M.	Christmas Seals first sold to help fight tuberculosis, 1907 • Tides {10.9 9.8 •	*Our*
10	Tu.	**New ●** • First Nobel Prizes awarded, 1901 • {11.3 10.1 •	*chestnuts*
11	W.	☾ runs low • Indiana became 19th state, 1816 • Tides {11.7 10.3 •	*are*
12	Th.	☌ ☿ ☾ • ☌ ♃ ☾ • ☾ at perig. •	*roasting —*
13	Fr.	**St. Lucy** • ☌ ♆ ☾ • ☌ ♅ ☾ • Tides {10.4 11.7 •	*more*
14	Sa.	George Washington died, 1799 • Alabama became 22nd state, 1819 •	*like*
15	**F**	**3rd S. in Advent** • ☿ Gr. Elong. (20°E.) •	*April*
16	M.	Boston Tea Party, 1773 • Halcyon Days • Tides {10.4 10.6 •	*Fool*
17	Tu.	☾ on Eq. • ☾ at ☋ • ☌ ♄ ☾ • Tides {10.3 10.1 •	*than*
18	W.	Ember Day • First giant panda imported to San Francisco zoo, 1936 • {10.3 9.7 •	*Yule.*
19	Th.	Ben Franklin began publishing *Poor Richard's Almanack,* 1732 • Tides {10.4 9.5 •	*Wintry*
20	Fr.	Ember Day • Louisiana Purchase, 1803 • Beware the Pogonip. •	*blast,*
21	Sa.	**St. Thomas** • **Winter Solstice** • Ember Day • Tides {10.6 9.4 •	*snow*
22	**F**	**4th S. in Advent** • U.S. Golf Assoc. founded, 1894 •	*at*
23	M.	☿ stat. • *It is in living wisely and fully that one's soul grows.* • {10.7 9.4 •	*last!*
24	Tu.	☾ rides high • **Full Long Nights** ○ • Kit Carson born, 1809 •	*Count*
25	W.	**Christmas Day** • *Christmas in snow, Easter in mud.* •	*down*
26	Th.	**St. Stephen** • Boxing Day (Canada) • Tides {— 10.5 •	*minutes*
27	Fr.	**St. John** • Carrie Nation attacked her first saloon, Wichita, Kansas, 1900 •	*from*
28	Sa.	**Holy Innocents** • Iowa became 29th state, 1846 • {9.3 10.1 •	*eleven:*
29	**F**	**1st S. af. C.** • ☾ at apo. • Tides {9.2 9.8 •	*Here's a*
30	M.	-42° F, New York City, 1917 • Tides {9.1 9.4 •	*cheer for*
31	Tu.	*Be at war with your vices, at peace with your neighbors, and let every new year find you a better man.* (Franklin)	*'97!*

Farmer's Calendar

Children like to eat snow, of course, but the rest of us, as we get older, generally grow away from the stuff. We shouldn't, perhaps. We eat a lot of worse things, and snow on the palate has its own subtle character, as I have discovered in a brief and self-directed course of snow connoisseurship — a snow tasting, you could say.

I find fresh, dry, powdery snow is for me entirely without taste, but in heavier, wetter snow, and in snow that has lain for a while, I detect a more or less fleeting flavor, a tartness. It's a little like the taste of steel, of a nail, say, but that isn't it exactly. The fact is that with snow as with any other material, each thing tastes like itself and nothing tastes like anything else, which must be why wine tasting, for example, is such a racket. You are left, not with useful, repeatable distinctions, but with vague associations. Or with not-so-vague associations. For me, snow's faint metallic flavor is the taste of the forbidden.

When I was little, my mother didn't like me to eat snow. It was dirty, she said. Well, it was. I grew up in a big city where everybody, at the time, burned soft coal for heat. Black soot covered everything all winter. The snow was gray. My mother, naturally, didn't want her only child eating anything like that. I ate it anyway, and I thought the peculiar snow taste was the wicked taste of coal. Now for years I have lived in the country, where the snow is comparatively clean. And yet it tastes the same. No sense endures in memory with the liveliness of taste; I'm quite sure of my recollection. I can hear her: "Don't eat that. For John's sake. Come on!"

"NEVER TAKE NO CUTOFFS"

This year marks the 150th anniversary of the most horrible mistake ever made by a group of people heading for California. Here's what happened...

BY DAYTON DUNCAN

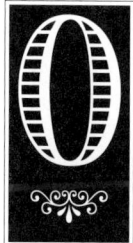

One hundred and fifty years ago, in the spring of 1846, mountain man James Clyman, a grizzled veteran of the western wilderness, was on his way back east when he started encountering wagon train after wagon train of American pioneers heading in the opposite direction. He found it "remarkable and strange" that so many people would have abandoned their comfortable homes to make such a long and dangerous journey to settle in a land they had never seen.

"But such," he concluded, "is the character of my countrymen."

Much happened that year in the West. The United States went to war with Mexico, eventually adding all of the Southwest and California to our borders. A boundary dispute with England was settled, securing what is now Oregon, Washington, and Idaho. The Mormons began their long odyssey to Utah. It was, in the words of historian Bernard DeVoto, our "year of decision," when the United States focused its collective eyes on the West and became a continental nation.

But 1846 was — and is — remembered for something else: It was the year a collection of pioneers known as the Donner party got stuck in the Sierra Nevada Mountains and, in the greatest tragedy of the overland migrations, resorted to cannibalism to survive.

When they started out on April 14 from Springfield, Illinois, no one would have predicted such a terrible fate. George and Jacob Donner and their neighbor, James Frazier Reed, were prosperous men. Each bought three new wagons and teams of oxen and hired drivers for the trip west. Reed had a customized, two-story covered wagon — a "pioneer palace car," his daughter Virginia called it — with bunk beds, cushioned seats, a stove, and a cook. Sewed into a quilt in one of George Donner's wagons, it was said, was $10,000 in cash.

And in Jacob Donner's saddlebag was a book that would cause them all so

Opposite page: *Delayed by taking the Hastings Cutoff, the Donner party struggled to cross the Sierra Nevadas before winter. But deep snow quickly made the route impassable.*

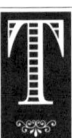

The "shortcut" they had followed turned out to be . . . 125 miles

At the Platte River

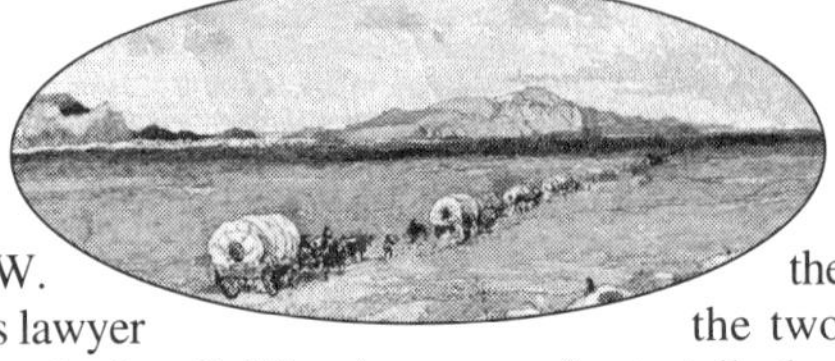

much grief. *The Emigrants' Guide, to Oregon and California,* written by Lansford W. Hastings, an ambitious lawyer with big plans for developing California, promised a shortcut — the Hastings Cutoff — that would shave nearly 400 miles from the regular route. Hastings' enthusiastic descriptions of its virtues did not mention the fact that he had never personally set eyes on the "direct route" he so heartily recommended.

By June 27 the Donners and Reeds were near Fort Laramie on the North Platte River in Wyoming, a little behind schedule. At a pace of 15 miles a day, anything that could reduce the distance to California and get them over the Sierras before winter was sounding better and better.

By chance they met James Clyman, who had just traveled Hastings Cutoff in reverse. He had served with Reed in Abraham Lincoln's company during the Black Hawk War, and the two old friends shared a campfire to talk about the route ahead.

"I told him to take the regular wagon track and never leave it," Clyman wrote in his diary. Hastings' route, he warned, crossed "the most desolate country perhaps on the whole globe."

They parted the next morning. For whatever reasons, Reed had already decided to trust the guidebook instead of the mountain man.

By July 20 they had crossed the Continental Divide at South Pass and veered off from the main route to start down toward Hastings Cutoff. After a few days' rest at Fort Bridger they entered Hastings Cutoff on July 31. There were 87 of them now —

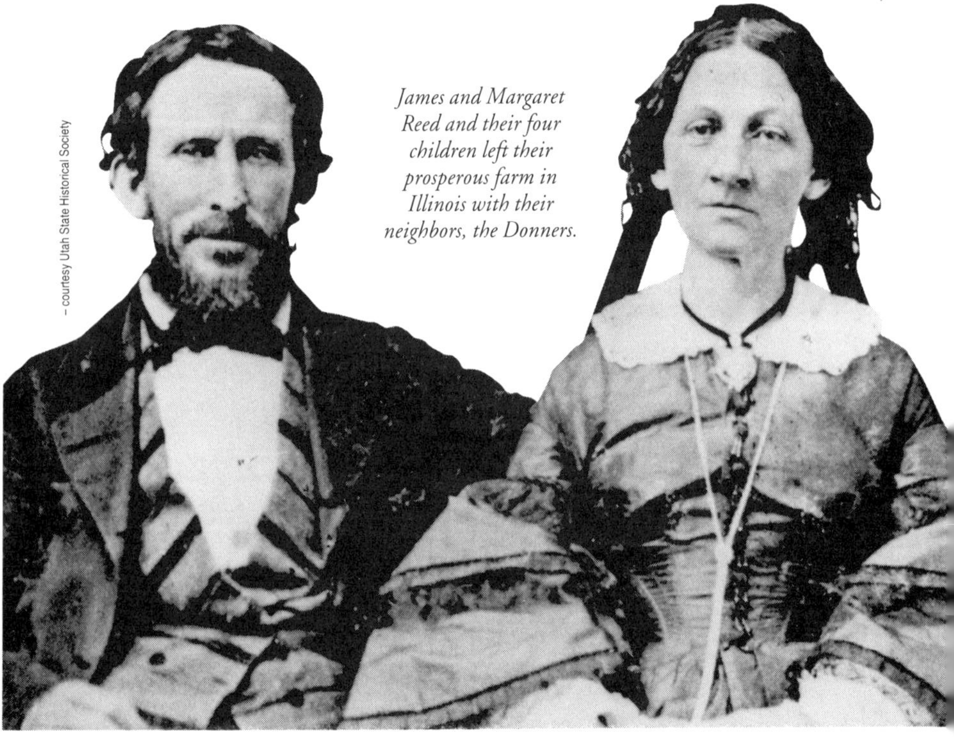

James and Margaret Reed and their four children left their prosperous farm in Illinois with their neighbors, the Donners.

– courtesy Utah State Historical Society

longer. A kind of chilly panic began to spread through their ranks.

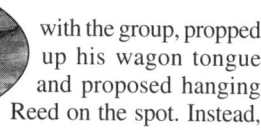
Great Salt Lake

families mostly, with children of all ages, and a handful of bachelors. They fully expected to be in California within eight weeks.

But the going was difficult. The wagon train had to make its own road — backbreaking labor, hard on the oxen, and excruciatingly slow. By the time they reached the Great Salt Lake, it was late August — and a barren desert stretched before them.

"It was a dreary, desolate, alkali waste," Virginia Reed wrote. "Not a living thing could be seen; it seemed as though the hand of death had been laid upon the country."

Hastings had written that the desert was 40 miles across. It turned out to be 80 miles and took them five agonizing days. On September 30, the weary group finally reached the point in eastern Nevada where Hastings Cutoff rejoined the main trail. By this time, virtually every other overland party had already reached California safely. All of Nevada lay before the Donner party, and the Sierras as well. The "shortcut" they had just followed turned out to be not only more arduous than the regular route, it was also 125 miles *longer*.

A kind of chilly panic began to spread through their ranks. Tempers got short. On October 5 an argument between Reed and one of the teamsters turned into a fight and ended with the teamster dead from a knife wound. Lewis Keseberg, a German traveling with the group, propped up his wagon tongue and proposed hanging Reed on the spot. Instead, the party voted to banish Reed from the group and sent him off the next morning on horseback, leaving his wife and four children with the others.

Things unraveled even further. As supplies ran low, Keseberg abandoned a 60-year-old man traveling with him, and no one bothered to go back for him. Paiute Indians killed 21 oxen with poisoned arrows. More wagons had to be left behind. One man was shot by Indians; another died in a gun accident. George Donner's axle broke, and he badly cut his hand trying to fix it.

But near the end of October, it seemed as if their bad luck had finally run its course. Two Indian employees from John Sutter's fort at Sacramento arrived with a few emergency supplies.

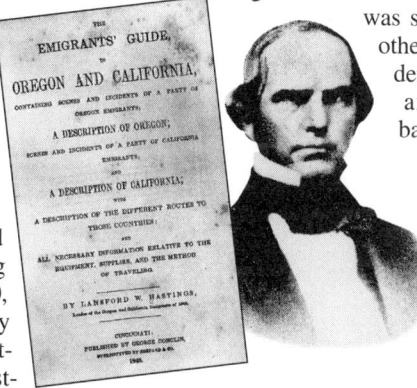
Lansford Hastings and his popular — if misleading — guidebook and travelogue.

The Sierra Nevada summits were in sight just ahead and the skies were clear, so they rested a few days to prepare for the mountain crossing that would bring them to their destination at last. They climbed up the foothills and stopped at a high, clear lake only a few miles from the pass.

That night, October 28, it began to snow — the start of the worst winter ever recorded in the Sierras.

They tried to get over the next day, but five feet of snow had fallen on the summit.

– Lansford Hastings photo courtesy Utah State Historical Society / booklet photo courtesy Bancroft Library, University of California, Berkeley

hey carefully separated the meat into different bundles so that no

They retreated to the lake and began preparing a winter camp: three cabins holding 60 people, including 29 children, six of them babies; and farther downhill from the lake, three tentlike structures sheltering George and Jacob Donner's group, 21 in all, a dozen of them children.

Two more attempts at crossing failed. On December 15, the first of their number, one of the Reeds' hired men, died of malnutrition.

On the sixth day, their food ran out. On the ninth day, crazed and weakened by hunger and snow blindness, they realized they were lost. One man died, then another and another. Christmas Day came and went.

When the storm passed, the survivors managed to set a dead pine tree on fire, but the only available food was the bodies of their fallen comrades. They roasted the flesh of Patrick Dolan's arms and legs, averting their eyes from each other and weeping as they ate. Then, as they butchered the other corpses, they carefully separated the meat into different bundles so that no one would end up devouring his or her kinfolk. (This bit of wilderness decorum proved small comfort in the end. Sarah Fosdick watched as her husband's heart was removed from his dead body and cooked on a stick by the others.)

On they stumbled. When their grisly food ran out again, someone killed Sutter's two Indians to replenish the supply. One month after leaving the lake, the survivors of the Forlorn Hope — only two of the 12 men, but all five women — made it to a settlement, where relief parties began organizing to rescue the people still trapped on the other side of the Sierras.

The next day, a group of the most able-bodied men and women, including the two Indians, set out once more for help, this time on snowshoes constructed by two New Englanders among them. It was slow going — some drifts were 20 feet high — but in two days they reached the summit and started down the broad west slopes of the Sierras, where the snow was even deeper. They began calling themselves the "Forlorn Hope."

Meanwhile, back at the lake, the snows now covered the cabins. The standard meal

one would end up devouring his or her kinfolk.

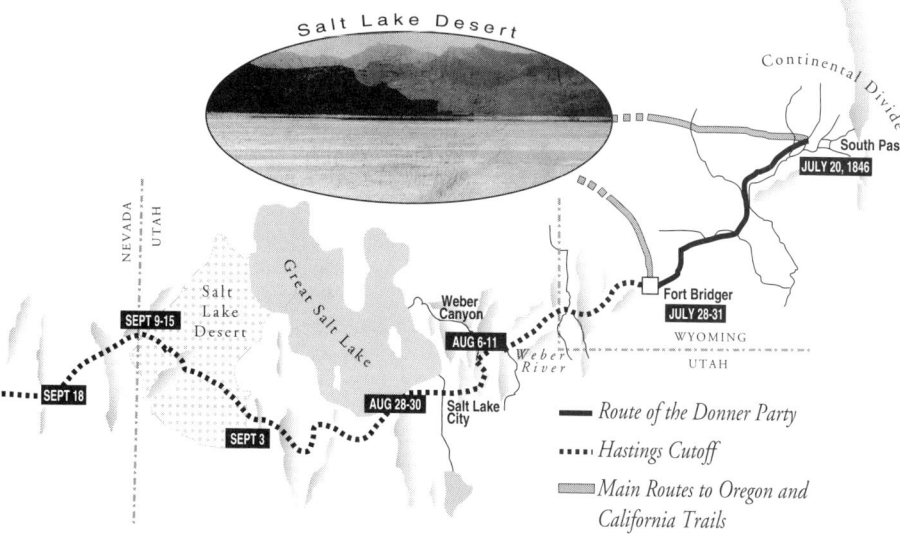

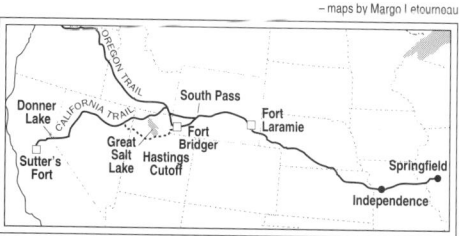

was a sickening gruel made from boiled cow hides (although on Christmas, Mrs. Reed had treated her children to some tripe, a cup of beans, some rice, a few dried apples, and small piece of bacon she had hoarded for the occasion). By mid-February, a dozen more people had succumbed — a few of the babies and some of the men, including Jacob Donner. Their bodies were hauled out of the shelters and dragged up steep slopes to the top of the snow.

Inside one of the cabins, Virginia Reed read aloud from a book about Daniel Boone's wilderness exploits; privately she promised God that if she survived, she would become a Catholic.

They heard voices calling from the frozen lake, and a few of them, emaciated and woozy from hunger, staggered slowly out of their snow caves to see what it was. Seven men stood there.

"Are you from California," one woman asked them, "or do you come from heaven?"

Donner Lake as seen from the Old Sacramento Trail in a 1890 engraving.

In mid-April, the last group of rescuers reached the lake. The only person they found left alive was Lewis Keseberg.

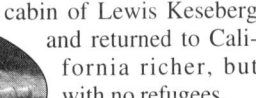

It was a rescue party, but the rugged crossing had meant it could bring only a few supplies. It needed to start back before another storm closed in — and it could safely take along only 23 of them. Thirty-one were left at the camps.

Over the next two months, as three more relief parties came and went, the refugees' cabins and the trail over the mountains would be the scene of remarkable heroism and incredible cowardice, supreme sacrifice and pure greed — and much more horror.

Eight-year-old Patty Reed would bravely volunteer to turn back from the first rescue attempt, when it was determined that her 3-year-old brother Tommy was too small to continue on the crossing.

Those left behind in the camps would soon resort to cannibalizing the dead. "Mrs. Murphy said here yesterday that she thought she would commence on Milt and eat him," said Patrick Breen's diary of late February. Jacob Donner's children hung on by devouring their father's corpse.

Having frantically attempted a rescue earlier in the winter, only to be turned back by the fierce storms, James Reed himself would lead one of the relief parties and bring out Patty and young Tommy and many others.

Tamsen Donner would refuse to leave the side of her injured husband, George, but offered two rescuers a handsome fee to escort her three youngest children to safety. The men abandoned the children at the cabin of Lewis Keseberg and returned to California richer, but with no refugees.

The third relief party would include two fathers from the Forlorn Hope who would learn on their arrival at the cabins that Keseberg had eaten their sons.

Finally, in mid-April, the last group of rescuers reached the lake. The only person they found left alive was Lewis Keseberg. Tamsen Donner had steadfastly remained with her wounded husband, but when he died had gone crazy and then died herself, Keseberg claimed. Others suspected he had killed her. There was no denying that he had lived off their corpses, hidden some of their money, and admitted that he had found Tamsen's flesh "the best he had ever tasted."

Keseberg, the last member of the Donner Party to reach California, was brought over the Sierras in late April — almost exactly one year after the ill-fated party had first left Springfield. Eighty-seven of them had decided to take the Hastings Cutoff to speed their way to California. Only 47 of them made it alive.

Among the statistics now fascinating social scientists, two-thirds of the women survived the ordeal; more than two-thirds of the men did not. And the emigrants traveling alone proved more likely to die than those in family units.

The two Donner families were an ex-

Lewis Keseberg was the last survivor to leave Donner Lake.

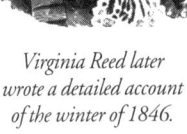

Virginia Reed later wrote a detailed account of the winter of 1846.

A true statement by Paul B.* of San Pedro, California

"I earned $1,000 on just 12 VCR repairs in one week!"

*Last name withheld by request.

How to cash in on the skyrocketing field of Electronics!

You too can earn up to $85 an hour, pocket $200 a day in one of many high profit electronics fields. There are over 77 million VCR's currently in use in America. More than 60 million personal computers. Countless new mini dishes are just starting to be utilized.

Here is a once-in-a-lifetime opportunity to go into a booming business of your own. Be your own boss and enjoy the financial freedom and security it brings.

It's easy to learn these electronic careers at home in just a few short weeks. Foley-Belsaw's unique method emphasizes the very basics involved in 90% of all electronics repairs.

Whether as a pro or only part-time, these practical hands-on courses were developed and proven over a long period of time. They combine simple step-by-step lessons with easy-to-follow video cassettes. No special experience or electronics background is necessary. And when you complete the course you will receive the School's official diploma attesting to your expertise.

Send coupon today for FREE Fact Kit. No obligation.

Don't miss out! Send in the coupon NOW. There's absolutely no obligation and no salesmen will call on you.

"I started 3 months ago, now earn over $900 a week."
D.K., New York, NY

"Took in over $3,200 in the past 10 days!"
H.H., Denver, CO

"Doubled my income within 6 weeks."
R.B., Bakersfield, CA

MAIL TODAY FOR FREE INFORMATION PACKET

Foley-Belsaw Institute
6301 Equitable Road
Kansas City, MO 64120-1395

FOLEY BELSAW — Since 1926

Please Check Only ONE of the Following:

- ☐ VCR Repair- 62378
- ☐ Computer Repair- 64270
- ☐ TV/Satellite Repair- 31149
- ☐ PC Programming- 35097
- ☐ PC Specialist- 38002
- ☐ Locksmith- 12695
- ☐ Small Engine- 52579
- ☐ Upholstery- 81129
- ☐ Woodworking- 43461
- ☐ Gunsmithing- 92181
- ☐ Vinyl Repair- 71063
- ☐ Saw & Tool Sharpening- 21523

Name _____
Address _____
City _____
State _____ Zip _____

Call toll-free 1-800-487-2100

ception. Most of them were dead. But the Reeds all made it through and prospered in California. As she had promised (and to the consternation of her family), Virginia converted to Catholicism. Little Patty had astonished everyone when she stumbled out of the mountains, clutching a tiny doll that can be seen today at Sutter's Fort.

Lewis Keseberg — the only survivor to talk openly about the cannibalism back in the fearsome cabins — eventually opened a restaurant in Sacramento.

The sensational news of the Donner party's travails at first reduced the stream of overland emigrants to California. But it quickly picked up again a few years later when gold was discovered at Sutter's Mill. The Gold Rushers named the pass in the Sierras and the nearby lake for the Donners and pushed right on through. Virginia Reed could appreciate their pragmatic attitude. Her advice to those following her family's way west was eminently practical. "Never take no cutoffs," she wrote to a cousin, "and hurry along as fast as you can." □□

Patty Reed's precious doll can be seen at the Sutter's Fort Museum.

AUTHOR'S NOTE: *The single best source for information on the Donner party is found in* Ordeal by Hunger: The Story of the Donner Party *by* GEORGE R. STEWART *(Houghton Mifflin, 1988).*

WINDCHILL TABLE

As wind speed increases, the air temperature against your body falls. The combination of cold temperatures and high winds creates a cooling effect so severe that exposed flesh can freeze. (Inanimate objects, such as cars, do not experience windchill.)

To gauge wind speed: at 10 miles per hour you can feel wind on your face; at 20 small branches move, and dust or snow is raised; at 30 large branches move and wires whistle; at 40 whole trees bend.   *– courtesy Mount Washington Observatory*

Wind Velocity (MPH)	Temperature (° F)										
	50	41	32	23	14	5	–4	–13	–22	–31	–40	–49	–58
	Equivalent Temperature (° F) (Equivalent in Cooling Power on Exposed Flesh under Calm Conditions)										
5	48	39	28	19	10	1	–9	–18	–27	–36	–51	–56	–65
10	41	30	18	7	–4	–15	–26	–36	–49	–60	–71	–81	–92
20	32	19	7	–6	–18| –31	–44	–58	–71	–83	–96	–108| –121
30	28	14	1	–13	–27	–40	–54	–69	–81	–96	–108	–123	–137
40	27	12	–2	–17	–31	–45	–60	–74	–89	–103	–116	–130	–144
50	25	10	–4	–18	–33	–47	–62	–76	–90	–105	–119	–134	–148
	Little Danger			**Increasing Danger**				**Great Danger**				
	Danger from Freezing of Exposed Flesh (for Properly Clothed Person)										

Highest Quality Vitamins Lowest Prices

Product	Size	Price
Beta Carotene 10,000 I.U.	100 caps	1.99
Beta Carotene 25,000 I.U.	100 caps	2.99
ULTRA ENERGY	60 tabs	3.29
Ginseng 1000 mg	60 tabs	2.99
E 200 IU NATURAL BLEND (MAIL ORDER COUPON, LIMIT 1 PER ORDER FALM96)	100 caps	1.99
FLATE-X COMPARE TO BEANO	30 tabs	3.89
Biotin 300 MCG	100 tabs	1.29
Biotin 800 MCG	100 tabs	2.29
B-6 50 MG	100 tabs	79¢
B-6 100 MG	100 tabs	99¢
C 1000 MG w/ROSE HIPS (MAIL ORDER COUPON, LIMIT 1 PER ORDER FALM96)	100 tabs	2.49
VITAMIN B-12 100 MCG	100 tabs	99¢
VITAMIN B-12 500 MCG	100 tabs	1.49
Odorless GARLIC 300 MG COMPARE TO Kwai	100 tabs	4.79
ZINC 50 MG	100 tabs	99¢
ZINC 100 MG	100 tabs	1.39
B-1 100 MG	100 tabs	1.19
B-1 500 MG	60 tabs	1.99
Magnesium 500 mg (MAIL ORDER COUPON, LIMIT 1 PER ORDER)	100 tabs	99¢
COENZYME Q-10 10 mg	60 caps	5.69
C 500 MG w/Rose Hips (MAIL ORDER COUPON, LIMIT 1 PER ORDER FALM96)	100 tabs	1.29
Grapefruit	90 tabs	2.49
GINKGO BILOBA 60 MG	60 caps	9.99
Ferrous Sulfate 325 mg	100 tabs	99¢
Bee Pollen 1000 MG	100 tabs	2.29
HAIR VITES	50 tabs	1.99
Niacin 500 mg Sustained Release	60 tabs	2.29
Chromium Picolinate 200 MCG	100 tabs	3.49
Potassium 99 MG	100 tabs	99¢
SELENIUM 50 MCG	100 tabs	89¢
SELENIUM 100 MCG	100 tabs	1.39
Pycnogenol 25 MG	60 tabs	11.99
PAPAYA (MAIL ORDER COUPON, LIMIT 1 PER ORDER FALM96)	100 tabs	59¢
Citrinate COMPARE TO CITRIMAX (MAIL ORDER COUPON, LIMIT 1 PER ORDER FALM96)	90 tabs	7.99
NIACIN 50 MG	100 tabs	69¢
NIACIN 100 MG	100 tabs	89¢
Lysine 500 mg	100 tabs	1.89
Lysine 1000 mg	100 tabs	2.39
PMS Tabs	60 tabs	5.99
Shark Cartilage 500 mg.	60 caps	12.99
Mega Multiple #6 COMPARE TO CENTRUM	100 tabs	2.49
Celebrity Tabs COMPARE TO STAR CAPS	60 tabs	28.99
KELP	500 tabs	1.99
Spirulina 500 MG	100 tabs	3.49
Chewable Antioxidant	60 tabs	3.99
Bromelain 500 mg	90 tabs	6.99
Oyster Shell 1000 MG Calcium	100 tabs	1.49
Folic Acid 400 MCG	100 tabs	79¢
Folic Acid 800 MCG	100 tabs	1.09
Chewable Cherry C 500 mg	100 tabs	3.49

CALL 1-800-619-1199

Or send this ad with Check or M.O. Plus $1.50 Shipping To:
THE VITAMIN FACTORY, 201 ROUTE 22, HILLSIDE, NJ 07205
OFFER EXPIRES SEPTEMBER 30, 1996!

FALM96

Yes, Virginia, There IS AN APHRODISIAC

Casanova championed oysters. Napoleon treasured truffles. Hulk Hogan swears by yohimbine. Then there are advocates of ginseng, rooster pills, and dried beetle bodies. Do any of these sorts of things have any real effect? Well, read on and maybe you'll be surprised.

IT IS A DELICATE MATTER — one, perhaps, you'd rather not discuss. We all get tired, all find ourselves now and then lacking the excitement we once did upon preparing for bed. Face it: You could use a little help, a little stimulation.

Suppose you had just what the doctor ordered — a dose of bear gallbladder, a dusting of Spanish fly — that would result in the erotic experience of your life? Would you give $20,000 for an ounce of potent love potion? Would you descend into a cave of tarantulas and snakes and bird guano for an absolutely amazing aphrodisiac? Would you risk disease? Death? Be honest. You might, just once, to see what you've been missing.

You are not alone. People from the most ordinary of places have tried the most bizarre of stimulants: powder from the horns of rhinos, ground heelbones from the Austrian Alpine ibex, snake bile laced with kaolin, bat blood mixed with whiskey. And wait, there's more! Crocodile dung. Shark fin soup. Turtle eggs. Siberian tiger penises. Deer penises steeped in rice wine with wolfberries (makes you drool, doesn't it?).

You get the idea: the more exotic, the more erotic. If it's hard to get, it must be good. And if it's good, it must cost

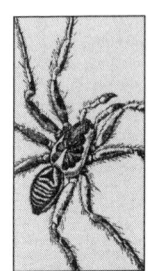

by Christine Schultz

THAT REALLY WORKS

In Elizabethan times, prunes were so highly regarded as aphrodisiacs that they were served free in brothels.

lots. You want a pair of Alaskan walrus tusks? That'll cost you $8,000. An ounce of bear gallbladder? Hand over $10,000. A rhino horn? Twenty thousand. On the cheap end we can get you a little Chattanooga beluga — that bluish-gray caviar from freshwater paddlefish — for $500 a pound. After you've spent enough dough, you'll be sure to stay awake to get your money's worth. Whatever happens, you're *bound* to find it memorable.

The down side to this exotic aphrodisiac business is that rare species are being decimated. "Our wildlife is under siege," said the director of the United States Fish and Wildlife Service to *Newsweek* in 1990. At that time officials had estimated the trade in illegal animal parts had reached $2.1 billion a year — up nearly 100 percent from a decade before. And it has been going up ever since, second only to the global drug trade in illegal profits.

Money and moral issues aside, the big question is this: Do aphrodisiacs really work? Hope is a great stimulant. And people have hoped for sexual euphoria since ancient times. The very word, *aphrodisiac,* traces all the way back to the Greek goddess of love, that queen of beauty and sensuality, Aphrodite. She has inspired cultures throughout the ages to achieve her legendary heights of delight.

For example, one of the first great Hindu physicians, Susruta, recommended that impotent Hindus consume animals' testicles to raise their testosterone levels. Pliny the Elder recommended hippopotamus snout and hyena eyes, while Horace touted dried marrow and liver. In Elizabethan times, prunes

1996   OLD FARMER'S ALMANAC   91

"POWER is the great aphrodisiac."
— Henry Kissinger

were so highly regarded as aphrodisiacs that they were served free in brothels. More dramatically, in 1889 a daring French physiologist named Charles Edouard Brown-Sequard injected himself with a mixture of dog testicles, guinea pig testicles, and saline solution in the purely scientific interests of sexology. He was happy to report "a remarkable return of my physical endurance." A month later he was, unfortunately, dead.

That was neither the first time death would be linked with sex, nor the last. It seems that even the possibility of death has heightened love affairs throughout the ages; that erotic urgency has sparked countless wartime romances, has tweaked endless spy thrillers, and charged illicit affairs. The presence of danger, in fact, is its own aphrodisiac. Secrecy gets the juices flowing, too. But so does the brain

chemical called PEA. You may know that PEA (or phenylethylamine, as the scientists call it) is also the stimulant that the brain releases during the early stages of infatuation. It's the revver-upper that allows us to stay awake all night and lose our appetites. But scientists have learned that PEA is also what races through the system of the thrill seeker. By raising the blood pressure and sending the heart racing, PEA allows the adventurer to feel alert, self-assured, and ready for whatever challenge awaits.

That thrill can come from love or conquest — or chocolate. Chocolate is the love drug, that luscious and indulgent melting in the mouth that makes amphetamines spurt and stirs up all sorts of sexy feelings. Chocolate was the virility-booster of choice for the Mexican emperor Montezuma, who drank 50 cups a day before visiting his harem of 600 women. But despite its sensual appeal and PEA content, the true effect of chocolate on the libido is still scientifically debated. When taken in large quantities, chocolate may even have a negative effect on sexual prowess, reports Dr. Wayne Meikle of the University of Utah. He found that men who consume too much high-fat food had a 30-percent drop in testosterone level.

Speaking of testosterone, modern research has shown, in

a surprising twist, that giving testosterone to older women has a more remarkable effect than it does on men. Small doses of testosterone prescribed to postmenopausal women by psychologist Barbara Sherwin at McGill University dramatically increased the women's sexual desire and energy levels. It was so effective, in fact, that some husbands whined about their wives' "overcharged" sex drive.

For those guys with flagging libidos, we offer a few tips from the great romantics of past and present. Casanova championed oysters; Napoleon treasured truffles; Popeye performed manly feats on a can or two of spinach; the Maharajah of Bikaner ingested crushed diamonds; many professional basketball players swear by ginseng; wrestler Hulk Hogan and many other celebrity bodybuilders praise "Hot Stuff," a protein powder made from yohimbine, the bark of an African tree (veterinarians use it in bull breeding, but high doses in humans can be lethal).

To be perfectly honest, the fact remains that the U.S. Food and Drug Administration declared all sex drugs lame. In 1989 they banned advertisers

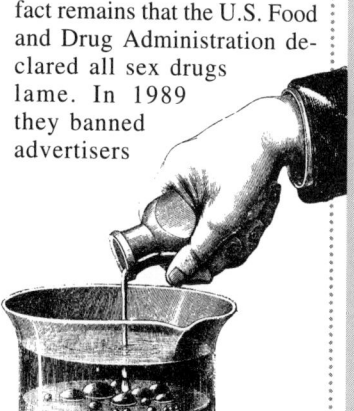

The FOOTSIE Survey

☞ Psychologist Daniel Wegner at the University of Virginia set out to test the theory that secrecy is especially thrilling. Randomly pairing 96 college students with members of the opposite sex, he instructed them to play a game of cards (not by its nature a stimulating exercise). He divided the couples into three groups. The couples in the first group can talk to each other, but are not allowed any physical contact. The couples in the second group must communicate nonverbally by secretly playing footsie under the table. The couples in the third group may also touch feet, but can be very open about it.

After the game, Wegner checked the students' attraction toward their card-playing partners. He discovered that those who had simply talked to each other and those who had touched feet openly were much less attracted to their partners than those who had been forced to conceal their foot caresses. The risk of detection had indeed heightened their erotic feelings for one another.

> There are women who say that money is the true aphrodisiac, that power is sexy, that there is nothing more alluring than a man holding a baby.

from promoting rooster pills or potions because their testing had shown that none worked no matter what the contents — fennel or strychnine or dried beetle bodies. The FDA said the love potions were only placebos. Any that appeared to work did so only because the user *believed* they would. The stimulant lay only in the user's mind.

In other words, it is the imagination that creates its own exciting possibilities and the body that leaps forward to fulfill the fantasies. Perhaps that's why a recent survey by the University of Chicago's National Opinion Research Center showed that of all possible sexual activities, Americans' second favorite was watching their mates undress. The anticipation, it seems, is almost as sweet as the culmination.

To men who are still lacking in oomph, go forth and make yourself rich or powerful or the caretaker of a baby. For there are women who say that money is the true aphrodisiac, that power is sexy, that there is nothing more alluring than a man holding a baby. In the end, arousal has most to do with believing that a particular man will fulfill your fantasies not only in the bedroom but beyond — by offering diamonds or fame or the perfect father for your kids.

The final stimulant is love, the most magnificent of aphrodisiacs. If properly applied, love can raise sexual intimacy to a height more explosive and enduring than could ever be reached through any amount of rhinoceros powder. And though love is certainly no easier to get hold of, it's a heck of a lot cheaper and more environmentally friendly. *(continued on page 96)*

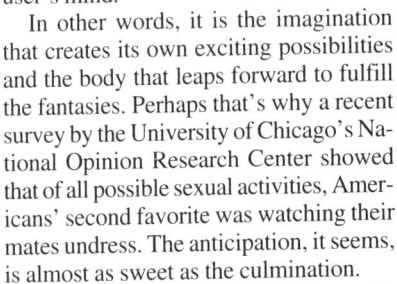

Announcing a Breakthrough For Adults of All Ages...
THE SUPPLEMENT THAT MAKES ANY RELATIONSHIP EXCITING AGAIN!

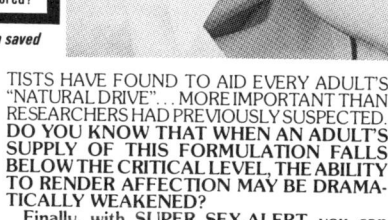

If you can answer YES to any of the following questions, you should order SUPER SEX-ALERT™ right now!
- Do you lack vigor and stamina?
- Do you lack vitality and desire?
- Has your lover lost interest in you?
- Are you easily exhausted?
- Do people think you act older than your years?
- Do you want the feeling of youth restored?

"I feel like a new person. I think it even saved my marriage." A NEW YORK MAN (on file)

It's happened to you. Happened to your friends. Happened to most everyone.
You want to be "loving". Provide affection for your partner. But somehow you are unable to "do it."
Perhaps it's nerves. Pressure at work. Worry. Fatigue. A headache. **Strangely, you lack the desire.** And it's happened more than once.
And something tells you this problem can only get worse.
Don't kid yourself either: **Loss of desire IS a problem!** Never dismiss lack of a healthy physical appetite as "normal" ... as something that **must** happen from time to time ... or as just "getting old."
**(Thousands of older couples in their seventies and eighties have the ability and desire to satisfy each other every day of their lives. WHAT EXCUSE CAN THERE BE FOR YOU?)
NOW, YOU CAN IMPROVE YOUR LOVE LIFE AND THRILL YOUR PARTNER EVERY TIME YOU WANT.**
Now everyone can look forward to a life enhanced with love and passion thanks to this extraordinary formula developed for adult men & women of all ages.
Attention reader: SUPER SEX-ALERT is not some type of dangerous prescription hormone supplement (which can give you harmful side effects). Laboratory formulated to bring into perfect balance concentrated micro-nutrients and specific sex-utilized vitamins, SUPER SEX-ALERT is expected to become an important tool of therapists and psychological counselors in the near future.
The ability to provide love, to arouse passion and to become rapturously revitalized WITHOUT USE OF DANGEROUS DRUGS is considered one of today's most important challenges. And SUPER SEX-ALERT meets this challenge.
AS POTENT AS THIS FORMULA IS NO PRESCRIPTION IS NEEDED!
You can use SUPER SEX-ALERT with confidence. It is all-natural and 100% safe. There are **no** addictive agents. **No dangerous "hormones." No** harmful substances found in many popular so called Love Products.
YET SUPER SEX-ALERT CONTAINS A CERTAIN FORMULATION THAT MEDICAL SCIENTISTS HAVE FOUND TO AID EVERY ADULT'S "NATURAL DRIVE"... MORE IMPORTANT THAN RESEARCHERS HAD PREVIOUSLY SUSPECTED. **DO YOU KNOW THAT WHEN AN ADULT'S SUPPLY OF THIS FORMULATION FALLS BELOW THE CRITICAL LEVEL, THE ABILITY TO RENDER AFFECTION MAY BE DRAMATICALLY WEAKENED?**
Finally, with SUPER SEX-ALERT, you can have **ALL THE VITAMINS AND NUTRIENTS YOU NEED**...
Whether you're young or old ... if you have a dull, drab life that doesn't meet your expectations ... if you find your drive and desire for love has diminished ... if you find it difficult to fulfill an affectionate relationship, SUPER SEX-ALERT is a **must** for your medicine cabinet.
You can reach for it daily — and know that help is always a moment away. Why endure the frustration and depression that comes from an unhappy love life? Mail the coupon now. You'll be delighted at the results this amazing formula can provide for you. YOU MUST BE TOTALLY SATISFIED — OR YOUR MONEY PROMPTLY REFUNDED (no explanation necessary).

For Our Fastest Service
Call 919-554-4014

▄▄▄▄▄NO-RISK **RUSH** COUPON ▄▄▄▄▄▄
T.E. HOLDING LABS INC. Dept. F
206 E. Jones Street, Holding Building
P.O. Box 1529, Wake Forest, NC 27588

Please rush me the remarkable SUPER SEX-ALERT™ backed by your No-Risk 30 day money back guarantee.
☐ Month supply (30 Tablets), only $15.43 plus $2.75 P&H.
☐ **SAVE $4.48** Two bottles (60 Tablets) for only $28.38 plus $3.50 P&H.
☐ **SUPER SAVINGS. SAVE $23.94.** Four bottles only $48.80.
We pay postage and handling.

Name _____
Address _____
City _____ State ____ Zip ____
N.C. Residents Add 6% Sales Tax
Quality • Research • Integrity • Since 1888

THE FOODS OF LOVE

In over 500 literary seduction scenes, the Aphrodisiac Growers Quarterly reported, 98 percent begin with a succulent meal. The list of foods thought to stir passion is long and seemingly random. But chances are the food is considered an aphrodisiac for one or more of the following four reasons:

☞ **Because** of its sensuous, fleshy texture and taste of the sea (oysters, mussels, caviar, herring, lobster, that sort of thing).

☞ **Because** the food (such as asparagus, carrots, mandrake root, ginseng root, and lupines) grows in the shape of the male sex organ and therefore falls within the Doctrine of Signatures — "that every plant bears some mark of the use to which it can be put."

☞ **Because** the food acts as a sort of a sexual smelling salt (think of chili peppers, garlic, and onions) that tingles the tongue and makes the nostrils flare.

☞ **Because** it's a natural rejuvenator, an herb or food with properties that enhance vigor and vitality or supply missing minerals. In the words of the *Kama Sutra:* "A man should eat strengthening foods, such as aromatic plants, meat, honey, and eggs. A robust constitution is indispensable . . ." A man lacking zinc is a man lacking a high sperm count. Feed him oysters, or asparagus, or the dark meat of turkey.

Just beware that you don't overdo it with any one food. In the words of Dr. Frederick Hollick, a roving medical expert in the 1840s, "In all cases, avoid constipation, the handmaiden of impotence and derangement." And further, be advised, as Dr. Hollick noted, that "Sexual indulgence just after eating is nearly certain to be followed by indigestion, even if it does not cause immediate vomiting."

What you are aiming for is well-moderated, plain, and simple good health. Take it from the Kinsey Institute for the Study of Human Sexuality, which advocates not only a good diet, but plenty of rest and regular exercise to keep the circulation pumping. When the body feels fit, the impulse to procreate will follow. ☐☐

Excerpted from the forthcoming *Old Farmer's Almanac Book of Romance* by Christine Schultz.

A WORD to the WISE

Just one word of advice on aphrodisiacs:

☞ Before you spend the money on the goods, spend the time on your partner. Otherwise nothing will work. In the words of Prince Charles, who was offered an arousing cup of camel's milk post-Diana: "Fat lot of use it's going to be to me now!"

Are You in Pursuit of Love & Happiness

or the Best Darn Tomatoes This Side of the Mississippi?

Now You Can Have It All–With The Expert Advice From A Psychic Friend.

Who says you can't have everything? Sure you can – provided, of course, you take the necessary steps along the way.

Like planting the best seeds. Cultivating the right relationships. Building the proper foundations. In short, getting the professional, personal guidance you desire – and deserve – from your very own Master Psychic at **The Psychic Friends Network!**℠

Over the past five years TV's **Psychic Friends Network** has become the most popular self-help, self-revelation movement in the country. It's as much a part of the American landscape as blue jeans and apple pie – an important part of what makes America a land of hope and opportunity. Every day millions of people from all walks of life call **The Psychic Friends Network** to get advice on things that matter most to them.

In other words, with **The Psychic Friends Network** Americans are getting the advice they need to take control of their lives & loves.

Men & Women all over America are turning to The Psychic Friends Network brought to you by Dionne Warwick & Linda Georgian.

So why not their *lima beans*, too? You see, there is really no limit to what kind of problems a Master Psychic can help you solve.

Want to cultivate the perfect garden? Just call **The Psychic Friends Network**. A Master Psychic, professionally trained in the astrological pattern of the moon, stars and tides can tell you which plants, flowers or vegetables are most likely to sprout – and which ones are most likely to shrivel.

Want to cultivate the perfect relationship. *Ditto.* The Psychic Friends Network can connect you directly to a Master Psychic specializing in marriage and romance.

As Linda Georgian, a premier psychic and founder of **The Psychic Friends Network** said, "Whether you're looking for love, money, career advancement – *or even a picture perfect tomato* – now there's a Master Psychic waiting to guide your every step of the way."

Call Now!
1-900-740-0445

(Only $3.99 per minute) You must be at least 18 years of age. Sponsored by Inphomation Communications, Inc. Baltimore, MD

★ **Psychic Friends Network** ★ **1-900-740-0445** ★

Getting Rid of PAPER CLUTTER

There's hardly a paper-clutter junkie alive who won't benefit from perusing the following hints, expert advice, and commonsense ideas.

by Maude Salinger

"You'd think that paper clutter would be easy to deal with. After all, paper comes boldly through the front door in broad daylight. It's not surreptitious, like a mouse. Actually, it's probably easier to get rid of the mouse — at least you can set a trap for it."

– Jeff Campbell of the Clean Team and author of *Clutter Control*

Picture this scene: You're rummaging through a pile of paper stacked on top of the kitchen counter (since you long ago ran out of room to store stuff on your desk), searching in vain for those theater tickets you need tonight. Do you find the tickets? No. But you do find six months' worth of bank statements neatly wrapped with a rubber band, last week's mail, all those recipes you clipped and have been meaning to try, catalogs (same company, four different seasons), school notices, bills (there's that credit card statement you thought you'd lost!), newspapers, magazines (there might be an important article you'll want to save), receipts, notes, and "to do" lists.... Why does all of this stuff seem to accumulate faster than you can read it, file it, pay it, give it away, or throw it out?

If clutter is the bane of your existence, take heart — you are not alone. Getting rid of clutter may take some time and effort, but remember, for every mess there is hope. Here are the basic principles, straight from the experts.

CLUTTER BUSTING:
Two Simple Steps

The problem of clutter can be broken down into two simple elements:

☞ **ONE: Too much stuff.**   ☞ **TWO: No place to put it.**

– illustrated by Abby Carter

The solution to # One (reducing the stuff) helps, but until — and unless — you set up a system for organizing the stuff, you'll be right back where you began, shuffling through those mounds of paper again. So, let's begin with #Two.

☞ **PROBLEM:** No place to put it. ☞ **SOLUTION:** Use a file cabinet.

IDEAS
for File Categories

✔ Bills
✔ Car
✔ Catalogs
✔ Checking Accounts
✔ Correspondence
✔ Coupons
✔ Documents (insurance policies, medical documents)
✔ Instruction Manuals (attach product warranties and purchase receipts to each manual)
✔ Recipes (Subheads: Appetizers, Main Dishes, Desserts, etc.)
✔ Savings Accounts
✔ School Records
✔ Taxes

Most of us spend at least as much time handling paper as we do preparing food. We wouldn't think of going without a kitchen, so why pretend we don't need a desk? Set up a permanent work center — in the bedroom, kitchen, or den — that will be available to you at all times. If you absolutely don't have room for a desk, use the dining room table. But get a file cabinet. Buy one with built-in metal frames for hanging file folders, or purchase add-on frames for each drawer. Also, get a supply of hanging folders.

Set Up a Filing System

First, gather up everything you want to store in your file cabinet. Then begin sorting it into stacks or general categories such as bills, instruction booklets, correspondence, school records, and so forth. Each stack will become a separate file, so pay attention to how big the pile gets. If a stack does get too bulky, subdivide it. For example, "School Records" can be broken down by each individual child.

File According to Usage and Alphabet

Seldom needed files (old tax returns, insurance policies) can go in the back of the drawer; files you will use often (checking account, bills) go toward the front.

To help figure out where to file each piece of paper, consider how you will use it. A Caribbean travel brochure should be filed under "Vacation Ideas," not "Caribbean." (Don't save the brochure at all if you plan on never leaving your hometown.)

Be specific, but not too specific, or you'll end up with lots of skinny files. Are you saving an article on how to fix a leaky faucet? Then file it under "Household Repairs," not "Leaky Faucet."

Begin file headings with nouns rather than adjectives. That's "Job Applications — Current," not "Current Job Applications."

Ask yourself what word would first enter your mind if you were searching for the information. The test of the system is to be able to retrieve something.

Make a file index — an alphabetical list of all your file headings — and update it every few months.

HINT: Keep a few extra folders at the back of your file cabinet so that it will be easy to start a new file when you need to.

FEELING OVERWHELMED?

You can buy someone else's system. Here are a few ready-made kits on the market:

- **Homefile** ($19.95, 800-695-3453)

- **File Solutions**, P.O. Box 516381, Dallas, TX 75251; 214-488-0100. File kits for home, business, student, or salesperson include guidebook, color-coded labels and a filing index. Home Filing System $30.

- Photo files and storage boxes, schoolwork savers, warranty and manual organizers, household inventory albums, and a variety of other organizational tools are available from your local stationery store and through catalogs such as:

Current, The Current Building, Colorado Springs, CO 80941; 800-525-7170.

Lillian Vernon, Virginia Beach, VA 23479-0002; 800-285-5555.

☞ **PROBLEM: Too much stuff.**
(Research shows that 80 percent of the material in most files is never used.)

☞ **SOLUTION: Get a wastebasket.**
(If you generate a lot of recyclable paper, get two.) This philosophy is also known as "When in doubt, toss it out."

If "keeping things for a rainy day" is ingrained in your character, ask yourself, "What is the worst thing that could happen if I threw this away?" If the answer is "Nothing much," throw it out. (Note: There are definitely items you need to keep — and we'll give you that list.)

If you're not using something, get rid of it. (Notice present tense.) Ask yourself, "How long has it been since I've used it?" "Do I need this many?" If you want to save magazines or newspapers, stash only those that fit in a single basket or in a stack on one shelf. Clip and file useful articles, then recycle the rest of the magazine. (Did you know that as of September 1991 there were approximately 3.784 billion copies of *National Geographic* in print, and just about every one of them is still in somebody's basement?)

Don't handle paper over and over again. When you open mail, don't leave it lying on top of the counter "for now." Sort it into four categories: "To Do," "To File," "To Pay," and "Toss." "Toss" goes in the trash — now.

Reduce unwanted mail at the source. If you want to eliminate your name from national advertising lists, send your name, address, and zip code to this address:

**Mail Preference Service
Direct Marketing Association
11 West 42nd St.
P.O. Box 3861
New York, NY 10163-3861**

(Include commonly used variations in the spelling of your name and in the format of your address.)

What You Can Safely Throw Away*

✔ **Expired insurance policies** (with no possibility of a claim).

✔ **Nontax-related checks** more than three years old.

✔ **Records for items you no longer own** (cars, boats).

✔ **Pay stubs going back more than two years.**

(* Note: If you are not sure about whether you should save a particular item, consult your CPA or lawyer first.)

WHAT TO SAVE
(For a While or Forever)

✔ **KEEP** canceled checks that substantiate tax deductions or major purchases. Pull out these checks when you get your bank statement each month. File tax-related checks under "taxes" (charitable giving, medical expenses); file big purchase checks with product warranties.

✔ **KEEP** a file with purchase and sale documents (including tax form 2119) for every home you've owned.

✔ **KEEP** a file of capital home-improvement expenditures. This will *increase* the home's cost

100   OLD FARMER   1996

Advertisement

IRRITABLE BOWEL?

(Special) If you suffer problems such as constipation, bloating, diarrhea, gas, stomach cramps, heartburn, pain and discomfort associated with foods, you should know about a new book, *The Irritable Bowel Syndrome & Gastrointestinal Solutions Handbook.*

The book contains the latest up-to-date information on the bowel—how it functions, what can go wrong, how it can best be treated, and how to protect yourself from irritable bowel problems. The book gives you specific facts on the latest natural and alternative remedies that can bring prompt and lasting relief without the use of dangerous drugs. You'll learn all about these new remedies and find out how and why they work. You'll discover what you can do to avoid irritable bowel and stomach problems, what foods actually promote healing, and what to avoid at all costs. The book even explains a simple treatment that has helped thousands rid themselves of irritable bowel problems, yet is little-known to most people—even doctors.

The book also explains how the gastrointestinal system works, how food is digested, how specific foods affect the bowel, why certain foods and activities cause problems, why over 20 million people suffer irritable bowel problems—and how most people are now able to overcome their problems.

Many Americans are putting up with troublesome irritable bowel and stomach problems because they are unaware of new natural treatments and the welcome relief that is now available.

Get all the facts. Order this book today. It is being made available for only $12.95 *(plus $3 postage and handling)*. To order, send name and address with payment to United Research Publishers, 103 N. Highway 101, Dept. FAS-3, Encinitas, CA 92024. You may return the book within 30 days for a refund if not satisfied.

FLATTEN YOUR BELLY!

If you want to flatten your stomach and trim your waist, you should know about a new book, *3 Simple Steps to Flatten Your Belly!* The book shows you a simple and fast way to give yourself a flat, firm stomach—even if other attempts to lose your pot belly failed.

Why It's So Hard to Get Rid of a Pot Belly

Incredibly, some stomach programs only make your pot belly worse. You see, some stomach programs may actually build up and swell the muscles in your stomach without removing the fat—making your stomach appear larger and puffier. What's more, exercises that work on your "love handles" (the sides of your waist) can actually build muscle and increase the overall size of your waist. Even worse, some so-called stomach exercises don't even work your stomach—they can merely strain your back and neck.

Why This Program Will Flatten Your Belly

This book shows you a simple program that won't bulge out or puff up your stomach but actually flattens it out, so your stomach becomes slimmer, trimmer and firmer. And this program is designed to flatten your stomach without straining your back or neck. What's more, this program shows you how to remove layers of fat around your belly. The book tells you about "fat melting" foods that work in conjunction with the exercise program to break down and flush away pockets of flab and fat around your midsection. This program launches an all-out attack on the bulging fat cells around your waistline.

Following this program should transform your pot belly from unsightly flab to a flat, trim and sexy waistline. A firm, flat belly makes you look and feel better. Your posture often improves while nagging back problems often disappear.

Forget about expensive exercise equipment, health spas and starvation diets. This belly-flattening program must work for you or you pay nothing. This book is being made available for only $12.95 *(plus $3 postage and handling)*. To order, send name and address with payment to United Research Publishers, 103 North Highway 101, Dept. FAF-3, Encinitas, CA 92024. You may return the book anytime for refund if not satisfied.

for tax purposes, thereby *decreasing* your capital gain later. (Routine repairs and maintenance don't count; new roofs, remodeled kitchens or baths, and landscaping do.)

✔ **KEEP** credit card records for six years.

✔ **KEEP** health records forever.

✔ **KEEP** contracts for seven years past the expiration date.

✔ **KEEP** loan papers for three years after final payment.

✔ **KEEP** records of all contributions to nondeductible IRAs, including form 8606.

✔ **KEEP** records of investments, with separate files for each mutual fund or brokerage account.

✔ **WILLS:** Don't put your will in a safe-deposit box; many states limit access when the holder dies. Keep a copy at home and leave the original with your attorney. Destroy outdated versions.

✔ **TAX RETURNS:** At the end of the tax season, save copies of federal and state returns and all supporting documents in a single folder. Store six years' worth: the IRS has three years to examine your return, six if there is substantial underreporting of income.

What to Keep in a
SAFE-DEPOSIT BOX

✔ Photocopy valuable, hard-to-replace papers. Place originals in a safe-deposit box and keep photocopies at home with a list of safe-deposit contents.

✔ Deeds and other records of ownership. Include material that documents the condition of your home: written inventory, appraisals, photos, receipts.

✔ Birth and marriage certificates.

✔ Passports.

✔ Stock and bond certificates.

✔ List of all insurance policies and agents (store actual documents at home).

✔ Adoption papers.

✔ Divorce decrees.

✔ Custody agreements.

LAST RESORTS

☞ Is a chronic case of chaos driving you nuts? Maybe you need:

Messies Anonymous
5025 S.W. 114 Ave.
Miami, FL 33165
305-271-8404

☞ Yes, there is a national Organize Your Home Office Day. It occurs annually on the fourth Tuesday in March (but don't wait that long to get started!). For information:

Lisa Kanarek
Organizational Consultant
660 Preston Forest Ctr., Suite 120
Dallas, TX 75230
214-361-0556

☞ Can't possibly organize the mess yourself? Contact:

National Association of Professional Organizers
1033 La Posada Dr. #220
Austin, TX 78752-3880
512-454-8626

Begun in 1985, the organization lists over 700 members in 44 states and can supply names and specialties of nearby members.

Books

CLUTTER CONTROL (Jeff Campbell, Dell, 1992, $6.99)

CLUTTER'S LAST STAND (Don Aslett, Writer's Digest Books, 1984, $10.95)

STEPHANIE WINSTON'S BEST ORGANIZING TIPS (Simon & Schuster, 1995, $20)

TAMING THE PAPER TIGER (Barbara Hemphill, The Kiplinger Washington Editors, 1992, $11.95)

Advertisement

Vinegar Can Be Used For WHAT?

If you're like me, you will be amazed at the multitude of uses for vinegar.

This common household product is *packed* with essential amino acids and helpful vitamins, minerals, and enzymes. Apple cider vinegar was found to be an almost universal preservative and cure-all. The healthy goodness of apples is concentrated into a teaspoon of golden liquid — a teaspoon of which supplies a generous portion of the building blocks needed for a healthy body.

The new book "The Vinegar Book" by natural remedies author Emily Thacker, shows you over 300 ways to use vinegar for fighting germs, easing pain, improving health, cutting grease, and cleaning tips for a natural sparkle! She gives you recipes to make your own flavored vinegar that will perk up the taste of your food!

Pain Relief
- Relieve varicose veins
- Fade headaches away
- Kill infection
- Soothe sore throats & coughs
- Calm nausea

Nature's Aid To A Healthier Body
- Control appetite to lose weight
- Protect skin from the ravages of the sun
- Fade age spots
- Minimize memory loss

Your House Will Be Ready For The "White-Glove Test!"
- Use as a disinfectant—some hospitals do!
- Use in the laundry — brightens colors! Whitens whites! Fades perspiration stains!
- Removes carpet stains—absorbs odors
- Repairs wood scratches & makes an excellent furniture polish
- Countertops, floors, windows & fixtures will shine!

Did You Know . . .
- Vinegar is credited for saving the lives of thousands of soldiers during the U.S. Civil War?
- In 400 B.C. Hippocrates, considered the father of medicine, used vinegar to treat his patients?
- Vinegar was used as a healing dressing on wounds and sores in Biblical times?

Research Shows . . .
- When fresh apples are allowed to ferment organically, the result is a vinegar that contains natural sediment with pectin, trace minerals, beneficial bacteria and enzymes.

Order your copy of "The Vinegar Book" TODAY. All you have to do is write the word "Vinegar" along with your name and address on a plain piece of paper. Mail your remittance of only $12.95 plus $2 postage & handling payable to: The Vinegar Book, 718 - 12th St. N.W., Dept. F5563, Canton, Ohio 44703.

Order an extra copy for family and friends and SAVE. You can order 2 for only $20 postpaid!

You may charge to your VISA or MasterCard by including your card number, expiration date and signature. For even faster service on VISA/MasterCard, call toll free 1-800-772-7285, Ext. F5563.

If you're dissatisfied for any reason, you may return the cover only within three months for a full refund. Act promptly and you will also receive a FREE copy of "Brain & Health Power Foods" Report. Supplies are limited so you must act now. ©1995 TRESCO TF701-3

by Howard Mansfield

Thanks to Henry Ford (and others), we are celebrating the 100th anniversary of the automobile in 1996. But we'd be stuck in eternal gridlock if not for an eccentric named WILLIAM PHELPS ENO, known to posterity as . . .

The Father of ALL TRAFFIC LAWS

New York City was stalked by a deadly peril at the turn of the century: traffic. "Careless Drivers Make Death Traps of Our Thoroughfares and Fill Hospital Beds with Maimed Men, Women, and Children," said a headline in the *New York Herald*. One person a day was killed in the streets, half the toll by trolleys, the rest by horse-drawn wagons, the new automobile, runaway horses, and bicycles. The streets were a free-for-all. There were no traffic laws. In sensational headlines and sermons, the press and the clergy called for reform.

Then, in 1900, one quiet man with a penchant for order delivered the motorized world from the confusion. An avid horseman, William Phelps Eno introduced the traffic rules that were to conquer the world in a small equestrian magazine, *Rider & Driver*. In the January 20, 1900, issue, he set down the rules of the road we know today: Drivers must

From chaos to order — thanks to William Eno (shown *at right* in Paris in 1935), who deplored traffic congestion in cities like Philadelphia *(above)* at the turn of the century and devoted his life to promoting what the French would call *"le Système Eno."*

– photos courtesy Eno Transportation Foundation, Inc.

The rules of the road were adopted by New York in 1903 and declared a success: stay to the right and signal for turns and when slowing down or stopping. Drivers should be licensed and "the speed of cars . . . should be regulated by law." Further refinements quickly followed. Eno proposed a ten-mile-per-hour limit for cars and bicycles; three miles per hour when turning or crossing a busy street. Cyclists and drivers protested, advocating 12 miles per hour. Eno also asked for one-way streets, one-way traffic rotaries, traffic tickets, pavement markings, traffic signs, taxi stands, off-street parking, rules of right-of-way at intersections, special traffic police, and a traffic commissioner.

Born in 1858, William Eno had grown up in a wealthy household in New York City. His life's work had been revealed to him in 1867, when he was only nine years old and stuck in traffic on lower Broadway near Grand Street for a half hour.

"That very first traffic jam will always remain in my memory," Eno later recalled. "There were only about a dozen horses and carriages involved, and all that was needed was a little order to keep the traffic moving. Yet nobody knew exactly what to do; neither the drivers nor the police knew anything about traffic control."

An average student at Yale, Eno had gone into his father's real estate business. His father owned property in Times Square and on Fifth Avenue and was said to be worth $20 million in the 1890s. Eno came into his inheritance at age 41 and retired to do what he loved best: regulate traffic.

Rest assured, Eno was not all work and no play. He summered at Judah Rock, his 30-room "cottage" on Long Island Sound in Saugatuck, Connecticut. There he docked his 152-foot steam yacht *Aquilo*

Eno's Apollo Squad in New York City used an elite team of horses and riders to enforce the new traffic rules, including the idea of keeping to the right side of the road.

and enjoyed billiards, boxing, collecting art, going to the opera and theater, and horseback riding. Eno was a natty dresser. He habitually wore a dark three-piece suit with a gold button in his lapel and a gold watch chain across his vest, a high starched collar, a tie, and a black derby. His gray Vandyke beard was always carefully groomed. He spent winters in Washington, D.C., and had his horses shipped there. When he traveled in this country, he usually used a private railroad car.

Most of his time was spent fighting people who were opposed to his new ideas. In Washington it would take Eno 25 years to get them adopted. Traffic in the nation's capital was "worse than in any other place in America," said an exasperated Eno. "And it is absolutely the fault of the police department or the boss commissioner. They are responsible for

Eno reported that he saw no traffic "blockade" of more than a minute.

those lives just as though they shot the people. They are killing more than twice as many people here, in proportion to the population, as they are in New York. There is no reason for it except pigheadedness and stupidity." The rules of the road were adopted by New York in 1903 and declared a success: Eno reported that he saw no traffic "blockade" of more than a minute. To enforce the rules, he helped start America's first mounted police unit, the Apollo Squad in New York. (He also donated a prized horse that the police named Eno.)

traffic all moving one way, for Piccadilly Circus in London.

Across the Channel, the French at first balked at having an American meddle with their driving, but Eno won them over with his book, *Le Problème de la Circulation*. The French, who could always appreciate an elegant set of ideas, praised "le Système Eno." Paris cabbies threatened to strike if the system was not adopted. The cabbies won, and Paris instituted one-way streets, mounted police officers, and a rotary for traffic around the Arc de Triomphe.

Eno was a familiar figure in Paris, even to the point of being kidded on stage in variety shows. In 1910 the cabbies made him an honorary member of their organization, the Chambre Syndicale des Cochers et Chauffeurs des Voitures de la Place de la Seine. Other Eno improvements followed, including pedestrian crosswalks on the Champs-Élysées.

A bicycle cop in 1906 was "like a snail after a greyhound" when trying to stop high-powered cars on Lafayette Boulevard along the Hudson River.

Eno diligently promoted his ideas. Working with his loyal secretary, each year he wrote 2,000 letters and articles. He wrote six books on traffic control, traveled the country preaching reform, and made nine trips to Europe to promote the cause. In 1921 Eno established the world's first traffic institute. Over the door he placed a stone medallion with the date of his first traffic jam — 1867 — and the motto *Ex Chao Ordo,* out of chaos, order.

Overseas the English, whom he admired for their orderliness, experimented with his "gyratory system," a rotary with

The French even credited *le Système Eno* with helping them win World War I. The Germans had expected to overrun the French at Verdun and then push on to Paris. But thanks to Eno's traffic regulations, the French were able to mass 60,000 troops at the front. "One is astonished at the facility with which the intense and uninterrupted traffic is maintained on the roads," reported a war correspondent. For bringing order to Paris, the French awarded

Mussolini implemented all of Eno's traffic-control ideas and forbade horn blowing, for which he won the latter's admiration.

Eno the Cross of the Legion of Honor in 1925.

But back home, Eno was fighting a losing battle against the spread of automatic traffic lights, which had been introduced before World War I. Eno insisted that preset lights were blind to actual traffic volume and encouraged a series of stops and dashes up the avenue that was dangerous to pedestrians. It was like a doctor giving the same remedy to all patients no matter what their illness, he said. "What is good for one intersection may not be appropriate for another," he noted.

In Washington at cherry blossom time and other crowded events, the police turned off the lights to speed traffic. When Eno testified before a Senate committee in 1929, he urged: "Eliminate all automatic traffic signals."

Rotaries were the answer, "the most important principle for the control of traffic so far advanced." They were a "no-stop system" that didn't bunch up vehicles and ran so smoothly that traffic officers were not required. But Washington never adopted Eno's plan for rotaries.

The most rapid and complete success Eno witnessed was in Italy. It took a dictator to impose order. Mussolini implemented all of Eno's traffic-control ideas and forbade horn blowing, for which he won the latter's admiration. "I have always had the highest admiration of Premier Mussolini and his great ability for thoroughness," said Eno. (On this point he differed with his barber, John Santella of Saugatuck. The Italian-born Santella thought that "Il Duce was too dictatorial." Even so, Eno was an excellent customer with a "good head" of gray hair, who paid $2 for his 25¢ haircut and gave the barber one of his traffic-control books every Christmas.)

In his later years Eno waged an anti-noise campaign. Once again, he was successful in Paris, where two dozen French papers endorsed the idea. At the outset of the motor age, French law had *required* drivers to honk their horns in warning each time they came to a bend in the road. In a few short years the French had become expressive horn blowers. Eno imposed order, restoring quiet to Paris and lowering accident rates.

Eno had other successes with his campaign against "nerve-cracking" car horns. New York's Mayor Fiorello La Guardia proclaimed "noiseless nights" in October 1935, which pleased Eno and his colleagues at the League for Less Noise in New York. In Switzerland, Zurich declared a "Silence Week," and Finland went the furthest, barring all street sound, including hand organs, noisy newsboys, sidewalk preachers, and street bells.

By the 1940s, in his eighties, Eno was in poor health, his eyesight failing. His foundation in Westport, Connecticut, carried on his work, developing a predecessor of the radar gun, the Enoscope, to catch speeders. (The Eno Transportation Foundation moved to Lansdowne, Virginia, in 1993.) Eno, anticipating the interstate highway system, called for a system of military highways to connect the states, but his heart was never in the automotive age. He thought cars should go no faster than 45 miles per hour under any conditions.

Eno died in 1945. Through his long life, the "Father of Traffic Regulation," the man the press called "a scientific doctor of traffic problems," remained a gentleman of the old order. When out in his carriage, he never traveled without a footman and coachman. In a car he always had a chauffeur. In fact, Eno never got a driver's license. He never liked cars.

☐ ☐

Amazing VITASEX ® Formula for MEN & WOMEN

GUARANTEED TO RENEW VIGOR

No Prescription Needed

REVIVE "YOUR" LOVE LIFE

This amazing formula renews your vigor and may be the fastest, safest, and surest vitamin, mineral tonic and stimulant formula ever released by medical science. Yes, many men and women who have taken these miracle tablets after a tiring working day have found new strength and potency to the point it has made the relationship come alive again. These potent VitaSex tablets are the reason many couples are enjoying a happier home life after years of dragging through each day.

REVITALIZE ENERGY, POTENCY, AND VIGOR

Start today to renew your strength, potency and vigor with the first tablets you take. You don't have to wait days to get results. You get almost immediate new surges of energy because this revolutionary new product is designed to start working instantly. And you won't experience hypertension and jittery energy that accompanies other drugs that you see advertised in certain magazines and newspapers.

AMAZING RESULTS

VITASEX® is a **scientifically formulated** tonic and stimulant that gives you the EXTRA measure of nutrients and stimulant that you may need to revitalize vigor, energy and stamina. Therefore, you'll also experience the exhilarating, rewarding lift of HEALTHY BODY FUNCTION.

Yes, now instead of being left out of the "good times" you can:

- Restore healthy body function . . .
- Improve your desire and performance . . .
- Renew your strength, potency and vigor . . .
- And win the desire of your mate regardless of age, or age differences.

Results with VITASEX have **proven** that it gets guaranteed results! Anyone in good health can renew their strength, stamina and vigor with VITASEX®. **Yes, success in every case.**

VITASEX®— A Personal Relations™ Health Product sold in drug stores. Ask your Pharmacist or order direct. Druggist inquiries appreciated.

RENEW VIGOR WITH THE FASTEST, SUREST, AND SAFEST TONIC AND STIMULANT FORMULA OUR MEDICAL SCIENTISTS HAVE EVER DEVELOPED — ABSOLUTELY GUARANTEED!

In fact, the only way VitaSex® won't work for you is by not using them! It's guaranteed to work for you, even if you've had a problem for years. Even if other formulas have failed you. Even if nothing you've tried in the past had any lasting effect!

That's why we can make this 100% no-risk guarantee. This potent formula must work for you or your money will be refunded (less postage of course), and you can keep the first bottle free. ACT NOW!

For Our Fastest Service
Call 919-554-4014

------- NO-RISK **RUSH** COUPON -------
T.E. HOLDING LABS INC. Dept. F
206 E. Jones Street, Holding Building
P.O. Box 1529, Wake Forest, NC 27587
Please rush me the amazing fast-acting VITASEX" backed by your 30 day No-Risk Guarantee.

☐ Month supply (30 Tablets), only $11.43 plus $2.75 postage & handling.
☐ SAVE $3.23 Two bottles only $21.88 plus $3.25 postage & handling.
— SPECIAL INTRODUCTORY OFFER —
☐ **SUPER SAVINGS. SAVE $15.92** Four bottles only $40.80 (we pay postage & handling)

Name _____
Address _____
City _____ State _____ Zip _____
N.C. Residents Add 6% Sales Tax

Quality • Research • Integrity • Since 1888

Some scientists are beginning to believe that standard tests used to measure animal intelligence are often about as meaningful as giving an American a multiple-choice exam in a foreign language.

Who's Smarter:
CATS OR DOGS OR HUMAN BEINGS?

by Sy Montgomery
– illustrated by Randy Verougstraete

QUESTION: Our dog often takes the posture of Rodin's famous statue, *The Thinker*. He sits there, chin on paw, thinking . . . what?

ANSWER: Owing to the artificially complex life led by city dogs of the present day, they frequently lapse into what comes very close to mental perplexity. I myself have known some very profoundly thoughtful dogs. . . .

■ THE QUESTION AND THE ANSWER WERE MADE UP BY HUmorist James Thurber, but they illustrate a thought common to all dog and cat owners: What strange beast is this that comes slouching forth at dinnertime? In other words, just how smart are they? And which — dog or cat — is the smarter?

Psychologists stepped in to solve the mystery. If human intelligence can be measured, why not animal IQ? So modeling their experiments after those used to test the intelligence of prespeaking children, they set about their task.

The psychologists were in for a shock.

One early test was designed to measure how fast one dog could learn from watching another. One dog was taught to jump onto a box at a given signal to receive a food reward. A second dog watched all the while. Dog One repeated the trick 110 times. Dog Two never got even a glimmer of the idea.

Then there was the animal version of "It's Academic." An oft-cited 1967 experiment pitted cats against minks, ferrets, and skunks in a test of how long it would take them to figure out that they would be rewarded for choosing one of two different-looking objects in a set, but not the other. After 200 problems, minks got the idea, and after 350 trials, their scores were almost perfect. Ferrets performed similarly. But after attempting 600 problems, the cats had barely begun to score higher than chance. At this task they stunk even worse than the skunks. At least the skunks eventually got about 70 percent of the problems right.

In another classic test, an animal faced four doors arrayed in an arc. One door was unlocked so the animal could go through it and get food. The door unlocked in the previous trial was never unlocked in the succeeding one. The

A maze experiment pitted 27 white rats against 38 college students. The rats learned the maze three times faster than the college students.

animal was supposed to learn to avoid the last door that worked.

People and our kin, the monkeys, do well on this test. After 100 trials we all get the idea and avoid the previous door.

But only 14 percent of the dogs tested got it, and a mere nine percent of the cats. Of all the creatures tested, only horses and gophers fared worse. None of them figured it out at all.

The psychologists' verdict was in: "Certain animals are numskulls," animal psychologist Vance Packard summed up in his 1950 book, *Animal IQ,* "grade-A morons." Lassie was dismissed as a lamebrain and Kitty labeled a knucklehead. Cats and dogs, it seemed, were about equally stupid.

Pet owners were horrified. An angry executive wrote Packard in defense of dogs: "I have an old setter dog that can tell a Buick from a Cadillac by its sound. I know because when I come home in a Buick he appears, but Cadillacs can go by all day, and he pays no attention to them. Are your chimpanzees and orangutans that mechanical?"

Even in the face of data giving the dog a slight numerical edge over the cat in IQ tests, the great dog lover Albert Payson Terhune

was finally convinced that the cat was smarter from watching a thirsty cat and a thirsty dog at a water faucet. The dog sat beneath the faucet waiting for a person to turn it on for him. The cat leapt up and pushed the tap open with her paws.

The psychologists responded that these animals only seemed to be thinking and learning, remembering and reasoning. What they were really doing was behaving by instinct. In other words, when they did something smart outside the laboratory, it didn't count.

But as the psychologists continued testing other species, they began to note some confusing results.

A startling experiment carried out at a well-known university pitted 27 white rats against 38 college students. Both species set about learning their way through a large, enclosed maze. The results were a disgrace to the human race: The rats learned the way three times faster than the college students.

Similarly disturbing results were obtained on other tests as well. On some visual tasks, chickens outperformed dolphins. On a test of short-term memory, wasps outscored all the mammals.

Results like these suggested that there might be something going on that the psychologists didn't understand. Perhaps, in these battles of wits, the losing contestants weren't stupid. Perhaps the tests were.

Ethologists, scientists who study animals' natural behavior (usually outside the laboratory) offered some obvious facts the psychologists had ignored. How could rats outscore college students? Because rats have lived in labyrinthine underground burrows for millennia. Why did Flipper flub? Because out of water, dolphins don't see as well as chickens do.

Why do dogs and cats fare so poorly on IQ tests? "These are artificial, human-centered tasks," says Randall Lockwood, a vice president of the Humane Society of the United States. Such tests may be perfectly fine for predicting how high a typical human toddler might later score on exams in a typical American grade school. But as for testing the intelligence of cats and dogs, the tests were about as useful as giving an American a multiple-choice exam in a foreign language.

The situation is like one once pictured in a "Far Side" cartoon: notebook-toting animal psychologists stand perplexed before a dolphin tank. "Matthews," says one scientist to his colleague, "we're getting another of those strange 'aw blah es span yol' sounds."

The problem with these IQ tests is that cats and dogs interpret and understand the world differently than we do. We live in a world dominated by images. To see something is to believe it. So most of the tests we make up measure ability to solve visual problems — like figuring out whether a teacup or a saucer will elicit a food reward.

Cats and dogs do have good vision: Though their eyes lack a fovea, an area of the retina that lets people quickly distinguish objects at a distance, they have better peripheral vision and see better at night than we do. But vision pales beside their ability to smell. In the membrane lining the nose, cats have 19 million nerve endings devoted to smelling; dogs, with 220 million such nerve endings, can identify the scent of a human fingerprint that's six weeks old.

Humans, with a paltry five million such nerve endings, could well be considered "nasally challenged," to use the modern euphemism. As author, philosopher, and animal trainer Vicki Hearne puts it, "A dog who did comparative psychology might easily worry about our consciousness or lack thereof, the way we worry about the consciousness of a squid."

Further, cats and dogs are as different from one another socially as we are from

> Humans, with a paltry five million such nerve endings, could well be considered "nasally challenged . . ."

WIN
AUSTRALIAN TAX-FREE, LUMP-SUM LOTTERIES NOW

PLAY FOR 5 WEEKS FOR ONLY $5.00 AND WIN UP TO $49 MILLION ... ORDER RIGHT NOW!

Is Your FUTURE Worth Investing Just $5? A Message From J. Michael Husk, President:

Will YOU be flying to Australia within 5 weeks on a Expense-Paid Holiday to collect a $MILLION DOLLARS or more? 527,839 CASH PRIZES have already been claimed. I want you to INVEST just $5 so that you'll have 5 WEEKS of play! WIN up to $49,000,000.00 (yes, $49 MILLION!) at a crack. GO FOR IT! Order right now.

I Love To Give Financial Freedom To My American Friends ... Will YOU Be A Millionaire in 5 Weeks?

AUSTRALIAN LOTTO 6/45

$1,270,294.46 WINNER	$5,000,246.70 WINNER	$1,249,971.51 WINNER	$1,432,294.51 WINNER	$7,000,972.42 WINNER	$3,800,167.00 WINNER	$2,000,826.22 WINNER

FILL OUT THIS GAMEBOARD & MAIL TODAY
Place an **X** in any 6 Boxes with your Pen.

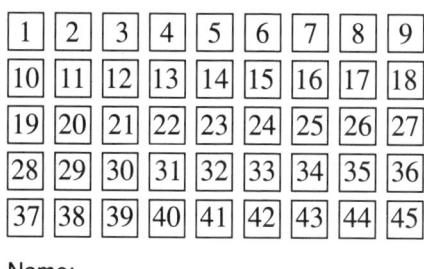

ALWS
AUSTRALIAN LOTTERY WINNERS SERVICE
P.O. Box 6017, G.C. Mail Centre
QLD 4217 Australia

No strings attached, simply return this Order Form. Our Computer Logic Win System has now chosen 6 LUCKY NUMBERS for you with over $9,000,000.00 weekly Payout. We PHONE immediately when you hit the JACKPOT! Your Phone No., please:

( )_____

Please include $1 to cover Postage & Handling.

❏ **Play for 5 WEEKS for Only $5**
I ENCLOSE ❏ CHECK ❏ MONEY ORDER
(PAYABLE TO ALWS) OR BILL MY ❏ VISA
❏ AMERICAN EXPRESS ❏ DINERS CLUB
❏ MASTERCARD
Card No:...
Expires:......... Signature:..................

Name:..
Address:..
City:............State:............Zip:..........
Please enter me in the Birthday Club. My Birthdate is:
Month............ Day.............. Year............

OLFA 96

them sensually. Cats are stealthy, solitary ambush hunters; dogs live in well-organized packs and hunt cooperatively. And this explains, at least partly, why a dog will work — well, doggedly — for hours solving laboratory experiments, and cats will walk away in the middle. (In her university studies, Vicki Hearne learned what the message in all this was for animal psychologists: "Don't use cats," the professors warned. "They'll screw up your data.") Cats and dogs can't be simply compared or equated.

Not only do our simpleminded tests underestimate the intelligence of dogs and cats, but new evidence from the leading-edge theorists of artificial intelligence suggests we may also be underestimating the nature of intelligence itself.

Efforts to build an "intelligent" machine have long focused on duplicating those human abilities we hone in classrooms. Systems have already been developed that solve geometrical analogy problems and play games like checkers and chess.

Vision, on the other hand, was thought to be so simple a process to duplicate by machine that the director of MIT's Artificial Intelligence laboratory is said to have assigned "solving the vision problem" to an undergraduate student as a summer project. Mental skills such as the processes by which creatures sort, interpret, and analyze information gathered with eye, ear, and nose were dismissed as "only" senses.

But 20 years later, we have computers that can beat champions at chess; meanwhile, no one has yet invented a computer that knows how to see.

Today, researchers are exploring each sense as a kind of intelligence in itself. In the realm of the senses, dogs and cats excel. Cats can hear two octaves higher than people (and one octave higher than dogs) and can hear a fly buzzing in another room. A dog can smell human sweat in concentrations as low as one part per million and hear the ticking of a watch 40 feet away. Some new research shows that dogs even have infrared detectors in their noses — which may be why Saint Bernards are able to tell whether a climber buried in an avalanche is alive or not.

Both species may possess senses of which we are not yet aware, allowing them to solve problems that would baffle a person. Animals' high-level survival skills are just as impressive as humans' abilities to play complicated board games — and just as worthy of exploration. A German zoologist once borrowed some cats from their owners, placed them in covered boxes, and drove around and around the city of Kiel. Finally he drove to a field where he had constructed a large, enclosed maze with 24 passages. Here, in turn, he let each cat go. The majority of the cats instantly chose the exit passage pointing them directly toward home.

Rather than creating more championship chess programs, suggests Beth Preston, a philosopher at the University of Georgia's artificial-intelligence program, "Artificial intelligence might find itself profitably devoting its energies to the construction of a better mousetrap in the form of an artificial feline intelligence."

As scientists are wising up to dogs' and cats' minds, we once again find ourselves impressed and humbled by our canine and feline companions. After all, as one researcher put it, "dogs and cats have got many thousands of years on us on the biggest IQ test going — survival." □□

FREE CATALOG
All-In The-Ear Hearing Aid

Nothing over, under or behind the ear.
No Cords • No Tubes • No Wires
Simple slip-in fit. Full-range volume control.
45 Day Trial • No Salesman will call on you.

REQUEST YOUR FREE CATALOG!
Write Rhodes Hearing Today.
RHODES HEARING
20115 Ohio, Brookport, IL 62910
1-800-453-4811 (24 Hrs.)

MEET FRIENDS WORLD-WIDE

CHERRY BLOSSOMS
190FA Rainbow Ridge
Kapaau, Hawaii 96755
1(408)980-7488

FREE 32 page Photo Catalog
WORLD FAMOUS SINCE 1974

United Country®

America's Catalog Of Country Real Estate

Over 200 pages of Descriptions & Photos, Plus Premier Properties In Full-Color!

Farms, Estates, Wilderness Kingdoms, Country Businesses & More...
No One Knows The Country Like We Do!®
Send $4.95, or Call Toll-Free to order the latest edition of United Country.
(Visa/MC accepted).

Also available: Free Regional Catalogs & Brochures tailored to the property and area of your choice!

(800) 999-1020

United National Real Estate
1600-BLF N. Corrington Ave
Kansas City, MO 64120

UNITED NATIONAL REAL ESTATE

• Helps Protect Animals
• Antiseptic all-purpose ointment

BAG BALM Ointment
An all time favorite that helps in fast healing of cuts, scrapes, chapping, galls, hobble burns. A great sweat. Stays on! At tack shops, farm, drug, hardware stores.
If unavailable in your area, order direct: 4 1/2 lb. pail $34.50; 10 oz. can $5.15; 1 oz. can $3.50.

GREEN MOUNTAIN Hoof Softener
For softening hardened, dry, pinched, or contracted hoofs and quarter cracks. Loaded with lanolin. Remember, "NO HOOF - NO HORSE!" At tack shops, farm, hardware stores.
If unavailable in your area, order direct: 10 oz. can $5.25; 28 oz. pail $7.50, $5.50 non-freeze liquid pint.

TACKMASTER
leather cleaner, conditioner, preservative. Penetrates leather thoroughly, helps restore original life with natural oils. Works on all leather except suede, and in one easy step! If unavailable in your area, order direct: Gallon $15.00; quart $6.75; pint $4.30; 4 oz. $2.45.

Add $2.00 handling for your order. Prices subject to change without notice.
To order, send check or money order to:

Dairy Assoc. Co., Inc.
P.O. Box 145, Dept. OFA6
Lyndonville, VT 05851
West of Rockies:
Smith Sales Service • 16372 S.W. 72nd St.
Portland, OR 97223

THE HEAT WAVE THAT

■ Even on the "cool" Eastern seaboard in July of 1936, it was the heat wave that made the news. In midcoast Maine, where only the hardiest swim, all-wool bathing trunks were advertised for a dollar or three dollars for those with detachable tops. In Boston the price of cream skyrocketed as the combination of the drought in the Midwest and the hot weather in the East made for a "very short cream market." Wholesale prices rose from $11 for a 40-quart can of cream in 1935 to $17.28 a can in July of 1936.

Central Park in New York City hit 106° F on July 9. The next day, Waterbury, Connecticut, saw 103° F, while many other New England towns hit over 100° F. Those who could left the steaming asphalt of the cities. Others stood under sprinklers or slept on roofs. In New York City, mayor Fiorello LaGuardia declared public beaches open all night for the duration, promising not to arrest anyone. City swimming pools lengthened their hours.

Nearly 1,000 deaths nationwide — 76 in New York City — were attributed to the ten-day heat wave, some from heat stroke or lung ailments, others from accidental drownings as non-swimmers desperately attempted to cool off. Cana-

Remember the hot summer of 1936? It set some blistering records.

by Martha White

MELTED DENTURES

dian towns and cities also felt the severity of the sun. Ontario alone marked over 500 deaths from the heat.

In the vast Dust Bowl region that spread from North Dakota southward into Texas, with its heart over Kansas and Oklahoma, black-dust blizzards had been common since about 1932. The heat wave of 1936 that broke all records in 15 states during July and August was the final blow to many midwestern farmers who had fought against economic hardship and unparalleled heat and drought. The 1936 heat gave new energy to the smothering dust storms that blackened skies. Trains missed their scheduled stops because they couldn't see the towns as they passed through them. Doors and windows had to be sealed with adhesive tape to keep out the dust. Dishes had to be washed after a meal and again before the next one because dust had sifted into cupboards. Ceilings collapsed from the weight of dust that had collected in attics. Seeded crops blew out of the soil, and white chickens were dyed the color of dust.

The chief of the Iowa Weather and Crop Bureau called July 1936 the hottest July in 117 years (although the single-day high had been reached in July 1934, at 118° F). On July 14, 1936, Iowa reported readings of more than 108° F at 113 separate weather stations. Kansas City, Missouri, saw temperatures of over 100° F on 53 days that summer. Parts of Kansas and North Dakota soared to 121° F; South Dakota, Arkansas, Texas, and Oklahoma saw 120° F. Indiana, Louisiana, Maryland, Michigan, Minnesota, Nebraska, New Jersey, West Virginia, and Wisconsin also hit their record highs in July or August of 1936.

Fortunately, humor increased with the heat and drought. According to a recent history called *The Dust Bowl* (Millbrook Press, Brookfield, Connecticut, 1993), one tall tale described a midwestern man so overwhelmed by a single drop of rain that he had to be revived by dumping a pail of dust over his head. *The New York Times* reported that a Syracuse housewife successfully fried an egg on the sidewalk. And in New York, a man left his dentures on the windowsill, only to return an hour later to find them melted.

Now, that's hot. □□

– photo: H. Armstrong Roberts

GENERAL WEATHER FORECAST
1995-1996

(For details see regional forecasts beginning on page 120.)

NOVEMBER THROUGH MARCH will be characterized by above-normal temperatures, particularly over the northeast quadrant of the country (from the eastern Great Lakes to the Ohio River valley and east to the Atlantic), and including much of the rest of the country. Only central Florida, the desert Southwest, the southwestern Rockies, and the Pacific coast will be cooler than normal. Precipitation will be variable: Expect well above normal amounts on the Atlantic seaboard from New England to the Carolinas, western sections of Oregon and northern California, and isolated sections of north-central Texas. The Northwest, northern portions of the central Great Plains, and eastern portions of Texas and Oklahoma will also get above-normal precipitation. North Florida, southern and western Texas, the southern Rockies, and southern California will be dry. January, in particular, will be mild overall, as will February from the central Great Plains to the Northeast and the Eastern seaboard.

Snowfall is expected to be well above normal in mountainous areas of the country: the Appalachian and Adirondack mountains, Rockies, Wasatch, Cascades, and Sierra Nevada and San Gabriel mountains of California. The northernmost tier, from northern New England across the northern Great Lakes through the northern Great Plains and Northwest, as well as the Colorado Plateau, will receive normal snowfall. However, below-normal amounts are expected in non-mountainous areas from southern New England across the southern Great Lakes through the lower Great Plains.

APRIL THROUGH JUNE: In marked contrast, much of the country will average cooler than normal temperatures in the spring. The Northeast, the Eastern seaboard, the South, the Gulf coast, and the southern Great Plains will be warmer than normal. Precipitation will be above normal in varying degrees over most of the country except for a swath through the middle from the Carolinas west through the Ohio River valley, the central Great Plains, and the central and southern Rockies, where rainfall will be below normal. Much of Texas and southern Florida will be very dry.

JULY THROUGH SEPTEMBER will be warmer than normal over most of the country. Only the far West may be somewhat cooler than normal. Precipitation is expected to be below normal over all of the country except in the northern Great Plains, east Texas, Louisiana, and southern Florida. Central Florida through Georgia may receive excessive amounts due to possible Gulf and offshore Atlantic hurricanes. Serious drought may occur in sections of the southern Great Plains and lower Ohio River valley.

Early fall may see a continuation of the warm and dry weather over much of the central and eastern part of the country. Serious drought may persist in central regions until the end of October. The far West will continue to be cooler than normal and the Northwest will receive well above normal rainfall.

U.S. WEATHER REGIONS

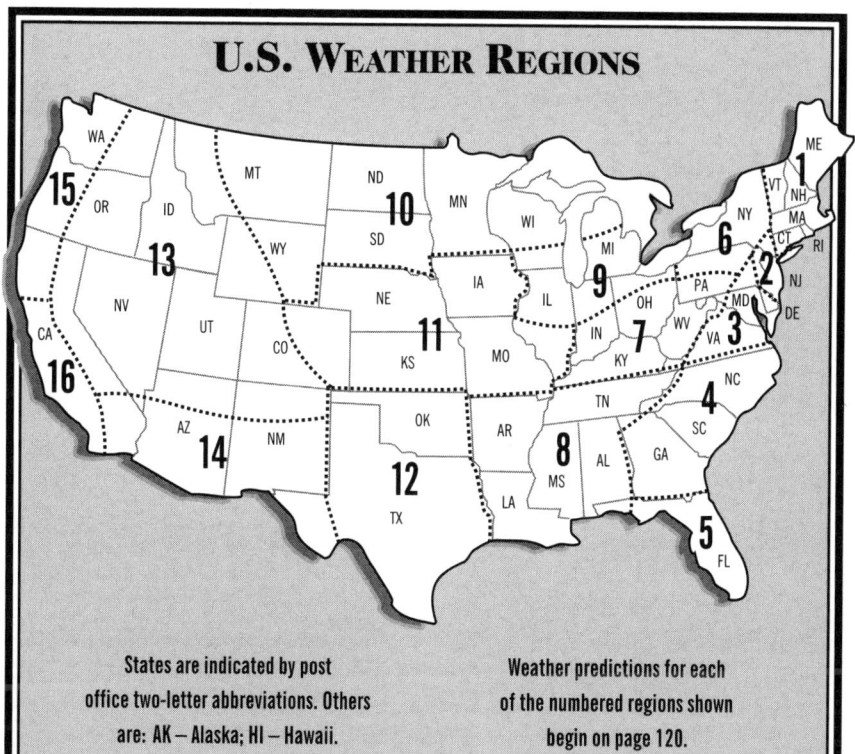

States are indicated by post office two-letter abbreviations. Others are: AK – Alaska; HI – Hawaii.

Weather predictions for each of the numbered regions shown begin on page 120.

1996
SUMMER OLYMPICS FORECAST
JULY 19 - AUGUST 4, ATLANTA, GEORGIA

JULY 19-21	Heavy showers; daytime high temperatures rising to the mid-80s, nighttime low temperatures near 70°.
JULY 22-24	Sunny; daytime highs in the mid-80s, sprinkles.
JULY 25-26	Heavy showers, daytime highs in the high 80s.
JULY 27-30	Sunny and warm, daytime highs near 90°.
JULY 31-AUGUST 1	Light showers, daytime highs in the mid-80s.
AUGUST 2-4	Clear and warm; daytime highs rising from mid-80s to mid-90s, nighttime lows rising from near 70° to mid-70s. Possible sprinkles at the close.

REGION 1
NEW ENGLAND
FORECAST

SUMMARY: *The period from November through March is expected to be 3 to 4 degrees warmer than normal with above-normal precipitation, but with considerable variability from month to month. Snowfall will be as much as 10 percent above normal in the north, but 15 percent below normal south. November will be mild early and late, but cold in between. December may be cold early and just before Christmas. A storm just after midmonth will bring snow to the north, rain to the south. January and February may be mild. January will be wet and snowy, February less so except for a northeaster the third week. After a cool first half, March will turn mild and wet, with possible floods.*

Spring temperatures will be variable, but will average close to normal. Mid-May and mid-June will be warm; the latter half of April and early May and June will be cool. April will be wet, with a snowstorm after midmonth, as will the first half of May, followed by a shift to drier conditions. Watch for drought conditions in some areas in June.

Summer will be warmer than usual, but with considerable variability. Expect cool periods from mid-July well into August, then a heat wave from late August to the first third of September. Drought conditions may continue in some areas. October will be mostly warm and dry. Watch for a northeaster at month's end.

NOV. 1995: Temp. 46° (0.5° above avg.; 2° above inland); Precip. 2" (2" below avg.). 1-4 Cold and rainy, snow north. 5-7 Mild, sunny. 8-11 Cold, sleet; then normal. 12-16 Cold, snow. 17-20 Sunny, milder. 21-22 Sleet. 23-25 Sunny, mild. 26-28 Heavy rain. 29-30 Warm.

DEC. 1995: Temp. 36° (3° above avg.; 5° above inland); Precip. 4" (Avg.; 2" above inland). 1-3 Light snow. 4-6 Clear, cold. 7-9 Sunny, milder. 10-12 Heavy rain, snow north. 13-15 Mild. 16-18 Snow, rain south. 19-21 Sprinkles. 22-26 Cold. 27-29 Rain, snow north. 30-31 Milder.

JAN. 1996: Temp. 33° (5° above avg.); Precip. 6" (2" above avg.; avg. north). 1-5 Cold, flurries. 6-8 Mild, rain. 9-13 Flurries, seasonable. 14-18 Snow, then freezing rain. 19-21 Sunny, mild. 22-23 Snow. 24-27 Mild. 28-30 Rain, warm. 31 Cold.

FEB. 1996: Temp. 34° (4° above avg.); Precip. 4" (0.5" above avg.). 1-5 Mild then seasonable, flurries. 6-9 Cold, snow. 10-11 Sunny, mild. 12-14 Freezing rain, snow north. 15-19 Warming, showers. 20-21 Northeaster. 22-25 Warm. 26-29 Flurries, then mild.

MAR. 1996: Temp. 39.5° (1° above avg.); Precip. 6.5" (3" above avg.; avg. inland). 1-2 Sunny, mild. 3-6 Cold, flurries. 7-9 Rain, snow mountains. 10-14 Severe cold. 15-20 Milder, rain. 21-24 Cool, sprinkles. 25-27 Clear, warm. 28-31 Rain, mild.

APR. 1996: Temp. 48.5° (0.5° above avg.); Precip. 6" (3" above avg.). 1-4 Rain, mild. 5-15 Warm, showers. 16-18 Rain, snow north; cold. 19-20 Seasonable. 21-24 Cold, sprinkles. 25-27 Sunny, warm. 28-30 Rain, cool.

MAY 1996: Temp. 59° (Avg.; 1° above inland); Precip. 3.5" (Avg.). 1-4 Cool. 5-7 Cold, heavy rain. 8-12 Warm, few showers. 13-15 Clear, warm. 16-19 Cool, sprinkles. 20-22 Rainy, warm. 23-25 Showers, cool. 26-28 Sunny, warm. 29-31 Showers, cool.

JUNE 1996: Temp. 68° (Avg.); Precip. 1" (2" below avg.). 1-5 Clearing, cool. 6-8 Sunny, warm. 9-13 Rain, warm, then sprinkles. 14-17 Sunny, cool. 18-24 Seasonable, then hot. 25-27 Sprinkles, seasonable. 28-30 Hot, rain.

JULY 1996: Temp. 73° (Avg.); Precip. 3" (Avg.). 1-5 Showers, warm. 6-8 Sunny, mild. 9-11 Hot, light rain. 12-15 Sunny. 16-18 Rain, cool. 19-23 Clear, hot, then cooling. 24-26 Rain, cool. 27-31 Light rain, warming.

AUG. 1996: Temp. 71° (1° below avg.); Precip. 2" (1" below avg.; 1" above west). 1-6 Sunny, warm, then cool. 7-9 Rain, heavy inland; cool. 10-12 Sunny, warm. 13-15 Rain. 16-22 Cool, showers. 23-27 Sunny, warm. 28-31 Warm, few showers.

SEPT. 1996: Temp. 68° (3° above avg.); Precip. 2.5" (0.5" below avg.). 1-8 Clear and hot. 9-11 Rain, heavy inland; cool. 12-14 Clear. 15-17 Rain, heavy east. 18-21 Showers, mild. 22-24 Sunny, warm. 25-26 Cold, rain. 27-30 Clear, warm.

OCT. 1996: Temp. 57° (2° above avg.); Precip. 3.5" (Avg.; 1" below inland). 1-3 Cool. 4-8 Sunny, warm. 9-11 Cold, rain. 12-16 Cool, then showers. 17-23 Clear, warm. 24-28 Seasonable. 29-31 Northeaster, then clear and warm.

50 Legendary Songs Of The Old West

From out of the Golden West we bring you a giant memory-stirring treasury of unforgettable cowboy favorites. Here are America's beloved singing cowboys with all the romantic western songs that helped build the legends of the Old West.

Settle back and close your eyes – hear the jingle of spurs and the gentle clippity-clop of horses on the range as the famous cowboys of yesteryear bring you 50 classic hits. Legends like Gene Autry, Tex Ritter, Rex Allen and the Sons of the Pioneers will serenade you with their plaintive harmonies and the easy rhythms of the trail. Imagine having all the great western stars of radio and the movies right in your own home. It's a goldmine of musical memories. Don't miss out! Be sure to order now.

I'M BACK IN THE SADDLE AGAIN
Gene Autry

TUMBLING TUMBLEWEEDS
Sons Of The Pioneers

CATTLE CALL
Eddy Arnold

BURY ME NOT ON THE LONE PRAIRIE
Tex Ritter

NEW SAN ANTONIO ROSE
Bob Wills

THE LAST ROUNDUP
Rex Allen

COOL WATER
Sons Of The Pioneers

RIDERS IN THE SKY
Vaughn Monroe

HIGH NOON
Tex Ritter

SOMEDAY YOU'LL WANT ME TO WANT YOU
Elton Britt

HOME ON THE RANGE
Gene Autry

THE SHIFTING, WHISPERING SANDS
Jim Reeves

WHOOPIE TI YI YO (GET ALONG LITTLE DOGGIE)
Sons Of The Pioneers

EL RANCHO GRANDE
Gene Autry

NOBODY'S DARLIN' BUT MINE
Jimmie Davis

MEXICALI ROSE
Jim Reeves

THE STREETS OF LAREDO
Marty Robbins

DON'T FENCE ME IN
Bing Crosby

GOODNIGHT IRENE
Ernest Tubb & Red Foley

I WANT TO BE A COWBOY'S SWEETHEART
Patsy Montana

I'M AN OLD COWHAND
Patsy Montana

EMPTY SADDLES
Sons Of The Pioneers

DOWN IN THE VALLEY
Slim Whitman

WHEN IT'S SPRINGTIME IN THE ROCKIES
Montana Slim

SOUTH OF THE BORDER
Patsy Cline

I'M THINKING TONIGHT OF MY BLUE EYES
The Carter Family

ALONG THE NAVAJO TRAIL
Sons Of The Pioneers

SIOUX CITY SUE
Bing Crosby

BEAUTIFUL, BEAUTIFUL BROWN EYES
Jimmy Wakely

RED RIVER VALLEY
Slim Whitman

MULE TRAIN
Frankie Laine

DEEP IN THE HEART OF TEXAS
Bob Wills

MY LITTLE CHEROKEE MAIDEN
Bob Wills

JEALOUS HEART
Tex Ritter

TAKE ME BACK TO MY BOOTS AND SADDLE
Jimmy Wakely

HAVE I TOLD YOU LATELY THAT I LOVE YOU
Gene Autry

PISTOL PACKIN' MAMA
Al Dexter

YOU ARE MY SUNSHINE
Jimmie Davis

WAGON WHEELS
Sons Of The Pioneers

HAPPY TRAILS
Roy Rogers & Dale Evans

AND MORE!

The Beautiful Music Company, Dept. CW-153
320 Main Street, Northport, NY 11768

WE SHIP FREE! No Postage or Handling Fees!

Please rush my *Wagon Wheels* Treasury on your unconditional money-mack guarantee.

☐ I enclose $19.98. Send 2 Cassettes..
☐ I enclose $19.98. Send 3 Records.
☐ I enclose $24.98. Send 2 Compact Discs.

Or Charge To: ☐ Visa ☐ MasterCard ☐ American Express ☐ Discover

Card No. _____ Exp. Date _____
Name _____
Address _____
City _____
State _____ Zip _____

REGION 2
GREATER NEW YORK-NEW JERSEY
FORECAST

SUMMARY: *The period from November through March is expected to be much milder and wetter than normal, with below-normal snowfall. November will begin cool and dry, then turn mild and wet. December will continue the mild and wet weather except for a cold wave and snowstorm the first week. Watch for an Alberta Clipper to bring cold and snow early in January, and another cold wave early in February. Despite these stormy periods, the winter as a whole is expected to be mild, with overall snowfall below normal but precipitation generally above normal, especially in the north. March will be warm and wet, despite cold and snowy weather during the first half of the month.*

Spring will be warm and wet overall, with considerable changeability. April will be warm and wet until Canadian polar air brings cold and cold to many sections. After another cold front in early May, warm and wet weather is expected, with frequent thunderstorms extending into June, which should be sunny and warm overall.

Summer will be warmer and drier than normal. Watch for a severe heat wave at the end of August extending into early September. Despite frequent thundershowers during July and August, drought conditions may appear by late September. Early fall will be sunny, warm, and dry, with possible drought conditions in many sections.

NOV. 1995: Temp. 49° (1.5° above avg.); Precip. 3" (0.5" below avg.). 1-3 Cold, snow west. 4-7 Sunny, warm. 8-9 Cold, rain. 10-13 Clear, cool. 14-15 Rain. 16-19 Clear, cold. 20-24 Showers, mild. 25-27 Rain. 28-30 Sunny, seasonable.

DEC. 1995: Temp. 39° (2.5° above avg.); Precip. 4.5" (1" above avg.). 1-3 Clear, mild. 4-8 Cold, snow. 9-11 Heavy rain, mild. 12-14 Sunny. 15-17 Heavy rain, mild. 18-20 Cold. 21-24 Clear, mild. 25-28 Freezing rain and snow. 29-31 Clearing, mild.

JAN. 1996: Temp. 35° (4° above avg.); Precip. 5" (2" above avg.). 1-4 Cold, snow. 5-7 Freezing rain, seasonable. 8-10 Clear, seasonable. 11-16 Cold, heavy sleet and snow. 17-21 Clear, warm. 22-28 Sun, intermittent rain. 29-31 Rain, mild.

FEB. 1996: Temp. 36° (3° above avg.); Precip. 3" (Avg.). 1-3 Mild; rain, heavy north. 4-6 Clearing and mild. 7-10 Cold snap. 11-13 Rain, mild. 14-18 Cold, snow, freezing rain. 19-21 Heavy rain. 22-25 Clear, mild. 26-29 Rain, seasonable.

MAR. 1996: Temp. 42.5° (1° above avg.); Precip. 5" (4" above avg.). 1-3 Mild, clear. 4-8 Cold, heavy rain. 9-11 Mild; rain north. 12-14 Sleet and snow. 15-20 Some rain, mild. 21-24 Seasonable, light rain. 25-27 Sunny, mild. 28-31 Heavy rain.

APR. 1996: Temp. 51° (Avg.); Precip. 5.5" (2" above avg.). 1-5 Sprinkles, seasonable. 6-9 Mild, showers. 10-12 Heavy rain, cool. 13-15 Sunny, mild. 16-18 Cold, rain, snow. 19-21 Seasonable, showers. 22-24 Cold wave, rain. 25-30 Clearing, mild, then rain.

MAY 1996: Temp. 63° (1° above avg.); Precip. 4" (0.5" above avg.). 1-4 Clearing, seasonable. 5-8 Cold; rain, locally heavy. 9-13 Rain, seasonable. 14-16 Clear, mild. 17-21 Rain, cooler. 22-25 Showers, mild. 26-27 Heavy rain. 28-31 Sunny, mild, then rain.

JUNE 1996: Temp. 71° (Avg.); Precip. 1.5" (2" below avg.). 1-5 Cold, then heavy rain. 6-9 Clear, warm. 10-12 Rain, locally heavy; seasonable. 13-15 Sunny, mild. 16-18 Cold, rain. 19-25 Warming. 26-27 Thundershowers. 28-30 Sunny, normal.

JULY 1996: Temp. 77.5° (1° above avg.); Precip. 4" (Avg.). 1-3 Rain, cool. 4-7 Hot, clear, then rain. 8-10 Sunny. 11-13 Showers, cool. 14-18 Mild, sprinkles north. 19-22 Sunny, hot. 23-25 Showers, seasonable. 26-28 Heavy rain, cool. 29-31 Clear, warm.

AUG. 1996: Temp. 75° (Avg.); Precip. 4" (Avg.). 1-3 Sunny, then showers, warm. 4-11 Cool, sprinkles. 12-14 Rain, cool. 15-17 Sunny, warm. 18-21 Rain, possible offshore hurricane. 22-26 Cool. 27-31 Dry; heat wave developing.

SEPT. 1996: Temp. 70° (2° above avg.); Precip. 3" (1" below avg.). 1-8 Heat wave, dry. 9-11 Rain, seasonable. 12-15 Clear, pleasant. 16-18 Showers, cool. 19-23 Showers, then clear. 24-26 Rain. 27-30 Clear, cool.

OCT. 1996: Temp. 60.6° (3° above avg.); Precip. 4" (1" above avg.). 1-8 Clear, dry. 9-11 Cold, rain. 12-14 Seasonable, clear. 15-17 Sprinkles, cooler. 18-24 Pleasant. 25-27 Seasonable. 28-31 Rain, showers south.

Natural Prostate Relief

It's a natural fact. If you are a male over 40 and don't already suffer from prostate gland disorder, the odds are 2 to 1 that you will before you are 59. As the years pass, mild discomforts can become disabling.

Prescription drugs may halt the swelling, but rarely end the suffering. They also may have side-effects, like weak erections and low sex drive.

Many doctors feel that prostate disorders can be treated or prevented by giving the prostate gland the nutrition it lacks.

Recent scientific research has shown how to remedy the underlying problems associated with prostate disorders...safely and effectively. They reveal that several vitamins, minerals and natural herbs can dramatically shrink the prostate and improve urinary performance in older men.

The most modern application of these healthy ingredients is found in **Prostsafe** from Whitewing Labs.

Prostsafe is the nutritional "tool kit" for men with benign prostate problems, *and those who wish to prevent them.* It is a mixture of zinc, serenoa serrulata, ginseng, certain amino acids, bee pollen and vitamins A, B-6 and E. Working as a team, these ingredients have been shown to shrink a swollen prostate.

Dr. Michael Rosenbaum, M.D. says "Prostsafe supplies essential vitamins, minerals and herbs needed to nourish and maintain a healthy prostate."

The reasons why men over 50 use **Prostsafe** are clear. If you are looking for relief, **order Prostsafe today!** If for some reason you are not satisfied, just return the unused portion within 30 days for a full refund.

Order by phone or mail.

Whitewing Labs, Dept 149
17939 Chatsworth St., Suite 408, Granada Hills, CA 91344

❏ PS1 1 month supply of Prostsafe only **$34.95** plus $4.50 S&H
❏ PS2 2 month supply only **$59.95** (Save $9.95) plus $4.50 S&H
❏ PS6 6 month supply only **$119.95** (Save $89.75) plus $4.50 S&H
Check Encl. $_____ CA res. add 8.25% & AZ res. add 5.50%
Visa/MC/AmEx/Disc._____ Exp._____
Name:_____
Address:_____
Ship to:_____
City _____ State___ Zip_____ Ph: (___)_____

or call **1-800-950-3030** Dept. 149

REGION 3
MIDDLE ATLANTIC COAST FORECAST

SUMMARY: *The period from November through March is expected to be a few degrees above normal, with well above normal precipitation, but extremely variable. November's most dramatic weather will come near the end of the month, when a storm brings heavy snow to the west. December will continue November's swings from cold and wet to mild and sunny. January will start cool and wet, then turn mild. The relatively mild weather will continue on through February with well below normal snowfall. March will have a cold first half, with well above normal snowfall, and a milder latter half.*

The spring months are predicted to be close to normal in temperature on the average, with variable precipitation over the region. April will see above-normal rainfall in western sections, below normal east of the mountains. May will be warm after the first week, with considerable variability in rainfall. June will see some cold, wet weather, but will be mostly sunny and warm.

Summer will be cooler than normal with near-normal rainfall in western and mountain sections, but warmer and drier than normal east of the Blue Ridge Mountains. Drought conditions may develop in August in many sections. A possible offshore hurricane may bring above-normal rainfall to eastern sections, but a severe heat wave from late August to early September may extend the drought in other sections. Drought conditions over much of the region may continue through most of October.

NOV. 1995: Temp. 49.5° (0.5° below avg.); Precip. 5" (2" above avg.). 1-3 Cold, sprinkles. 4-7 Sunny, warm. 8-10 Rain, cold. 11-14 Sunny, warm. 15-17 Cold, rain. 18-21 Clear, cold nights; then rain. 22-24 Warm. 25-27 Heavy rain, snow west, cold. 28-30 Clear, seasonable.

DEC. 1995: Temp. 39.5° (Avg.); Precip. 2.5" (0.5" below avg.). 1-3 Warm, showers. 4-11 Freezing rain and snow. 12-14 Sunny, seasonable. 15-16 Rain, mild. 17-20 Cold. 21-23 Sunny, milder. 24-27 Sleet, snow. 28-31 Clearing, mild.

JAN. 1996: Temp. 38.5° (4° above avg.); Precip. 4.5" (2" above avg.). 1-3 Cold wave. 4-11 Clear, then freezing rain, seasonable. 12-17 Heavy rain and snow. 18-21 Clear, warm. 22-23 Cold, sleet. 24-26 Sunny, mild. 27-29 Rain. 30-31 Clear, mild.

FEB. 1996: Temp. 40° (2.5° above avg.); Precip. 2.5" (Avg.). 1-2 Snow. 3-6 Sunny, mild. 7-10 Seasonable, sprinkles. 11-13 Rain, mild. 14-18 Cold, then rain. 19-21 Rain and snow. 22-24 Clear, cold nights. 25-27 Rain, warm. 28-29 Seasonable.

MAR. 1996: Temp. 47° (Avg.); Precip. 6" (3" above avg.). 1-4 Sprinkles, then sunny, mild. 5-7 Snowstorm. 8-11 Sunny, mild. 12-14 Cold, snow. 15-20 Rain, then cooler. 21-23 Sun then rain, mild. 24-26 Clear. 27-30 Rain. 31 Clear, cold.

APR. 1996: Temp. 55.5° (1° below avg.); Precip. 3.5" (1" above avg.). 1-3 Clear, cold. 4-6 Warm, rain. 7-9 Sunny, mild. 10-12 Rain, cool. 13-15 Sunny, warm. 16-18 Cold, rain. 19-21 Sunny, cold. 22-25 Cold, rain. 26-30 Warm; then rain.

MAY 1996: Temp. 69.5° (3° above avg.); Precip. 7" (3" above avg.; 0.5" below south). 1-3 Clear, cold. 4-9 Rain, then clear. 10-13 Rain. 14-18 Clear, hot. 19-21 Warm, showers. 22-24 Heavy rain. 25-27 Clear, hot. 28-31 Few showers, warm.

JUNE 1996: Temp. 73° (2.5° below avg.; avg. south); Precip. 4" (0.5" above avg.). 1-5 Cool, few showers. 6-10 Clear, hot. 11-15 Rain, milder. 16-20 Cold, light rain. 21-27 Rain, hot. 28-30 Sunny, seasonable.

JULY 1996: Temp. 80° (Avg.; 1° above south); Precip. 4" (Avg.; 2" below southwest). 1-4 Warm, showers. 5-7 Clear, hot. 8-12 Showers, cooler. 13-18 Cool, dry. 19-22 Clear, hot. 23-27 Showers, milder. 28-31 Clear, pleasant.

AUG. 1996: Temp. 76.5° (2° below avg.; avg. south); Precip. 4" (Avg.; 2" below south). 1-3 Sunny, hot. 4-13 Showers, cool; then sunny, warm. 14-16 Clear, seasonable. 17-18 Possible offshore hurricane. 19-21 Hot, clear. 22-26 Cool, showers. 27-31 Heat wave.

SEPT. 1996: Temp. 71° (Avg.); Precip. 4" (0.5" above avg.; 3" above south). 1-8 Heat wave, drought. 9-11 Heavy rain, cool. 12-15 Sunny. 16-18 Few showers, cool. 19-23 Clear, seasonable. 24-26 Heavy showers. 27-30 Clear, cool, then showers.

OCT. 1996: Temp. 62° (2° above avg.); Precip. 2" (1" below avg.; 3" below south). 1-5 Clear, warm. 6-9 Clear, seasonable. 10-13 Cold, showers. 14-17 Clear, seasonable. 18-24 Clear, warm. 25-31 Seasonable, few showers.

Presenting...
The DR® FIELD and BRUSH MOWER
-- the amazing walk-behind brush cutter that --

- **CLEARS & MAINTAINS** meadows, pastures, roadsides, fences, wooded and rough non-lawn areas with ease. Mows over 1/2 acre per hour!
- **CUTS** tall grass, weeds, brush, brambles, sumac - even tough saplings up to 1" thick!
- **Plus CHOPS/MULCHES** most everything it cuts; leaves NO TANGLE of material to trip over or to pick up like hand-held brushcutters and sicklebar mowers.
- **POWERFUL** 8 HP Briggs & Stratton engine; *optional Electric-Starting*. BIG 20" SELF-PROPELLED WHEELS roll through ditches, furrows, over bumps and logs with ease.

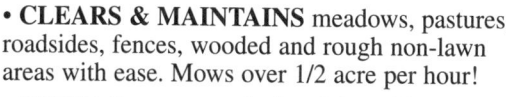

So, **WHY MESS** with hand-held brushcutters that are so dangerous, slow and tiring to use... OR with sicklebar mowers that shake unmercifully and leave such a tangled mess?

TOLL FREE 1(800) 215-1600

Please mail coupon below today for complete **FREE DETAILS** all about the Amazing **DR® FIELD and BRUSH MOWER!**

- **Perfect for** *low-maintenance wildflower meadows...* European-style woodlots free of undergrowth... walking paths... or any area that you only want to mow once a month... or once a season!

YES! Please rush complete FREE DETAILS of the **DR® FIELD and BRUSH MOWER** including prices, specifications of Manual and ELECTRIC-STARTING Models and "Off-Season" Savings now in effect.

Name _____
Address _____
City _____ State ____ ZIP _____
To: **COUNTRY HOME PRODUCTS®**
Dept. 577F, Box 89, Ferry Road
Charlotte, VT 05445

ALM
© 1995 CHP, Inc.

REGION 4: PIEDMONT & SOUTHEAST COAST FORECAST

SUMMARY: *The period from November through March is expected to be warmer than normal. Precipitation will be slightly above normal in the north, but well below south. Drought conditions may persist through the first part of November before sporadic cold fronts bring light rains after mid-November and in December. Aside from a dry spell at midmonth, January will be wet, with warm temperatures during the latter half before closing with a cold snap. The first half of February will be warm, after which cold and wet periods will alternate with warm and sunny ones through March.*

Spring will be slightly warmer than normal and particularly wet in the south. April will be cool; May and June will be warm. April may be drier than normal in the north, wet in the south. May will be dry except for showers at midmonth, and June will see frequent rains and thundershowers.

The summer months may be close to normal in temperature overall. Dry conditions in the north may bring drought to many sections; the south will have ample rain. July will begin and end with hot weather. August will see variable temperatures, resulting in temperatures slightly below normal for the month, and drought conditions may develop in many sections. A hurricane in the Gulf may bring heavy rains to the south at the end of September. Early fall will be sunny and warm, with little rainfall.

NOV. 1995: Temp. 52° (Avg.); Precip. 2" (1" below avg.). 1-4 Cold, dry. 5-8 Sunny, mild. 9-13 Mild days; cold nights. 14-17 Rain, then clear; cold nights. 18-23 Showers, then clear; warm. 24-27 Rain, cool. 28-30 Mild.

DEC. 1995: Temp. 42.5° (Avg.; 2° below south); Precip. 2.5" (1" below avg.). 1-2 Rain. 3-5 Cold, sprinkles. 6-9 Cold, rainy. 10-13 Clear, warm. 14-16 Seasonable, rain. 17-20 Clear, cold. 21-23 Sunny, warm. 24-27 Rain, cool. 28-31 Clearing, mild.

JAN. 1996: Temp. 43° (4° above avg.); Precip. 5" (1" above avg.; avg. south). 1-3 Clear, cold nights. 4-7 Rain, seasonable. 8-11 Flurries, cold. 12-14 Heavy rain, mild. 15-18 Clear, seasonable. 19-21 Sunny, warm. 22-28 Rain, warm. 29-31 Cold, clear.

FEB. 1996: Temp. 45.5° (3° above avg.); Precip. 5" (1.5" above avg.; avg. south). 1-3 Mild, rain. 4-9 Sunny, warm; then cool, sprinkles. 10-12 Rain, warm. 13-17 Warm, showers. 18-19 Rain. 20-23 Clear, cold. 24-26 Warm, rain. 27-29 Cold, rain.

MAR. 1996: Temp. 52° (1° above avg.); Precip. 5" (0.5" above avg.; 1" below south). 1-4 Clear, warm. 5-7 Cold, rain and snow. 8-11 Sunny, warm. 12-15 Cold, rain. 16-19 Warm, showers. 20-23 Sprinkles, mild. 24-27 Rain, cool. 28-31 Clear, frigid.

APR. 1996: Temp. 58.5° (1° below avg.); Precip. 1.5" (1" below avg.; 1" above south). 1-5 Warm, sprinkles. 6-8 Rain, cool. 9-12 Warm, rain south. 13-19 Cold, rain. 20-22 Clear, cold. 23-27 Sunny, warm; sprinkles. 28-30 Clear, cold.

MAY 1996: Temp. 71.5° (4° above avg.); Precip. 3.5" (Avg.; 1" above south.). 1-7 Rain, mild. 8-10 Cold; heavy rain. 11-17 Clear, warm. 18-21 Rain, heavy south; mild. 22-27 Sunny, hot. 28-30 Clear, cooling. 31 Warm.

JUNE 1996: Temp. 76.5° (1° above avg.); Precip. 4.5" (1" above avg.). 1-2 Clear, hot. 3-6 Clear, cool. 7-11 Rain, heavy north; warm. 12-17 Showers, cold. 18-24 Sunny, warm; thundershowers. 25-28 Light rain, seasonable. 29-30 Clear, warm.

JULY 1996: Temp. 79° (Avg.); Precip. 2" (2" below avg.; 4" above south). 1-9 Showers, locally heavy; hot. 10-12 Sunny, seasonable. 13-16 Clear, cool. 17-22 Sunny, warm; showers south. 23-27 Mild; showers, locally heavy. 28-31 Clear, hot.

AUG. 1996: Temp. 78° (Avg.); Precip. 2" (1.5" below avg.). 1-5 Hot; few showers. 6-8 Showers; hot and humid south. 9-12 Rain, heavy south. 13-19 Clear, hot; possible offshore hurricane. 20-25 Cold; rain, clearing. 26-31 Clear, hot.

SEPT. 1996: Temp. 72° (0.5° below avg.); Precip. 3.5" (Avg.; Gulf hurricane may bring excess). 1-4 Hot, showers south. 5-9 Cold, possible offshore hurricane, rain. 10-15 Clear, cool nights. 16-18 Sunny, hot. 19-26 Rain, heavy south. 27-30 Gulf hurricane, cold.

OCT. 1996: Temp. 64° (3° above avg.); Precip. 0.5" (3" below avg.; 1" below south). 1-3 Hot, then rain. 4-7 Clear, warm. 8-11 Cold, sunny. 12-14 Clear, warm. 15-17 Cold, rain. 18-23 Sunny. 24-27 Cold, then warm. 28-31 Sprinkles.

EMERGENCY FLASHLIGHT
No Batteries! No Recharging!
Lasts a Lifetime! Keeps on working 5...15... 100 years from now!

Only $7.95

Never be caught in the dark without the unique **100% reliable Dynamo Flashlight** with Nite-Glow locator strip. Uniquely powered by a mini-generator. *Simply press lever...Presto! Darkness turns into light.*

A "must" for car, garage, basement, nightstand, tent, tool box, etc.
Use it for fire, flood, power failure & more. Save a bundle on batteries and re-charge units.
Lightweight, compact, durable, shock resistant, waterproof and guaranteed to light every time.
Order Today! Only $7.95....Save More! Buy 3 (tool box, nightstand & car) only $19.95.

------ **30-DAY MONEY BACK GUARANTEE** ------

☐ Dynamo Flashlight (Lights Every Time!) Only $7.95 + $2.50 S & H
☐ *Bonus!* Buy 3 (tool box, nightstand, car) Only $19.95 + $4.95 S & H
Send To: Next Generation, Dept. DF223SB, 75 Albertson Ave., Albertson, NY 11507
Or Charge It! Call Toll Free: **1-800-947-2248**

FREE! Nite-Glow Strip Locate Your Flashlight In The Dark!

Change Tiny Small Print
Into
Large Sharp Print
Miracle Magnifying Glasses

Don't strain your eyes to read fine print, road maps, thread needles, etc. These fantastic low priced magnifying specs may be all you need! Everything increases in size from 2½ times to 4 times depending on the strength you need. You get a stylish look at an incredible low, low price.

Rich Gold Tone XL Sturdy © Metal Frames with high impact resistant optical lenses fit both men and women.

SEE THE ACTUAL DIFFERENCE!!!

ORIGINAL SIZE	SELECT STRENGTH	MAGNIFIED RESULTS
From This	2½X	To This!
From This	3X	To This!
From This	3½X	To This!
From This	4X	To This!

© Rush Ind., Inc. 1989

These truly attractive glasses are yours for as low as $9.98. Order by magnification strength.

------ **30 DAY MONEY BACK GUARANTEE** ------

Send To: Rush Inc., Optical Div. Dept. MG223SB, 75 Albertson Ave., Albertson, NY 11507
QTY.   *Satisfaction Guaranteed or Money Back! (Less shipping & handling.)*

____ 2½X Magnification Strength Only $9.98 + $2.00 Shipping, Handling & Insurance.
____ 3X Magnification Strength Only $10.98 + $2.00 Shipping, Handling & Insurance.
____ 3½X Magnification Strength Only $11.98 + $2.00 Shipping, Handling & Insurance.
____ 4X Magnification Strength Only $12.98 + $2.00 Shipping, Handling & Insurance.
____ A convenient 5" long slip-on pocket case is available for an extra $1.00.
____ Special Bonus! Order 2 or more pairs of glasses and deduct $1.00 from each pair.

Name _____
Address _____
City _____ State _____ Zip _____

REGION 5

FLORIDA FORECAST

SUMMARY: *The period from November through March is expected to be warmer than normal. Precipitation will be normal in the south, below normal in the north. Cold waves with rain will begin and end November and return after mid-December, but the balance of the two months will be warm and fairly dry. Watch for snow in the far north in December. January will begin cool, with a heavy storm before midmonth, then turn unseasonably warm, particularly in the north. February through March will become progressively warmer than normal except for a cool spell after mid-February. Rainfall is expected in early February and at the end of March.*

The spring months will be on average warmer than normal in the north, near normal south, with above-normal rainfall central and north, but below normal south. April temperatures will see wide swings; rainfall will be heavy in the north. May will experience hot and dry conditions, followed by a near-normal June with frequent thundershowers but below-normal rainfall. Some rain may come from a possible tropical storm in the Gulf.

The summer months will be close to normal in temperature, with well above normal rainfall. Expect heavy thundershower activity from mid-July on. Slackening in the rainfall may occur near mid-August and mid-September, but may be quite heavy otherwise. Early fall will be wet due to a possible tropical storm in the Gulf at the end of September and a possible hurricane across the southern tip before mid-October.

NOV. 1995: Temp. 66° (2° below avg.; avg. south); Precip. 1" (1.5" below avg.). 1-4 Cold, clear. 5-8 Warm, sprinkles. 9-13 Clear, cold nights. 14-15 Sunny, warm. 16-18 Showers, mild. 19-22 Warm. 23-28 Rain, cold. 29-30 Clear, warm.

DEC. 1995: Temp. 60° (2° below avg.); Precip. 0.5" (1.5" below avg.; avg. south). 1-5 Sunny; sprinkles south. 6-9 Few showers. 10-15 Clear, cold nights, then warm. 16-22 Rain, snow; then clear, cold. 23-25 Warm, sprinkles. 26-28 Cold. 29-31 Clear, warm.

JAN. 1996: Temp. 60° (Avg.; 2° above north); Precip. 4" (1" above avg.; 2" above south). 1-4 Showers, cool, then rain. 5-9 Rain, cold. 10-14 Clear, warm, then rain. 15-17 Cold. 18-26 Sunny, warm, few sprinkles. 27-29 Rain, cool. 30-31 Cold.

FEB. 1996: Temp. 63° (2° above avg.); Precip. 2.5" (1.5" above avg.; 1.5" below north). 1-4 Showers, cool. 5-7 Warm, rain. 8-11 Rain, then clear, cold. 12-14 Rain, warm. 15-19 Sunny, mild. 20-23 Cold. 24-27 Rain, warm, then cooler. 28-29 Clear.

MAR. 1996: Temp. 70° (3.5° above avg.); Precip. 3.5" (Avg.; 1" below north and south). 1-4 Clear, warm. 5-8 Sunny, hot. 9-11 Showers, mild. 12-14 Clear, cool. 15-19 Warm, showers. 20-23 Clear, warm. 24-27 Rain, heavy central, mild. 28-31 Cold, clear.

APR. 1996: Temp. 70° (1° below avg.); Precip. 5.5" (4" above avg.; 1" above south). 1-3 Cold, clear. 4-9 Warm, showers. 10-13 Rain, heavy north, then clear. 14-17 Warm; rain. 18-23 Heavy showers, mild. 24-27 Cold. 28-30 Warm, rain.

MAY 1996: Temp. 79° (2° above avg.; 4° above north); Precip. 1.5" (2" below avg.). 1-3 Clearing, cold. 4-9 Warm. 10-13 Rain, warm. 14-19 Clear, dry, cold nights. 20-23 Seasonable. 24-26 Rain south, warm. 27-31 Clear, hot.

JUNE 1996: Temp. 81° (Avg.; 1° above north); Precip. 6" (1" below avg.; 3" below south). 1-5 Turning hot, showers south. 6-10 Gulf storm, showers. 11-16 Sunny, showers. 17-21 Thundershowers, hot south. 22-25 Showers, hot. 26-30 Thundershowers, warm.

JULY 1996: Temp. 83° (0.5° above avg.); Precip. 7" (2" above avg.; 1" below central). 1-3 Showers south. 4-8 Showers, hot. 9-12 Hot, showers north. 13-17 Thundershowers. 18-24 Few showers, mild. 25-31 Thundershowers.

AUG. 1996: Temp. 82° (Avg.); Precip. 9.5" (2" above avg.; 6" above central). 1-3 Thunderstorms, warm. 4-8 Showers, hot. 9-15 Thundershowers, mild. 16-19 Few showers. 20-25 Showers, seasonable. 26-31 Showers, cooler.

SEPT. 1996: Temp. 80° (1° above avg.); Precip. 10" (4" above avg.). 1-5 Thundershowers, warm. 6-9 Showers, hot. 10-16 Showers, heavy south; cool. 17-19 Few showers, cool. 20-27 Heavy thundershowers, cool central. 28-30 Possible Gulf hurricane; warm.

OCT. 1996: Temp. 74° (1° below avg.); Precip. 3.5" (1" above avg.; 5" above south). 1-4 Showers, seasonable. 5-9 Thundershowers. 10-11 Clear, warm. 12-14 Possible hurricane south. 15-22 Showers, mild. 23-31 Sunny.

FACT: Septic Helper works

"An ounce of prevention is worth a pound of cure"

to prevent septic tank and cesspool problems and saves you $$$$!

FINALLY... SEPTIC MAINTENANCE MADE EASY

CUT DOWN: re-doing drain fields • pumpouts • wet spots • costly expenses • clogged drains • offensive odors

100% GUARANTEED

Septic tanks/cesspools can eventually clog-up, back up and become malodorous. Slow drainage can set in and become a constant problem. Now there is a product available that will help maintain your system and also help it reach maximum efficiency. **Septic Helper** goes to work in your system, activates the bacteria and begins to change organic solids into liquids. Let **Septic Helper** work to keep your septic system trouble free.

A beneficial bacteria additive that is safe and easy to use

For More Information Call Toll Free

1-800-533-2445

OR Fill Out Coupon

Keep your septic tank and cesspool in great shape. Use SEPTIC HELPER!

SEPTIC TANK BEFORE
(INLET — SCUM — SLUDGE — OUTLET)

SEPTIC TANK AFTER
(INLET — OUTLET)

DRAIN LINES BEFORE/AFTER

A drain pipe loses part of its diameter in 5 years due to organic build-up.

SEPTIC HELPER helps to restore the pipe to original after a few months of treatment.

I am interested in more information on **SEPTIC HELPER**

Name _____

Address _____

Town _____ State _____

Zip _____ Tel. (___) _____

How many septic tanks/cesspools? _____

Mail in coupon to: **Big K Inc**
P.O. Box 568144 Atlanta, GA 31156-8144

OFA

REGION 6
UPSTATE NEW YORK
FORECAST

SUMMARY: *The period from November through March will see large and frequent swings in temperature, with the mild spells dominating cold. Precipitation will be well above normal east and north, but below in the west; snowfall will be generally below normal. Cold Canadian air will dominate the first half of November, early December, and the week before Christmas, with heavy December snows. January will start cold, then turn unusually mild; most of February will also be mild. Precipitation in both months will be frequent but generally light. March will be cold and snowy the first half and warm and wet thereafter.*

Spring is expected to be cool in the west, mild in the east; precipitation will be close to normal west, above normal east. Cold spells with rain and snow after mid-April will change to a warm and wet period. Following a cold and wet start, May will be warm and wet, then turn cold and wet into early June. Thereafter it will be quite dry with variable temperatures.

The summer months will average slightly above normal in temperature and below in rainfall, but with considerable variability. Rain at the start of July may relieve some of the June drought, but little rainfall is then expected for several weeks. A severe heat wave in late August will last through the first week of September, after which mild, showery weather should prevail. Early fall will start off sunny and warm, with a cool and wet mid-October.

NOV. 1995: Temp. 41° (1° above avg.; 3° above west); Precip. 3" (0.5" below avg.; 1.5" below west). 1-3 Cold; rain, snow. 4-6 Clear, warm. 7-11 Cold, rain. 12-15 Snow, cold. 16-19 Clear; cold nights. 20-23 Rain, mild. 24-27 Rain, warm. 28-30 Cool.

DEC. 1995: Temp. 30.5° (4° above avg.); Precip. 4" (1" above avg.; avg. west). 1-4 Cold, rain, then snow. 5-7 Cold, snow. 8-11 Snow, mild. 12-15 Rain, warm. 16-20 Heavy snow, seasonable. 21-24 Sunny, mild. 25-31 Freezing rain, snow.

JAN. 1996: Temp. 26.5° (6° above avg.); Precip. 3.5" (1" above avg.; avg. west). 1-3 Severe cold. 4-8 Mild, flurries. 9-14 Cold, snow, turning heavy. 15-20 Warm, sprinkles. 21-25 Sleet, cool. 26-28 Rain. 29-31 Cold, snow.

FEB. 1996: Temp. 27.5° (4° above avg.); Precip. 2" (Avg.). 1-3 Mild, snow. 4-5 Sunny, warm. 6-9 Snow; then clear, cold. 10-12 Mild. 13-15 Light snow. 16-18 Mild, sprinkles. 19-22 Cold, snow. 23-25 Sunny, warm. 26-29 Cold, then mild.

MAR. 1996: Temp. 35° (1° above avg.); Precip. 5" (2" above avg.). 1-2 Mild, sprinkles. 3-5 Cold, flurries. 6-8 Rain, warm. 9-13 Cold, light snow. 14-16 Warm, rain. 17-22 Seasonable, showers; then sunny, mild. 23-27 Sunny, warm. 28-31 Rain, cold.

APR. 1996: Temp. 46° (Avg.; 2° below west); Precip. 4" (2" above avg.; 0.5" below west). 1-4 Rain, cool. 5-8 Sunny, warm. 9-11 Cool, rain. 12-14 Mild, sprinkles. 15-17 Cold, rain; snow mountains. 18-19 Sunny, dry. 20-24 Rain, snow; cold. 25-30 Mild, rain.

MAY 1996: Temp. 59° (1.5° above avg.; avg. west); Precip. 7" (3" above avg.). 1-2 Cold, rain. 3-6 Mild, then heavy rain, cold. 7-15 Frequent rain, warm. 16-20 Cold, heavy rain. 21-25 Sunny, warm, few showers. 26-31 Cold, heavy rain.

JUNE 1996: Temp. 67° (Avg.); Precip. 1" (2.5" below avg.). 1-3 Cold, showers. 4-7 Clear, warm. 8-12 Sunny, warm; few showers. 13-17 Clear, cool, few showers. 18-21 Sunny, warm. 22-25 Hot, showers. 26-28 Clear, cool. 29-30 Showers, hot.

JULY 1996: Temp. 72.5° (0.5° above avg.); Precip. 3" (Avg.). 1-6 Rain, then showers; hot. 7-9 Cold, few showers. 10-12 Sprinkles, warm. 13-15 Clear, cold nights. 16-18 Sprinkles, cool. 19-25 Clear, hot; showers. 26-31 Cool, then warm.

AUG. 1996: Temp. 69° (0.5° below avg.); Precip. 3" (0.5" below avg.). 1-3 Showers, seasonable. 4-8 Showers, mild. 9-13 Clear, cool; then rain. 14-19 Sunny, warm. 20-25 Clear days, cold nights. 26-31 Sunny, hot; sprinkles.

SEPT. 1996: Temp. 64° (3° above avg.); Precip. 3" (Avg.). 1-7 Hot, little rain. 8-10 Cold; rain, heavy east. 11-13 Sunny. 14-17 Showers, cool. 18-23 Sunny, warm; then cool, showers. 24-30 Sunny, cold; then seasonable.

OCT. 1996: Temp. 53° (3° above avg.); Precip. 3" (Avg.; 2" below west). 1-7 Sunny, pleasant. 8-10 Cold; rain east. 11-13 Clear, cold nights. 14-17 Showers, then cold. 18-23 Clear, warm. 24-27 Mild, showers. 28-31 Cool, rain.

The Songs America Sang
Mairzy Doats
Plus
43 More Wacky Hits from the Fun 40's
The Original Hits!
The Original Stars!

4 Big Records, 3 Big Cassettes & 2 Compact Discs

Mairzy Doats The Merry Macs • **Aba Daba Honeymoon** Debbie Reynolds & Carleton Carpenter • **Rag Mop** The Ames Brothers • **Chickory Chick** Sammy Kaye • **Civilization (Bongo, Bongo, Bongo)** Danny Kaye & The Andrews Sisters • **Woody Woodpecker** The Sportsmen & Mel Blanc • **The Thing** Phil Harris • **Manana** Peggy Lee • **Cocktails For Two** Spike Jones • **Buttons And Bows** Dinah Shore • **Too Fat Polka** Arthur Godfrey • **I've Got A Lovely Bunch Of Coconuts** Freddy Martin with Merv Griffin • **Cement Mixer (Put-ti Put-ti)** Alvino Rey • **I'm My Own Grandpa** Guy Lombardo • **Pistol Packin' Mama** Bing Crosby & The Andrews Sisters • **I'm Looking Over A Four Leaf Clover** Art Mooney • **Huggin' And Chalkin'** Hoagy Carmichael • **Chattanoogie Shoe Shine Boy** Red Foley • **Twelfth Street Rag** Pee Wee Hunt • **Deep In The Heart Of Texas** Alvino Rey • **Beer Barrel Polka** Will Glahe • **Bell Bottom Trousers** Jerry Colonna • **Across The Alley From The Alamo** The Mills Brothers • **The Hut-Sut Song** Freddy Martin • **Hey! Ba-Ba-Re-Bop** Tex Beneke & The Glenn Miller Orchestra • **Three Little Fishies** Kay Kyser • **Doctor, Lawyer, Indian Chief** Betty Hutton • **I Never See Maggie Alone** Kenney Roberts • **Doin' What Comes Naturally** Dinah Shore... and 16 more just as great.

Those crazy wonderful songs of the 40's will bring tears of joy to your eyes and rekindle your fondest memories. The 40's were the war years, the waiting years. It was a time for falling in love, sacrificing... and we held on. We had our friends, our families and our music. And often it was the music that saw us through those unforgettable times with hope in our hearts.

This Mairzy Doats Wacky Hits collection brings back all those memorable moments with 44 great songs by the great stars that gave our country a laugh when it needed it most. It's a collection you'll enjoy again and again and it's not available in any store.

OUR GUARANTEE: If for any reason you are not 100% satisfied with your purchase, you may return it within 30 days for a complete refund. So order with confidence!

The Good Music Record Co., Dept. 053835, P.O. Box 11060, Des Moines, IA 50336-1060
YES please rush me MAIRZY DOATS collection on your unconditional money-back guarantee.

☐ 4 Records $19.95 #115238
☐ 3 Cassettes $19.95 #115212
☐ 2 Compact Discs $24.95 #115220
☐ Check Enclosed
☐ VISA ☐ MASTERCARD ☐ DISCOVER
(Enclose $3.50 for mailing and handling)
NY, NJ & IA res. add sales tax.

Acct. No. _____ Exp. Date _____
Name _____
Address _____
City _____
State _____ Zip _____

REGION 7
GREATER OHIO VALLEY
FORECAST

SUMMARY: *The period from November through March will average warmer and drier than normal with below-normal snowfall, but with considerable variability from month to month. Canadian fronts bringing cold and snow during November and December will be relieved by warm spells, sometimes with heavy rain. January will begin cold and snowy, then turn warm and wet. February will be largely warm and dry. March will be cold and snowy the first half, then turn warm.*

The spring months may be cool, especially during April, with below-normal precipitation in western and central sections, above normal in the east. April will have above-normal snowfall, particularly in the east. May should see a few more mild spells, while frequent warm spells will dominate June.

Summer will be warmer and considerably drier than normal, particularly in central and eastern sections, with drought in some sections. Both July and August will begin with heat waves, then moderate at midmonth. A heat wave at the end of August extending into September will increase the drought until relief arrives later in September. The warm and dry weather will continue in the early fall.

NOV. 1995: Temp. 49° (3° above avg.); Precip. 2" (1" below avg.). 1-3 Cold, flurries. 4-6 Clear, warm. 7-9 Cold, snow; then sunny, mild. 10-15 Canadian cold, snow. 16-19 Clear, mild. 20-22 Showers, warm. 23-28 Rain, cool. 29-30 Showers, warm.

DEC. 1995: Temp. 36° (2° above avg.); Precip. 4" (1" above avg.; 0.5" below east). 1-7 Cold, snow. 8-10 Clear, seasonable. 11-13 Sunny, mild. 14-16 Cold, stormy. 17-19 Cold, snow. 20-23 Clear, mild. 24-28 Rain, heavy west. 29-31 Flurries.

JAN. 1996: Temp. 34° (5° above avg.); Precip. 3" (0.5" above avg.). 1-2 Cold, flurries. 3-6 Mild, freezing rain. 7-11 Very cold, snow. 12-16 Mild; rain. 17-20 Clear, warm. 21-23 Rain, snow north. 24-27 Flurries. 28-31 Rain, snow; then cold.

FEB. 1996: Temp. 37° (4° above avg.); Precip. 2" (0.5" below avg.). 1-3 Rain then snow, cold. 4-9 Warm, sprinkles; then cold. 10-13 Rain, then clearing; mild. 14-17 Rain, cold. 18-19 Sunny, mild. 20-22 Flurries, cold. 23-25 Warm, rain. 26-29 Clear.

MAR. 1996: Temp. 45° (1° above avg.); Precip. 3.5" (0.5" below avg.). 1-3 Rain, mild. 4-8 Snowstorm, cold. 9-12 Snow, cold. 13-16 Warm, sprinkles. 17-19 Heavy rain. 20-23 Mild, light rain. 24-26 Rain, warm. 27-31 Sprinkles, cold.

APR. 1996: Temp. 50° (4° below avg.); Precip. 3" (0.5" below avg.). 1-5 Cool, showers, then rain. 6-9 Light rain, cold. 10-12 Warm, showers. 13-15 Cold, snow. 16-21 Clear, then showers, cool. 22-24 Cold, snowstorm. 25-29 Sunny, warm. 30 Cold.

MAY 1996: Temp. 65° (1° above avg.; 1° below west); Precip. 5.5" (1" above avg.; 1" below west). 1-6 Warm, showers. 7-10 Cool, rain. 11-15 Warm, few showers. 16-22 Heavy rain; cool. 23-25 Clear, warm. 26-29 Rain. 30-31 Warm.

JUNE 1996: Temp. 74° (2° above avg.); Precip. 2.5" (1" below avg.; 0.5" below east). 1-9 Cold then warm, rain east. 10-14 Warm, showers. 15-18 Cool, showers. 19-24 Sunny, seasonable, then hot. 25-30 Hot, then showers.

JULY 1996: Temp. 76° (Avg.); Precip. 4" (Avg.; 1" below east). 1-4 Hot, showers. 5-8 Mild, locally heavy rain. 9-11 Cool, showers. 12-15 Clear. 16-19 Sunny, warm. 20-26 Intermittent rain, mild then warm. 27-31 Clear, mild.

AUG. 1996: Temp. 76° (1° above avg.); Precip. 2.5" (1" below avg.). 1-5 Few showers, hot. 6-9 Hot then mild, showers. 10-13 Thundershowers, mild. 14-19 Sunny, warm. 20-24 Clear, sprinkles. 25-31 Hot and dry.

SEPT. 1996: Temp. 70° (2° above avg.); Precip. 1" (2" below avg.). 1-7 Heat wave, dry. 8-11 Seasonable; few showers. 12-14 Clearing, warm. 15-17 Cool, rain. 18-22 Sunny, warm. 23-25 Rain, cool. 26-30 Clear, warm.

OCT. 1996: Temp. 60° (4° above avg.); Precip. 1.5" (1.5" below avg.). 1-7 Clear, dry; hot. 8-11 Cold, rain. 12-14 Clear, warm. 15-17 Sunny, seasonable. 18-23 Sunny, warm. 24-27 Cool. 28-31 Showers, cold.

Wife's Confession:
"I had to trick him... and he's happy I did!"

"I had really begun to wonder about him," says Sally S*, 26, who asked that her last name not be published!

"At first I thought it was another woman. Then I wondered if maybe it was something worse."

The problem was her husband, George. "We used to have such good times," Sally recalled fondly of her dating days. "We went dancing and to parties and he could stay up all night."

But, after three years together, the romance began to fade.

George was bringing home a paycheck that should have made them happy, but he was clearly leaving something behind at the job.

"I dreamed of an affair," Sally admits. "But I couldn't picture myself with anyone else."

That's when Sally heard about a pill her best friend's husband was using. "He gets it sent to the office," Laura explained, "so I won't know he buys it. Of course," Laura added with a wicked grin, "if he ever stopped using it, I'd leave him in a minute! That pill has changed my life!"

Pill for men

What was this pill? Amazingly, thousands of men, like Laura's husband, have used it ever since it was first released to men in 1981.

It is called "NSP- 270" and stories about it have appeared in leading publications. At one time it even received a critical assessment by the Navy. It has been widely used by both young men and older men — in fact, there are men in their 60's and 70's who count on it.

A happy trick

Laura agreed to "borrow" a few pills for Sally — and find out where her husband was getting them.

At the market, Sally bought a bottle of ordinary vitamins, emptied them out, and put the NSP-270 inside the bottle. The next morning at breakfast, Sally offered George a "vitamin." He took it and the rest is history. Later that night when Sally told George what she had done, he offered to buy a six month supply. George now takes his "vitamins" regularly, Sally has her affair (with George, of course!), and both Sally and Laura are making extra money selling NSP-270 to their friends!

Men should Know!

If a man doesn't yet know about NSP-270, it may be because, like certain personal products, you can't buy it in local stores. But you can order it by mail, if you are over 18.

Write to Frank E. Bush, Inc., Dept. NE-82, Box 5009, Monticello, NY 12701. Be sure to include your name and address. Both checks and money orders are accepted. For orders of $25 or more you may request C.O.D. if your order is to a street address (not a P.O. box).

Send $12.95 for one bottle of NSP-270 (30-day supply), $18.95 for 2 bottles, $24.95 for 3 bottles, $42.95 for 6 bottles or $62.00 for 10 bottles. The company will pay the postage & handling charges on your first order.

If you are ordering 3 bottles or more, they will also send you an interesting book about NSP-270. The product carries a 30-day money back guarantee. ##

---

*Sally S. represents a compilation of letters received from many satisfied customers over a period of years. NSP-270 is a healthful multivitamin-mineral formulation that provides a measure of "nutritional insurance" to subjects in need of the same.
© 1991 Frank E. Bush, Inc.

REGION 8
DEEP SOUTH FORECAST

SUMMARY: *The period from November through March is expected to average a couple of degrees warmer than normal with below-normal precipitation. Heavy rains in mid-November will bring some relief to a fall drought. However, warm and dry spells may still dominate the rest of November before a cold front brings heavy rains in early December. The rest of December will be variable before closing on a seasonable note. January will be warm despite a brief cold wave at midmonth, with normal precipitation. After a warm first half, February will become cool and wet. A warm March will have heavy shower activity, particularly in the north.*

The spring months will average near normal in temperature in the north, with well above normal rainfall, and above normal in both temperature and rainfall in the south. April and May will see several periods of cold and stormy weather before a relatively dry and hot spell arrives and persists until the end of June. A brief mild spell will bring rain primarily to southern sections.

The summer months may see above-normal temperatures over most of the region, with milder spells in mid-July and briefly before and after mid-August and mid-September. Precipitation may be well below normal, with most rain occurring after mid-July. Early fall will begin warm and dry, with cool weather and rain after mid-October.

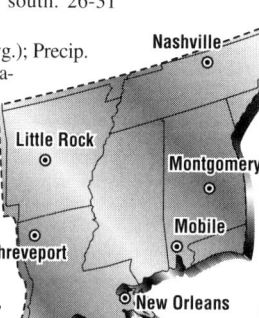

NOV. 1995: Temp. 52.5° (Avg.); Precip. 4" (1" below avg.; 0.5" above west). 1-3 Clear, cold. 4-6 Sunny. 7-12 Mild, cold nights. 13-15 Cold, rain. 16-18 Warming, cold nights. 19-22 Clear, warm. 23-26 Cold, heavy rain. 27-30 Warm, clear.

DEC. 1995: Temp. 43° (0.5° below avg.); Precip. 3.5" (2" below avg.; avg. south). 1-6 Cold; rain, snow north. 7-9 Showers, warming. 10-13 Clear, warm. 14-16 Showers, normal. 17-20 Cold, hard frost. 21-25 Mild; rain, heavy south. 26-31 Sprinkles.

JAN. 1996: Temp. 45° (5° above avg.); Precip. 3.5" (Avg.). 1-3 Clear, cool. 4-6 Seasonable, showers. 7-9 Clear, frost. 10-12 Clear, warm. 13-15 Heavy rain, cold. 16-19 Sunny, warm. 20-26 Cold; rain, then milder. 27-29 Rain, mild. 30-31 Cold.

FEB. 1996: Temp. 46° (2° above avg.); Precip. 5.5" (1.5" above avg.). 1-3 Sprinkles, warm. 4-6 Rain, seasonable. 7-9 Clear, warm. 10-13 Showers, cool. 14-16 Rain, warm. 17-20 Cold; rain, heavy south. 21-23 Clear, cold. 24-26 Rain, mild. 27-29 Cold, rain.

MAR. 1996: Temp. 55° (2° above avg.); Precip. 7.5" (2" above avg.; 0.5" below south). 1-4 Clear, warming. 5-7 Warm, showers. 8-11 Mild, cold nights. 12-14 Cold. 15-24 Showers; warm. 25-27 Heavy rain, warm. 28-31 Cold, showers.

APR. 1996: Temp. 59° (4° below avg.; 2° below south); Precip. 5" (0.5" below avg.). 1-4 Clearing, warm. 5-9 Showers, heavy north; cool. 10-12 Sunny, warm. 13-16 Cold, sprinkles. 17-24 Showers, cold. 25-28 Seasonable, rain. 29-30 Cold.

MAY 1996: Temp. 71° (1° below avg.; 1° above south and east); Precip. 10" (5" above avg.; 1" above east). 1-5 Heavy rain, mild. 6-9 Cold, rain. 10-16 Showers, warm. 17-22 Rain; cool then seasonable. 23-31 Sunny, hot; dry north.

JUNE 1996: Temp. 84° (5° above avg.); Precip. 1" (2.5" below avg.; 1" above east). 1-5 Hot, dry. 6-12 Sunny, then hot. 13-15 Hot, sprinkles. 16-23 Clear, near-record heat. 24-30 Hot, then seasonable; showers south, drought north.

JULY 1996: Temp. 83° (Avg.); Precip. 4.5" (1" above avg.; 1" below central). 1-3 Sunny, hot; rain south. 4-11 Clear, hot. 12-14 Mild, light rain. 15-19 Showers, warm. 20-22 Sunny, seasonable. 23-26 Heavy rain. 27-31 Clear, warm.

AUG. 1996: Temp. 81° (Avg.); Precip. 1.5" (2" below avg.; 0.5" above Gulf). 1-5 Clear, hot; showers south. 6-10 Sunny, sprinkles north. 11-13 Sunny, mild; showers south. 14-18 Clear, hot. 19-27 Few showers, mild. 28-31 Sunny, seasonable.

SEPT. 1996: Temp. 75° (1° above avg.); Precip. 1" (2.5" below avg.). 1-3 Clear, hot; rain south. 4-7 Sprinkles, hot. 8-12 Cold, rain south. 13-18 Clearing, hot. 19-22 Showers, hot. 23-25 Sunny, seasonable. 26-30 Sunny, cool.

OCT. 1996: Temp. 66° (3° above avg.); Precip. 2" (1" below avg.). 1-7 Hot, dry. 8-13 Cold, light rain. 14-16 Warm, dry. 17-21 Clear; warm, cool nights. 22-27 Warm. 28-31 Cold, heavy rain.

Works So Fast, The Very First Weekend Alone, Patients Report It

DISSOLVES UP to 3 POUNDS OF FAT and 2 INCHES OF FLAB EVERY 24 HOURS!

Doctor's Wonder-Treatment for Obesity

— then, BURNS AWAY 50% OF ALL EXCESS BODY FAT IN AS LITTLE AS 14 DAYS!

In Fact — Clinical Tests Prove NOT EVEN TOTAL STARVATION CAN SLIM YOU DOWN AND FIRM YOU UP THIS FAST!

MELTS DOWN FAT JUST LIKE HOT WATER MELTS DOWN ICE!

Just recently, at the nationally famous obesity research medical center in Miami, Florida...where even the most hopeless, grossly obese, lifetime prisoners of fat fly in from all over to LOSE as much as 6 to 9 LBS. IN A SINGLE WEEKEND — 15 to 21 LBS. IN A SINGLE WEEK — SLIM DOWN AS MUCH AS 4 SIZES SMALLER IN JUST 14 DAYS...the doctor in charge announced the results of one of the most successful weight-loss tests performed by medical science. A clinically proven way to safely speed up your metabolism after every time you eat...and actually STOP YOUR SYSTEM FROM PRODUCING A SINGLE OUNCE OF EXCESS FAT, as your entire body starts to grow THINNER, TRIMMER, FIRMER IN JUST 3 TO 5 DAYS!

PATIENTS REPORT LOSSES OF UP TO 3 POUNDS A DAY — SHRINKING DOWN A FULL SIZE SMALLER EVERY 72 HOURS!

Yes, medical science's incredible new "Slim For Life" program that produces weight-loss results that absolutely stagger the imagination!

As much as 10–15–even 20 pounds dissolved and gone in just one week — 20, 30 even 40 pounds dissolved and gone in just one month — and most mind-boggling of all, as much as 107 POUNDS and 16 WAISTLINE INCHES GONE FOREVER without a single moment of torturous diet or a single minute of brutal, back-breaking exercise!

In short — THERE IS NO FASTER, SURER, SAFER WEIGHT-LOSS METHOD NOW KNOWN TO MEDICAL SCIENCE!

DRAMATIC PROOF FROM LEADING U.S. MEDICAL SCHOOL

But the most startling proof of all comes from California's leading medical school. Based upon extensive research at this prestigious institution, this proven wonder-treatment for obesity actually BURNS AWAY MORE FAT EACH AND EVERY DAY than:

- *Running as much as 100 miles a week!*
- *or, up to 3,000 sit-ups and push-ups a day*
- *or, 19 solid hours of weight-lift workouts*
- *or, even as much as 10 hours of non-stop Marine Corps calisthenics!*

And that's only the beginning of this weight-loss wonder-development!

IF YOU READ NOTHING ELSE — READ THIS MESSAGE FROM THE DOCTOR:

"The incredible losses of both pounds and inches you see above...and the incredible speed at which they came off, (as much as 21 lbs. IN A SINGLE WEEK), are atypical results from all test subjects who tried this 'Lifetime Slimness' program. How much will you lose? And how fast will you lose it? Well, here's the good news. While results vary from person to person, medical research indicates, the more overweight you are, the more weight you will lose and THE FASTER YOU WILL LOSE IT. And remember this...as stated above and I feel compelled to repeat: Not even total starvation can slim you down and firm you up this fast and this safely!"

NOW A LIFETIME OF SLIMNESS WITHOUT A MOMENT OF GNAWING HUNGER!

You see, what medical science has developed is a proven way to SAFELY SPEED UP YOUR FAT-BURNING METABOLISM all day, all night, even while you sleep...plus rev up your body's rate of calorie burn-off AFTER EVERY TIME YOU EAT! The miracle result? Even while you enjoy 3 solid meals a day...even while you snack, nibble and treat yourself to all sorts of between-meal "goodies"... thanks to your newly fired-up metabolism you safely, surely steadily:

- *BURN AWAY 40–60–80–100–even 150 LBS. OR MORE faster than you ever dreamed possible*

LIKE GROWING A BRAND NEW BODY IN JUST 2 WEEKS

- *SHRINK DOWN your waistline as much as 4, 5 even 6 inches smaller in a single week*
- *MELT AWAY fat by the hour...carve away inches by the week... all without missing a single meal, without giving up snacks.*

A DOCTOR EXPLAINS MEDICAL SCIENCE'S FINAL VICTORY IN THE WAR AGAINST FAT

MEDICAL FACT #1: In your body there are exist natural fat-burners...powerful digestive enzymes able to melt down and flush away clinging pockets of fat — PLUS, burn away all the calories in the food you consume after every time you eat.

MEDICAL FACT #2: In naturally slim people, the action of these metabolic fat-burners is so effective they AUTOMATICALLY STOP ALL THE FOOD THESE PEOPLE TAKE IN FROM TURNING TO LAYERS OF FAT. Which is why these "lifetime skinnies" seem to eat all they want and never gain an ounce. B-U-T...

MEDICAL FACT #3: In overweight people caloric excess overwhelms the body's natural fat-destroying system...and instead of turning all the food you eat into burned away energy, allows it to turn into bulging pounds and inches.

MEANING: To conquer fat build-up, what medical science had to do was find a way to create a continual caloric deficit in each overweight person's system...step up their fat-burning metabolism... speed up the flow of your body's own natural fat-burners...and AUTOMATICALLY start to dissolve fat by the hour...pounds by the day...and inches by the week!

DOCTOR'S WONDER-TREATMENT FEATURING THE ULTIMATE WEIGHT-LOSS DIET PILL TURNS YOUR ENTIRE BODY INTO A GIANT FAT-BURNING FURNACE!

And this is precisely what medical science now makes available to the public for the first time without a prescription from a doctor. An incredibly simple way to step up the flow of your body's own natural fat-burners...and through the use of a tiny, golden, once-a-day, time-released tablet and a 'round the clock high-burn dietary regime, turn your system into a GIANT FAT-BURNING MACHINE!

WORKS LIKE A "FURNACE IN A PILL" HELPS TRIGGER THE MOST DYNAMITE FAT-BURN SPREE OF YOUR LIFE!

And here's the most exciting news of all — the release to the public of a new wonder-capsule called "Theraslim/MD" that works before meals, during meals and between meals to help you lower your system's caloric intake and BURN AWAY ALL THE CALORIES IN ALL THE FOOD YOU TAKE IN AFTER EVERY TIME YOU EAT!

Yes, medical science's new wonder-capsule that throughout the day releases into your system tiny grains of biologic stimulators that safely, surely continually TURN UP the level of your fat-burning metabolism...and send your fat-burning chain-reaction going in your body NON-STOP all day, all night, even while you sleep.

Meaning: All the food you take in on this wonder weight-loss program, all the thousands of calories you enjoy, are all burned away by your stepped up metabolism starting in as little as 2 to 3 hours after every time you eat! So, you not only start to grow slimmer the very first day...BUT, after your very first meal...and every meal thereafter, as excess fat and unwanted inches start to disappear BY THE HOUR!

THE FOOD YOU EAT NO LONGER TURNS TO FAT!

Right now, look at your figure in the mirror and ask yourself:

How would I look one week from today as much as 10 to 15 pounds thinner and 2 waistline sizes smaller?

How would I look 2 weeks from now up to 20 pounds lighter and 4 sizes smaller?

BUT DON'T STOP THERE — if you need to lose still more pounds and still more inches, then continue the Doctor's 'Theraslim/MD' Lifetime Slimness program until you've won the magnificent body and figure you've always dreamed of all your life...with as much as:

6 INCHES CARVED OFF YOUR HIPS
ANOTHER 3 INCHES CARVED OFF YOUR THIGHS
ANOTHER 4 INCHES OFF YOUR BUTTOCKS
ANOTHER 6 INCHES OFF YOUR STOMACH
ANOTHER 6 INCHES OFF YOUR WAISTLINE!

Because as proven in clinical tests...as proven by extensive medical school research...**THERE IS NO FASTER, SAFER, SURER WEIGHTLOSS METHOD NOW KNOWN TO MEDICAL SCIENCE. In fact, not even total starvation can slim you down and firm you up this fast!**

And since we invite you to prove every lost ounce, every lost inch entirely at our risk...with this special trial-offer...you have nothing to lose but unwanted fat and a lifetime of slimness to gain. Isn't this the dream-announcement from medical science you've been waiting for all your life? Now the final step is up to you. So take advantage of this strictly limited, introductory, no-risk trial offer — ACT NOW!

CALL NOW FOR IMMEDIATE DELIVERY!

Operators are standing by 24 hours a day, 7 days a week.

1-800-851-6633

Visa/MC and CHECKS ACCEPTED BY PHONE
(Have your checkbook ready when calling.)

INTRODUCTORY OFFER

Theraslim/M.D. Research Project Dept. FA
100 Fusion Way, Country Club Hills, IL 60478

30 Day Supply $29.95...only $19.95 (save $10)
60 Day Supply $59.95...only $34.95 (save $25)
Please add $4.95 shipping & handling on any size order. Florida residents add 7% sales tax.

© Theraslim/MD Research Center, Aventura, FL 33181

REGION 9

CHICAGO & SOUTHERN GREAT LAKES
FORECAST

SUMMARY: The period from November through March is expected to be much milder than normal, with below-normal precipitation and snowfall. Expect great variability from month to month. Dry conditions during the first half of November will be alleviated by ample rainfall the latter half, while warm periods will relieve frequent Canadian cold fronts. December will see both wintry weather and unusually mild periods. Cold and snowy weather the second week of January will be followed by generally mild weather until late February when stormy weather will return, with reappearances throughout March.

The spring months overall will be cooler than normal with below-normal precipitation in the south, but near normal north. April will be cold, particularly after midmonth, but end with a warm and rainy spell, while May will be extremely variable, with frequent storms. Frequent hot spells are anticipated in June, with temperatures reaching 100° near the end of the month.

The summer will be warmer and drier than normal, with drought developing in much of the south and west. July will begin hot and showery, then turn cool until closing with a hot spell that continues into early August. After a mild, showery period, watch for a dry heat wave from late August through the first week of September, after which temperatures and precipitation will be closer to normal. Early fall will be mostly warm, sunny, and dry.

NOV. 1995: Temp. 45° (3.5° above avg.); Precip. 2.5" (0.5" below avg.; avg. east). 1-3 Cold, flurries. 4-6 Clear, warm. 7-15 Frequent Canadian cold waves. 16-20 Clear, warm. 21-23 Rain, cooling. 24-28 Cold; rain east. 29-30 Rain, snow.

DEC. 1995: Temp. 30° (2° above avg.); Precip. 2" (1" below avg.). 1-2 Rain, snow north. 3-5 Cold, flurries. 6-10 Snow, seasonable. 11-14 Clear, warm; rain east. 15-19 Cold, light snow. 20-22 Sunny, mild. 23-25 Snow. 26-31 Mild, then cold; light snow.

JAN. 1996: Temp. 28° (5° above avg.); Precip. 1.5" (Avg.). 1-3 Clearing, mild. 4-6 Freezing rain. 7-11 Cold, snow. 12-16 Freezing drizzle, then clearing. 17-19 Warm. 20-24 Snow, seasonable. 25-27 Mild. 28-31 Snow, then cold.

FEB. 1996: Temp. 30° (3° above avg.); Precip. 1.5" (Avg.; 0.5" below south). 1-4 Cold; then snow. 5-7 Cold, flurries. 8-10 Mild, rain. 11-17 Seasonable, flurries. 18-19 Sunny, warm. 20-23 Cold, snow. 24-26 Rain, warm. 27-29 Cold, then mild.

MAR. 1996: Temp. 38° (Avg.); Precip. 3.5" (0.5" above avg.). 1-3 Sprinkles, mild. 4-11 Cold, flurries. 12-14 Sunny, warm. 15-19 Rain, cool. 20-23 Sunny, then cool, showers. 24-27 Very warm, rain. 28-31 Freezing drizzle.

APR. 1996: Temp. 46° (4° below avg.); Precip. 3" (1" below avg.; avg. east). 1-4 Rain west; cool. 5-9 Rain. 10-12 Warm, showers. 13-16 Cold, rain and snow. 17-19 Rain, cool. 20-23 Cold, snow. 24-28 Warm, sprinkles. 29-30 Rain, cold.

MAY 1996: Temp. 59° (1° below avg.; avg. east); Precip. 3" (0.5" below avg.). 1-4 Warm, showers. 5-9 Cold, rain. 10-15 Sunny, warm; few showers. 16-20 Cold, rain. 21-24 Sunny, warm. 25-27 Cold, heavy rain. 28-31 Warm, then rain.

JUNE 1996: Temp. 72.5° (2° above avg.); Precip. 4.5" (0.5" above avg.; 0.5" below south). 1-3 Warm, rain. 4-7 Cold, then warm. 8-20 Brief warm and cool periods, few showers. 21-24 Clear, hot. 25-27 Rain, mild. 28-30 Rain; hot south.

JULY 1996: Temp. 76° (1° above avg.); Precip. 3" (1" below avg.; 0.5" below east). 1-4 Showers, then hot. 5-7 Cool, rain. 8-10 Showers, warm. 11-14 Clear. 15-19 Sunny, hot. 20-25 Rain, hot. 26-28 Clear, warm. 29-31 Showers, hot.

AUG. 1996: Temp. 75° (1.5° above avg.); Precip. 2.5" (1" below avg.). 1-6 Thundershowers, hot south. 7-13 Showers, locally heavy, mild. 14-18 Clear, warm. 19-23 Sunny, sprinkles. 24-27 Clear, hot. 28-31 Heat wave, dry.

SEPT. 1996: Temp. 68° (2° above avg.); Precip. 2.5" (1" below avg.; 0.5" below east). 1-7 Heat wave, showers north. 8-11 Sunny, few showers. 12-14 Showers, warm. 15-18 Cool, showers. 19-22 Warm, rain. 23-26 Clear, cool. 27-30 Rain, warm.

OCT. 1996: Temp. 56° (5° above avg.); Precip. 1.5" (1" below avg.). 1-6 Sunny, warm. 7-11 Cold, rain. 12-17 Warm, then seasonable. 18-27 Warm, clear; light rain north. 28-31 Rain, cool.

Be Your Own Boss... IN YOUR OWN BUSINESS!

Work Part Time OR Full Time

Get Into This Booming High-Profit Business That's Easy To Learn — Easy to Do — Easy On You!

START YOUR OWN MONEY MAKING BUSINESS & BEAT INFLATION!

Never before have money-making opportunities been so great for qualified Locksmiths. Now lucrative regular lock and key business has multiplied a thousandfold as millions seek more protection against zooming crime. Yet there's only one Locksmith for every 17,000 people!

Make Up to $26.00 an Hour — even while learning! Train FAST at Home!

You're "in business" ready to earn $10 to $26.00 an hour a few days after you begin Foley-Belsaw's shortcut training. Take advantage of today's unprecedented opportunities in locksmithing for year-round EXTRA INCOME in spare time — or full time in a high-profit business of your own. Hundreds we've trained have done it. So can YOU! All tools plus professional Key Machine given you with course. These plus practice materials and equipment, plus simple, illustrated lessons, plus expert supervision, plus business-building guidance will enable you to **KEEP THE MONEY COMING IN!** Ideal for retirement — good jobs, too.

No Extra Cost! Included With Your Locksmith Training

BURGLAR ALARM and SECURITY SYSTEMS training. Covers all phases of Burglar, Hold-Up and Fire Alarm servicing and installation. ONLY Foley-Belsaw offers such extensive training in this rapidly expanding field as a part of your Locksmith training. **PLUS... ADVANCED Locksmithing!**

How to change combinations, install and service Safe, Vault and Bank Safe-Deposit Box locks. You'll find it fascinating and highly profitable work.

Just fill in and mail coupon (or send postcard) to receive full information and details by return mail. FOLEY-BELSAW INSTITUTE
6301 EQUITABLE RD., DEPT. 12694
KANSAS CITY, MO 64120

RUSH COUPON TODAY FOR THIS FACT-FILLED FREE BOOKLET!
30-DAY NO RISK TRIAL!
SEND FOR FACTS TODAY!

BE A LOCKSMITH

ALL SPECIAL TOOLS AND EQUIPMENT INCLUDED!

PRO KEY MACHINE YOURS TO KEEP!

This Pro Key Machine can alone add up to $200 a month to your income... and it won't cost you a penny extra with your training.

NO OBLIGATION... NO SALESMAN WILL CALL

FOLEY-BELSAW INSTITUTE
6301 EQUITABLE RD., DEPT. 12694
KANSAS CITY, MO 64120

☐ YES, please send me the FREE booklet that gives full details about starting my own business in Locksmithing. I understand there is no obligation and that no salesman will call.

Name _____

Address _____

City _____

State _____ Zip _____

REGION 10
NORTHERN GREAT PLAINS-GREAT LAKES
FORECAST

SUMMARY: *The period from November through March is expected to be warmer than normal, with above-normal precipitation in the west but below normal in the east. Drought conditions may persist through the first three weeks of November before cold, snowy weather arrives to last through early December. Warm and dry conditions will then continue through the first week of January. Brief cold fronts will appear at mid- and late December. It should then get progressively colder and snowier, with frequent cold fronts during January, February, and March, with warm and wet weather in between.*

The spring months will be colder and wetter than normal, with above-normal snowfall. Cold waves will dominate in April and the first half of May, with only brief warm spells. The balance of May and the month of June will see wide swings in temperature, with frequent rain.

The summer will be warmer than normal, with near-normal rainfall in southern sections, below normal in the north. Following a hot, dry start, mild weather will prevail until mid-July. A milder than normal first half of August will be offset by a heat wave from late in the month into September, after which warm and dry spells will dominate. Early fall will be warm and dry, with only the far west having above-normal precipitation.

NOV. 1995: Temp. 37° (4° above avg.); Precip. 1.5" (Avg.). 1-2 Cold, clear. 3-5 Sunny, warm. 6-9 Showers, then clear, warm. 10-14 Cold, flurries. 15-20 Sunny. 21-24 Rain, east; cold. 25-28 Seasonable, snow west. 29-30 Snowstorm east.

DEC. 1995: Temp. 21° (3° above avg.); Precip. 0.5" (0.5" below avg.). 1-5 Snow ending; cold, clear. 6-9 Light snow, seasonable. 10-13 Sunny, warm. 14-18 Snow, cold. 19-20 Clear, warm. 21-27 Flurries, then mild. 28-31 Cold.

JAN. 1996: Temp. 16° (4° above avg.); Precip. 0.5" (0.5" below avg.). 1-4 Sunny, mild; cold nights. 5-8 Flurries. 9-11 Cold, snow. 12-17 Clearing, warm west. 18-20 Cold, blizzard. 21-24 Seasonable, light snow. 25-31 Flurries, mild.

FEB. 1996: Temp. 17° (1° below avg.; avg. west); Precip. 1.2" (0.5" above avg.). 1-4 Flurries, cold, then mild. 5-7 Snow, cold. 8-13 Sleet and snow. 14-18 Snow, then clear, seasonable. 19-23 Snow. 24-26 Blizzard. 27-29 Clear, seasonable.

MAR. 1996: Temp. 29.5° (1.5° below avg.); Precip. 1.5" (0.5" below avg.). 1-3 Light snow. 4-7 Cold, snow. 5-10 Very cold, flurries. 11-15 Mild, sprinkles. 16-19 Cold, snow. 20-25 Mild, clear; then rain. 26-29 Cold, snow. 30-31 Mild.

APR. 1996: Temp. 41.5° (5° above avg.); Precip. 2" (0.5" below avg.). 1-5 Sprinkles, mild; cold west. 6-8 Cold, snow. 9-11 Sunny, seasonable. 12-14 Snowstorm. 15-18 Clear, seasonable. 19-22 Cold, snow west. 23-27 Clear, warm. 28-30 Cold, snow.

MAY 1996: Temp. 56° (2.5° below avg.); Precip. 2.5" (1" below avg.; avg. west). 1-2 Sunny, mild. 3-6 Freezing rain. 7-12 Clear, warm. 13-16 Cold; heavy rain, snow west. 17-23 Showers, warm. 24-31 Rain; cold, then warm.

JUNE 1996: Temp. 69° (1° above avg.); Precip. 6" (2" above avg.). 1-3 Rain, heavy west; warm. 4-6 Sunny, warm. 7-9 Cold, showers west. 10-12 Cold, rain. 13-16 Showers, warm. 17-20 Thundershowers. 21-23 Clear, hot. 24-30 Cool, few thundershowers.

JULY 1996: Temp. 73° (0.5° below avg.; 2° below west); Precip. 5" (1.5" above avg.; 0.5" below west). 1-5 Hot, showers. 6-11 Cool, few showers. 12-14 Clear, cool. 15-18 Thundershowers, warm. 19-23 Hot, showers. 24-31 Mild, thundershowers.

AUG. 1996: Temp. 72° (1.5° above avg.); Precip. 3" (0.5" below avg.). 1-4 Showers, warm. 5-8 Thundershowers, mild. 9-12 Cool; showers. 13-16 Warm then hot; showers. 17-19 Sprinkles, warm. 20-26 Clear, warm. 27-31 Heat wave, showers.

SEPT. 1996: Temp. 63° (2.5° above avg.); Precip. 1.5" (1" below avg.). 1-3 Hot, showers. 4-5 Clear, hot. 6-8 Mild, thundershowers. 9-13 Sunny, warm. 14-16 Cool, showers. 17-22 Sunny. 23-30 Light rain; cool, then warm.

OCT. 1996: Temp. 55° (6° above avg.); Precip. 1" (1" below avg.). 1-5 Clear, hot. 6-8 Sprinkles, seasonable. 9-11 Cold, clear. 12-17 Sunny, warm. 18-23 Warm, sprinkles. 24-27 Cold; rain, snow west. 28-31 Rain; clearing west.

Storage • Shops • Offices • Etc.
Pre-packaged Steel Frame Buildings

- Buy Factory Direct and SAVE THOUSANDS
- Build it yourself and save even more!

Special Limited Offer

Packages include #1 grade steel frames and endwalls, high strength sheeting, deluxe trim package and easy step-by-step assembly plans.

34'x48' - $13,135 Value	48'x72' - $27,196 Value
NOW ONLY - $6,699	**NOW ONLY - $13,899**

Some other sizes available

CALL 1-800-843-8275
FAX 1-612-544-1835

MIRACLE TRUSS®

OFA

Complete First Year Set Of...
SHORTEST U.S. DOLLAR SERIES SINCE 1795!

The Susan B. Anthony Dollar was issued only 3 years! The only other U.S. Dollar with a shorter life was the 1794-95 Flowing Hair Dollar — America's 1st Dollar!

This is *your* opportunity to get the complete First Year All-Mint Set of the historic 1979 Susan B. Anthony Dollar. One Uncirculated coin from each U.S. Mint — Philadelphia, San Francisco, Denver. Purchased individually these 3 coins would cost $11.50, but this offer saves you money. YOURS FOR ONLY $5 per set!

Ridiculed by the public as the "Carter Quarter" the mini-dollar is fast becoming a *prized collectible*. Hard to put together now, a First Year Set will get even harder. Clip the coupon below and send today! You'll also receive our free fully illustrated catalog, plus other offers on approval. Satisfaction guaranteed. DON'T DELAY! (Limit 4 sets.)

☐ **YES!** Please send me the **First Year All-Mint Set** of 1979 Susan B. Anthony Dollars for **ONLY $5.00**.

$_____ How Many? *(Limit 4)*
$_____ Total enclosed

Send coupon with payment to: Mr./Mrs./Ms. _____
Address _____

Littleton Coin Company
Dept. LZT209,
Littleton, NH 03561

City _____ State ___ ZIP _____ - ____

Full 45-Day Money Back Guarantee of Satisfaction ©LCC

REGION 11
CENTRAL GREAT PLAINS
FORECAST

SUMMARY: *The period from November through March will be milder than normal, with above-normal precipitation in the north, below normal central and south. Warm and dry conditions may persist through much of November, before the weather turns wet and cold into the first week of December. Warm and dry conditions may then return until a cold and snowy spell occurs in late December. The first half of January will be seasonable, but then mild periods will dominate through February, particularly in southern sections. Cold waves and snow after mid-January, in late February, and in mid- and late March will bring more wintry weather.*

Spring will be colder than normal in the north, warm in the southwest; precipitation will be below normal across the region. April will be cold over the region, despite one or two brief warm spells, with above-normal precipitation, except in the west. May will be mostly cool and dry. June will be very warm and dry, with possible drought in central and southern sections.

The summer months will be warmer than normal with well below normal rainfall, causing serious drought in southern sections. Some respite in temperature is expected in mid-July and briefly before and after mid-August and mid-September. Early fall may see a continuation of warm and dry conditions except for a cold wave before mid-October and another at the close of the month.

NOV. 1995: Temp. 42° (3° above avg.); Precip. 4" (2" above avg.; avg. south). 1-2 Cold. 3-5 Warm and dry. 6-9 Cold, clear; then mild. 10-14 Sunny, cold; rain south. 15-20 Clear, warm. 21-23 Rain. 24-27 Clearing, mild. 28-30 Rain turning to snow.

DEC. 1995: Temp. 26° (2° above avg.; 1° below southwest); Precip. 1" (Avg.; 1" below east). 1-4 Cold, snow. 5-8 Flurries, cold. 9-12 Clear, warm. 13-15 Cool, sprinkles. 16-18 Cold, flurries. 19-21 Clear, warm. 22-27 Snowstorm. 28-31 Cold, flurries.

JAN. 1996: Temp. 22° (3° above avg.; 5° above east); Precip. 1" (Avg.; 0.5" below south). 1-5 Clear, seasonable. 6-9 Flurries, snow west. 10-12 Cold, snow north. 13-18 Clearing, warm. 19-21 Severe cold. 22-28 Light snow. 29-31 Clear, warm.

FEB. 1996: Temp. 28° (4° above avg.; 5° above south); Precip. 1.5" (0.5" above avg.; 0.5" below east). 1-3 Clear, warm. 4-6 Cold north; warm south. 7-9 Clear, warm. 10-23 Cold wave, then mild, flurries. 24-26 Cold, snowstorm. 27-29 Clear, warm; then rain.

MAR. 1996: Temp. 37° (Avg.; 2° above south and west); Precip. 1" (1" below avg.). 1-3 Rain ending, mild. 4-7 Cold, snow. 8-11 Mild, then snow. 12-16 Mild, showers. 17-19 Rain, sleet. 20-24 Sunny, warm. 25-27 Rain, snow north. 28-31 Clear, mild.

APR. 1996: Temp. 46° (5° below avg.); Precip. 3.5" (Avg.; 0.5" below east). 1-5 Rain, cold. 6-11 Sunny; cold nights. 12-14 Rain, cold. 15-17 Sunny, seasonable. 18-22 Rain, snow north. 23-26 Clear, warm. 27-30 Rain, cold.

MAY 1996: Temp. 60° (2° below avg.); Precip. 3" (0.5" below avg.; 1" below south and east). 1-4 Warm, rain. 5-7 Cold, rain. 8-13 Sunny, warm. 14-16 Rain, cold. 17-21 Mild, showers. 22-24 Clear, warm. 25-28 Cool, rain. 29-31 Sunny, hot; then showers.

JUNE 1996: Temp. 74° (2° above avg.; 6° above south); Precip. 4" (0.5" below avg.; 2" below south). 1-3 Clear, warm. 4-8 Showers, hot. 9-12 Rain, cool. 13-18 Showers, hot. 19-22 Clear, then hot. 23-30 Warm, showers.

JULY 1996: Temp. 76° (Avg.; 2° below southwest); Precip. 2" (1.5" below avg.; 3" below south). 1-3 Hot; rain south. 4-7 Sprinkles. 8-13 Sunny, rain west. 14-22 Few showers, then hot. 23-26 Showers, warm. 27-31 Sprinkles, hot.

AUG. 1996: Temp. 75° (1° above avg.; avg. southwest); Precip. 1" (3" below avg.; 1" below west). 1-5 Sunny, hot. 6-11 Mild, showers. 12-17 Seasonable, few showers. 18-23 Mild, sunny. 24-27 Clear, hot. 28-31 Very hot, drought southeast.

SEPT. 1996: Temp. 67° (2° above avg.; 4° above south); Precip. 1.5" (2" below avg.; 3" below south and west). 1-5 Clear, hot. 6-9 Mild, showers. 10-14 Clear, hot; few showers. 15-20 Sunny, warm. 21-24 Cool, showers. 25-27 Sunny, warm. 28-30 Light rain.

OCT. 1996: Temp. 60° (6° above avg.); Precip. 1" (1.5" below avg.). 1-5 Clear, hot. 6-10 Sprinkles, rain south; cold. 11-15 Sunny. 16-18 Warm. 19-23 Showers, heavy west; warm. 24-27 Cold; showers. 28-31 Rain south; cold.

The professional weather station for people curious about the weather.

WEATHER MONITOR II
- Inside & Outside Temperature
- Wind Speed
- Wind Direction
- Wind Chill
- Barometer
- Inside Humidity
- Time & Date
- Highs & Lows
- Alarms

OPTIONAL ACCESSORIES
- Rain Collector
- Outside Humidity/Dew Point Sensor
- IBM or Mac Interface

For a free catalog, call
1-800-678-3669

DAVIS INSTRUMENTS 3465 Diablo Ave., Hayward, CA 94545 • OF257E

60% MORE JUICE FROM YOUR APPLES!

The secret is the "APPLE EATER" grinder which reduces the fruit to a fine pulp. Has stainless steel knives and will grind a box of whole apples in less than five minutes. Makes 2 to 3 gallons of cider per tub. Heavy 1½" acme screw and cast iron cross beam. All hardwood construction. Four models -from single tubs to double tub. Completely assembled or low cost kits. Send $1.00 or call 913-849-3103 for catalog.

EXCLUSIVE FEATURE
THE "APPLE EATER" GRINDER WILL GRIND WHOLE APPLES WITH EASE. YOU DO NOT HAVE TO SLICE THEM OR PUSH THEM DOWN!

HAPPY VALLEY RANCH
Dept. A, 16577 W. 327th St.
Paola, KS 66071

You Can Save Up To 50% On Home Heating Cost
And never have to buy fuel, wood, oil, gas, kerosene ever again.

REPLACE OLD & INEFFICIENT HEAT

Hydro-Sil is a unique zone heating system that can **save you hundreds of dollars** in home heating costs.
It can replace or supplement your electric heat, oil or gas furnace. Your kerosene heaters and woodstoves.

Your benefits with Hydro-Sil
- Slash Heating Cost – Up to 50%
- Lifetime Warranty - no service calls
- Safe for children & furniture
- Clean – no fumes – no smoke
- U.L. Listed
- Preassembled – ready to use
- No furnaces – ducts – chimney
- Portable (110V) or permanent (220V)
- Whole House Heating or Single Room
- Room by Room Control

Hydro-Sil works like this: inside the heater case is a sealed copper tube filled with a harmless silicone fluid that will never spill, leak, boil or freeze. **It's permanent. You'll never run out.** Running through the liquid is a hydroelectric element that, when the thermostat is turned on, quickly warms the liquid. The silicone liquid with its heat retention qualities continues to heat after the Hydro element shuts off, **saving you money.** The heat radiating from the tube is directed into a gentle convection flow that delivers warm, comfortable heat into the room. It's just that simple. The principle is the same as hot water heating and provides the same benefits.

Credit Orders–Toll Free
1-800-627-9276 (M/C-VISA)
Or Mail Check To: **Hydro-Sil**
PO Box 662, Fort Mill, SC 29715

SPRING DISCOUNT FACTORY SALE

LIFETIME WARRANTY–U.L. LISTED

TWO MODELS TO CHOOSE FROM:
PORTABLE 110 V or PERMANENT 220 V

220 Volt Permanent	Approx. Area To Heat	Discount Price	Quantity
8' 2000 watts	300 sq. ft.	$239	
6' 1500 watts	250 sq. ft.	$219	
5' 1250 watts	200 sq. ft.	$199	
4' 1000 watts	175 sq. ft.	$179	
3' 750 watts	150 sq. ft.	$169	
2' 500 watts	100 sq. ft.	$149	
110 Volt Portable			
5' Dual watt 750-1500 W		$199	
3' 750 watts	150 sq. ft.	$169	
4' Dual Convector 750-1500 W		$169	
$15.00 shipping per heater		$	
Total Amount		$	

Acct No. _____ Ex. _____
Name _____
Address _____
Phone _____

REGION 12

TEXAS-OKLAHOMA
FORECAST

SUMMARY: *The period from November through March will be warmer than normal over the region, with above-normal precipitation in the north and east, below normal in the south. The first three weeks of November will be warm despite brief cold waves. A cold, wet, and snowy period at the end of November and into early December will relieve drought over much of the north. Generally warm and dry weather will then persist until mid-February, except for cold and stormy spells at the ends of December and January. The last half of February will again be cold, wet, and snowy. March will be warm and fairly dry south, but wet central and north.*

The spring months will average close to normal in temperature, with well below normal precipitation except for the northeast. April through mid-May will be dominated by frequent cold waves with heavy precipitation and flooding, but then hot and dry weather will prevail through June in most sections, with serious drought in the west.

Summer will average slightly cooler than normal central and north, warm in the Gulf region. Rainfall will be below normal over the region except for a wet southeast. Central and northeastern sections will see a mild mid-July, with heavy rains in the north, but generally seasonal temperatures will prevail except for brief hot spells. Early fall is expected to be considerably warmer and drier than normal, except for above-normal rainfall in the west.

NOV. 1995: Temp. 58° (1° above avg.); Precip. 3" (0.5" above avg.; 4" above central). 1-3 Clear, cold. 4-6 Sunny, warm. 7-9 Cold, rain. 10-12 Clear, warm. 13-15 Rain, heavy south; cold. 16-21 Warm, clear. 22-26 Rain, snow north. 27-30 Rain, cold.

DEC. 1995: Temp. 46° (2° below avg.); Precip. 2.5" (0.5" above avg.; 1" below northeast). 1-7 Rain south, snow north; cold. 8-10 Clear, warm; rain south. 11-15 Sunny, warm. 16-19 Cold, flurries north. 20-24 Rain, warm. 25-31 Rain, snow north.

JAN. 1996: Temp. 49° (4° above avg.; 5° above west); Precip. 1.5" (Avg.; 1" below south). 1-4 Warm; rain south. 5-14 Clear, warm; snow north. 15-19 Warm. 20-22 Cold, snow; rain south. 23-25 Warm, clear. 26-28 Rain. 29-31 Warm, sunny.

FEB. 1996: Temp. 50° (1° above avg.; 4° above north); Precip. 1.5" (0.5" below avg.). 1-9 Clear, warm; rain south. 10-12 Seasonable, sprinkles. 13-15 Rain, cold. 16-18 Clearing, cold. 19-24 Showers, seasonable. 25-29 Cold; snow, rain south.

MAR. 1996: Temp. 60° (2° above avg.; 4° above south); Precip. 3" (Avg.; 1" above northeast). 1-3 Sunny, mild. 4-7 Rain north, cold. 8-11 Sunny, warm. 12-14 Rain, cold. 15-18 Warm; rain north. 19-24 Showers, warm. 25-28 Cold. 29-31 Rain, seasonable.

APR. 1996: Temp. 63° (4° below avg.; avg. south); Precip. 3" (1" below avg.; 3" above northeast). 1-5 Rain, seasonable. 6-10 Cold; rain, heavy north. 11-14 Sunny, warm. 15-18 Showers, cold. 19-21 Mild. 22-24 Rain, cold. 25-30 Rain, mild.

MAY 1996: Temp. 72° (2° below avg.; avg. south); Precip. 5" (Avg.; 3" above southeast, 1" below west and north). 1-4 Mild; rain. 5-9 Cold, sprinkles. 10-12 Clear, warm. 13-19 Rain, cold. 20-22 Mild, few showers. 23-31 Clear, hot.

JUNE 1996: Temp. 86° (4° above avg.; 2° above south); Precip. 0.5" (3" below avg.). 1-7 Sunny, hot. 8-10 Warm, rain north. 11-14 Clear, hot. 15-24 Few showers, hot. 25-27 Sunny, hot; showers north. 28-30 Milder, sunny.

JULY 1996: Temp. 85° (1° below avg.; 1° above south); Precip. 1.5" (1" below avg.; 1" above northeast). 1-4 Mild, showers. 5-10 Clear, hot. 11-17 Cool; showers. 18-23 Mild; showers, heavy north. 24-31 Hot then seasonable, showers.

AUG. 1996: Temp. 84.5° (1° below avg.; avg. south); Precip. 1.5" (1" below avg.; 1" above south). 1-4 Clear, warm. 5-10 Showers, mild. 11-15 Showers north, hot. 16-19 Mild, sprinkles. 20-25 Rain, heavy south; cool. 26-31 Warm; showers, heavy south.

SEPT. 1996: Temp. 79° (1° above avg.; avg. south); Precip. 2" (1.5" above avg.; 0.5" above southeast). 1-5 Rain, seasonable. 6-9 Cold, showers. 10-18 Hot and dry. 19-21 Mild, sprinkles. 22-24 Showers, hot. 25-30 Mild, then warm.

OCT. 1996: Temp. 71° (3° above avg.); Precip. 3.3" (0.5" below avg.; 1" above west). 1-6 Clear, hot. 7-11 Cold; rain, heavy west. 12-14 Sunny, hot. 15-22 Warm, sunny. 23-29 Cold, heavy rain. 30-31 Clear, cold.

Advertisement

Mother's Thin Hair Problem
By John Peters

My mother's hair was extremely thin. She was terribly embarrassed by it. You could look right through the hair and see large spots of exposed scalp; and she had split ends. She tried everything available but nothing worked. Today, my mother's hair looks thick and gorgeous; she looks younger, and you would never know she had a problem.

She credits her new hair look to Neutrolox™ hair thickening cream. I told my mother about this great product. I also have a severe hair thinning problem and was at my wits end until I discovered **Neutrolox™**.

The product is so effective that we both are getting compliments on the appearance of our hair for the first time in years. We honestly believe in **Neutrolox™**. We know you will too! It's great for men and women and can be used on color-treated or processed hair. Try **Neutrolox™**, if you don't agree I'll send every penny of your money back—no one can beat a 100% no-risk money-back guarantee. **To order send $11.95 for a small or SAVE money by sending $15.95 for a medium, or the most savings come with the large for $24.95.** Please add $1.00 S&H for each order. Send to:

Neutrolox, Dept. FRM-N
Box 366, Taylor, MI 48180

Mother's Wrinkle Problem
By James Brothers

My dear mother's face was covered with wrinkles, she had severe prune lips, crows feet and dark age spots that were getting worse. *Tears would come to her eyes when she spoke of the old days when her face glowed with perfection.* She was so embarrassed by her appearance, she had nearly given up hope when we discovered a cream, **NEW FACE WRINKLE AND AGE SPOT™** and the **New Face Plan™**.

In just a few weeks, we could see a remarkable transformation in the appearance of her skin. **My mother's wrinkles began disappearing, her facial muscles tightened up and she no longer had severe drooping jowls. The age spots had faded; and she looked like a million dollars without those horrible deep-seated prune lips.**

Today mother looks years younger. She is getting honest compliments for the first time in years on how great she looks. She swears by the cream and the plan and recommends it to everyone. It's 100% guaranteed to work for you or your money back. **To order NEW FACE™** send $16.95 plus $3.00 S&H to: **Total Research, Inc., Dept NF-FRM, Box 667, Taylor, MI 48180**

Say you saw it in the OFA!

- Wildflowers are gorgeous, easy to grow, and they attract birds and butterflies!
- They return every spring and bloom through fall!
- One sack covers 750 sq. ft.! • 15 varieties in all!

```
MICHIGAN BULB COMPANY          S96
1950 WALDORF, N.W., GRAND RAPIDS, MICHIGAN 49504
MR.
MRS.                     BX 8130 A 4
MS.
MISS_____
             PLEASE PRINT
ADDRESS_____
CITY_____STATE____ZIP_____
☐ 1 Sack of Wildflowers  $12.95*  #20644
☐ 2 Sacks of Wildflowers $24.90*  Save $1.00
Add $2.90 postage and handling no matter how many you order.
    * MI res. add 6% sales tax.  * TN res. add 8.25% sales tax.
         * MO res. add 5.725% sales tax.
  $              .       TOTAL AMOUNT
```

REGION 13

ROCKY MOUNTAINS
FORECAST

SUMMARY: *The period from November through March will be warmer and wetter than normal in central and northern sections, but near normal or slightly below west and south. Snowfall will be above normal. The first half of November will be warm and dry, but then wintry weather will arrive and persist through December. Warmer than normal weather should then appear and persist through mid-February, with central and northern sections receiving well above normal precipitation due primarily to a snowstorm shortly after mid-January. The latter half of February and parts of March will also be cold, wet, and snowy.*

Spring is expected to be colder than normal over the region, with above-normal precipitation and snowfall in the north, below normal in the south. A cold and snowy period after the first week of April and cool and wet weather through much of May and the first half of June will be relieved by mild and dry periods in each month.

The summer months will vary only slightly from normal in temperature across the region, with below-normal rainfall. Northern and western sections will be cool in early and mid-July and especially at the end of August and early September, but will be otherwise warm and dry. The rest of the region will see brief variations about the mean, with frequent showers. Early fall will start warm and dry, then turn cold, wet, and snowy.

NOV. 1995: Temp. 39° (2° below avg.); Precip. 1" (Avg.; 1" below north). 1-4 Warm; sprinkles north. 5-7 Cold; rain south. 8-11 Sunny, mild. 12-14 Cold, rain south, snow mountains. 15-18 Mild, cold nights. 19-22 Snow. 23-26 Cold. 27-30 Snow, cold.

DEC. 1995: Temp. 30° (Avg.); 2° below south); Precip. 1" (0.5" below avg.; 0.5" above west). 1-4 Clear, cold. 5-8 Sleet, snow. 9-11 Sunny, mild. 12-14 Rain, snow north. 15-19 Clear, mild. 20-24 Cold, flurries. 25-27 Snow. 28-31 Clear, cold.

JAN. 1996: Temp. 35° (7° above avg.; 4° above south); Precip. 2.5" (1.5" above avg.; avg. south). 1-3 Clear, mild. 4-6 Snow, cold. 7-10 Sunny, mild. 11-13 Snow, then rain. 14-17 Clear, warm. 18-20 Snow, cold. 21-25 Warm, rain. 26-31 Cold then clear, warm.

FEB. 1996: Temp. 36° (2° above avg.; avg. south); Precip. 0.7" (0.5" below avg.). 1-4 Showers, mild. 5-8 Clear, warm. 9-12 Rain, mild. 13-17 Light snow, cold. 18-22 Showers, snow north. 23-26 Clear, cold; snow east. 27-29 Light snow.

MAR. 1996: Temp. 42° (Avg.); Precip. 1.5" (0.5" below avg.). 1-3 Clear, warm. 4-7 Cold; snow. 8-10 Sunny, warm. 11-14 Clear, warm; showers south. 15-17 Cold, snow north. 18-22 Clear, mild. 23-26 Cold; rain, snow. 27-31 Sunny, warm.

APR. 1996: Temp. 48° (2° below avg.); Precip. 2" (Avg.; 0.5" below south). 1-3 Seasonable, light snow. 4-8 Sunny, warm. 9-11 Cold, snow. 12-15 Heavy snow north. 16-19 Clear, warm. 20-22 Rain central, cool. 23-27 Warm; showers. 28-30 Warm.

MAY 1996: Temp. 63° (6° below avg.); Precip. 2" (Avg.; 0.5" above north). 1-5 Cold, rain, snow mountains. 6-10 Sunny, warm. 11-14 Cold; rain, snow. 15-20 Sunny, milder; snow south. 21-24 Cold, rain, snow mountains. 25-31 Cold, showers.

JUNE 1996: Temp. 65° (4° below avg.; 7° below north and west); Precip. 1" (Avg.; 0.5" above north). 1-2 Cold, rain. 3-6 Cool, rain north and west. 7-11 Showers. 12-15 Warm. 16-18 Showers, mild. 19-24 Warm; showers. 25-27 Sunny, warm. 28-30 Cold.

JULY 1996: Temp. 78° (Avg.; 1° below north); Precip. 0.8" (Avg.). 1-5 Hot; showers north and east. 6-12 Clear, hot. 13-15 Mild, showers; hot west. 16-22 Warm, rain; clear north. 23-26 Showers. 27-31 Warm, few showers.

AUG. 1996: Temp. 76° (Avg.); Precip. 1" (Avg.; 2" above northwest). 1-6 Mild; showers, heavy central. 7-11 Clear, warm. 12-14 Thundershowers, mild. 15-18 Hot, clear. 19-22 Few showers, hot. 23-27 Sprinkles. 28-31 Showers, mild.

SEPT. 1996: Temp. 68° (3° above avg.; 1° above south); Precip. 0.5" (1" below avg.). 1-3 Mild; showers. 4-7 Clear, cool. 8-11 Sunny, warm. 12-14 Sprinkles. 15-18 Clear, warm. 19-21 Few showers. 22-25 Sunny. 26-30 Seasonable, clear.

OCT. 1996: Temp. 55° (2° above avg.; 1° below south); Precip. 1" (0.5" below avg.). 1-3 Mild; showers north. 4-8 Clear, then cold. 9-13 Sunny, warm. 14-21 Seasonable, showers. 22-28 Cold, snow mountains. 29-31 Clear, warm.

REGION 14

SOUTHWEST DESERT FORECAST

SUMMARY: *The period from November through March will be cooler and wetter than normal in the north, near normal in the south, and warmer and drier than normal in the east. After a warm and dry first half of November, cold fronts with heavy rains will dominate the weather through early December. The weather will be mostly cold and wet from mid-December through early January, turn warm and dry until mid-February, and then return to a pattern of cold fronts bringing rain and snow until early March. Thereafter, look for warm spells with a few showers the second and final weeks, with seasonable temperatures in between.*

The spring months will be cooler than normal, especially in the west, with close to normal precipitation. April will be cold and clear at midmonth, cold and wet at the end. May will be dominated by cold periods after midmonth. June will also have some cold snaps, but end with a hot spell.

The summer overall is expected to be drier than normal; it will be cooler than normal in the north, warmer in the south. Following a heat wave the first week of July, the summer rains will arrive, with heavy showers and milder temperatures extending into early August. Thereafter, hot temperatures will prevail through September, with light showers in August and virtually none in September. Early fall will be sunny and pleasant.

NOV. 1995: Temp. 61° (1° below avg.; avg. south and east); Precip. 2" (1.5" above avg.; avg. east). 1-5 Clear, warm. 6-10 Sunny, warm; showers east. 11-14 Rain, mild. 15-18 Clear, pleasant. 19-21 Rain, cool. 22-26 Clear, cold nights. 27-30 Cold, rain.

DEC. 1995: Temp. 52° (2° below avg.); Precip. 1" (Avg.). 1-3 Clear, freezing. 4-6 Mild, rain. 7-11 Cold nights; frost. 12-15 Warm; cold nights. 16-19 Unseasonably warm, sunny. 20-23 Rain, seasonable. 24-26 Showers, cold. 27-31 Clear, frost.

JAN. 1996: Temp. 53.5° (Avg.; 4° above east); Precip. 0.3" (0.4" below avg.). 1-3 Cool; showers east. 4-6 Cold, rain. 7-10 Clear, warm. 11-13 Cool, rain. 14-17 Sunny, warm. 18-21 Showers, cold. 22-25 Warm, clear. 26-28 Cold. 29-31 Sunny, warm.

FEB. 1996: Temp. 55° (3° below avg.; 1° below south); Precip. 0.3" (0.4" below avg.). 1-3 Warm, cold nights. 4-12 Clear, warm. 13-17 Cold, showers, then clear. 18-22 Warm; cold nights. 23-25 Cold. 26-29 Mild; then rain, snow.

MAR. 1996: Temp. 61° (1° below avg.; 1° above south and east); Precip. 1" (Avg.). 1-2 Clear, seasonable. 3-6 Rain, cold. 7-10 Warming. 11-14 Seasonable, few showers. 15-19 Sunny, cold nights. 20-23 Showers. 24-29 Clear, warm. 30-31 Cold, showers.

APR. 1996: Temp. 67° (3° below avg.; 1° below south); Precip. 0" (0.2" below avg.; 0.5" above east). 1-3 Cold, few showers. 4-7 Clear, warm. 8-16 Cold, few showers. 17-23 Sunny, warm. 24-26 Cold; rain. 27-30 Clear, warm.

MAY 1996: Temp. 74° (5° below avg.); Precip. 0.7" (0.5" above avg.; avg. south and east). 1-3 Cold, rain. 4-6 Clear, cold. 7-10 Seasonable. 11-17 Clear, cold. 18-20 Rain north; cold. 21-26 Sunny, warm. 27-31 Showers, cold.

JUNE 1996: Temp. 95° (3° below avg.; avg. south, 1° above east); Precip. 0" (Avg.). 1-5 Cold, then warming. 6-12 Sunny, warm. 13-16 Rain, hot. 17-20 Clear, hot. 21-23 Clear, mild; rain east. 24-30 Sunny, hot.

JULY 1996: Temp. 92° (1.5° below avg.; 1° above south); Precip. 0.6" (0.2" below avg.). 1-5 Clear, hot. 6-10 Mild, light rain. 11-15 Showers, hot. 16-21 Rain, mild. 22-26 Sunny, hot; showers east. 27-31 Showers, mild.

AUG. 1996: Temp. 90° (1.5° below avg.; avg. south); Precip. 0.5" (0.5" below avg.). 1-4 Rain, mild. 5-10 Clear, hot; cool nights. 11-14 Mild, sprinkles. 15-21 Hot. 22-28 Seasonable; sprinkles. 29-31 Mild, rain.

SEPT. 1996: Temp. 85° (Avg.; 2° above south); Precip. 0" (1" below avg.). 1-2 Rain. 3-6 Clear, mild. 7-18 Clear, hot; sprinkles. 19-21 Sunny, seasonable. 22-28 Clear, hot. 29-30 Sunny, seasonable.

OCT. 1996: Temp. 73° (1.5° below avg.); Precip. 0" (0.5" below avg.). 1-2 Warm; cool nights. 3-6 Sunny, hot. 7-11 Clear; cold nights. 12-21 Warm. 22-27 Mild; cold nights. 28-31 Clear, cool.

REGION 15
PACIFIC NORTHWEST FORECAST

SUMMARY: *The period from November through March will be warmer and drier than normal in the north, close to normal in temperature, and wetter than normal in central and southern sections. Expect significant variability over the region from month to month. Snowfall will be below normal over the region.* November will be mostly mild and dry past midmonth, followed by rain and then a cold, dry spell extending into December. Thereafter, relatively mild and wet weather will prevail through most of January before cooler weather with frequent showers becomes dominant, particularly during the latter half of February and much of March.

The spring months will be cold and wet central and south, with above-normal snowfall, and closer to normal in temperature and precipitation in the north. It may get progressively cooler and wetter through May and June, broken only by brief hot and dry spells.

The summer will be warmer than normal in the north, but cooler than normal in central and southern sections, with below-normal rainfall over the region. Hot spells are predicted for early July, mid-August, and throughout September. The latter half of July and early and late August will be cool. Drier than normal conditions will prevail, particularly in September, except for heavy rains central and south at the end of August. Early fall will be warmer and much wetter than normal.

NOV. 1995: Temp. 44° (2° below avg.; 2° above north); Precip. 2" (3" below avg.). 1-5 Rain, cold. 6-10 Sunny, showers north. 11-13 Clear, cold nights. 14-19 Rain, snow mountains. 20-22 Clear, cold. 23-25 Showers. 26-30 Clear, cold.

DEC. 1995: Temp. 40° (Avg.; 3° above north); Precip. 6" (Avg.; 2" below north). 1-4 Cold, clear. 5-8 Snow then rain, mild. 9-13 Rain, locally heavy. 14-17 Rain, warm. 18-24 Cold then seasonable, showers. 25-27 Rain. 28-31 Cold.

JAN. 1996: Temp. 45° (5° above avg.); Precip. 11" (6" above avg.). 1-5 Rain, mild. 6-8 Rain, mild. 9-11 Clear, cold. 12-17 Heavy rain, mild. 18-20 Light rain, cool. 21-25 Heavy rain, floods. 26-28 Showers, warm. 29-31 Cold; rain, snow.

FEB. 1996: Temp. 45° (1° above avg.); Precip. 4" (Avg.; 1" below north). 1-5 Rain, mild. 6-12 Rain, warm south. 13-15 Cold, sunny. 16-18 Showers, cold north. 19-23 Rain, snow mountains; cold. 24-27 Showers, flurries. 28-29 Clear, cold.

MAR. 1996: Temp. 46° (1° below avg.; avg. north); Precip. 3.5" (Avg.; 0.5" below north). 1-6 Cold; showers. 7-13 Sprinkles then clear, warm. 14-18 Rain, then cold. 19-26 Rain, cold. 27-29 Showers, warm. 30-31 Cool, showers north.

APR. 1996: Temp. 50° (1° below avg.); Precip. 2" (0.5" below avg.). 1-4 Cold; rain, snow mountains. 5-7 Sunny, mild. 8-11 Showers, cold. 12-14 Sunny, seasonable. 15-18 Rain, cool. 19-23 Sunny, warm. 24-26 Cool, rain. 27-30 Warm, rain.

MAY 1996: Temp. 55° (2° below avg.; 1° above north); Precip. 3" (1" above avg.). 1-5 Rain, cold. 6-10 Warm, sunny. 11-13 Cold, rain. 14-16 Clear, warm. 17-21 Cool, showers. 22-28 Rain, cold. 29-31 Mild, rain.

JUNE 1996: Temp. 60° (3° below avg.); Precip. 1.5" (Avg.). 1-3 Cold, showers. 4-8 Showers, cool. 9-11 Rain, cold. 12-14 Clear, warm. 15-17 Cold, rain. 18-20 Sunny, seasonable. 21-24 Cold, showers. 25-30 Cold; rain.

JULY 1996: Temp. 67° (1° below avg.; avg. north); Precip. 0.5" (Avg.). 1-3 Rain, cold. 4-7 Sunny, seasonable. 8-10 Clear, hot. 11-14 Showers, mild. 15-18 Sprinkles, cool. 19-23 Warm, then showers, cold. 24-25 Clear, mild. 26-31 Cool.

AUG. 1996: Temp. 66.5° (2° below avg.); Precip. 1.5" (0.5" above avg.). 1-4 Sunny, warm. 5-7 Cold, sprinkles. 8-12 Rain, cool. 13-17 Clear, hot. 18-19 Showers, cool. 20-22 Sunny, warm. 23-26 Cool, sprinkles. 27-31 Rain.

SEPT. 1996: Temp. 63° (Avg.; 2° above north); Precip. 0.5" (1" below avg.). 1-5 Cool, rain. 6-8 Clear, hot. 9-11 Mild, sprinkles. 12-14 Sunny, warm. 15-18 Sprinkles, mild. 19-21 Clear, cool. 22-24 Sunny. 25-30 Rain, then clear.

OCT. 1996: Temp. 54.5° (Avg.; 2° above north); Precip. 2.5" (2" above avg.). 1-5 Heavy rain, cold. 6-11 Clear, warm. 12-14 Rain, seasonable. 15-19 Mild. 20-24 Rain, seasonable. 25-28 Clear, cold. 29-31 Sunny, mild.

REGION 16 CALIFORNIA FORECAST

SUMMARY: *The period from November through March is expected to be warmer than normal in the north, cooler than normal in the south. Precipitation will be above normal west, below south and east. Snowfall will be well above normal in the northern mountains and close to normal central and south. After a warm first half, November will have heavy rain and snow in the mountains. December will also have heavy rain and snow, particularly in the north. January will be warm with possible floods in the northwest, while February will be dry. Cold in the second half of February and in March will bring frosts to the central valley.*

Spring will be cooler than normal, particularly inland, with above-normal precipitation. April through early May will be particularly variable in temperature. A cold wave in May will bring heavy rain and snow to the north. It will be cold through mid-June, with light rain south and heavy rain north, before turning warm and dry.

Summer will be cooler than normal along the coast, but close to normal inland, with below-normal rainfall over the region. July and September both may see lengthy hot spells inland. August will be mostly seasonal. Early fall will see generally cooler than normal temperatures, with below-normal precipitation the latter half of October.

NOV. 1995: Temp. 57° (2° above avg.; 2° below south); Precip. 2" (1" below avg.). 1-6 Cool coast; warm inland. 7-11 Sunny, warm. 12-16 Seasonable, sprinkles. 17-20 Rain, snow mountains. 21-25 Clear, mild. 26-30 Showers south, cool.

DEC. 1995: Temp. 51° (1.5° above avg.; 1° below south); Precip. 7" (4" above avg.; avg. south). 1-3 Cold. 4-7 Heavy rain, snow. 8-10 Clear, mild. 11-14 Rain and snow, heavy north. 15-17 Clear; hot south. 18-25 Cold, then heavy rain, snow. 26-31 Showers, cool.

JAN. 1996: Temp. 52° (3° above avg.; avg. south); Precip. 4.5" (Avg.). 1-6 Rain; cool south. 7-9 Clear; hot south. 10-14 Cold, showers, then clear. 15-21 Light rain, cool. 22-25 Rain, floods north. 26-31 Clear; warm, then cool.

FEB. 1996: Temp. 53° (1° above avg.); Precip. 1" (2" below avg.). 1-2 Clear, cold nights. 3-5 Sunny, warm. 6-9 Cool, sprinkles. 10-13 Showers; warm south. 14-18 Warm coast, cold nights. 19-23 Cool, few showers. 24-29 Showers south; cold nights inland.

MAR. 1996: Temp. 53° (Avg.; 1° below south); Precip. 2" (1" below avg.). 1-3 Warm. 4-6 Showers, frost inland. 7-12 Clear, warm. 13-16 Cold, rain north, snow mountains. 17-20 Clear, cool. 21-24 Rain, snow mountains. 25-27 Clear, warm. 28-31 Sunny, cool.

APR. 1996: Temp. 53.5° (2° below avg.); Precip. 2.5" (1" above avg.). 1-2 Seasonable; showers south. 3-9 Cool; warm inland. 10-14 Rain, snow mountains. 15-19 Clear, mild. 20-24 Rain south, cool. 25-29 Clear. 30 Cold.

MAY 1996: Temp. 57° (1° below avg.); Precip. 0.7" (0.5" above avg.). 1-5 Rain, snow mountains. 6-9 Warm. 10-13 Cool, showers. 14-16 Sunny. 17-20 Light rain, cool. 21-23 Seasonable. 24-27 Light rain, cool. 28-31 Cold, showers.

JUNE 1996: Temp. 58° (3.5° below avg.; 2° below south); Precip. 0.5" (0.5" above avg.). 1-5 Showers, cold. 6-9 Seasonable. 10-13 Showers, cool. 14-19 Sunny, warming. 20-23 Showers, cool. 24-30 Sunny, warm.

JULY 1996: Temp. 60° (3° below avg.; 1° above south, inland); Precip. 0" (Avg.). 1-5 Clear, warm. 6-10 Clear, hot inland; sprinkles north. 11-13 Sprinkles. 14-19 Cool, hot south. 20-31 Cool; hot inland.

AUG. 1996: Temp. 60.5° (3° below avg.); Precip. 0" (Avg.). 1-4 Seasonable. 5-8 Cool; sprinkles north. 9-12 Warm, clear. 13-17 Cool; warm inland. 18-24 Cool, sprinkles north; warm inland. 25-31 Cold.

SEPT. 1996: Temp. 62.5° (2° below avg.); Precip. 0" (0.2" below avg.). 1-3 Cold; rain. 4-8 Hot inland; cool coast. 9-12 Seasonable. 13-17 Clear, hot. 18-24 Cool; clear inland. 25-30 Mild.

OCT. 1996: Temp. 61° (Avg.; 1° below south); Precip. 0.5" (0.5" below avg.). 1-5 Cool; mild inland. 6-10 Hot, clear. 11-14 Few showers, mild. 15-21 Clear, cool; sprinkles. 22-28 Showers, mild. 29-31 Clear, warm.

The Beauty of Boxwood

"The glory of Lebanon shall come unto thee, the pine tree, the box, to beautify the place of my sanctuary."

– Isaiah 60:13

EMMA EDMUNDS remembers the boxwood of her Virginia childhood and tells how to grow this most ancient and satisfying of plants in gardens as far north as USDA Zone 4.

❦ WHEN I LOOKED OUT OF THE BEDROOM window of my childhood, the plant that defined the landscape was boxwood. Boxwood formed the boundaries of my grandmother's garden, with borders of iris, larkspur, hollyhocks, and roses. A single row of boxwood against a white rail fence kept back the orchard; a double row of ancient boxwood formed a path to a circle of wisteria-draped cedar trees.

In the summer my sisters and I played hide-and-seek in the boxwood, finding places to burrow down under the low branches in the holes the hunting dogs dug in the soil to keep cool. I got my first kiss at 14, when an opportunistic fellow visiting from another town asked me to go for an evening stroll along the boxwood path.

Ours was not the only home bejeweled with boxwood. When I walked the mile to downtown, I passed boxwood adorning the landscape of the village's grandest mansions and lining the walkways of the most modest of white frame homes. We were Virginians all, and if you lived in Virginia, boxwood was the shrub of your heritage.

Some claim boxwood first came to North America in 1652, brought by Nathaniel Sylvester to Sylvester Manor, his Long Island estate. But Virginians knew boxwood must  have been brought to Jamestown in 1619 on the boat that brought such mainstays of southern life as honeysuckle, English sparrows, wild onions, and women.

" The gardens of the old South were built to a great extent around the wonderful boxwood," writes Don Hastings in *Gardening in the South*. "No other plant has all its characteristics of being a near-perfect foundation, small background, or border plant."

There are over 100 species of boxwood worldwide, in a variety of sizes and colorations. It grows in the temperate and tropical climates in Korea, Japan, and China. In South Africa, *Buxus macowani* thrives in the wooded sand dunes of the Eastern Cape. France and Italy have natural stands of boxwood. Hardy in USDA Zones 4 through 9, it can be cultivated successfully in parts of Canada, as well as in most regions of the United States.

Blissfully ignorant of the wealth of choices in the outside world, we in Halifax, Virginia, knew only of English and American boxwood. English — a slow-growing, beautiful dwarf variety — was always the boxwood of choice. It is vivid green, compact, elegant, refined, with small elliptical leaves; its Latin name is *Buxus sempervirens* 'Suffruticosa' (shrubby).

The second

The background photo on these two pages shows the boxwood garden at the author's family home. *Inset: Buxus sempervirens* 'Graham Blandy,' a naturally columnar form, in the garden of Mr. and Mrs. Charles Waltz, Charlottesville, Virginia.

– Background photo by Beth Robertson / inset photo by Decca G. Frackelton

type was the faster-growing so-called American boxwood, *Buxus sempervirens* 'Arborescens' (treelike). Its leaf is much the same as the English box, but the Arborescens can grow ten to 15 feet over the decades. Perhaps, as only staid Virginians can, we looked down our noses a bit on anything that changed so dramatically.

When I look out the bedroom window of my Atlanta condo, the dominant pattern in my tiny garden is made by English boxwood transplanted from my parents' home in Virginia, where my father tends hundreds of boxwoods from the tiniest sprouts that will survive all of us to the giant mounds of green that are older than anyone I know.

THE LEGACY

Virginians have no claim to boxwood exclusivity, and even English boxwood is not English; American, not American. Consider the plant's rich history:

🌿 Evidence of the pollen of boxwood has been found in digs of Pliocene Ice Age sites in 20 locations in Europe.

🌿 When King Midas's tomb was discovered in 1957, an eighth-century B.C. table made of boxwood with a juniper inlay and walnut top was among the findings.

🌿 The early Greeks and Romans planted boxwood for decorative purposes and also used the dense, pale wood for tablets, flutes, and spinning tops. The highly prized wood is still used by wood engravers and in furniture inlays.

🌿 At the end of the 1500s, garden designers such as Mollet began to make the first edgings of box. Its advantage: unlike santolina and thyme, it did not have to be replaced every three years. Gradually box came to be accepted on European royal estates as the basis for complex "embroidered" arabesques, such as those at Versailles, Vaux, and Chantilly.

🌿 In the late 1600s English gardeners began reacting against French formality, calling geometric clipped hedges and avenues "unnatural." Boxwood, the backbone of those hedges, went out of fashion in England for a couple of centuries, although American gardeners, particularly in the South, continued to prefer the traditional formal layout of boxwood knots and edgings.

PLANTING and

Though some people make a fuss about boxwood being difficult, you can follow these guidelines and choose plants suited to your climate to ensure a less-taxing experience.

🌿 Plant in a well-drained location with some shade.

🌿 Because boxwood roots feed on the surface, don't dig a hole any deeper than the root ball. Water well when planting.

🌿 Mulch with about one inch of shredded bark, pine needles, or other nonclogging materials. Never let the mulch touch the main trunk or lowest branches.

🌿 Maintain at least an inch of mulch under boxwood to keep weeds down (feeder roots are close to the surface and can be severely damaged by any cultivation). Weed by hand only.

Because English boxwood grows by producing an extremely dense outer foliage, it does well in a natural, billowing form, rather than as clipped hedging and topiary.

He refuses to sell one of them. He gives them to his children, and he grows them with hope for his grandchildren. He instructs his family to clip them for Christmas wreaths, and he supervises as we decorate the mantels with them.

He presents boxwood at proper occasions as gifts to people whom he believes deserve the honor. When his church got a new minister, my father didn't ruminate for a second over his gift of welcome. He dug up a little boxwood, put it in a bushel basket, and placed the basket on the front pew as his present for the Rev. Michael Coleman. To the basket he attached a note with a quote from Keats: "A Thing of Beauty Is a Joy Forever."

GROWING GUIDELINES

Boxwood thrives in the lacy shade of locust trees; locusts also produce nitrogen, which boxwood likes. The plants are deeper green in color when grown in partial shade.

- Water deeply at least once a week if you don't get rain. Continue until the plant is established (about two years). A very small plant needs to be babied for three to four years.

- Fertilize new plants in late winter. Established boxwood should not be fertilized every year. Do not fertilize in spring.

- Boxwood tolerates, even welcomes, thinning. Clean out the center of the plant at least once a year, preferably in spring. English boxwood, in particular, produces a very dense canopy of outer foliage, which you must thin so sunlight and air will penetrate to the middle. Thin or pluck inside twigs and branches so new growth will develop. Remove dead leaves and debris by hand or by squirting a strong stream of water from the hose.

Buxus microphylla 'Compacta' at Willow Oaks, the Harriman family home in Virginia.

This lush specimen of *Buxus harlandii* at the College of William and Mary is 7 feet tall and 4 feet wide.

MORE *Boxwood*, PLEASE!

❦ The simplest way to propagate boxwood is to take cuttings in late summer and stick them in the ground, protected from the wind, on the north side of large existing boxwood. The length of the cutting depends on the size of the plant (small for small plants). Take a cutting of at least three inches; strip leaves off bottom inch, and trim with a pocket knife. Use a soilless mix for the rooting medium — shredded pine bark and perlite or perhaps half and half of coarse sand and peat moss. (Use no topsoil; shovel it away and use four to five inches of peat moss.) Don't let the cuttings dry out.

BOXWOOD SPECIES GROWN IN THE U.S.

There are at least 100 species of boxwood worldwide, but four are most commonly used in the United States. In Zone 4 and in cold spots in Zone 5, Korean boxwood tends to be the hardiest and is most successful in coastal areas. Favorable local conditions (protected locations, ample moisture, and other amenities) can make nearly a whole zone's difference.

❦ **Buxus microphylla.** A fast-growing Oriental boxwood, introduced to America after 1860 and often seen on the West Coast. Zones 5-9.

B. microphylla var. *japonica*, or Japanese little-leaf boxwood. Used heavily in Charleston and Savannah because it withstands heat and shearing. Its leaves are shinier and more leathery and have a yellowish cast. Zone 6.

❦ **Buxus sempervirens,** or common boxwood. The basic European species. Many European species will not withstand intense heat. Zones 6-9.

B. sempervirens 'Suffruticosa' (suffruticosa — "shrubby"), or true dwarf boxwood. Commonly called English boxwood, this dwarf variety produces a dense canopy of outer foliage, is a slow grower, and will not withstand intense heat.

B. sempervirens 'Arborescens' (arborescens — "treelike"), or true tree boxwood. Commonly known as American boxwood, this variety grows taller and at a faster rate than Suffruticosa, though the leaves are similar.

B. sempervirens 'Vardar Valley' (after a river in Yugoslavia). Blue-green leaves, low, spreading.

B. sempervirens 'Fastigiata.' An upright, vertical-growing plant with dark shiny green leaves. May reach eight feet in 15 years.

B. sempervirens 'Graham Blandy.' A narrow columnar boxwood that grows vertically and tightly and seldom gets more than 18 inches wide.

❦ **Buxus sinica.** A Chinese species with many varied forms. Tiny-leafed type grows slowly into a tight, compact mound suitable for bonsai. Zones 4-8.

B. sinica var. *insularis*. Korean boxwood, used frequently in the last ten years. Some Korean boxes are slow growing and willowy.

B. sinica var. *insularis* 'Justin Browers.' Has a dainty leaf; excellent dark color; maximum height, 30 inches.

B. sinica var. *insularis* 'Tide Hill.' Needs shade. Soft, fluffy, low-growing, spreading plant; two feet high with unlimited width. Plant on north side of house.

❦ **Buxus harlandii.** Chinese boxwood, also used in Charleston and Savannah because it withstands heat. Beautiful plant with long slender leaves. Needs a protected location out of the wind. Zone 8.

(continued on page 154)

The Big New Park Seed® Catalog

"With color so real you can almost smell the beautiful flowers and taste the luscious vegetables!"

Our big, 124 page catalog is chock-full of delights for your garden... Artichokes to Zucchini — Ageratum to Zinnia — from the most advanced new varieties and the rare, to your long-time favorites. Here in one big color catalog you'll find over **1,800 quality products**: flower and vegetable seed, bulbs, plants and garden supplies — many available only from Park. We back each and every one with a solid guarantee of complete satisfaction.

Have more fun gardening this year with **Park High Performer® varieties** — flowers more beautiful and easier to grow, vegetables with better taste and higher yield. Park tests thousands each year to make sure you get only the best. **Send for your free copy today and let Park Help You Grow!**

Complete Satisfaction Guaranteed
"Home Garden Seed Specialists Since 1868"

❑ *Send FREE Color Catalog*

Please Print   BZ 706

Name _____

Address _____

_____ Apmt. ____

City _____

State _____ Zip _____

Park Seed Co.
Cokesbury Rd. PO Box 46
Greenwood, SC 29648-0046

PESTS AND PESTILENCE

🌿 *Boxwood leaf miner.* This insect is the worst pest, nesting and tunneling between the upper and lower surface of the leaf. Larvae develop and emerge, creating big holes in the leaves. The leaf miner can kill boxwood. American boxwood is most susceptible. Call your cooperative extension agent for local remedies.

🌿 *Boxwood psyllid.* This is the next most dangerous pest. The psyllid feeds on very early new growth and causes new leaves to curl. Very unsightly, but easy to control. Call your cooperative extension agent.

🌿 *English boxwood decline.* This disease applies only to 'Suffruticosa.' The preventive remedy is to thin English boxwood once a year to allow light and air to penetrate to the center. If an English boxwood is destroyed by the disease, another cannot be planted in its place.

WHERE TO SEE Boxwood

🌿 **American Boxwood Society's Memorial Garden,** State Arboretum of Virginia, Blandy Experimental Farm, Boyce, VA 22620; 703-837-1458. Garden landscaped with 100 *Buxus* species and cultivars.

🌿 **Colonial Williamsburg,** P.O. Box C, Williamsburg, VA 23187; 804-229-1000. With 4½ miles of boxwood in the historic area, the plant is hard to miss.

🌿 **Green Animals Topiary Gardens,** Cory's Lane, Portsmouth, RI 02871; 401-683-1267. Fantastical animals and mazes of boxwood.

🌿 **North Carolina State University Arboretum,** 4301 Beryl Rd., Raleigh, NC 27695; 919-515-7641.

🌿 **Oatlands Plantation,** Rte. 2, Leesburg, VA 22075; 703-777-3174. A 260-acre property with historic gardens.

🌿 **Old Westbury Garden,** 71 Old Westbury Rd., Old Westbury, NY 11568; 516-333-0048. The 88-acre grounds were built in 1906 to re-create an English country estate.

🌿 **United States National Arboretum,** 3501 New York Ave. NE, Washington, D.C.; 202-245-2726. Over 150 varieties in the Boxwood Collection.

Buxus sempervirens topiary graces the Bryan House garden at Colonial Williamsburg, Virginia.

RESOURCES

🌿 **The American Boxwood Society,** P.O. Box 85, Boyce, VA 22620. Sponsors research projects, publishes *The Boxwood Bulletin* quarterly, sponsors workshops and seminars, and maintains a Memorial Garden. $15 membership includes subscription to *The Boxwood Bulletin*.

🌿 *Boxwood Handbook: A Practical Guide to Knowing and Growing Boxwood* ($15), published by the American Boxwood Society.

🌿 *Boxwood Buyer's Guide* ($8), also published by the American Boxwood Society. Lists people all over the U.S. who sell boxwood.   ☐☐

What does it take to be "The World's Best Aerobic Exerciser®"?

It takes a total-body exerciser.
A machine capable of exercising all the major muscle groups in your body, not simply your legs like treadmills, exercise bikes and stairsteppers.

It takes a cardiovascular exerciser.
A machine that uses enough muscle mass to readily exercise your heart, not simply specific muscle groups like weight machines.

It takes a weight-bearing exerciser.
A machine that uses the standing position to exercise the joints and long bones of the skeleton, not simply a few muscle groups like sit-down exercisers.

It takes a safe exerciser.
A machine that can't damage your knees like stairsteppers, or your back like hydraulic-cylinder rowers, or throw you off like treadmills.

NordicTrack Pro® model

It takes a calorie burning exerciser.
A machine capable of burning up to 1,100 calories per hour. And able to burn more fat than stairsteppers, treadmills and exercise bikes.

It takes an exerciser that you'll use.
Studies show that 7 out of 10 owners still use their NordicTrack® exerciser an average of three times a week after five years. Join the over 3 million NordicTrack users — Call today!

It takes a NordicTrack.

30-day in-home trial!

NordicTrack®

©1995 NordicTrack, Inc., A CML Company • All rights reserved.

- **Independently Adjustable Upper-Body Exerciser**
  works extensor muscles of the back, trunk, rotators, biceps, triceps, shoulders, chest and upper back.

- **Patented Flywheel and One-Way Clutch Mechanism**
  ensures maximum workout efficiency and virtually eliminates the risk of injury.

- **Independently Adjustable Lower-Body Exerciser**
  works hip flexors, gluteus muscles, thighs, hamstrings, knee extensors, ankles and calves.

- **Stand-Up Position**
  exercises muscles and the skeleton.

- **Rugged Wooden Skis**
  glide on hard, rubber rollers to ensure smooth, quiet operation.

- **Adjustable Elevation**
  raises the front legs to intensify your workout.

FREE VIDEO & BROCHURE
CALL: 1-800-441-7891
Ext. TF615

❏ Please send me a FREE video & brochure
My main fitness goal is (check one) ❏ Weight loss
❏ Shaping & toning ❏ Cardiovascular fitness ❏ Overall health

Name _____
Street _____
City _____ State _____ Zip _____
Phone ( ) _____

Call or send to: NordicTrack, Dept. TF615
104 Peavey Road, Chaska, MN 55318-2355

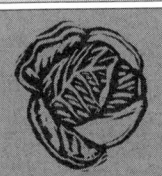

First Guess

_____ Apple
_____ Artichoke
_____ Asparagus
_____ Avocado
_____ Bean (String)
_____ Beet
_____ Broccoli
_____ Brussels Sprouts
_____ Cabbage
_____ Carrot
_____ Cauliflower
_____ Celery
_____ Corn
_____ Cucumber
_____ Eggplant
_____ Grape
_____ Lettuce
_____ Onion
_____ Parsnip
_____ Pea
_____ Peach
_____ Pear
_____ Pepper
_____ Plum
_____ Potato
_____ Radish
_____ Raspberry
_____ Squash
_____ Tomato
_____ Watermelon

– illustrated by Carol O'Malia

IS IT A Fruit? OR IS IT A VEGETABLE?

(AND DOES IT MATTER?)

A game of botany, cooking, and common sense by Georgia Orcutt

There was a time not so very long ago when schoolteachers and other people of authority frequently spoke of doing things "according to Hoyle." If, as a small child, you were caught misbehaving, chances are Mr. Hoyle's sense of rightness was invoked by a governing adult.

Hoyle, in fact, was an Englishman who spent a good part of his life prescribing rules and regulations for all sorts of indoor games. He died in 1769. And we sorely miss him today, as we set out to play a game that might be easier if we could simply refer to his rules to settle any disputes that might occur. The game is called "Fruit or Vegetable?"

The object of this exercise is educational in nature. As you make your choices, think about the differences between fruits and vegetables. How do they grow, what parts of the plant do you eat? Since we don't have Mr. Hoyle's rules to follow, we'll use reference books to guide us through several versions of the game. These are *The New Garden Encyclopedia* (A) and *Wyman's Gardening Encyclopedia* (B).

Now let's get started. Read through the list

at left and decide whether each food mentioned is a fruit or a vegetable. In the space provided to the left of each item, write V next to those that you think of as vegetables and F next to those that you think of as fruits. (Use a pencil with an eraser.)

• • •

Now that you've categorized these familiar fruits and vegetables, let's consider several ways to judge your answers.

The Botanically Correct Version

■ If you've ever taken a botany course, you know that every part of a plant, whether fruit or vegetable, has a name. There's a science to it all, the sort of thing Mr. Hoyle would appreciate. So let's look at some definitions. "Botanically and strictly, fruit is the ripened ovary of a flower, including its contents and any closely adhering parts. Examples are cucumber, pepper, tomato, apple, plum, raspberry" (see source A). Or even more to the point, fruit is "the seed-bearing product of a plant" (source B).

According to the botanists, the parts of squash, eggplant, watermelon, cucumber, and pepper that we eat are actually very large berries, so we are correct to call them fruit. With this light to guide us, we can safely determine that avocado, string bean, grape, peach, and pear are also, of course, fruit. Corn and peas also have seeds, so we may as well include them. Maybe we ought to rename that plot out back the fruit garden.

Wait, you wail. You've never called a cucumber or a string bean or a squash a fruit in your life, and you're not about to start now. You don't *like* that version of the game.

Maybe it's time to consider fruits and vegetables from the cook's point of view.

The Culinary Version

■ Let's play another way, starting with a definition for vegetable as "any plant whose edible part is used in some culinary way, as distinguished from a 'fruit,' which is used as a dessert" (source A).

Look back over that list one more time and think about how you would prepare those foods in your kitchen. What is dessert and what isn't? Surely asparagus is a vegetable, apple a fruit, avocado goes in salads so that must be a vegetable, artichokes, beans, broccoli, Brussels sprouts are surely vegetables . . . is this starting to feel better? Now carrots we bake in carrot cake, so they must be fruit. That sets us to thinking about squash pie, so we'll call squash a fruit, too.

What's that you're yelling? You want to play by some other rules? There is another possibility.

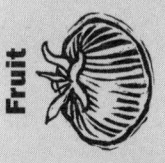
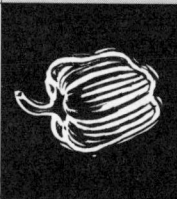

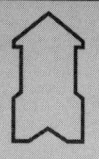

  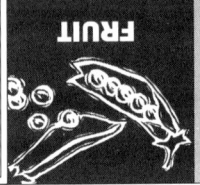 

Common Sense Version

■ In the name of sportsmanship, let's consider one more way to look at fruits and vegetables. "According to L. H. Bailey, a vegetable is 'in horticultural usage, an edible herbaceous plant or part thereof that is commonly used for culinary purposes.' In common usage, the fruits of the tomato, cucumber, squash, etc., are considered as vegetables, grown with other vegetables in the home garden, although of course each one is a seed-bearing organ and hence, under strict usage of the language, might be considered a fruit" (source B). It is also, as popularly understood, any plant cultivated for its edible parts. This loose definition includes roots (beet, carrot), tubers (potato), stems (celery), leaves (lettuce), flower buds and heads (cauliflower), fruits (tomato), and seeds (peas, corn) (source A).

Looking back to the list, we can easily slip into familiar habits: artichoke, asparagus, avocado, bean, beet, broccoli, Brussels sprouts, cabbage, carrot, cauliflower, celery, corn, cucumber, eggplant, lettuce, onion, parsnip, pea, pepper, potato, radish, squash, and tomato are vegetables; all the others are fruits.

In other words, if you call it a vegetable, and your neighbor calls it a vegetable, and your local grocer calls it a vegetable, then it must be a vegetable. You like the sound of this? Fine with us. And deep in our hearts, we suspect that's the best way to play, according to Hoyle.

Advice from Hope, Arkansas

No, not from the president. But it's a pretty good diplomatic solution . . .

■ In 1979 Ivan Bright and his son, Lloyd, of Hope, Arkansas, harvested a watermelon weighing 200 pounds, then the largest ever grown (the current record is 262 pounds). Their horticultural prowess attracted garden writers aplenty, and the Brights generously conducted tours of their farm and talked openly about their secrets. Standing in the middle of a sea of sprawling vines, with huge watermelons all around, Ivan was asked if a watermelon was a fruit or a vegetable. A look of pure surprise came into his eyes. He slowly shook his head. "I dunno," he said in a soft voice. "To me it's jess watermelon."

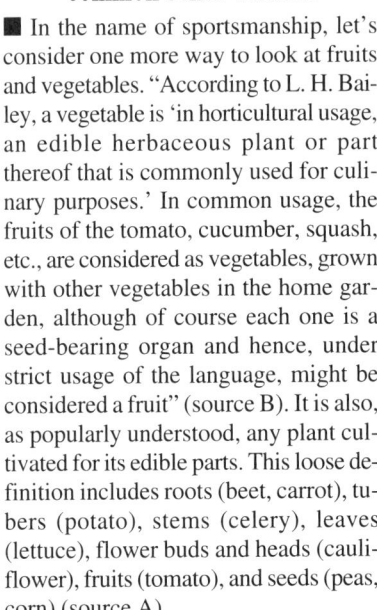

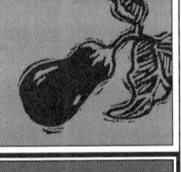

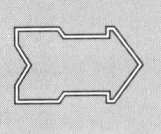   

 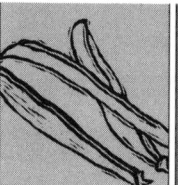   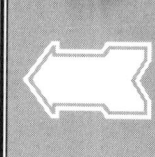

	Botanical	Culinary	Common Sense (see "First Guess")
Apple	F	F	F
Artichoke	V	V	V
Asparagus	V	V	V
Avocado	F	V	F/V
Bean (String)	F	V	V
Beet	V	V	V
Broccoli	V	V	V
Brussels Sprouts	V	V	V
Cabbage	V	V	V
Carrot	V	F/V	V
Cauliflower	V	V	V
Celery	V	V	V
Corn	F	V	V
Cucumber	F	V	V
Eggplant	F	V	V
Grape	F	F	F
Lettuce	V	V	V
Onion	V	V	V
Parsnip	V	V	V
Pea	F	V	V
Peach	F	F	F
Pear	F	F	F
Pepper	F	V	V
Plum	F	F	F
Potato	V	V	V
Radish	V	V	V
Raspberry	F	F	F
Squash	F	F/V	V
Tomato	F	V	V
Watermelon	F	F	F

In the Eyes of the Law

In 1893 the U.S. Supreme Court decided that a tomato was a vegetable!

■ While it may seem frivolous to ponder the differences between fruits and vegetables, more than 100 years ago the tomato's status became legal fodder for the U.S. Supreme Court in the case of Nix v. Hedden.

In 1887 a businessman importing tomatoes from the West Indies tried to sue the Port of New York to recover back duties he'd been forced to pay to bring his produce into the country. He was, in fact, trying to elude a tariff imposed on vegetables by claiming that tomatoes were fruits. (Fruits were not subject to the tariff.)

He fought hard, and his case spiraled up through the judicial system until it reached the Supreme Court in 1893. Definitions of fruits and vegetables from several dictionaries were read at the trial, and two professional fruit and vegetable sellers who served as witnesses for the plaintiff were asked to reflect on the matter. The Court's decision: Tomatoes are "vegetables" and not "fruit" within the meaning of the Tariff Act of March 3, 1883.

In the opinion of the court, "Botanically speaking, tomatoes are the fruit of a vine, just as are cucumbers, squashes, beans, and peas. But in the common language of the people, whether sellers or consumers of provisions, all these are vegetables, which are grown in kitchen gardens, and which, whether eaten cooked or raw, are, like potatoes, carrots, parsnips, turnips, beets, cauliflower, cabbage, celery, and lettuce, usually served at dinner in, with, or after the soup, fish, or meats which constitute the principal part of the repast, and not, like fruits generally, as dessert." ❏❏

Frosts and Growing Seasons

Courtesy of National Climatic Center

Dates given are normal averages for a light freeze (32° F); local weather and topography may cause considerable variations. The possibility of frost occurring after the spring dates and before the fall dates is 50 percent. The classification of freeze temperatures is usually based on their effect on plants, with the following commonly accepted categories: **Light freeze:** 29° F to 32° F — tender plants killed, with little destructive effect on other vegetation. **Moderate freeze:** 25° F to 28° F — widely destructive effect on most vegetation, with heavy damage to fruit blossoms, tender, and semihardy plants. **Severe freeze:** 24° F and colder — heavy damage to most plants.

CITY	Growing Season (Days)	Last Frost Spring	First Frost Fall	CITY	Growing Season (Days)	Last Frost Spring	First Frost Fall
Mobile, AL	272	Feb. 27	Nov. 26	North Platte, NE	136	May 11	Sept. 24
Juneau, AK	133	May 16	Sept. 26	Las Vegas, NV	259	Mar. 7	Nov. 21
Phoenix, AZ	308	Feb. 5	Dec. 15	Concord, NH	121	May 23	Sept. 22
Tucson, AZ	273	Feb. 28	Nov. 29	Newark, NJ	219	Apr. 4	Nov. 10
Pine Bluff, AR	234	Mar. 19	Nov. 8	Carlsbad, NM	223	Mar. 29	Nov. 7
Eureka, CA	324	Jan. 30	Dec. 15	Los Alamos, NM	157	May 8	Oct. 13
Sacramento, CA	289	Feb. 14	Dec. 1	Albany, NY	144	May 7	Sept. 29
San Francisco, CA	*	*	*	Syracuse, NY	170	Apr. 28	Oct. 16
Denver, CO	157	May 3	Oct. 8	Fayetteville, NC	212	Apr. 2	Oct. 31
Hartford, CT	167	Apr. 25	Oct. 10	Bismarck, ND	129	May 14	Sept. 20
Wilmington, DE	198	Apr. 13	Oct. 29	Akron, OH	168	May 3	Oct. 18
Miami, FL	*	*	*	Cincinnati, OH	195	Apr. 14	Oct. 27
Tampa, FL	338	Jan. 28	Jan. 3	Lawton, OK	217	Apr. 1	Nov. 5
Athens, GA	224	Mar. 28	Nov. 8	Tulsa, OK	218	Mar. 30	Nov. 4
Savannah, GA	250	Mar. 10	Nov. 15	Pendleton, OR	188	Apr. 15	Oct. 21
Boise, ID	153	May 8	Oct. 9	Portland, OR	217	Apr. 3	Nov. 7
Chicago, IL	187	Apr. 22	Oct. 26	Carlisle, PA	182	Apr. 20	Oct. 20
Springfield, IL	185	Apr. 17	Oct. 19	Williamsport, PA	168	Apr. 29	Oct. 15
Indianapolis, IN	180	Apr. 22	Oct. 20	Kingston, RI	144	May 8	Sept. 30
South Bend, IN	169	May 1	Oct. 18	Charleston, SC	253	Mar. 11	Nov. 20
Atlantic, IA	141	May 9	Sept. 28	Columbia, SC	211	Apr. 4	Nov. 2
Cedar Rapids, IA	161	Apr. 29	Oct. 7	Rapid City, SD	145	May 7	Sept. 29
Topeka, KS	175	Apr. 21	Oct. 14	Memphis, TN	228	Mar. 23	Nov. 7
Lexington, KY	190	Apr. 17	Oct. 25	Nashville, TN	207	Apr. 5	Oct. 29
Monroe, LA	242	Mar. 9	Nov. 7	Amarillo, TX	197	Apr. 14	Oct. 29
New Orleans, LA	288	Feb. 20	Dec. 5	Denton, TX	231	Mar. 25	Nov. 12
Portland, ME	143	May 10	Sept. 30	San Antonio, TX	265	Mar. 3	Nov. 24
Baltimore, MD	231	Mar. 26	Nov. 13	Cedar City, UT	134	May 20	Oct. 2
Worcester, MA	172	Apr. 27	Oct. 17	Spanish Fork, UT	156	May 8	Oct. 12
Lansing, MI	140	May 13	Sept. 30	Burlington, VT	142	May 11	Oct. 1
Marquette, MI	159	May 12	Oct. 19	Norfolk, VA	239	Mar. 23	Nov. 17
Duluth, MN	122	May 21	Sept. 21	Richmond, VA	198	Apr. 10	Oct. 26
Willmar, MN	152	May 4	Oct. 4	Seattle, WA	232	Mar. 24	Nov. 11
Columbus, MS	215	Apr. 8	Oct. 29	Spokane, WA	153	May 4	Oct. 5
Vicksburg, MS	250	Mar. 13	Nov. 18	Parkersburg, WV	175	Apr. 25	Oct. 18
Jefferson City, MO	173	Apr. 26	Oct. 16	Green Bay, WI	143	May 12	Oct. 2
Fort Peck, MT	146	May 5	Sept. 28	Janesville, WI	164	Apr. 28	Oct. 10
Helena, MT	122	May 18	Sept. 18	Casper, WY	123	May 22	Sept. 22
Blair, NE	165	Apr. 27	Oct. 10				

*Frosts do not occur every year

Stark Bro's Wants To Give You Both Of These!

Send today for your **FREE** copy of Stark Bro's Fruit Trees and Landscaping Catalog and receive a $5.00 Discount Coupon.

Full-color catalog features a broad selection of fruit and nut trees, berries, grapes, shade and ornamental trees and much more!
Quality products since 1816!

1-Year Promise of Satisfaction

Mail this coupon today or call TOLL FREE **1-800-775-6415**. Ask for offer A2369R.
Stark Bro's Nurseries & Orchards Co., Box 10, Dept. A2369R, Louisiana, MO 63353-0010

A2369R

Mail today for your FREE catalog and $5.00 discount coupon

Print Name _____
Address _____
_____
City _____
State _____ Zip _____
Home Phone (____) _____

LEARN THE SECRETS TO GUARANTEED SUCCESS
From information on tree selection, to a simple-to-use planting zone map, Stark Bro's Catalog offers all you'll need for successful landscaping and luscious fruit trees.

Sorry, catalogs not mailed outside continental U.S.

OUTDOOR PLANTING TABLE
1996

The best time to plant flowers and vegetables that bear crops above the ground is during the *light* of the Moon; that is, between the day the Moon is new to the day it is full. Flowering bulbs and vegetables that bear crops below ground should be planted during the *dark* of the Moon; that is, from the day after it is full to the day before it is new again. The dates given here are based on the safe periods for planting in areas that receive frost, and the Moon's phases for 1996. Consult page 160 for dates of frosts and length of growing season. See calendar pages 52-78 for the exact days of the new and full Moons.

☞ Above-Ground Crops Marked (*)   ☞ E means Early   ☞ L means Late

	Planting Dates	Moon Favorable	Planting Dates	Moon Favorable	Planting Dates	Moon Favorable
*Barley	5/15-6/21	5/17-6/1, 6/15-21	3/15-4/7	3/19-4/3	2/15-3/7	2/18-3/5
*Beans (E)	5/7-6/21	5/17-6/1, 6/15-21	4/15-30	4/17-30	3/15-4/7	3/19-4/3
(L)	6/15-7/15	6/15-30, 7/15	7/1-21	7/15-21	8/7-31	8/14-28
Beets (E)	5/1-15	5/4-15	3/15-4/3	3/15-18	2/7-28	2/7-17
(L)	7/15-8/15	7/31-8/13	8/15-31	8/29-31	9/1-30	9/1-11, 9/27-30
*Broccoli (E)	5/15-31	5/17-31	3/7-31	3/19-31	2/15-3/15	2/18-3/5
Plants (L)	6/15-7/7	6/15-30	8/1-20	8/14-20	9/7-30	9/12-26
*Brussels Sprouts	5/15-31	5/17-31	3/7-4/15	3/19-4/3	2/11-3/20	2/18-3/5, 3/19-20
*Cabbage Plants	5/15-31	5/17-31	3/7-4/15	3/19-4/3	2/11-3/20	2/18-3/5, 3/19-20
Carrots (E)	5/15-31	5/15-16	3/7-31	3/7-18	2/15-3/7	2/15-17, 3/6-7
(L)	6/15-7/21	7/1-14	7/7-31	7/7-14, 7/31	8/1-9/7	8/1-13, 8/29-9/7
*Cauliflower (E)	5/15-31	5/17-31	3/15-4/7	3/19-4/3	2/15-3/7	2/18-3/5
Plants (L)	6/15-7/21	6/15-30, 7/15-21	7/1-8/7	7/15-30	8/7-31	8/14-28
*Celery Plants (E)	5/15-6/30	5/17-6/1, 6/15-30	3/7-31	3/19-31	2/15-28	2/18-28
(L)	7/15-8/15	7/15-30, 8/14-15	8/15-9/7	8/15-28	9/15-30	9/15-26
*Collards (E)	5/15-31	5/17-31	3/7-4/7	3/19-4/3	2/11-3/20	2/18-3/5, 3/19-20
(L)	7/1-8/7	7/15-30	8/15-31	8/15-28	9/7-30	9/12-26
*Corn, Sweet (E)	5/10-6/15	5/17-6/1, 6/15	4/1-15	4/1-3	3/15-31	3/19-31
(L)	6/15-30	6/15-30	7/7-21	7/15-21	8/7-31	8/14-28
*Cucumber	5/7-6/20	5/17-6/1, 6/15-20	4/7-5/15	4/17-5/3	3/7-4/15	3/19-4/3
*Eggplant Plants	6/1-30	6/15-30	4/7-5/15	4/17-5/3	3/7-4/15	3/19-4/3
*Endive (E)	5/15-31	5/17-31	4/7-5/15	4/17-5/3	2/15-3/20	2/18-3/5, 3/19-20
(L)	6/7-30	6/15-30	7/15-8/15	7/15-30, 8/14-15	8/15-9/7	8/15-28
*Flowers (All)	5/7-6/21	5/17-6/1, 6/15-21	4/15-30	4/17-30	3/15-4/7	3/19-4/3
*Kale (E)	5/15-31	5/17-31	3/7-4/7	3/19-4/3	2/11-3/20	2/18-3/5, 3/19-20

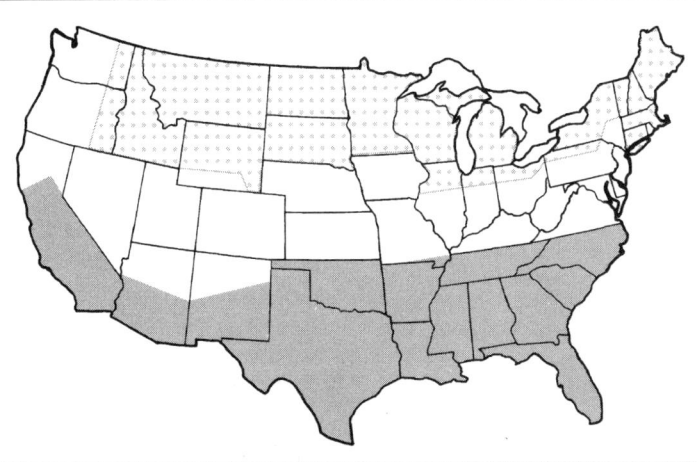

	Planting Dates	Moon Favorable	Planting Dates	Moon Favorable	Planting Dates	Moon Favorable
*Kale (L)	7/1-8/7	7/15-30	8/15-31	8/15-28	9/7-30	9/12-26
Leek Plants	5/15-31	5/15-16	3/7-4/7	3/7-18, 4/4-7	2/15-4/15	2/15-17, 3/6-18, 4/4-15
*Lettuce	5/15-6/30	5/17-6/1, 6/15-30	3/1-31	3/19-31	2/15-3/7	2/18-3/5
*Muskmelon	5/15-6/30	5/17-6/1, 6/15-30	4/15-5/7	4/17-5/3	3/15-4/7	3/19-4/3
Onion Sets	5/15-6/7	5/15-16, 6/2-7	3/1-31	3/6-18	2/1-28	2/5-17
*Parsley	5/15-31	5/17-31	3/1-31	3/19-31	2/20-3/15	2/20-3/5
Parsnips	4/1-30	4/4-16	3/7-31	3/7-18	1/15-2/4	1/15-19
*Peas (E)	4/15-5/7	4/17-5/3	3/7-31	3/19-31	1/15-2/7	1/20-2/4
(L)	7/15-31	7/15-30	8/7-31	8/14-28	9/15-30	9/15-26
*Pepper Plants	5/15-6/30	5/17-6/1, 6/15-30	4/1-30	4/17-30	3/1-20	3/19-20
Potato	5/1-31	5/4-16	4/1-30	4/4-16	2/10-28	2/10-17
*Pumpkin	5/15-31	5/17-31	4/23-5/15	4/23-5/3	3/7-20	3/19-20
Radish (E)	4/15-30	4/15-16	3/7-31	3/7-18	1/21-3/1	1/19, 2/5-17
(L)	8/15-31	8/29-31	9/7-30	9/7-11, 9/27-30	10/1-21	10/1-11
*Spinach (E)	5/15-31	5/17-31	3/15-4/20	3/19-4/3, 4/17-20	2/7-3/15	2/18-3/5
(L)	7/15-9/7	7/15-30, 8/14-28	8/1-9/15	8/14-28, 9/12-15	10/1-21	10/12-21
*Squash	5/15-6/15	5/17-6/1, 6/15	4/15-30	4/17-30	3/15-4/15	3/19-4/3
Sweet Potatoes	5/15-6/15	5/15-16, 6/2-14	4/21-30	none	3/23-4/6	4/4-6
*Swiss Chard	5/1-31	5/17-31	3/15-4/15	3/19-4/3	2/7-3/15	2/18-3/5
*Tomato Plants	5/15-31	5/17-31	4/7-30	4/17-30	3/7-20	3/19-20
Turnips (E)	4/7-30	4/7-16	3/15-31	3/15-18	1/20-2/15	2/5-15
(L)	7/1-8/15	7/1-14, 7/31-8/13	8/1-20	8/1-13	9/1-10/15	9/1-11, 9/27-10/11
*Watermelon	5/15-6/30	5/17-6/1, 6/15-30	4/15-5/7	4/17-5/3	3/15-4/7	3/19-4/3
*Wheat, Winter	8/11-9/15	8/14-28, 9/12-15	9/15-10/20	9/15-26, 10/12-20	10/15-12/7	10/15-26, 11/10-24
Spring	4/7-30	4/17-30	3/1-20	3/19-20	2/15-28	2/18-28

The Pure Pleasures of Country Cooking

BY JAMES HALLER

Forget periwinkle pâté and red pepper polenta, and remember instead the kind of food that made one Indiana grandmother a legend among her neighbors — and in the eyes of her grandson.

♥ THE FIRST TIME I EVER SAW MY GRANDMA HAZEL, SHE was killing chickens for dinner. I was four years old at the time and thought it was about the most interesting thing I'd ever seen: Grandma Hazel in the chicken yard backing a generous-looking hen into a corner, swooping it up by the feet, then scoping out a second victim. She grabbed a head and swung the body in a circle above her like David with his sling until it flew disconnected from the neck, then repeated the show with the second bird.

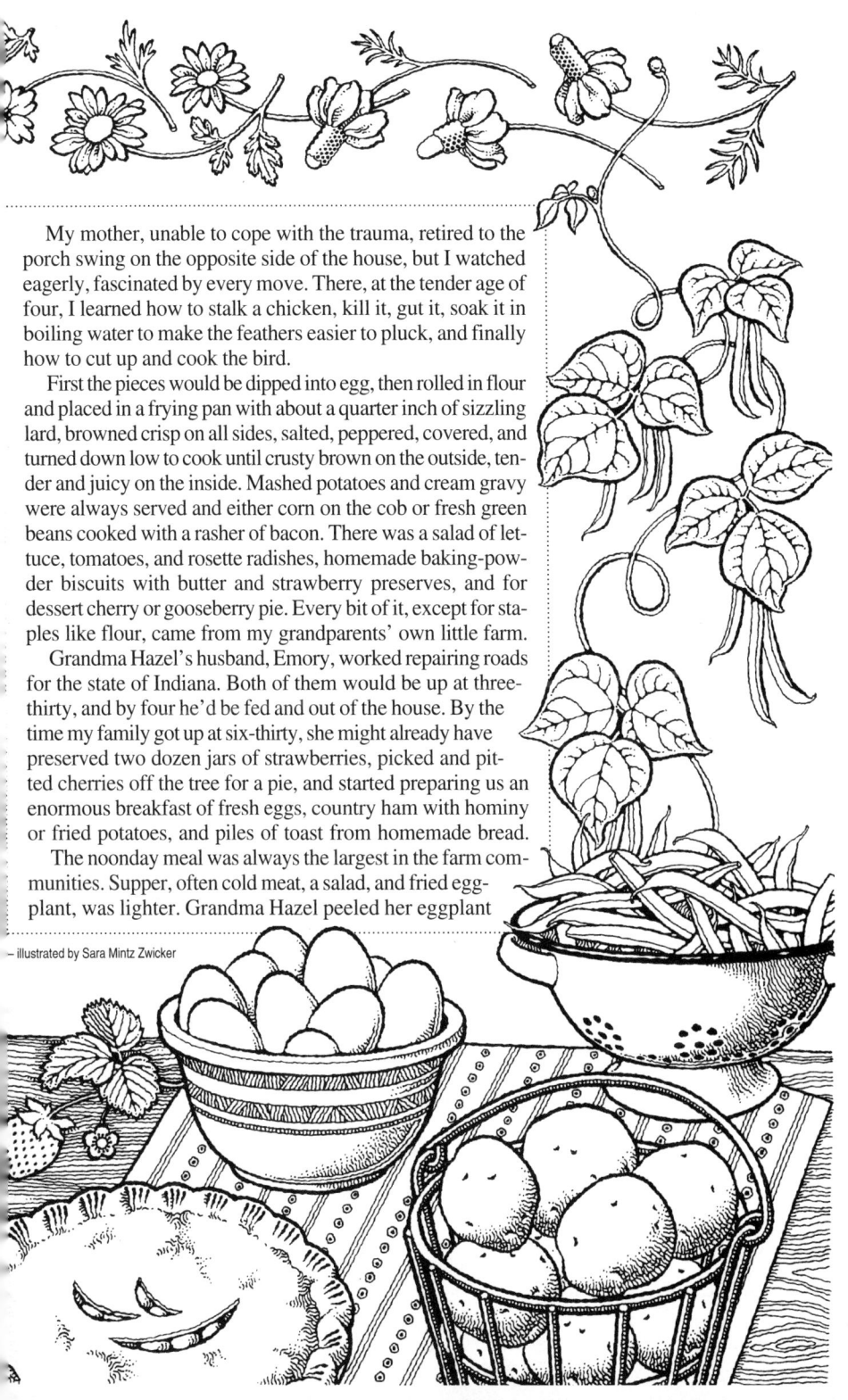

My mother, unable to cope with the trauma, retired to the porch swing on the opposite side of the house, but I watched eagerly, fascinated by every move. There, at the tender age of four, I learned how to stalk a chicken, kill it, gut it, soak it in boiling water to make the feathers easier to pluck, and finally how to cut up and cook the bird.

First the pieces would be dipped into egg, then rolled in flour and placed in a frying pan with about a quarter inch of sizzling lard, browned crisp on all sides, salted, peppered, covered, and turned down low to cook until crusty brown on the outside, tender and juicy on the inside. Mashed potatoes and cream gravy were always served and either corn on the cob or fresh green beans cooked with a rasher of bacon. There was a salad of lettuce, tomatoes, and rosette radishes, homemade baking-powder biscuits with butter and strawberry preserves, and for dessert cherry or gooseberry pie. Every bit of it, except for staples like flour, came from my grandparents' own little farm.

Grandma Hazel's husband, Emory, worked repairing roads for the state of Indiana. Both of them would be up at three-thirty, and by four he'd be fed and out of the house. By the time my family got up at six-thirty, she might already have preserved two dozen jars of strawberries, picked and pitted cherries off the tree for a pie, and started preparing us an enormous breakfast of fresh eggs, country ham with hominy or fried potatoes, and piles of toast from homemade bread.

The noonday meal was always the largest in the farm communities. Supper, often cold meat, a salad, and fried eggplant, was lighter. Grandma Hazel peeled her eggplant

– illustrated by Sara Mintz Zwicker

and sliced it into half-inch-thick pieces, which she salted and let sit overnight. This leached out the excess water and made the vegetable more firm. To cook it, she would dry it off, dip it in egg and cracker crumbs, then fry it in shortening to a toasty brown on both sides. Salt and pepper were the only seasonings she ever used. The taste was unmistakably eggplant. No herbs, no spice, not even garlic. We ate mounds of it.

On Sunday morning she baked the communion bread for the little Christian church to which they belonged, where Emory was a deacon. The "communion" was a large, crisp, thin bread, perfectly round and about 18 inches in diameter. There were always two, wrapped respectfully in white linen and carried on silver trays. The bread was passed from member to member along with a tray of tiny glasses of grape juice. Even nonmembers were invited to join.

The highlight of any local occasion was Grandma's angel food cake. Grandma Hazel could beat 13 egg whites into a meringue with just a fork. They were the highest angel food cakes I've ever seen, elegantly decorated with a "seven-minute icing" that never failed.

A seven-minute or "boiled" icing, as some people used to call it, is simpler than it sounds. The sugar and water and egg whites must be whipped together in a double boiler over rapidly boiling water for seven minutes. People did this using hand beaters, flat wire whisks, or like Grandma Hazel, forks. Imagine the relief that must have greeted the electric beater, which didn't become a common household item until the 1950s.

Grandma Hazel swirled her seven-minute icing lavishly over that tall, heavenly cake and decorated it with fresh strawberries. It surely was the best angel food cake ever, made by a woman who found great joy in her culinary ability to evoke a smile of awed satisfaction from the small grandson sitting at her table.

Every now and again I'll taste something — a piece of cake, or a bite of mashed potatoes and gravy, a chunk of fried eggplant — and I see that wide green field next to her white farmhouse, with the line of trees along the dusty road that ended at the back porch and her kitchen door. And for just a moment, an instant, it's all still there, and me with it.

Fried Chicken with Cream Gravy

1 egg
1 cup milk
1 frying chicken, cut up
2 cups flour
1/4 to 1/2 inch shortening or vegetable oil

❤ Whip egg and milk together. Dip the chicken pieces into the egg mixture, then roll them in flour. Heat shortening or oil in frying pan until it begins to sizzle, then add the chicken. Brown on all sides, salt and pepper lightly, cover pan, and turn heat to medium low. Cook for 30 to 40 minutes, turning the pieces at least once. Remove to a plate to keep warm.

Cream Gravy: Drain off all but about 2 tablespoons of the grease in the frying pan. Sprinkle 2 to 3 tablespoons flour into the pan and stir over medium heat until the flour begins to brown. Add, ¼ cup at a time, 2 cups milk, stirring well to keep the gravy smooth. Salt and pepper to taste.

Real Mashed Potatoes

5 pounds potatoes, peeled and halved
2 tablespoons butter
1 cup milk

❤ Put the cut-up potatoes into a pan and cover with cold water. Add a tablespoon of salt and bring to a boil. Cook until tender when poked with a fork. Drain off water and add butter and milk to the pan. With a masher or ricer, mash in the butter and milk until potatoes are smooth. Add extra milk if desired. Serve in a large bowl with a lump of butter, a sprinkle of pepper, and a little chopped parsley on top.

Just Plain Fried Eggplant

2 medium, firm eggplants
salt
2 eggs, beaten
2 cups cracker crumbs
1/4 cup shortening

♥ Peel eggplants and cut into ½-inch slices. Sprinkle with salt, cover, and let sit overnight in the refrigerator. Rinse and dry the eggplant, then dip each piece into the egg, then the cracker crumbs. Fry in melted shortening until crispy brown on both sides. Salt and pepper to taste.

Gooseberry Pie

2 cups gooseberries
1 cup brown sugar
1 cup white sugar
1 tablespoon flour
1 egg, well beaten
3 tablespoons melted butter
1/2 to 1 teaspoon cloves
pastry for 2 8-inch crusts
1 egg yolk beaten with
   1 tablespoon of water

♥ Mix gooseberries, sugars, and other ingredients and turn into an unbaked pie shell. Cover with the other crust and poke a few air holes to let out the steam. Paint the top crust with the egg wash and sprinkle generously with sugar. Bake at 450° F for 15 minutes, then reduce heat to 350° F and bake another 30 minutes.

Angel Food Cake

13 egg whites at room temperature
2 teaspoons cream of tartar
1/2 cup granulated sugar
2 teaspoons pure vanilla
1/4 teaspoon salt
1 cup all-purpose flour
2 cups powdered sugar

♥ Whip the egg whites and cream of tartar into stiff peaks while adding the granulated sugar 2 or 3 tablespoons at a time. Add the vanilla and salt. The egg whites should be stiff and shiny. Mix together the flour and powdered sugar and fold into the egg whites about ¼ cup at a time until completely mixed, then pour into an ungreased tube pan. Run a knife through the mixture a couple of times to get rid of any air pockets. Bake on the bottom rack of a preheated 375° F oven for 30 to 40 minutes, until the top springs back lightly when you touch it and the cake feels dry. Immediately invert the pan onto the neck of a glass bottle or funnel and let it hang there until the cake is completely cool (about 2 hours). Remove from the pan and ice.

Seven-Minute Icing

4 egg whites
3 cups sugar
10 tablespoons ice water
1/2 teaspoon cream of tartar
3 teaspoons corn syrup

♥ Combine ingredients in a double boiler and stir well. (If you don't have a double boiler, place a bowl on top of a saucepan of water.) Bring the water to a rolling boil, set your timer, and whip the mixture with a hand beater, electric beater, wire whisk, or even a fork for 7 minutes. The mixture will expand and turn a beautiful white. When the 7 minutes are up, remove from the heat and mix in 1 tablespoon vanilla. Whip for a few more minutes until the frosting is the desired consistency for spreading. Be generous!

□□

Master chef James Haller is the author of *Cooking in the Shaker Spirit* (with Jeffrey Paige, Yankee Books); *The Blue Strawberry Cookbook* (Harvard Common Press, 1976); *Another Blue Strawberry* (Harvard Common Press, 1983).

His latest project, a cookbook for people whose appetite is dulled by serious illness, grew out of 12 years' experience as a volunteer with Seacoast Hospice in Exeter, New Hampshire. *What to Eat When You Don't Feel Like Eating* is a small book filled with ideas for fresh, simple, and nutritious foods that will appeal to people who are sick and those who are on the road to recovery. It is distributed in the U.S. by the author (James Haller, Three Hills Distribution, P.O. Box 110, South Berwick, ME 03908; $10.60 including shipping).

WHAT YOU CAN EAT TO ACHIEVE PEACE OF MIND

TRUE

QUESTION:

What looks like a big green bean on the vine, takes up to five years to grow and process (making it the most labor-intensive agricultural product in the world), and is quickly becoming the hottest marketing concept of the decade? (Hint: the imitation product sometimes goes by the name of hydroxy-4 methoxy-3 benzaldehyde.)

It's VANILLA!

■ What was once a metaphor for things ordinary is suddenly on the cutting edge of fragrance and flavor. Four-star chefs are featuring it in desserts *and* main-dish fare (Wolfgang Puck of Spago fame likes it with lobster). The titans of Big Food are tallying up big sales with new vanilla-flavored coffees, yogurts, cake mixes, and frostings. With big profits riding on it, industry is doing all it can to catch the first whiff of the next vanilla craze. It could be in low-fat foods; flavor consultants say vanilla masks the off-taste that comes when you pull fat out of certain foods. And the cosmetics industry — buoyed by vanilla's alleged aphrodisiacal properties — is tripping all over itself to introduce the next in a stampede of new vanilla fragrances.

One trend watcher contends that the vanilla boom reflects America's yearning for a return to a less frenzied past. And there's at least circumstantial evidence that the link between vanilla and a peaceful state of mind is more than a figment of the imagination. In a recent hospital study of 85 patients conducted at New York's Memorial Sloan-Kettering Cancer Center, researchers found that a sweet vanilla scent reduced anxiety and lowered stress among 65 percent of patients who were undergoing magnetic-resonance-imaging (MRI) testing.

The bean responsible for all this brouhaha is a native of Central America, unknown on any other continent before its discovery there. The first to claim a piece of the vanilla action were the Aztecs, who became so smitten with the bean that they used it as tribute to the emperor, as trading currency, as perfume, and in chocolate drinks.

BY KEN

– Illustrated by Steve Buchanan

The vanilla orchid is a member of the plant family known as *Orchidaceae* and is the only orchid that produces edible fruit. The beans grow on a thick vine that flourishes in warm, moist climates within 25 degrees of the equator. The vanilla plant begins to bear fruit when it is three or four years old. Eight to nine months after pollination, the beans are golden yellow and ready for harvest and curing.

It takes about five to six pounds of green, freshly picked vanilla beans to make one pound of properly cured beans. There are basically two ways to cure the beans: in the sun or over a fire. Using the solar method, beans are spread in the hot sun by day and wrapped in blankets and placed in wooden boxes by night. The sweating process is repeated over and over for six months, until the beans have lost up to 80 percent of their moisture content. This method produces superior results and is used in Madagascar, Mexico, the former Bourbon Islands, Tonga, and Tahiti.

The wood-fire curing method, used in Indonesia and Bali, takes only two to three weeks, but produces a dry, brittle bean with a smoky flavor, generally considered inferior.

When you buy a vanilla bean at your market, the black, oily, smooth pod you're buying is a cured bean. When you purchase a bottle of pure vanilla extract, you're buying beans whose flavor components have been dissolved in a solution of water and alcohol. By law, pure vanilla extract must contain at least 35 percent alcohol by volume. Anything less is labeled a flavor. Pure vanilla extracts come in a variety of folds, or strengths. The Food and Drug Administration has established that a fold of vanilla is the extractive matter of 13.35 ounces of vanilla beans to a gallon of liquid. Strong, pure extracts, such as four-fold, are primarily used in mass food production.

WHAT ABOUT Imitation Vanilla?

■ Not only is pure vanilla expensive, but demand also far exceeds the world's supply of the real thing. Stepping in to fill the void is the chemist, who has come up with a variety of imitations made from synthetic

vanillin, the organic component that gives vanilla its distinctive flavor and fragrance. Most synthetic vanillin is a by-product of the paper industry, made by cooking and treating wood-pulp effluent. But since vanillin is only one of more than 150 flavor and fragrance compounds found in pure vanilla, the chemist has yet to match the subtlety with which Mother Nature has endowed the real thing.

How to Tell a GOOD BEAN When You See One

■ Quality is key. To truly experience all the flavor and fragrance vanilla has to offer, you have to seek out quality beans and extracts. Generally speaking, look for beans that are supple and aromatic. Tahitian beans are moister and relatively short and plump, with thin skins and a floral aroma. Bourbon beans (so called because they originate in Madagascar, Réunion, and the Comoros, formerly known as the Bourbon Islands) are slightly dryer, contain more natural vanillin, and have thick skins (the flavor has nothing to do with bourbon whiskey). Stay away from dry, brittle, or smoky-smelling beans. Depending on quality and variety, single vanilla beans retail from about $1.50 to $10 apiece. Vanilla beans should be kept at room temperature in an airtight container. Don't refrigerate them or they may develop mold. Vanilla beans last up to two years.

Especially if you cook with it often, it is more economical to buy pure vanilla extract by the pint, or even the quart, and share it with a friend (see Vanilla Sources). The best pure extracts contain no caramel and artificial color and little or no sugar. Store extract at room temperature, tightly closed. It will keep for up to five years.

Whether or not the vanilla boom will last as long as the beans themselves is anybody's guess. Enjoy it while you can. And don't be surprised if the next low-fat sausage you bite into tastes a bit like you know what.

USING VANILLA IN THE KITCHEN

■ Vanilla beans can be used more than once, though they tend to lose their potency with repeated use. Rinse the bean after using it, wipe dry, and store in an airtight container. Use it to flavor fruit compotes, custards, ice creams, rice puddings, tapioca, and hot drinks (chocolate, tea, coffee, or hot buttered rum).

■ To make your own vanilla extract, split and chop five or six long beans and put them in a quart of good vodka. Cover tightly and store in a dark, cool place for at least a month (preferably three), shaking the bottle occasionally. Brandy or cognac may also be used.

■ To make vanilla sugar for dusting on cakes or rolling freshly baked cookies in, put 4 cups of sugar and 1 long vanilla bean (split lengthwise and cut in pieces) in a food processor. Process until the bean pieces are well chopped. Store in an airtight container and use as needed, putting the sugar through a sieve or sifter first.

■ To make vanilla oil for salads or sautés — try it with poultry, delicately seasoned meats, seafood, and vegetables — place a long, split bean in a pint of good-quality cooking oil. Steep for a week or so and use as needed.

(continued on page 172)

10 Healthy Reasons to Send for your FREE! HERBALIST CATALOG

4 Men Over 50 (Saw Palmetto)

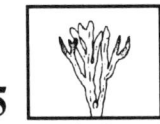
5 Weight Control (Bladderwrack)

6 Energy (Burdock)

7 Vascular Health (Garlic)

3 Vision (Bilberry)

8 Glowing Skin (Aloe Vera)

2 Memory (Ginkgo)

9 Breathe Easy (Mullein)

1 Antioxidant (Rosemary)

10 Healthy Hair (Kelp)

Herbs! The 1996 Herbalist Catalog features over 500 different herbs for helping you lead a healthier, more active life! These ancient healers have been used by mankind for over 4,000 years to soothe pain, increase energy and just look & feel better. Herbs work safely & gently so they do not have dangerous side-effects on your body as many drugs do.

Join the millions of people who have discovered the health benefits of natural and delicious herb teas...without the side-effects and costly doctor bills! Choose from over 500 different herb remedies, all backed by The Herbalist's famous guarantee--*your money back if you are not completely satisfied.*

Send for your FREE Big Herb Catalog TODAY!

THE HERBALIST CATALOG

☐ **YES! Send me my FREE 1996 Herbalist Catalog**
HERBALIST, P.O. Box 5 Dept OFMN
Hammond, IN 46325

Mr.
Mrs.
Ms. _____

Address _____

City _____

State _____ Zip _____

"Keeping America Healthy Since 1910" FC34

VANILLA AND DRIED PEAR GRANOLA

6 cups rolled oats
1 cup wheat germ
1 cup sliced almonds
1/2 cup flaked sweetened coconut
1/4 teaspoon ground cardamom or cinnamon
1/4 cup water
1/4 teaspoon salt
1/2 cup packed light brown sugar
1/4 cup flavorless vegetable oil
2 tablespoons pure vanilla extract
1 cup finely chopped dried pears

■ Mix oats, wheat germ, almonds, coconut, and spice in a large bowl. Bring water and salt to a boil in a small saucepan, lower heat, stir in brown sugar and oil, and stir for 1 minute over medium heat. Remove from heat and blend in vanilla. Pour hot liquid over oat mixture and mix well. Spread granola in a thin layer on 1 or 2 greased baking sheets. Toast at 250° F, stirring and rotating the sheets every 10 minutes for about 30 minutes, or until golden brown. Cool on the baking sheets, mix in pears, and store in sealed plastic bags.

Makes about ½ gallon.

VANILLA SOURCES

■ **KCJ VANILLA CO.**, P.O. Box 126-OF, Norwood, PA 19074. The most complete source of vanilla in the country. KC Jurchak sells single-, double-, and quadruple-strength vanilla extracts, all from premium vanilla beans and containing no artificial ingredients. Tahitian, Madagascar, and Mexican vanilla beans, pure vanilla powder, and pure vanilla sugar are also for sale. Catalog $1, includes 50 recipes.

■ **PATRICIA RAIN**, specialty food distributor, 116 Forest Ave., Dept. V, Santa Cruz, CA 95062; 408-457-0902; fax 408-457-2521. Ms. Rain is an expert on vanilla, has written a vanilla cookbook, and sells top-notch beans and extracts by mail. Write or call for her price list and product information.

■ **PENZEYS, LTD. SPICE HOUSE**, P. O. Box 1448, Waukesha, WI 53187; 414-574-0277. Sellers of pure vanilla extract and vanilla beans. Catalog free. MC, VISA.

The Old Farmer's Almanac REFERENCE CHARTS

ANNOUNCING
Our Newest Household Chart:

100 Unexpected Uses for Common Household Items from Vinegar, Salt, and Baking Soda to Lemon and Soap

Did you know that hot lemon juice will remove dried paint from glass, and that a little salt in the water will keep cut flowers fresh longer? Try a little vinegar in the water when rinsing your hair for extra shine and softness.

Guide to Spices & Herbs

Add spice to your life with our handy wall chart listing dozens of spices and herbs, their recommended uses in cooking and baking, interesting folklore, plus recipes for making your own special blends.

Useful Kitchen Reference Chart

Do you remember what to substitute if you've run out of baking powder or chocolate? Can you convert an ounce of flour to tablespoons? Send for our useful chart of substitutions for common ingredients and how to measure fruits and vegetables, plus a helpful table of weights and measures.

Handy Storage Chart

This handy chart lists how to store everything from onions to hockey pucks. Did you know that coffee keeps best in your refrigerator or freezer while bread should be kept at room temperature?

Guide to Weather Proverbs and Prognostics

In response to your questions about weather folklore, we have assembled a wide-ranging collection of time-honored weather proverbs and traditional weather-forecasting charts.

🍂 These decorative and informative charts are printed on sturdy stock. Please send $3 for each chart ordered to *The Old Farmer's Almanac*, Dept. Charts OFA96, P.O. Box 520, Dublin, NH 03444.

SPECIAL OFFER to *Old Farmer's Almanac* readers! GET ALL FIVE CHARTS FOR $12.

Introducing the Revolutionary **NEW!**

DR® POWER WAGON™

- HAULS 800 LBS!
- BIG POWER-DRIVEN WHEELS & 4 speed transaxle.
- Power Reverse!
- Dump bed. • *Made to order for suburban/rural property owners, businesses of any size; pays for itself over and over in time and labor saved!* Please write or call for complete FREE DETAILS of the Revolutionary **DR® POWER WAGON** including prices, specifications and "Off-Season" Savings now in effect.

TOLL FREE 1(800)215-1600

To: **COUNTRY HOME PRODUCTS®**, Dept. 577N Ferry Road, Box 89, Charlotte, VT 05445

HERNIA APPLIANCES
FOR COMFORT!
You can enjoy heavenly comfort night and day at work or at play! Send for FREE illustrated booklet.

BROOKS APPLIANCE COMPANY
120 State St., Marshall, Mich. 49068

Earn $4,000 Per Month From Your Home With A Computer!

Begin part-time and still retain the security of your present position. We offer 20 services you can perform for your community from your home. No experience necessary–easy to learn. We provide training and computer. For FREE explanation cassette and literature call:

1-800-343-8014, ext. 1194
Computer Business Services, Inc.

Your Fresh Fruits and Vegetables Need Water!
FREE INFO!

Now, find all the water you need with a water well you drilled yourself!

Since 1962, thousands of happy gardeners and homeowners around the world have discovered the **Hydra-Drill™** secret. They drilled their own wells and their gardens prove it! You can, too. Call or write us today and we'll send you a big, free package of information about drilling your own well with the **Hydra-Drill™**. We carry everything you need for your home water requirements, including pumps, tanks, and water purification products. We can even have your water tested for you.

Ask about our "How To..." video!

Call Today for FREE Water Well Drilling Information Package
1-800-333-7762
(Ask for Operator 7741)

DeepRock 7741 Anderson Road
Opelika, AL 36802

❑ **YES!** Send the **FREE INFORMATION PACKAGE** and the illustrated guide **HOW TO DRILL YOUR OWN WATER WELL.**

| Print Name |
| Address |
| City/State/Zip |
| Phone (must have) | © 1995 DeepRock |

Winning Recipes

in the **1995 RECIPE CONTEST**

Family-Tradition Ethnic Desserts

First Prize

Cardamom-Scented Carrot-Rice Pudding (Gajar Ki Kheer)

This recipe is originally from Pakistan and is a favorite everyday dessert. Rice puddings with a variety of styles are popular in both India, where I was born, and Pakistan. I have adjusted the recipe to my family's tastes.

- 1 quart half-and-half cream
- 1 quart milk
- 1/2 cup short-grain or pearl rice (do not use long-grain rice)
- 6 carrots, grated
- 1 cup sugar (or more to taste)
- 4 cardamom pods, lightly crushed, or 1 to 1-1/2 teaspoons ground cardamom
- blanched, slivered almonds

In a large, heavy pan over medium-high heat, bring cream, milk, and rice to a boil. Reduce heat to low and let simmer for 30 minutes, stirring often. In a separate pot bring 6 cups water to a boil. Blanch carrots in boiling water for 3 minutes and drain well. Add to milk-rice mixture. Add sugar and cardamom. Cook until mixture has thickened slightly, about 15 minutes. Cool and serve in individual bowls, sprinkled with almonds. **Serves 8 to 10.**

Farah Ahmed, Sunnyvale, California

Second Prize

Serbian Plum Dumplings

When my grandmother left Serbia in the early 1920s, she brought very little with her to the United States. One thing she brought was her recipe for plum dumplings. Handed down for generations, this is an heirloom our family can enjoy as often as we like without diminishing its value.

- 1-1/2 pounds potatoes (about 5 medium potatoes)
- 2 eggs, beaten
- 1 teaspoon salt
- 2 cups (approximately) flour
- 1/2 cup sugar
- 1 teaspoon cinnamon
- 14 small purple plums
- 1/2 stick butter, melted
- 1/4 cup toasted bread crumbs

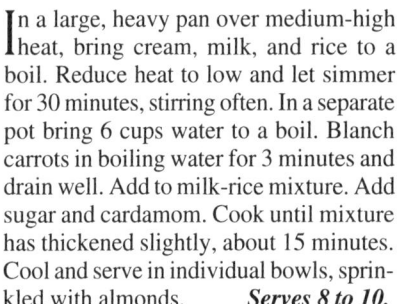

Peel potatoes and cut into quarters. Boil until tender. Cool, then mash until smooth. Add eggs and salt; mix well. Work enough flour into potato mixture to make a smooth, firm dough. In a separate bowl mix sugar and cinnamon. Pit plums and fill each cavity with 1 teaspoon of the cinnamon-and-sugar mixture.

Take a piece of dough and pat it into a round cake 2½ inches wide and about ¼ inch thick. Put one sugared plum in it, fold the dough over the plum, and pinch edges to seal, making a round dumpling. Repeat with the remaining plums and dough.

Drop dumplings one at a time into a large pot of boiling salted water, until water returns to the boil with all dumplings in the pot. Boil gently for 5 minutes, then turn down heat and simmer for about 15 minutes longer. Scoop out with a slotted spoon and place in serving bowl. Drizzle with melted butter, sprinkle with bread crumbs, and serve hot.

Makes 14 dumplings.

Marcelle LaMaster-Skelton, Bloomington, Indiana

(EDITOR'S NOTE: If fresh plums are not available, canned ones may be used if well drained and blotted dry. Dumplings also may be shaped into half-circles and may be prepared ahead, then reheated in hot water or the microwave oven.)

Third Prize

Norwegian Fruit Soup (Sot Suppe)

Served as dessert every Christmas Eve at our home, this recipe came from Norway in 1913 when my husband's parents arrived in this country. Any combination of dried fruits may be used, and every year my recipe changes. This is the basic recipe.

1/2 pound dark raisins
1/2 pound light raisins
1 pound small pitted prunes
3 cinnamon sticks, broken up
1 tablespoon whole cloves
6 cups water
4 tablespoons Minute tapioca
1/2 cup sugar
1 seedless orange, peeled, thinly sliced, then quartered
1 to 2 cups applesauce
1 cup orange juice or water as needed

Slowly bring raisins, prunes, cinnamon sticks, cloves, water, and tapioca to a boil, stirring occasionally. Cook gently until tapioca is transparent. Add sugar, orange slices, and applesauce. Add orange juice or water to thin the soup. Serve warm or chilled in bowls. Also delicious over sponge cake or ice cream. *Serves 8.*

Mary Linstad, Porterfield, Wisconsin

(EDITOR'S NOTE: Whole cinnamon and cloves may be tied first into a cheesecloth bag, then removed before serving.)

Our thanks go to Sylvia Wright and Rich Roth for their expertise in recipe judging and testing.

SPECIAL OFFER
to OLD FARMER'S ALMANAC READERS

Your response to this recipe contest was wonderful! Thank you for sharing your family treasures. We regret that we have space to publish only the three winning recipes. However, if you'd like to receive the ten recipes we selected (i.e., tested, tasted, argued over, and loved as much as the winners) for Honorable Mention, including Irish Potato Pie, Indian Saffron Bread Pudding, Hungarian Nut Torte, Raspberry-Orange Mazurkas, and six others, please send $2 and a self-addressed business-size envelope to Bonus Ethnic Recipes, *The Old Farmer's Almanac*, P.O. Box 520, Dublin, NH 03444.

ANNOUNCING
The 1996 RECIPE CONTEST

Salads

For 1996, cash prizes (first prize, $50; second prize, $25; third prize, $15) plus baskets of *Old Farmer's Almanac* brand-name foods will be awarded for the best original recipes for fresh salads (please include recipes for any accompanying dressings). All entries become the property of Yankee Publishing Incorporated, which reserves all rights to the materials submitted. Winners will be announced in the 1997 edition of *The Old Farmer's Almanac.* Deadline is February 1, 1996. Address: Recipe Contest, *The Old Farmer's Almanac*, P.O. Box 520, Dublin, NH 03444.

in the **1995 ESSAY CONTEST**

The Best Tried-and-True Way to Cure a Headache

First Prize

The best way to cure a headache (you'll have to judge how tried-and-true it is) was confided to me on his deathbed by my uncle Scotty (Clarence Scott). Scotty was an Albuquerque sheet-metal man who inherited about $1.1 million from a long-lost Canadian uncle in 1951.

He went into the greyhound dog racing business a few years later in Tampa, and he always said, "Those dogs are a devil of a headache." When Scotty was dogged out (his phraseology), he'd put a rolled-up kudzu vine between two flats of wood, hit that wooden sandwich with his sledge, suck up the juice with a natural bay sponge, and squeeze it into a half-glass of Florida orange juice.

Scotty swore that this recipe always fixed him right up, but I need to tell you that he expired in 1982 of emphysema while feeding a flock of really ugly Muscovy ducks with an oxygen tank on his back.   *Frederick O. Kiel, Cincinnati, Ohio*

Second Prize

The best tried-and-true way to get rid of a headache is to use a cocker spaniel. My cocker spaniel is black and white, but I don't think it's the color that matters. What matters is that his feet are big and he's not. In order for the treatment to work, I first have to figure out where the headache is located. This is important, since I need to rest my head just so. The paw rests on my eye on the affected side. If both sides of my head are affected, I rotate eyes and paws every five minutes. Obviously I do this lying down in a nice bed with soft pillows. Also, the room should be sort of dark. What's not so clear is that the dog's feet have to be nice and cool to have the best results. Therefore, having the dog walk on cold cement or frozen grass previous to headache work is best. Having a dog who is calm and flexible helps, too. I have found this method to be quite effective — and it lets me get a nap.

J. A. Strasser, Baltimore, Maryland

Third Prize

Headaches are really a pain. Wouldn't it be great if you could just wish them away and they would be gone? According to my grandpa, you can almost do just that. He says that all you have to do is with one hand squeeze the soft pad on the other hand in between your thumb and index finger (putting your thumb on the top and your index finger on the palm pad, squeezing really hard), and it will be gone in minutes.

Another way to get rid of your headache is to rotate your big toe until it feels loose. The headache should go away soon.

Stephen Gulasey (age 13), Littleton, Colorado
(continued on page 178)

Country Magazine Has Something for Everyone

THAT'S RIGHT—the upbeat, *positive* articles in *Country* are sure to please just about everyone...country *and* city folk alike! If you haven't seen this unique magazine (full-color, high-quality paper, *no advertising*—just good reading cover to cover), here's your chance to order a sample copy.

Each issue features more than 100 gorgeous rural photos...heartwarming "reader-written" stories about real people living country lives...old-fashioned, hearty recipes on handy clip-and-save recipe cards...and more!

More than *2 million* folks like you have already subscribed to *Country*, and nearly *10,000 more* sign up each month!

So why not order a *free copy* and see what so many people love about this *ad-free, photo-packed* magazine? Just complete the form below, mail it to us and we'll rush your free sample copy of *Country* to you.

If you like it, you can extend your subscription to a full year for just $12.98—a **$4.00 savings!** If you're not delighted, mark our invoice "no thanks" and return it. The FREE COPY is yours to keep...no matter what.

Country

❑ **Please send me a FREE issue of *Country* magazine as described above.**

Name _____ Address _____
　　　　　(please print)
City _____ State _____ Zip _____

Mail this coupon to: *Country*, PO Box 5280, Harlan IA 51593-0780

*Country is published bimonthly at the regular rate of $16.98 per year. Canadian subs $23.52 CDN (includes GST). Please allow 4-6 weeks for delivery of your free copy.　　**1298/S5003J**

And we can't resist sharing the following excerpts from other essays on the same subject:

■ "When my father-in-law Clyde had a throbbing headache, he would roll up his pants legs and sit on the edge of a bathtub with his feet in the hottest water he could bear. On his head he would place a well-filled ice bag." *(Betty Ramey-Martin, Richmond, Indiana)*

■ "Get 50 dandelions, put them in a blender until they're mushy paste, mash them through a sieve, add minced garlic, and make a compress. Guaranteed success." *(Roz Davidson, Redwood City, California)*

■ "I steep white willow bark in boiling water for five minutes, then strain it and drink the tea." *(Louise Trail, Yuma, Arizona)*

■ "My mother put a bandanna on the table, stretched out. Then she put sliced raw potatoes across the bandanna and tied it around her forehead. This was a sure cure for headaches." *(Jean Templeman, Monson, Massachusetts)*

■ "You take a glass of 7-Up, warm or cold; to that add one tablespoon of Autocrat coffee-flavored syrup. Then add a crushed-up aspirin — Bayer works best. Lightly shake it once, then drink it down in two gulps. If that doesn't cure you, I suppose you'll be needing to wash your shirt!" *(Joseph Zuchero, Hyannis, Massachusetts)*

■ "After years of headaches, I got a divorce, and my headaches disappeared like magic." *(Robert Jansson, Portland, Connecticut)*

■ "I wolf down a large bowl of ice cream, inducing a cold headache, which, when it passes after a minute or so, takes the original headache with it." *(Dan Roberts, Surrey, British Columbia)*

■ "I use alcohol rubs on the forehead and cold packs. My mother used mustard on our foreheads." *(Helen Harter, Rome, New York)*

■ "Quit doing whatever it is that causes the head to ache . . . do something different." *(Joanne Larkins, Storrs, Connecticut)*

■ "Gently massage a loved one as you would wish to be massaged yourself. It may be your family dog, cat, or a relative." *(Dan Van Blaircom, Rensselaer, Indiana)*

■ "My mother-in-law told me to rub a dab of Vicks Vapo-Rub on the middle of my forehead and on each side at the temples. Then lie down with an ice pack on the back of my head." *(Nancy Vondrak, Sagamore Hills, Ohio)*

■ "I hit my finger with a hammer. It hurt so bad my head quit hurting." *(Hursle Burns, Oneida, Kentucky)*

■ "Eat chocolate and go to bed." *(Lizbe Walker, Savannah, Georgia)*

■ "I take off my clothes. I wrap a towel around me. I also use this time to tint my hair." *(Doris Williams, Fort Worth, Texas)*

■ "A whiskey sour and a plate of marinated herring — this bizarre combination has stood me in good stead over the years." *(Dennis Dix Jr., Avon, Connecticut)*

■ "I wrap an Ace bandage around my head. For super bad headaches, I place a domino against my temple before wrapping my head." *(Kathy Benner, Haines City, Florida)*

■ "Apply drops of lavender oil to the temples and to the back of the neck." *(Rebecca Malila, Milton, Vermont)*

■ "The best remedy for a headache is a blow dryer." *(Eleanor Chamberlain, Olean, New York)*

■ "Place a cat on your stomach." *(Tracy Meddaugh, Wagoner, Oklahoma)*

ANNOUNCING
The 1996 ESSAY CONTEST
My Best Summer Memory as a Child

For 1996, cash prizes (first prize, $50; second prize, $25; third prize, $15) will be awarded for the best 200-word essays on this topic: "My Best Summer Memory as a Child." All entries become the property of Yankee Publishing Incorporated, which reserves all rights to the materials submitted. Winners will be announced in the 1997 edition of *The Old Farmer's Almanac*. Deadline is February 1, 1996. Address: Essay Contest, *The Old Farmer's Almanac*, P.O. Box 520, Dublin, NH 03444.

WISDOM YOU CAN WEAR

Comfort, practical philosophy, and timeless fashion from your friends at The Old Farmer's Almanac.

Get back to basics in our fluffy, 9oz., 80% cotton, natural fleece sweatshirts for only $35.00!!

"LABEL LOGO"

"EARTHDAY"

"SUNFLOWER LOGO"

Rather have a T-shirt? Call 1·800·418·6075 for a catalog of our equally cool T-shirts.

"OLD LOGO"

TO PLACE AN ORDER, CALL 1·800·418·6075

Operators are standing by, sunup to sundown.
Or if you prefer, send your check or money order to:

IOCOM
P.O. Box 2900
Cocoa, FL 32922

Alaska residents must add $2.00 to delivery charges.
Canadian residents must add $5.00.
Kentucky residents must add 5% Sales Tax.

Shipping and handling charges		
0 — $40.00		$3.50
$40.01 — $75.00		$4.50
$75.01 — $110.00		$5.00
$110.01 — $180.00		$6.50
$180.01 — $250.00		$9.00
$250.01 — & over		$11.50

The OLD FARMER'S GENERAL STORE

A special section featuring unique mail order products for all our readers who shop by mail.

KITES
FREE COLOR CATALOG
Call Toll Free!
1-800-724-7267

HOME GARDENER'S CATALOG

- We offer over 500 vegetable varieties
- Herb seeds and herb plants
- Potpourri and wreath supplies
- Wine and beer making supplies
- FREE 70 page catalog filled with gardening tips and cooking hints

NICHOLS GARDEN NURSERY
1194 North Pacific Albany, Oregon 97321

MAKE YOUR OWN
WINES and BEERS
FREE CATALOG
E. C. KRAUS
P.O. BOX 7850-FD
INDEPENDENCE, MO 64054
816-254-0242

FREE BUY 1...GET 1 FREE

THAYERS SLIPPERY ELM LOZENGES

Send: Name, Address, $1.75 & Flavor (unflavored or cherry)
Mail to: Henry Thayer & Co.
P.O. Box 56
Westport, CT 06881

Prized by Opera Singers

HERNIA APPLIANCES
FOR COMFORT!
You can enjoy heavenly comfort night and day at work or at play! Send for FREE illustrated booklet.

BROOKS APPLIANCE COMPANY
120 State St., Marshall, Mich. 49068

Work at Home
Earn up to $25,000 a year typing medical histories!

No experience needed. Work the hours you choose. The medical profession needs skilled transcriptionists. So if you type, or can learn, we can train you at home to type medical histories from audio cassettes dictated by doctors. Get free facts! Call Toll-Free...1-800-475-0100...or write At-Home Professions, 2001 Lowe St., Dept. GXM95, Fort Collins, CO 80525.

Celebrate July 4th & All Events
CARBIDE CANNON
BIG BANG! $119.95

Mammoth Cannons shoot with terrific BANG! Have a bang-up time at special events. Uses powdered carbide ammo. Hundreds of shots for few cents. All metal construction with large, rugged cast-iron wheels. Machined brass mechanism for easy loading and firing. Authentic turn-of-century design. Handsome decor when not in use. Made in USA to last a lifetime. Available in 3 sizes: 9" cannon, **$49.95 postpaid;** 17" cannon, **$89.95 postpaid;** 25" cannon (shown here) with rapid firing and automatic loading, **$119.95 postpaid.** The larger the cannon the louder the bang! **Carbide ammo, about 100 shots, $6.00; 3 packs for $15.00.** Send check, money order or call. Visa, MasterCard accepted by mail or phone. Give card number & expiration. Money-back guarantee. Send for **FREE CATALOG!**
The Conestoga Co., Inc., Dept OFA, PO Box 405, Bethlehem, PA 18016
★★ Call **1-800-987-BANG** (2264) ★★

CUSTOM COOKBOOKS
- Low Minimum Order
- Many Free Features
- Competitive Prices
- Helpful & Friendly Customer Service

FREE KIT BOOK!
1-800-383-1679

G&R Publishing Co.
Dept. OFA
507 Industrial St.
Waverly, IA 50677

Create your own cookbook. It's **FUN** and **EASY** to do. Plus it makes a **GREAT** fund-raiser for your church, school or for yourself!

The OLD FARMER'S GENERAL STORE

Order this
Hand-Pressed Glass Medallion,
only $6.00 *postpaid* & we will include a catalog of our other designs. This approx. 3 1/2 x 4 1/4" medallion was made in the historic glass-making region of southwestern New Hampshire. We use centuries old techniques & recycled glass [O.F.A. pressed in yellow glass]. Purchase this limited "Old Farmer" medallion & our catalog for $6 postpaid or send $1 for catalog only. Mail your check, phone your order - or visit - Your humble servant, Prop. Old Hancock Glassworks.

Old Hancock Glassworks
375 Keene Road, Route 9
Antrim, New Hampshire 03440
1-800-693-8004   9am to 5pm ET

 YOU'LL NEVER FORGET GARBAGE DAY AGAIN!
Place this handy device on your shelf - It will start beeping at the right time each and every week to let you know it's time to take the can to the curb. Set it only once. So simple a four year old can do it. Unconditional 90 day guarantee. 3 inches tall.
$13.50 post paid.
A. Watson POB 21991 Carson City NV 89721

SAY YOU SAW IT IN THE OFA

HAVE AN IDEA?
If so, we are a company that can help you obtain patent services and submit your ideas, inventions and new products to industry.
Call Toll Free 1-800-288-IDEA
Ask for operator FA
Invention Submission Corp. FA
217 Ninth Street
Pittsburgh, PA 15222-3506
© ISC 1994

UNIVERSITY TESTED   **Dr. T's** Nature Products   EPA REGISTERED

SNAKE-A-WAY®
SNAKE REPELLENT
HIGHLY EFFECTIVE AGAINST POISONOUS & NON-POISONOUS SNAKES.

 **Cobweb Eliminator** Discourages Reformation

• NON-TOXIC
• ALL NATURAL
• LAST UP TO 4 MONTHS

FOR MORE INFORMATION CALL:
DR. T's NATURE PRODUCTS
1-800-299-NATURE (6288)

SLEEP WARM – SAVE FUEL

Automatic Bed Warmer makes electric blankets obsolete. All sizes, dual controls, plus 12V for RV's. Also foot, back & pet warm-ers. Free booklet explains advantages & savings. Special prices direct from factory (our 55th year). **Patented Products, Box A/F96**. Danville, Ohio 43014
Phone 614-599-6842

Mail Box Name & Street Number
2 sides (12" wide) & one front (5"wide)
Computer cut and spaced for that professional look. You just peel & stick.
Specify – Block, ROMAN, or *Casual* style.
Black or White color, Check or Money Order

B.A. Wright
1828 S.700 W.

ONLY $ 9.95   Plus $ 2.00 Shipping & Handling TO ---   B.A. Wright
1828 S. 700 W.
Anderson, IN 46011

---

4 WHEEL BIKE
DRIVES LIKE A CAR!
• Easy to Pedal • Fun
• Multi-speed • Stable
• Golf Bag-Cargo Carrier
• 1, 2 & 4 Seater • Street Legal
Free Literature 24 hr. 1 (615) 822-2737 Ext. 2681

RHOADES CAR DEPT. 2681 • 125 RHOADES LN
HENDERSONVILLE, TN 37075

KITES
FREE COLOR CATALOG
Choose from over 200 exciting kites.
• Many unusual & innovative designs.
Call or write for your catalog today!
Into The Wind • (800) 541-0314
1408-FA Pearl St., Boulder, CO 80302

PUBLISH YOUR BOOK!

Our FREE step-by-step Self Publishing Guide gives you all features and prices up-front so you're never in the dark! Prices include typesetting, art service, printing, binding, and more! Call or write for our FREE guide.

800-650-7888, ext. OFA9

 **MORRIS** PUBLISHING   3212 East Highway 30 • Kearney, NE 68847

The OLD FARMER'S GENERAL STORE

Invest In America!
Buy 1995 Silver Eagles
For Only $7.95 ea.
When you buy 20 coin roll

For Limited Time Only, Eastern Numismatics is offering the new 1995 American Silver Eagle. The purchase price is $7.95 per coin. Each coin is Brilliant Uncirculated and contains **One Oz. of Pure Silver .999 Fine.** Protective display holders are available for individual coins for additional $1.00 each.

1 Coin $8.49 + $1.00 P&H ....(Total $9.49)
10 Coins $72.50+$2.50 P&H ....(Total $82.00)
20 Coin roll in Original U.S. Mint tube with Treasury Seal. for $159.00 + $5.00 P&H ....(Total $164.00)

I understand I may charge my coins if my minimum order is $50.00 or more. Prices are subject to change without notice.

EASTERN NUMISMATICS INC.
642 Franklin Ave., Garden City N.Y. 11530
Order Toll Free 1-800-835-0008

Since 1892 the most famous natural salve that is ideal as an aid toward the relief of **Chapped Lips** and skin, **Blemishes, Diaper Rash**, etc. Other quality products, **Smith's Mentholated Salve, Strawberry Lip Balm, Grandpa's Tar Soap, Cloverine Salve & Jewelry.** Send a stamped self-addressed envelope for a **Product Brochure.**
ROSEBUD CO., 6 N. Main St.
Box OFA-96, Woodsboro, MD 21798
Phone: 301-845-8788
ROSEBUD SALVE

Forecasts, Fun, and Folklore Plus an Exclusive 4-for-1 Offer!

To mark the release of the 204th consecutive issue, the publishers have authorized a special limited-edition printing of the 1996 *Old Farmer's Almanac Collector's Hardcover Edition.* This exclusive 4-for-1 offer includes historic reprints from 1796 and 1896 plus the 1996 *Old Farmer's Almanac* Gardening Calendar— more than a $5.95 value!

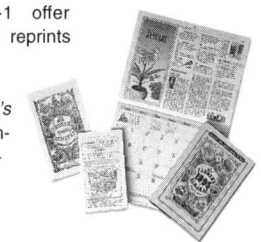

To order call: 800-223-3166
1996 OFA Collector's
Hardcover Edition 4-for-1 Offer
OF96BHC $14.95
plus $3.95 S&H

Steam Models
"FASCINATING WORKING STEAM MODELS!"
Complete "WILESCO & MAMOD" line. Over 100 different models. Trains, Marine, Cars, Trucks, Stationary Fire Engines & Accessories. Stunning, large 34 page colored Catalog $6.95 Refundable.
SALES • PARTS • SERVICE   PHONE
LARGE DISCOUNTS   (613) 475-1771
YESTERYEAR TOYS & BOOKS, INC.
Dept. FAT Box 537, Alexandria Bay, NY 13607
Kits or Assembled

For infomation about advertising in the General Store call **603-563-8111** x141

Cook's Pure Vanilla Powder
The Ultimate Coffee condiment and much, much more.

Convenience never tasted so good...Sprinkle on crepes, French Toast, Waffles or bake with it just like all of our other famous extracts, measure for measure. For free catalog and recipes call 800-735-0545 or write PO Box 890 Tacoma WA 98401.
Visa and MC accepted.

BeYour Own Boss!

Start your own high-paying A/C, Heating, and Refrigeration business. Study at your own pace with NRI at-home training that includes professional equipment. Get the hands-on skills you need to succeed!
Call 1-800-321-4634 Ext. 1249 or write:

NRI Schools
McGraw-Hill Continuing Education Center
4401 Connecticut Ave. NW, Washington, DC 20008

The OLD FARMER'S GENERAL STORE

SCHOOL AT HOME
Kindergarten through Grade 8
- teach your child at home
- complete curriculum
- no experience necessary
- traditional, classical education
- accredited, nonprofit program
- advisory teachers available
- all materials included
- French, art, music courses offered
- send for free information

CALVERT **SCHOOL**
Since 1897
Dept. OF5, 105 Tuscany Road, Baltimore, MD 21210
(410) 243-6030 fax (410) 366-0674

America's Oldest & Largest Rare Breed Hatchery
Free Color Catalog
Over 140 varieties Baby Chicks, Bantams, Turkeys, Game Birds, Peacocks, Waterfowl, Guineas, plus Books, Equipment, Eggs, Incubators, & Medicine.
1-800-456-3280 (24 hours a day)
Murray McMurray Hatchery
C100, Webster City, Iowa 50595-0458

BURIED TREASURE
- Locate From a Long Distance
- Most Sensitive Equipment Available
- For FREE Brochure write to:

SIMMONS SCIENTIFIC
BOX 10057Q WILMINGTON, NC 28405

NOURISH DRY SKIN NATURALLY
Use **Farmer's Friend** Hand Salve before & after garden or barn work. Made from natural oils, herbs, beeswax and rosemary.

- Farmer's Friend Hand Salve $5.95
- Gardener's Soap w/ Cornmeal $4.95
- Beeswax Moisturizing Creme $9.95

Add $3.50 s/h and mail to:
Running Rabbit Farm
14660 NW Sellers Rd.
Banks, OR 97106

FREE CATALOG

ENERGY-SAVING SUN-PORCH®
CONVERTIBLE SUNSPACE

INSULATED WINTER SUNROOM CONVERTS TO A SUMMER SCREEN ROOM!

MOUNTS READILY ON DECKS, PATIOS, OR LANDSCAPE TIES.

☐ QWIK® window/screen change system ☐ Do-it-yourself kit, no contractors needed ☐ Meets building codes for snow & wind loads ☐ Unique Climate Control System ☐ No extras, comes complete ☐ Buy factory direct & save ☐ America's #1 value since 1974.

Send $2 for Color Catalogue, Prices, SENT FIRST CLASS MAIL.

SUN-PORCH® DIVISION
VEGETABLE FACTORY, INC.
P.O. Box 1353, Dept. OFA
Stamford, CT 06904-1353

INVENTORS!
Can You Patent and Profit from Your Idea?
We have a full range of patenting and marketing services. Confidentiality guaranteed. Call for a free info. kit.
American Institute for Research & Development
1-800-582-2473

PUBLISH YOUR COOKBOOK

- Organizations
- Churches
- Families

AND RAISE FUNDS!

Call For FREE Cookbook Information
1-800-445-6621, ext. 4909

Cookbooks by Morris Press
P.O. Box 2110 • Kearney, NE 68848

Secrets of the Zodiac

Famous Debowelled Man of the Signs

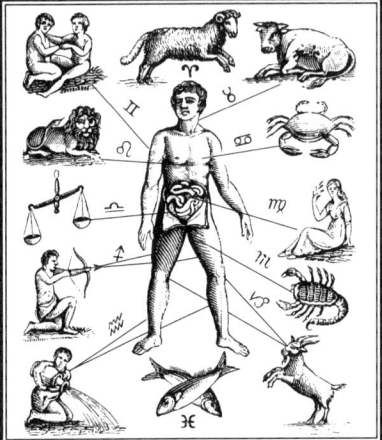

Ancient astrologers associated each of the signs with a part of the body over which they felt the sign held some influence. The first sign of the zodiac — Aries — was attributed to the head, with the rest of the signs moving down the body, ending with Pisces at the feet.

♈	Aries, head. ARI Mar. 21-Apr. 20
♉	Taurus, neck. TAU Apr. 21-May 20
♊	Gemini, arms. GEM May 21-June 20
♋	Cancer, breast. CAN June 21-July 22
♌	Leo, heart. LEO July 23-Aug. 22
♍	Virgo, belly. VIR Aug. 23-Sept. 22
♎	Libra, reins. LIB Sept. 23-Oct. 22
♏	Scorpio, secrets. SCO Oct. 23-Nov. 22
♐	Sagittarius, thighs. SAG Nov. 23-Dec. 21
♑	Capricorn, knees. CAP Dec. 22-Jan. 19
♒	Aquarius, legs. AQU Jan. 20-Feb. 19
♓	Pisces, feet. PSC Feb. 20-Mar. 20

Astrology and Astronomy

Astrology is a tool we use to time events according to the *astrological* placement of the two luminaries (the Sun and Moon) and the eight known planets in the 12 signs of the zodiac. Astronomy, on the other hand, is the charting of the actual placement of those planets and constellations, taking into account precession of the equinoxes. As a result, *the placement of the planets in the signs of the zodiac are not the same astrologically and astronomically.* (The Moon's *astronomical* place is given in the Left-Hand Calendar Pages [52-78] and its *astrological* place is given in Gardening by the Moon's Sign, page 187.)

Modern astrology is a study of synchronicities. The planetary movements do not *cause* events. Rather, they explain the "flow" or trajectory events will tend to follow. Just as with waves or tides in the oceans, your own free will gives you the choice to swim with or against the currents. But those who choose to can plan a schedule in harmony with the flow.

The dates given in the Month-by-Month Astrological Timetable (page 186) have been chosen with particular care to the astrological passage of the Moon. However, since other planets also influence us, it's best to take a look at all indicators before seeking advice on *major* life decisions. A qualified astrologer can study the current relationship of the planets and your own personal birth chart in order to assist you in the best possible timing for carrying out your plans.

Planet Mercury Does What?

Sometimes when we look out from our perspective here on Earth, the other planets appear to be traveling backward through the zodiac. (They're not actually moving backward, it just looks that way to us.) We call this *retrograde*.

Mercury's retrograde periods, which occur three or four times a year, can cause travel delays and misconstrued communications. Plans have a way of unraveling, too. However, this is an excellent time to be researching or looking into the past. Intuition is high during these periods, and unplanned coincidences can be extraordinary.

When Mercury is retrograde, astrologers advise us to keep plans flexible, allow extra time for travel, and avoid signing contracts. It's OK and even useful to look over projects and plans, because we may see them with different eyes at these times. However, our normal system of checks and balances might not be active, so it's best to wait until Mercury is direct again to make any final decisions. In 1996 Mercury will be retrograde from January 9 to 30, May 3 to 27, September 4 to 26, and after December 23.

MORE BOOKS from *The Old Farmer's Almanac*

Always useful...
Always familiar...
And always fun!

1996 Gardener's Companion

(AVAILABLE JANUARY 16, 1996)

An entertaining and informative quick-reference guide full of useful gardening tips. The 1996 edition will feature "How to Grow Terrific Tulips," "The Best-Tasting Vegetable Varieties," "Pruning Tips from the Pros," and "Should You Buy Bugs by Mail?" plus lots more.

1996 HomeOwner's Companion

(AVAILABLE MARCH 5, 1996)

A full compendium of expert advice, how-to articles, and do-it-yourself projects. Feature stories include "How to Thatch Your Roof," "The Language of the Hardware Store," "Ten Projects Not to Do Yourself," "Your Lawn and the Law."

Each book is only $2.99 (plus $1.95 per book for shipping and handling). After release date, all orders will be shipped within two to three days of receipt.

Send payment with order to:
The Old Farmer's Almanac
Dept. SO, P.O. Box 520, Dublin, NH 03444

A Month-by-Month Astrological Timetable for 1996

Herewith we provide the following yearlong chart, based on the Moon signs, showing the most favorable times each month for certain activities. BY CELESTE LONGACRE

	JAN.	FEB.	MAR.	APR.	MAY	JUNE	JULY	AUG.	SEPT.	OCT.	NOV.	DEC.
Give up smoking	8, 13	9, 13	11, 15	7, 16	9, 14	5, 9	2, 11	3, 7	4, 9	1, 6	2, 7	9, 27
Begin diet to lose weight	8, 13	9, 13	11, 15	7, 16	9, 14	5, 9	2, 11	3, 7	4, 9	1, 6	2, 7	9, 27
Begin diet to gain weight	24, 25	1, 28	1, 28	24, 29	22, 27	18, 28	25, 29	12, 21	13, 26	15, 23	16, 20	17, 22
Cut hair to encourage growth	27, 28	23, 24	29, 30	9, 10	7, 8	8, 9	5, 6	1, 2	25, 26	26, 27	23, 24	3, 4
Cut hair to discourage growth	12, 13	8, 9	7, 8	29, 30	26, 27	22, 23	20, 21	24, 25	20, 21	22, 23	18, 19	16, 17
Dental care	10, 11	6, 7	4, 5	1, 2, 28	26, 27	22, 23	19, 20	15, 16	11, 12	9, 10	5, 6	2, 3
End old projects	18, 19	17, 18	17, 18	16, 17	15, 16	14, 15	13, 14	12, 13	11, 12	10, 11	9, 10	8, 9
Start a new project	21, 22	19, 20	20, 21	18, 19	18, 19	17, 18	16, 17	15, 16	13, 14	13, 14	12, 13	11, 12
Entertain	7, 8	3, 4	29, 30	25, 26	7, 8	3, 4	27, 28	24, 25	20, 21	17, 18	14, 15	11, 12
Fishing	16, 17	13, 14	11, 12	7, 8	5, 6	1, 2, 29	26, 27	22, 23	19, 20	16, 17	12, 13	9, 10
Breed	14, 15	11, 12	9, 10	5, 6	2, 3	26, 27	24, 25	20, 21	16, 17	13, 14	10, 11	7, 8
Planting above-ground crops	22, 23, 27, 28	19, 20, 23, 24	22, 23, 27, 28	18, 19, 23, 24	4, 5, 9, 10	1, 2, 5, 6, 10	2, 3, 7, 8	3, 4, 8, 9	4, 5, 27, 28	5, 6, 28, 29	2, 3, 25, 26	3, 4, 26, 27
Planting below-ground crops	5, 6, 10, 11	6, 7, 11, 12	4, 5, 9, 10	2, 3, 14, 15	21, 22, 26, 27	18, 19, 22, 23	15, 16, 20, 21	12, 13, 16, 17	12, 13, 17, 18	10, 11, 15, 16	11, 12, 16, 17	13, 14, 18, 19
Destroy pests/weeds	25, 26	21, 22	20, 21	16, 17	13, 14	9, 10	7, 8	3, 4	27, 28	24, 25	20, 21	18, 19
Graft or pollinate	5, 6, 23	1, 2	27, 28	23, 24	20, 21	7, 8	14, 15	10, 11	6, 7	4, 5	1, 27, 28	25, 26
Prune to encourage growth	25, 26	21, 22	20, 21	9, 10	7, 8	3, 4	9, 10	5, 6	2, 3	26, 27	4, 5	1, 2
Prune to discourage growth	7, 8	13, 14	11, 12	18, 19	15, 16	20, 21	17, 18	14, 15	10, 11	17, 18	14, 15	11, 12
Harvest above-ground crops	27, 28	23, 24	22, 23	18, 19	1, 2	22, 23	19, 20	15, 16	16, 17	13, 14	23, 24	20, 21
Harvest root crops	10, 11	6, 7	4, 5	1, 2	15, 16	12, 13	9, 10	5, 6	2, 3	9, 10	5, 6	2, 3
Cut hay	25, 26	21, 22	20, 21	16, 17	13, 14	9, 10	7, 8	3, 4	27, 28	24, 25	20, 21	18, 19
Begin logging	18, 19	15, 16	13, 14	9, 10	7, 8	3, 4	1, 28, 29	24, 25	21, 22	18, 19	14, 15	11, 12
Set posts or pour concrete	18, 19	15, 16	13, 14	9, 10	7, 8	3, 4	1, 28, 29	24, 25	21, 22	18, 19	14, 15	11, 12
Slaughter	14, 15	11, 12	9, 10	5, 6	2, 3	26, 27	24, 25	20, 21	16, 17	13, 14	10, 11	7, 8
Wean	16, 17	13, 14	11, 12	7, 8	5, 6	1, 2, 29	26, 27	22, 23	19, 20	16, 17	12, 13	9, 10
Castrate animals	20, 21	17, 18	15, 16	5, 6	9, 10	5, 6	30, 31	26, 27	23, 24	20, 21	16, 17	13, 14

Gardening by the Moon's Sign

It is important to note that *the actual placements of the planets through the signs of the zodiac are not the same in astronomy and astrology.* The *astrological* placement of the Moon, by sign, is given in the chart below. (The *astronomical* placement is given in the Left-Hand Calendar Pages 52-78.)

For planting, the most fertile signs are the three water signs: Cancer, Scorpio, and Pisces. Taurus, Virgo, and Capricorn would be good second choices for sowing.

Weeding and plowing are best done when the Moon occupies the signs of Aries, Gemini, Leo, Sagittarius, or Aquarius. Insect pests can also be handled at those times. Transplanting and grafting are best done under a Cancer, Scorpio, or Pisces Moon. Pruning is best done under an Aries, Leo, or Sagittarius Moon, with growth encouraged during the waxing stage (between new and full Moon) and discouraged during waning (day after full to the day before new Moon). (The dates of the Moon's phases can be found on pages 52-78.) Clean out the garden shed when the Moon occupies Virgo so the work will flow smoothly. Fences or permanent beds can be built or mended when Capricorn predominates. Avoid indecision when under the Libra Moon.

Moon's Place in the Astrological Zodiac

	NOV. 95	DEC. 95	JAN. 96	FEB. 96	MAR. 96	APR. 96	MAY 96	JUNE 96	JULY 96	AUG. 96	SEPT. 96	OCT. 96	NOV. 96	DEC. 96
1	PSC	ARI	TAU	CAN	CAN	VIR	LIB	SAG	CAP	PSC	TAU	GEM	CAN	LEO
2	PSC	ARI	GEM	CAN	LEO	VIR	SCO	SAG	AQU	PSC	TAU	GEM	LEO	VIR
3	PSC	TAU	GEM	LEO	LEO	LIB	SCO	CAP	AQU	ARI	TAU	CAN	LEO	VIR
4	ARI	TAU	GEM	LEO	VIR	LIB	SCO	CAP	PSC	ARI	GEM	CAN	LEO	VIR
5	ARI	TAU	CAN	LEO	VIR	SCO	SAG	AQU	PSC	TAU	GEM	CAN	VIR	LIB
6	TAU	GEM	CAN	VIR	LIB	SCO	SAG	AQU	ARI	TAU	CAN	LEO	VIR	LIB
7	TAU	GEM	LEO	VIR	LIB	SAG	CAP	PSC	ARI	GEM	CAN	LEO	LIB	SCO
8	GEM	CAN	LEO	LIB	LIB	SAG	CAP	PSC	ARI	GEM	CAN	VIR	LIB	SCO
9	GEM	CAN	LEO	LIB	SCO	CAP	AQU	ARI	TAU	GEM	LEO	VIR	LIB	SAG
10	GEM	CAN	VIR	SCO	SCO	CAP	AQU	ARI	TAU	CAN	LEO	VIR	SCO	SAG
11	CAN	LEO	VIR	SCO	SAG	AQU	PSC	TAU	GEM	CAN	VIR	LIB	SCO	CAP
12	CAN	LEO	LIB	SCO	SAG	AQU	PSC	TAU	GEM	LEO	VIR	LIB	SAG	CAP
13	CAN	VIR	LIB	SAG	CAP	AQU	ARI	TAU	GEM	LEO	VIR	SCO	SAG	AQU
14	LEO	VIR	SCO	SAG	CAP	PSC	ARI	GEM	CAN	LEO	LIB	SCO	CAP	AQU
15	LEO	VIR	SCO	CAP	AQU	PSC	TAU	GEM	CAN	VIR	LIB	SCO	CAP	PSC
16	VIR	LIB	SAG	CAP	AQU	ARI	TAU	CAN	LEO	VIR	SCO	SAG	AQU	PSC
17	VIR	LIB	SAG	AQU	PSC	ARI	TAU	CAN	LEO	LIB	SCO	SAG	AQU	PSC
18	LIB	SCO	CAP	AQU	PSC	TAU	GEM	CAN	LEO	LIB	SAG	CAP	PSC	ARI
19	LIB	SCO	CAP	PSC	ARI	TAU	GEM	LEO	VIR	LIB	SAG	CAP	PSC	ARI
20	LIB	SAG	AQU	PSC	ARI	GEM	CAN	LEO	VIR	SCO	SAG	AQU	ARI	TAU
21	SCO	SAG	AQU	ARI	ARI	GEM	CAN	LEO	LIB	SCO	CAP	AQU	ARI	TAU
22	SCO	CAP	PSC	ARI	TAU	GEM	CAN	VIR	LIB	SAG	CAP	PSC	ARI	GEM
23	SAG	CAP	PSC	TAU	TAU	CAN	LEO	VIR	SCO	SAG	AQU	PSC	TAU	GEM
24	SAG	AQU	PSC	TAU	GEM	CAN	LEO	LIB	SCO	CAP	AQU	ARI	TAU	GEM
25	CAP	AQU	ARI	TAU	GEM	LEO	VIR	LIB	SCO	CAP	PSC	ARI	GEM	CAN
26	CAP	PSC	ARI	GEM	CAN	LEO	VIR	SCO	SAG	AQU	PSC	TAU	GEM	CAN
27	AQU	PSC	TAU	GEM	CAN	LEO	LIB	SCO	SAG	AQU	ARI	TAU	CAN	LEO
28	AQU	ARI	TAU	CAN	CAN	VIR	LIB	SAG	CAP	PSC	ARI	GEM	CAN	LEO
29	PSC	ARI	GEM	CAN	LEO	VIR	LIB	SAG	CAP	PSC	TAU	GEM	CAN	VIR
30	PSC	ARI	GEM	—	LEO	LIB	SCO	CAP	AQU	ARI	TAU	GEM	LEO	VIR
31	—	TAU	GEM	—	VIR	—	SCO	—	AQU	ARI	—	CAN	—	VIR

The True Story

– photo: National Baseball Library, Cooperstown, N.Y.

When Connie Mack saw the young boy pitch, he compared him to Lefty Grove, arguably the greatest left-handed pitcher of all time. But then the young boy went to war. In Italy he barely survived an explosion that killed nine of his buddies and mangled his legs. The rest is unbelievable . . .

■ THE CAREER OF LELAND VICTOR ("Lou") Brissie Jr. occupies little space in the *Baseball Encyclopedia*. He won 44 major-league games. He lost 48. One year he won 16 games and pitched in the All-Star game. Unless you followed the old Philadelphia Athletics in the late 1940s or the Cleveland Indians in the early 1950s, and unless you're from Savannah, where for a few blazing months he held that city as few athletes have ever held their fans, you probably do not remember Lou Brissie. Unless, that is, you were torn up in the war, or unless you loved someone who was torn up in the war. Then you remember Lou Brissie.

He was barely 19 in 1943 when he went to war, a rawboned six-foot-four-inch South Carolinian with a whip of a left arm that struck out nearly 20 batters a game and made him the sensation of army-camp baseball. Soldiers knew his name long before the nation's sportswriters. He had a new bride and a promise from Connie Mack of the Philadelphia Athletics. Lou Brissie knew that when the war ended, the A's would be waiting.

But his war ended like this: At 11:20 A.M., December 7, 1944, squad leader Corporal Lou Brissie, 351st Infantry, 88th Division, leaped from a truck winding its way through the mountains of northern Italy and shouted to his men to take cover from a storm of German artillery.

A shell exploded at Lou Brissie's feet. Nine of his men died almost immediately. Brissie's left leg split open "like a ripe watermelon," he said later. He clawed along the snow-covered ground, then collapsed in a creek bed. He lay motionless for six hours, blood trickling from his mouth and ears, given up for dead by the passing corpsmen. Finally, in the fading light, someone leaned over him and found he was breathing. He was rushed to a field hospital. His left leg was hopelessly mangled and caked with dirt. Doctors said they needed to amputate. Through his pain he fought to sit up. "You can't take the leg off," he said. "I'm a ballplayer."

"You will die if we don't," the doctors said.

# of a Hero

by Mel R. Allen

Lou (at right) and another G.I. in Italy early in 1944 (above); *Ted Williams, another decorated veteran, connecting with a pitch.*

Through the pain he fought to sit up. "You

He wrote a friend: "I'll play again, but it will be quite a while. If God lets me walk again, I'll play. That's my ambition."

"Once I knew I wasn't going to lose my leg, it never once occurred to me that I wasn't going to be able to play again," Lou Brissie says today. "But the big question was how?"

He'd grown up knowing about pain and endurance. He'd seen his father, a motorcycle barnstormer at county airports and fairgrounds, tape up a broken hand and say, "Well, you've got to do it." When rheumatic fever crippled Lou's arms at age ten, his father gave him two lard buckets and told him to walk with them every day, until the arms grew straight and strong. When he was 12, his family moved to the textile town of Ware Shoals, South Carolina. All the mills fielded baseball teams, and by 16 Lou, already as big as a grown man, was striking out the men. The Dodgers offered $25,000. But his father had other plans.

"Don't worry about the money," he said. "Don't do anything until Mr. Mack sees you."

By 1941 Connie Mack was nearly 80. His kindnesses were legendary, and people across the country rooted for his A's. He had won world championships with players like Jimmie Foxx and Lefty Grove

Brissie replied, "I'll take my chances." Four days after being wounded, Brissie arrived at the 300th General Hospital in Naples. There Dr. Wilbur K. Brubaker took over the case. "He so desperately wanted us to save his leg," recalls Dr. Brubaker, who lives today in Florida. "He was willing to take a big risk. He had tremendous courage. I cannot ever remember a patient with his courage. He fought for his recovery."

Dr. Brubaker had a new miracle drug that fought infections, and Lou Brissie became a test case, the first soldier in the Mediterranean theater to be placed on around-the-clock penicillin.

He would not walk for nearly nine months. Twenty-three times doctors operated to remove splintered bone and shrapnel. With both legs in casts, he was shipped home. Doctors in veterans' hospitals told him he would never really heal. Osteomyelitis, an infection of the bone, could flare up at any time, threatening his life. A fall, a bump, anything could set off a potentially lethal infection.

can't take the leg off," he said. "I'm a ballplayer."

and Mickey Cochrane, but that had been years ago. When Lou was just a boy, his father told him, "You're going to grow up, and you're going to help the old man win another championship."

So in 1941, at age 17, Lou Brissie tried out for Connie Mack. The coach's eyes lit up. He had always said that Lefty Grove was the greatest left-handed pitcher of all time, and this kid had all the makings of another Grove. But he was young and raw. Connie Mack said he would pay for Lou to go to Presbyterian College for two years. The baseball coach there would make certain Lou Brissie developed properly. After two years, if all went well, Lou would join the A's for spring training.

It wasn't until the late summer of 1945 that Lou finally came back to Shibe Park to see Connie Mack. It was a sight the old man never forgot.

"I didn't have the heart to tell him how pitiful he appeared," Connie Mack later said. "His leg was broomstick thin. He didn't have the strength to throw. But he kept on trying, balancing himself on one crutch and throwing with his free arm. I had never seen anything like it. I felt like crying."

With his wife and new daughter, Lou moved in with his parents back in Ware Shoals. He'd wake early and try to walk. He moved from crutches to a cane, and he started throwing again, as slow as a child almost. He could not lift his left foot, the foot a left-hander needs to push off the mound.

"It all came back to how?" he said. "How? What do I have to do to be more like I was? I kept asking everyone who remembered me — 'Am I throwing the way I used to?' "

Lou with his mentor, legendary coach Connie Mack (above), and pitching for the A's, his shattered left leg in a brace (right).

Brissie celebrated his first win in the hospital, receiving massive doses of penicillin.

Lou Brissie started over in the spring of 1946, pitching again for the Riegel Textile team. At a Shriner's hospital he had a brace fitted over his scarred, fragile, and utterly vulnerable leg. His first game back he threw only ten pitches, giving up two home runs and seven hits. He got nobody out. "I thought, is this what I struggled for?" he said.

But then in July he struck out 14. He told the A's he was ready. He went to Philadelphia, threw one day of batting practice, and tried to ignore the throbbing in his leg. Osteomyelitis. He returned to the hospital. The A's said to wait until spring training.

In the spring of 1947 Connie Mack sent him to Savannah in the Class A Sally League. "We have to see if your leg can stand up to a season," he said. In Savannah infection disabled him again. Six weeks went by and Lou could not pitch. The team floundered in last place. When he was finally able to pitch, he lost. And lost again. Then he caught fire. He won 12 in a row, and the team surged toward the pennant.

When Lou pitched, people jammed together on the edge of the outfield. Once he drew over 11,000 fans to a field that held only 8,500. That season the Savannah team drew over 200,000 fans, a mark never equaled. When the season ended, Lou Brissie had won 23 games and lost only five. He also set a modern strikeout record of 278.

"Lou Brissie spoiled Savannah fans," says Tom Coffey, longtime writer and editor for the *Savannah Morning News and Evening Express*. "They keep waiting for another Brissie. But he was heroic. He was unique."

When the 1948 season began, he was still only 23 years old. Connie Mack told reporters Lou Brissie would one day be the equal of Lefty Grove. He named the rookie to open the season on Patriots Day against the Boston Red Sox.

On opening day he was leading 4-2 when Ted Williams came to bat in the sixth inning. Williams always maintained that Lou Brissie was one of the five hardest lefties he ever faced. This time he drove a bullet back to the mound. The ball smashed into the top corner of Brissie's brace and bounced 50 feet in the air. Brissie crumpled to the ground as Fenway Park hushed. Everyone knew what the rookie had gone through to get back to baseball. Williams, himself a decorated veteran, kicked angrily at the first-base bag. He walked over to the mound where Brissie lay. For a minute Lou could not speak. But when he saw Ted Williams leaning over him, he managed, "Next time, Williams, next time pull the damn ball." Williams laughed. A few months later Williams hit a towering right-field home run off Brissie. As he rounded the bases, he hollered, "Did I pull that one enough?"

"I didn't mean that far," Brissie shouted back.

He insisted on finishing the game. In the ninth inning Ted Williams came to bat again. Brissie struck him out. Connie Mack said after the game that he had never been so exhausted watching a baseball game, his heart was pounding so hard.

Brissie celebrated his first win in the hospital, receiving massive doses of penicillin. He woke the next morning to find himself a national hero. A Boston writer called Lou "as game a kid as ever hit the majors." The Associated Press called him "one of the most courageous and determined players of all time." Another writer called Lou Brissie "the most dramatic story in sports."

The sudden fame made Brissie uncomfortable. "Writers called me a hero," he said, "but I wasn't a hero. I left a lot of guys in hospitals, guys fighting bigger battles without anyone cheering for them. I thought just by showing I could do it, I could help them, too." When Hollywood asked to make a

He woke the next morning to find himself a national hero.

movie of his life, Lou said no.

He had a fine season, winning 14 games and finishing fourth for rookie of the year. The next year he made the All-Star team. But he told nobody that as soon as he left the ballpark, he went to bed. He got up only to play baseball. The next season he lost 19 games, even though he was among the league leaders in innings pitched. He was only 26, but he did not have much more to give.

At the end of the 1950 season Connie Mack retired. The next year the Cleveland Indians, battling for the pennant, needed left-handed pitching. They traded for Lou Brissie. Two years later Hank Greenberg, the Indians' general manager, sold him to their minor-league team in Indianapolis.

"Hank didn't believe I'd quit. He just didn't understand where I was coming from," Lou Brissie explained to a reporter.

"Where were you coming from?"

"Italy. 1944. Hank never understood that. I felt if I went to the minors, I would have failed all those guys still in the hospital."

So Lou Brissie walked away from baseball on his own terms, and soon after became director of American Legion Junior Baseball. He watched youngsters throwing their arms out during playoff games and drafted the rule that limited the number of innings young pitchers could work in a week, a rule that has filtered down to youth leagues everywhere.

He is 71 today. He lives in North Augusta, South Carolina, a tall, dignified man. He walks with difficulty and always with pain. Because of pain he cannot remember sleeping through the night. He lives within minutes of the Master's Golf Course, but he cannot play because walking on rough ground can flare up his chronic infection. His first wife died at age 42. Yet he tells people he is blessed. He speaks of his great fortune.

He is asked if his is not, instead, a story of misfortune: a potentially great career reduced to 44 wins and a life of incessant pain.

Gentleman, athlete, and hero Lou Brissie, in a recent photograph.

He looks at his questioner. Then he speaks of boyhood friends who went to war and did not return. He says that 50 years after he was carried from a creek bed in Italy, he went back. The graves stretched beyond his vision. He came to pay his respects but admits, "I could not finish. I had to walk away."

"I'm here," he said finally. "I'm here. I feel privileged just to have made it." Then he can say no more. □□

READY, SET, GO!!

1897 The first Boston Marathon was held April 19 — Patriots Day in Massachusetts, commemorating the battle of Lexington and Concord in 1775. Olympic sprinter Tom Burke drew a line in the dirt. At 12:19 P.M. he said "Go!" and all 18 runners went.

The winner in 2:55:10 was John J. McDermott, whose weight dropped from 123½ to 114½ during the race. Early leader Dick Grant of Harvard wore black leather shoes with leather soles.

Clarence DeMar

1899 The first ad for running shoes appeared ($2 a pair). The race drew 17 entrants plus a hound dog named Prince.

1900 Headlines in the Boston *Herald* on April 18:

"No weaklings will be permitted to start in the marathon tomorrow." Physicians examined each of the 29 entrants just to be sure.

1909 Temperatures hit 83.4° F — deadly to runners. The winner was Henri Renaud, whose job in a hot, humid cotton mill in Manchester, New Hampshire, accustomed him to the heat.

1911 "I did not let my eagerness to pass them get the better of me."
– winner Clarence DeMar, to a *Boston Post* reporter

1912 The race was bumped from the headlines on April 15, when the *Titanic* sank with 1,500 people aboard.

1913 Andrew Sockalexis, an Indian from Old Town, Maine, would win the hand of his sweetheart, Pauline Shay, if he won the race. Andrew came in second, two minutes behind the first-place finisher. Pauline married him anyway.

1918 War on Germany had been declared, and the marathon was replaced with a military relay. Uniformed servicemen raced the course carrying batons promoting Liberty Bonds.

1922 Clarence DeMar, 1911 winner, returned to set a new course record (2:18:10 for the 24.5-mile course). The press began calling him "Mr. DeMarathon" and "Mister DeMarvelous."

1927 Hot — up to 84° F by afternoon. The roads on the course had just been tarred. The *Boston Post* reported, "At frequent intervals yesterday the erstwhile macadam was a sea of live sticky tar." Clarence DeMar ran along the dirt walkways to win, setting yet another course record. Official marathon distance of 26 miles, 385 yards was adopted.

1930 "Mr. DeMarathon" won for the seventh time — an unsurpassed record of triumphs.

Johnny Kelley

1935 Johnny Kelley finished his third Boston Marathon and won. He would go on to run in 61 Boston marathons.

– photos this page courtesy the Trustees of the Boston Public Library

1996 will see the 100th running of the famous Boston Marathon, the oldest marathon in the country. Here are a few of the highlights, zigzags, and wrong turns along the way.   by Jamie Kageleiry

1946 Greek runner Stylianos Kyriakides determined to win in Boston so he could plead for food and medicine for his starving countrymen. In the final stage of the race Kyriakides pulled ahead of Johnny Kelley to win in 2:29:27. His emotional victory inspired many contributions to war-torn Greece.

1954 Clarence DeMar finished 78th. He was 66 years old.

1955 The Boston Marathon was televised for the first time.

1964 The number of runners went over 300 for the first time. Winner Aurele Vandendriessche beat the field on the hills to win in 2:19:59.

1966 From the moment Bobbi Gibb jumped out of the bushes and joined the starting lineup, runners had been asking each other, "Is that a girl?" Somewhere before Wellesley the cheers began. Against regulations, a woman was running the Boston Marathon. The crowd went wild. Roberta Gibb finished (unofficially) in 3:21:40.

Nina Kuscsik

Bill Rodgers

— courtesy of the Trustees of the Boston Public Library

1972 Women could race officially for the first time. Nina Kuscsik of Huntington, New York, was the women's winner in 3:10:26.

1975 Bill Rodgers beat the pack of 2,340 runners in an unprecedented 2:09:55.

1976 "Run for the Hoses" in 90° F sunshine saw exhausted runners struggling through rainbows of spray from Hopkinton to Boston.

1980 Boston's Bill Rodgers won his fourth marathon, and a woman named Rosie Ruiz slipped into the pack of runners about a mile before the finish and temporarily fooled everyone into thinking she had broken Joan Benoit's 1979 record (with barely breaking a sweat!).

Rosie Ruiz

1993 One hundred and one male runners finished under 2:38. John McDermott's winning time in 1897, on a shorter course, was 2:55.

1996 Race officials expect 25,000 entrants in this year's 100th marathon. □ □

The crowd loved Roberta Gibb in 1966.

TIME CORRECTION TABLES

The times of sunrise/sunset, moonrise/moonset, and the rising and setting times of the planets and bright stars are given for **Boston only** on pages 52-78, 40, and 44. Use the **Key Letter** shown to the right of each time on those pages with these tables to find the number of minutes that should be added to or subtracted from Boston time to give the correct time for your city. (Because of the complexities of calculation for different locations, times may not be precise to the minute.) If your city is not listed, find the city closest to you in both latitude and longitude and use those figures. **Boston's latitude is 42° 22' and longitude is 71° 03'**. Canadian cities appear at the end of the list. For a more complete explanation of the usage of Key Letters and these tables, see "How to Use This Almanac," page 30.

Time Zone Code: Atlantic Std. is -1; Eastern Std. is 0; Central Std. is 1; Mountain Std. is 2; Pacific Std. is 3; Alaska Std. is 4; Hawaii-Aleutian Std. is 5.

City	North Latitude ° '	West Longitude ° '	Time Zone Code	Key Letters				
				A min.	B min.	C min.	D min.	E min.
Aberdeen, SD	45 28	98 29	1	+37	+44	+49	+54	+59
Akron, OH	41 5	81 31	0	+46	+43	+41	+39	+37
Albany, NY	42 39	73 45	0	+ 9	+10	+10	+11	+11
Albert Lea, MN	43 39	93 22	1	+24	+26	+28	+31	+33
Albuquerque, NM	35 5	106 39	2	+45	+32	+22	+11	+ 2
Alexandria, LA	31 18	92 27	1	+58	+40	+26	+ 9	– 3
Allentown-Bethlehem, PA	40 36	75 28	0	+23	+20	+17	+14	+12
Amarillo, TX	35 12	101 50	1	+85	+73	+63	+52	+43
Anchorage, AK	61 10	149 59	4	–46	+27	+71	+122	+171
Asheville, NC	35 36	82 33	0	+67	+55	+46	+35	+27
Atlanta, GA	33 45	84 24	0	+79	+65	+53	+40	+30
Atlantic City, NJ	39 22	74 26	0	+23	+17	+13	+ 8	+ 4
Augusta, GA	33 28	81 58	0	+70	+55	+44	+30	+19
Augusta, ME	44 19	69 46	0	–12	– 8	– 5	– 1	0
Austin, TX	30 16	97 45	1	+82	+62	+47	+29	+15
Bakersfield, CA	35 23	119 1	3	+33	+21	+12	+ 1	– 7
Baltimore, MD	39 17	76 37	0	+32	+26	+22	+17	+13
Bangor, ME	44 48	68 46	0	–18	–13	– 9	– 5	– 1
Barstow, CA	34 54	117 1	3	+27	+14	+ 4	– 7	–16
Baton Rouge, LA	30 27	91 11	1	+55	+36	+21	+ 3	–10
Beaumont, TX	30 5	94 6	1	+67	+48	+32	+14	0
Bellingham, WA	48 45	122 29	3	0	+13	+24	+37	+47
Bemidji, MN	47 28	94 53	1	+14	+26	+34	+44	+52
Berlin, NH	44 28	71 11	0	– 7	– 3	0	+ 3	+ 7
Billings, MT	45 47	108 30	2	+16	+23	+29	+35	+40
Biloxi, MS	30 24	88 53	1	+46	+27	+11	– 5	–19
Binghamton, NY	42 6	75 55	0	+20	+19	+19	+18	+18
Birmingham, AL	33 31	86 49	1	+30	+15	+ 3	–10	–20
Bismarck, ND	46 48	100 47	1	+41	+50	+58	+66	+73
Boise, ID	43 37	116 12	2	+55	+58	+60	+62	+64
Brattleboro, VT	42 51	72 34	0	+ 4	+ 5	+ 5	+ 6	+ 7
Bridgeport, CT	41 11	73 11	0	+12	+10	+ 8	+ 6	+ 4
Brockton, MA	42 5	71 1	0	0	0	0	0	– 1
Brownsville, TX	25 54	97 30	1	+91	+66	+46	+23	+ 5
Buffalo, NY	42 53	78 52	0	+29	+30	+30	+31	+32
Burlington, VT	44 29	73 13	0	0	+ 4	+ 8	+12	+15
Butte, MT	46 1	112 32	2	+31	+39	+45	+52	+57
Cairo, IL	37 0	89 11	1	+29	+20	+12	+ 4	– 2
Camden, NJ	39 57	75 7	0	+24	+19	+16	+12	+ 9
Canton, OH	40 48	81 23	0	+46	+43	+41	+38	+36
Cape May, NJ	38 56	74 56	0	+26	+20	+15	+ 9	+ 5
Carson City–Reno, NV	39 10	119 46	3	+25	+19	+14	+ 9	+ 5

City	North Latitude ° '		West Longitude ° '		Time Zone Code	Key Letters				
						A min.	B min.	C min.	D min.	E min.
Casper, WY	42	51	106	19	2	+19	+19	+20	+21	+22
Chadron, NE	42	50	103	0	2	+ 5	+ 6	+ 7	+ 8	+ 9
Charleston, SC	32	47	79	56	0	+64	+48	+36	+21	+10
Charleston, WV	38	21	81	38	0	+55	+48	+42	+35	+30
Charlotte, NC	35	14	80	51	0	+61	+49	+39	+28	+19
Charlottesville, VA	38	2	78	30	0	+43	+35	+29	+22	+17
Chattanooga, TN	35	3	85	19	0	+79	+67	+57	+45	+36
Cheboygan, MI	45	39	84	29	0	+40	+47	+53	+59	+64
Cheyenne, WY	41	8	104	49	2	+19	+16	+14	+12	+11
Chicago-Oak Park, IL	41	52	87	38	1	+ 7	+ 6	+ 6	+ 5	+ 4
Cincinnati-Hamilton, OH	39	6	84	31	0	+64	+58	+53	+48	+44
Cleveland-Lakewood, OH	41	30	81	42	0	+45	+43	+42	+40	+39
Columbia, SC	34	0	81	2	0	+65	+51	+40	+27	+17
Columbus, OH	39	57	83	1	0	+55	+51	+47	+43	+40
Cordova, AK	60	33	145	45	4	−55	+13	+55	+103	+149
Corpus Christi, TX	27	48	97	24	1	+86	+64	+46	+25	+ 9
Craig, CO	40	31	107	33	2	+32	+28	+25	+22	+20
Dallas-Fort Worth, TX	32	47	96	48	1	+71	+55	+43	+28	+17
Danville, IL	40	8	87	37	1	+13	+ 9	+ 6	+ 2	0
Danville, VA	36	36	79	23	0	+51	+41	+33	+24	+17
Davenport, IA	41	32	90	35	1	+20	+19	+17	+16	+15
Dayton, OH	39	45	84	10	0	+61	+56	+52	+48	+44
Decatur, AL	34	36	86	59	1	+27	+14	+ 4	− 7	−17
Decatur, IL	39	51	88	57	1	+19	+15	+11	+ 7	+ 4
Denver-Boulder, CO	39	44	104	59	2	+24	+19	+15	+11	+ 7
Des Moines, IA	41	35	93	37	1	+32	+31	+30	+28	+27
Detroit-Dearborn, MI	42	20	83	3	0	+47	+47	+47	+47	+47
Dubuque, IA	42	30	90	41	1	+17	+18	+18	+18	+18
Duluth, MN	46	47	92	6	1	+ 6	+16	+23	+31	+38
Durham, NC	36	0	78	55	0	+51	+40	+31	+21	+13
Eastport, ME	44	54	67	0	0	−26	−20	−16	−11	− 8
Eau Claire, WI	44	49	91	30	1	+12	+17	+21	+25	+29
El Paso, TX	31	45	106	29	2	+53	+35	+22	+ 6	− 6
Elko, NV	40	50	115	46	3	+ 3	0	− 1	− 3	− 5
Ellsworth, ME	44	33	68	25	0	−18	−14	−10	− 6	− 3
Erie, PA	42	7	80	5	0	+36	+36	+35	+35	+35
Eugene, OR	44	3	123	6	3	+21	+24	+27	+30	+33
Fairbanks, AK	64	48	147	51	4	−127	+ 2	+61	+131	+205
Fall River–New Bedford, MA	41	42	71	9	0	+ 2	+ 1	0	0	− 1
Fargo, ND	46	53	96	47	1	+24	+34	+42	+50	+57
Flagstaff, AZ	35	12	111	39	2	+64	+52	+42	+31	+22
Flint, MI	43	1	83	41	0	+47	+49	+50	+51	+52
Fort Scott, KS	37	50	94	42	1	+49	+41	+34	+27	+21
Fort Smith, AR	35	23	94	25	1	+55	+43	+33	+22	+14
Fort Wayne, IN	41	4	85	9	0	+60	+58	+56	+54	+52
Fresno, CA	36	44	119	47	3	+32	+22	+15	+ 6	0
Gallup, NM	35	32	108	45	2	+52	+40	+31	+20	+11
Galveston, TX	29	18	94	48	1	+72	+52	+35	+16	+ 1
Gary, IN	41	36	87	20	1	+ 7	+ 6	+ 4	+ 3	+ 2
Glasgow, MT	48	12	106	38	2	− 1	+11	+21	+32	+42
Grand Forks, ND	47	55	97	3	1	+21	+33	+43	+53	+62
Grand Island, NE	40	55	98	21	1	+53	+51	+49	+46	+44
Grand Junction, CO	39	4	108	33	2	+40	+34	+29	+24	+20
Great Falls, MT	47	30	111	17	2	+20	+31	+39	+49	+58
Green Bay, WI	44	31	88	0	1	0	+ 3	+ 7	+11	+14
Greensboro, NC	36	4	79	47	0	+54	+43	+35	+25	+17

City	North Latitude ° '		West Longitude ° '		Time Zone Code	Key Letters				
						A min.	B min.	C min.	D min.	E min.
Hagerstown, MD	39	39	77	43	0	+35	+30	+26	+22	+18
Harrisburg, PA	40	16	76	53	0	+30	+26	+23	+19	+16
Hartford-New Britain, CT...	41	46	72	41	0	+ 8	+ 7	+ 6	+ 5	+ 4
Helena, MT	46	36	112	2	2	+27	+36	+43	+51	+57
Hilo, HI	19	44	155	5	5	+94	+62	+37	+ 7	−15
Honolulu, HI	21	18	157	52	5	+102	+72	+48	+19	− 1
Houston, TX	29	45	95	22	1	+73	+53	+37	+19	+ 5
Indianapolis, IN	39	46	86	10	0	+69	+64	+60	+56	+52
Ironwood, MI	46	27	90	9	1	0	+ 9	+15	+23	+29
Jackson, MI	42	15	84	24	0	+53	+53	+53	+52	+52
Jackson, MS	32	18	90	11	1	+46	+30	+17	+ 1	−10
Jacksonville, FL	30	20	81	40	0	+77	+58	+43	+25	+11
Jefferson City, MO	38	34	92	10	1	+36	+29	+24	+18	+13
Joplin, MO	37	6	94	30	1	+50	+41	+33	+25	+18
Juneau, AK	58	18	134	25	4	−76	−23	+10	+49	+86
Kalamazoo, MI	42	17	85	35	0	+58	+57	+57	+57	+57
Kanab, UT........................	37	3	112	32	2	+62	+53	+46	+37	+30
Kansas City, MO	39	1	94	20	1	+44	+37	+33	+27	+23
Keene, NH	42	56	72	17	0	+ 2	+ 3	+ 4	+ 5	+ 6
Ketchikan, AK	55	21	131	39	4	−62	−25	0	+29	+56
Knoxville, TN	35	58	83	55	0	+71	+60	+51	+41	+33
Kodiak, AK......................	57	47	152	24	4	0	+49	+82	+120	+154
LaCrosse, WI	43	48	91	15	1	+15	+18	+20	+22	+25
Lake Charles, LA	30	14	93	13	1	+64	+44	+29	+11	− 2
Lanai City, HI	20	50	156	55	5	+99	+69	+44	+15	− 6
Lancaster, PA...................	40	2	76	18	0	+28	+24	+20	+17	+13
Lansing, MI......................	42	44	84	33	0	+52	+53	+53	+54	+54
Las Cruces, NM	32	19	106	47	2	+53	+36	+23	+ 8	− 3
Las Vegas, NV.................	36	10	115	9	3	+16	+ 4	− 3	−13	−20
Lawrence-Lowell, MA	42	42	71	10	0	0	0	0	0	+ 1
Lewiston, ID	46	25	117	1	3	−12	− 3	+ 2	+10	+17
Lexington-Frankfort, KY..	38	3	84	30	0	+67	+59	+53	+46	+41
Liberal, KS.......................	37	3	100	55	1	+76	+66	+59	+51	+44
Lihue, HI	21	59	159	23	5	+107	+77	+54	+26	+ 5
Lincoln, NE......................	40	49	96	41	1	+47	+44	+42	+39	+37
Little Rock, AR................	34	45	92	17	1	+48	+35	+25	+13	+ 4
Los Angeles incl. Pasadena and Santa Monica, CA ...	34	3	118	14	3	+34	+20	+ 9	− 3	−13
Louisville, KY	38	15	85	46	0	+72	+64	+58	+52	+46
Macon, GA	32	50	83	38	0	+79	+63	+50	+36	+24
Madison, WI....................	43	4	89	23	1	+10	+11	+12	+14	+15
Manchester-Concord, NH...	42	59	71	28	0	0	0	+ 1	+ 2	+ 3
McAllen, TX	26	12	98	14	1	+93	+69	+49	+26	+9
Memphis, TN	35	9	90	3	1	+38	+26	+16	+ 5	− 3
Meridian, MS	32	22	88	42	1	+40	+24	+11	− 4	−15
Miami, FL........................	25	47	80	12	0	+88	+57	+37	+14	− 3
Miles City, MT	46	25	105	51	2	+ 3	+11	+18	+26	+32
Milwaukee, WI	43	2	87	54	1	+ 4	+ 6	+ 7	+ 8	+ 9
Minneapolis-St. Paul, MN	44	59	93	16	1	+18	+24	+28	+33	+37
Minot, ND........................	48	14	101	18	1	+36	+50	+59	+71	+81
Moab, UT.........................	38	35	109	33	2	+46	+39	+33	+27	+22
Mobile, AL	30	42	88	3	1	+42	+23	+ 8	− 8	−22
Monroe, LA	32	30	92	7	1	+53	+37	+24	+ 9	− 1
Montgomery, AL..............	32	23	86	19	1	+31	+14	+ 1	−13	−25
Muncie, IN.......................	40	12	85	23	0	+64	+60	+57	+53	+50
Nashville, TN...................	36	10	86	47	1	+22	+11	+ 3	− 6	−14
New Haven, CT	41	18	72	56	0	+11	+ 8	+ 7	+ 5	+ 4

City	North Latitude ° '	West Longitude ° '	Time Zone Code	Key Letters				
				A min.	B min.	C min.	D min.	E min.
New London, CT	41 22	72 6	0	+ 7	+ 5	+ 4	+ 2	+ 1
New Orleans, LA	29 57	90 4	1	+52	+32	+16	– 1	–15
New York, NY	40 45	74 0	0	+17	+14	+11	+ 9	+ 6
Newark–Irvington–East Orange, NJ	40 44	74 10	0	+17	+14	+12	+ 9	+ 7
Norfolk, VA	36 51	76 17	0	+38	+28	+21	+12	+ 5
North Platte, NE	41 8	100 46	1	+62	+60	+58	+56	+54
Norwalk-Stamford, CT	41 7	73 22	0	+13	+10	+ 9	+ 7	+ 5
Oakley, KS	39 8	100 51	1	+69	+63	+59	+53	+49
Ogden, UT	41 13	111 58	2	+47	+45	+43	+41	+40
Ogdensburg, NY	44 42	75 30	0	+ 8	+13	+17	+21	+25
Oklahoma City, OK	35 28	97 31	1	+67	+55	+46	+35	+26
Omaha, NE	41 16	95 56	1	+43	+40	+39	+37	+36
Orlando, FL	28 32	81 22	0	+80	+59	+42	+22	+ 6
Ortonville, MN	45 19	96 27	1	+30	+36	+40	+46	+51
Oshkosh, WI	44 1	88 33	1	+ 3	+ 6	+ 9	+12	+15
Palm Springs, CA	33 49	116 32	3	+28	+13	+ 1	–12	–22
Parkersburg, WV	39 16	81 34	0	+52	+46	+42	+36	+32
Paterson, NJ	40 55	74 10	0	+17	+14	+12	+ 9	+ 7
Pendleton, OR	45 40	118 47	3	– 1	+ 4	+10	+16	+21
Pensacola, FL	30 25	87 13	1	+39	+20	+ 5	–12	–26
Peoria, IL	40 42	89 36	1	+19	+16	+14	+11	+ 9
Philadelphia-Chester, PA	39 57	75 9	0	+24	+19	+16	+12	+ 9
Phoenix, AZ	33 27	112 4	2	+71	+56	+44	+30	+20
Pierre, SD	44 22	100 21	1	+49	+53	+56	+60	+63
Pittsburgh-McKeesport, PA	40 26	80 0	0	+42	+38	+35	+32	+29
Pittsfield, MA	42 27	73 15	0	+ 8	+ 8	+ 8	+ 8	+ 8
Pocatello, ID	42 52	112 27	2	+43	+44	+45	+46	+46
Poplar Bluff, MO	36 46	90 24	1	+35	+25	+17	+ 8	+ 1
Portland, ME	43 40	70 15	0	– 8	– 5	– 3	– 1	0
Portland, OR	45 31	122 41	3	+14	+20	+25	+31	+36
Portsmouth, NH	43 5	70 45	0	– 4	– 2	– 1	0	0
Presque Isle, ME	46 41	68 1	0	–29	–19	–12	– 4	+ 2
Providence, RI	41 50	71 25	0	+ 3	+ 2	+ 1	0	0
Pueblo, CO	38 16	104 37	2	+27	+20	+14	+ 7	+ 2
Raleigh, NC	35 47	78 38	0	+51	+39	+30	+20	+12
Rapid City, SD	44 5	103 14	2	+ 2	+ 5	+ 8	+11	+13
Reading, PA	40 20	75 56	0	+26	+22	+19	+16	+13
Redding, CA	40 35	122 24	3	+31	+27	+25	+22	+19
Richmond, VA	37 32	77 26	0	+41	+32	+25	+17	+11
Roanoke, VA	37 16	79 57	0	+51	+42	+35	+27	+21
Roswell, NM	33 24	104 32	2	+41	+26	+14	0	–10
Rutland, VT	43 37	72 58	0	+ 2	+ 5	+ 7	+ 9	+11
Sacramento, CA	38 35	121 30	3	+34	+27	+21	+15	+10
Salem, OR	44 57	123 1	3	+17	+23	+27	+31	+35
Salina, KS	38 50	97 37	1	+57	+51	+46	+40	+35
Salisbury, MD	38 22	75 36	0	+31	+23	+18	+11	+ 6
Salt Lake City, UT	40 45	111 53	2	+48	+45	+43	+40	+38
San Antonio, TX	29 25	98 30	1	+87	+66	+50	+31	+16
San Diego, CA	32 43	117 9	3	+33	+17	+ 4	– 9	–21
San Francisco incl. Oakland and San Jose, CA	37 47	122 25	3	+40	+31	+25	+18	+12
Santa Fe, NM	35 41	105 56	2	+40	+28	+19	+ 9	0
Savannah, GA	32 5	81 6	0	+70	+54	+40	+25	+13
Scranton–Wilkes Barre, PA	41 25	75 40	0	+21	+19	+18	+16	+15
Seattle-Tacoma-Olympia, WA	47 37	122 20	3	+ 3	+15	+24	+34	+42

City	North Latitude ° '	West Longitude ° '	Time Zone Code	Key Letters A min.	B min.	C min.	D min.	E min.
Sheridan, WY	44 48	106 58	2	+14	+19	+23	+27	+31
Shreveport, LA	32 31	93 45	1	+60	+44	+31	+16	+ 4
Sioux Falls, SD	43 33	96 44	1	+38	+40	+42	+44	+46
South Bend, IN	41 41	86 15	0	+62	+61	+60	+59	+58
Spartanburg, SC	34 56	81 57	0	+66	+53	+43	+32	+23
Spokane, WA	47 40	117 24	3	−16	− 4	+ 4	+14	+23
Springfield, IL	39 48	89 39	1	+22	+18	+14	+10	+ 6
Springfield-Holyoke, MA	42 6	72 36	0	+ 6	+ 6	+ 6	+ 5	+ 5
Springfield, MO	37 13	93 18	1	+45	+36	+29	+20	+14
St. Johnsbury, VT	44 25	72 1	0	− 4	0	+ 3	+ 7	+10
St. Joseph, MI	42 5	86 26	0	+61	+61	+60	+60	+59
St. Joseph, MO	39 46	94 50	1	+43	+38	+35	+30	+27
St. Louis, MO	38 37	90 12	1	+28	+21	+16	+10	+ 5
St. Petersburg, FL	27 46	82 39	0	+87	+65	+47	+26	+10
Syracuse, NY	43 3	76 9	0	+17	+19	+20	+21	+22
Tallahassee, FL	30 27	84 17	0	+87	+68	+53	+35	+22
Tampa, FL	27 57	82 27	0	+86	+64	+46	+25	+ 9
Terre Haute, IN	39 28	87 24	0	+74	+69	+65	+60	+56
Texarkana, AR	33 26	94 3	1	+59	+44	+32	+18	+ 8
Toledo, OH	41 39	83 33	0	+52	+50	+49	+48	+47
Topeka, KS	39 3	95 40	1	+49	+43	+38	+32	+28
Traverse City, MI	44 46	85 38	0	+49	+54	+57	+62	+65
Trenton, NJ	40 13	74 46	0	+21	+17	+14	+11	+ 8
Trinidad, CO	37 10	104 31	2	+30	+21	+13	+ 5	0
Tucson, AZ	32 13	110 58	2	+70	+53	+40	+24	+12
Tulsa, OK	36 9	95 60	1	+59	+48	+40	+30	+22
Tupelo, MS	34 16	88 34	1	+35	+21	+10	− 2	−11
Vernal, UT	40 27	109 32	2	+40	+36	+33	+30	+28
Walla Walla, WA	46 4	118 20	3	− 5	+ 2	+ 8	+15	+21
Washington, DC	38 54	77 1	0	+35	+28	+23	+18	+13
Waterbury-Meriden, CT	41 33	73 3	0	+10	+ 9	+ 7	+ 6	+ 5
Waterloo, IA	42 30	92 20	1	+24	+24	+24	+25	+25
Wausau, WI	44 58	89 38	1	+ 4	+ 9	+13	+18	+22
West Palm Beach, FL	26 43	80 3	0	+79	+55	+36	+14	− 2
Wichita, KS	37 42	97 20	1	+60	+51	+45	+37	+31
Williston, ND	48 9	103 37	1	+46	+59	+69	+80	+90
Wilmington, DE	39 45	75 33	0	+26	+21	+18	+13	+10
Wilmington, NC	34 14	77 55	0	+52	+38	+27	+15	+ 5
Winchester, VA	39 11	78 10	0	+38	+33	+28	+23	+19
Worcester, MA	42 16	71 48	0	+ 3	+ 2	+ 2	+ 2	+ 2
York, PA	39 58	76 43	0	+30	+26	+22	+18	+15
Youngstown, OH	41 6	80 39	0	+42	40	+38	+36	+34
Yuma, AZ	32 43	114 37	2	+83	+67	+54	+40	+28
CANADA								
Calgary, AB	51 5	114 5	2	+13	+35	+50	+68	+84
Edmonton, AB	53 34	113 25	2	− 3	+26	+47	+72	+93
Halifax, NS	44 38	63 35	−1	+21	+26	+29	+33	+37
Montreal, PQ	45 28	73 39	0	− 1	+ 4	+ 9	+15	+20
Ottawa, ON	45 25	75 43	0	+ 6	+13	+18	+23	+28
Peterborough, ON	44 18	78 19	0	+21	+25	+28	+32	+35
Saint John, NB	45 16	66 3	−1	+28	+34	+39	+44	+49
Saskatoon, SK	52 10	106 40	1	+37	+63	+80	+101	+119
Sydney, NS	46 10	60 10	−1	+ 1	+ 9	+15	+23	+28
Thunder Bay, ON	48 27	89 12	0	+47	+61	+71	+83	+93
Toronto, ON	43 39	79 23	0	+28	+30	+32	+35	+37
Vancouver, BC	49 13	123 6	3	0	+15	+26	+40	+52
Winnipeg, MB	49 53	97 10	1	+12	+30	+43	+58	+71

THE TWILIGHT ZONE

How to Determine the Length of Twilight and the Times of Dawn and Dark

Twilight begins (or ends) when the Sun is about 18 degrees below the horizon, and the latitude of a place, together with the time of year, determines the length of the twilight. To find the latitude of your city or the city nearest you, consult the **Time Correction Tables**, page 196. Check the figures against the chart at right for the appropriate date, and you will have the length of twilight in your area.

It is also possible to determine the times dawn will break and darkness descend by applying the length of twilight taken from the chart at right, to the times of sunrise and sunset at any specific place. (Follow the instructions given in "How to Use This Almanac," page 30, to determine sunrise/sunset times for a given locality.) **Subtract** the length of twilight from the time of sunrise for dawn. **Add** the length of twilight to the time of sunset for dark.

Latitude	25° N to 30° N	31° N to 36° N	37° N to 42° N	43° N to 47° N	48° N to 49° N
	H M	H M	H M	H M	H M
Jan. 1 to Apr. 10	1 20	1 26	1 33	1 42	1 50
Apr. 11 to May 2	1 23	1 28	1 39	1 51	2 04
May 3 to May 14	1 26	1 34	1 47	2 02	2 22
May 15 to May 25	1 29	1 38	1 52	2 13	2 42
May 26 to July 22	1 32	1 43	1 59	2 27	—
July 23 to Aug. 3	1 29	1 38	1 52	2 13	2 42
Aug. 4 to Aug. 14	1 26	1 34	1 47	2 02	2 22
Aug. 15 to Sept. 5	1 23	1 28	1 39	1 51	2 04
Sept. 6 to Dec. 31	1 20	1 26	1 33	1 42	1 50

	Boston, MA (latitude 42° 22')	Dallas, TX (latitude 32° 47')
Sunrise, August 1	4:37 A.M.	5:48 A.M.
Length of twilight	−1:52	−1:38
Dawn breaks	2:45 A.M., EST	4:10 A.M., CST
Sunset, August 1	7:03 P.M.	7:31 P.M.
Length of twilight	+1:52	+1:38
Dark descends	8:55 P.M., EST	9:09 P.M., CST

TIDAL GLOSSARY

Apogean Tide: A monthly tide of decreased range that occurs when the Moon is farthest from the Earth (at apogee).

Diurnal: Applies to a location that normally experiences one high water and one low water during a tidal day of approximately 24 hours.

Mean Lower Low Water: The arithmetic mean of the lesser of a daily pair of low waters, observed over a specific 19-year cycle called the National Tidal Datum Epoch.

Neap Tide: A tide of decreased range occurring twice a month when the Moon is in quadrature (during the first and last quarter Moons, when the Sun and Moon are at right angles to each other relative to the Earth).

Perigean Tide: A monthly tide of increased range that occurs when the Moon is closest to the Earth (at perigee).

Semidiurnal: Having a period of half a tidal day. East Coast tides, for example, are semi-diurnal, with two highs and two lows in approximately 24 hours.

Spring Tide: Named not for the season of spring, but from the German *springen* (to leap up). This tide of increased range occurs at times of syzygy (q.v.) each month. A spring tide also brings a lower low water.

Syzygy: Occurs twice a month when the Sun and Moon are in conjunction (lined up on the same side of the Earth at the new Moon) and when they are in opposition (on opposite sides of the Earth at the full Moon, though usually not so directly in line as to produce an eclipse). In either case, the gravitational effects of the Sun and Moon reinforce each other and tidal range is increased.

Vanishing Tide: A mixed tide of considerable inequality in the two highs or two lows, so that the "high low" may become indistinguishable from the "low high" or vice versa. The result is a vanishing tide, where no significant difference is apparent.

Tide Corrections

Many factors affect the time and height of the tides: the coastal configuration, the time of the Moon's southing (crossing the meridian) at the place, and the phase of the Moon. This table of tidal corrections is a sufficiently accurate guide to the times and heights of the high water at the places shown. (Low tides occur approximately 6.25 hours before and after high tides.) No figures are shown for the West Coast or the Gulf of Mexico, since the method used in compiling this table does not apply there. For such places and elsewhere where precise accuracy is required, consult the Tide Tables published annually by the National Ocean Service, 1305 E. West Highway, Silver Spring, MD 20910; telephone 301-713-2815.

The figures for Full Sea on the Left-Hand Calendar Pages 52-78 are the times of high tide at Commonwealth Pier in Boston Harbor. (Where a dash is shown under Full Sea, it indicates that time of high water has occurred after midnight and so is recorded on the next date.) The heights of these tides are given on the Right-Hand Calendar Pages 53-79. The heights are reckoned from Mean Lower Low Water, and each day listed has a set of figures — upper for the morning, lower for the evening. To obtain the time and height of high water at any of the following places, apply the time difference to the daily times of high water at Boston (pages 52-78) and the height difference to the heights at Boston (pages 53-79).

	Time Difference: Hr. Min.	Height Feet
MAINE		
Bar Harbor	–0 34	+0.9
Belfast	–0 20	+0.4
Boothbay Harbor	–0 18	–0.8
Chebeague Island	–0 16	–0.6
Eastport	–0 28	+8.4
Kennebunkport	+0 04	–1.0
Machias	–0 28	+2.8
Monhegan Island	–0 25	–0.8
Old Orchard	0 00	–0.8
Portland	–0 12	–0.6
Rockland	–0 28	+0.1
Stonington	–0 30	+0.1
York	–0 09	–1.0
NEW HAMPSHIRE		
Hampton	+0 02	–1.3
Portsmouth	+0 11	–1.5
Rye Beach	–0 09	–0.9
MASSACHUSETTS		
Annisquam	–0 02	–1.1
Beverly Farms	0 00	–0.5
Boston	0 00	0.0
Cape Cod Canal:		
East Entrance	–0 01	–0.8
West Entrance	–2 16	–5.9
Chatham Outer Coast	+0 30	–2.8
Inside	+1 54	*0.4
Cohasset	+0 02	–0.07
Cotuit Highlands	+1 15	*0.3
Dennis Port	+1 01	*0.4
Duxbury (Gurnet Pt.)	+0 02	–0.3
Fall River	–3 03	–5.0
Gloucester	–0 03	–0.8
Hingham	+0 07	0.0
Hull	+0 03	–0.2
Hyannis Port	+1 01	*0.3
Magnolia (Manchester)	–0 02	–0.7
Marblehead	–0 02	–0.4
Marion	–3 22	–5.4
Monument Beach	–3 08	–5.4
Nahant	–0 01	–0.5
Nantasket	+0 04	–0.1
Nantucket	+0 56	*0.3
Nauset Beach	+0 30	*0.6
New Bedford	–3 24	–5.7
Newburyport	+0 19	–1.8
Oak Bluffs	+0 30	*0.2
Onset (R.R. Bridge)	–2 16	–5.9
Plymouth	+0 05	0.0
Provincetown	+0 14	–0.4
Revere Beach	–0 01	–0.3
Rockport	–0 08	–1.0
Salem	0 00	–0.5
Scituate	–0 05	–0.7
Wareham	–3 09	–5.3
Wellfleet	+0 12	+0.5
West Falmouth	–3 10	–5.4
Westport Harbor	–3 22	–6.4
Woods Hole Little		
Harbor	–2 50	*0.2
Oceanographic Institute	–3 07	*0.2
RHODE ISLAND		
Bristol	–3 24	–5.3
Sakonnet	–3 44	–5.6
Narrangansett Pier	–3 42	–6.2
Newport	–3 34	–5.9
Pt. Judith	–3 41	–6.3
Providence	–3 20	–4.8
Watch Hill	–2 50	–6.8
CONNECTICUT		
Bridgeport	+0 01	–2.6

	Time Difference: Hr. Min.	Height Feet
Madison	−0 22	−2.3
New Haven	−0 11	−3.2
New London	−1 54	−6.7
Norwalk	+0 01	−2.2
Old Lyme (Highway Bridge)	−0 30	−6.2
Stamford	+0 01	−2.2
Stonington	−2 27	−6.6
NEW YORK		
Coney Island	−3 33	−4.9
Fire Island Lt	−2 43	*0.1
Long Beach	−3 11	−5.7
Montauk Harbor	−2 19	−7.4
New York City (Battery)	−2 43	−5.0
Oyster Bay	+0 04	−1.8
Port Chester	−0 09	−2.2
Port Washington	−0 01	−2.1
Sag Harbor	−0 55	−6.8
Southampton (Shinnecock Inlet)	−4 20	*0.2
Willets Point	0 00	−2.3
NEW JERSEY		
Asbury Park	−4 04	−5.3
Atlantic City	−3 56	−5.5
Bay Head (Sea Girt)	−4 04	−5.3
Beach Haven	−1 43	*0.24
Cape May	−3 28	−5.3
Ocean City	−3 06	−5.9
Sandy Hook	−3 30	−5.0
Seaside Park	−4 03	−5.4
PENNSYLVANIA		
Philadelphia	+2 40	−3.5
DELAWARE		
Cape Henlopen	−2 48	−5.3
Rehoboth Beach	−3 37	−5.7
Wilmington	+1 56	−3.8
MARYLAND		
Annapolis	+6 23	−8.5
Baltimore	+7 59	−8.3
Cambridge	+5 05	−7.8
Havre de Grace	+11 21	−7.7
Point No Point	+2 28	−8.1
Prince Frederick (Plum Point)	+4 25	−8.5
VIRGINIA		
Cape Charles	−2 20	−7.0
Hampton Roads	−2 02	−6.9
Norfolk	−2 06	−6.6
Virginia Beach	−4 00	−6.0
Yorktown	−2 13	−7.0
NORTH CAROLINA		
Cape Fear	−3 55	−5.0
Cape Lookout	−4 28	−5.7
Currituck	−4 10	−5.8
Hatteras:		
Ocean	−4 26	−6.0
Inlet	−4 03	−7.4
Kitty Hawk	−4 14	−6.2
SOUTH CAROLINA		
Charleston	−3 22	−4.3
Georgetown	−1 48	*0.36
Hilton Head	−3 22	−2.9
Myrtle Beach	−3 49	−4.4
St. Helena Harbor Entrance	−3 15	−3.4
GEORGIA		
Jekyll Island	−3 46	−2.9
Saint Simon's Island	−2 50	−2.9
Savannah Beach:		
River Entrance	−3 14	−5.5
Tybee Light	−3 22	−2.7
FLORIDA		
Cape Canaveral	−3 59	−6.0
Daytona Beach	−3 28	−5.3
Fort Lauderdale	−2 50	−7.2
Fort Pierce Inlet	−3 32	−6.9
Jacksonville Railroad Bridge	−6 55	*0.10
Miami Harbor Entrance	−3 18	−7.0
St. Augustine	−2 55	−4.9
CANADA		
Alberton, P.E.I.	−5 45**	−7.5
Charlottetown, P.E.I.	−0 45**	−3.5
Halifax, N.S.	−3 23	−4.5
North Sydney, N.S.	−3 15	−6.5
Saint John, N.B.	+0 30	+15.0
St. John's, Nfld.	−4 00	−6.5
Yarmouth, N.S.	−0 40	+3.0

* Where the difference in the "Height/Feet" column is so marked, height at Boston should be multiplied by this ratio.
** Varies widely; accurate only within 1½ hours. Consult local tide tables for precise times and heights.

Example: The conversion of the times and heights of the tides at Boston to those of Norfolk, Virginia, is given below:

Sample tide calculation July 10, 1996:

High tide Boston (p. 68)	7:00 A.M., EST
Correction for Norfolk	−2:06 hrs.
High tide Norfolk	4:54 A.M., EST
Tide height Boston (p. 69)	9.1 ft.
Correction for Norfolk	−6.6 ft.
Tide height Norfolk	2.5 ft.

HAND-CARVED CUCKOO CLOCK

"FOREST CREATURES"

Deluxe Clock features deeply hand-carved owls, squirrels and songbirds with nest. Cuckoos on the hour and half hour with one day weight-driven movement. Carved from select lindenwood in the Black Forest region of Germany. Cuckoo, case, dial and hands are wood. Hand-stained and rubbed antique finish. Facade 13.75"
#15386..........................$265.00
plus $15.00 shipping. N.Y.S. + tax C.O.D. + $4.50.   M/C VISA
1-800-632-8105
or write: Terre Celeste Gallery
Box 4125
Kenmore, N.Y. 14217

Best Fishing Days, 1996
(and other fishing lore from the files of *The Old Farmer's Almanac*)

Probably the best fishing time is when the ocean tides are restless before their turn and in the first hour of ebbing. All fish in all waters — salt or fresh — feed most heavily at that time.

Best temperatures for fish species vary widely, of course, and are chiefly important if you are going to have your own fish pond. Best temperatures for brook trout are 45° to 65° F. Brown trout and rainbows are more tolerant of higher temperatures. Smallmouth black bass do best in cool water. Horned pout take what they find.

Most of us go fishing when we can get time off, not because it is the best time. But there are best times:

☞ One hour before and one hour after high tide, and one hour before and one hour after low tide. (The times of high tides are given on pages 52-78 and corrected for your locality on pages 202-203. Inland, the times for high tides would correspond with the times the Moon is due south. Low tides are halfway between high tides.)

☞ "The morning rise" — after sunup for a spell — and "the evening rise" — just before sundown and the hour or so after.

☞ Still water or a ripple is better than a wind at both times.

☞ When there is a hatch of flies — caddis or mayflies, commonly. (The fisherman will have to match the hatching flies with *his* fly — or go fishless.)

☞ When the breeze is from a westerly quarter rather than north or east.

☞ When the barometer is steady or on the rise. (But, of course, even in a three-day driving northeaster the fish isn't going to give up feeding. His hunger clock keeps right on working, and the smart fisherman will find something he wants.)

☞ When the Moon is between new and full.

Moon Between New & Full, 1996

Jan. 1-5	June 15-30
Jan. 20-Feb. 4	July 15-30
Feb. 18-March 5	Aug. 14-29
March 19-April 3	Sept. 12-26
April 17-May 3	Oct. 12-26
May 17-June 1	Nov. 10-24
Dec. 10-24	

Classified Advertising

ASTROLOGY/OCCULT

ASTROLOGY. Personalized, comprehensive natal chart $12. Progressed chart for current year $12. Both $18. Send name, birthdate, birth time, birthplace. Cycles, Dept. FAA, 2251 Berkely Ave., Schenectady NY 12309

AMERICA'S PSYCHIC HOT LINE. Fast, astonishing answers from warm, friendly professionals. Call today! 900-420-2444 ext. 515, $2.99/minute. 18+ Avalon.

CATALOG: Complete spiritual, self-help needs. Oils, incense, books, etc. $2. Power Products, Box 442-F, Mars Hill NC 28754

THE MOST COMPLETE metaphysical, magical, psychic-power correspondence course ever. Become a recognized professional. Earn unlimited income with our university doctoral degree program. Reasonable rates. Priesthood, 2401 Artesia Blvd. 12-188FA, Redondo Beach CA 90278

LARGEST WITCHCRAFT CATALOG! Gain love, money & power! Send $2, refundable. PO Box 667, Jamestown NY 14702

BEST LIVE PSYCHICS, accurate & powerful, 800-756-4733. Canadian callers, dial 900-451-3885. 24 hours, 18+, $1.99 1/2 minute.

PSYCHIC CAN influence others. Removes spells. Restores nature. Brings luck: Rev. Carson Weaver. Telephone 703-439-8495

LOVE, LUCK, AND MONEY can be yours. Send now for free catalog. Church Goods, Dept. F, 801 W. Jackson, Chicago IL 60607

WITCHCRAFT POWERS for protection, success, and happiness can be yours. Seven home-study courses and personal instruction. Free information: PO Box 1366, Nashua NH 03061. 603-880-8237

WANT MORE from Celeste Longacre? Daily guidance in *Sweet Fern* (quarterly magazine). $14 annually. RR 1 Box 566-F, Walpole NH 03608

LOOKING EAGERLY for institution dealing in magic carbon with lucky numbers that reappear on same even when burned. Interested all information related this kind of business. Kennedy, PO Box 4663, Curacao, Netherlands Antilles

BIORHYTHMS. Your physical, emotional, intellectual cycles charted in color. Interpretation guide. Six months $12. Twelve months $18. Send name, birthdate. Cycles, Dept. FAB, 2251 Berkely Ave., Schenectady NY 12309

AMAZING OCCULT discoveries develop supernatural powers safely, easily! Free experiments. Williamsburg, Box 3483-FAL, New York NY 10008

FREE LUCKY NUMBERS. Send birthdate, self-addressed stamped envelope. Mystic, Box 2009-R, Jamestown NC 27282

WORLD'S LARGEST OCCULT, New Age, witchcraft, voodoo. 220 pages of thousands of fascinating curios and gifts. 1996 issue, $2. By airmail, $3. Worldwide Curio House, Box 17095-A, Minneapolis MN 55417

FIND OUT what's in your future! Live physic line 24-hours/day. 900-226-4345 ext. 1548. $3.95/min., average call 3/min., 18+, touch-tone phone. TeleService USA inc., Hagerstown MD. 301-797-2323

FREE NATAL CHART. Prepared by one of America's best ten top metaphysicians, Stacey Dean. Send birthdate, time, and place. Please enclose $1 for postage. I.A.P.A. Network, PO Box 17070 Dept. SD, Las Vegas NV 89114

AUTOMOTIVE

AUTOMOBILE LITERATURE WANTED, 1900-1975. I buy automobile sales brochures, manuals, etc. Walter Miller, 6710 Brooklawn, Syracuse NY 13211. 315-432-8282 or fax 315-432-8256

WANTED: Porcelain license plates, especially from southern states and cities. Chuck Westphal, 246 E. Broadway, Port Jefferson NY 11777

GOVERNMENT AUCTIONS, your area: Cars, trucks, computers, more! Must sell! Great deals now! 800-601-2212, ext. sp8440

BEER & WINE MAKING

HOMEMADE LIQUEURS, wine, beer recipes; book $4. Homemade sausage recipes; book $4. 3 books $10. Homemade Recipes, Box 53 RR 3, Yorkton, SK S3N 2X5

WINE IS CHEAPER than ever to make. One quart 50¢. Recipe $3. Conco, 16796 Malibu Dr., Flint TX 75762-9231

WINEMAKERS-BEERMAKERS. Free illustrated catalog. Fast service. Large selection. Kraus, Box 7850-YB, Independence MO 64054. 816-254-0242

HOME BREWERS. Great beginner's kit. Free catalog. James Page Brewery, 1310 Quincy, Minneapolis MN 55413. 800-234-0685

BOAT KITS & PLANS

BOAT KITS & PLANS. Boatbuilding supplies. 250 designs. Catalog only $3. Clarkcraft, 16-29 Aqualane, Tonawanda NY 14150

BOOKS/MAGAZINES/CATALOGS

PERSONALIZED BOOKS starring your child! For catalog, write CCAB(OFA), PO Box 526, Owings MD 20736

FREE BOOKLETS. Life, death, soul, resurrection, pollution crisis, hell, Judgment Day, restitution. Bible Standard (OF), PO Box 67, Chester Springs PA 19425-0067

PIONEER HISTORICAL ROMANCE novels. Free book with purchase. Free list. Hermit Press, 2675 Choctaw Trail, Marianna FL 32446

PHOTOWORK NEWSLETTER readers make better pictures. Four issues $10. Photowork, 317 E. Winter #J, Danville IL 61832-1857

FREE CATALOG. Minnetonka Moccasins, the No. 1 brand in America. Available men's, women's, children's. Your satisfaction guaranteed. Write: Moccasin House, PO Box 16235A, St. Paul MN 55116

MOOSE LOVERS! Free catalog of fine handcrafted items with *Mostly Moose* in mind. Call or write: Mostly Moose, 166 Shephard Rd., Dept. G1, Gibsonia PA 15044. 800-488-6674

PUBLISH YOUR BOOK! All subjects invited. Attractive publicity, advertising, quality service, covering 5 decades of satisfied authors. Send for fact-filled booklet and free manuscript evaluation. Carlton Press, Dept. OA11, W. 32nd St., New York NY 10001

FREE GIFT catalog. Send for catalog to A.L.L. Novelties; PO Box 2920-FA1, Wendover NV 89883

WIN CONSISTENTLY at slot machines! Free report. Write: JSA Publications, Box 919, North Arlington NJ 07031

CLASSIFIEDS

HOW TO get out of debt fast! Send SASE for free information. Magi, Box 1508, Airway Hts. WA 99001. 509-244-5949

FREE! World's most unusual novelty catalog: 2,000 things you never knew existed. Johnson-Smith, F-625, Bradenton FL 34200

CHILDREN'S personalized books, personalized pop-up books. Write for free catalog. United Publication, Box 5215, Brookfield CT 06804

MANY GRACE LIVINGSTON HILL books. List free. Arnold Publications-A, 2440 Bethel Rd., Nicholasville KY 40356. Phone 800-854-8571

REPAIR SUPPLIES FOR CHINA, pottery, dolls, figurines, and glass. Catalog $2. Restoration Materials, Ltd., PO Box 186, Webster City IA 50595-0186

HOW-TO BOOKS AND VIDEOS on self-reliance, practical survival, personal and financial freedom, and more! 72-page catalog describes over 600 titles. Send $2 to: Paladin Press, Box 1307-6AZ, Boulder CO 80306

HOME STORAGE CHECKLIST. Practical workbook shows how much food, clothing, hygienic and first-aid items to store. Send $6.45 to Griffin Publishing, PO Box 1645, Ogden UT 84402

TRICKS YOUR BUTCHER USES. Unique book reveals them. Plus how to cut your meat budget in half. 100 plus pages. Send $9.95 plus $3 S&H to: Shop Smart Books, Ste. 7, PO Box 323, Baldwinsville NY 13027

SENIOR/CATALOG BUYERS! Amway products. Free "Priority Service Catalog." 1-800 Ordering. UPS delivery. Harris, 1137 W. 140 Pl., Gardena CA 90247. 24 hours, 310-323-1137

FULCRUM PUBLISHING. Gardeners across America swear by our gardening books and calendars, including *The Undaunted Garden* (Lauren Springer), *Edible Flowers* (Cathy Barash), *Easy Gardening* (Jack Kramer), and *Greenhouse Gardener's Companion* (Shane Smith). Order your *1996 Gardening Guide* calendar today – the only gardening calendar with region-specific advice (7 U.S. regions) and luscious garden photography. Cal 800-992-2908 to order or for a copy of our catalog.

BUSINESS OPPORTUNITIES

$1,000 WEEKLY POSSIBLE: $2 for each envelope you stuff. Rush SASE for free details: Postscripts, PO Box 39608, Los Angeles CA 90039

HERBALIFE DISTRIBUTOR. Marie Van Stokkum, Business Opportunity, Products. 619-320-9421 or 800-246-8312 (USA). Leave message. Compuserve 72223.640.

WE BUY magazine/newspaper clippings. $781.23 weekly. Send stamped envelope. Edwards, Box 467159FA, Atlanta GA 31146

LET THE GOVERNMENT FINANCE your small business. Grants/loans to $500,000. Free recorded message: 707-448-0270. (KE1)

WATKINS PRODUCTS since 1868, has steady and sincere ways to help you have a successful home-based business. Call 800-828-1868.

JOIN HOME-WORKER'S ASSOCIATION. Get guaranteed legitimate home-employment offers! Many choices! Write: Association-FA96, Alexandria Bay NY 13607-0250.

EARN UP TO $15,000 per month, guaranteed. Rush SASE for free details: BHCS, 4470 Sunset Blvd. Ste. 580, Los Angeles CA 90027

START A MONEYMAKING plumbing-repair business. Free exciting details. Distance Learning, 33227 Bainbridge, Cleveland OH 44139

HOW TO start your own profitable wholesale business. $1, refundable. KG Specialty Merchandise, 1779 Jane #705-FA, Toronto, Ontario, Canada M9N 3V7

HOME TYPING. Hand addressing. $500 weekly possible! Details free: National, Box 104-A G, Island Park NY 11558-0104

RECORD VIDEOTAPES at home. $5,000 monthly possible. No pornography. Free details. Write: CMS Video Co., 210 Lorna Sq. #163FA, Birmingham AL 35216

GOOD WEEKLY INCOME processing our mail! Free supplies! Genuine opportunity! Rush SASE to: GSECO, 11220 W. Florissant-DE, Florissant MO 63033

WORLDWIDE LOTTO CLUB. 100 chances every week. Send large SASE. Club, Box 1701(FA), Fairborn OH 45324. Order: 800-323-5025; sponsor #2905.

MAKE $25 PER POUND from free aluminum scrap? Yes! Free report! Ameriscrap-FA96, Alexandria Bay NY 13607-0107

BE YOUR OWN BOSS. Buy below wholesale. Sell over 2,500 fast-selling items at swap meets, retail stores, parties. Free info: Supreme Products, Dept. G, PO Box 4821, Warrington FL 32507

$27,000 IN BACKYARD. Grow new specialty plants. Start with $100. Free booklet. Growers, Box 1058-FA, Bellingham WA 98227-1058

MONEYMAKING BOOKS. Great selection! Write: Brickyard Publishing, Dept. A, PO Box 1103, Hudson NH 03051

NEW! 2,000% PROFITS in mold making/casting. Free information: Castcraft, Box 17000(FA), Memphis TN 38187-0000

YOUR OWN BUSINESS. Complete package. Guaranteed moneymaker. Free information. SASE: Parrish Enterprises, 3352 R.O. Peach Rd., Columbia TN 38401

INDEPENDENT FULLER BRUSH distributors. Earn amazing profits. Get the facts. Free information package. Catalog 800-445-0761

900 TURNKEY. Complete, profitable TV/print advertising program; 30-day pay out. Free information: 800-574-5099. T.M.P., 2609 S. Highland Dr. Dept. OFA, Las Vegas NV 89109

COLLECTIBLES/NOSTALGIA

WARREN'S ILLUSTRATED AMERICANA GUIDE lists over 20,000 prices in 250 categories of American collectibles. Invaluable reference for collectors, flea-markets, etc. Send $14.40 plus $2.50 s/h. The O'Learys, 30 Independence, Montpelier VT 05602

WANTED. Glass swirl marbles, sulphide marbles. Top prices paid. Write: Bertram Cohen, 169 Marlborough St., Boston MA 02116. 617-247-4754

A FREE LIST: High-quality antique pocket knives. Case, Primble, and other superior brands. Ideal for investment return and memorable gifts. Reasonably priced. Send LSASE. Bill Penley, Box 818-OFA, Fletcher NC 28732

POSTCARDS. Do you have a collection of early postcards you wish to dispose of, add to, or have appraised? Request a free Dealer Directory that lists over 300 reputable postcard dealers who will be glad to assist you, plus other helpful information concerning postcards as a hobby. To cover P/H in U.S. send $1.25 (stamps preferred), Canada $2 (U.S.) & Europe $2.50 (U.S.) to: International Federation of Postcard Dealers, Attn-FA, PO Box 1765, Manassas VA 22110.

CRAFTS

BEADS, BEEDS, beades, beyds, bieds, beadds, bbeads, boyds, boids, byeds, byods, beezds, beadz, beades, beatds, beydds, bbbs, beezts, beads, and more beads. Catalog $1. Terre Celeste, Box 4125FA, Kenmore NY 14217

INDIAN CRAFTS. Free brochure showing materials used. Recommended to Indian guides, scout troops, etc. Cleveland Leather, 2629 Lorain Ave., Cleveland OH 44113

EXOTIC/TROPICAL PLANTS

CARNIVOROUS (insect-eating) plants, seeds, supplies, and books. Peter Paul's Nurseries, Canandaigua NY 14424-8713

CLASSIFIEDS

CALADIUM BULBS. Send a gift to cheer someone with bright-colored caladiums. Use in your yard for beautiful color all summer. Send for brochure. Fancy Leaf Caladiums Aim, 704 CR 621 East, Lake Placid FL 33852. 813-465-0044

FREE CATALOG. Exotic, tropical, unusual, and rare seeds worldwide. 400+ varieties. Seeds, 3421 Bream, Gautier MS 39553

EDUCATION/INSTRUCTION

LEARN TAX PREPARATION. Approved home study. Free career literature. P.C.D.I., Atlanta, Georgia. 800-362-7070, Dept. TPK554

LEARN LANDSCAPING at home. Free brochure. Call 800-326-9221 or write Lifetime Career Schools, Dept. OBO116, 101 Harrison St., Archbald PA 18403

DOLLS! Learn to make, repair, and dress dolls. Free brochure on homestudy program. Call 800-326-9221 or write Lifetime Career Schools, Dept. OBO416, 101 Harrison St., Archbald PA 18403

BECOME A PARALEGAL. Attorney-instructed home study. P.C.D.I., Atlanta, Georgia. 800-362-7070, Dept. LLK554

COMPLETE HIGH SCHOOL AT HOME. Diploma awarded. Low tuition. Est. 1897. Telephone 800-228-5600 for free information or write American School, Dept. #348, 850 E. 58th St., Chicago IL 60637

LEARN SEWING/DRESSMAKING at home. Latest factory shortcuts and methods. Free information. Call 800-326-9221 or write Lifetime Career Schools, Dept. OBO316, 101 Harrison St., Archbald PA 18403

BECOME AN ELECTRICIAN. Approved home study. Free career literature. P.C.D.I., Atlanta, Georgia. 800-362-7070, Dept. TEK554

COLLEGE DEGREES WITHOUT classrooms. Complete information on hundreds of accredited schools. Free recorded message: 707-447-3053. (6KE1)

LEARN FLOWER ARRANGING! Start business or hobby. Free brochure on Home Study Program. Call 800-326-9221 or write Lifetime Career Schools, Dept. OBO216, 101 Harrison St., Archbald PA 18403

LEARN VCR REPAIR. Great profits. Home study. P.C.D.I., Atlanta, Georgia. Free literature. 800-362-7070, Dept. VRK554

LEARN FLORAL DESIGN/FLOWER BUSINESS. Home study. Free literature. P.C.D.I., Atlanta, Georgia. 800-362-7070, Dept. FLK554

ELECTRICITY/ELECTRONICS TRAINING series used by U.S. military, 24 volumes; other courses available. Free catalog. Federal Technical Publishers, Box 1218 R, Glen Lake MN 55345

BECOME A MEDICAL transcriptionist. Home study. Free career literature. P.C.D.I., Atlanta, Georgia. 800-362-7070, Dept. YYK554

UNIVERSITY DEGREES without classes! Accredited bachelor's, master's, doctorates. Free revealing facts! Thornson-FA6, Box 470886, Tulsa OK 74147

VETERINARY ASSISTANT/ANIMAL CARE careers. Home study. P.C.D.I., Atlanta, Georgia. Free literature. 800-362-7070, Dept. CCK554

BECOME A HOME INSPECTOR. Approved home study. Free literature. P.C.D.I., Atlanta, Georgia. 800-362-7070, Dept. PPK554

FARM AND GARDEN

TROYBILT OWNERS. Discount parts catalog. Send stamp. Replacement tines $57. Kelly's, Manilla IN 46150. 317-398-9042

SAFE, EASY LAWN CARE Guide. Send $2. V.L. Price Horticultural, 506 Grove Ave., Catawissa PA 17820

FREE CATALOG. Finest-quality flower, herb, and vegetable seeds obtainable. Burrell, PO Box 150-FA, Rocky Ford CO 81067

LIVE FISH, pond stocking, 20 species, also lilies. Colored catalog $2. Zetts Fish Hatcheries, Drifting PA 16834

FREE GARDENING CATALOG. 4,000 items! Seeds, trees, shrubs, supplies, greenhouses, beneficial insects. Mellinger's, Dept. 720K, Range Rd., North Lima OH 44452-9731

HOME CANNERS. Order everything you need: canners, jars, rubber rings, spices, more. Send $1 for catalog. Home Canning Supply, PO Box 1158-OF, Ramona CA 92065

SAWMILL $3,795. Saw logs into lumber. Free information. Silvacraft Sawmills, 90 Curtwright #3, Amherst NY 14221. 800-661-7746

WE DESIGN ANYTHING. Barns. Houses. Aviaries. SASE/$3. Biljon Corp., FA PO Box 420, Jonesboro AR 72403-0420

HYDROELECTRIC SYSTEMS since 1973. Free brochure, guide. U.S. $15. WPM, c/o Box 9723, Midland TX. 915-697-6955

PAYING TOP DOLLAR for wildcrafted roots, herbs, leaves, and barks. Send for a free price list and more information to Wilcox Natural Products, PO Box 391 Dept. FA, Boone NC 28607. Five locations nationwide.

BONSAI PLANTS, pots, tools, books. Send $1 for catalog to: The Bonsai Farm, PO Box 130F, LaVernia TX 78121

FLAGS

FLAGS, FLAGS! American, state, MIA/POW, Confederate, historical, more. For color catalog, send $2 to: Flags & Things, PO Box 356, Dillsburg PA 17019

FOOD AND RECIPES

MEAT-LOAF DINNERS. Cook and serve all in one pan. Send $2. Ginny, PO Box 113, Gloucester NC 28528

FAMILY TREASURE Recipes: Pennsylvania Dutch Shoo-fly Pie and deluxe, delicious, raspberry/chocolate delights. Send $1 with SASE to: PO Box 1214, Oak Park IL 60304

CANDY MAKING. Complete line of candy supplies, chocolate, molds, boxes, etc. Send SASE for price lists. Ferncliff House, Box 177, Tremont City OH 45372

SCANDINAVIAN DESSERTS. Eight delicious recipes. SASE, $2. Robert Salberg, 3714 Beverly Ave. NE, Salem OR 97305

SOURDOUGH SECRETS plus 4 exciting recipes. SASE, $3. Aunt Mottney, 1225 Maple Springs Ch. Rd., Shelby NC 28152

SPICES-SPICES-SPICES. Buy direct and save for all your cooking and crafting needs. Quart-size containers. Send one dollar for free sample and price list. Dealers welcomed. J. & L. Spice Plus, PO Box 117, Terryville CT 06786-0117. 806-582-1121

DO YOUR PANCAKES leave you flat? Tug Hill Buttermilk Pancake Recipe. $1 and SASE: Recipe, Box 87, Union Hill NY 14563

MOUTH WATERING: Broccoli casserole New England style. Send $3 with stamped envelope to Natalia's Recipes, 880 Bristol St., New Bedford MA 02745

CHOCOLATE POTPOURRI LTD. Handcrafted chocolate made with tender loving care. As featured in *Bon Appetit* magazine. Catalog available. 800-466-3353. 1880 Johns Dr., Glenview IL 60025

DEER, DUCK, RABBIT. 15 easy recipes $4. Nancy's, Box 1318-B, Florence SC 29503

PREWAR PLANTATION cooking book, bonus recipe $6.95. Harper Enterprises, PO Box 180, Hobson TX 78117

COOKING WITH BEER. Fantastic new cookbook has over 130 recipes. Only $9.50 delivered. Patco, Box 190-A, Florence SC 29503. Credit card orders 800-562-6053

CLASSIFIEDS

MONTEREY COUNTY GRAND-PRIZE winners' nutritious, delicious, sugarless Apple Pie, Big Sur Turkey Chili. SASE $1. Wildflower, Pacific Valley Ctr., Big Sur CA 93920

GOOD COOKING SECRETS. Tips. Recipes. $15 to J. Doggette, PO Box 52, Belle Chasse LA 70037

FOR THE HOME

CUCKOO, KUCKOO, kuckuck, coocoo, kuukuu, coucou, khukhu, ucucuu and more hand-carved cuckoo clocks. Catalog $1. Terre Celeste Gallery, Box 4125F, Kenmore NY 14217

NEW! HURRICANE, STORM-TRACKING system/weather station. Simply beautiful! For home, office, gifts. Free brochure: Magnetracker, PO Box 675, E. Freetown MA 02717

BEAUTIFUL dried-flower wall pieces. Send LSASE to: L. Enterprises (FA1), PO Box 1948, Andover MA 01810

HOW TO BUILD your dream home for 1/3 the cost. Guaranteed! $4.95 complete details. Ron Viveiros, 125 Jerome St., Berkley MA 02779-1006

ALADDIN MANTEL LAMPS and parts. Practical and beautiful. Free catalog. M.S.I., 201 W. Commerce St., Lewisburg TN 37091-3337 or 615-270-6962

GINSENG AND HERBS

GINSENG 1st-year roots $18/100, stratified seed $12/oz. Complete information $1. Ginseng OFAG, Flagpond TN 37657

$80,000 FROM ONE ACRE! Grow ginseng. Sell $60/pound. Information: Leeland's, 5712-FB Cooper Rd., Indianapolis IN 46208

GOVERNMENT SURPLUS

GOVERNMENT-SEIZED VEHICLES! Buy dirt cheap! Your area! Free details. Surplus, Box 3321, Ft. Smith AR 72913

GREENHOUSES

SUPER-STRONG GREENHOUSE, pond-liner plastic. Resists hail, windstorms, yellowing. Box 42FA, Neche ND 58265. 204-327-5540, daily.

FREE CATALOG. Lowest prices: pots, flats, lights. Wholesale/retail. Three stamps postage: Plant Collectibles, 103FAM Kenview, Buffalo NY 14217

HEALTH/BEAUTY

FREE VIDEO CATALOG information herbal/patent medicines. Champion's Rx-Herbs, 2369-Fa Elvis Presley, Memphis TN 38106

FREE CATALOG! Name-brand natural vitamins, herbs, and nutritional supplements. Prices up to 60% below suggested retail. Brands include Country Life, Enzymatic Therapy, Kal, Nature's Life, Schiff, Twinlab, and more! 800-858-2143

HERBS FOR YOUR HEALTH. Many proven, safe medicinal uses. Also great for cooking. Free catalog: Herbs, PO Box 2115, Naples FL 33939

I SMOKED 4 packs/day. *How I Quit.* Startling. $5. FAB, Box 189-FA, Hilton NY 14468

MIRACULOUS CURE of mange. For detailed instructions send $4, SASE to: Cure, PO Box 6547, San Juan PR 00914

EXOTIC SOUTH PACIFIC PERFUME sachets. U.S. $5, check/m.o. for 3. J. Hermes, 36 Aubrey Road, Silverdale RD3, Auckland, New Zealand.

ALLERGY SUFFERERS: Try our natural raw honey produced from organic floral sources. Six large 40-oz. jars $39.95 postpaid. Buffalo Creek Honey Farm, Rte. One, Box 147, Nahunta GA 31553. 912-462-5068

NATURAL MEDICINE for your common ailments with no side effects. Homeopathic medicines are safe for you. Free catalog: Luyties, Box 8080 (Dept. 06), St. Louis MO 63156

1,300 NATURAL HOME REMEDIES. All-purpose health book. Shipped 48 hours. MC/VISA. Send $16 Almanac, 6709 LaTijera Ste. 447-F, Los Angeles CA 90045. 800-697-9739

KOMBUCHA TEA BEVERAGE. Wonderful health benefits. Complete starter package $10. Wildflower, Pacific Valley Ctr., Big Sur CA 93920

HELP WANTED

READ BOOKS FOR PAY! $95 each. Free report. Send #10/SASE: BES, Box 4579-FA, Walnut Creek CA 94596-0579

WARNING! Don't fall for home-working scams. Free consumer newsletter helps you find legitimate home employment. Send LSASE: Consumer Publications, Box 1250-F, Medford OR 97501

INDEPENDENT SALES AGENTS. Goodwill ambassadors to market *Greatest Story Ever Told.* Commission. Reply: BHPP, PO Box 489, Spearfish SD 57783

$329.84 WEEKLY assembling products at home. Receive free information! Call toll free: 800-460-WABC ext. 1292 (message).

EXCELLENT EXTRA INCOME! Assemble simple craft products at home! Program guaranteed! Call now! 800-377-6000, ext. 8440

INVENTION/PATENTS

FREE INVENTION PACKAGE. Davison & Associates offers customized development, patenting, and licensing. Proven results: 800-677-6382

PATENT IT ECONOMICALLY! Free details. Licensed since 1958. Ranere Associates, 2008 Fondulac, Richmond VA 23229

INVENTORS: If you have an invention for sale or license, write for free booklet explaining how we can help you. Kessler Sales Corp., C-42-5, Fremont OH 43420

INVENTIONS, IDEAS, new products! Presentation to industry/exhibition at national innovation exposition. Patent services. 800-288-IDEA

JEWELRY

ZODIAC PENDANTS. 14kt gold layered $14.95 (send sign), or $3 unique gifts catalog and free crystal pendant. Visionary Enterprises, PO Box 117, Findlay OH 45839-0117

JEWELRY: 14kt gold bracelets, earrings, necklaces, and rings with semiprecious stones. Big savings! For brochure, call 800-729-2521, toll free. 24-hour service.

COPPER BRACELETS: Solid copper chain link. Beautifully hand polished. specify 8-, 9-, or 10-inch length. $12.50 each. Touch of Excellence, 75 Forest Ridge Dr., Columbus OH 43235-1410

SHARK-TOOTH NECKLACE, authentic 1" tooth $5. Rattlesnake fang, genuine, $3. Rattlesnake fang necklace $9.99. $2 S/H. Catalog $1. Rarities, Box FA7000-134, Redondo Beach CA 90277

LOANS BY MAIL/FINANCIAL

SMALL BUSINESS government loans available nationwide! It's easy when you know how. Call 800-226-3601, BF8440

VISA/MASTERCARD. Guaranteed approval. No credit, bad credit, no problem! Lowest interest rates. Call toll free 800-382-0868, 24 hours.

MUSIC/RECORDS/TAPES

ACCORDIONS, CONCERTINAS, button boxes. New, used, buy, sell, trade, repair. Hohners, Martin guitars, lap harps, hammer dulcimers. Catalog $5. Castiglione, Box 40, Warren MI 48090. 313-755-6050

DISCOVERY... REAL MUSIC! *Borderline* by Keith Curtis. CD $16.50, Cassette $12.50, check or MO: KC-Music, PO Box 10998, Glendale AZ 85318-0998

TRADITIONAL MUSIC. Hammer and mountain dulcimer. Celtic, old-time, and more! Recordings, dulcimers, instruction, accessories. Catalog $2. Fishbite Recordings, Box 280632-FA6, San Francisco CA 94128-0632

MOUNTAIN DULCIMER. America's own folk instrument, handcrafted, from $60. Sweetland Dulcimers, 1686 Sweetland Acres, Muscatine IA 52761. 319-262-0407

CLASSIFIEDS

PLAY GOSPEL SONGS by ear! Ten lessons $7.98. *Learn Gospel Music!* Chording, runs, fills. $8.98. Both $15. Davidsons, 6727FA Metcalf, Shawnee Mission KS 66204

NURSERY STOCK

GINSENG! GOLDENSEAL! Profitable, good demand. Quality planting stock. Comfrey. Information $1. William Collins, Viola IA 52350

EVERGREEN TREE SEEDLINGS. Direct from grower. Free catalog. Carino Nurseries, Box 538 Dept. AL, Indiana PA 15701

OF INTEREST TO ALL

BELLS IN YOUR EARS? Amazing natural remedy: 100 capsules $13.95. International Concepts, 60 Martin Creek Ct., Stockbridge GA 30281

JUST MARRIED bumper stickers solve many car-decorating problems. Free details. Reasonable prices. Prompt service. 1776 Enterprises, PO Box 374FG6, Sudbury MA 01776

BE GOOD to yourself. Practice the universal basics of life. For more information: 800-992-ATOM

IRISH, AMERICAN ALMANACS! Mail order groceries, merchandise, books. Megaselection! Catalog $3. Smith's, RR 1 Box 54, Blain PA 17006

TO BUY, or not to buy! Amazing booklet *How to Inspect a Used Car* helps you decide! Save money, grief! Only $3. Order now! RHW, Box 570092FA, Whitestone NY 11357

AVOID PROBATE! Save attorney's fees, protect your family. Free information. Wildwood, 195 E. Main St. #466F, Milford MA 01757

RESOURCE GUIDES giving resources available for specific illnesses and disabilities. SASE. Ondricek's, PO Box 535, Plymouth CA 95669

END PROBLEMS WITH OTHERS forever! Order two powerful booklets today: *How to Handle Difficult People!* and *Your Power to Say NO.* $2. Dr. Frank Cassidy MD, PO Box 2230-W, Pine AZ 85544

UP TO $10,000 cash benefits! Help your loved ones with the burden of your final expenses. Whole Life Insurance Policy, series 3-602. Free information with details and limitations for ages 40-85. Unavailable GA, NH, NY, OR, VT, and WV. Guarantee Reserve Life Insurance Company, 530 River Oaks W. Dept. 896W, Calumet City IL 60409

GIFTS BY MAIL for all occasions. For free, colorful catalog write to V.P. Enterprises, PO Box 1196, Hightstown NJ 08520

HAVE YOU DONE ENOUGH to be saved? Write: DL, Box 121, Republic MO 65738

PHOTOS, HOME MOVIES, SLIDES transferred to video. Relive the memories! For information call or write: Movieland, 20 Main St., Lisbon Falls ME 04252. 207-353-4143

FOUNDATION GRANTS for individuals, to $180,000 for widely varied uses. Free recorded message: 707-448-2668. (2KE1)

WHISPERING ORACLE New Age readings and more. Catalog $1. PO Box 691, Milton NH 03851-0691

KEEP SIDEWALKS AND DRIVEWAYS clear of ice with our heavy-duty chopper. Free information. SASE. Chopper, Box 353, Allston MA 02134

TWELVE-MONTH BIORHYTHM CHARTS. $6. Send birthdate and year. John Morgan, 1208 Harris, Bartlesville OK 74006

SAVE 50%. Discount on travel cost sworldwide. Guaranteed. Information $1: Small, Box 50366, Atlanta GA 30302

ESSENTIAL OILS, 142 SCENTS + designer's 1/3 oz. $8.95 plus S/H. List, sample $3, cash/money order. Amore Oils, Box 1232, Brooklyn NY 11202

RECHARGEABLE prepaid phone card. 30 minutes $22. Includes one time $10 activation fee. TCK, 70 Macomb Ste. 207, Mt. Clemens MI 48043

FRESH, CLEAN AIR inside and total odor removal for house, shop, barn, store, car. Eliminates pollutants and odors from smoking, cooking, animals, paints, solvents, detergents, moisture, fire, locker rooms, mildew, toilets, many more. 100% effective, proven environmentally safe! One 8 oz. for 200-300 sq. ft. $8.95, two $14.95, three $19.95 plus $4.50 S/H. Check or money order. Technoport International, Box 545, Holicong PA 18928

PERSONALS

SMOKE FREE conquered, plus valuable moneymakers $12. J.E.P., PO Box 28305, Moncton NB, E1C 9N4 Canada

NICE SINGLES with Christian values. Free magazine. Send age, interests. Singles, Box 310-OFA, Allardt TN 38504

JAPANESE, ASIAN, European pen pals seek correspondence! All ages! Information: Inter-Pacific, Box 304-K, Birmingham MI 48012

WONDERING ABOUT TOMORROW? Find out today! Let Sister Hope help you with love, marriage, business, good luck. Whatever your problem may be, call today, for tomorrow may be too late. 706-548-8598

BEAUTIFUL GIRLS WORLDWIDE desire correspondence with gentlemen for friendship, marriage. Free brochure. A&P Gems, PO Box 6464F, Portland OR 97228-6464

MEET LATIN AMERICAN BEAUTIES! Videos, tours, free photo brochure! TLC, PO Box 924994SS, Houston TX 77292-4994. 713-896-9224

NEED HELP DESPERATELY? Mrs. Stevens, Astrologer. Lonely? Unlucky? Unhappy? Helps all. Marriage, love, business, health, stress. I will give you options you never considered, never dreamed of. Immediate results. Call or write now. Mrs Stevens, PO Box 207, Laurens SC 29360. 803-682-3669

RUSSIAN LADIES, truly beautiful, educated, seek companionship. Beautiful color-photo catalogs, live videos, Moscow tours. Free color-photo brochure. Russia182, PO 888851, Atlanta GA 30356. 404-458-0909

ATTENTION: SISTER LIGHT, Spartanburg, S.C. One free reading when you call. I will help in all problems. 803-576-9397

NEW AGE contacts, occultists, circles, wicca, companionship, love, etc. America/worldwide. Dollar bill: Dion, Golden Wheel, Liverpool L15 3HT, England

THAI, ASIAN, worldwide ladies desire correspondence, friendship! 24-page, 271-photo catalog. Free brochure! World's #1 service. TAWL, Box 937(FA), Kona Hawaii 96745-0937. 808-329-5559

MOTHER DOROTHY, reader and adviser. Advice on all problems – love, marriage, health, business, and nature. Gifted healer, she will remove your sickness, sorrow, pain, bad luck. ESP. Results in 3 days. Write or call about your problems. 404-755-1301. 1214 Gordon St., Atlanta GA 30310

FREE LIST! Singles dateline! 800-764-0901. Toll free, 24 hours. All areas and lifestyles.

ASIAN WOMEN desire romance! Overseas. $2 for details, photos! Sunshine International, Box 5500-YH, Kailua-Kona HI 96745-5500

GORGEOUS ASIAN WOMEN! Correspondence, romance! Details, color-photo brochure $2. P.I.C., Box 461873-FA, Los Angeles CA 90046

FREE INFORMATION PACKET! Unmarried Catholics. Large membership. Unlimited choice. Established 1980. Sparks, Box 872-F, Troy NY 12181

PAPA JOHN AND SISTER JOHN Spiritualist. Solve all your problems. Love, money, health. Specialist in court cases. Write: 89-27 165 St., Jamaica NY 11432. 800-278-1768 or 718-657-8426

CLASSIFIEDS

ANN HILL, PSYCHIC, helps in all problems of life. Specializing in re-uniting lovers. Guarantees immediate results. 817-536-3407 ro 817-536-9033

SISTER ADAMS. Spiritual reader and healer will solve all problems: love, marriage, business, health. 8287 Spanish Ft. Blvd., Spanish Ft. Al 36527. Call 334-626-7997

PET AND PET SUPPLIES

LLAMAS, INTELLIGENT AND FUN to raise. Pearson Llamas, Ellijay, Georgia. 706-276-3658

UNCOMMON/UNUSUAL dogs! Breeder directory, $2. International Rare Breed Dog Club, PO Box 757-OFA, Blooming Prairie MN 55917-0757

POULTRY

GOSLINGS, DUCKLINGS, chicks, turkeys, guineas, books. Picture catalog $1, deductible. Pilgrim Goose Hatchery, OF-96, Williamsfield OH 44093

AMERICAN POULTRY ASSOCIATION, promoting all breeds domestic poultry and waterfowl. $10/year, $25/3 years. Free brochure. Karen Porr, 7 Springer Ln., Dept. OF, New Cumberland PA 17070

GOSLINGS, DUCKLINGS, chicks, turkeys, guineas, bantams, pheasants, swans, books, medications, equipment. Hoffman Hatchery, Gratz PA 17033

REAL ESTATE

ARKANSAS – FREE CATALOG. Natural beauty. Low taxes. The good life for families and retirement. Fitzgerald-Olsen Realtors, PO Box 237-A, Booneville AR 72927. Call toll-free 800-432-4595, Ext. 641A

OZARK MOUNTAIN or lake acreages, from $30/month, nothing down. Environmental protection codes, huge selection. Free catalog. Woods & Waters, Box 1-FA, Willow Springs MO 65793. 417-469-3187

GOVERNMENT LAND now available for claim. Up to 160 acres/person. Free recorded message: 707-448-1887. (4KE1)

OIL INCOME? Secrets your brother-in-law, the investment banker, won't tell you! Free details. SASE: Oil Income, Box 21567, Oklahoma City OK 73156

ARKANSAS LAND. Free lists! Recreational, investment, retirement homes, acreages. Gatlin's, Box 790, Waldron AR 72958. Toll-free 800-562-9078 XOFA

RELIGION

FREE: Three booklets of Bible verses: Vernon-OFA, 11613 N. 31st Dr., Phoenix AZ 85029-3201

INSPIRATIONAL TAC PINS. Guardian angel. Footprints. Praying hands & cross. $2.50 each. $6.50 all. Include $2 s/h to Echo, 4400 Crystal Springs Dr., Los Angeles CA 90027

BLACK HILLS PASSION PLAY. Acclaimed drama of Christ. Florida, February-March-April 800-622-8383, S.D. June-July-August 800-457-0160. Bring ad, save $2.

LAST DAYS? Seventy revealing Bible lessons. Rush $1. Write: Dr. Hido, 33227 Brainbridge, Solon OH 44139

FREE ADULT OR CHILDREN'S Bible-study courses. Project Philip, Box 35-A, Muskegon MI 49443

WHY DOES GOD PERMIT suffering, disasters, violence? What is this world coming to? Prophetic outcome of present world perplexities. Free packet. Clearwater Bible Students, PO Box 8216, Clearwater FL 34618

JAMAICA RELIGIONS. Bibles, candles, oils, robes, incense, etc. Call 800-278-1768 or 718-657-8426.

JESUS SAID, "With God all Things are Possible." Are you facing difficult problems? Health, money, family? Life-Study Fellowship, founded in 1939, has news for you of a remarkable new way of prayer that is helping thousands. Send your name, address, and $1 for postage and handling to: Life-Study Fellowship, Dept. F-8960, Noroton CT 06820

SEEDS

GROW YOUR OWN TOBACCO products at home! Five varieties of seeds for cigarettes, cigars, pipe, chewing, insecticides. Instructions for growing, harvesting, curing. Satisfaction guaranteed. $12.95. Southern, 3421 Bream, Gautier MS 39553

1000'S OF EXOTIC SEEDS. All kinds! For listings send SASE with 2 stamps. Strikes Seeds, 819 W. Main St., Blytheville AR 72315

RARE HILARIOUS peter, female, and squash pepper seeds. $3 per pkg. Any two $5. All three $7.50, and over 100 rare peppers. Seeds, Rte. 2 Box 246, Atmore AL 36502

WANTED

WANTED: AUTOGRAPHS, signed photos, letters, documents of famous people. Gray, Box 5084, Cochituate MA 01778 or 617-426-4912

INDIAN ARTIFACTS: CASH for authentic prehistoric and historic items. Arrowheads, stone tools, beadwork, baskets, moccasins, pipes, rugs, any thing Indian. Single pieces or collections. Please contact Derek, Box 1115, Afton NY 13730. 607-639-2052

OLD FOUNTAIN PENS wanted by collector. Write to Morris, Box 790503, San Antonio TX 78279

1000'S OF COMMON ITEMS WANTED. Read *Finders & Pickers Newsletter.* Sample copy, $5. Antiques & Collectibles, 2421 W. Pratt Blvd. Suite #307, Chicago IL 60645

SALT & PEPPER SHAKER Collections purchased (novelty). Vera, PO Box 572, Plainville CT 06062. 203-828-4097

WE BUY ROYALTIES and minerals in producing oil and gas wells. Please write Marienfield Royalty Corp., PO Box 25914, Houston TX 77265, or call 800-647-2580.

BUYING PINBALL GAMES, arcade and baseball machines. FAO, 1010 Grayson St., Berkeley CA 94710. 510-548-2300

KNIFE COLLECTIONS WANTED. Cash. Sensitive to private and estate situations. Small or large quantities. Send list and price. Reference available. Bill Penley, Box 818-OFA, Fletcher NC 28732

WORK CLOTHES

OSHKOSH B'GOSH Men's work clothes! Regular, big, and tall. Sizes to 74. Children's basics. Bohlings, 159 Starks, Randolph WI 53956-1291. 800-922-3533

WORK CLOTHES. Save 80%. Shirts, pants, coveralls. Free folder. Write: Galco, 4004 East 71st St., Dept. OF-3, Cleveland OH 44105

MISCELLANEOUS

TRAVEL FREE in luxurious motor home, earn $600 weekly. Blackthorn Associates, Box 1190-I, Biddeford ME 04005

NIGHT FLYERS, 8x10 color photo print of UFO. Fantastic! Send $10 and return address to: Night Flyers, PO Box 105, Thompson Ridge NY 10985-0105

BURIED TREASURE, water, mineral deposits. Sensitive equipment allows locating from distance. Brochure free. Simmon Scientific, Box 10057PA, Wilmington NC 28405

LET THE GOVERNMENT FINANCE your career in writing or the arts. Free recorded message: 707-448-0200. (5KE1)

CASH FOR OLD RECORDS! Illustrated 72-page catalog, including thousands of specific prices we pay for 78s on common labels (Columbia, Decca, Victor, etc.), information about scarce labels, shipping instruction, etc. Send $2 (refundable). Discollector, Box 691035(FA), San Antonio TX 78269

WATKINS. Free catalog. Free call. Great products. 800-354-0386

CLASSIFIEDS

DID YOU SELLER-FINANCE the sale of your property? Tired of receiving payments? Need cash? We buy-mortgages, land contracts, trust deeds. Nationwide? 800-839-YES

PHONED BUSINESS CARDS. Save time. Convenient, promotional item.

MJ Phonecard Co, 5450 Slauson Ave. Ste. 212, Culver City CA 90230

POEMS WANTED for national contest. $15,000 in prizes. Be a published poet. Send one poem, 20 lines or less, any subject, any style, to: Sparrow Grass Poetry Forum, PO Box 193FA, Sisterville WV 26175

PITTSBURGH IRISH Mysteries and Music. Video $19.95. Zimcom, Inc., PO Box 101262 Dept. A, Pittsburgh PA 15237

FREE OCCULT CATALOG! Over 5,000 books, jewelry, incense, candles, music, etc. ABYSS 48-OFA, Chester Rd., Chester MA 01011. 413-623-2155.

The Old Farmer's Almanac accepts classified ads for products and services we feel will be of interest to our readers. However, we cannot verify the quality or reliability of the products or services offered.

ATTENTION, CLASSIFIED ADVERTISERS!

Reach a circulation of 4,400,000 with your classified ad in *The Old Farmer's Almanac, The Old Farmer's Almanac Good Cook's Companion, The Old Farmer's Almanac Gardener's Companion,* and *The Old Farmer's Almanac HomeOwner's Companion.* Or try all four! For special multi-ad rates or more information, call 800-747-6400 or write to: *The Old Farmer's Almanac,* P.O. Box 520, Dublin, NH 03444.

CLOSING DATES:

The 1996 Old Farmer's Almanac Gardener's Companion . . . . October 27, 1995

The 1996 Old Farmer's Almanac HomeOwner's Companion . . . . December 20, 1995

The 1997 Old Farmer's Almanac Good Cook's Companion . . . . April 8, 1996

The 1997 Old Farmer's Almanac . . . . May 3, 1996

New on the Horizon

AN HERBAL COLD, FLU & SORE THROAT MEDICINE

1st SNEEZE!™
ECHINACEA

Safe & Effective with no side effects

Take at 1st sign of cold symptoms for excellent results!

Available at Eckerd's, Thrift & other fine drug stores

FLORA LABORATORIES, INC.• TROUT LAKE, WASHINGTON • 1 (800) 395 6093

ANECDOTES and PLEASANTRIES

A motley collection of useful (and useless) facts, stories, advice, and observations compiled mostly from reader correspondence received over the past 12 months.

Five Pieces of Swell News for '96

1 The Scent of Little Green Apples Helps Claustrophobia

■ Although some might wonder why anyone would even suspect that the sense of smell might be connected to claustrophobia, not so the folks at the Smell & Taste Treatment and Research Foundation of Chicago. They recently conducted a study in which volunteers were placed in a coffinlike cylinder that was only 2.5 feet in diameter and 4.5 feet in height. In this confined environment, they were then exposed to smells of evergreen, vanilla, buttered popcorn, the seashore, barbecue smoke, cucumber, coconut, and green apples.

The results were that little green apples made the space seem bigger. Barbecue smoke, on the other hand, made the space seem even smaller. Other odors had little effect one way or the other.

Courtesy of Denise Faher of the Smell & Taste Treatment and Research Foundation, Chicago, Illinois

2 Cows and Sheep Will Do Less Burping

■ You've probably heard the dire reports that the depletion of the Earth's ozone layer is caused in part by cows and sheep belching

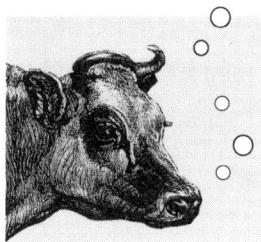

methane gas into the atmosphere. So the good news is that a group of scientists in Australia has apparently come up with a substance to feed cows and sheep (they won't say what it is until further testing) that cuts down on the amount of burping they do. How about that?

Courtesy of Ritt Sidney, San Diego, California

3 UFOs Might Actually Be Earthquake Warnings

■ At a meeting of the Seismological Society of America, John Derr, a geophysicist in Albuquerque, New Mexico, said he believes some UFO sightings may actually be "earthquake lights" — glowing globes of electricity generated by rock movements or groundwater flow changes as underground stress accumulates in the months prior to an earthquake. If true, such sightings in the future might constitute useful, if somewhat imprecise, earthquake warnings.

Clipping sent by Rodney Haverhill, Des Moines, Iowa

4 Coming (Maybe): A Clock That's Easier to Read

■ In place of the two hands on a standard clock, an Arlington, Virginia, man, Scott L. Sullivan, has invented one with only one hand. "You don't have to stare at the clock and decide which hand is the smaller of the two," he says. Instead, his clock features a circle that moves around the face to each hourly position. At the same time, the circle also rotates on its own axis so that a mark on said circle depicts the passing of minutes in each hour. (His patent is number 5,103,434 registered at the Patent and Trademark Office, Washington, DC 20231.)

What about digital clocks? Well, they're OK as is. (Except the numbers in most of them are too small. *Ed.*)

New York Times *clipping sent by Romaine Lattis, New York City*

5 Baseball Is Good for Marriages

■ According to a study by the Center for Marital and Family Studies at the University of Denver, it seems that cities with major-league baseball teams have a divorce rate 23 percent lower than cities without teams. Specifically, the census figures studied show the divorce rate in major-league baseball cities is 4.6 per 1,000 people. For cities without teams — Buffalo, Miami, Denver, Indianapolis, Orlando, Nashville, Phoenix, Tampa, and Washington, D.C. — the mean rate of divorce is 6 per 1,000.

However, the director of the center, Howard Markman, called the findings "speculation rather than science at this point."

Clipping sent by Rhonda Ashley, Miami, Florida

Surprise! Southern Accents Are the Sexiest

Southern accents may be the sexiest, but Boston accents are the smartest. Those are two results of a survey conducted for Hyundai Motor America to help launch its new car, the Accent. Some additional findings:

In addition to being the sexiest, southern accents were also the most liked and most recognizable.

New Yorkers, on the other hand, scored highest in two categories — the most intimidating and least-liked American accent.

The Los Angeles "Valley" accent was rated lowest on the intelligence scale.

The most popular foreign accent was Australian. Larry Moss, a Hollywood dialect coach, attributes the choice to the outgoing and adventurous impressions made by actors such as Mel Gibson and Paul Hogan.

The most recognizable cartoon-character accent belonged to Bugs Bunny, with Pepe LePue a distant runner-up. (Goodness, haven't they ever heard Donald Duck's accent?)

by Richard P. Carpenter of Boston, Massachusetts (reprinted courtesy of the Boston Globe)

An Old-Fashioned (and Clean) Joke

Bill Jones, the local athletic "champion," was bragging about his physical prowess at the local bar. None of the regulars challenged him. But a visitor piped up, "I'll bet you 20 dollars that I can wheel something in a wheelbarrow for one block and you can't wheel it back."

Bill looked the visitor over and decided that whatever the stranger could do, he could do better. "I'll take you on," he said.

The visitor, Bill, and a number of the regulars borrowed a wheelbarrow and took it to the corner.

The challenger smiled smugly, rubbed his hands, picked up the handles, and turned to Bill. "OK, get in, Bill," he said.

From Anne Victoria Baynas, Holiday, Florida

A Short (But Tricky) Almanac Quiz

If you can correctly answer even two of these three questions, you'll be entitled to (but, alas, will not receive) an absolutely fabulous prize . . .

1. **After the Bible, what is the second-best-selling book in all of history? Hint: No, it's not *Gone with the Wind*, Webster's Dictionary, or Peyton Place.**

2. **Name the title — in either French or English — of the world's longest novel. HINT: The abridged version was published in 14 volumes from 1933 to 1946.**

3. **Whose signature is the most valuable historical autograph in America? HINT: There are only about 50 documents known to bear this man's signature, each worth $100,000 or more. (Most of his papers were destroyed in a smallpox plague and a hurricane.) One more hint: He was killed in a duel.**

<small>Questions 1 and 2 are courtesy of Gregory McNamee, Tucson, Arizona</small>

ANSWERS: 1.) The *Guinness Book of World Records*, with a total reported sale of about 70 million. 2.) Jules Romains's *Les Hommes de Bonne Volonté (Men of Good Will)*, which runs about two million words and was first published in 27 volumes. 3.) Button Gwinnett, who, shortly before being killed in a duel, signed the Declaration of Independence.

Ten Things (among many) That Happened Exactly 100 Years Ago

■ **The world's first automobile** accident occurred. It happened in New York when a Duryea car, driven by Henry Wells, collided with a bicycle. The bicycle rider, Evylyn Thomas, was taken to a Manhattan hospital with a fractured leg. Mr. Wells spent the night in jail awaiting the report on the extent of the injuries. (But everyone was right in thinking that the coming of the automobile would mean the virtual end of all those horrible horse-and-buggy accidents.)

■ **The zipper** (also known as the "clasp locker and unlocker for shoes") was improved by Whitcomb L. Judson of Chicago. He obtained Patent No. 557,207 on a fastening for shoes, consisting of two metal chains that could be fastened together by moving a slider. Most people found it impractical.

■ **Henry Ford's very first car** was actually driven. Ford built the two-cylinder "quadricycle" with his own hands, then had to tear down a barn wall to get it out so he could drive it around the darkened streets of Detroit.

Automotive pioneer Henry Ford and his Quadricycle, 1896.

■ **New York's first showing of motion pictures.** One, entitled *The Execution of Mary, Queen of Scots*, lasted only 30 seconds (the film, that is), while the other, entitled *The Kiss*, was a bit longer. Both films were by Thomas Edison.

■ **Gold was discovered** in Rabbit Creek (later Bonanza Creek) near the Klondike River in Yukon Territory in Canada.

■ **Chop suey was first** cooked and served in the United States. The dish was created by a chef working for the Chinese statesman Li Hung-Chang, who was visiting New York City. Asked by guests what the dish was called, the chef said, "Chop suey, that's what we call hash in China." As a result chop suey parlors became popular all over the States.

■ **Idaho became the first** state in the United States to grant women the right to vote. (The vote to do so was taken by men only.)

■ **The NEW ORLEANS PICAYUNE was the first** daily newspaper to run a personal advice column. The column of advice to the lovelorn, "Dorothy Dix Talks," became one of the best-known columns in the early 1900s.

■ **The first X-ray photograph** in the U.S. was taken by Dr. Henry Louis Smith at Davidson College in North Carolina. He fired a bullet into a hand of a corpse and then took a 15-minute exposure. After it was developed, it revealed the exact location of the bullet.

Leo Hirschfield's first Tootsie Roll delivery van.

■ **Tootsie Rolls were invented** and sold for a penny each in Leo Hirschfield's candy store in New York City. ("Tootsie" was the name of his little daughter.) Mr. Hirschfield brought the recipe with him from his native Austria and made the candies in his living quarters in the rear of his small store.

Roosters: Do They Go "Cock-a-doodle-doo"? Yes or No?

The Chinese would say "no." Roosters in China, you see, go "gu-gu-gu." In Portugal, they go "cocoracoco." In Holland, "Kukeleku."

Pigs? The ones we know go "oink-oink." But in Japan they go "bu-bu." Pigs in Swahili go "nkru-nkru." (Hard enough for us to say. How could a pig?)

Our dogs go "woof-woof." But Japanese dogs go "wan-wan," and Portuguese dogs go "au-au."

Well, at least we can all pretty much agree on what cats say. Almost everywhere in the world cats say something sounding very much like our cats' "meow." Chinese: "miao." Dutch: "miauw." Swahili: "nyau-nyau." Portuguese: "miau-miau."

On the other hand, while our cats have nine lives, Swahili cats have only three.

Can't we all just get along?

Courtesy of Margot Gurainick

cocoracoco

An Almanac Exposé!
How Each Dollar in the Federal Budget Is Really Spent

☞ Let's say all the billions our government spends each year become exactly one hundred pennies. One dollar. If that were the case, here's how, in 1994, for instance, those hundred pennies were budgeted to be spent . . .

Social Security	21.1 cents
National defense	17.4 cents
Unemployment benefits, Medicaid, other welfare	14.2 cents
Interest on the national debt	14.0 cents
Medicare	9.7 cents
Health (immunization, disease control, etc.)	7.6 cents
Education	3.4 cents
Transportation (mostly federal highways)	2.5 cents
Veterans' benefits	2.4 cents
Natural resources and environment	1.3 cents
International affairs (including foreign aid)	1.2 cents
Science, space, technology	1.1 cents
Agriculture (including farm subsidies)	1.1 cents
Justice (federal courts, prisons, FBI)	1.0 cent
Running the White House, Congress, etc.	0.9 cent
Commerce	0.8 cent
Community and regional development	0.5 cent
Energy	0.2 cent

Now we have a problem. As of 1994 we collected only 83 cents of revenue to pay for that dollar. (The 1995 spending and revenue figures are about the same.) So to balance the budget, we have to cut 17 cents from the above. Or add 17 cents to the annual revenue figures below. (Or some of both.)

Individual income tax	37 cents
Social Security and other payroll tax	31 cents
Corporate income tax	8 cents
Excise tax (on alcohol, tobacco, gasoline, etc.)	3.4 cents
Customs and other miscellaneous receipts	2.3 cents
Estate and gift tax	1.0 cent

So what would you do? If you can compile a better budget, don't send it to the Almanac. Send it to your elected representatives in Washington. They'd probably appreciate a little help.

Condensed from an article by Donella H. Meadows, an adjunct professor of environmental studies at Dartmouth College, New Hampshire

Why Four Toronto Women Decided to Have Nine Babies (in ten years)

At his death in 1926, 70 years ago, Toronto lawyer Charles Vance Millar bequeathed shares in breweries to teetotalers and racetrack shares to anti-gamblers. But the self-described "uncommon and capricious" document's strangest clause, Number

9, stipulated that the Toronto woman who gave birth to the most babies in the decade following Vance's death would receive $750,000. The unorthodox last testament sparked what newspapers promptly dubbed the Great Stork Derby, with about a dozen or so families in contention for the great prize. It also unleashed a flurry of legal action by Ontario's cash-strapped provincial government, which wanted to nullify the will and channel the money into provincial coffers. The courtroom wrangling went all the way to the federal Supreme Court, but to no avail: In 1936, the derby ended in a tie. Four Toronto mothers, who gave birth to nine babies apiece during the decade, were each awarded $125,000.

by Alec Ross, Kingston, Ontario

GET IN ON THE PROFITS OF SMALL ENGINE SERVICE AND REPAIR
START YOUR OWN MONEY MAKING BUSINESS & BEAT INFLATION!

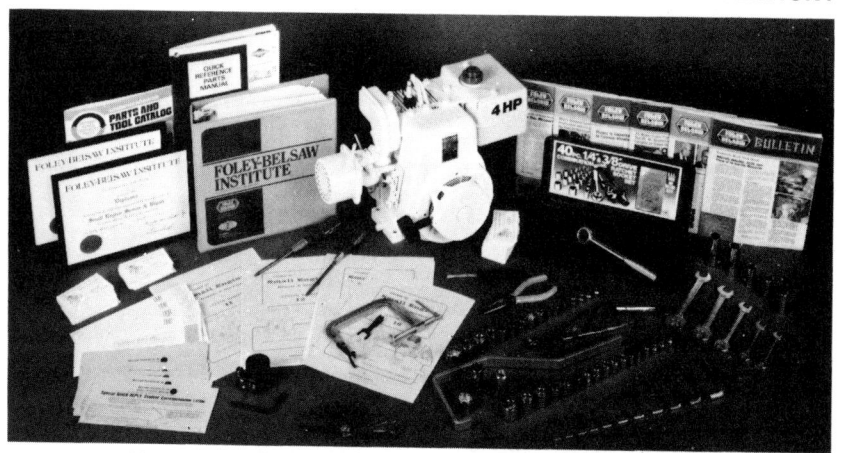

You get all this Professional equipment with your course, PLUS 4 H.P. Engine... ALL YOURS TO KEEP... All at NO EXTRA COST.

Work part time, full time right at home. In just a short time, you can be ready to join one of the fastest growing industries in America... an industry where qualified men are making from **$25.00 to $30.00 per hour.** Because the small engine industry has grown so quickly, an acute shortage of qualified Small Engine Professionals exists throughout the country. When you see how many small engines are in use today, it's easy to understand why qualified men command such high prices — as much as $49.95 for a simple tune-up that takes less than an hour.

65-million small engines are in service today!
That's right — there are over sixty-five million 2-cycle and 4-cycle small engines in service across the U.S.A.! With fully accredited and approved Foley-Belsaw training, you can soon have the skill and knowledge to make top money servicing these engines. Homeowners and businessmen will seek you out and pay you well to service and repair their lawn mowers, tillers, edgers, power rakes, garden tractors, chain saws, mini-bikes, go-carts, snowmobiles... the list is almost endless.

No experience necessary.
We guide you every step of the way, including tested and proven instructions on how to get business, what to charge, how to get free advertising, where to get supplies wholesale... all the 'tricks of the trade'... all the inside facts you need to assure success right from the start.

Send today for FREE facts!
You risk nothing by accepting this offer to find out how Foley-Belsaw training can give you the skills you need to increase your income in a high-profit, recession-proof business of your own.
Just fill in and mail coupon below (or send postcard) to receive full information and details by return mail. DO IT TODAY!

FOLEY-BELSAW INSTITUTE
6301 EQUITABLE RD., DEPT. 52578
KANSAS CITY, MO 64120

NO OBLIGATION... NO SALESMAN WILL CALL

RUSH COUPON TODAY FOR THIS FACT-FILLED FREE BOOKLET!

Tells how you quickly train to be your own boss in a profitable Spare time or Full time business of your own PLUS complete details on our 30 DAY NO RISK Trial Offer!

```
FOLEY-BELSAW INSTITUTE
6301 EQUITABLE RD., DEPT. 52578
KANSAS CITY, MO 64120

☐ YES, please send me the FREE booklet that gives full details
  about starting my own business in Small Engine Repair. I under-
  stand there is no obligation and that no salesman will call.

NAME _____
ADDRESS _____
CITY _____
STATE _____ ZIP _____
```

The Great "Miss Liberty" Scandal

If you can find a 1916 quarter in your piggy bank today, one on which Miss Liberty is rather "exposed," well, you're rich! Fabulously rich! (Well, maybe not as rich as winning Megabucks, but . . .)

For more than 200 years Miss Liberty has been depicted on United States coins standing, seated, and walking. In 1916 she appeared seminude on a quarter-dollar and caused a sensation. Examples of these naughty coins may still be found in stashes of old pocket change, and they're certainly worth more than two bits.

A decade earlier, sculptor Hermon Atkins MacNeil had been selected by the Treasury Department to create a new look for the quarter. His design — a standing figure of Liberty holding an olive branch in her right hand, a shield in her upraised left hand, with an eagle in flight on the reverse side of the coin — was "a beautiful departure from its predecessor, the rather nondescript Liberty head profile," says coin dealer James A. Simek of Chicago, an authority on U.S. quarters.

The new coin was approved, and in December 1916 the mint began striking the silver coins. Immediately a controversy erupted. Critics, protesting that Miss Liberty's right breast was not covered by the drapery over her upper body, said the quarter was immoral and obscene.

The mint capitulated in 1917 by redesigning the coin, covering up Miss Liberty's chest with chain-mail combat armor. But 52,000 of the racy quarters had been struck in 1916, making even poor specimens worth about $1,000 each today. Just over 12 million of the MacNeil quarters were struck in 1917 before the design was changed, and those coins range in value from a few dollars to several hundred dollars, depending on their condition.

One controversy remains: Who was the model for Miss Liberty? Actresses Doris (Doree) Doscher and Irene MacDowell both claimed to have been the beauty who posed for MacNeil's design. The naked truth may never be known.

by Donn Pearlman, Skokie, Illinois

Happy 150th Birthday, Dear Smithsonian Institution, Happy Birthday to You

Created in Washington, D.C., by an act of Congress in 1846, the Smithsonian, the largest museum complex in the whole world, owes its origins to a wealthy English scientist named James Smithson, who willed his entire fortune to the United States in order to found the Smithsonian Institution. No one knows exactly why. He'd never even *been* to the United States. But, hey, it was a real nice gift and we appreciate it. Smithson finally arrived, posthumously, in 1904, when Alexander Graham Bell brought his remains from Italy and installed them near the main entrance.

And finally...

Watch your thoughts.
They become words.
Watch your words.
They become actions.
Watch your actions.
They become habits.
Watch your habits.
They become character.
Watch your character.
It becomes your destiny.

by Frank Outlaw
Submitted by Tom Macfie, Atlanta, Georgia

Advertisement

The Most Important Money/Power/Romantic-Love Discovery Since The Industrial Revolution © 1995

Receive Free — The valuable, 8000-word Neo-Tech Information Package

An entire new field of knowledge has been discovered by Dr. Frank R. Wallace, a former Senior Research Chemist for E.I. du Pont de Nemours & Co. For over a decade, Dr. Wallace researched Psychous Advantages to uncover a powerful array of new knowledge called Neo-Tech. That new knowledge allows any person to prosper monetarily, personally, romantically, and financially anywhere in the world, even during personal or financial hard times, inflation, boom times, recession, depression, war.

No one can spot the Neo-Tech man. The constant invisible advantages obtained by Neo-Tech appear completely natural, yet are unbeatable. Neo-Tech puts one in the ultimate catbird seat.

Neo-Tech is a new, scientific method for capturing major financial and personal advantages everywhere. Neo-Tech is a new knowledge that has nothing to do with positive thinking, religion, or anything mystical. Once a person is exposed to Neo-Tech, he can quietly profit from anyone — anywhere, anytime. He can prosper almost anywhere on earth and succeed under almost any economic or political condition. Combined with Psychous Advantages, Neo-Tech applies to all money and power gathering techniques — to all situations involving the transfer of money, power, or love.

Neo-Tech has its roots in the constant financial pressures and incentives to develop the easiest, most profitable methods of gaining advantages. Over the decades, all successful salesmen, businessmen, politicians, writers, lawyers, entrepreneurs, investors, speculators, gamers and Casanovas have secretly searched for shortcuts that require little skill yet contain the invisible effectiveness of the most advanced techniques. Dr. Wallace identified those shortcuts and honed them into practical formats called Neo-Tech. Those never-before-known formats transfer money, power, and prestige from the uninformed to the informed. Those informed can automatically take control of most situations involving money and power.

Who is The Neo-Tech Man? He is a man of quiet power — a man who cannot lose. He can extract money at will. He can control anyone unknowledgeable about Neo-Tech — man or woman.

The Neo-Tech man has the power to render others helpless, even wipe them out, but he wisely chooses to use just enough of his power to give himself unbeatable casino-like advantages in all his endeavors for maximum long-range profits. His Neo-Tech maneuvers are so subtle that they can be executed with casual confidence. His hidden techniques let him win consistently and comfortably — year after year, decade after decade. Eventually, Neo-Tech men and women will quietly rule everywhere.

The Neo-Tech man can easily and safely beat any opponent. He can quickly impoverish anyone he chooses. He can immediately and consistently acquire large amounts of money. He has the power to make more money in a week than most people without Neo-Tech make in a full year. He commands profits and respect. He controls business deals and emotional situations to acquire money and power...and to command love. He can regain lost love. He can subjugate a business or personal adversary. He wins any lover at will. He can predict stock prices — even gold and silver prices. He quietly rules all.

Within a week, an ordinary person can become a professional Neo-Tech practitioner. As people gain this knowledge, they will immediately begin using its techniques because they are irresistibly easy and overwhelmingly potent. Within days after gaining this knowledge, a person can safely bankrupt opponents — or slowly profit from them, week after week. He can benefit from business and investment endeavors — from dealing with the boss to the biggest oil deal. He can also benefit from any relationship — from gaining the respect of peers to inducing love from a partner or regaining lost love from an ex-partner. He will gain easy money and power in business, investments, the professions, politics, and personal life.

Indeed, with Neo-Tech, a person not only captures unbeatable advantages over others, but commands shortcuts to profits, power, and romance. The ordinary person can quickly become a Clark Kent — a quiet superman — taking command of all. He can financially and emotionally control whomever he deals with. He becomes the man-on-the-hill, now. He is armed with an unbeatable weapon. All will yield to the new-breed Neo-Tech man, the no-limit man....All except the Neo-Tech man will die unfulfilled...without ever knowing wealth, power, and romantic love.

Readers of *Farmer's Almanac* can obtain the valuable, 8000-word Neo-Tech Information Package without charge by sending this Special-Offer coupon to the address below.

☐ Please rush to me, free of charge, the 8000-word Neo-Tech Information Package.

Name_____

Address_____

City_____

State/Zip_____

Mail To: **Neo-Tech, Dept. FM-1
850 S. Boulder Hwy., Henderson, Nevada 89015**
Fax to: (702) 795-8393   Or call: (702) 891-0300
Note: Available as long as supply lasts.   0474-G

The GRANDFATHER PARADOX:

BY MICHAEL MCNIERNEY

Is Travel to the Past Possible?

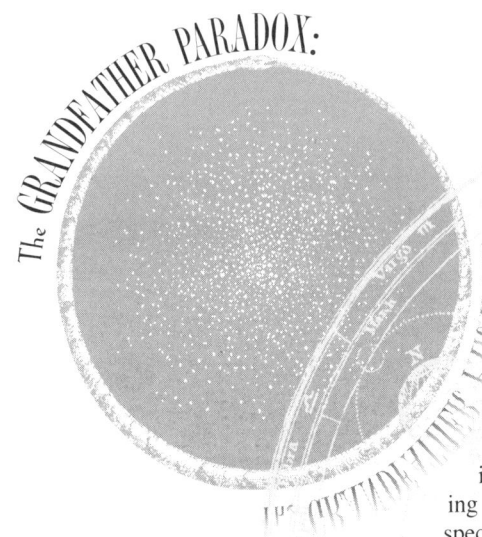

All you need to do to

The 1993 movie *Time Cop* concerns travel backward in time. People traveling to the past cause so many problems that a special police force must be set up to deal with them. Travel to the future is dismissed out of hand by one character with the remark that it is impossible because the future hasn't happened yet.

So much for Hollywood's knowledge of physics. The situation is in fact the opposite. Travel forward in time is theoretically possible, according to the predictions of Albert Einstein's special theory of relativity (1905), which has been proven experimentally many times. All you need to travel into the future is to be able to move at a reasonable fraction of the speed of light (about 186,282 miles per second). Neither the laws of classical physics nor the dictates

travel into the future is to be able to move somewhere close

to the speed of light. Theoretically, that's possible.

Traveling into the past is a bit more complicated.

But very intriguing . . .

– photo: Photofest

of logic and common sense forbid it.

Traveling backward in time, however, seems impossible because of what is known formally as the inconsistency paradox and informally as the "grandfather paradox." This paradox could just as accurately be called the grandmother paradox or the ancestor paradox. It is simply explained. If you travel back in time, meet any of these ancestors, and kill them — or kill them all, if your taste runs to mass murder — you will never come into existence and be available to go back in time and do the dirty deed. Yet you just did it! Hence, a paradox, and our logic and common sense and classical physics, too, all yell "Stop!" at this point.

Yet special relativity does allow for backward time travel. If you could move *faster* than light, you would go back in time. This outrageous idea was given popular expression by Arthur Buller's famous limerick that appeared in 1923 in the British magazine *Punch*:

> *There was a young lady named Bright,*
> *Whose speed was far faster than light;*
> *She set out one day*
> *In a relative way*
> *And returned home the previous night.*

Of course, special relativity also maintains that nothing can travel faster than light because to accelerate any mass to light speed would require an infinite amount of energy, and there just isn't that much available in the universe.

Too bad. But Einstein again comes to the rescue of would-be time travelers with his general theory of relativity (1915). Like the special theory, it has been experimentally proven many times to be true. Ramifications of it allow travel to the past because of something called "warped space-time."

In the universe of general relativity, time does not exist as an isolated phenomenon. It is part of space-time. Space, as we ordinarily think of it, is three dimensional and consists of points — one point here, one there. Space-time is four dimensional: the three dimensions of space plus the fourth dimension of time. It consists of "spatiotemporal points" or events. Each event is at a specific place at a specific time.

Everything that exists — including you (and me) — forms a sort of worm through space-time. The tail of the worm is your birth and the head of the worm is your death. The line that your worm makes is called your world-line. Some world-lines are relatively short, like yours and mine, and some are very long, like that of a piece of granite billions of years old. Our world-lines are squiggles as we move here and there in space. Time, as we measure it with clocks, also has a world-line that goes in one direction, forward, and is straight.

However odd this talk of world-lines may seem, it is just a way of describing our ordinary reality in different terms.

The general theory of relativity predicts that massive bodies such as stars and black holes warp space-time and bend world-lines. This is, in fact, what is happening when we notice the effects of gravity. The reason the Earth is bound in an orbit around the Sun is not that there is a mysterious force emanating from the Sun, but that the mass of the Sun bends the Earth's world-line around it. Space-time is warped near the Sun.

What if an object, say a black hole or neutron star, is so massive that it dramatically warps space-time so that world-lines actually

The famous "quantum leap" is when an electron moves from one "orbit" around a nucleus to another without ever occupying the space in between.

This paradox is why most physicists don't like to even think about time travel.

bend back on themselves, forming a loop? This phenomenon is possible and is called a closed timelike curve (CTC). If you were present at any point along the loop, time would seem to "flow" normally. *But* the closed loop would be a pathway into the past.

If you traveled all the way around the loop, you would run into your own world-line in the past — that is, you would run into yourself! And if the loop were large enough, you could go around and come back before your world-line started, meet your ancestors, and if you wanted to, *kill them.*

The paradox! Classical physics is totally deterministic: It doesn't actually say you can't travel around the CTC and meet your grandfather, but it does say that however much you may want to kill your grandfather, you can't. Something will stop you. What could this something be? Nobody has a clue. This paradox is why most physicists don't like to even think about time travel.

But help is on the way. It lies in one particular theory that has evolved to explain the weirdness of the quantum world of subatomic particles. Things are very different down there. They do not obey the laws of the macroworld we live in. They boggle the mind, in fact.

A few examples are enough to give you a taste. A photon can be in two places at the same time. The famous "quantum leap" is when an electron moves from one "orbit" around a nucleus to another *without ever occupying the space in between.* Light is at the same time both particles and a wave. The quantum world simply doesn't exist in a definite state until we observe it.

The best-known explanation of quantum weirdness is the Copenhagen interpretation of Werner Heisenberg and Niels Bohr that says, among other things, that objective reality is a fiction and that the quantum world is not as real as our macroscopic world.

Another interpretation was first proposed by Hugh Everett III in 1957 and provides a way around the grandfather paradox. It is the "many worlds" or "multiverse" interpretation. It is a minority view, but has a respectable and increasing following of physicists.

According to this theory, if something can happen, it will — if not in this universe, then in another. For example, if we look for light to behave like particles, it will. If we look for it to behave like a wave, it will. But there is no contradiction. The moment we choose, the universe splits. In one universe at that moment, the light we observe is a collection of particles; in another, it is a wave. This splitting happens every time we observe or make a decision or act. Reality is constantly splitting into an infinite number of universes.

The way out of the grandfather paradox is now clear. You travel back in time and murder your grandfather. The universe splits at that moment. In the future of one universe, you never exist. In the future of another, you do.

If the multiverse interpretation of reality is correct, we could someday travel into the past once we learned how to harness the power of warped space-time, of CTCs. This raises many questions, of course, but ask yourself this one: Has someone from the future come back and interfered with your life? You will never know. Or will you? ☐☐

Send for FREE FACTS
Train at home for a better career
58 ways ICS can help improve your life

Get Your Specialized Associate Degree or Career Diploma at Home in Spare Time

The decision to invest time, energy and money in preparing for a new career is not an easy one. Yet it may be the most important decision you will ever make. It can offer you the opportunity to qualify for the job you want...more money, more prestige, a better way of life.

At ICS we've spent more than one hundred years training people for exciting, profitable careers. Since 1890 more than 10,000,000 students have enrolled with us and over 2,000 major corporations have chosen the ICS training system for their own employees!

No Need to Attend Technical School, College or University
If you've always wanted your Specialized Associate Degree, now you can get it without ever setting foot on a college campus! Or if specialized career training is your goal, now you can have that, too...no need to attend trade or technical school. Home study makes it possible to get the education you want, yet never quit your job or change your lifestyle. You study at home, the hours you choose...go as fast or slow as you like.

And our lessons make it easy because they're clearly written and include drawings, diagrams and photos. Tools, calculators, electronic instruments, computers, drawing materials, fabric swatches, reference books... whatever you need to complete your training is included with your program at no extra cost!

——— CALL TOLL FREE ———
1-800-595-5505 Ext. 9193
CALL ANYTIME—24 hours a day, 7 days a week.
OR MAIL COUPON TODAY.

828ZI

ICS Over 100 Years of Excellence SINCE 1890

International Correspondence Schools, Dept. AA2S95S
925 Oak Street, Scranton, Pennsylvania 18515

Please send me free facts, color brochure and full information on how I can train at home for the career I have chosen. I understand I am under no obligation and no salesman will visit me. **CHECK ONE BOX ONLY.**

ASSOCIATE IN SPECIALIZED BUSINESS DEGREE PROGRAMS
☐ Business Management
☐ Accounting
☐ Business Management with option in Finance
☐ Business Management with option in Marketing
☐ Applied Computer Science
☐ Hospitality Management

ASSOCIATE IN SPECIALIZED TECHNOLOGY DEGREE PROGRAMS
☐ Civil Engineering Technology
☐ Mechanical Engineering Technology
☐ Electrical Engineering Technology
☐ Industrial Engineering Technology
☐ Electronics Technology

——— CAREER DIPLOMA COURSES ———

☐ Computer Programming
☐ Computer Programming/COBOL
☐ Personal Computer Specialist
☐ Computer-Assisted Bookkeeping
☐ PC Repair
☐ Desktop Publishing & Design
☐ Secretary with Computer
☐ High School
☐ Catering/Gourmet Cooking
☐ Medical Office Assistant
☐ Dental Office Assistant
☐ Auto Mechanics
☐ Bookkeeping

☐ Hotel/Restaurant Mgmt.
☐ Drafting
☐ Animal Care Specialist
☐ Travel Agent
☐ Air Conditioning & Refrigeration
☐ Electronics
☐ Secretary
☐ Electrician
☐ Police Sciences
☐ Private Security Officer
☐ Art

☐ Small Business Mgmt.
☐ Interior Decorating
☐ TV/VCR Repair
☐ Child Day Care
☐ Wildlife/Forestry Conservation
☐ Legal Secretary
☐ Diesel Mechanics
☐ Fashion Merchandising
☐ Gun Repair
☐ Motorcycle Repair
☐ Surveying & Mapping

☐ Fitness & Nutrition
☐ Legal Assistant
☐ Photography
☐ Journalism/Short Story Writing
☐ Dressmaking & Design
☐ Florist
☐ Teacher Aide
☐ Home Inspector
☐ Medical Transcriptionist
☐ Real Estate Appraiser
☐ Professional Locksmithing
☐ Appliance Repair

NAME_____ AGE_____
ADDRESS_____ APT. #____
CITY/STATE_____ ZIP_____
PHONE (_____)_____

1995

JANUARY
S	M	T	W	T	F	S
1	2	3	4	5	6	7
8	9	10	11	12	13	14
15	16	17	18	19	20	21
22	23	24	25	26	27	28
29	30	31	—	—	—	—

FEBRUARY
S	M	T	W	T	F	S
—	—	—	1	2	3	4
5	6	7	8	9	10	11
12	13	14	15	16	17	18
19	20	21	22	23	24	25
26	27	28	—	—	—	—

MARCH
S	M	T	W	T	F	S
—	—	—	1	2	3	4
5	6	7	8	9	10	11
12	13	14	15	16	17	18
19	20	21	22	23	24	25
26	27	28	29	30	31	—

APRIL
S	M	T	W	T	F	S
—	—	—	—	—	—	1
2	3	4	5	6	7	8
9	10	11	12	13	14	15
16	17	18	19	20	21	22
23	24	25	26	27	28	29
30	—	—	—	—	—	—

MAY
S	M	T	W	T	F	S
—	1	2	3	4	5	6
7	8	9	10	11	12	13
14	15	16	17	18	19	20
21	22	23	24	25	26	27
28	29	30	31	—	—	—

JUNE
S	M	T	W	T	F	S
—	—	—	—	1	2	3
4	5	6	7	8	9	10
11	12	13	14	15	16	17
18	19	20	21	22	23	24
25	26	27	28	29	30	—

JULY
S	M	T	W	T	F	S
—	—	—	—	—	—	1
2	3	4	5	6	7	8
9	10	11	12	13	14	15
16	17	18	19	20	21	22
23	24	25	26	27	28	29
30	31	—	—	—	—	—

AUGUST
S	M	T	W	T	F	S
—	—	1	2	3	4	5
6	7	8	9	10	11	12
13	14	15	16	17	18	19
20	21	22	23	24	25	26
27	28	29	30	31	—	—

SEPTEMBER
S	M	T	W	T	F	S
—	—	—	—	—	1	2
3	4	5	6	7	8	9
10	11	12	13	14	15	16
17	18	19	20	21	22	23
24	25	26	27	28	29	30

OCTOBER
S	M	T	W	T	F	S
1	2	3	4	5	6	7
8	9	10	11	12	13	14
15	16	17	18	19	20	21
22	23	24	25	26	27	28
29	30	31	—	—	—	—

NOVEMBER
S	M	T	W	T	F	S
—	—	—	1	2	3	4
5	6	7	8	9	10	11
12	13	14	15	16	17	18
19	20	21	22	23	24	25
26	27	28	29	30	—	—

DECEMBER
S	M	T	W	T	F	S
—	—	—	—	—	1	2
3	4	5	6	7	8	9
10	11	12	13	14	15	16
17	18	19	20	21	22	23
24	25	26	27	28	29	30
31	—	—	—	—	—	—

1996

JANUARY
S	M	T	W	T	F	S
—	1	2	3	4	5	6
7	8	9	10	11	12	13
14	15	16	17	18	19	20
21	22	23	24	25	26	27
28	29	30	31	—	—	—

FEBRUARY
S	M	T	W	T	F	S
—	—	—	—	1	2	3
4	5	6	7	8	9	10
11	12	13	14	15	16	17
18	19	20	21	22	23	24
25	26	27	28	29	—	—

MARCH
S	M	T	W	T	F	S
—	—	—	—	—	1	2
3	4	5	6	7	8	9
10	11	12	13	14	15	16
17	18	19	20	21	22	23
24	25	26	27	28	29	30
31	—	—	—	—	—	—

APRIL
S	M	T	W	T	F	S
—	1	2	3	4	5	6
7	8	9	10	11	12	13
14	15	16	17	18	19	20
21	22	23	24	25	26	27
28	29	30	—	—	—	—

MAY
S	M	T	W	T	F	S
—	—	—	1	2	3	4
5	6	7	8	9	10	11
12	13	14	15	16	17	18
19	20	21	22	23	24	25
26	27	28	29	30	31	—

JUNE
S	M	T	W	T	F	S
—	—	—	—	—	—	1
2	3	4	5	6	7	8
9	10	11	12	13	14	15
16	17	18	19	20	21	22
23	24	25	26	27	28	29
30	—	—	—	—	—	—

JULY
S	M	T	W	T	F	S
—	1	2	3	4	5	6
7	8	9	10	11	12	13
14	15	16	17	18	19	20
21	22	23	24	25	26	27
28	29	30	31	—	—	—

AUGUST
S	M	T	W	T	F	S
—	—	—	—	1	2	3
4	5	6	7	8	9	10
11	12	13	14	15	16	17
18	19	20	21	22	23	24
25	26	27	28	29	30	31

SEPTEMBER
S	M	T	W	T	F	S
1	2	3	4	5	6	7
8	9	10	11	12	13	14
15	16	17	18	19	20	21
22	23	24	25	26	27	28
29	30	—	—	—	—	—

OCTOBER
S	M	T	W	T	F	S
—	—	1	2	3	4	5
6	7	8	9	10	11	12
13	14	15	16	17	18	19
20	21	22	23	24	25	26
27	28	29	30	31	—	—

NOVEMBER
S	M	T	W	T	F	S
—	—	—	—	—	1	2
3	4	5	6	7	8	9
10	11	12	13	14	15	16
17	18	19	20	21	22	23
24	25	26	27	28	29	30

DECEMBER
S	M	T	W	T	F	S
1	2	3	4	5	6	7
8	9	10	11	12	13	14
15	16	17	18	19	20	21
22	23	24	25	26	27	28
29	30	31	—	—	—	—

1997

JANUARY
S	M	T	W	T	F	S
—	—	—	1	2	3	4
5	6	7	8	9	10	11
12	13	14	15	16	17	18
19	20	21	22	23	24	25
26	27	28	29	30	31	—

FEBRUARY
S	M	T	W	T	F	S
—	—	—	—	—	—	1
2	3	4	5	6	7	8
9	10	11	12	13	14	15
16	17	18	19	20	21	22
23	24	25	26	27	28	—

MARCH
S	M	T	W	T	F	S
—	—	—	—	—	—	1
2	3	4	5	6	7	8
9	10	11	12	13	14	15
16	17	18	19	20	21	22
23	24	25	26	27	28	29
30	31	—	—	—	—	—

APRIL
S	M	T	W	T	F	S
—	—	1	2	3	4	5
6	7	8	9	10	11	12
13	14	15	16	17	18	19
20	21	22	23	24	25	26
27	28	29	30	—	—	—

MAY
S	M	T	W	T	F	S
—	—	—	—	1	2	3
4	5	6	7	8	9	10
11	12	13	14	15	16	17
18	19	20	21	22	23	24
25	26	27	28	29	30	31

JUNE
S	M	T	W	T	F	S
1	2	3	4	5	6	7
8	9	10	11	12	13	14
15	16	17	18	19	20	21
22	23	24	25	26	27	28
29	30	—	—	—	—	—

JULY
S	M	T	W	T	F	S
—	—	1	2	3	4	5
6	7	8	9	10	11	12
13	14	15	16	17	18	19
20	21	22	23	24	25	26
27	28	29	30	31	—	—

AUGUST
S	M	T	W	T	F	S
—	—	—	—	—	1	2
3	4	5	6	7	8	9
10	11	12	13	14	15	16
17	18	19	20	21	22	23
24	25	26	27	28	29	30
31	—	—	—	—	—	—

SEPTEMBER
S	M	T	W	T	F	S
—	1	2	3	4	5	6
7	8	9	10	11	12	13
14	15	16	17	18	19	20
21	22	23	24	25	26	27
28	29	30	—	—	—	—

OCTOBER
S	M	T	W	T	F	S
—	—	—	1	2	3	4
5	6	7	8	9	10	11
12	13	14	15	16	17	18
19	20	21	22	23	24	25
26	27	28	29	30	31	—

NOVEMBER
S	M	T	W	T	F	S
—	—	—	—	—	—	1
2	3	4	5	6	7	8
9	10	11	12	13	14	15
16	17	18	19	20	21	22
23	24	25	26	27	28	29
30	—	—	—	—	—	—

DECEMBER
S	M	T	W	T	F	S
—	1	2	3	4	5	6
7	8	9	10	11	12	13
14	15	16	17	18	19	20
21	22	23	24	25	26	27
28	29	30	31	—	—	—

Special Bookstore Supplement for 1996

226
I. In Praise of Local Heroes, 1996
Eight profiles of public-spirited citizens prove that the individual really *can* make a difference in community life. *by Jim Collins*

238
II. A Reference Compendium
Compiled by Sarah Hale and Mare-Anne Jarvela

Weather
Is It Raining, Drizzling, or Misting? **238**
A Table Foretelling the Weather Through All the Lunations of Each Year (Forever) **238**
Where the Sun Rises and Sets **239**
1996 Atlantic and Caribbean Hurricane Names **239**
Average Monthly Temperatures for Selected U.S. Cities ... **240**
Full Moon Names **242**
Phases of the Moon **242**
Temperature Conversion Formula **242**
Heat Index **243**
Glossary of Almanac Oddities **243**

Government
Abbreviations Approved by the U.S. Postal Service to Be Used in Addressing Mail **245**
Canadian Province and Territory Postal Codes ... **245**
U.S. Postage Rates **246**
Dear Congressman **246**
Federal Agencies **246**
Government Telephone Numbers **247**
Federal Information Center .. **248**
The Sequence of Presidential Succession **248**
Presidents of the United States **249**
States of the United States .. **250**
America's Seacoasts **252**

The Kitchen
Seasonal Guide to Fresh Fruits and Vegetables **253**
Substitutions for Common Ingredients **254**
Measuring Vegetables **254**
Measuring Fruits **255**

Egg Equivalents **256**
Dairy Definitions **256**
Freezer Storage Time Chart .. **257**
Beef Cuts **259**
Cake Mistake? **260**
What Counts as a Serving? .. **260**
Dietary Guidelines **261**
Food for Thought **261**

The Home
Guide to Lumber and Nails .. **262**
How Long Household Items Last **263**
How Much Electricity Is Used? **263**
How Much Water Is Used? . **263**
The Right Wood for the Job .. **264**

The Garden
General Rules for Pruning .. **265**
Flowers That Attract Hummingbirds **265**
Plants That Attract Butterflies **266**
Fall Palette **266**
Manure Guide **266**
Forcing Indoor Blooms **267**
Herbs to Plant in Lawns **267**
Planning Your Garden **268**
Herb Companions in Garden and Kitchen **268**
Plant a 1792 Flower and Herb Garden **270**

Animals & Birds
Gestation and Mating Table .. **271**
Animal Terminology **272**
More Animal Collectives ... **273**
Birdseed Chart **274**
How Old Is Your Dog? **274**

Health
Where to Find Vitamins and Minerals in Your Diet **275**

What Should You Weigh? .. **277**
How Fat Are You? **277**
Recommended Daily Dietary Allowances of Calories ... **277**
Average Time Spent Sleeping at Different Ages **278**
Calorie Burning **278**

Sports
Safe Ice Thickness **279**
Sports Halls of Fame **279**
Participation in Sports **280**
Acceptable Two-Letter Words in Scrabble **280**
The Most Landed-on Spaces on the Monopoly Game Board **281**
The Rank of Poker Hands ... **281**
Sports Quiz **281**

Miscellaneous
Decibels **282**
Makeshift Measurers **282**
Richter Scale for Measuring Earthquakes **282**
Metric Conversion **283**
How to Find the Day of the Week for Any Given Date .. **283**
Formula for Determining the Date of Easter for Any Year **284**
Another Way to Determine the Date of Easter **284**
Principal Religions of the World **285**
The Golden Rule **285**
Every Minute Counts **285**
Good Luck or Bad Luck? Here's How to Tell **286**
Rules of Introduction **287**
Military Rank **287**
Having Tea with the Queen? **287**
A Handy Chart for Identifying Five Generations of Blood Relatives **288**

The Old Farmer's Almanac hereby recognizes eight citizens and groups who have recently created and sustained the spirit of community within their neighborhoods and towns. So anytime you get discouraged about all the bad news in the daily newspapers, read one of these stories as an antidote.

In Praise of LOCAL HEROES

1 9 9 6

■ When Alexis de Tocqueville visited the United States in the 1830s, he was curious. How, he wondered, had this new country achieved such unprecedented success making democracy work? The key, he decided, was that "Americans of all ages, all stations of life, and all types of disposition, are forever forming associations. There are not only commercial and industrial associations in which all take part, but others of a thousand different types — religious, moral, serious, futile, very general and very limited, immensely large and very minute." In a way, de Tocqueville was describing the word *community*. That sense of common fellowship, of people coming together for the common good, has been a cornerstone in the foundation of American life. ■ Lately, there has been a growing sense that the foundation is cracking. For any number of reasons — the loss of family-scale agriculture, changing economics, suburbanization, strip malls, television, mistrust of government, a transient, fragmented populace — Americans fear that we are losing our sense of community. ■ Around the country, though, people are not only clinging to their communities, but are actively strengthening them. Acting out of a mix of idealism, pragmatism, faith, and enlightened self-interest, they are effecting positive changes in everyday life. In their stories, we can see a new, hopeful vision of our future. We can see new cornerstones being laid.

by   J i m   C o l l i n s

Inner City Earth Woman

Not many could imagine inner-city children in a racially divided Central Los Angeles neighborhood planting fruit trees and community gardens. Lois Arkin was an exception.

■ When Lois Arkin first dreamed of creating an ecological community — a garden — in central Los Angeles, she set her sights on a large, vacant lot that had once been a landfill. In that open space, she envisioned people working together, growing their own food, being stewards of their own environment. Sixty percent of Los Angeles is paved. The city has dirty air and water and few food sources of its own.

As Lois tried generating support for her landfill project, she discovered barriers beyond pavement and pollution. Within just two blocks from her home on White House Place lived 13 different ethnic groups speaking four different languages. Tension, mistrust, and suspicion greeted Lois's early attempts. She shifted her focus to building friendships and trust among the diverse groups. In the process, she reconsidered her plan for the vacant land and decided to focus on her immediate neighborhood, which already had some amenities in place. When two large fires burned the fringes of the two-block area during the riots in April of 1992, it became even clearer to Lois that her work was needed close to home.

In the beginning, it was children who brought the community together. Lois and other adult volunteers helped the children plant fruit trees along the barren streets — and made each planting a social and spiritual occasion. Lois talked to the children about the economics and nutrition of the trees, how the fruit could be harvested and eaten, where the surplus could be sold to bring in a little extra money. She talked about the difference between ownership and stewardship and assigned a different child to be responsible for each tree. They created a half-dozen community gardens overseen by teams of adult and child stewards. They organized a small-scale compost program and a junior recycling co-op. Every other week, Lois leads a string of neighborhood kids to the local recycling center, the children pulling their loaded wagons behind them. They divide the proceeds from the recyclables according to how much each one has contributed.

Lois Arkin began to draw her neighborhood together with this first tree-planting ceremony.

— courtesy Lois Arkin

A lot of the projects, originally promoted by word-of-mouth, are now advertised in a newsletter, *Bimini & White House Place Neighborhood News,* and a growing sense of hope and pride is spreading throughout the community. And another type of integration is taking root alongside the fruit trees and vegetable gardens. Recently, weekly community dinners have started in the neighborhood, both within and across the various ethnic groups. In 1992 racial tension and violence threatened to destroy this part of central Los Angeles. Today, in the integrated neighborhood around Lois Arkin's home, children pick oranges together and learn why it pays to cooperate.

Let's Go Bowling Again

League bowling is another indicator of community spirit — and its decline troubled Roger Robinson. Here's what he did about it in his Detroit suburb.

■ In the January 1995 issue of the *Journal of Democracy,* Harvard professor Robert Putnam described America's declining involvement in civic activities. "The most whimsical yet discomfiting bit of evidence of social disengagement in contemporary America that I have discovered is this," he wrote. "More Americans are bowling today than ever before, but bowling in organized leagues has plummeted. Between 1980 and 1993 the total number of bowlers in America has increased by ten percent, while league bowling decreased by 40 percent. . . . I should note that nearly 80 million Americans went bowling at least once during 1993, *nearly a third more than voted in the 1994 congressional elections* and roughly the same number as claim to attend church regularly. The rise of solo bowling threatens the livelihood of bowling-lane proprietors because those who bowl as members of leagues consume three times as much beer and pizza as solo bowlers, and the money in bowling is in the beer and pizza, not the balls and shoes. The broader social significance, however, lies in the social interaction and even occasionally civic conversations over beer and pizza that solo bowlers forgo. Bowling teams illustrate yet another vanishing form of social capital."

This wasn't news to Roger Robinson. He had noticed the decline in league play at his five centers in the suburbs of Detroit — long considered the capital city of U.S. bowling. He'd been in the business since 1958 and had watched attendance at his lanes ebb and flow with the changing tides of the auto industry. But the drop

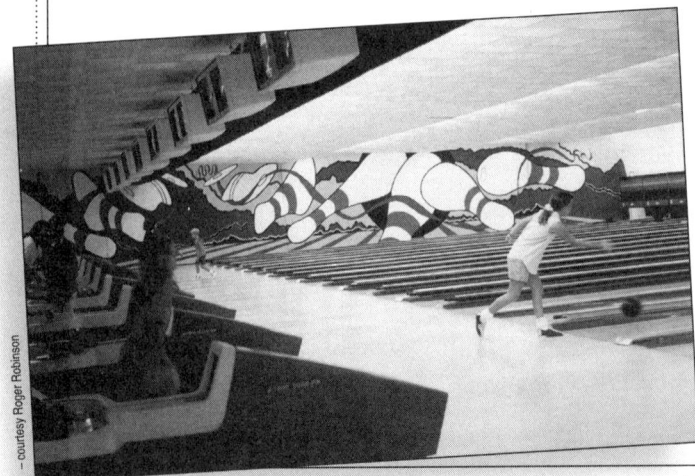

League play is up at Roger Robinson's suburban Detroit bowling alleys.

in league play during the 1980s seemed more serious than a cyclical dip.

Faced with changing times and falling attendance, Roger innovated. Besides the standard league structure of five-member teams bowling a 36-week season, he let teams pick their own numbers, one to five people, and bowl however many weeks they wanted. He created an eight-week singles league — with a party at the end of the season. (One couple met that way and got married.) He created special leagues for seniors. At the 50-lane center in Sterling Heights, his wife, a graphic artist, painted wild murals on the walls — huge floating lips, crazy geometric shapes, bright, electric colors, five-foot-tall fingers in the form of a V. He added video-game machines to the billiards room and bar and put in automatic scoring.

Attendance in league play jumped five percent, then another two percent the next year. In the summer at the 40-lane center in Livonia, he closed the center for "Rock 'n' Bowl" nights for kids ten to 15 years old, bringing in a DJ for dancing and donating proceeds to D.A.R.E., a drug prevention program. League play, thanks partly to young bowlers, has grown by ten percent over the past two years. Last year charity fund-raisers at his centers brought in close to $100,000.

"There's no doubt that numbers around the country are off," says Roger. "But I can't remember when things around here have been this exciting. People still like to get together and bowl."

Everybody Loves a Parade

When Dorothy Behlen Heinrichs moved into a suburban block in Bethesda, Maryland, she was astonished to learn that no one ever bothered to plan anything for the Fourth of July.

■ It was a neighborhood where nobody talked. The beltway had cut through a few miles away and intersected with I-270, making this part of Bethesda a kind of huge residential traffic island. Commuters moved in and out as jobs came and went. Fewer and fewer residents' memories stretched back to when the modest, compact houses were built in the 1950s.

But a nice little park framed the end of Lone Oak Drive, and sidewalks and red maples and flowering trees lined the street. When Dorothy Behlen Heinrichs moved there ten years ago, she was astonished that none of the neighbors welcomed her. Back home in Cincinnati, neighbors greeted newcomers with baskets of bread and wine. She was surprised, too, that no one was planning any celebration for the Fourth of July. The kids' parade on Independence Day had been a regular part of her childhood. She couldn't imagine that all places didn't have one.

She became friends with another young mother, Elin Haaga, who lived a few doors down.

Miss Liberty (Dorothy Watson Heinrichs) marched in that first parade, July 4, 1986.

Dorothy brought up the idea of organizing a kids' Fourth of July parade, and Elin, though Welsh, became an instant accomplice. The two women spread the word to everyone they met. They tacked up posters around the block. Dorothy found cookie cutters shaped like the United States and the Statue of Liberty. The kids helped her and Elin decorate the cookies and make lemonade.

Neither woman had any idea how many people would show up for the parade. But on the morning of the Fourth, Elin looked out her window and saw a few neighbors walking toward the gathering spot at the top of the hill. One of them was carrying a huge American flag. A couple of the kids rode bikes decorated with red, white, and blue crepe-paper streamers. When Dorothy and Elin got to the top of the hill, they saw dozens of people gathered — trikes and strollers, three-year-olds dressed in tri-corner hats, kids as ballerinas and leopards, kids holding pots and pans and wooden noisemakers.

The woman with the flag led the parade back down the block, and Elin played her recorder. Kids banged on their pots and rang the bells on their bikes. Older residents stepped out and waved from their porches as the kids marched by on the sidewalk. The parade passed the houses on Dickens Avenue, then Edward, then back up Lone Oak Drive. It lasted maybe ten minutes, but everyone gathered afterward for cookies and lemonade on Elin's lawn and lingered and laughed and got to know each other. They had never seen anything like it there.

Something in the neighborhood changed that day. Before long, the young mothers had organized a play group and a baby-sitting co-op. They printed their own yellow "money" in units of time, exchanging the currency among themselves and presenting it as gifts to new neighbors. In the summer, residents roped off the streets and had giant block parties. At Christmas they held music recitals. The parade became a much-anticipated annual event, attracting kids and onlookers, even from other parts of town.

The neighborhood has continued to be somewhat transient, but the community spirit that was sparked by that first parade took hold. When Birgit Chrambach was operated on for breast cancer earlier this year, her phone rang and kept on ringing: neighbors offering prayers and well wishes, sending flowers, organizing rides for her kids, taking shifts to cook her meals, arranging visits to keep her company — neighbor reaching out to neighbor in a time of need.

Don't Like Your Government? Then Set Up Your Own

That's what a community of fishing families on an island in Maine did a couple of years ago. And are they ever happy now!

■ At the turn of the century, there were 300 islands in Maine supporting year-round populations. Today just 14 remain. Many of the 170 year-round residents of Long Island, in Casco Bay off Portland, didn't want their community to be the next to go. So on election day three years ago, the residents of Long Island gathered to vote on breaking their 206-year tie with the city of Portland. Portland's recent revaluation had doubled and even tripled some of the island property taxes, and islanders worried that their traditional, fishing-based community would become nothing more than a summer playground for the rich. They'd heard stories of that happening up and down the coast: Waterfront property became too valuable for local homeowners to afford the taxes, so they were forced to sell, and the only people who could pay the new prices were wealthy "summer people" from the mainland. Without a local year-round economy, without enough children to sustain a school, vibrant, living island communities were bound to die. During the first stirrings of secession on Long Island, the fishermen practically took over Channel 73 on the VHF and turned it into an open forum on the topic. Excitement grew — you could almost feel it as you walked from the dock past the tiny post office, past the two-room K-5 schoolhouse, and up Beach Avenue. Inside the small, wood-frame houses, people were preparing to take their fate into their own hands: set up their own government, raise their own money, and decide for themselves how to spend it; assume responsibility for their school and their roads, their water, and their waste.

By the time the vote came up in November, the islanders had organized meetings with representatives from similar-sized islands and had consulted with experts in town planning, budgets, and municipal services. They had proved that Long Island could make a go on its own, at least on paper. But what started out as an issue over property taxes had become something much more important: a referendum on self-governance and self-reliance. The vote, 144-29, was overwhelmingly in favor.

Bob Brayley and Don McVane, lobstermen who grew up together on the island, were elected as selectmen. They had both learned a thing or two about pulling together in their 65-odd years of friendship. "There were 25 lobster fishermen on the island," says Bob, "and 18 boats. We've always helped each other out because we've had to, to survive — but now it wasn't just the fishermen. It felt like the whole town was pulling together.

Don McVane (left) and Bob Brayley, lobstermen and lifelong friends, served as selectmen in the new town of Long Island, Maine.

"We had selectmen's meetings every Saturday after the vote, and 20 or 25 people showed up at every one," Don says. "Why, it used to be you wouldn't see 25 people in a week. Every committee was filled, everyone wanted to get involved." (Today Bob Brayley is still a selectman, though Don McVane chose not to run for reelection.)

On July 1, 1993, Long Island officially became the first new town in Maine in 70 years. Property taxes dropped in each of the town's first two years, and another drop is anticipated this year, even as Portland's rates have risen. The islanders — most of them second and third generation — have never felt more tightly drawn together. Committees are filled, volunteers continue to put in long hours as they struggle to make a new government run smoothly. More important, Bob Brayley points out, 18 boats and 25 fishermen still work from the island.

Women of the Butterfly Circle

In Chicago, 500 low-income women entrepreneurs have been able to start small businesses through an innovative "bank" that loans seed money to anyone with enough peer support and determination. The success rate? It's 93 percent — much higher than conventional banks achieve.

■ Around the culturally diverse housing projects in the Englewood area of Chicago, residents have gotten used to this daily sight: Omiyala Dupart, larger than life, walking the streets wearing brightly colored African clothes, selling butter cookies from a wide wicker basket. She's usually smiling — and has good reason to be. Married, the mother of seven children, Omiyala no longer works at the tedious polishing job she held in a lamp factory. Today, she runs her own business called Global Bee Trading Company — an eclectic purveyor of used furniture, Afrocentric clothing, collectibles, jewelry, and the best butter cookies this side of the Loop.

She got her start five years ago when she joined "Les Papillons" ("The Butterflies"), a group of five low-income women from the same community. They were just one of dozens of similar "circles" from the poorest neighborhoods in the city. As in the other circles, the women of Les Papillons were able to borrow money through Chicago's Women's Self-Employment Project. Modeled on the Grameen Bank in Bangladesh, the project loans money to small groups of poor women who promise peer pressure and support instead of the conventional collateral and good credit ratings. The women must create their group from the same neighborhood and meet biweekly for support and assistance. The circle approves all of the loans; each borrower must make three timely payments before another circle sister can take out a loan. The project provides advice, technical assistance, and any other help the women may need in setting up their businesses. Once good credit and an ongoing business are established, many of the women leave the circle and join the mainstream small-business community.

The success of the project has been remarkable. More than 500 women (85 percent of them African-American, four percent Latina, and 11 percent Caucasian) have borrowed money from the circle fund since 1986. The success rate on repayments has been 93 percent — about ten points higher than conventional banks. In Omiyala's circle, one woman created an ethnic jewelry business; another, Arinez Gilyard, set up a day-care center in her home; another, Philonese Simmons, became a

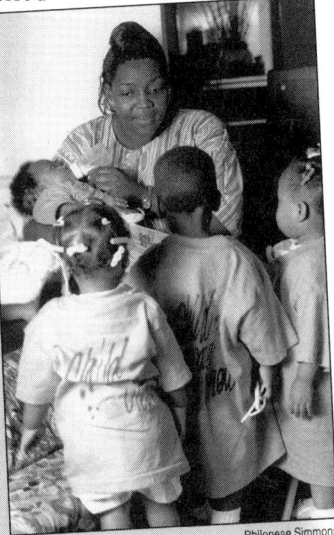

Arinez Gilyard of Les Papillons got a circle loan to start a day-care center in her home.

— Philonese Simmons

professional photographer. (See her photo at left.) In all of the cases, the seed money from the circle was crucial.

The circle loans were established to help low-income women become economically self-sufficient. But the impact has gone deeper. For many of the women, the circles have provided a fundamental sense of community where survival depends on group incentive and support. They have drawn strength from two ingredients: a sense of necessity and shared adversity. When people in Englewood see Omiyala Dupart's smile and wicker basket coming down the street, they feel a little better about their world.

The Noisiest Library in the Country

At Roger Faris's Seattle, Washington, "tool library," people check out everything from electric drills and scaffolding to hydraulic jacks in order to help out their neighbors.

■ It was a scene out of the Amish country of rural Ohio or 19th-century small-town New England. Mary Dreisbach, in her seventies and living alone in an old house, needed her rotten porch replaced, and a bunch of neighbors gathered on a fine summer weekend and pitched in with hammers and nails and cedar boards. By afternoon, they'd finished the final part — an extra-solid handrail. Mary put down her hammer (she was swinging one right along with the rest of them), brought cold drinks out from the house, and thanked her neighbors for their help.

Mary's house is a little bungalow near the Phinney Ridge section of Seattle. In a city known for its civic involvement, few organized groups have done as much to bring people together as has the Phinney Neighborhood Association. Mary had been active in the association, and she had been part of work parties at other people's houses. She'd helped a family put in insulation. At another house, she showed up for a plumbing project, even though she knew little about plumbing.

– courtesy Roger Faris

Volunteer Ladell Black operates a power mitre saw while Mary Dreisbach and another helper take a break during her porch renovation project.

"That's the way the thing worked," she says. "We were all there to learn as well as to help each other." When she needed help of her own, the word spread. The work party for her new porch was advertised in the association's monthly newsletter and also on the bulletin board of the Well Home Program, a remarkable neighborhood resource started in 1977.

Roger Faris was a general contractor when he was hired to coordinate a new "tool library" and home repair program. The idea was simple: to provide basic tools and instruction for area residents. The program got funding and a place to house tools from the local Methodist Church. The innovative program eventually became part of the Phinney Neighborhood Association.

Today, the tool library has grown to include "in the high hundreds" of tools: extension ladders and Sawz-alls, bolt-cutters, scaffolding, table saws, hammers, electric drills, pressure washers, hydraulic jacks, all manner of tools and supplies for plumbing, gardening, electrical work, carpentry, and painting. Members check out the tools for a modest fee, along with instructional books or videos. They pick through the salvaged and recycled materials pile, get advice on home repairs and improvements, get referrals for dependable contractors, check the bulletin board for work swaps and sale items. Classes and workshops offer basic instruction; guest instructors include building inspectors, earthquake experts, plumbers, and electricians. Members organize work and painting parties to help elderly or disabled neighbors who can't do the work themselves. Some go along just to watch and learn.

And for more than 15 years, Roger Faris has continued to direct the center and its neighbor-helping-neighbor philosophy. He has been described in the local paper as a grown-up version of the small-town teen-age gas-station attendant, someone who knows most of his customers by name, remembers their problems, and gives free advice laced with humor. And the neighborhood is looking fine these days.

Living with the Giants

In the Coulee region of west-central Wisconsin, downtown merchants and farmers have learned how to compete with the retail giants of the world. In Viroqua, it all started when Nancy Rhodes-Seevers organized an all-day retreat to figure out how to save the downtown.

■ A magazine article described the Viroqua, Wisconsin, of ten years ago: "By the mid-1980s, the four-block-long downtown business district had a dingy, let-it-slide look. Storefronts on the two-story brick buildings deteriorated, awnings sagged, and it felt like nobody cared. Merchants, the city council, the professionals, and the farmers went their separate ways; the same seven or eight people turned up at every meeting."

Like hundreds of rural places across the country, the area had lost a lot of its dairy farms — and creameries, cheese factories, and tobacco farms — and young people moved away as soon as they finished school. And then something happened. Or rather, a couple of things happened around the same time.

In the spring of 1986, the first signs appeared announcing the arrival of a large Wal-Mart store on Highway 14 north of downtown Viroqua. The discount giant had priced out many local businesses across the South and Midwest, but in Viroqua the businesses rallied together in order to compete. Bed-and-breakfast owner Nancy Rhodes-Seevers organized an all-day retreat that attracted close to 70 people. Acting together — for the first time any of them could remember — the business owners talked

Elbow grease and imagination refurbished downtown Viroqua's Main Street.

— courtesy Viroqua Chamber of Commerce

about what was wrong with downtown, how it could be strengthened, where expertise and funding were available, how the town could attract more visitors and businesses. The energy from that initial meeting spread like a fever.

Over the next several months, an unprecedented fund-raising campaign brought in close to $150,000, the town qualified for guidance under the National Historic Trust's "Main Street" program, and an energetic young woman named Theresa Washburn was hired to coordinate the downtown revitalization. Merchants refurbished their storefronts and devised strategies to stay competitive, the city council funded new, 1930s-era street lights, and the town was energized and optimistic. The more people saw what was happening, the more people got involved; the revitalization took off.

Wal-Mart opened on schedule, even contributing to Main Street projects and participating in special events. Downtown, a few miles away, civic pride and support not only kept old businesses open, but also attracted new ones. Half a decade later, the success story continues. The latest project involves the restoration of the old vaudeville theater. Towns throughout the Midwest now look to Viroqua for ideas and advice.

Around the same time that Wal-Mart was moving in, a small group of vegetable farmers gathered in the kitchen of George Siemon, about 15 miles east of Viroqua. Like the downtown merchants, they were being forced out of a market increasingly dominated by large, mass-market producers and retailers. George, a newcomer to the area, had a commitment to organic farming — growing produce without the use of pesticides or chemicals. He also had the idea of pooling the produce of small, independent farmers in order to take advantage of the marketing and transportation efficiencies usually enjoyed by large producers. In his kitchen, the seeds of the Coulee Region Organic Produce Pool were planted.

Lifetime resident and dairy farmer Jim Wedeberg attended the group's organizational meeting at the county courthouse in Viroqua and talked with George about including milk and cheese producers in the pool. Like other milk producers in the area, Jim was worried about chronically low milk prices and the impact of Bovine Growth Hormone (BGH). He and George became unlikely allies — newcomer and native — and the cooperative, now known nationally as Organic Valley, has grown and flourished. More than 100 farmers have become part of the pool, including ex-hippie vegetable growers and old-time dairymen, Amish chicken farmers, and the state's largest organic apple orchard. The cooperative has provided a modern solution to an age-old problem: keeping the rural tradition of the family farm vibrant and profitable.

Keeping the Faith in Rural Minnesota

Everyone assumed that St. Peter's Elementary School in Canby would have to close. But the Reverend Paul Van de Crommert resolved to save the school — and in the process lifted the whole town's morale.

■ Five years ago, when the Reverend Paul Van de Crommert became pastor at the Church of St. Peter in Canby, Minnesota, the local Catholic elementary school was in trouble. Enrollment in the six grades was down to about 85 and sinking fast. The building had been badly neglected and was desperate for repair, the administration was foundering, and teacher morale was low. Most folks around town took it for granted that the school, founded 35 years earlier, would soon go the way of so many other abandoned parochial schools scattered around the Midwest.

The new pastor, only 28 years old, was fully aware of the social and demographic trends behind so many rural school closings. But he also knew how important the school was to this parish and this farming community of 1,800 people near the South Dakota border. St. Peter's School employed 15 people and pumped much-needed money into the local economy. It put on annual pageants and social events; it fostered a healthy sense of rivalry and competition with the town's public school; it spread the faith. He was convinced that a little creativity and a lot of hard work could revitalize the school.

With the recommendation of the pastoral council, Father Paul became the principal of the school. He immediately reorganized the administration, saving money in salaries and overhead. His combined role of pastor/principal streamlined the administration and taught him about all aspects of the school. He actively promoted the school in the area, recruiting volunteers for fund-raising and work projects. Kids gained a visible presence in the town and support from downtown merchants through walkathons, raffles, and auctions. Classes visited nursing homes. Father Paul added a kindergarten and enrolled non-Catholic students. The first summer, volunteers painted walls that hadn't seen a paintbrush in 20 years. He later wrote, "Like the Amish, who hold barn-raisings without degrees in architecture or carpentry, the faithful and I worked together to build up our school."

Father Paul, who had grown up in the small town of Slayton about an hour south of Canby, knew about the economic issues that threatened the health of small towns everywhere. In renovating the school, he sought out local businesses, using local contractors and suppliers even when they hadn't submitted the lowest bids, negotiating for the best deal. For example, he bought the school's new windows from the town lumberyard, pumping $30,000 into the local economy.

Morale in the school rose and spilled over into the community. "It's not the issue of faith," Father Paul says. "It's giving people the choice of education. When you have more than one institution of learning in such a small town, when people work to create their own opportunities, that does a lot for a community's morale."

Attendance in church has increased, and two or three masses a week are now offered for the grade-school children instead of one. Parishioners are united again, not divided over the wisdom of pouring funding into a dying school. Not all towns are as lucky. In the diocese that Canby belongs to, two of the 21 Catholic elementary schools have closed, and at least two more are in danger. In Canby, 110 students are expected to enroll in the fall of 1995.

The Reverend Paul Van de Crommert knew that saving a school would boost the whole town of Canby, Minnesota.

"In a small community," says the Reverend Paul Van de Crommert, "you do need leadership, someone who will keep pushing. It's very hard to find those people. We're always looking for a hero."

"Discover a *Guaranteed** Way to
Boost Your Mental Energy
and
Feel More Alive Than You Have in Years!"

"I want to retain my mental and physical well-being into a ripe old age. So I started using Ginkgo Biloba about 1 1/2 years ago. Since then I have noticed a marked improvement in my mental health."
—Ann Romano, Newington, CT

Do you suffer from low energy, mental fatigue, or cold hands and feet?

Join over 20 million people who have used GINKGO BILOBA, a remarkable herbal extract that helps:

GUARANTEED POTENCY

- **Increase Energy**
- **Support Healthy Circulation**
- **Promote Better Memory & Mental Alertness**

*100% SATISFACTION GUARANTEED
You take no risk in ordering. If you're not pleased with the results of Ginkgo Biloba, we'll refund 100% of your money, no questions asked.

Statements included herein by Amrion, Inc., shall not be construed to imply claims or representations that these products treat or prevent any disease, but rather are dietary supplements intended solely for nutritional support.

$9.99 ea.

ORDER GINKGO BILOBA Today and SAVE up to 45%!

TO ORDER BY CREDIT CARD, JUST CALL TOLL FREE **1-800-627-7775** M-F 6:30 a.m.- 9:00 p.m. SAT. & SUN. 8 a.m.- 5 p.m. (Mountain time zone) OR MAIL IN THIS COUPON!	Rush Me: (Check a box)	Regular Price	Special Offer Price	Number Bottles		Ttl. Bottle Price	You Pay	You Save
	☐ 60 capsules	$13.99	$ 9.99	x 1	=	$ 9.99	$	$ 4.00
	☐ 60 capsules	$13.49	$ 9.49	x 2	=	$18.98	$	$ 9.00
	☐ 60 capsules	$12.99	$ 8.99	x 4	=	$35.96	$	$20.00
	☐ 120 capsules	$23.99	$14.99	x 1	=	$14.99	$	$ 9.00
	☐ 120 capsules	$22.99	$13.99	x 2	=	$27.98	$	$20.00
	☐ 120 capsules	$21.99	$12.99	x 4	=	$51.96	$	$44.00
	ALL CAPSULES 40 mg		Colorado Residents Add 3% Tax				$	
			Shipping and Handling				$ 3.00	
			Send check or money order to:			**TOTAL**	$	

Name_____
Address_____
City_____ State___ Zip___
Phone (___)_____
© 1994 Amrion, Inc.   Key Code: A6OFGB

BIOENERGY NUTRIENTS
Bioenergy Nutrients
6565 Odell Place
Boulder, CO 80301-3330

Is It Raining, Drizzling, or Misting?

	Drops (per sq. ft. per second)	Diameter of Drops (mm)	Intensity (in. per hr.)
Cloudburst	113	2.85	4.00
Excessive Rain	76	2.40	1.60
Heavy Rain	46	2.05	.60
Moderate Rain	46	1.60	.15
Light Rain	26	1.24	.04
Drizzle	14	.96	.01
Mist	2,510	.10	.002
Fog	6,264,000	.01	.005

A Table Foretelling the Weather Through All the Lunations of Each Year (Forever)

This table is the result of many years' actual observation and shows what sort of weather will probably follow the Moon's entrance into any of its quarters. For example, the weather for the week following May 3, 1996, would be windy and rainy because the Moon becomes full that day at 6:49 A.M., EST.

Editor's note: *While the data in this table are taken into consideration in the yearlong process of compiling the annual long-range weather forecasts for* The Old Farmer's Almanac, *we rely far more on our projections of solar activity.*

Time of Change	Summer	Winter
Midnight to 2 A.M.	Fair	Hard frost, unless wind is south or west
2 A.M. to 4 A.M.	Cold, with frequent showers	Snow and stormy
4 A.M. to 6 A.M.	Rain	Rain
6 A.M. to 8 A.M.	Wind and rain	Stormy
8 A.M. to 10 A.M.	Changeable	Cold rain if wind is west; snow if east
10 A.M. to noon	Frequent showers	Cold with high winds
Noon to 2 P.M.	Very rainy	Snow or rain
2 P.M. to 4 P.M.	Changeable	Fair and mild
4 P.M. to 6 P.M.	Fair	Fair
6 P.M. to 10 P.M.	Fair if wind is northwest; rain if south or southwest	Fair and frosty if wind is north or northeast; rain or snow if wind is south or southwest
10 P.M. to midnight	Fair	Fair and frosty

This table was created more than 160 years ago by Dr. Herschell for the Boston Courier; *it first appeared in* The Old Farmer's Almanac *in 1834.*

WEATHER

Where the Sun Rises and Sets

By using the table below and a compass, you can determine accurately where on the horizon the Sun will rise or set on a given day. The top half of the table is for those days of the year, between the vernal and autumnal equinoxes, when the Sun rises north of east and sets north of west. March 21 through June 21 are listed in the left column, June 21 through September 22 appear in the right column. Similarly arranged, the bottom half of the table shows the other half of the year when the Sun rises south of east and sets south of west. Here's how it works: Say you live in Gary, Indiana, and need to know where the Sun will rise or set on October 10. Use the Time Correction Tables (p. 196-200) to determine the latitude of your city or the listed city nearest to you. Gary is at 41° latitude. Find the 40° latitude column, and you see that on October 10 the Sun rises 8° south of east and sets 8° south of west. Of course, you can determine figures for other latitudes and days not actually shown in the table by using extrapolation.

Latitude Date	0°	10°	20°	30°	40°	50°	60°	Latitude Date
Mar. 21	0°	0°	0°	0°	0°	0°	0°	Sept. 22
Mar. 31	4° N	4° N	4° N	4° N	5° N	6° N	8° N	Sept. 14
Apr. 10	8° N	8° N	8° N	9° N	10° N	12° N	15° N	Sept. 4
Apr. 20	11° N	12° N	12° N	13° N	15° N	18° N	23° N	Aug. 24
May 1	15° N	16° N	16° N	17° N	20° N	23° N	31° N	Aug. 14
May 10	17° N	18° N	19° N	20° N	23° N	28° N	37° N	Aug. 4
May 20	20° N	21° N	21° N	23° N	26° N	32° N	43° N	July 25
June 1	22° N	22° N	23° N	26° N	29° N	36° N	48° N	July 13
June 10	23° N	24° N	24° N	27° N	31° N	37° N	51° N	July 4
June 21	23½° N	25° N	25° N	27° N	31° N	38° N	53° N	June 21
Sept. 22	0°	0°	0°	0°	0°	0°	0°	Mar. 21
Oct. 1	3° S	3° S	3° S	3° S	4° S	5° S	6° S	Mar. 14
Oct. 10	6° S	7° S	7° S	7° S	8° S	10° S	13° S	Mar. 5
Oct. 20	10° S	11° S	11° S	12° S	13° S	16° S	20° S	Feb. 23
Nov. 1	15° S	15° S	15° S	16° S	18° S	22° S	29° S	Feb. 12
Nov. 10	17° S	18° S	18° S	20° S	22° S	27° S	36° S	Feb. 2
Nov. 20	20° S	21° S	21° S	23° S	26° S	31° S	42° S	Jan. 23
Dec. 1	22° S	23° S	23° S	25° S	29° S	35° S	48° S	Jan. 13
Dec. 10	23° S	24° S	24° S	27° S	30° S	37° S	51° S	Jan. 4
Dec. 21	23½° S	25° S	25° S	27° S	31° S	38° S	53° S	Dec. 21

1996 Atlantic and Caribbean Hurricane Names

Since 1950, hurricane names have been selected and approved by the World Meteorological Organization and reflect a variety of cultures and languages. Hurricanes were given only women's names until 1979, when men's names were added to eliminate gender bias. The National Hurricane Center near Miami, Florida, assigns names for hurricanes in the Atlantic and Caribbean regions. The names are rotated every six years; however, in the event of a particularly destructive hurricane, such as Andrew in 1992, a name is often retired.

Arthur	Edouard	Isidore	Nana	Wilfred
Bertha	Fran	Josephine	Omar	Sally
Cesar	Gustav	Kyle	Paloma	Teddy
Dolly	Hortense	Lili	Rene	Vicky
		Marco		

WEATHER

Average Monthly Temperatures for Selected U.S. Cities

Daily maximum (**bold numbers**) and minimum averages in ° Fahrenheit

	JAN.	FEB.	MAR.	APR.	MAY	JUNE	JULY	AUG.	SEPT.	OCT.	NOV.	DEC.
Mobile, Alabama	**59.7** 40.0	**63.6** 42.7	**70.9** 50.1	**78.5** 57.1	**84.6** 64.4	**90.0** 70.7	**91.3** 73.2	**90.5** 72.9	**86.9** 68.7	**79.5** 57.3	**70.3** 49.1	**62.9** 43.1
Anchorage, Alaska	**21.4** 8.4	**25.8** 11.5	**33.1** 18.1	**42.8** 28.6	**54.4** 38.8	**61.6** 47.2	**65.2** 51.7	**63.0** 49.5	**55.2** 41.6	**40.5** 28.7	**27.2** 15.1	**22.5** 10.0
Phoenix, Arizona	**65.9** 41.2	**70.7** 44.7	**75.5** 48.8	**84.5** 55.3	**93.6** 63.9	**103.5** 72.9	**105.9** 81.0	**103.7** 79.2	**98.3** 72.8	**88.1** 60.8	**74.9** 48.9	**66.2** 41.8
Little Rock, Arkansas	**49.0** 29.1	**53.9** 33.2	**64.0** 42.2	**73.4** 50.7	**81.3** 59.0	**89.3** 67.4	**92.4** 71.5	**91.4** 69.8	**84.6** 63.5	**75.1** 50.9	**62.7** 41.5	**52.5** 33.1
San Francisco, California	**55.6** 41.8	**59.4** 45.0	**60.8** 45.8	**63.9** 47.2	**66.5** 49.7	**70.3** 52.6	**71.6** 53.9	**72.3** 55.0	**73.6** 55.2	**70.1** 51.8	**62.4** 47.1	**56.1** 42.7
Denver, Colorado	**43.2** 16.1	**46.6** 20.2	**52.2** 25.8	**61.8** 34.5	**70.8** 43.6	**81.4** 52.4	**88.2** 58.6	**85.8** 56.9	**76.9** 47.6	**66.3** 36.4	**52.5** 25.4	**44.5** 17.4
Hartford, Connecticut	**33.2** 15.8	**36.4** 18.6	**46.8** 28.1	**59.9** 37.5	**71.6** 47.6	**80.0** 56.9	**85.0** 62.2	**82.7** 60.4	**74.8** 51.8	**63.7** 40.7	**51.0** 32.8	**37.5** 21.3
Washington, D.C.	**42.3** 26.8	**45.9** 29.1	**56.5** 37.7	**66.7** 46.4	**76.2** 56.6	**84.7** 66.5	**88.5** 71.4	**86.9** 70.0	**80.1** 62.5	**69.1** 50.3	**58.3** 41.1	**47.0** 31.7
Miami, Florida	**75.2** 59.2	**76.5** 60.4	**79.1** 64.2	**82.4** 67.8	**85.3** 72.1	**87.6** 75.1	**89.0** 76.2	**89.0** 76.7	**87.8** 75.9	**84.5** 72.1	**80.4** 66.7	**76.7** 61.5
Atlanta, Georgia	**50.4** 31.5	**55.0** 34.5	**64.3** 42.5	**72.7** 50.2	**79.6** 58.7	**85.8** 66.2	**88.0** 69.5	**87.1** 69.0	**81.8** 63.5	**72.7** 51.9	**63.4** 42.8	**54.0** 35.0
Honolulu, Hawaii	**80.1** 65.6	**80.5** 65.4	**81.6** 67.2	**82.8** 68.7	**84.7** 70.3	**86.5** 72.2	**87.5** 73.5	**88.7** 74.2	**88.5** 73.5	**86.9** 72.3	**84.1** 70.3	**81.2** 67.0
Boise, Idaho	**36.4** 21.6	**44.2** 27.5	**52.9** 31.9	**61.4** 36.7	**71.0** 43.9	**80.9** 52.1	**90.2** 57.7	**88.1** 56.7	**77.0** 48.2	**64.6** 39.0	**48.7** 31.1	**37.7** 22.5
Chicago, Illinois	**29.0** 12.9	**33.5** 17.2	**45.8** 28.5	**58.6** 38.6	**70.1** 47.7	**79.6** 57.5	**83.7** 62.6	**81.8** 61.6	**74.8** 53.9	**63.3** 42.2	**48.4** 31.6	**34.0** 19.1
Indianapolis, Indiana	**33.9** 17.2	**38.2** 20.3	**50.0** 30.9	**62.4** 41.2	**73.2** 51.6	**82.3** 61.1	**85.6** 65.4	**83.8** 62.9	**78.0** 55.8	**65.8** 43.4	**52.2** 34.4	**39.2** 23.1
Des Moines, Iowa	**28.1** 10.7	**33.7** 15.6	**46.9** 27.6	**61.8** 40.0	**73.0** 51.5	**82.2** 61.2	**86.7** 66.5	**84.2** 63.6	**75.6** 54.5	**64.3** 42.7	**48.0** 29.9	**32.6** 16.1
Wichita, Kansas	**39.8** 19.2	**45.9** 23.7	**57.2** 33.6	**68.3** 44.5	**76.9** 54.3	**86.8** 64.6	**92.8** 69.9	**90.7** 67.9	**81.4** 60.3	**70.6** 46.6	**55.3** 33.9	**43.0** 23.0
Louisville, Kentucky	**40.3** 23.2	**44.8** 26.5	**56.3** 36.2	**67.3** 45.4	**76.0** 54.7	**83.5** 62.9	**87.0** 67.3	**85.7** 65.8	**80.3** 58.7	**69.2** 45.8	**56.8** 37.3	**45.1** 28.6
New Orleans, Louisiana	**61.3** 44.1	**64.5** 47.1	**71.8** 54.2	**78.7** 60.9	**84.5** 67.5	**89.4** 73.0	**90.8** 74.9	**90.5** 74.8	**87.1** 71.7	**80.0** 61.8	**71.5** 54.1	**64.8** 47.6
Portland, Maine	**30.3** 11.4	**33.1** 13.5	**41.4** 24.5	**52.3** 34.1	**63.2** 43.4	**72.7** 52.1	**78.8** 58.3	**77.4** 57.1	**69.3** 48.9	**58.7** 38.3	**47.0** 30.4	**35.1** 17.8
Boston, Massachusetts	**35.7** 21.6	**37.5** 23.0	**45.8** 31.3	**55.9** 40.2	**66.6** 49.8	**76.3** 59.1	**81.8** 65.1	**79.8** 64.0	**72.8** 56.8	**62.7** 46.9	**52.2** 38.3	**40.4** 26.7
Detroit, Michigan	**30.3** 15.6	**33.3** 17.6	**44.4** 27.0	**57.7** 36.8	**69.6** 47.1	**78.9** 56.3	**83.3** 61.3	**81.3** 59.6	**73.9** 52.5	**61.5** 40.9	**48.1** 32.2	**35.2** 21.4
Minneapolis-St. Paul, Minnesota	**20.7** 2.8	**26.6** 9.2	**39.2** 22.7	**56.5** 36.2	**69.4** 47.6	**78.8** 57.6	**84.0** 63.1	**80.7** 60.3	**70.7** 50.3	**58.8** 38.8	**41.0** 25.2	**25.5** 10.2

WEATHER

	JAN.	FEB.	MAR.	APR.	MAY	JUNE	JULY	AUG.	SEPT.	OCT.	NOV.	DEC.
Jackson,	55.6	60.1	69.3	77.4	84.0	90.6	92.4	92.0	88.0	79.1	69.2	59.5
Mississippi	32.7	35.7	44.1	51.9	60.0	67.1	70.5	69.7	63.7	50.3	42.3	36.1
St. Louis,	37.7	42.6	54.6	66.9	76.1	85.2	89.3	87.3	79.9	68.5	54.7	41.7
Missouri	20.8	25.1	35.5	46.4	56.0	65.7	70.4	69.7	60.5	48.3	37.7	26.0
Butte,	28.5	33.9	39.9	50.4	60.3	70.2	80.1	78.4	66.4	55.5	39.3	29.4
Montana	5.0	10.0	16.7	25.9	34.0	41.7	45.7	44.0	35.1	26.4	16.0	5.5
Omaha,	29.7	35.0	47.6	62.4	72.8	82.4	86.5	84.0	74.9	64.0	47.7	32.9
Nebraska	11.2	16.6	27.8	40.3	51.8	61.4	66.5	63.8	54.7	43.0	29.7	15.9
Reno,	45.1	51.7	56.3	63.7	72.9	83.1	91.9	89.6	79.5	68.6	53.8	45.5
Nevada	20.7	24.2	29.2	33.3	40.1	46.9	51.3	49.6	41.3	32.9	26.7	19.9
Albuquerque,	46.8	53.5	61.4	70.8	79.7	90.0	92.5	89.0	81.9	71.0	57.3	47.5
New Mexico	21.7	26.4	32.2	39.6	48.6	58.3	64.4	62.6	55.2	43.0	31.2	23.1
Buffalo,	30.2	31.6	41.7	54.2	66.1	75.3	80.2	77.9	70.8	59.4	47.1	35.3
New York	17.0	17.4	25.9	36.2	47.0	56.5	61.9	60.1	53.0	42.7	33.9	22.9
Charlotte,	49.0	53.0	62.3	71.2	78.3	85.8	88.9	87.7	81.9	72.0	62.6	52.3
North Carolina	29.6	31.9	39.4	47.5	56.4	65.6	69.6	68.9	62.9	50.6	41.5	32.8
Bismarck,	20.2	26.4	38.5	54.9	67.8	77.1	84.4	82.7	70.8	58.7	39.3	24.5
North Dakota	-1.7	5.1	17.8	31.0	42.2	51.6	56.4	53.9	43.1	32.5	17.8	3.3
Columbus,	34.1	38.0	50.5	62.0	72.3	80.4	83.7	82.1	76.2	64.5	51.4	39.2
Ohio	18.5	21.2	31.2	40.0	50.1	58.0	62.7	60.8	54.8	42.9	34.3	24.6
Tulsa,	45.4	51.0	62.1	73.0	79.7	87.7	93.7	92.5	83.6	73.8	60.3	48.8
Oklahoma	24.9	29.5	39.1	49.9	58.8	67.7	72.8	70.6	63.0	50.7	39.5	28.9
Portland,	45.4	51.0	56.0	60.6	67.1	74.0	79.9	80.3	74.6	64.0	52.6	45.6
Oregon	33.7	36.1	38.6	41.3	47.0	52.9	56.5	56.9	52.0	44.9	39.5	34.8
Philadelphia,	37.9	41.0	51.6	62.6	73.1	81.7	86.1	84.6	77.6	66.3	55.1	43.4
Pennsylvania	22.8	24.8	33.2	42.1	52.7	61.8	67.2	66.3	58.7	46.4	37.6	28.1
Charleston,	57.8	61.0	68.6	75.8	82.7	87.6	90.2	89.0	84.9	77.2	69.5	61.6
South Carolina	37.7	40.0	47.5	53.9	62.9	69.1	72.7	72.2	67.9	56.3	47.2	40.7
Huron,	24.1	29.7	42.1	58.6	70.4	80.3	87.1	84.8	74.2	61.5	43.0	28.3
South Dakota	2.3	9.1	21.7	34.0	44.8	55.5	61.7	58.8	47.3	35.4	21.8	7.8
Nashville,	45.9	50.8	61.2	70.8	78.8	86.5	89.5	88.4	82.5	72.5	60.4	50.2
Tennessee	26.5	29.9	39.1	47.5	56.6	64.7	68.9	67.7	61.1	48.3	39.6	30.9
Houston,	61.0	65.3	71.1	78.4	84.6	90.1	92.7	92.5	88.4	81.6	72.4	64.7
Texas	39.7	42.6	50.0	58.1	64.4	70.6	72.4	72.0	67.9	57.6	49.6	42.2
Salt Lake City,	36.4	43.6	52.2	61.3	71.9	82.8	92.2	89.4	79.2	66.1	50.8	37.8
Utah	19.3	24.6	31.4	37.9	45.6	55.4	63.7	61.8	51.0	40.2	30.9	21.6
Burlington,	25.1	27.5	39.3	53.6	67.2	75.8	81.2	77.9	69.0	57.0	44.0	30.4
Vermont	7.5	8.9	22.0	34.2	45.4	54.6	59.7	57.9	48.8	38.6	29.6	15.5
Richmond,	45.7	49.2	59.5	70.0	77.8	85.1	88.4	87.1	80.9	70.7	61.3	50.2
Virginia	25.7	28.1	36.3	44.6	54.2	62.7	67.5	66.4	59.0	46.5	37.9	29.9
Seattle-Tacoma,	45.0	49.5	52.7	57.2	63.9	69.9	75.2	75.2	69.3	59.7	50.5	45.1
Washington	35.2	37.4	38.5	41.2	46.3	51.9	55.2	55.7	51.9	45.8	40.1	35.8
Charleston,	41.2	45.3	56.7	66.8	75.5	83.1	85.7	84.4	78.8	68.2	57.3	46.0
West Virginia	23.0	25.7	35.0	42.8	51.5	59.8	64.5	63.4	56.5	44.2	36.3	28.0
Madison,	24.8	30.1	41.5	56.7	68.9	78.2	82.4	79.6	71.5	59.9	44.0	29.8
Wisconsin	7.2	11.1	23.0	34.1	44.2	54.2	59.5	56.9	48.2	37.7	26.7	13.5
Cheyenne,	37.7	40.5	44.9	54.7	64.6	74.4	82.2	80.0	71.1	60.0	46.8	38.8
Wyoming	15.2	18.1	22.1	30.1	39.4	48.3	54.6	52.8	43.7	33.9	23.7	16.7

(courtesy Dr. Richard Head and National Climatic Data Center)

WEATHER

Full Moon Names

Historically the Indians of what are now the northern and eastern United States kept track of the seasons by distinctive names given to each recurring full Moon, these names being applied to the entire month in which it occurred. With some variations, the same Moon names were used throughout the Algonquin tribes from New England to Lake Superior.

Name	Month	Other Names Used
Full Wolf Moon	January	Full Old Moon
Full Snow Moon	February	Full Hunger Moon
Full Worm Moon	March	Full Crow Moon, Full Crust Moon, Full Sugar Moon, Full Sap Moon
Full Pink Moon	April	Full Sprouting Grass Moon, Full Egg Moon, Full Fish Moon
Full Flower Moon	May	Full Corn Planting Moon, Full Milk Moon
Full Strawberry Moon	June	Full Rose Moon, Full Hot Moon
Full Buck Moon	July	Full Thunder Moon, Full Hay Moon
Full Sturgeon Moon	August	Full Red Moon, Full Green Corn Moon
Full Harvest Moon*	September	Full Corn Moon
Full Hunter's Moon	October	Full Travel Moon, Full Dying Grass Moon
Full Beaver Moon	November	Full Frost Moon
Full Cold Moon	December	Full Long Nights Moon

* The Harvest Moon is always the full Moon closest to the autumnal equinox. If it occurs in October, the September full Moon is usually called the Corn Moon.

Phases of the Moon

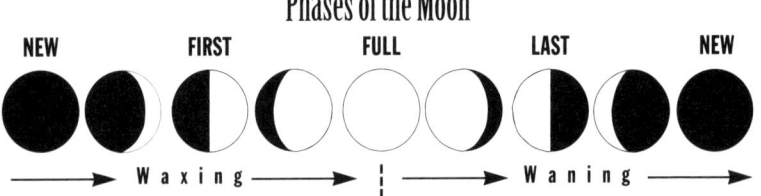

NEW   FIRST   FULL   LAST   NEW

⟶ Waxing ⟶ | ⟶ Waning ⟶

Temperature Conversion Formula

To convert Fahrenheit to Celsius, subtract 32 and multiply by .5556 (or 5/9).
Example: 50° F - 32 x .5556 = 10° C

To convert Celsius to Fahrenheit, multiply by 1.8 (or 9/5) and add 32.
Example: 30° C x 1.8 + 32 = 86° F

WEATHER

Heat Index

As humidity increases, the air temperature feels hotter to your skin. The combination of hot temperature and high humidity reduces your body's ability to cool itself. For example, the heat you feel when the actual temperature is 90 degrees Fahrenheit with a relative humidity of 70 percent is 106 degrees.

Humidity (%)	Temperature (°F)									
	70	75	80	85	90	95	100	105	110	115	120
	Equivalent Temperature (°F)									
0	64	69	73	78	83	87	91	95	99	103	107
10	65	70	75	80	85	90	95	100	105	111	116
20	66	72	77	82	87	93	99	105	112	120	130
30	67	73	78	84	90	96	104	113	123	120	148
40	68	74	79	86	93	101	110	123	137	135	
50	69	75	81	88	96	107	120	135	150		
60	70	76	82	90	100	114	132	149			
70	70	77	85	93	106	124	144				
80	71	78	86	97	113	136					
90	71	79	88	102	122						
100	72	80	91	108							

Glossary of Almanac Oddities

Many readers have expressed puzzlement over the rather obscure notations that appear on our Right-Hand Calendar Pages (pages 53-79). These "oddities" have long been fixtures in the Almanac, and we are pleased to provide some definitions. (Once explained, it would seem that they are not so odd after all!)

■ **Beware the Pogonip (December)**

The word *pogonip* is a meteorological term used to describe an uncommon occurrence — frozen fog. The word was coined by American Indians to describe the frozen fogs of fine ice needles that occur in the mountain valleys of the western United States. According to Indian tradition, breathing the fog is injurious to the lungs.

■ **Cat Nights Begin (August)**

The term harks back to the days when people believed in witches. An old Irish legend has it that a witch could turn herself into a cat eight times and then regain herself, but on the ninth time — August 17 — she couldn't change back. Hence the saying, "A cat has nine lives." Since August is a "yowly" time for cats, this may have prompted the speculation about witches on the prowl in the first place.

■ **Cornscateous Air (July)**

A term first used by the old almanac makers signifying humid, warm, damp air. While it signals ideal climatic conditions for growing corn, it also poses a danger to those affected by asthma, pneumonia, and other respiratory problems.

■ **Dog Days (July-August)**

The hottest and most unhealthy days of the year. Also known as "Canicular Days," the name derives from the Dog Star, Sirius. The Almanac lists the traditional timing of Dog Days: The 40 days beginning July 3 and ending August 11, coinciding with the heliacal (at sunrise) rising of Sirius.

(continued on next page)

WEATHER

■ Ember Days (and Ember Weeks)

The four periods set apart by the Roman Catholic and Anglican churches for special prayer and fasting and the ordination of clergy. The Ember Weeks are the complete weeks following 1) the First Sunday in Lent; 2) Pentecost (Whit Sunday); 3) the Feast of the Holy Cross (September 14); and 4) the Feast of St. Lucy (December 13). The Wednesdays, Fridays, and Saturdays of these weeks are the Ember Days — days marked for fasting. (The word *ember* is thought to derive from an Old English term that refers to the revolution of time.)

Folklore has it that the weather on each of the three days foretells weather for three successive months — that is, in September Ember Days, Wednesday forecasts weather for October, Friday for November, and Saturday for December.

■ Halcyon Days (December)

A period (about 14 days) of calm weather, following the blustery winds of autumn's end. The ancient Greeks and Romans believed them to occur around the time of the winter solstice when the halcyon, or kingfisher, was brooding. In a nest floating on the sea, the bird was said to have charmed the wind and waves so the waters were especially calm during this period.

■ Harvest Home (September)

In both Europe and Britain, the conclusion of the harvest each autumn was once marked by great festivals of fun, feasting, and thanksgiving known as "Harvest Home." It was also a time to hold elections, pay workers, and collect rents. These festivals usually took place around the time of the autumnal equinox. Certain ethnic groups in this country, particularly the Pennsylvania Dutch, have kept the tradition alive.

■ Indian Summer (November)

A period of warm weather following a cold spell or a hard frost. While there are differing dates for the time of occurrence, for 204 years the Almanac has adhered to the saying, "If All Saints brings out winter, St. Martin's brings out Indian Summer." Accordingly, Indian Summer can occur between St. Martin's Day, November 11, and November 20. As for the origin of the term, some say it comes from the early Indians who believed the condition was caused by a warm wind sent from the court of their southwestern God, Cautantowwit.

■ Midsummer Day (June 24)

While it occurs near the summer solstice, to the farmer it is the midpoint of the growing season, halfway between planting and harvest, and an occasion for festivity. The English church considered it a "Quarter Day," one of the four major divisions of the liturgical year. It also marks the feast day of St. John the Baptist.

■ Plough Monday (January)

The first Monday after the Epiphany (January 6); so called because it was the end of the Christmas holidays when men returned to their plough — or daily work. It was customary for farm laborers to draw a plough through the village, soliciting money for a "plough-light," which was kept burning in the parish church all year. In some areas, the custom of blessing the plough is maintained.

■ St. Luke's Little Summer (October)

A spell of warm weather occurring about the time of the saint's feast day, October 18. This period is sometimes referred to as "Indian Summer."

■ Three Chilly Saints (May)

Pancratius, Mammertius, and Gervatius, three early Christian saints, whose feast days occur on May 11, 12, and 13, respectively. Because these days are traditionally cold (an old French saying goes: "St. Mammertius, St. Pancras, and St. Gervais do not pass without a frost"), they have come to be known as the Three Chilly Saints.

GOVERNMENT

Abbreviations Approved by the U.S. Postal Service to Be Used in Addressing Mail

Alabama .... AL	North Dakota .... ND	East .... E
Alaska .... AK	North Mariana Islands MP	Estates .... EST
American Samoa ..... AS	Ohio .... OH	Expressway ...... EXPY
Arizona .... AZ	Oklahoma .... OK	Extension .... EXT
Arkansas .... AR	Oregon .... OR	Freeway .... FWY
California .... CA	Pennsylvania .... PA	Gardens .... GDNS
Colorado .... CO	Puerto Rico .... PR	Grove .... GRV
Connecticut .... CT	Rhode Island .... RI	Heights .... HTS
Delaware .... DE	South Carolina .... SC	Highway .... HWY
District of Columbia .. DC	South Dakota .... SD	Island .... IS
Florida .... FL	Tennessee .... TN	Junction .... JCT
Georgia .... GA	Texas .... TX	Lake .... LK
Guam .... GU	Trust Territory .... TT	Lane .... LN
Hawaii .... HI	Utah .... UT	Manor .... MNR
Idaho .... ID	Vermont .... VT	Mountain .... MTN
Illinois IL	Virgin Islands, U.S. ... VI	North .... N
Indiana .... IN	Virginia .... VA	Park .... PK
Iowa .... IA	Washington .... WA	Parkway .... PKY
Kansas .... KS	West Virginia ...... WV	Place .... PL
Kentucky .... KY	Wisconsin .... WI	Plaza .... PLZ
Louisiana .... LA	Wyoming .... WY	Point .... PT
Maine .... ME		Road .... RD
Maryland .... MD	Alley .... ALY	Room .... RM
Massachusetts ...... MA	Apartment .... APT	Rural .... R
Michigan .... MI	Arcade .... ARC	South .... S
Minnesota .... MN	Avenue .... AVE	Square .... SQ
Mississippi .... MS	Boulevard ...... BLVD	Station .... STA
Missouri .... MO	Branch .... BR	Street .... ST
Montana .... MT	Bypass .... BYP	Suite .... STE
Nebraska .... NE	Causeway .... CSWY	Terrace .... TER
Nevada .... NV	Center .... CTR	Trail .... TRL
New Hampshire ..... NH	Circle .... CIR	Turnpike .... TPKE
New Jersey .... NJ	Court .... CT	Viaduct .... VIA
New Mexico .... NM	Courts .... CTS	Vista .... VIS
New York .... NY	Crescent .... CRES	Valley .... VLY
North Carolina ...... NC	Drive .... DR	West .... W

Canadian Province and Territory Postal Codes

Alberta .... AB	Northwest Territories .... NT
British Columbia .... BC	Ontario .... ON
Manitoba .... MB	Prince Edward Island .... PE
New Brunswick .... NB	Quebec .... PQ
Newfoundland .... NF	Saskatchewan .... SK
Nova Scotia .... NS	Yukon Territory .... YT

GOVERNMENT

U.S. Postage Rates

Single-Piece Letter Rates

First ounce $0.32
Each additional
  ounce $0.23

**For pieces not
exceeding (oz.). . . . . . The rate is**

1	$0.32
2	0.55
3	0.78
4	1.01
5	1.24
6	1.47
7	1.70
8	1.93
9	2.16
10	2.39
11	2.62

For pieces over 11 ounces consult postmaster.

Card Rates

Single postcards . . $0.20

Note: To qualify for card rates, a card may not be larger than 4¼ by 6 inches, nor smaller than 3½ by 5 inches. The thickness must be uniform and not less than 0.007 inch.

Size Standards for Domestic Mail

Minimum Size

Pieces that do not meet the following requirements are prohibited from the mails:

A. All pieces must be at least 0.007 inch thick.

B. All pieces (except keys and identification devices) that are ¼ inch or less in thickness must be:

1) Rectangular in shape,
2) At least 3½ inches high, **and**
3) At least 5 inches long

Note: Pieces greater than ¼ inch thick can be mailed even if they measure less than 3½ by 5 inches.

Nonstandard Mail

First-class mail, except presort first-class and carrier route first-class, weighing one ounce or less, and all single-piece rate third-class mail weighing one ounce or less, is nonstandard (and subject to a $0.11 surcharge in addition to the applicable postage and fees) if:

1) Any of the following dimensions are exceeded:

  Length — 11-1/2 inches
  Height — 6-1/8 inches
  Thickness — 1/4 inch, OR

2) The length divided by the height is not between 1.3 and 2.5, inclusive.

Dear Congressman...

Address a letter to your senator or representative as follows:

[Senator's name]
United States Senate
Washington, DC 20510

[Representative's name]
United States House of
Representatives
Washington, DC 20515

Federal Agencies

Advisory Council on Historic Preservation . . . (202) 254-3974
Consumer Product Safety Commission 800-638-2772
Environmental Protection Agency . . . . (202) 260-2090
Farm Credit Administration . . . . (703) 883-4000
Federal Communications Commission . . . . . . (202) 418-0200
Federal Maritime Commission . . . . (202) 523-5707
General Services Administration . . . . (202) 708-5082
National Science Foundation . . . . (703) 306-1234
Peace Corps 800-424-8580
Small Business Administration 800-827-5722
Smithsonian Institution . . . . (202) 357-1300
U.S. Information Agency . . . . (202) 619-4700
U.S. Postal Service . . . . (202) 268-2000

GOVERNMENT

Government Telephone Numbers

This list includes a general information number for each of the departments within the Executive Department and information numbers for selected branches of those departments. Information numbers for selected Federal agencies are on page 246. For a complete list of government telephone numbers and addresses, refer to a directory at your library.

AGRICULTURE DEPARTMENT .... **(202) 720-2791**
   Agricultural Marketing Service .... (202) 720-8998
   Animal and Plant Health Inspection Service .... (202) 720-2511
   Extension Service .... (202) 720-3029
   Farmers Home Administration .... (202) 720-4323
   Food and Nutrition Service .... (703) 305-2276
   Forest Service .... (202) 205-8333
COMMERCE DEPARTMENT .... **(202) 482-2000**
   National Institute of Standards and Technology .... (301) 975-2000
   National Oceanic and Atmospheric Administration .... (301) 413-0900
   Patent and Trademark Office .... (703) 557-4636
   U.S. Travel and Tourism Administration .... (202) 482-2000
DEFENSE DEPARTMENT .... **(703) 545-6700**
   Air Force .... (703) 695-5554
   Army .... (703) 695-4462
   Navy .... (703) 695-0965
   Marines .... (703) 614-1492
EDUCATION DEPARTMENT .... **(202) 401-1576**
ENERGY DEPARTMENT .... **(202) 586-5000**
HEALTH AND HUMAN SERVICES DEPARTMENT .... **(202) 619-0257**
   Food and Drug Administration .... (301) 443-3170
   Health Resources and Services Administration .... (301) 443-2086
   Social Security Administration 800-772-1213
HOUSING AND URBAN DEVELOPMENT DEPARTMENT .... **(202) 708-1422**
INTERIOR DEPARTMENT .... **(202) 208-3100**
   National Park Service .... (202) 208-4747
   U.S. Fish and Wildlife Service .... (202) 208-5634
JUSTICE DEPARTMENT .... **(202) 514-2000**
   Environment and Natural Resources Division .... (202) 616-2765
   Immigration and Naturalization Service .... (202) 514-4316
LABOR DEPARTMENT .... **(202) 219-6666**
   Bureau of Labor Statistics .... (202) 606-7828
   Employment Standards Administration .... (202) 219-8743
STATE DEPARTMENT .... **(202) 647-4000**
TRANSPORTATION DEPARTMENT .... **(202) 366-4000**
   U.S. Coast Guard .... (202) 267-2229
TREASURY DEPARTMENT. .... **(202) 622-2000**
   Internal Revenue Service .... (800) 829-1040
VETERANS AFFAIRS DEPARTMENT .... **(202) 273-5400**

GOVERNMENT

Federal Information Center

If you have a question about the federal government, but don't know whom to call, start with the Federal Information Center. Following is a list of numbers for major metropolitan areas. If you are outside the areas listed, call **(301) 722-9000**.

(800) 347-1997
Connecticut: Hartford, New Haven
Florida: Fort Lauderdale, Jacksonville, Miami, Orlando, St. Petersburg, Tampa, West Palm Beach
Georgia: Atlanta
Indiana: Indianapolis
Kentucky: Louisville
Maryland: Baltimore
Massachusetts: Boston
Michigan: Detroit, Grand Rapids
New Jersey: Newark, Trenton
New York: Albany, Buffalo, New York, Rochester, Syracuse
North Carolina: Charlotte
Ohio: Akron, Cinncinnati, Cleveland, Columbus, Dayton, Toledo

Pennsylvania: Philadelphia, Pittsburgh
Rhode Island: Providence
Tennessee: Chattanooga
Virginia: Norfolk, Richmond, Roanoke

(800) 366-2998
Alabama: Birmingham, Mobile
Arkansas: Little Rock
Illinois: Chicago
Indiana: Gary
Louisiana: New Orleans
Minnesota: Minneapolis
Missouri: St. Louis
Nebraska: Omaha
Oklahoma: Oklahoma City, Tulsa
Tennessee: Memphis, Nashville
Texas: Austin, Dallas, Fort Worth, Houston, San Antonio
Wisconsin: Milwaukee

(800) 359-3997
Arizona: Phoenix
Colorado: Colorado Springs, Denver, Pueblo
New Mexico: Albuquerque
Utah: Salt Lake City

(800) 726-4995
California: Los Angeles, Sacramento, San Diego, San Francisco, Santa Ana
Oregon: Portland
Washington: Seattle, Tacoma

(800) 733-5996
Hawaii: Honolulu

(800) 729-8003
Alaska: Anchorage

(800) 735-8004
Iowa: all locations
Kansas: all locations

The Sequence of Presidential Succession

1. Vice President
2. Speaker of the House
3. President Pro Tempore of the Senate
4. Secretary of State
5. Secretary of the Treasury
6. Secretary of Defense
7. Attorney General
8. Secretary of the Interior
9. Secretary of Agriculture
10. Secretary of Commerce
11. Secretary of Labor
12. Secretary of Health and Human Services
13. Secretary of Housing and Urban Development
14. Secretary of Transportation
15. Secretary of Energy
16. Secretary of Education

GOVERNMENT

Presidents of the United States — Service

1. George Washington (1732-1799) 1789-1797
2. John Adams (1735-1826) 1797-1801
3. Thomas Jefferson (1743-1826) 1801-1809
4. James Madison (1751-1836) 1809-1817
5. James Monroe (1758-1831) 1817-1825
6. John Quincy Adams (1767-1848) 1825-1829
7. Andrew Jackson (1767-1845) 1829-1837
8. Martin Van Buren (1782-1862) 1837-1841
9. William Henry Harrison (1773-1841) 1841
10. John Tyler (1790-1862) 1841-1845
11. James K. Polk (1795-1849) 1845-1849
12. Zachary Taylor (1784-1850) 1849-1850
13. Millard Fillmore (1800-1874) 1850-1853
14. Franklin Pierce (1804-1869) 1853-1857
15. James Buchanan (1791-1868) 1857-1861
16. Abraham Lincoln (1809-1865) 1861-1865
17. Andrew Johnson (1808-1875) 1865-1869
18. Ulysses S. Grant (1822-1885) 1869-1877
19. Rutherford B. Hayes (1822-1893) 1877-1881
20. James A. Garfield (1831-1881) 1881
21. Chester A. Arthur (1830-1886) 1881-1885
22. Grover Cleveland (1837-1908) 1885-1889
23. Benjamin Harrison (1833-1901) 1889-1893
24. Grover Cleveland (1837-1908) 1893-1897
25. William McKinley (1843-1901) 1897-1901
26. Theodore Roosevelt (1858-1919) 1901-1909
27. William H. Taft (1857-1930) 1909-1913
28. Woodrow Wilson (1856-1924) 1913-1921
29. Warren G. Harding (1865-1923) 1921-1923
30. Calvin Coolidge (1872-1933) 1923-1929
31. Herbert C. Hoover (1874-1964) 1929-1933
32. Franklin D. Roosevelt (1882-1945) 1933-1945
33. Harry S Truman (1884-1972) 1945-1953
34. Dwight D. Eisenhower (1890-1969) 1953-1961
35. John F. Kennedy (1917-1963) 1961-1963
36. Lyndon B. Johnson (1908-1973) 1963-1969
37. Richard M. Nixon (1913-1994) 1969-1974
38. Gerald R. Ford (1913-) 1974-1977
39. James (Jimmy) Carter (1924-) 1977-1981
40. Ronald Reagan (1911-) 1981-1989
41. George Bush (1924-) 1989-1993
42. William (Bill) Clinton (1946-) 1993-

States of the United States

STATE	ORIGIN OF NAME	CAPITAL	POPULATION (1993)	FARMS (1,000)	FARM ACREAGE (million)
Alabama	Native American, "I make a clearing"	Montgomery	4,186,806	47	10
Alaska	Aleut, "land that is not an island"	Juneau	599,151	1	1
Arizona	Native American: Pima, "little spring place"; Aztec, "silver-bearing"	Phoenix	3,936,142	8	36
Arkansas	Native American, "downstream people"	Little Rock	2,424,418	46	15
California	Spanish, name of imaginary island, an earthly paradise, in Montalvo's "Las Serges de Esplandian"	Sacramento	31,210,750	76	30
Colorado	Spanish, "color red"	Denver	3,565,959	26	33
Connecticut	Native American, "beside the long tidal river"	Hartford	3,277,316	4	(-)*
Delaware	for Lord De La Warr, early governor of Virginia	Dover	700,269	3	1
District of Columbia	for Christopher Columbus		578,448	(-)*	(-)*
Florida	Named by Ponce de Leon on Pascua Florida, "feast of flowers"	Tallahassee	13,678,914	39	10
Georgia	for King George II of England	Atlanta	6,917,140	45	12
Hawaii	Native word for homeland or place of the gods	Honolulu	1,171,592	4	2
Idaho	Native American (invented), "gem of the mountains"; or Kiowa Apache term for the Comanche	Boise	1,099,096	21	14
Illinois	French, "land of Illini"; Native American, "men" or "warriors"	Springfield	11,697,336	80	28
Indiana	"Land of the Indians"	Indianapolis	5,712,799	63	16
Iowa	Native American, "one who puts to sleep" or "beautiful land"	Des Moines	2,814,064	100	33
Kansas	Native American, "south wind people"	Topeka	2,530,746	65	48
Kentucky	Native American, "dark and bloody ground," "meadow land," or "land of tomorrow"	Frankfort	3,788,808	91	14
Louisiana	for King Louis XIV of France	Baton Rouge	4,295,477	29	9
Maine	Ancient French province or "mainland"	Augusta	1,239,448	7	1
Maryland	for Queen Henrietta Maria, wife of Charles I of England	Annapolis	4,964,898	15	2
Massachusetts	Native American, "near the great hill"	Boston	6,012,268	7	1
Michigan	Native American, "great water"	Lansing	9,477,545	52	11
Minnesota	Native American, "cloudy water" or "sky-tinted water"	St. Paul	4,517,416	87	30

GOVERNMENT

State	Etymology	Capital	Population		
Mississippi	Native American, "great river" or "gathering-in of all the waters"	Jackson	2,642,748	39	13
Missouri	Native American, "river of the big canoes"	Jefferson City	5,233,849	106	30
Montana	Latin or Spanish, "mountainous"	Helena	839,422	25	60
Nebraska	Native American, "broad water" or "flat river"	Lincoln	1,607,199	55	47
Nevada	Spanish, "snow-clad"	Carson City	1,388,910	2	9
New Hampshire	for Hampshire County, England	Concord	1,125,310	3	(-)*
New Jersey	for Isle of Jersey, England	Trenton	7,849,164	8	1
New Mexico	for Mexico	Santa Fe	1,616,483	14	44
New York	for Duke of York and Albany, brother of Charles II of England	Albany	18,197,154	38	8
North Carolina	Carolina, for King Charles I of England	Raleigh	6,945,180	59	9
North Dakota	Native American, "friend" or "ally"	Bismarck	634,935	33	40
Ohio	Native American, "fine or good river"	Columbus	11,091,301	76	15
Oklahoma	Native American, "red man"	Oklahoma City	3,231,464	71	34
Oregon	Unknown; possibly from "Ouaricon-sint" denoting Wisconsin River on French map	Salem	3,031,867	37	18
Pennsylvania	for William Penn, plus *sylvania* meaning woodland	Harrisburg	12,048,271	51	8
Rhode Island	Unknown; possibly Dutch, "red clay"	Providence	1,000,012	1	(-)*
South Carolina	(see North Carolina)	Columbia	3,642,718	24	5
South Dakota	(see North Dakota)	Pierre	715,392	35	44
Tennessee	from "tanasi," the name of Cherokee villages on the Little Tennessee River	Nashville	5,098,798	86	12
Texas	Native American, "friends" or "allies"	Austin	18,031,484	185	130
Utah	Native American, "upper" or "higher up"	Salt Lake City	1,859,582	13	11
Vermont	French, "green mountain"	Montpelier	575,691	7	2
Virginia	for Queen Elizabeth I, the Virgin Queen of England	Richmond	6,490,634	43	9
Washington	for George Washington	Olympia	5,255,276	36	16
West Virginia	so named when western counties of Virginia refused to secede from Union, 1863	Charleston	1,820,137	20	4
Wisconsin	Native American, "grassy place"	Madison	5,037,928	79	17
Wyoming	Native American, "large prairie place"	Cheyenne	470,242	9	35
Total			**257,907,937**	**2071**	**978**

* (-) indicates less than 500,000

GOVERNMENT

America's Seacoasts

STATE	LENGTHS IN STATUTE MILES	
	1. General Coastline	2. Tidal Shoreline
Atlantic Coast		
Maine	228	3,478
New Hampshire	13	131
Massachusetts	192	1,519
Rhode Island	40	384
Connecticut	–	618
New York	127	1,850
New Jersey	130	1,792
Pennsylvania	–	89
Delaware	28	381
Maryland	31	3,190
Virginia	112	3,315
North Carolina	301	3,375
South Carolina	187	2,876
Georgia	100	2,344
Florida (Atlantic)	580	3,331
Total	**2,069**	**28,673**
Gulf Coast		
Florida (Gulf)	770	5,095
Alabama	53	607
Mississippi	44	359
Louisisana	397	7,721
Texas	367	3,359
Total	**1,631**	**17,141**
Pacific Coast		
California	840	3,427
Oregon	296	1,410
Washington	157	3,026
Hawaii	750	1,052
Alaska (Pacific)	5,580	31,383
Total	**7,623**	**40,298**
Arctic Coast		
Alaska (Arctic)	1,060	2,521
Total	**1,060**	**2,521**
UNITED STATES TOTAL	**12,383**	**88,633**

1. Figures are lengths of general outline of seacoast. Measurements made with unit measure of 30 minutes of latitude on charts as near scale of 1:1,200,000 as possible. Coastline of bays and sounds is included to point where they narrow to width of unit measure, and distance across at such point is included.

2. Figures obtained in 1939-1940 with recording instrument on largest-scale maps and charts then available. Shoreline of outer coast, offshore islands, sounds, bays, rivers, and creeks is included to head of tidewater, or to point where tidal waters narrow to width of 100 feet.

Source: Department of Commerce, National Oceanic and Atmospheric Administration, National Ocean Service

THE KITCHEN

Seasonal Guide to Fresh Fruits and Vegetables

● = Good supply ◗ = Fair supply ○ = Low supply

	JAN	FEB	MAR	APR	MAY	JUN	JUL	AUG	SEPT	OCT	NOV	DEC
Apples	◗	◗	◗	◗	◗	○	○	○	●	●	●	●
Apricots	○	○	○	○	○	●	●	○	○	○	○	○
Artichokes	○	○	◗	●	●	●	◗	◗	◗	◗	○	○
Asparagus	○	○	●	●	●	◗	○	○	○	○	○	○
Bananas	●	●	●	●	●	●	●	◗	◗	●	●	●
Beans, snap	◗	◗	◗	◗	●	●	●	●	◗	◗	◗	◗
Beets	○	○	◗	◗	●	●	●	●	●	●	◗	○
Blueberries	○	○	○	○	○	●	●	●	○	○	○	○
Broccoli	●	●	●	●	◗	◗	○	○	●	●	●	●
Brussels sprouts	●	●	◗	◗	○	○	○	○	◗	●	●	●
Cabbage	●	●	●	●	●	●	●	◗	●	●	●	●
Cantaloupes	○	○	○	○	◗	●	●	●	●	○	○	○
Cauliflower	◗	◗	◗	◗	○	○	○	○	●	●	●	◗
Celery	●	●	●	●	●	●	●	◗	◗	●	●	●
Cherries	○	○	○	○	◗	●	●	◗	○	○	○	○
Corn	○	○	○	◗	●	●	●	●	●	●	○	○
Cranberries	○	○	○	○	○	○	○	○	◗	●	●	●
Cucumbers	○	○	○	◗	●	●	●	●	◗	◗	◗	◗
Grapefruit	●	●	●	●	◗	◗	○	○	○	◗	●	●
Grapes	○	○	○	○	○	◗	●	●	●	●	●	◗
Lemons	◗	◗	◗	◗	●	●	●	●	◗	◗	◗	◗
Lettuce	●	●	●	●	●	●	●	●	●	●	◗	●
Limes	○	○	○	○	○	●	●	●	◗	◗	◗	◗
Mushrooms	●	●	●	●	●	◗	◗	◗	●	●	●	●
Nectarines	○	○	○	○	○	●	●	●	●	○	○	○
Onions	●	◗	●	●	●	●	●	●	●	●	●	●
Oranges	●	●	●	●	●	◗	○	○	○	○	◗	●
Peaches	○	○	○	○	○	●	●	●	●	○	○	○
Pears	◗	◗	◗	◗	○	○	○	●	●	●	●	◗
Peas	◗	●	◗	●	●	●	●	◗	◗	○	○	○
Peppers	◗	◗	◗	◗	◗	●	●	●	●	◗	◗	◗
Pineapples	◗	◗	●	●	●	●	●	◗	○	○	●	●
Plums	○	○	○	○	○	●	●	●	●	○	○	○
Potatoes	●	●	●	●	●	●	●	●	●	●	●	●
Pumpkins	○	○	○	○	○	○	○	○	◗	●	◗	○
Radishes	◗	◗	●	●	●	●	●	◗	◗	◗	◗	◗
Spinach	●	●	●	●	◗	◗	◗	○	◗	◗	◗	◗
Squash	◗	◗	◗	◗	◗	●	●	●	●	●	●	◗
Strawberries	○	○	◗	●	●	●	◗	○	○	○	○	○
Sweet potatoes	◗	◗	◗	◗	○	○	○	●	●	●	●	●
Tomatoes	◗	◗	◗	◗	●	●	●	●	◗	○	○	○
Watermelons	○	○	○	○	●	●	●	●	◗	○	○	○

Note: Based on commercial supplies. Native crops have shorter, more intense seasons.

Substitutions for Common Ingredients

ITEM	QUANTITY	SUBSTITUTION
Allspice	1 teaspoon	½ teaspoon cinnamon plus ⅛ teaspoon ground cloves
Arrowroot, as thickener	1½ teaspoons	1 tablespoon flour
Baking powder	1 teaspoon	¼ teaspoon baking soda plus ⅝ teaspoon cream of tartar
Bread crumbs, dry	¼ cup	1 slice bread
soft	½ cup	1 slice bread
Buttermilk	1 cup	1 cup plain yogurt
Chocolate, unsweetened	1 ounce	3 tablespoons cocoa plus 1 tablespoon butter or fat
Cracker crumbs	¾ cup	1 cup bread crumbs
Cream, heavy	1 cup	¾ cup milk plus ⅓ cup melted butter (this will not whip)
Cream, light	1 cup	⅞ cup milk plus 3 tablespoons melted butter
Cream, sour	1 cup	⅞ cup buttermilk or plain yogurt plus 3 tablespoons melted butter
Cream, whipping	1 cup	⅔ cup well-chilled evaporated milk, whipped; **or** 1 cup nonfat dry milk powder whipped with 1 cup ice water
Egg	1 whole	2 yolks
Flour, all-purpose	1 cup	1⅛ cups cake flour; **or** 5/8 cup potato flour; **or** 1¼ cups rye or coarsely ground whole grain flour; **or** 1 cup cornmeal
Flour, cake	1 cup	1 cup minus 2 tablespoons sifted all-purpose flour
Flour, self-rising	1 cup	1 cup all-purpose flour plus 1¼ teaspoons baking powder plus ¼ teaspoon salt
Garlic	1 small clove	⅛ teaspoon garlic powder or instant minced garlic
Herbs, dried	½ to 1 teaspoon	1 tablespoon fresh, minced and packed
Honey	1 cup	1¼ cups sugar plus ½ cup liquid

Measuring Vegetables

Asparagus: 1 pound = 3 cups chopped
Beans (string): 1 pound = 4 cups chopped
Beets: 1 pound (5 medium) = 2-1/2 cups chopped
Broccoli: 1/2 pound = 6 cups chopped
Cabbage: 1 pound = 4-1/2 cups shredded
Carrots: 1 pound = 3-1/2 cups sliced or grated
Celery: 1 pound = 4 cups chopped
Cucumbers: 1 pound (2 medium) = 4 cups sliced
Eggplant: 1 pound = 4 cups chopped (6 cups raw, cubed = 3 cups cooked)

Garlic: 1 clove = 1 teaspoon chopped
Leeks: 1 pound = 4 cups chopped (2 cups cooked)
Mushrooms: 1 pound = 5 to 6 cups sliced = 2 cups cooked
Onions: 1 pound = 4 cups sliced = 2 cups cooked
Parsnips: 1 pound unpeeled = 1-1/2 cups cooked, pureed
Peas: 1 pound whole = 1 to 1-1/2 cups shelled
Potatoes: 1 pound (3 medium) sliced = 2 cups mashed
Pumpkin: 1 pound = 4 cups chopped = 2 cups cooked and drained
Spinach: 1 pound = 3/4 to 1 cup cooked

THE KITCHEN

ITEM	QUANTITY	SUBSTITUTION
Lemon	1	1 to 3 tablespoons juice, 1 to 1½ teaspoons grated rind
Lemon juice	1 teaspoon	½ teaspoon vinegar
Lemon rind, grated	1 teaspoon	½ teaspoon lemon extract
Milk, skim	1 cup	⅓ cup instant nonfat dry milk plus about ¾ cup water
Milk, whole	1 cup	½ cup evaporated milk plus ½ cup water; **or** 1 cup skim milk plus 2 teaspoons melted butter
Milk, to sour	1 cup	Add 1 tablespoon vinegar or lemon juice to 1 cup milk minus 1 tablespoon. Stir and let stand 5 minutes.
Molasses	1 cup	1 cup honey
Mustard, prepared	1 tablespoon	1 teaspoon dry or powdered mustard
Onion, chopped	1 small	1 tablespoon instant minced onion; **or** 1 teaspoon onion powder; **or** ¼ cup frozen chopped onion
Sugar, granulated	1 cup	1 cup firmly packed brown sugar; **or** 1¾ cups confectioners' sugar (do not substitute in baking); **or** 2 cups corn syrup; **or** 1 cup superfine sugar
Tomatoes, canned	1 cup	½ cup tomato sauce plus ½ cup water; **or** 1⅓ cups chopped fresh tomatoes, simmered
Tomato juice	1 cup	½ cup tomato sauce plus ½ cup water plus dash each salt and sugar; **or** ¼ cup tomato paste plus ¾ cup water plus salt and sugar
Tomato ketchup	½ cup	½ cup tomato sauce plus 2 tablespoons sugar, 1 tablespoon vinegar, and ⅛ teaspoon ground cloves
Tomato purée	1 cup	½ cup tomato paste plus ½ cup water
Tomato soup	1 can (10¾ oz.)	1 cup tomato sauce plus ¼ cup water
Vanilla	1-inch bean	1 teaspoon vanilla extract
Yeast	1 cake (⅗ oz.)	1 package active dried yeast
Yogurt, plain	1 cup	1 cup buttermilk

Squash (summer): 1 pound = 4 cups grated = 2 cups salted and drained
Squash (winter): 2 pounds = 2-1/2 cups cooked, pureed
Sweet Potatoes: 1 pound = 4 cups grated = 1 cup cooked, pureed
Swiss Chard: 1 pound = 5 to 6 cups packed leaves = 1 to 1-1/2 cups cooked
Tomatoes: 1 pound (3 or 4 medium) = 1-1/2 cups seeded pulp
Turnips: 1 pound = 4 cups chopped = 2 cups cooked, mashed

Measuring Fruits

Apples: 1 pound (3 or 4 medium) = 3 cups sliced
Bananas: 1 pound (3 or 4 medium) = 1-3/4 cups mashed
Berries: 1 quart = 3-1/2 cups
Dates: 1 pound = 2-1/2 cups pitted
Lemon: 1 whole = 1 to 3 tablespoons juice; 1 to 1-1/2 teaspoons grated rind
Lime: 1-1/2 to 2 tablespoons juice
Orange: 1 medium = 6 to 8 tablespoons juice; 2 to 3 tablespoons grated rind
Peaches: 1 pound (4 medium) = 3 cups sliced
Pears: 1 pound (4 medium) = 2 cups sliced
Rhubarb: 1 pound = 2 cups cooked
Strawberries: 1 quart = 4 cups sliced

Egg-quivalents

Most states classify hen eggs according to the U.S. Grade Standards as follows:

Classification	Net weight per dozen (oz)
Jumbo	30
Extra Large	27
Large	24
Medium	21
Small	18
Peewee	15

An egg is approximately one-third yolk, two-thirds white. The yolk of a large egg is about 1 tablespoon plus one teaspoon; the white is about 2 tablespoons. In one cup there are approximately:

	Whole	Whites	Yolks
Jumbo	4	6	12
Extra Large	4	6	12
Large	5	7-8	13
Medium	5-6	9	14
Small	6-7	10	16

In recipes that call for eggs, use large eggs or adjust according to the following equivalents:

Jumbo	Extra Large	Large	Medium	Small
1	1	1	1	1
2	2	2	2	3
2	3	3	3	4
3	4	4	5	5
4	4	5	5-6	6-7
5	5	6	7	8

White eggs come from the Single Comb White Leghorn. Brown eggs come from Rhode Island Red, New Hampshire, and Plymouth Rock. There is no difference in the quality or nutritional value.

Dairy Definitions

Straight from the cow, milk is approximately 87% water and 13% solids (3.7% fat and 9% solids-not-fat). Federal Definitions and Standards of Identity specify the minimum levels of milkfat and solids-not-fat for the various milks shipped in interstate commerce:

Milk

Whole Milk: Contains at least 3.25% milkfat; 8.25% solids-not-fat. Addition of vitamins A and D is optional.

Lowfat Milk: Contains either 0.5%, 1.5%, or 2.0% milkfat; at least 8.25% solids-not-fat. Must contain vitamin A. Addition of vitamin D is optional.

Skim or Nonfat Milk: Contains less than 0.5% milkfat; at least 8.25% solids-not-fat. Must contain vitamin A. Addition of vitamin D is optional.

Cultured Milks: Produced by culturing any of the milks listed above with appropriate characterizing bacteria. The addition of certain characterizing ingredients and lactic-acid-producing bacteria may permit, for example, the product to be labeled "cultured buttermilk," "cultured lowfat buttermilk," or "cultured skim milk (or nonfat) buttermilk," depending upon the level of milkfat in the finished product.

Cream

Half-and-Half: A mixture of milk and cream containing at least 10.5% milkfat, but not more than 18%.

Light Cream: Contains at least 18% milkfat, but not more than 30%. Also called "coffee cream" or "table cream."

Light Whipping Cream: Contains at least 30% milkfat, but not more than 36%. Also called "whipping cream."

Heavy Cream: Contains at least 36% milkfat. Also called "heavy whipping cream."

Sour Cream

Sour Cream: The product resulting from the addition of lactic-acid-producing bacteria to pasteurized cream containing at least 18% milkfat. Also called "cultured sour cream."

Acidified Sour Cream: The product resulting from the addition of acidifiers to pasteurized cream containing at least 18% milkfat. May or may not contain lactic-acid-producing bacteria.

Sour Half-and-Half: The product resulting from the addition of lactic-acid-producing bacteria to pasteurized half-and-half. Contains at least 10.5% milkfat, but less than 18% milkfat. May or may not contain lactic-acid-producing bacteria.

Cottage Cheese

Dry Curd Cottage Cheese: A soft, unripened cheese made from skim milk and/or reconstituted nonfat dry milk. The cheese curd is formed by the addition of either lactic-acid-producing bacteria or acidifiers. The latter process is called direct acidification. Rennet and/or other suitable enzymes may be used to assist curd formation. Contains less than 0.5% milkfat and not more than 80% moisture. Also called "cottage cheese dry curd."

Cottage Cheese: The product resulting from the addition of a creaming mixture (dressing) to dry curd cottage cheese. Contains at least 4% milkfat and not more than 80% moisture.

Lowfat Cottage Cheese: The product resulting from the addition of a creaming mixture (dressing) to dry curd cottage cheese. Contains either 0.5%, 1%, or 2% milkfat and not more than 82.5% moisture.

Yogurt

Yogurt: The product resulting from the culturing of a mixture of milk and cream products with the lactic-acid-producing bacteria, *Lactobacillus bulgaricus* and *Streptococcus thermophilus*. Sweeteners, flavorings, and other ingredients may also be added. Contains at least 3.25% milkfat and 8.25% solids-not-fat.

Lowfat Yogurt: Similar in composition to yogurt except that it contains either 0.5%, 1%, 1.5%, or 2% milkfat.

Nonfat Yogurt: Similar in composition to yogurt and lowfat yogurt except that it contains less than 0.5% milkfat.

Source: National Dairy Council

Freezer Storage Time Chart

(Freezer Temperature 0° F or Colder)

Product	Months in Freezer
Fresh meat	
Beef	6 to 12
Veal	6 to 9
Pork	3 to 6
Lamb	6 to 9
Ground beef, veal, and lamb	2 to 4
Ground pork	1 to 2
Sausage, fresh pork	2
Frankfurters	2
Ready-to-serve luncheon meats	not recommended
Cured, cured and smoked	
Bacon	1
Smoked ham, whole or slices	2
Beef, corned	1

(continued on next page)

Product	Months in Freezer
Cooked meat	
Leftover cooked meat	1 to 2
Frozen combination foods	2 to 3
Poultry	
Chicken or turkey (whole)	6 to 12
Chicken or turkey (parts), Rock Cornish game hens, game birds	6 to 9
Duck, cooked poultry (in gravy), smoked chicken and turkey	6
Goose, squab	4 to 6
Cooked poultry (breaded, fried)	4
Giblets	2 to 3
Cooked poultry (plain meat)	1
Fresh fruits (prepared for freezing)	
All fruits except those listed below	10 to 12
Avocados, bananas	3
Lemons, limes, plantains	not recommended
Fresh vegetables (prepared for freezing)	
Beans, beets, black-eyed peas, bok choy, broccoli, brussels sprouts, cabbage, carrots, cauliflower, celery, corn, green onions, greens, kale, kohlrabi, leeks, mushrooms, okra, sliced onions, parsnips, peas, peppers, soybeans, spinach, sprouts, summer squash, Swiss chard	10 to 12
Asparagus, rutabagas, turnips	8 to 10
Artichokes, eggplant	6 to 8
Tomatoes (overripe or sliced)	2
Bamboo shoots, celery root, cucumbers, endive, lettuce, radishes, water chestnuts, watercress	not recommended
Cheese (except those listed below)	6
Cottage cheese, cream cheese, cremes, feta, goat, fresh mozzarella, Neufchatel, Parmesan, pot cheese, processed cheese (opened)	not recommended
Dairy products	
Butter	6 to 9
Margarine (not diet)	12
Milk	3
Cream, half-and-half	4
Ice Cream	1 to 2
Yogurt	1 to 1½
Juice	8 to 12
Bread	
Yeast bread (sliced), tortillas, pita	4
Quick bread, rolls, raised doughnuts	3
Yeast bread (whole loaves)	6 to 9
Nuts	
Almonds, filberts, pecans, pistachios, sunflower seeds, walnuts, mixed nuts	12
Chestnuts (shelled), macadamia nuts, peanuts (in shell)	9 to 12
Brazil nuts, cashews	9
Coconut (shelled, dried — opened), peanuts (shelled), pine nuts (shelled)	6

THE KITCHEN

Beef Cuts

SIRLOIN *
- Top Sirloin Steak
- Sirloin Steak
- Tenderloin Roast / Steak
- Beef Tri-Tip

The tri-tip roast is a boneless cut from the bottom sirloin. It is also called a "triangle" roast because of its shape.

ROUND *
- Round Steak
- Top Round Roast
- Top Round Steak
- Bottom Round Roast
- Tip Roast Cap Off
- Eye Round Roast
- Tip Steak
- Boneless Rump Roast

SHORT LOIN *
- Top Loin Steak, boneless
- T-Bone Steak
- Porterhouse Steak
- Tenderloin Roast / Steak

FLANK *
- Flank Steak
- Flank Steak Rolls

RIB
- Rib Roast, large end
- Rib Roast, small end
- Rib Steak, small end
- Rib Eye Steak
- Rib Eye Roast
- Back Ribs

PLATE
- Skirt Steak

CHUCK
- Chuck Eye Roast, boneless
- Top Blade Steak, boneless
- Arm Pot Roast
- Shoulder Pot Roast, boneless
- Mock Tender Roast
- Blade Roast
- Under Blade Pot Roast
- 7-Bone Pot Roast
- Short Ribs
- Flanken-Style Ribs
- Cross Rib Pot Roast

BRISKET
- Whole Brisket
- Brisket, point half, corned
- Brisket, flat half

SHANK
- Shank Crosscut

* Beef primals that feature cuts lowest in fat.

— courtesy the Beef Industry Council

Cake Mistake?

If the cake...	Too much flour	Too little flour	Too much sugar	Too much fat	Too little fat	Eggs beaten too much	Eggs beaten too little
Is too small						X	X
Has peaks or cracks	X						
Is sunken		X	X	X			
Is too dark or too pale							
Tastes flat							
Tastes bitter or unpleasant							
Is coarse				X		X	
Is too dense						X	X
Is crumbly							
Has tunnels							
Has thick, hard crust	X		X				
Is dry	X				X	X	
Is soggy		X		X			
Is tough	X				X		

What Counts as a Serving?

Bread Group
1 slice of bread
1 ounce of ready-to-eat cereal
½ cup of cooked cereal, rice, or pasta

Vegetable Group
1 cup of raw leafy vegetable
½ cup of other vegetables, cooked or chopped raw
¾ cup of vegetable juice

Fruit Group
1 medium apple, banana, orange
½ cup of chopped, cooked or canned fruit
¾ cup of fruit juice

Milk Group
1 cup of milk or yogurt
1½ ounces of natural cheese
2 ounces of processed cheese

Meat Group
2 to 3 ounces of cooked lean meat, poultry, or fish
½ cup of cooked dry beans, 1 egg, or 2 tablespoons of peanut butter count as 1 ounce of meat (about ⅓ serving)

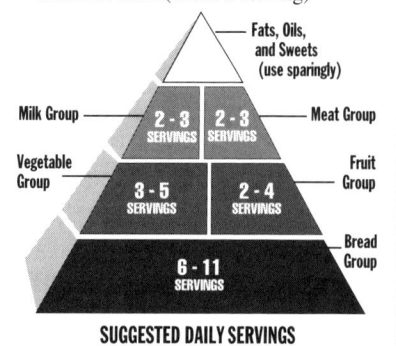

SUGGESTED DAILY SERVINGS

THE KITCHEN

Mixed too much	Mixed too little	Poor quality ingredients	Oven too hot	Oven too cool	Underbaking	Overbaking	Wrong-sized pan
			X	X			X
			X				
				X	X		
			X	X	X	X	X
		X					
		X					
X				X			
X			X				
	X						
X			X				
				X		X	
						X	
	X				X		
X			X		X		

The best Dietary Guidelines for a healthful diet from the USDA (United States Department of Agriculture) and HHS (Department of Health and Human Services) are:

- Eat a variety of foods
- Maintain healthy weight
- Choose a diet low in fat, saturated fat, and cholesterol
- Choose a diet with plenty of vegetables, fruits, and grain products
- Use sugars only in moderation
- Use salt and sodium only in moderation
- If you drink alcoholic beverages, do so in moderation

Food for Thought

☞ A piece of pecan pie = 580 calories
☞ Grilled cheese sandwich = 440 calories
☞ A chocolate shake = 364 calories
☞ Bagel with cream cheese = 361 calories
☞ 20 potato chips = 228 calories
☞ 10 French fries = 214 calories
☞ Half a cantaloupe = 94 calories
☞ Corn on the cob = 70 calories (no butter)
☞ One carrot = 30 calories

Guide to Lumber and Nails

Lumber Widths and Thickness in Inches

NOMINAL SIZE	ACTUAL SIZE Dry or Seasoned
1 x 3	¾ x 2½
1 x 4	¾ x 3½
1 x 6	¾ x 5½
1 x 8	¾ x 7¼
1 x 10	¾ x 9¼
1 x 12	¾ x 11¼
2 x 3	1½ x 2½
2 x 4	1½ x 3½
2 x 6	1½ x 5½
2 x 8	1½ x 7¼
2 x 10	1½ x 9¼
2 x 12	1½ x 11¼

Nail Sizes

The nail on the left is a 5d (penny) finish nail; on the right, 20d common. The numerals below the nail sizes indicate the approximate number of common nails per pound.

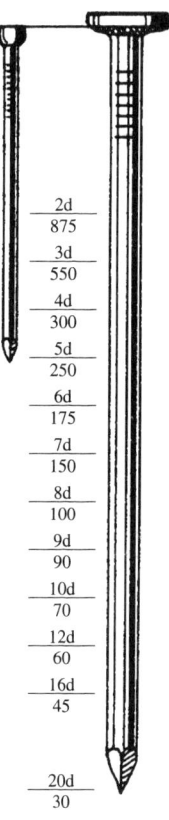

Size	Nails/lb
2d	875
3d	550
4d	300
5d	250
6d	175
7d	150
8d	100
9d	90
10d	70
12d	60
16d	45
20d	30

Lumber Measure in Board Feet

Size in Inches	12 ft.	14 ft.	16 ft.	18 ft.	20 ft.
1 x 4	4	4⅔	5⅓	6	6⅔
1 x 6	6	7	8	9	10
1 x 8	8	9⅓	10⅔	12	13⅓
1 x 10	10	11⅔	13⅓	15	16⅔
1 x 12	12	14	16	18	20
2 x 3	6	7	8	9	10
2 x 4	88	9⅓	10⅔	12	13⅓
2 x 6	12	14	16	18	20
2 x 8	16	18⅔	21⅓	24	26⅔
2 x 10	20	23⅓	26⅔	30	33⅓
2 x 12	24	28	32	36	40
4 x 4	16	18⅔	21⅓	24	26⅔
6 x 6	36	42	48	54	60
8 x 8	64	74⅔	85⅓	96	106⅔
10 x 10	100	116⅔	133⅓	150	166⅔
12 x 12	144	168	192	216	240

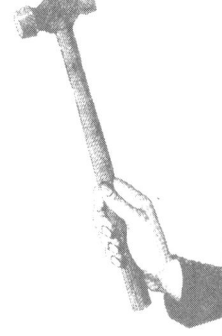

THE HOME

How Long Household Items Last

ITEM	YEARS (Approx. Averages)
Electric shavers	4
Personal computers	6
Lawn mowers	6
Automatic coffee makers	6
VCRs	6
Food processors	7
Electric can openers	7
CD players	7
Camcorders	7
Toasters	8
Stereo receivers	8
Color TV sets	8
Blenders	8
Room air conditioners	9
Vacuum cleaners	10
Microwave ovens	10
Dishwashers	11
Dehumidifiers	12
Washing machines	13
Electric dryers	13
Refrigerators	14
Gas dryers	14
Electric ranges	15
Gas ranges	18

The life span of a product depends not only on its actual durability but also on your desire for some new convenience found only on a new model.

– courtesy *Consumer Reports*

How Much Electricity Is Used?

The table below indicates the annual estimated energy consumption for various household electrical products. Note: One kilowatt equals 1,000 watts; a kilowatt-hour is the work done by one kilowatt in an hour.

APPLIANCE	ESTIMATED KILOWATT-HOURS
Water heater (standard)	4,219
Refrigerator (frost free)	1,591-1,829
Freezer (frost free)	1,820
Air conditioner (room)	1,389
Range (self-cleaning oven)	1,205
Clothes dryer	993
Television (color)	502
Computer	25-400
Dehumidifier	377
Dishwasher	165-363
Microwave oven	300
Fan (attic)	291
Frying pan	186
Iron	144
Coffee maker	106
Clothes washer	103
Broiler	100
Radio	86
Videocassette recorder (VCR)	10-70
Vacuum cleaner	46
Fan (circulating)	43
Garbage disposal	30
Clock	17
Blender	15
Hair dryer	14
Food mixer	13

How Much Water Is Used?

	Gallons
To brush your teeth (water running)	1-2
To flush a toilet	5-7
To run a dishwasher	9-12
To shave (water running)	10-15
To wash dishes by hand	20
To take a shower	15-30
By an average person daily	123
In the average residence during a year	110,000

Source: American Water Works

THE HOME

The Right Wood for the Job

Doors	Birch, oak
Cabinet doors	Maple, oak, birch, cherry
Shelving	Ash, birch, maple, oak, walnut, poplar, Douglas fir, redwood, ponderosa pine, sugar pine, Idaho white pine
Paneling	Oak, redwood, cypress, walnut, cedar, ash, birch, pine
Stairways	Oak, birch, maple, walnut, beech, ash, cherry
Interior trim, natural finish	Oak, birch, maple, cypress, cherry, sycamore, beech, walnut. Knotty surface: cedar, ponderosa pine, spruce, sugar pine, gum, lodgepole pine
Interior trim, painted finish	Northern and Idaho white pine, ponderosa pine, sugar pine, poplar
Exterior trim	Cedar, cypress, redwood, northern and Idaho white pine, ponderosa pine, sugar pine
Frames and sash	Cypress, cedar, redwood, northern and Idaho white pine, ponderosa pine, sugar pine
Siding	Western red cedar, cypress, redwood
Decking and outdoor steps	White oak, locust, walnut
Exposed platforms and porches	Redwood, locust, white oak
Shingles	Cedar, cypress, redwood
Plank roof decking	Southern yellow pine, Douglas fir, or other softwood
Fence posts	Black locust, Osage orange, white oak, cedar, cypress, redwood, catalpa, chestnut
Gates and fences	Douglas fir, western larch, southern yellow pine, redwood, white oak
Roof sheathing	Douglas fir, western larch, southern yellow pine
Wall sheathing	Cedar, hemlock, northern and Idaho white pine, redwood, aspen, spruce, balsam, white fir, basswood, lodgepole pine, poplar, sugar pine, ponderosa pine
Subfloors	Douglas fir, western larch, southern yellow pine, ash, oak

General Rules for Pruning

What	When	How
Apple	Early spring	Prune moderately. Keep tree open with main branches well spaced. Avoid sharp V-shaped crotches.
Cherry	Early spring	Prune the most vigorous shoots moderately.
Clematis	Spring	Cut weak growth. Save as much old wood as possible.
Flowering dogwood	After flowering	Remove dead wood only.
Forsythia	After flowering	Remove old branches at ground. Trim new growth.
Lilac	After flowering	Remove diseased, scaly growth, flower heads, and suckers.
Peach	Early spring	Remove half of last year's growth. Keep tree headed low.
Plum	Early spring	Cut dead, diseased branches; trim rank growth moderately.
Rhododendron	After flowering	Prune judiciously. Snip branches from weak, leggy plants to induce growth from roots.
Roses (except climbers)	Spring, after frosts	Cut dead and weak growth; cut branches or canes to four or five eyes.
Roses, climbers	After flowering	Cut half of old growth; retain new shoots for next year.
Rose of Sharon	When buds begin	Cut all winter-killed wood to swell growth back to live wood.
Trumpet vine	Early spring	Prune side branches severely to main stem.
Virginia creeper	Spring	Clip young plants freely. Thin old plants and remove dead growth.
Wisteria	Spring, summer	Cut new growth to spurs at axils of leaves.

Flowers That Attract Hummingbirds

Beard tongue . . . . *Penstemon*
Bee balm . . . . *Monarda*
Butterfly bush . . . . *Buddleia*
Catmint . . . . *Nepeta*
Clove Pink . . . . *Dianthus*
Columbine . . . . *Aquilegia*
Coral bells . . . . *Heuchera*
Daylily . . . . *Hemerocallis*
Delphinium . . . . *Larkspur*
Desert candle . . . . *Yucca*
Flag . . . . *Iris*
Flowering tobacco . . . . *Nicotiana alata*
Foxglove . . . . *Digitalis*
Lily . . . . *Lilium*
Lupine . . . . *Lupinus*
Petunia . . . . *Petunia*
Pincushion flower . . . . *Scabiosa*
Red-hot poker . . . . *Kniphofia*
Scarlet sage . . . . *Salvia splendens*
Scarlet trumpet honeysuckle . . . . . . *Lonicera sempervirens*
Soapwort . . . . *Saponaria*
Summer phlox . . . . *Phlox paniculata*
Verbena . . . . *Verbena*
Weigela . . . . *Weigela*

Note: Choose varieties in red and orange shades.

THE GARDEN

Plants That Attract Butterflies

Allium . . . . *Allium*	Helen's flower . . . . . . *Helenium*	Purple coneflower . . *Echinacea*
Aster . . . . *Aster*	Hollyhock . . . . *Alcea*	Purple loosestrife . . . . *Lythrum*
Bee balm . . . . *Monarda*	Honeysuckle . . . . *Lonicera*	Rock cress . . . . *Arabis*
Butterfly bush . . . . *Buddleia*	Lavender . . . . *Lavendula*	Sage . . . . *Salvia*
Catmint . . . . *Nepeta*	Lilac . . . . *Syringa*	Sea holly . . . . *Eryngium*
Clove Pink . . . . *Dianthus*	Lupine . . . . *Lupinus*	Shasta daisy . . *Chrysanthemum*
Cornflower . . . . *Centaurea*	Lychnis . . . . *Lychnis*	Snapdragon . . . . . . *Antirrhinum*
Daylily . . . . *Hemerocallis*	Mallow . . . . *Malva*	Stonecrop . . . . *Sedum*
False indigo . . . . *Baptisia*	Milkweed . . . . *Asclepias*	Sweet alyssum . . . . . *Lobularia*
Fleabane . . . . *Erigeron*	Mint . . . . *Mentha*	Sweet rocket . . . . *Hesperis*
Floss flower . . . . *Ageratum*	Pansy . . . . *Viola*	Tickseed . . . . *Coreopsis*
Globe thistle . . . . *Echinops*	Phlox . . . . *Phlox*	Zinnia . . . . *Zinnia*
Goldenrod . . . . *Solidago*	Privet . . . . *Ligustrum*	

Fall Palette

TREE	COLOR
Sugar maple and sumac	Flame red and orange
Red maple, dogwood, sassafras, and scarlet oak	Dark red
Poplar, birch, tulip tree, willow	Yellow
Ash	Plum purple
Oak, beech, larch, elm, hickory, and sycamore	Tan or brown
Locust	Stays green (until leaves drop)
Black walnut and butternut	Drops leaves before turning color

Manure Guide

		Primary Nutrients (pounds per ton)		
Type of Manure	Water Content	Nitrogen	Phosphate	Potash
Cow, horse	60%-80%	12-14	5-9	9-12
Sheep, pig, goat	65%-75%	10-21	7	13-19
Chicken: Wet, sticky, and caked	75%	30	20	10
Moist, crumbly to sticky	50%	40	40	20
Crumbly	30%	60	55	30
Dry	15%	90	70	40
Ashed	none		135	100

Type of Garden	Best Type of Manure	Best Time to Apply
Flower	cow, horse	early spring
Vegetable	chicken, cow, horse	fall, spring
Potato or root crop	cow, horse	fall
Acid-loving plants (blueberries, azaleas, mountain laurel, rhododendrons)	cow, horse	early fall or not at all

Forcing Indoor Blooms

Here is a list of shrubs and some trees that can be forced to flower indoors. (The trees tend to be stubborn, and their blossoms may not be as rewarding as those of the shrubs.) The numbers indicate the approximate number of weeks they will take to flower.

Buckeye	5
Cherry	4
Cornelian dogwood	2
Crabapple	4
Deutzia	3
Flowering almond	3
Flowering dogwood	5
Flowering quince	4
Forsythia	1
Honeysuckle	3
Horse chestnut	5
Lilac	4
Magnolia	3
Pussy willow	2
Red maple	2
Redbud	2
Red-twig dogwood	5
Spicebush	2
Spirea	4
Wisteria	3

Source: Purdue University Cooperative Extension Service

Herbs to Plant in Lawns

Choose plants that suit your soil and your climate. All these can withstand mowing and considerable foot traffic.

Ajuga or bugleweed *(Ajuga reptans)*
Roman chamomile *(Chamaemelum nobile)*
Dwarf cinquefoil *(Potentilla tabernaemontani)*
Corsican mint *(Mentha requienii)*
English pennyroyal *(Mentha pulegium)*
Thyme *(Thymus serpyllum)*
Pearly everlasting *(Anaphalis margaritacea)*
Rupturewort *(Herniaria glabra)*
Speedwell *(Veronica officinalis)*
White clover *(Trifolium repens)*
Wild strawberries *(Fragaria virginiana)*
Sweet violets *(Viola odorata* or *tricolor)*
Wintergreen or partridgeberry *(Mitchella repens)*
Green Irish moss *(Sagiona subulata)*
Stonecrop *(Sedum ternatum)*

THE GARDEN

Planning Your Garden

Sow or plant in cool weather	Beets/chard, cabbage, broccoli, brussels sprouts, lettuce, onions, parsley, peas, radishes, spinach, turnips
Sow or plant in warm weather	Beans, carrots, corn, cucumbers, eggplant, peppers, squash tomatoes, melons, okra
One crop per season	Corn, eggplant, melons, leeks, peppers, tomatoes, summer squash, winter squash, New Zealand spinach, potatoes
Resow for additional crops	Beans, beets, carrots, cabbage family, kohlrabi, lettuce, radishes, rutabagas, spinach, turnips

Herb Companions in Garden and Kitchen

Herbs are great companions to food in your culinary masterpieces, and they are great companions in the garden, too.

Anise

In the garden: Plant with coriander, which promotes its germination and growth.

In the kitchen: Use in cookies, cakes, fruit fillings, and breads, or with cottage cheese, shellfish, and spaghetti dishes.

Basil

In the garden: Plant with tomatoes. Repels flies and mosquitoes.

In the kitchen: Use in tomato dishes, pesto, sauces, and salad dressings.

Borage

In the garden: Plant with tomatoes, squash, and strawberries. Deters tomato worm.

In the kitchen: Use leaves in salads; flowers in soups and stews.

Caraway

In the garden: Plant here and there. Loosens soil.

In the kitchen: Use in rye breads, cheese dips and rarebits, soups, applesauce, salads, coleslaw, and over pork or sauerkraut.

Chervil

In the garden: Plant with radishes.

In the kitchen: Use with soups, salads, sauces, eggs, fish, veal, lamb, and pork.

Chives

In the garden: Plant with carrots.

In the kitchen: Related to the onion, chives enliven vegetable dishes, dressings, casseroles, rice, eggs, cheese dishes, sauces, gravies, and dips.

Dill

In the garden: Plant with cabbages. Keep away from carrots.

In the kitchen: Use seed for pickles and also to add aroma and taste to strong vegetables like cauliflower, cabbage, and turnips. Use fresh with green beans, potato dishes, cheese, soups, salads, seafood, and sauces.

Fennel

In the garden: Plant away from other herbs and vegetables.

In the kitchen: Use to flavor pastries, confectionery, sweet pickles, sausages, tomato dishes, soups, and to flavor vinegars and oils. Gives warmth and sweetness to curries.

Garlic

In the garden: Plant near roses and raspberries. Deters Japanese beetle.

In the kitchen: Use in tomato dishes, garlic bread, soups, dips, sauces, marinades, or with meats, poultry, fish, and vegetables.

Lovage

In the garden: Plant here and there to improve the health and flavor of other plants.

In the kitchen: It's a great flavoring for soups, stews, and salad dressings. Goes well with potatoes. The seeds can be used on breads and biscuits.

Marjoram

In the garden: Good companion to all vegetables.

In the kitchen: Excellent in almost any meat, fish, dairy, or vegetable dish that isn't sweet. Add near the end of cooking.

Mint

In the garden: Plant near cabbage and tomatoes. Deters white cabbage moth.

In the kitchen: It is common in Middle Eastern dishes. Use with roast lamb or fish and in salads, jellies, or teas.

Oregano

In the garden: Good companion to all vegetables.

In the kitchen: Of Italian origin, its taste is zesty and strong, good in any tomato dish. Try oregano with summer squash and potatoes, mushroom dishes, beans, or in a marinade for lamb or game.

Parsley

In the garden: Plant near asparagus, corn, and tomatoes.

In the kitchen: Use fresh parsley in soups, sauces, and salads. It lessens the need for salt in soups. You can fry parsley and use it as a side dish with meat or fish. It is, of course, the perfect garnish.

Rosemary

In the garden: Plant near cabbage, beans, carrots, and sage. Deters cabbage moth, bean beetles, and carrot fly.

In the kitchen: Use for poultry, lamb and tomato dishes, stews, soups, and vegetables. Try it finely chopped in breads and custards.

Sage

In the garden: Plant near rosemary, cabbage, and carrots; away from cucumbers. Deters cabbage moth and carrot fly.

In the kitchen: Use in cheese dishes, stuffings, soups, pickles, with beans and peas, and in salads. Excellent for salt-free cooking.

Summer Savory

In the garden: Plant with beans and onions to improve growth and flavor.

In the kitchen: Popular in soups, stews, stuffings, and with fish, chicken, green beans, and eggs.

Tarragon

In the garden: Good companion to most vegetables.

In the kitchen: Great with meat, eggs, poultry, seafood, and in salad dressings, marinades, and sauces.

Thyme

In the garden: Plant near cabbage. Deters cabbage worm.

In the kitchen: Use in casseroles, stews, soups, ragouts, and with eggs, potatoes, fish, and green vegetables.

THE GARDEN

Plant a 1792 Flower and Herb Garden

Selected Flowers and Herbs Grown in New England Before 1800

Note: From 1800 to 1840, many new plants were introduced to New England gardens. Not found here in 1792, but popular later, were double asters, fuchsias, gladioli, dahlias, French (and dwarf) marigolds, zinnias, petunias, snapdragons, forsythia, spirea, and weigela.

Perennial and Annual Flowers

Alyssum *(Alyssum saxatile)*
Anemone *(Anemone hortensis)*
Amaranth or love-lies-bleeding *(Amarantus caudatus)*
Baby's breath *(Gypsophila)*
Bee balm or Oswego tea *(Monarda didyma)*
Black-eyed Susan *(Rudbeckia hirta)*
Canterbury bells or bellflower *(Campanula)*
Candytuft, evergreen *(Iberis sempervirens)*
Cardinal flower *(Lobelia)*
Clove pinks or gillyflowers *(Dianthus)*
Columbine *(Aquilegia)*
Cornflower or bachelor's button *(Centaurea cyanis)*
Cranesbill *(Geranium)*
Daisy (Ox-eye, English, and others) *(Chrysanthemum)*
Daylily *(Hemerocallis)*
False indigo *(Baptisia)*
Feverfew *(Chrysanthemum parthenium)*
Flax *(Linum perenne)*
Forget-me-not *(Myosotis arvenis)*
Four o'clock *(Mirabilis jalapa)*
Foxglove *(Digitalis)*
Geranium, Martha Washington and scented *(Pelargonium)*
Heliotrope *(Heliotropium arborescens)*
Hollyhock *(Althea rosea)*
Honesty or moonwort *(Lunaria)*
Iris, Siberian or flag (not bearded) *(Iris)*
Jacob's ladder *(Polemonium caeruleum)*
Lavender cotton *(Santolina)*
Love-in-a-mist *(Nigella damascena)*
Lupine *(Lupinus)*
Marigold (not French or dwarf) *(Calendula)*
Mignonette *(Reseda odorata)*
Musk mallow *(Malva moschata)*
Nasturtium *(Tropaeolum)*

Peony *(Paeonia officinalis)*
Phlox *(Phlox divaricata* or *P. paniculata)*
Primrose or cowslip *(Primula vulgaris)*
Sneezewort *(Achillea ptarmica)*
Soapwort *(Saponica)*
Southernwood or wormwood *(Artemisia)*
Speedwell *(Veronica)*
Sunflower *(Helianthus)*
Sweet William *(Dianthus barbatus)*
Teasel *(Dipsacus fullonum)*
Tickseed *(Coreopsis tinctoria)*
Violets *(Viola odorata)*
Yarrow *(Achillea millefolium)*

Perennial Herbs

Anise *(Pimpinella asisum)*
Borage *(Borago officinalis)*
Camomile *(Anthemis tinctoria)*
Catmint or Catnip *(Nepeta)*
Chives *(Allium schoenoprasum)*
Clary *(Salvia sclarea)*
Hyssop *(Hyssopis officinalis)*
Lavender *(Lavandula officinalis)*
Marjoram *(Marjorana hortensis)*
Peppermint *(Mentha piperita)*
Rosemary *(Rosmarinus officinalis)*
Rue *(Ruta graveolens)*
Sage *(Salvia officinalis)*
Savory *(Satureia)*
Tansy *(Tanacetum vulgare)*
Tarragon *(Artemisia dracunculus)*
Thyme *(Thymus vulgaris)*
Wormwood *(Artemisia abrotanum)*

ANIMALS & BIRDS

Gestation and Mating Table

	Proper age for first mating	Period of fertility, in years	No. of females for one male	Period of gestation in days Range	Average
Ewe	90 lbs. or 1 yr.	6		142-154	147 / 151[8]
Ram	12-14 mos., well matured	7	50-75[2] / 35-40[3]		
Mare	3 yrs.	10-12		310-370	336
Stallion	3 yrs.	12-15	40-45[4] / Record 252[5]		
Cow	15-18 mos.[1]	10-14		279-290[6] 262-300[7]	283
Bull	1 yr., well matured	10-12	50[4] / Thousands[5]		
Sow	5-6 mos. or 250 lbs.	6		110-120	115
Boar	250-300 lbs.	6	50[2] / 35-40[3]		
Doe goat	10 mos. or 85-90 lbs.	6		145-155	150
Buck goat	Well matured	5	30		
Bitch	16-18 mos.	8		58-67	63
Male dog	12-16 mos.	8			
She cat	12 mos.	6		60-68	63
Doe rabbit	6 mos.	5-6		30-32	31
Buck rabbit	6 mos.	5-6	30		

[1]Holstein & beef: 750 lbs.; Jersey: 500 lbs. [2]Handmated. [3]Pasture. [4]Natural. [5]Artificial. [6]Beef; 8-10 days shorter for Angus. [7]Dairy. [8]For fine wool breeds.

Bird and Poultry Incubation Periods, in Days

Chicken......21　Goose......30-34　Guinea......26-28
Turkey......28　Swan......42　Canary......14-15
Duck......26-32　Pheasant......22-24　Parakeet......18-20

Gestation Periods, Wild Animals, in Days

Black bear......210　Seal......330
Hippo......225-250　Squirrel, gray......44
Moose......240-250　Whale, sperm......480
Otter......270-300　Wolf......60-63
Reindeer......210-240

Maximum Life Spans of Animals in Capitivity, in Years

Ant (queen)......18+　Eagle......55　Mussel (freshwater)......70-80
Badger......26　Elephant......75
Beaver......15+　Giraffe......36　Monarch butterfly......1+
Box turtle (Eastern)......138　Goat (domestic)......20　Octopus......2-3
Camel......35+　Goldfish......41　Oyster (freshwater)......80
Cat (domestic)......34　Goose (domestic)......20　Quahog......150
Chicken (domestic)　25　Gorilla......50+　Rabbit......18+
Chimpanzee......51　Horse......62　Squirrel, gray......23
Coyote......21+　Housefly......04 (17 days)　Tiger......26
Dog (domestic)......29　Kangaroo......30　Toad......40
Dolphin......25　Lion......29　Tortoise (Marion's)......152+
Duck (domestic)......23　Mouse (house)......6　Turkey (domestic)......16

	Recurs if not bred	Estrual cycle incl. heat period (days)		In heat for		Usual time of ovulation
	DAYS	AVG.	RANGE	AVG.	RANGE	
Mare	21	21	10-37	5-6 days	2-11 days	24-48 hours before end of estrus
Sow	21	21	18-24	2-3 days	1-5 days	30-36 hours after start of estrus
Ewe	16½	16½	14-19	30 hours	24-32 hours	12-24 hours before end of estrus
Goat	21	21	18-24	2-3 days	1-4 days	Near end of estrus
Cow	21	21	18-24	18 hours	10-24 hours	10-12 hours after end of estrus
Bitch	pseudo-pregnancy	24		7 days	5-9 days	1-3 days after first acceptance
Cat	pseudo-pregnancy		15-21	3-4 if mated	9-10 days in absence of male	24-56 hours after coitus

ANIMALS & BIRDS

Animal Terminology

Animal	Male	Female	Young
Ant	Male-ant (reproductive)	Queen (reproductive) worker (nonreproductive)	Antling
Antelope	Ram	Ewe	Calf, fawn, kid, yearling
Ass	Jack, jackass	Jenny	Foal
Bear	Boar, he-bear	Sow, she-bear	Cub
Beaver	Boar	Sow	Kit, kitten
Bee	Drone	Queen or queen bee, worker (nonreproductive)	Larva
Buffalo	Bull	Cow	Calf, yearling, spike-bull
Camel	Bull	Cow	Calf, colt
Caribou	Bull, stag, hart	Cow, doe	Calf, fawn
Cat	Tom, tomcat, gib, gibcat, boarcat, ramcat	Tabby, grimalkin, malkin, pussy, queen	Kitten, kit, kitling, kitty, pussy
Cattle	Bull	Cow	Calf, stot, yearling, bullcalf, heifer
Chicken	Rooster, cock, stag, chanticleer	Hen, partlet, biddy	Chick, chicken, poult, cockerel, pullet
Deer	Buck, stag	Doe	Fawn
Dog	Dog	Bitch	Whelp
Duck	Drake, stag	Duck	Duckling, flapper
Elephant	Bull	Cow	Calf
Fox	Dog	Vixen	Kit, pup, cub
Giraffe	Bull	Cow	Calf
Goat	Buck, billy, billie, billie-goat, he-goat	She-goat, nanny, nannie, nannie-goat	Kid
Goose	Gander, stag	Goose, dame	Gosling
Horse	Stallion, stag, horse, stud,	Mare, dam	Colt, foal, stot, stag, filly, hog-colt, hogget
Kangaroo	Buck	Doe	Joey
Leopard	Leopard	Leopardess	Cub
Lion	Lion, tom	Lioness, she-lion	Shelp, cub, lionet
Moose	Bull	Cow	Calf
Partridge	Cock	Hen	Cheeper
Quail	Cock	Hen	Cheeper, chick, squealer
Reindeer	Buck	Doe	Fawn
Seal	Bull	Cow	Whelp, pup, cub, bachelor
Sheep	Buck, ram, male-sheep, mutton	Ewe, dam	Lamb, lambkin, shearling, yearling, cosset, hog
Swan	Cob	Pen	Cygnet
Swine	Boar	Sow	Shoat, trotter, pig, piglet, farrow, suckling
Termite	King	Queen	Nymph
Walrus	Bull	Cow	Cub
Whale	Bull	Cow	Calf
Zebra	Stallion	Mare	Colt, foal

Animals & Birds

	Collective
	Colony, nest, army, state, swarm
	Herd
	Pace, drove, herd
	Sleuth, sloth
	Family, colony
	Swarm, grist, cluster, nest, hive, erst
	Troop, herd, gang
	Flock, train, caravan
	Herd
	Clowder, clutter (kindle or kendle of kittens)
	Drove, herd
	Flock, run, brood, clutch, peep
	Herd, leash
	Pack (cry or mute of hounds, leash of greyhounds)
	Brace, team, paddling, raft, bed, flock, flight
	Herd
	Leash, skulk, cloud, troop
	Herd, corps, troop
	Tribe, trip, flock, herd
	Flock (on land), gaggle, skein (in flight), gaggle or plump (on water)
	Haras, stable, remuda, stud, herd, string, field, set, pair, team
	Mob, troop, herd
	Leap
	Pride, troop, flock, sawt, souse
	Herd
	Covey
	Bevy, covey
	Herd
	Pod, herd, trip, rookery, harem
	Flock, drove, hirsel, trip, pack
	Herd, team, bank, wege, bevy
	Drift, sounder, herd, trip (litter of pigs)
	Colony, nest, swarm, brood
	Pod, herd
	Gam, pod, school, herd
	Herd

More Animal Collectives

army of caterpillars, frogs
bale of turtles
band of gorillas
bed of clams, oysters
brood of jellyfish
business of flies
cartload of monkeys
cast of hawks
cete of badgers
charm of goldfinches
chatter of budgerigars
cloud of gnats, flies, grasshoppers, locusts
colony of penguins
congregation of plovers
convocation of eagles
crash of rhinoceri
descent of woodpeckers
dole of turtles
down of hares
dray of squirrels
dule of turtle doves
exaltation of larks
family of sardines
flight of birds
flock of lice

gang of elks
hatch of flies
horde of gnats
host of sparrows
hover of trout
husk of hares
knab of toads
knot of toads, snakes
murder of crows
murmuration of starlings
mustering of storks
nest of vipers
nest or nide of pheasants
pack of weasels
pladge of wasps
plague of locusts
scattering of herons
sedge or siege of cranes
smuck of jellyfish
span of mules
spring of teals
steam of minnows
tittering of magpies
troop of monkeys
troubling of goldfish
volery of birds
watch of nightingales
wing of plovers
yoke of oxen

Birdseed Chart

Although most birds are perfectly happy with a variety of foods, here is a list of backyard birds and their favorite feeder fare.

Bird	Food
Blue jay	Peanut kernels, black oil sunflower
Cardinal	Peanut kernels, black oil sunflower
Chickadee	Black oil sunflower, niger thistle
Evening grosbeak	Black oil sunflower
Common grackle	Black-striped sunflower
American goldfinch	Hulled sunflower, niger thistle
House finch	Hulled sunflower, black oil sunflower
Purple finch	Black oil sunflower, niger thistle
Tufted titmouse	Peanut kernels
Brown-headed cowbird	White proso millet
House (English) sparrow	White proso millet
Mourning dove	White or red proso millet, black oil sunflower
White-throated sparrow	Peanut kernels
Nuthatch	Black oil sunflower
Redpoll	Niger thistle
Junco	Peanut kernels, proso millet
Starling	Cracked corn
Pheasant	Cracked corn
Pine Siskin	Niger thistle

How Old Is Your Dog?

Multiplying your dog's age by seven is easy, but doesn't always hold true. The more carefully graded system below has the human equivalency years piled onto a dog's life more quickly during the dog's rapid growth to maturity, after which each year for a dog becomes the equivalent of four human years, and after age 13 it slows down to 2½ years.

Dog Age	Equivalent Human Age	Dog Age	Equivalent Human Age
6 mos	10 yrs.	16	75½
1 year	15	17	78
2	24	18	80½
3	28	19	83
4	32	20	85½
5	36	21	88
6	40	22	90½
7	44	23	93
8	48	24	95½
9	52	25	98
10	56	26	100½
11	60	27	103
12	64	28	105½
13	68	29	108
14	70½	30	110
15	73		

Where to Find Vitamins and Minerals in Your Diet

VITAMINS

Vitamin A
Sources: Milk, eggs, liver, cheese, fish oil, yellow fruits, and dark green and yellow vegetables.
Benefits: Good vision; healthy skin and mucous membranes; strong bones and teeth, stress relief.

Vitamin C (ascorbic acid)
Sources: Citrus fruits and juices, berries, tomatoes, peppers, potatoes, kale, cauliflower, cantaloupe, and brussels sprouts.
Benefits: Healthy gums, teeth, and bones; formation and maintenance of connective tissue; healing of wounds; iron absorption.

Vitamin D
Sources: Fish, fish oils, milk, dairy products, and fortified margarine. (Also, exposure to sunlight.)
Benefits: Calcium absorption for strong bones and teeth; proper blood levels of calcium and phosphorus.

Vitamin E
Sources: Vegetable oils, nuts, margarine, soybeans, asparagus, olives, wheat germ, and leafy greens.
Benefits: Formation of red blood cells; proper digestion of polyunsaturated fats; proper function of circulatory, nervous, digestive, excretory, and respiratory systems.

Thiamin (B_1)
Sources: Whole grains, brewer's yeast, bran, most vegetables, steak, lean pork, nuts, beans, liver, and fish.
Benefits: Healthy brain, nerve cells, and heart; energy release from foods.

Riboflavin (B_2)
Sources: Dairy products, liver, lean meat, poultry, fish, eggs, beans, leafy greens, and enriched grain products.
Benefits: Healthy skin, mouth, and eyes; energy release from foods.

Niacin (B_3)
Sources: Fish, poultry, peanuts, dairy products, brewer's yeast, and liver.
Benefits: Healthy skin, mouth, and nervous system; energy release from foods.

B_6 (pyridoxine)
Sources: Whole grains, brewer's yeast, wheat germ, bananas, beans, nuts, liver, fish, and poultry.
Benefits: Breakdown of protein; proper function of brain, nervous system, and muscles; formation of red blood cells; cavity prevention.

B_{12} (cyanocobalamin)
Sources: Liver, beef, pork, poultry, shellfish, eggs, milk, cheese, yogurt, and fortified cereals.
Benefits: Development of red blood cells; proper function of nervous system.

Folacin (folic acid)
Sources: Deep green leafy greens, wheat germ, liver, beans, whole grains, citrus fruits and juices, avocados, broccoli, and asparagus.
Benefits: Proper development of cells; syntheseis of DNA; production of hemoglobin (with B_{12}).

Biotin
Sources: Eggs, liver, brewer's yeast, milk, mushrooms, tomatoes, bananas, and whole grains.
Benefits: Metabolism of protein, carbohydrates, and fats.

Pantothenic acid (B_5)
Sources: Whole grains, beans, milk, eggs, liver, and nuts.
Benefits: Energy release from foods; production of hormones.

(continued on next page)

HEALTH

MINERALS

Calcium
Sources: Milk, sardines and salmon (with bones), dark green leafy vegetables, shellfish.
Benefits: Strong bones and teeth; healthy heart, muscles, and nerves.

Chloride
Sources: Table salt, fish.
Benefits: Regulation of fluids; balanced blood pH; good digestion.

Chromium
Sources: Meat, cheese, whole grains, dried peas and beans, peanuts.
Benefits: Metabolism of glucose.

Copper
Sources: Shellfish, nuts, liver, cocoa powder, chocolate, kidneys, dried beans, raisins, corn-oil margarine.
Benefits: Formation of red blood cells; iron absorption.

Fluorine (fluoride)
Sources: Fluoridated water and foods grown or cooked in it; fish, tea, gelatin.
Benefits: Strong bones and teeth.

Iodine
Sources: Iodized salt, seafood, seaweed food products, vegetable oil.
Benefits: Proper function of thyroid gland; normal cell function; healthy skin, hair, and nails.

Iron
Sources: Liver, kidneys, red meats, egg yolks, peas, beans, nuts, dried fruits, green leafy vegetables, enriched grain products.
Benefits: Formation of hemoglobin; oxygen-carrying factor in blood.

Magnesium
Sources: Wheat bran, whole grains, raw leafy green vegetables, nuts, soybeans, bananas, apricots, spices.
Benefits: Bone growth; proper function of nerves and muscles; healthy heart rhythm.

Manganese
Sources: Nuts, whole grains, vegetables, fruits, instant coffee, tea, cocoa powder, beets, egg yolks.
Benefits: Bone growth and development; normal reproduction; proper cell function.

Molybdenum
Sources: Peas, beans, cereal grains, organ meats, dark green vegetables.
Benefits: Normal cell function; metabolism of carbohydrates.

Phosphorus
Sources: Meats, poultry, fish, cheese, egg yolks, dried peas and beans, milk and milk products, soft drinks, nuts.
Benefits: Strong bones and teeth; energy metabolism.

Potassium
Sources: Oranges and orange juice, bananas, dried fruits, peanut butter, dried peas and beans, potatoes, coffee, tea, cocoa, yogurt, molasses, meat.
Benefits: Normal muscle tone; regular heartbeat; water balance; transfer of nutrients to cells; regulation of blood pressure.

Selenium
Sources: Fish, shellfish, red meat, egg yolks, chicken, garlic, tuna, tomatoes.
Benefits: With vitamin E fights cell damage by oxygen-derived compounds.

Sodium
Sources: Table salt, salt added to prepared foods, baking soda.
Benefits: Water balance; helps maintain blood pressure.

Zinc
Sources: Oysters, crabmeat, beef, liver, eggs, poultry, brewer's yeast, whole wheat bread.
Benefits: Acute taste and smell; normal growth and sexual development; proper fetal growth; healing of wounds.

HEALTH

What Should You Weigh?

Women (Medium Frame)		Men (Medium Frame)	
Height	Weight	Height	Weight
5' 0"	113 - 126 lbs.	5' 2"	131 - 141 lbs.
5' 2"	118 - 132 lbs.	5' 4"	135 - 145 lbs.
5' 4"	124 - 138 lbs.	5' 6"	139 - 151 lbs.
5' 6"	130 - 144 lbs.	5' 8"	145 - 157 lbs.
5' 8"	136 - 150 lbs.	5' 10"	151 - 163 lbs.
5' 10"	142 - 156 lbs.	6' 0"	157 - 170 lbs.
6' 0"	148 - 162 lbs.	6' 2"	164 - 178 lbs.

How Fat Are You?

More accurate than a standard height/weight table is the body mass index (BMI), which measures the percentage of fat in the body. This formula is a quick way to determine your BMI:

1. Convert your weight to kilograms: Divide your weight in pounds (no clothes) by 2.2. _____ kilograms

2. Convert your height to meters: Divide your height in inches (no shoes) by 39.4, then square it (multiply it by itself). _____ meters

3. Divide (1) by (2). This is your BMI. _____

Men: **Desirable BMI: 22-24**
Overweight: 28.5 and over
Seriously overweight: Above 33

Women: **Desirable BMI: 21-23.**
Overweight: 27.5 and over
Seriously overweight: Above 31.5

Recommended Daily Dietary Allowances (RDAs) of Calories

Age	Calories needed	
	Male	Female
11-14	2,800	2,400
15-18	3,000	2,100
19-22	3,000	2,100
23-50	2,700	2,000
51+	2,400	1,800

PLEASE NOTE: If pregnant or nursing add 300 to 500 calories

HEALTH

Average Time Spent Sleeping at Different Ages

Age	Hours of sleep	Age	Hours of sleep
0-3 months	16-22	14-18 years	8.5
4-6 months	15	19-30 years	8
7-23 months	13	31-45 years	7.5
3-5 years	11	46-50 years	6.5
6-9 years	10	50+ years	6
10-13 years	9.5		

Calorie Burning

If you hustle through your chores to get to the fitness center, relax. You're getting a great workout already. The left-hand column lists "chore" exercises, the middle column shows number of calories you burn per minute per pound of your body weight, the right-hand column lists comparable "recreational" exercises. For example, a 150-pound person forking straw bales burns 9.45 calories per minute, the same workout he/she would get playing basketball.

Chore	Calories	Recreational
Ax chopping, fast	0.135	Skiing, cross country — up hill (0.125)
Climbing hills, with 44-pound load	0.066	Swimming, crawl — fast (0.071)
Digging trenches	0.065	Skiing, cross country — steady walk
Forking straw bales	0.063	Basketball
Chopping down trees	0.060	Football
Climbing hills, with 9-pound load	0.058	Swimming, crawl — slow
Sawing by hand	0.055	Skiing, cross country, moderate
Lawn mowing	0.051	Horseback riding, trotting (0.050)
Scrubbing floors	0.049	Tennis
Shoveling coal	0.049	Aerobic dance, medium
Hoeing	0.041	Weight training, circuit training (0.042)
Stacking firewood	0.040	Weight lifting, free weights (0.039)
Shoveling grain	0.038	Golf
House painting	0.035	Walking, normal pace — asphalt road
Weeding	0.033	Table tennis (0.031)
Food shopping	0.028	Cycling, 5.5 mph (0.029)
Mopping floors	0.028	Fishing
Window cleaning	0.026	Croquet
Raking	0.025	Dancing, ballroom (0.023)
Driving a tractor	0.016	Drawing, in standing position

SPORTS

Safe Ice Thickness *

Ice Thickness	Permissible load
2 inches	one person on foot
3 inches	group in single file
7½ inches	passenger car (2-ton gross)
8 inches	light truck (2½-ton gross)
10 inches	medium truck (3½-ton gross)
12 inches	heavy truck (8-ton gross)
15 inches	10 tons
20 inches	25 tons
30 inches	70 tons
36 inches	110 tons

* **Solid clear blue/black pond and lake ice**
☞ Slush ice has only one-half strength of blue ice.
☞ Strength value of river ice is 15 percent less.

Source: American Pulpwood Association

Sports Halls of Fame

Association of Sports Museums and Halls of Fame
101 West Sutton Place
Wilmington, DE 19810

Pro Football Hall of Fame
2121 George Halas Dr. N.W.
Canton, OH 44708
216-456-8207

National Football Foundation and Hall of Fame
1865 Palmer Ave.
Larchmont, NY 10538
914-834-0474

National Soccer Hall of Fame
5-11 Ford Ave.
Oneonta, NY 13820
607-432-3351

Pro Rodeo Hall of Fame
101 Pro Rodeo Dr.
Colorado Springs, CO 80919
719-528-4764

International Boxing Hall of Fame
P.O. Box 425
Canastota, NY 13032
315-697-7095

National Baseball Hall of Fame and Museum
P.O. Box 590
Cooperstown, NY 13326
607-547-7200

Naismith Memorial Basketball Hall of Fame
1150 W. Columbus Ave.
Springfield, MA 01101
413-781-6500

National Softball Hall of Fame
2801 N.E. 50th St.
Oklahoma City, OK 73111
405-424-5266

Hockey Hall of Fame and Museum
Yonge & Front Sts.
Toronto, Ontario
Canada M5E 1X8
416-360-7765

National Tennis Foundation and Hall of Fame
100 Park Ave.
New York, NY 10017
212-880-4179

International Swimming Hall of Fame
1 Hall of Fame Dr.
Fort Lauderdale, FL 33316
305-462-6536

Bowling Hall of Fame and Museum
111 Stadium Plaza
St. Louis, MO 63102
314-231-6340

International Checker Hall of Fame
220 Lynn Ray Rd.
(P.O. Box 365)
Petal, MS 39465
601-582-7090

National Freshwater Fishing Hall of Fame
1 Hall of Fame Dr.
(P.O. Box 33)
Hayward, WI 54843
715-634-4440

SPORTS

Participation in Sports

Here's a ranking of participation in recreational activities among Americans surveyed in 1992.

1. Exercise walking
2. Swimming
3. Bicycle riding
4. Camping
5. Bowling
6. Fishing (fresh water)
7. Exercising with equipment
8. Basketball
9. Aerobic exercising
10. Golf
11. Volleyball
12. Running/jogging
13. Hiking
14. Softball
15. Hunting with firearms
16. Tennis
17. Baseball
18. Fishing (salt water)
19. Target shooting
20. Calisthenics
21. Skiing (alpine/downhill)
22. Soccer
23. Backpacking and wilderness camping
24. Racquetball
25. Skiing (cross country)

For comparison, here are the top ten sports of two different age groups.

12-17 years

1. Swimming
2. Bicycle riding
3. Basketball
4. Camping
5. Bowling
6. Volleyball
7. Football
8. Fishing (freshwater)
9. Running/jogging
10. Softball

35-44 years

1. Exercise walking
2. Swimming
3. Camping
4. Bicycle riding
5. Fishing (freshwater)
6. Exercising with equipment
7. Bowling
8. Aerobic exercise
9. Hiking
10. Golf

Acceptable Two-Letter Words in Scrabble™

aa	aw	do	fa	it	my	op	sh	we
ad	ax	ef	go	jo	na	or	si	wo
ae	ay	eh	ha	ka	no	os	so	xi
ah	ba	el	he	la	nu	ow	ta	xu
ai	be	em	hi	li	od	ox	ti	ya
am	bi	en	ho	lo	oe	oy	to	ye
an	bo	er	id	ma	of	pa	un	
ar	by	es	if	me	oh	pe	up	
as	da	et	in	mi	om	pi	us	
at	de	ex	is	mu	on	re	ut	

SPORTS

The Most Landed-on Spaces on the Monopoly Game Board

1. Illinois Avenue
2. Go
3. B&O Railroad
4. Free Parking
5. Tennessee Avenue
6. New York Avenue
7. Reading Railroad
8. St. James Place
9. Water Works
10. Pennsylvania Railroad

The Rank of Poker Hands (without wild cards)

1. Royal flush — ace, king, queen, jack, ten of the same suit
2. Straight flush — five cards, same suit, in sequence
3. Four of a kind — four cards, same rank
4. Full house — three cards, same rank, and a pair of another rank
5. Flush — five cards, same suit
6. Straight — five cards in sequence (different suits)
7. Three of a kind — three cards, same rank
8. Two pairs — two of the same rank, and two cards of a different rank
9. One pair — two cards, same rank
10. High card — highest rank of five unmatched cards

Sports Quiz

Can you match each term with its correct sport? We bet even the most savvy fan will be stumped by some of these. (Answers below.)

1.	Pitchout		A.	Basketball
2.	Dink		B.	Billiards
3.	Sling		C.	Curling
4.	Catching a crab		D.	Golf
5.	Riposte		E.	Tennis
6.	Surplace		F.	Rowing
7.	Jerk		G.	Bowling
8.	Swisher		H.	Fencing
9.	Turkey		I.	Rugby
10.	Stutz		J.	Skiing
11.	Gimme		K.	Bike racing
12.	Maul		L.	Football
13.	Cradling		M.	Weight lifting
14.	Kiss		N.	Gymnastics
15.	Wedeln		O.	Badminton
16.	Hog		P.	Lacrosse

Answers: 1. L; 2. E; 3. O; 4. F; 5. H; 6. K; 7. M; 8. A; 9. G; 10. N; 11. D; 12. I; 13. P; 14. B; 15. J; 16. C

Decibels

Decibels (dB) are used to measure the loudness or intensity of sounds. One decibel is the smallest difference between sounds detectable by the human ear. Intensity varies exponentially: A 20 dB sound is 10 times louder than a 10 dB sound; a 30 dB sound is 100 times louder than a 10 dB sound; a 40 dB sound is 1,000 times louder than a 10 dB sound; and so on. A 120-decibel sound is painful.

10 decibels	light whisper
20	quiet conversation
30	normal conversation
40	light traffic
50	typewriter, loud conversation
60	noisy office
70	normal traffic, quiet train
80	rock music, subway
90	heavy traffic, thunder
100	jet plane at takeoff

Makeshift Measurers

When you don't have a measuring stick or tape, use what is at hand. To this list, add any other items that you always (or nearly always) have handy.

Credit card: 3-3/8" x 2-1/8"
Business card (standard): 3-1/2" x 2"
Floor tile: 12" square
Dollar bill: 6-1/8" x 2-5/8"
Quarter (diameter): 1"
Penny (diameter): 3/4"
Sheet of paper: 8-1/2" x 11"
   (legal size: 8-1/2"x 14")
Your foot/shoe: _____
Your outstretched arms, fingertip to
   fingertip: _____
Your shoelace: _____
Your necktie: _____
Your belt: _____

Richter Scale for Measuring Earthquakes

MAGNITUDE	POSSIBLE EFFECTS
1	Detectable only by instruments
2	Barely detectable, even near the epicenter
3	Felt indoors
4	Felt by most people; slight damage
5	Felt by all; damage minor to moderate
6	Moderately destructive
7	Major damage
8	Total and major damage

Devised by American geologist Charles W. Richter in 1935 to measure the magnitude of an earthquake.

MISCELLANEOUS

Metric Conversion

CONVENTIONAL TO METRIC, MULTIPLY BY		METRIC TO CONVENTIONAL, MULTIPLY BY		
inch	2.54	centimeter	0.39	inch
foot	30.48	centimeter	0.033	foot
yard	0.91	meter	1.09	yard
mile	1.61	kilometer	0.62	mile
square inch	6.45	square centimeter	0.15	square inch
square foot	0.09	square meter	10.76	square foot
square yard	0.8	square meter	1.2	square yard
square mile	0.84	square kilometer	0.39	square mile
acre	0.4	hectare	2.47	acre
ounce	28.0	gram	0.035	ounce
pound	0.45	kilogram	2.2	pound
short ton (2,000 pounds)	0.91	metric ton	1.10	short ton
ounce	30.0	milliliter	0.034	ounce
pint	0.47	liter	2.1	pint
quart	0.95	liter	1.06	quart
gallon	3.8	liter	0.26	gallon

If you know the conventional measurement and want to convert it to metric, multiply it by the numbers in the first column (**example: 1 inch equals 2.54 centimeters**). If you know the metric measurement, multiply it by the numbers in the second column (**example: 2 meters equals 2.18 yards**).

How to Find the Day of the Week for Any Given Date

To compute the day of the week for any given date as far back as the mid-18th century, proceed as follows:

Add the last two digits of the year to one-quarter of the last two digits (discard any remainder if it doesn't come out even), the given date, and the month key from the key-box below. Divide the sum by seven; the number left over is the day of the week (one is Sunday, two is Monday, and so on). If it comes out even, the day is Saturday. If you go back before 1900, add two to the sum before dividing; before 1800, add four; and so on. Don't go back before 1753. From 2000 to 2099, subtract one from the sum before dividing.

Example: **The Dayton Flood was on Tuesday, March 25, 1913.**

Last two digits of year:	13
One-quarter of these two digits:	3
Given day of month:	25
Key number for March:	4
Sum:	45

45/7=6, with a remainder of 3. The flood took place on Tuesday, the third day of the week.

KEY
- Jan. 1
- *leap yr.* 0
- Feb. 4
- *leap yr.* 3
- Mar. 4
- Apr. 0
- May 2
- June 5
- July 0
- Aug. 3
- Sept. 6
- Oct. 1
- Nov. 4
- Dec. 6

MISCELLANEOUS

Formula for Determining the Date of Easter for Any Year in the Gregorian Calendar

Step	N=Numerator	Denominator	Equation	Quotient	Remainder
1. Example:	N=The Year N=1994	19	N/19 1994/19	Discard	a a=18
2.	N=The Year N=1994	100	N/100 1994/100	b b=19	c c=94
3.	N=b N=19	4	N/4 19/4	d d=4	e e=3
4.	N=(b+8) N=27	25	N/25 27/25	Discard	f f=2
5.	N=(b-f+1) N=18	3	N/3 18/3	g 6	Discard
6.	N=(19a+b-d-g+15) N=366	30	N/30 366/30	Discard	h h=6
7.	N=c N=94	4	N/4 94/4	i i=23	j j=2
8.	N=(32+2e+2i-h-j) N=76	7	N/7 76/7	Discard	k k=6
9.	N=(a+11h+22k) N=216	451	N/451 216/451	L L=0	Discard
10.	N=(h+k-7L+114) N=126	31	N/31 126/31	m m=4	n n=2

m=month in which Easter occurs: m=4=April   n+1=day of month on which Easter occurs: n+1=3
Hence, Easter 1994 occurred on April 3.

March 22 is the earliest possible date for Easter. It has not been celebrated that early since March 22, 1818, and will not be again until 2133. The latest date on which Easter can fall is April 25, on which it was celebrated in 1943 and will be next in 2038.

Another (Simpler) Way to Determine the Date of Easter

Christian churches that follow the Gregorian calendar (Eastern Orthodox churches follow the Julian calendar) celebrate Easter on the first Sunday after the full Moon that occurs on or just after the vernal equinox.

In ...	Easter will fall on ...
1996	April 7
1997	March 30
1998	April 12
1999	April 4
2000	April 23

MISCELLANEOUS

Principal Religions of the World

The figures given for membership in each religious affiliation are estimates based on 1991 statistics.

Christians . . . . 1.8 billion
Muslims 1
Nonreligious . . . . 900 million
Hindus 750
Buddhists 325
Atheists 250
Chinese folk religionists . . 200
New-Religionists 150
Tribal religionists 100
Sikhs 19
Jews 18
Shamanists 10
Confucians 6
Baha'is 5.5
Jains 3.8
Shintoists 3.2
Other religionists 18

The Golden Rule
(It's True in All Faiths)

BRAHMANISM:
This is the sum of duty: Do naught unto others which would cause you pain if done to you. *Mahabharata 5:1517*

BUDDHISM:
Hurt not others in ways that you yourself would find hurtful. *Udana-Varga 5:18*

CONFUCIANISM:
Surely it is the maxim of loving-kindness: Do not unto others what you would not have them do unto you. *Analects 15:23*

TAOISM:
Regard your neighbor's gain as your own gain and your neighbor's loss as your own loss. *T'ai Shang Kan Ying P'ien*

ZOROASTRIANISM:
That nature alone is good which refrains from doing unto another whatsoever is not good for itself. *Dadistan-i-dinik 94:5*

JUDAISM:
What is hateful to you, do not to your fellowman. That is the entire Law; all the rest is commentary. *Talmud, Shabbat 31a*

CHRISTIANITY:
All things whatsoever ye would that men should do to you, do ye even so to them; for this is the law and the prophets. *Matthew 7:12*

ISLAM:
No one of you is a believer until he desires for his brother that which he desires for himself. *Sunnah*

– courtesy Elizabeth Pool

Every Minute Counts

The Tax Foundation gives a breakdown of the amount of time you work in an eight-hour day to pay for certain expenses as follows:

Federal and state taxes . . . . 2 hours, 45 minutes
Housing . . . . 1 hour, 25 minutes
Food, tobacco . . . . 57 minutes
Medical care . . . . 46 minutes
Transportation . . . . 39 minutes
Recreation . . . . 25 minutes
Other . . . . 1 hour, 3 minutes

MISCELLANEOUS

Good Luck or Bad Luck? Here's How to Tell

GOOD LUCK

To arise from slumber on your right side.

To have wine or any other kind of drink spilled on you.

Small spiders, especially black ones, bring good luck if not disturbed or injured.

To spit on the hands increases good luck.

Spitting on money brings good luck.

To see a frog is a sign of gold.

To be the seventh son of a seventh son.

To find a stone with a natural hole.

A bent or perforated coin brings good luck.

For a strange black cat to follow you or to come to your house will bring good luck.

To sneeze between midnight and noon.

To see a white rat.

To find a horseshoe.

To pick up a pin or a piece of coal.

To touch unfinished wood.

To keep a branch of mountain ash in your house.

To have crickets in your house.

A mole on the neck is a promise of health and riches.

To find pieces of old iron.

To be born on Good Friday.

To have a martin build its nest about your house.

To have a swallow build a nest in the chimney or eaves of your house.

A hawk flying overhead is a sign of good luck.

To see a white cricket means the return of an absent lover.

June and October are the luckiest months to be married.

The full Moon is considered lucky for matrimony or other important events.

For a bride to weep profusely at her wedding.

To throw a shoe or an old slipper after a bride and groom.

A cat sneezing is a lucky omen for a bride to be married the next day.

The right foot should be first on entering the church.

BAD LUCK

For two persons to pass each other on the stairs.

To open an umbrella in the house.

To get out of bed backward will bring ill luck for the whole day.

To place a knife and a fork crosswise.

To find a knife or a razor will bring disappointment.

To meet a fox.

To take a ring off another person's finger breaks friendship.

It is unlucky for two persons to wash their hands in the same bowl at the same time or with the same water.

To sweep out the house you are leaving.

To take the old broom to the new house.

To bring a hoe into the house.

To cut a new window in an old house.

To stumble in the morning or when starting a journey.

To enter a house by one door and leave by another is regarded as unlucky.

To see the new Moon for the first time through a window or over one's left shoulder.

To see a barefoot woman or break a shoelace before a journey.

To see a sow, hare, or a black cat cross your path.

To walk under a ladder.

To put on a garment with the wrong side out is unlucky.

To put on the left shoe before the right shoe.

To meet three nuns.

To wear old clothes on Easter Day.

To throw ashes or dirty water out of the house on New Year's Day.

It's a bad omen if the leaves of your bean plants turn white.

To sneeze while putting on your shoes.

To break a mirror.

To kill a wren or a robin or to destroy its nest will bring bad luck.

To have 13 persons sitting down together at a table.

The sudden falling of hens from the housetop is ominous.

Unseasonable cock-crowing denotes approaching trouble.

To carry a baby upstairs before it is carried downstairs.

To hear thunder in the winter.

To be married in May.

To marry in the waning of the moon.

To change the date for a wedding or a baptism.

The person who takes the last piece of bread or cake on the plate will never be married.

Excerpted from Ominous Secrets
(copyrighted 1894 by Pabst Brewing Co.)

MISCELLANEOUS

Rules of Introduction

Countless situations call for introductions. Here are some basic guidelines to help you through. Even if you can't remember the proper order of introduction, forget names, or make another mistake in your introduction, it is a far greater blunder to neglect this social courtesy altogether. To easily carry out a "proper" introduction, just remember to say first the name of the person who is having someone introduced *to* them. For example, you would say: "Mary, this is Tom Smith; Tom, Mary Jones."

A man	TO	a woman
A young person	TO	an older person
A less important person	TO	a more important person
A peer in your own company	TO	a peer in another company
A nonofficial person	TO	an official person
A junior executive	TO	a senior executive
A fellow executive	TO	a customer or client

Military Rank

Army, Air Force, and Marine Corps:
1. General
2. Lieutenant General
3. Major General
4. Brigadier General
5. Colonel
6. Lieutenant Colonel
7. Major
8. Captain
9. First Lieutenant
10. Second Lieutenant

Navy and Coast Guard:
1. Admiral
2. Vice Admiral
3. Rear Admiral
4. Captain
5. Commander
6. Lieutenant Commander
7. Lieutenant
8. Lieutenant, Junior Grade
9. Ensign

Note: A captain in the Navy or Coast Guard outranks a captain in the Army, Air Force, or Marine Corps.

Having Tea with the Queen?

On the off-chance that you may have the honor of conversing with members of the British Royal Family or members of the nobility, use these forms of address:

Your Majesty (to the queen or king)
Your Royal Highness (to the monarch's spouse, children, and siblings)
Your Highness (to nephews, nieces, and cousins of the monarch)
Duke or Duchess (to a duke or duchess if you are also among the nobility)
Your Grace (to a duke or duchess if you are a commoner; to an archbishop of the Church of England)
My Lord (to a peer below a duke; to a bishop of the Church of England)
Lord (to an earl, marquis, or viscount; an earl or marquis is usually "of" somewhere, but you don't say the "of," just Lord Derby for the Earl of Derby)
Lady (to a marchioness, countess, viscountess, or baroness; as in Lord, you don't say the "of")
Sir (to a baronet or knight, using his first name; i.e., Sir Thomas Lipton)
Lady (to the wife of a baronet or knight; in olden days, the title was Dame)

MISCELLANEOUS

A Handy Chart for Identifying Five Generations of Blood Relatives

Technically it's known as consanguinity. That is, the quality or state of being related by blood or descended from a common ancestor. These relationships are diagrammed herewith for the genealogy of five generations of one family.

– courtesy Frederick H. Rohles Jr., Ph.D.

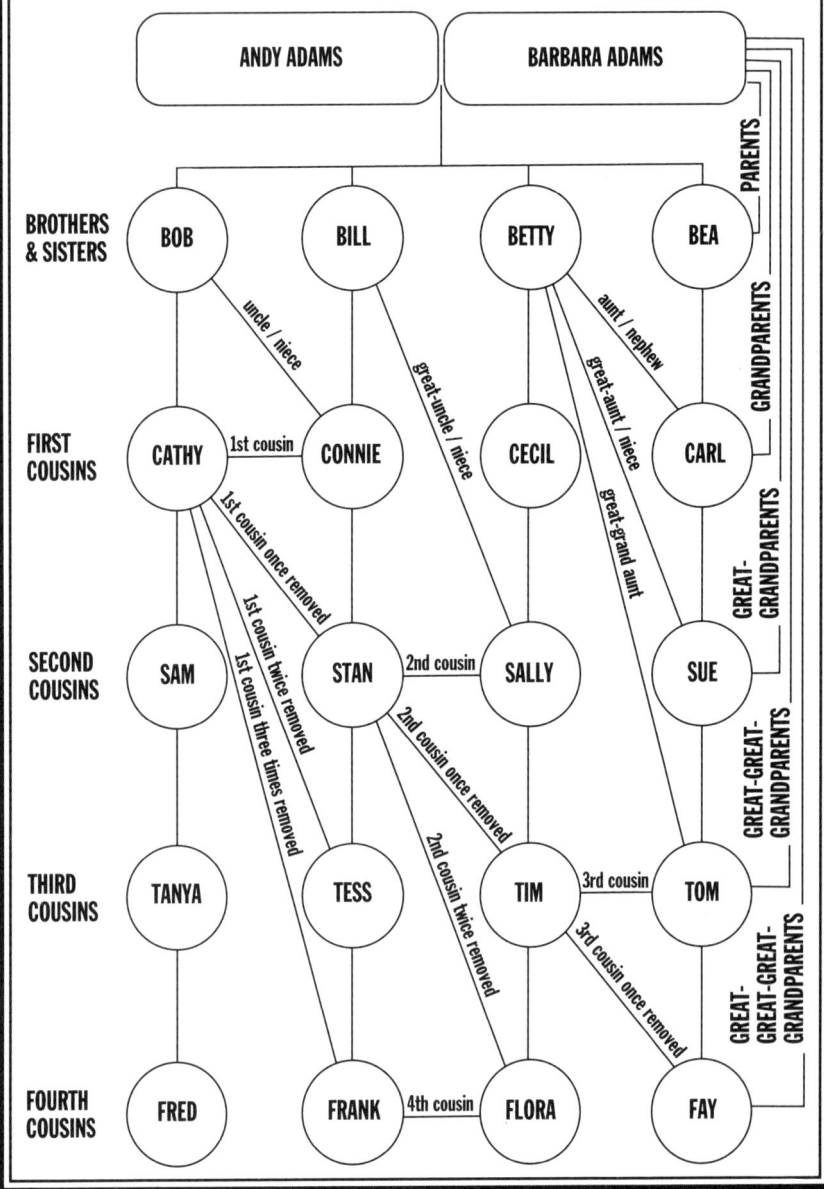